More Praise for *Chokepoints*

"How can America sustain its economic and financial advantage in the face of fierce geopolitical competition? *Chokepoints* provides the playbook. Edward Fishman traces the historical evolution of economic warfare, taking readers behind the scenes of the U.S. campaigns to counter China's economic aggression, Iran's nuclear ambitions, and Russia's revanchism. Along the way, Fishman uncovers valuable strategic lessons and makes compelling recommendations that leaders in government and business must implement urgently."

—Lieutenant General H. R. McMaster, U.S. Army (Ret.), former White House National Security Advisor, author of *Battlegrounds* and *At War with Ourselves*

"This peerless contemporary history of American sanctions, grounded in personal experience and thorough research, will guide all who wish to address global problems through the responsible and effective use of economic power."

—Timothy Snyder, author of *On Freedom* and *Bloodlands*

"This book should be required reading on both sides of the Atlantic as the West faces a geopolitical reckoning. Edward Fishman, a scholar-practitioner with deep insider knowledge from his time in government, provides a gripping account of the rise of a new form of economic warfare. *Chokepoints* is written with an eye to both the general and the specific, skillfully blending the Olympian big picture with wonderful vignettes of how the world economy works. Fishman argues convincingly that the West cannot have economic interdependence, economic security, and great power competition at the same time. We will have to make a choice quickly, before it is made for us."

—Brendan Simms, author of *Europe: The Struggle for Supremacy, from 1453 to the Present*

"Sanctions are vital weapons in the war for global power and influence. *Chokepoints* is a master class in how sanctions work—and why, sometimes, they don't. It is essential reading for anyone who wants to understand global competition today."

—Hal Brands, author of *The Eurasian Century*, co-author of *Danger Zone*

"*Chokepoints* is a compelling exploration of how economic infrastructure increasingly shapes geopolitics—illuminating the history, inner workings, and future stakes of this important twenty-first-century phenomenon. An excellent read for anyone seeking to understand how power will be wielded in the years to come."

—Patrick Collison, co-founder and CEO of Stripe

CHOKEPOINTS

CHOKEPOINTS

American Power in the
Age of Economic Warfare

≡

EDWARD FISHMAN

PORTFOLIO | PENGUIN

Portfolio / Penguin
An imprint of Penguin Random House LLC
1745 Broadway, New York, NY 10019
penguinrandomhouse.com

Most Portfolio books are available at a discount when purchased in quantity for sales
promotions or corporate use. Special editions, which include personalized covers, excerpts,
and corporate imprints, can be created when purchased in large quantities. For more information,
please call (212) 572-2232 or e-mail specialmarkets@penguinrandomhouse.com. Your local
bookstore can also assist with discounted bulk purchases using the Penguin Random House
corporate Business-to-Business program. For assistance in locating a participating retailer,
e-mail B2B@penguinrandomhouse.com.

Image credits may be found on pages 521–22.

Book design by Alissa Rose Theodor

Maps and charts by Jeffrey L. Ward

ISBN 9780593712979 (hardcover)
ISBN 9780593712986 (ebook)

Printed in the United States of America
1st Printing

The authorized representative in the EU for product safety and compliance is
Penguin Random House Ireland, Morrison Chambers, 32 Nassau Street,
Dublin D02 YH68, Ireland, https://eu-contact.penguin.ie.

For Lepi

Contents

≡

Part Three ≡ Russia's Imperial Land Grab

Cast of Characters

———

DAVID COHEN: Lawyer who served as the Treasury Department's second-ever undersecretary for terrorism and financial intelligence, succeeding Stuart Levey in 2011; oversaw efforts to ramp up pressure on Iran in 2012, including by targeting its central bank and oil revenues.

DAN FRIED: Veteran U.S. diplomat who served as the State Department's first-ever coordinator for sanctions policy from 2013 to 2017; led diplomacy with Europe to impose joint U.S.-EU sanctions on Russia after its 2014 annexation of Crimea.

MARK KIRK: Republican senator from Illinois who advocated for aggressive sanctions against Iran; co-sponsored the Menendez-Kirk amendment in 2011, which levied sanctions on the Central Bank of Iran and established a scheme to reduce Iran's oil sales.

SERGEI LAVROV: Russia's longtime foreign minister, appointed by Vladimir Putin in 2004; negotiated with Secretary of State John Kerry following Russia's 2014 seizure of Crimea and with Secretary of State Tony Blinken before Russia's 2022 full-scale invasion of Ukraine.

STUART LEVEY: Lawyer who served as the Treasury Department's first undersecretary for terrorism and financial intelligence, holding the post from 2004 to 2011; developed a strategy to isolate Iran from the international financial system and later served as chief legal officer of HSBC and CEO of the Diem Association.

JACK LEW: U.S. secretary of the treasury from 2013 to 2017; encouraged Treasury's sanctions officials to work with the department's international economists to develop penalties against Russia; gave a notable speech warning against the overuse of sanctions.

ROBERT LIGHTHIZER: Trade lawyer who served as the U.S. trade representative from 2017 to 2021; vocal critic of free trade and architect of the Trump administration's tariffs on Chinese imports.

BOB MENENDEZ: Democratic senator from New Jersey who pushed the Obama administration to impose harsher sanctions on Iran; co-sponsored the Menendez-Kirk amendment in 2011, which levied sanctions on the Central Bank of Iran and established a scheme to reduce Iran's oil sales.

STEVEN MNUCHIN: U.S. secretary of the treasury from 2017 to 2021 and former Goldman Sachs banker; advocate of free markets who was wary of an economic standoff with China and competed with Robert Lighthizer for control of Trump's trade negotiations with Beijing.

ELVIRA NABIULLINA: Governor of the Central Bank of Russia since 2013 and long-time economic advisor to Vladimir Putin; coordinated Russia's economic response to Western sanctions in both 2014 and 2022.

VICTORIA NULAND: Veteran U.S. diplomat who served as assistant secretary of state for European and Eurasian affairs from 2013 to 2017; played a central role in U.S. policy in response to Russia's 2014 annexation of Crimea and invasion of the Donbas.

MATT POTTINGER: Former China-based reporter who served as senior director for Asia and later deputy national security advisor on the National Security Council during the Trump administration; key architect of a more assertive U.S. policy toward China.

WILBUR ROSS: Veteran private equity investor who served as U.S. secretary of commerce from 2017 to 2021; oversaw Commerce's evolution into a command center for technological competition with China, particularly through the imposition of export controls.

BJOERN SEIBERT: Chief of staff and close advisor to European Commission President Ursula von der Leyen; coordinated EU sanctions policy in response to Russia's 2022 full-scale invasion of Ukraine.

DALEEP SINGH: Former Goldman Sachs trader who served at the Treasury Department during Russia's 2014 annexation of Crimea and later as deputy national security advisor for international economics in the Biden administration; key architect of sanctions against Russia in both 2014 and 2022.

JAKE SULLIVAN: U.S. national security advisor under President Joe Biden; coordinated U.S. policy in response to Russia's 2022 full-scale invasion of Ukraine and declared "small yard and high fence" strategy to keep critical U.S. technology away from China.

ADAM SZUBIN: Director of the Treasury Department's Office of Foreign Assets Control (OFAC) from 2006 to 2015 and later acting undersecretary for terrorism and financial intelligence; key architect of U.S. sanctions against Iran in the years leading up to the 2015 nuclear deal.

URSULA VON DER LEYEN: President of the European Commission since 2019; advocate of tough policy toward Russia, including sanctions and military assistance, following its full-scale invasion of Ukraine in 2022.

MENG WANZHOU: CFO of Huawei and daughter of company founder Ren Zhengfei; charged with violating U.S. sanctions and arrested by Canadian authorities in 2018.

VIKTOR YANUKOVYCH: President of Ukraine from 2010 until 2014, when he fled to Russia amid the Euromaidan protests; ally of Vladimir Putin and advocate of closer Ukrainian ties with Moscow.

JANET YELLEN: Veteran economist who served as chair of the U.S. Federal Reserve from 2014 to 2018 and later as secretary of the treasury in the Biden administration; played a central role in the 2022 sanctions on Russia, often as a voice of caution.

JAVAD ZARIF: Iran's foreign minister under President Hassan Rouhani from 2013 to 2021; led negotiations toward the 2015 nuclear deal with Secretary of State John Kerry and other foreign ministers from the P5+1.

REN ZHENGFEI: Founder and CEO of Huawei, who built the company into the world's leading manufacturer of telecommunications equipment; formerly an officer in China's People's Liberation Army.

Glossary

Blocking sanctions: The strongest form of sanctions deployed by the Treasury Department; the penalty includes both an asset freeze and a transaction ban, effectively cutting off targets from the U.S. financial system and access to the dollar.

CISADA: Comprehensive Iran Sanctions, Accountability, and Divestment Act, which was passed by Congress and signed by President Barack Obama in 2010; the law threatened foreign financial institutions with secondary sanctions if they continued transacting with most Iranian banks.

CHIPS: Clearing House Interbank Payments System, a U.S.-based payment system that is the world's primary mechanism for settling large dollar transactions.

Correspondent bank: A domestic bank that serves as an intermediary for a foreign bank, enabling the foreign bank to access domestic financial services; U.S.-based correspondent banks are particularly important because they allow foreign banks to hold dollar deposits, conduct transactions in dollars, and facilitate cross-border payments on behalf of clients without the need for a physical presence in the United States.

Entity List: Public list managed by the U.S. Commerce Department that identifies foreign companies and individuals subject to American export controls; U.S. firms require a license before selling goods or technology to anyone on the Entity List.

FDPR: Foreign Direct Product Rule, a measure deployed by the Commerce Department to ban the sale of goods to specific end users if they were made using U.S. technology; it rose to prominence when it was deployed against Huawei in 2020.

Foreign exchange reserves: Assets held by a country's central bank or monetary authority that consist of readily convertible currencies—such as the dollar, euro, pound, and yen—as well as gold; foreign exchange reserves are often used to support the value of a domestic currency, pay for imports, and service international debt obligations.

G7: The Group of Seven, a democratic bloc consisting of the United States, the European Union, Germany, France, Italy, the United Kingdom, Canada, and Japan (the EU participates in the G7 as a "non-enumerated member"); the group formerly included Russia and was known as the G8 until Russia's 2014 annexation of Crimea.

IA: Office of International Affairs, a division within the Treasury Department that focuses on promoting U.S. economic growth and preventing global financial instability; IA became increasingly involved in U.S. sanctions policy after Russia's 2014 annexation of Crimea.

IEEPA: International Emergency Economic Powers Act, which grants the U.S. president broad authority to declare a "national emergency" and wield extraordinary powers over the American economy; the law underpins all U.S. sanctions.

ILSA: Iran and Libya Sanctions Act, which Congress passed in 1996 to try to pressure foreign companies to stop investing in Iran's energy sector; later renamed the Iran Sanctions Act (ISA), the law was the first major U.S. attempt to wield secondary sanctions.

JCPOA: Joint Comprehensive Plan of Action, also known as the Iran nuclear deal; a diplomatic agreement reached in 2015 between Iran and the P5+1 exchanging sanctions relief for constraints on Iran's nuclear program.

Menendez-Kirk amendment: An amendment to the annual Defense Department spending bill that passed Congress in late 2011; it levied sanctions on the Central Bank of Iran and established a scheme to reduce Iran's oil sales.

OFAC: Office of Foreign Assets Control, the agency within the Treasury Department in charge of sanctions policy and enforcement.

P5+1: Negotiating bloc consisting of the five permanent members of the UN Security Council (the United States, China, France, Russia, and the United Kingdom) plus Germany, which participated in talks with Iran over its nuclear program, culminating in the JCPOA in 2015.

Petrodollars: U.S. dollars earned by oil-exporting countries through the sale of oil; typically used to invest in U.S. government debt, corporate bonds, and stocks; pay for imports; and accumulate foreign exchange reserves.

SDN List: Specially Designated Nationals and Blocked Persons List; a public list managed by OFAC that identifies foreign companies and individuals that are subject to U.S. blocking sanctions.

Secondary sanctions: Economic penalties aimed not at the primary target of sanctions but rather at foreign banks, companies, or individuals that do business with the primary target; for instance, if an Iranian bank is a primary target of U.S. sanctions, penalties on a Chinese bank that does business with that Iranian bank would constitute "secondary sanctions."

SWIFT: Society for Worldwide Interbank Financial Telecommunications, a Brussels-based financial messaging service that is widely used among banks to send and receive information about transactions; SWIFT is used to share payment instructions, not to settle payments.

TFI: Office of Terrorism and Financial Intelligence, a division within the Treasury Department that focuses on sanctions and counterterrorist financing; TFI oversees OFAC and Treasury's in-house intelligence agency.

U-turn transactions: Cross-border transactions between two non-U.S. financial institutions that use U.S.-based correspondent banks as an intermediary, either to complete a transaction in dollars or to use the dollar as a means of converting one foreign currency into another; often used as a chokepoint for U.S. financial sanctions.

INTRODUCTION

Win Without Fighting

There are places in the world that, owing to geography alone, appear repeatedly across the pages of history. The Bosphorus, the narrow waterway that cuts through the center of Istanbul and marks the boundary between Europe and Asia, is one such place. It is the passageway from the resource-rich Black Sea to the ports of the Mediterranean and the oceans beyond. It is a vital crossroads, a place where civilizations trade and jostle for power, where empires rise and fall.

In its golden age in the fifth century BC, Athens, the leading city-state of ancient Greece, depended on free navigation of the Bosphorus for access to food. Ships loaded grain from the fertile fields of Ukraine and dried fish from Crimea and sailed south through the Bosphorus toward Athens, protected on their journey by a string of imperial outposts and the fearsome Athenian navy. This fact was not lost on Athens's biggest rival, Sparta. The twenty-seven-year Peloponnesian War came to an end when the Spartan navy destroyed the Athenian fleet at Aegospotami and seized control of the Bosphorus, severing Athens's food supply and starving it into submission. The Bosphorus had been the Athenians' lifeline, and the Bosphorus was where their empire met its demise.

Seven centuries later, on the banks of the same strait, the Roman emperor Constantine founded the city of Constantinople, known today as Istanbul. Constantinople grew into Europe's largest and wealthiest metropolis, its skyline punctuated by the Hagia Sophia's majestic dome. It served as the capital of the eastern branch of the Roman Empire for more than a thousand years until coming under Ottoman attack in the fifteenth century. After a

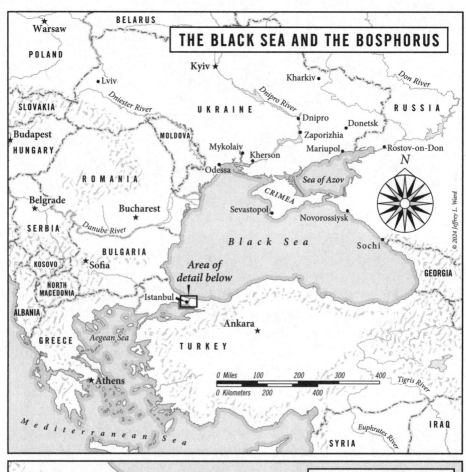

THE BLACK SEA AND THE BOSPHORUS

Warsaw
BELARUS
POLAND
Lviv
Kyiv
Kharkiv
Dnipro River
Don River
SLOVAKIA
UKRAINE
RUSSIA
Budapest
MOLDOVA
Dnipro
Donetsk
HUNGARY
Mykolaiv
Zaporizhia
Rostov-on-Don
Kherson
Mariupol
ROMANIA
Odessa
Sea of Azov
Belgrade
CRIMEA
Bucharest
Sevastopol
Novorossiysk
SERBIA
Danube River
Black Sea
Sochi
KOSOVO
BULGARIA
Sofia
GEORGIA
NORTH
MACEDONIA
Area of
detail below
Istanbul
ALBANIA
Ankara
GREECE
Aegean Sea
TURKEY
Athens
0 Miles 100 200 300 400
Tigris River
M e d i t e r r a n e a n   S e a
0 Kilometers 200 400
Euphrates River
IRAQ
SYRIA

© 2024 Jeffrey L. Ward

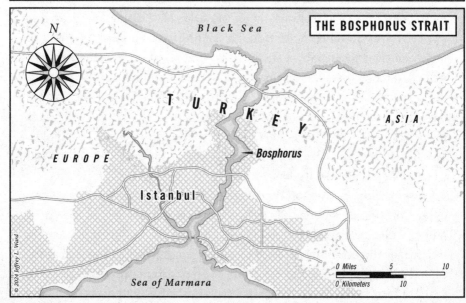

THE BOSPHORUS STRAIT

Black Sea
T U R K E Y
ASIA
Bosphorus
EUROPE
Istanbul
0 Miles 5 10
Sea of Marmara
0 Kilometers 10

© 2024 Jeffrey L. Ward

protracted siege, Constantinople fell, extinguishing the last embers of the Roman Empire. From its new capital on the Bosphorus, the Ottoman Empire flourished for centuries to come. The Ottomans, like their predecessors, fought hard to fend off other great powers that coveted the strait, from the Crimean War to World War I.

That history has so often been made in this one spot is no accident. The Bosphorus is the epitome of a chokepoint: a gateway so critical to international trade that controlling it confers immense power—and blocking it can bring an enemy to its knees.

On December 5, 2022, with Russia's brutal war against Ukraine raging a few hundred miles away, an ominous scene unfolded at the mouth of the Bosphorus. As far as the eye could see, a line of colossal oil tankers, some nearly a thousand feet long, formed a maritime traffic jam. Their transit through the strait was blocked. News of the standstill spread quickly. The Bosphorus is one of the busiest shipping lanes in the world today and an essential artery for the energy and food trade. Closing it for any prolonged period would unleash chaos on the global economy.

What was causing this gridlock?

It was not a hostile gunboat or battleship. Nor was it a shipping accident—an ever-present risk in the Bosphorus, whose sharp bends and fierce currents make it one of the world's hardest waterways to navigate. Gumming up the works on that December day were new regulations, issued by the United States and its closest allies, which had gone into effect at 12:01 a.m. that morning.

Under the regulations, U.S. and European firms could no longer ship, insure, or finance cargoes of Russian oil sold for any price above $60 per barrel. The policy, known as the "price cap," was intended to cut the Kremlin's oil revenues and thereby undermine its war effort in Ukraine. The price cap packed a punch because trading oil without using Western services and institutions was next to impossible. A typical barrel of Russian oil was shipped aboard a European tanker whose insurance was British and whose cargo was paid for in U.S. dollars. The West had a near-monopoly on maritime insurance, in particular: its insurers covered more than 95 percent of all oil cargoes. Now, Western governments were exploiting this dominance to stem the flow of petrodollars to the Kremlin.

Turkey did not formally support the price cap, but the Turkish officials monitoring traffic through the Bosphorus were acutely aware of its implications: if a tanker was in violation of the policy, it would likely lose its insurance coverage, leaving the Turkish government vulnerable in the event of an oil spill or any other catastrophic accident. As a result, skittish Turkish officials were demanding extra proof that each tanker was fully insured before it could transit the strait, a requirement that led to the mounting congestion. A few paragraphs of regulatory jargon, published on the website of the U.S. Treasury Department in Washington, had ground traffic to a halt at a vital waterway more than five thousand miles away.

It was the latest in a series of moves by Western governments to squeeze the Russian economy in the wake of Vladimir Putin's grisly invasion of Ukraine. Every economic penalty levied against Russia in this pressure campaign was like the price cap: simple regulations, issued at the stroke of a pen by little-known American and European bureaucrats. But their effects rippled far and wide. The measures reshaped trade and financial flows, re-wiring the global economy. They restructured relationships between world powers, sketching the blueprints of a new international order.

The economic offensive against Russia is part of an extraordinary evolu-tion in U.S. foreign policy. To address the most pressing global security challenges, the United States has come to rely on an arsenal of economic weapons, chief among them sanctions, over the use of military force. Eco-nomic weapons have existed for centuries, but in the past two decades, their sophistication and impact have grown by leaps and bounds. In a world econ-omy interconnected by half a century of globalization and neoliberal re-forms, the actions of U.S. officials can send shock waves across the globe at breathtaking speed.

This is economic warfare. It is how America fights its most important geopolitical battles today. From thwarting Iran's pursuit of nuclear weapons to checking Russian imperialism and China's bid for world mastery, the United States has reached into its economic arsenal to get the job done.

In the process, the world economy has become a battlefield. Its weapons take the form of sanctions, export controls, and investment restrictions. Its commanders are not generals and admirals but lawyers, diplomats, and economists. Its foot soldiers are not brave men and women who volunteer for military service but business executives who seek to maximize profits yet often find they have no option other than to obey Washington's marching orders. And America's strength in these battles stems not from its gargan-tuan defense budget but from its primacy in international finance and tech-nology.

This is a new kind of war. But economic warfare itself is as old as history.

In 1958, Thomas Schelling, the Nobel Prize–winning economist and nuclear strategist, defined economic warfare as "*economic* means by which damage is imposed on other countries or the threat of damage used to bring pressure on them." As Schelling pointed out, the distinction between economic and conventional war is *how* each is waged: Sanctioning an adversary's bank is an act of economic war, whereas bombing that same bank is an act of conventional war. Both may aim to shut the bank down, but they seek to accomplish this goal in very different ways. Herein lies the main reason policymakers are so tempted by economic warfare: its tactics are inherently *nonviolent*. What makes today's economic wars novel is the highly interdependent world economy, which amplifies their impact and makes their aftershocks hard to contain.

═

When asked which candidate he supported in America's 2008 presidential election, Alan Greenspan, the recently retired chairman of the U.S. Federal Reserve, neatly summarized the prevailing economic wisdom of the time. "National security aside, it hardly makes any difference who will be the next president," he said. "The world is governed by market forces." The post–Cold War neoliberal order was built by and for multinational corporations. Their CEOs were the new titans of history. Officeholders in Washington, Beijing, or any other world capital were mere onlookers and occasional administrators.

Greenspan was not alone in this assessment. The "galloping new system of international finance," the American financier Walter Wriston wrote in 1988, was "not built by politicians, economists, central bankers or finance ministers, nor did high-level international conferences produce a master plan." On the contrary, it was built by "the men and women who interconnected the planet with telecommunications and computers" and the bankers who "immediately drove their trades over the new global electronic infrastructure." Wriston was the most powerful banker of his time, leading Citibank from the late 1960s to the mid-1980s. He twice turned down offers to serve as the U.S. secretary of the treasury: as the top CEO on Wall Street, he knew public office would not confer any economic or political privilege he did not already enjoy.

In his 1992 manifesto *The Twilight of Sovereignty*, published a year after the collapse of the Soviet Union, Wriston predicted that national governments would grow obsolete as the twin forces of finance and information technology took command of the levers of history. Multinational corporations would stitch together global supply chains, further locking in the dominance of industry over politics. "As these alliances grow and strengthen over time," Wriston argued, "it will become harder and harder for politicians to unscramble the emerging global economy and reassert their declining power to regulate national life." Wriston was describing a process and system that we now call "globalization."

The globalized economy was a seemingly autonomous machine, operating beyond the reach of traditional state institutions, but it was by no means decentralized. The system that neoliberal reformers such as Greenspan created was centered on the U.S. dollar, whose role in everything from buying oil to investing capital would continue growing long after America's post–World War II dominance in trade began to decline. Meanwhile, CEOs such as Wriston built a centralized financial network that enabled banks and companies to move money around the world at the speed of light. Wriston's motivation, like that of other executives who try to build infrastructure and set standards, was simple: to collect a kind of toll and reap outsize profits.

But in developing and connecting these systems, Greenspan, Wriston, and other globalizers like them created something else, too: chokepoints. And these chokepoints, it turned out, lent themselves to political exploitation.

Great powers once rose and survived by controlling geographic chokepoints like the Bosphorus. American power in the globalized economy relies on chokepoints of a different kind. Among them is the U.S. dollar, the default currency for international trade and finance. Other chokepoints include the main banks and networks that move money around the world and the intellectual property and technical know-how that underpin a vast array of essential technologies, notably the advanced computer chips at the core of the digital economy. The United States has used its hold over these chokepoints to pioneer a new, hard-hitting style of economic warfare. The result has been a stunning resurgence of state power in a world supposedly governed by market forces.

═══

As a college student in the years after 9/11, I grappled with a contradiction. The United States was the most powerful country on earth, but it struggled to translate that power into solving global security problems. Few foreign policy disasters laid bare this paradox better than the U.S. wars in Afghanistan and Iraq, which cost America and its opponents untold blood and treasure with little to show for it. There had to be a better way.

"The acme of skill," Sun Tzu wrote in *The Art of War*, is not "to win one hundred victories in one hundred battles," but "to subdue the enemy without fighting." I have devoted much of my career to exploring how economic power can advance this goal. I served on the teams at the U.S. State Department that designed and negotiated Western sanctions against Russia after its 2014 annexation of Crimea, and whose economic pressure campaign against Iran led to a landmark nuclear deal in 2015. I've advised the secretary of state, the chairman of the Joint Chiefs of Staff, and the top sanctions official at the Treasury Department. I've written widely about economic warfare, counseled companies on how to navigate the sanctions landscape, and taught a graduate-level course on the subject at Columbia University. Through these experiences, I've participated directly in some of the history recounted in these pages and worked closely with many of the main characters.

But this book does not rely on my own memories. It blends research, analysis, and extensive interviews with more than one hundred of the key players in the events described, highlighting inflection points, interpreting their significance, and pulling back the curtain on the places where economic wars are fought—places like the windowless warren of the White House Situation Room, the gilded diplomatic halls of Europe, the gleaming banking headquarters of Wall Street and the City of London, the sprawling compounds of the Kremlin and Zhongnanhai, and the Strait of Hormuz, where tankers carrying one-fifth of the world's oil supply slip uneasily past Iranian warships. The narrative follows the protagonists in their moments of decision, as the fairest and most instructive way to assess choices made in the past is to do so without the benefit of hindsight. To that end, the book is structured chronologically.

Part One answers some of the most basic questions about economic warfare against the backdrop of globalization—*Why does the world economy work this way? How did we get here?*—with an emphasis on the people and events in the second half of the twentieth century and the early years of the twenty-first that created the system we have today.

Parts Two through Five detail four consequential episodes between 2006 and the present, a period I call the Age of Economic Warfare. These years saw the development of the most significant and novel economic weapons, which the United States first deployed against Iran (Part Two), then Russia

(Part Three), then China (Part Four), before combining them in overwhelming fashion against Russia again in 2022 (Part Five). The book ends by exploring the fragmented world economy left in the wake of these events (Part Six).

Economic fragmentation was not part of the plan. Indeed, America deployed its new economic weapons with an unspoken assumption that it could use them at relatively low cost—that they would not, for instance, remake the global economy itself. This assumption came under increasing strain throughout the 2010s and shattered on the anvil of Putin's 2022 war against Ukraine.

That war—and the massive economic penalties levied by the West in response—marks a hinge in history. In the years ahead, economic weapons will grow more pervasive and powerful. Economic warfare, now a baseline feature of our world, will permeate other areas of foreign policy, global economics, domestic politics, and business. The result will be a scramble for economic security that redraws the geopolitical map and ends globalization as we know it. Those who fear U.S. economic warfare and seek to insulate themselves from it will be pitted against those who harbor greater fear of China's potential to wield economic weapons of its own. A third group—the "swing states"—will try to straddle both camps, giving its members significant influence but also exposing them to danger.

The United States must prepare for this future. America's economic arsenal has demonstrated that it can inflict tremendous damage, but it has not proven that it can reliably advance U.S. strategic goals. Part of the reason for this mixed track record is that American economic warriors often shoot from the hip, forced to react to crises without much advance planning. While this ad hoc approach had few global repercussions when the targets were small and isolated adversaries such as Cuba and North Korea, today's economic wars against China and Russia are a different matter. America's current economic weapons are durable but not indestructible. If used recklessly, they could be broken forever or trigger unforeseen economic and political repercussions that come back to haunt us. It's little wonder that some veterans of America's economic wars have been urging caution: former Secretary of the Treasury Jack Lew, for one, has warned that the "overuse of sanctions could undermine our leadership position within the global economy." Yet simply discarding these powerful tools would leave Washington at a grave disadvantage in a world of intensifying geopolitical competition. For the United States to prevail in future economic wars, it will need to pair its economic might with strategic wisdom.

In 405 BC, stopping traffic at the Bosphorus required a stunning Spartan naval victory and the destruction of the once-dominant Athenian fleet. In 2022, all it took was a regulation posted online by the U.S. government. That is a fearsome power, made all the more chilling by its seeming inscrutability. This book aims to demystify that power by explaining how it came to be, how it works, and what it means for the world. It is also a book about the choices America has made—for good and for ill—and how it can do better.

PART ONE

Building the Chokepoints

1

The Old Way: A Brief History of Economic War from Pericles to Saddam

Go back to any moment in history and you'll find governments seeking to follow Sun Tzu's advice: win without fighting.

Economic warfare has always offered one path to this goal. Depriving an adversary of money, resources, and other fruits of commerce can sap its will, compelling it to make concessions. Such tactics can also exhibit one's own economic power for all to see and fear. Even if the enemy refuses to give in, economic warfare can degrade its industrial capacity and weaken its military, hindering its ability to fight should armed conflict break out.

One of the earliest documented economic wars unfolded in ancient Greece in 432 BC. As tensions boiled between Athens and Sparta, the Athenian leader Pericles issued a sweeping trade embargo on one of Sparta's allies, the city-state of Megara. The Megarian Decree barred the Megarians from both the market of Athens and all ports of the Athenian Empire, which included most of the major coastal and island powers of the Aegean. The embargo hit hard. The playwright Aristophanes wrote that it left the Megarians "slowly starving" and caused them to plead for help from the Spartans.

Historians disagree about Pericles's intentions, but the most persuasive account is that he used the embargo to try to deter a broader war. Megara had recently sided with Corinth in a battle against Corcyra, an Athenian ally, and Pericles wanted to impress on other Greek city-states, chief among them Sparta, the risks of opposing Athens and its vast naval power. By making an example of Megara, Pericles aimed to dissuade others from challenging Athens. As the English classicist Sir Alfred Zimmern put it, "Pericles determined to give a demonstration of what sea power really meant."

The Megarian Decree showed both the strengths and weaknesses of economic warfare. Thanks to Athens's naval dominance, compliance with the embargo was widespread, and it put immense economic pressure on the Megarians. But the measure ultimately failed to forestall war. In fact, it may have accelerated the descent into war by convincing the Spartans that peaceful coexistence with Athens was impossible. Pericles hoped to avoid war by threatening Athens's adversaries with starvation. Instead, he convinced them that Athens was reckless and needed to fall. War came, and Athens fell.

The episode points to an enduring problem in economic warfare: the harm it inflicts does not always elicit the hoped-for policy changes, and its unintended consequences can sometimes precipitate the very outcome it aimed to prevent. Indeed, the failures of economic warfare are better known than its successes.

In 1806, the French emperor Napoleon imposed a wide-ranging trade embargo on Britain, hoping to force his biggest rival to accept France's expanding European empire. Known as the Continental System, the policy prohibited British trade with all territories under Napoleon's control, including Austria, Belgium, the Netherlands, Poland, Spain, and much of Germany and Italy.

The embargo was a total bust. Unlike Periclean Athens, Napoleonic France did not control the seas—Britain did, so compliance was shoddy. British goods continued to find their way into Europe, and the British economy did not suffer as much as Napoleon had anticipated. "To keep the English away from the Continent by blockade without possessing fleets is just as impossible as to forbid the birds to build their nests in our country," concluded a contemporary report from Germany. The lands under French control bristled at the inconveniences of the embargo, as did other powers on the continent. After Tsar Alexander I stopped cooperating with the policy, Napoleon made the fateful decision to invade Russia, and the ensuing campaign so decimated his army that he was eventually forced into an ignominious retreat. The Continental System debacle illustrates another perennial challenge of economic warfare: for sanctions to be effective, they usually require the cooperation of other states—a difficult task, especially when those states are asked to make sacrifices.

Fast-forward a hundred years, and we find the world grasping for peaceful solutions to conflict. By 1919, the Great War had torn Europe apart, killing as many as 20 million people and unraveling European empires in quick succession. At the Paris Peace Conference that year, U.S. President Woodrow Wilson and other leaders conceived of a new organization called the League of Nations, whose purpose would be to preserve world peace. Under the auspices of the League, states would collectively commit to punish any would-be aggressor with devastating economic sanctions. If all member states unified behind such sanctions, they could, in Wilson's words, unleash "something more tremendous than war." Aggressors would back down without a shot being fired. "A nation that is boycotted is a nation that is in sight of surrender," Wilson declared. "Apply this economic, peaceful, silent, deadly remedy and there will be no need for force."

It did not take long for Wilson's dream to be dashed. Congress voted down America's entry into the League of Nations, meaning that an organization devoted in part to economic warfare would miss out on support from the world's largest economy. When Japan invaded Manchuria in 1931, the League's members could not agree on economic sanctions. Four years later, when Italian leader Benito Mussolini set out to conquer Ethiopia, the League cobbled together a halfhearted trade embargo that exempted key commodities such as oil, coal, and steel. The impact was negligible. Italy had stockpiled strategic materials before the invasion, and it continued to trade openly with both America and Germany, neither of which joined the embargo. Mussolini's troops soon captured Ethiopia's capital, Addis Ababa, and the League promptly lifted sanctions. Military force had succeeded, and what the League called the "economic weapon" had failed.

The ramifications went well beyond Ethiopia. Many scholars have pointed to the League's powerlessness as one of the factors that emboldened Adolf

*Pericles, Napoleon, and Woodrow Wilson: three leaders whose
plans for economic warfare did not turn out as they hoped.*

Hitler to launch his own war of conquest a few years later. If Britain, France, and other League members lacked the resolve to punish Italian aggression, surely they would not stand in the way of a German blitzkrieg, either. Whether this is true or not, the episode did much to discredit economic warfare. It mattered little if, in theory, a total economic boycott could deter war. At the time, bringing such pressure to bear still required unity among fractious world powers, each with its own narrow interests. It would be more than another half century before the global financial system evolved to render that elusive unity unnecessary.

=

Before the turn of the twenty-first century, most economic wars faced the same pitfalls that doomed the Megarian Decree, the Continental System, and the League of Nations. Imposing serious economic pressure required formidable naval power, a broad international coalition, or both. The first requirement, naval force, blurred the line between economic war and conventional war, making economic weapons more of a prelude or supplement to military action than a replacement for it. The second requirement, international unity, was hard to galvanize in all but the rarest of circumstances, and harder still to maintain for a prolonged period. Together, these conditions limited the efficacy of economic weapons, especially during peacetime.

Even when underwritten by naval power and international support, economic wars often proved costly and challenging. The United Nations' embargo against Iraq in the 1990s is a case in point. In August 1990, Iraqi dictator Saddam Hussein launched an invasion of Kuwait, Iraq's small, oil-rich neighbor. Iraqi forces rapidly occupied Kuwait, and Saddam summarily annexed it, designating Kuwait the nineteenth province of Iraq. It was a shameless land grab—and it happened at a moment when, as in 1919, world leaders believed they were opening a new era of peace.

Nine months earlier, the Berlin Wall had fallen. The Soviet Union would survive another year, but the geopolitical stalemate between East and West was coming to an end. Mikhail Gorbachev condemned the Iraqi invasion of Kuwait as a "blatant violation" of international law and pledged his support for global efforts to punish Saddam. Within days of the attack, the UN Security Council unanimously adopted a resolution banning all trade with Iraq. The UN's condition for lifting sanctions was the withdrawal of all Iraqi forces from Kuwait.

Because every UN member state was legally obligated to comply with the resolution and a U.S.-led naval blockade implemented the policy by force, the sanctions devastated Iraq's economy. Trade with Iraq plummeted. The country's oil sales, which accounted for 60 percent of its GDP and nearly all of its export earnings, were almost wiped out in a matter of months. For a moment, it seemed as if the post–Cold War United Nations could redeem Woodrow Wilson's vision and check military aggression by economic pressure alone. Speaking before Congress in September 1990, President George H. W. Bush struck a tone of accomplishment. "We're now in sight of a United Nations," he said, "that performs as envisioned by its founders." But he'd spoken too soon. Weeks dragged into months, and Saddam refused to reverse course. Eventually, the UN Security Council authorized military action to expel Iraqi troops from Kuwait.

The ensuing war wasn't much of a fight. It took just 100 hours for U.S. and allied forces to rout the Iraqi military in February 1991. Once again, military force had succeeded where economic pressure had failed.

Even after Kuwait regained its independence, the UN kept its economic embargo against Iraq in place, now with the declared aim of stopping Saddam's pursuit of a nuclear bomb and other weapons of mass destruction. Until inspectors could verify that Iraq had eliminated its nuclear, chemical, and biological weapons programs, the world would continue to ban trade with Iraq.

The embargo would last more than a decade, but it proved difficult to maintain. For one thing, enforcement required the continuous deployment of naval forces. Warships from more than twenty countries, commanded by U.S. naval officers, monitored maritime traffic in and out of Iraq's ports. Whenever the sailors grew suspicious of a vessel, they dispatched a team via boat or helicopter to board and inspect it. Starting in 1995, their work was made more complicated by the UN's decision to allow limited Iraqi oil exports to resume, a reprieve intended to mitigate the embargo's severe impact on ordinary Iraqis. The Oil-for-Food program, as it was known, permitted Iraq to sell oil so long as it used the proceeds to buy food, medicine, and other humanitarian products. To ensure compliance with these terms, U.S. officials had to scrutinize every Iraqi oil shipment, verifying that the petroleum was accurately labeled and that the proceeds were used appropriately. This complex task involved poring over contracts and occasionally even sending out oil samples for laboratory testing.

It was an arduous and costly operation, and not entirely effective. Smugglers

developed ever-more clandestine methods to evade detection. Swashbuckling oil traders saw the embargo as a moneymaking opportunity; if they
were caught violating it, they would chalk it up as a cost of doing business.
Saddam demanded kickbacks from oil customers, which they often paid
in secret. Saddam banked almost $2 billion from these side payments. The
Central Intelligence Agency (CIA) estimated that he collected as much as
$11 billion from oil smuggling. Iraq was under intense economic pressure,
but oil was leaking from every seam, and enough money was flowing back in
to keep Saddam on his feet.

Meanwhile, international support for the embargo withered. Iraq was
mired in a humanitarian crisis, a consequence not only of the embargo but
of the damage caused by the Gulf War and the pervasive corruption of Saddam's regime. Hunger and infant mortality spiked as Saddam opted to sell oil
via smugglers so that he could siphon off profits for himself instead of using
them under the terms of the Oil-for-Food program. By the time George W.
Bush entered the White House in 2001, the embargo was universally reviled,
condemned as inhumane by some and ineffective by others. Its perceived
failure contributed in no small part to Bush's disastrous decision to invade
Iraq in 2003.

The irony was that the embargo achieved its main objective: it crushed
Saddam's nuclear program. Despite the Iraqi government's relative success
in bypassing sanctions, it still lost hundreds of billions of dollars' worth of
oil proceeds along with access to important military equipment. The policy
did not temper Saddam's ambitions, but it undoubtedly hampered his ability
to realize them. As Hans Blix, the UN's chief weapons inspector in Iraq, put
it, "The UN and the world had succeeded in disarming Iraq without knowing it."

All told, the Iraq embargo was a messy, tragic lesson in modern economic warfare. On the one hand, it succeeded in kneecapping a dictator's
military and preventing the emergence of a new nuclear power in the Middle
East. On the other hand, it caused undue harm to Iraqi civilians; its enforcement required a thirteen-year naval blockade, which cost at least $1 billion
per year and kept American forces on a continuous war footing; and it
eroded the international unity at the UN that had emerged when Saddam
invaded Kuwait. Worst of all, even though it hollowed out Iraq's nuclear
program, it did not stop America's 2003 invasion of Iraq. Instead of offering
a viable alternative to war, the embargo merely served as a bridge from one
war to another.

The fiasco soured the United States and other world powers on economic warfare. The costs were too high and the benefits too low. Changing this equation would require a fundamental shift in the global financial system, a shift that would free economic warriors from past constraints. As it turned out, this change was well underway in the 1990s, though it would still be some years before its implications became clear. To wage the next economic war, U.S. officials would not need a naval blockade, nor would they need to rely so heavily on the UN. They would need only to map the pipes of the world economy laid by central bankers like Alan Greenspan and CEOs like Walter Wriston, find the chokepoints, and squeeze.

2

Invisible Infrastructure

Adam Smith, the eighteenth-century Scottish economist and pioneering theorist of capitalism, famously described the free market as guided by an "invisible hand." That unseen force—human self-interest—ensured a more efficient allocation of resources than any central planner could devise. Today's global economy relies on another unseen force, one that is far less theoretical: the invisible infrastructure that enables cross-border finance, which in turn underlies everything from commodity sales and global supply chains to international trade and foreign investment. Just about every major transaction in the global economy relies on this infrastructure, no matter which countries or companies are involved. If you do any business outside your home country, you use this infrastructure, whether you're aware of it or not.

At the heart of this infrastructure is a currency: the U.S. dollar. It has rightly become commonplace to think of the dollar as the global reserve currency and U.S. Treasuries as the safest asset for investors worldwide, attracting everyone from farmers in the Midwest to the Chinese Communist Party. The dollar is the world's preeminent store of value. Central banks hold 60 percent of all foreign exchange reserves in dollars, three times the share of the second-place euro and more than twenty times that of the Chinese renminbi. America is also home to the world's two largest stock markets, the New York Stock Exchange and the NASDAQ, both of which boast market capitalizations several times larger than those of their biggest foreign rivals. Valued at over $50 trillion, the U.S. bond market also dwarfs those of the rest of the world. And when firms anywhere turn to international capital markets for cash, they almost always borrow in dollars: 70 percent of foreign-currency debt is denominated in dollars.

Impressive as these stats are, they represent just the tip of the iceberg. The dollar is also the world's default unit of account and medium of exchange, which means that access to it is a necessity for participation in the global economy. When two firms based in different countries trade with each other, the buyer must first convert its currency to that of the seller. Consider an Indian farmer exporting rice to Saudi Arabia. To pay for the rice, the Saudi importer must convert Saudi riyals to Indian rupees. But there is no way for a bank to convert these two currencies directly. Saudi banks do not hold rupees, and Indian banks do not accept riyals. The global economy is too complex and the number of currencies too diverse for a single bank to hold in reserve every kind of currency it might encounter. Banks typically hold significant stocks of only two currencies: the currency of their home country and the U.S. dollar. To purchase the Indian rice, the Saudi importer's bank must first convert riyals to dollars and then use those dollars to buy rupees on the foreign exchange market. The dollar will have served as a way station even in a transaction that involved no American firms.

This explains why the U.S. dollar is involved in nearly 90 percent of foreign exchange transactions even though the United States accounts for less than 10 percent of global exports. Of the top ten most common currency pairings for foreign exchange trades, all but one include the dollar. Every day, traders swap U.S. dollars for Swiss francs more frequently than they swap the euro or the Chinese renminbi for any other currency besides the dollar.

In addition to the dollar itself, the invisible infrastructure undergirding the world economy includes banks and other middlemen that facilitate most cross-border transactions. Many of these institutions are American, and those that aren't still follow U.S. law because they depend on the ability to operate in the United States to function.

Now consider an Indian refinery that imports oil from Saudi Arabia. To pay for this purchase, the Indian refinery needs to wire dollars to the Saudi oil company. (For reasons we'll soon learn, oil, the world's most traded commodity, is priced in dollars.) Because most banks do not retain accounts with one another, the wire transfer would have to go through correspondent accounts at a major bank in New York. That bank—say, Citibank or JPMorgan Chase—would debit the account of the Indian refinery's bank and credit that of the Saudi oil company's bank. To do this, the wire would be cleared

through one of two U.S.-based payment systems—the Clearing House Interbank Payments System (CHIPS) or the Federal Reserve's Fedwire system. If
the Indian refinery, the Saudi oil company, or either of their banks were
barred from these systems, the deal could not be completed.

The U.S. government is the gatekeeper at each point along this invisible
infrastructure. With a simple executive order, the president can deny a foreign firm access to any or every part of it. (Typically, the president delegates
this power to officials at the Treasury and State Departments, many of whom
will be introduced in the pages that follow.) If banks ignore these decrees or
attempt clever schemes to circumvent them, they risk harsh punishments by
the Justice Department and other U.S. law enforcement agencies. In the past
fifteen years, the United States has hit multiple banks, including ones headquartered abroad, with huge penalties for violating U.S. sanctions. The
French bank BNP Paribas was fined nearly $9 billion in 2014; the UK-based
HSBC almost $2 billion in 2012—penalties too steep to be written off as
merely a cost of doing business. In both cases, the Justice Department also
installed independent monitors at the banks to supervise compliance reforms for years thereafter. And even though both banks were headquartered
outside the United States, they had little choice but to pay up and comply
with the U.S. government's orders: the alternative—permanently losing
access to the dollar and the rest of the invisible infrastructure—would be
far worse.

The result is that global banks—whether based in New York, London,
Frankfurt, Hong Kong, or elsewhere—have become reliable infantrymen on
the front line of U.S. sanctions enforcement. In recent years, Washington
has started conscripting firms outside the financial sector, too. U.S. authorities have smacked the Chinese telecom giant ZTE with more than $2 billion
in fines for violating U.S. law by reselling American technology to Iran, and
it has made clear that it will aggressively enforce U.S. sanctions regulations
even when the only touchpoint with America is a server in a computer network. This expansion of power will undoubtedly continue in the years ahead
as businesses in every industry rewire their operations to placate the world's
sanctions police.

≡

These developments have immense ramifications. They have radically reduced the cost of deploying economic weapons while simultaneously super-

charging their impact. The United States no longer needs to commit to an expensive and risky naval blockade to make sanctions bite, nor does it need political unity at the UN. At the stroke of a pen, the U.S. president can impose economic penalties far more severe than the blockades and embargoes of old.

Critically, the invisible infrastructure allows America to wield economic weapons even against fellow great powers. Unless it's ready to fight a nuclear-armed adversary, the United States would recoil at imposing a blockade of Chinese or Russian ports, which those countries would view as an act of war. UN-backed sanctions against China or Russia are impossible since Beijing and Moscow possess veto power as permanent members of the UN Security Council. But over the past decade, America has targeted both China and Russia by weaponizing its control over the global economy, leaving the rest of the world scrambling to adapt.

How did the United States come by these economic superpowers? The answer lies in the transformation of the world economy that began in the 1970s and accelerated in the 1990s after the end of the Cold War. It is the story of globalization—first of finance, then of supply chains. And paradoxically, it begins with a fateful decision at a moment when the U.S. economy seemed at risk of inexorable decline.

3

Finance Unchained

On a warm morning in early August 1971, a French warship slipped out of the mists of the Atlantic Ocean and into the waters of New York Harbor. In its hold was something potentially more menacing than ammunition: empty space. The French government had sent the warship to pack up a literal pile of gold from the vaults of the Federal Reserve Bank of New York and haul it back to France. A few days later, Britain asked the United States to backstop all British holdings at the New York Fed by transferring $3 billion in gold from Fort Knox to New York. France and Britain had both lost confidence in the strength of the dollar, so they were racing to convert their dollars into gold before America's hoard of the shiny metal ran out.

U.S. President Richard Nixon retreated to Camp David with his economic team to devise a response. This would prove to be a crucial moment in the economic history of the twentieth century. Complying with the French and British demands could trigger the mother of all bank runs, draining America's gold reserves and making it impossible for the United States to fulfill its obligations at the center of the world financial system. The alternative would be no less dramatic: denying the requests, ending the convertibility of dollars into gold at a fixed rate, and allowing the U.S. currency to float, its value set by the whims of the market. The former option risked chaotic upheaval in the global economy. The latter might stave off chaos, but it would be an admission that the United States had relinquished the driver's seat. Both options were bad, but Nixon had to choose. At stake was nothing less than the rules of the global economy, which had stood strong since the end of World War II.

To grasp why the prospect of delinking the dollar from gold was so momentous, it's necessary to understand how the two came to be linked in the first place. In 1944, with World War II still raging, officials from Allied nations gathered at the Mount Washington Hotel in Bretton Woods, New Hampshire, to discuss how economic dysfunction contributed to the war's outbreak—and how better rules might prevent the same thing from happening again. The Allies agreed that after World War I, structural flaws in the international economy had sown discord among nations. The unraveling of the gold standard amid the Great Depression ushered in an ever-shifting patchwork of exchange rates, which enabled governments to engage in competitive currency devaluations, throw up tariffs, and pursue other beggar-thy-neighbor policies. All the while, speculators rapidly moved money from one country to another, spreading financial panic. The result was poverty, political strife, and, finally, war. With a more rigorous, rules-based economic system in place, perhaps World War II could have been avoided.

From these insights arose what would become known as the Bretton Woods system, the rules of the road for the post–World War II economy. At the heart of Bretton Woods were fixed exchange rates: the dollar was pegged to gold at $35 an ounce, and all other currencies were pegged to the dollar. These exchange rates were adjustable only within a narrow band; anything beyond a 1 percent move required consultations with the newly created International Monetary Fund (IMF). Bretton Woods also included restrictions on the movement of money across borders, walling off a key route through which financial instability had spread during the Great Depression. The dollar was now at the center of the world economy. But by fixing exchange rates and limiting cross-border capital flows, the Allies created a heavily constrained international financial system—which is exactly what John Maynard Keynes, the renowned British economist and a principal architect of Bretton Woods, thought was necessary.

Keynes believed that barriers to cross-border capital movements were particularly important for maintaining postwar stability. Without such barriers, capital would flow swiftly to wherever interest rates were highest, reducing governments' control over their domestic economic policies. This was problematic because governments needed to be free to set their own interest rates, pursue social spending, and build national welfare states to recover from the devastation of war. Each country therefore had to be able to stop foreign currency from arriving at its shores by imposing capital controls, ranging from hefty taxes on foreign investments to outright bans on currency conversions. "Not merely as a feature of the transition, but as a permanent arrangement, the plan accords to every member government the explicit right to control all capital movements," Keynes explained. As Henry Morgenthau, Franklin D. Roosevelt's treasury secretary, put it in closing remarks at the Bretton Woods conference, the goal was to "drive the usurious moneylenders from the temple of international finance."

For two decades, Bretton Woods was a stunning success, facilitating the rebirth of the global economy after the most destructive war in history. But by the late 1960s, cracks began to develop. The first source of pressure was a reaction to the fixed dollar-to-gold exchange rate. Charles de Gaulle, the French president, bristled at the notion that the U.S. dollar was automatically as good as gold. His finance minister, Valéry Giscard d'Estaing, decried the dollar's international status as America's "exorbitant privilege." To assert France's independence from the United States, de Gaulle's government began exchanging France's dollar reserves en masse for gold. France's actions, in turn, raised doubts about America's ability to continue redeeming dollars for gold at $35 per ounce.

A second crack in the façade stemmed from backlash to the constraints on cross-border capital movements. In London during the 1960s, a new market emerged in which firms could deposit, borrow, and exchange dollars. As it was based outside the United States, the so-called Eurodollar market was free from regulation and thus gave banks and multinational corporations an avenue to evade the strict capital controls of the time. Although the Eurodollar market was something of a Wild West, the British government embraced it as a way to preserve the City of London's role as a world financial center. The U.S. government could have taken steps to shut the market down, but Washington also ended up supporting it out of its own self-interest: the Eurodollar market increased the appeal of dollar holdings, effectively enticing foreigners to finance American deficits, which were growing rapidly amid the Vietnam War. It didn't matter that the Eurodollar market undermined Bretton Woods; the prospect that Washington could run big deficits and avoid spending cuts trumped all.

In a manner that today's cryptocurrency enthusiasts could only dream of, the Eurodollar market started as an unauthorized monetary experiment and then evolved, with the blessing of the U.S. and British governments, into a piece of critical infrastructure for the world economy. Gradually, the capital controls of Bretton Woods eroded, and money began moving across borders more freely.

Escalating doubts about the strength of the dollar converged with the breakdown of capital controls at the moment the French warship entered New York Harbor. By itself, France's repatriation of its gold may not have been enough to cause a crisis. Add to it Britain's faltering confidence in the dollar, however, and Nixon had a full-blown catastrophe on his hands. As Paul Volcker, then a U.S. Treasury official and later chairman of the Federal Reserve, described, "If the British, who had founded the system with us, and who had fought so hard to defend their own currency, were going to take gold for their dollars, it was clear the game was indeed over."

After a weekend of deliberations at Camp David, Nixon delivered a televised address on the evening of Sunday, August 15. To confront the "speculators" who were "waging all-out war on the American dollar," Nixon declared that the United States would no longer honor requests to convert dollars for gold. In one fell swoop, the announcement cut down the central pillar of Bretton Woods and essentially forced the global financial system to adopt floating exchange rates. Under Bretton Woods, currency values had been set by agreement among governments; after the "Nixon shock," they were set by the market. It was the dawn of a new era for the world economy— one in which financial markets, contrary to Keynes's wishes, would reign supreme.

Many contemporary observers viewed the Nixon shock as the end of U.S. economic hegemony. From World War II through 1971, the United States had led the global economy on paper and in practice, and the dollar was as good as gold. After the Nixon shock, America became just another normal member of the world economy. The ensuing decade was disastrous for the U.S. economy, plagued by stagnant growth and high inflation, or "stagflation." America's share of global GDP fell from 40 percent in 1960 to 25 percent in 1980, roughly the level it stands today. But in an ironic turn, this decline marked only a new phase of U.S. economic dominance. America's preeminence in manufacturing and trade was fading, but its supremacy in international finance was about to begin.

4

The Deal in the Desert

The year 1973 was rough for the United States. The economy was in the dumps. The end of Bretton Woods and the new system of floating exchange rates had caused the dollar to plunge. Years of heavy spending on the Vietnam War had degraded America's financial health. Inflation soared to heights last seen in the 1940s. Instead of focusing on confronting these headwinds, Richard Nixon floundered to contain the Watergate scandal.

To make matters worse, America was rapidly declining as an energy superpower and losing its traditional status as the swing producer in the global oil market. U.S. oil production peaked in 1970 and would not reach the same level again for nearly fifty years. For the first time, the country became dependent on oil imports, largely from the Middle East.

On October 6, 1973—the Jewish holy day of Yom Kippur—a coalition of Arab states attacked Israel. Two weeks later, in response to a request by Nixon to Congress for emergency aid for Israel, Saudi Arabia and the other members of the Organization of Petroleum Exporting Countries (OPEC), the oil-producers' cartel, cut production and imposed an oil embargo on the United States. All told, the Saudis and their allies removed some five million barrels per day from global oil markets, amounting to almost 10 percent of worldwide production.

The result was a wrenching energy crisis. Henry Kissinger, the U.S. secretary of state, feared that the world was at risk of "a vicious cycle of competition, autarchy, rivalry, and depression such as led to the collapse of world order in the thirties." The man charged with avoiding that outcome was Nixon's energy czar, William Simon. A chain-smoking New Jersey native described by a peer as "far to the right of Genghis Khan," Simon had joined the administration after a career as a bond trader on Wall Street, and his gruff style and short temper suited the confrontational nature of his new job. Not everyone could have made the fraught decision to ration gasoline, that American lifeblood, and allocate scarce oil supplies to factories over motorists. But that's what Simon did.

By the end of the year, Americans were waiting hours to fill their tanks. ("I'm the guy that caused the lines at the gas stations," Simon admitted.) Prices at the pump surged by 40 percent. Even after OPEC lifted the embargo in March 1974, oil prices did not fall back to earth. In 1970, the price of a barrel of oil was about $1.80. By 1980, the price was $39—an increase of more than 2,000 percent. America's import bills skyrocketed, and deficits spiked. On top of the energy crisis, America was on the brink of a full-fledged financial meltdown.

With Nixon fighting for political survival over Watergate, William Simon was as good a choice as any for treasury secretary, the new role he took up in May 1974. Simon's solution for the strain that higher oil prices were putting on America's finances was to convince Saudi Arabia to invest its windfall oil profits in U.S. government debt. This way, the Saudis would essentially recycle the dollars America paid them for oil, plugging the U.S. deficit.

In July 1974, Simon boarded a plane at Andrews Air Force Base and headed for the Saudi coastal city of Jeddah. En route, he indulged in copious amounts of whiskey. By the time he got off the plane, he was noticeably drunk. The liquor had no apparent effect on his negotiating ability, however. Simon was no Kissinger; he was not schooled in the art of diplomacy. But he was a damn good bonds salesman, and he left the desert kingdom with a deal in hand: In exchange for American military assistance and continued oil purchases, the Saudis would funnel their oil money into U.S. Treasury bonds, which they would be permitted to buy in secret outside the normal auctions. Simon had secured a commitment by a foreign country to finance American deficits—and the petrodollar was born.

In the years that followed, there were moments when Simon's deal risked coming apart. As the dollar continued to plunge throughout the 1970s, the real value of Saudi oil profits fell in lockstep. The weakening dollar was effectively reducing the global price of oil. As a result, in 1975, OPEC resolved to

William Simon: the ex–bond trader
who cut the deal that created the petrodollar.

stop pricing oil in dollars, opting instead for a basket of currencies. But before the plan could be implemented, Simon's successor at Treasury, Michael Blumenthal, cut a fresh deal with Riyadh. The United States promised to help Saudi Arabia obtain more voting rights at the IMF, and in exchange, the Saudis and their OPEC partners would continue to price oil in dollars. Over time, Simon's arrangement crystallized into a structural feature of the world economy. Oil is still priced in dollars, and foreigners still finance American deficits. Petrodollars became a key ingredient in an increasingly global financial system—a system dominated by the United States.

5

Our Currency, Your Problem

William Simon was both a maker of history and a product of his times. If the former was apparent in his pathbreaking diplomacy with the Saudis, the latter was apparent in his embrace of the ascendant economic ideology of his day. Like a growing number of his colleagues, Simon was a devoted, unquestioning believer in the power of the free market. His 1978 bestselling capitalist manifesto, *A Time for Truth*, included a preface by none other than the University of Chicago economist Milton Friedman, the chief ideologue of neoliberalism.

Elevated to positions of influence, Friedman's acolytes took an axe to regulations and taxes and disassembled the last remaining restrictions on cross-border financial movements that the architects of Bretton Woods had deemed so vital. In Britain, Margaret Thatcher's government went so far as to destroy official files on capital controls so that successors would struggle to reimpose them. In the United States, Ronald Reagan deregulated vast parts of the financial industry and created gaping budget deficits by slashing taxes at the same time as he boosted military spending.

These policies created conditions under which new technologies—the computer, the standardized shipping container, and eventually the internet— could knit together the global economy into one giant web, and they granted Thatcher and Reagan admission into the neoliberal pantheon. But in the United States, in particular, neoliberalism's ascendancy started before Reagan entered the White House, and it crested well after he departed. In fact, what made the free-market philosophy so transformative was its eventual adoption even by leaders of the Left. It was Reagan's Democratic predecessor, Jimmy Carter, who deregulated the airline, railroad, and trucking industries and who declared in his 1978 State of the Union address that "Government cannot solve our problems." It was one of Reagan's Democratic successors, Bill Clinton, who entrenched neoliberalism in the United States and endeavored to spread it all over the world.

In history, timing is everything. Just as neoliberal ideas came to dominate Western economic policy, a geopolitical earthquake struck: the end of the Cold War. That the Soviet Union disintegrated without a violent conflict seemed so miraculous that many saw it as ordained by history—the triumph of noble ideas over an "evil empire." For many, it went without saying that those noble ideas included neoliberal dogma. As the Soviet Union crumbled, George H. W. Bush awarded the Presidential Medal of Freedom to Friedrich Hayek, another intellectual godfather of neoliberalism. "How magnificent it must be for him to witness his ideas validated before the eyes of the world," Bush gushed as Hayek accepted his prize.

With the Soviet Union gone, a huge swath of the world opened up to American financiers, corporate executives, and neoliberal reformers. Now, the free-market policies embraced by the West could spread everywhere, turning "globalization" from an abstract concept into an omnipresent reality. Bill Clinton signed a free-trade pact with Canada and Mexico (the North American Free Trade Agreement, or NAFTA) and backed the creation of a global free-trade system (the World Trade Organization, or WTO). In approaching the former Communist states, his government preached the "Washington Consensus," a set of free-market reforms to be adopted via "shock therapy." As Lawrence Summers, Clinton's treasury secretary, confessed, "Any honest Democrat will admit that we are all Friedmanites now."

Clinton also completed Reagan's deregulation of the financial sector, allowing the banking industry to become bigger and more globalized than ever. He signed the law that repealed the Glass-Steagall Act, which had walled off commercial banking from investment banking since 1933. For the key post of Federal Reserve chair, Clinton twice renominated Reagan appointee and fellow neoliberal crusader Alan Greenspan, whose command over U.S. monetary policy thus stretched into a second decade.

Business initiatives and government policy worked in tandem to drive globalization forward. In finance, the growth of the Eurodollar market helped precipitate the end of capital controls, which in turn led banks to create new technologies for cross-border finance, including CHIPS (the world's leading system for settling payments) and the Society for Worldwide Interbank Financial Telecommunications, or SWIFT (a messaging service for banks that became a lingua franca for international finance). In trade, the emergence of the standardized shipping container and just-in-time manufacturing allowed firms to capitalize on lower tariff barriers negotiated under the auspices of NAFTA and the WTO. Time and again, removing obstacles to cross-border economic activity created demand for new technologies that would help conduct such activity, which incentivized additional globalization-friendly policies, and so on.

The United States was hardly alone in driving this process. Over the course of the 1990s, the European Union launched a common currency, the euro, and paved the way for the accession of more than a dozen new members, turning the bloc into the world's largest single market. Japan and the so-called "Asian tiger" economies of South Korea and Taiwan became export powerhouses. Corporate giants such as Sony, Samsung, and Taiwan Semiconductor Manufacturing Corporation (TSMC) churned out the electronic components that powered the digital revolution. Most important of all, China emerged as the workshop of the world. The country's economy had boomed ever since the onset of market reforms under Deng Xiaoping in the late 1970s, and its expansion was now reaching dizzying speeds, with Chinese exports growing fivefold during the 1990s. By 2010, China had amassed more than a trillion dollars' worth of U.S. debt, in large part due to ballooning U.S. trade deficits with China. William Simon's 1974 deal with Saudi Arabia to funnel petrodollars into U.S. Treasuries initially enabled surging American deficits and an explosion in dollar lending; the ascent of "Chimerica" in the 1990s extended this trend into the twenty-first century.

Undergirding the entire system, however, was the U.S. dollar. No data point better illustrates this than the meteoric rise of the foreign exchange market to become the biggest financial market of all. In the 1950s, global foreign exchange trading was minimal. By the 1990s, it had reached almost $1 trillion *per day*, roughly forty times the daily value of global trade. Today, foreign exchange trading eclipses $7 trillion each day—a staggering volume that is more than eighty times the daily value of world trade. (If you don't have a calculator handy, that's equal to an annual market volume of around $2.5 *quadrillion*.) A whopping 90 percent of these foreign exchange transactions involve the dollar.

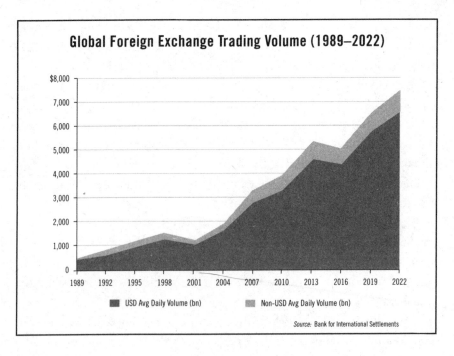

Global Foreign Exchange Trading Volume (1989–2022)

Legend: USD Avg Daily Volume (bn) | Non-USD Avg Daily Volume (bn)

Source: Bank for International Settlements

The dollar's dominance gave Washington immense economic and geopolitical power. Without the need for congressional approval, an American president could issue sanctions that cut off any individual or company from access to the dollar. And trying to navigate the global economy without access to the dollar is like trying to travel the world without a passport. As a former U.S. treasury secretary once told a group of foreign counterparts, "The dollar is our currency, but it's your problem."

By the 1990s, everything was in place for the United States to wield high-potency weapons of economic warfare. The world economy was intensely globalized and financialized, allowing for goods and, above all, money to move across borders more freely than ever before. The dollar's importance in the global economy gave the United States control of a chokepoint of unparalleled strategic value. And the collapse of the Soviet Union made America the world's sole superpower, giving the United States license to throw its weight around while attracting more and more countries into its orbit.

America's new economic leverage was sitting on the table like a loaded gun. But the U.S. government chose not to fire it. Within the Clinton administration, Robert Rubin, the powerful treasury secretary and former Goldman Sachs co-chairman, worried that any measures to instrumentalize the dollar for overtly political ends might "undermine the role of the dollar as the reserve currency" and push other countries away from the U.S. financial system. "Once you do it once," Rubin said, "you become a less reliable supplier." The U.S. economy was booming, the Cold War was over, and the geopolitical environment was mostly benign, so why take any risks? What's more, the debacle of the UN embargo on Iraq appeared to validate the idea that economic sanctions didn't work, while American military power seemed to be working just fine. With minimal risk of U.S. casualties and relatively low costs, air strikes and cruise missiles were Clinton's weapons of choice.

This calculus changed, as with so much else in U.S. foreign policy, on a single day: September 11, 2001.

6

"Guerrillas in Gray Suits"

S tuart Levey, a young lawyer at the Justice Department, was sitting in his office at 950 Pennsylvania Avenue in Washington on the morning of September 11, 2001, when he received a phone call. On the line was a colleague, who uttered a simple instruction: "Turn on the TV."

The North Tower of the World Trade Center was already in flames. Minutes later, a second plane hit the South Tower.

Levey, a slight man with intense dark eyes and salt-and-pepper hair, worked primarily on immigration issues. Some of his colleagues just a few doors down the hall were involved in terrorism investigations, but as he looked at the surreal images of the burning towers, he couldn't piece together their meaning. "I had not been read into the threat stream," Levey said. "There were a few people who were read into it at the time, but I had no idea. So when 9/11 happened, I was completely shocked."

Levey gathered with his colleagues in the command center at the top floor of the Justice Department to track the unfolding catastrophe. Soon, news came in that there could be additional hijacked planes in the air, targets unknown. Then, word came that a colleague's wife had called from aboard American Airlines Flight 77, trying to reach her husband. The plane crashed into the Pentagon.

Fearing an attack on the Justice Department, Levey and other DOJ lawyers moved to an alternate location that was designated in advance for moments of extreme threat. The new spot was safer but had too few phone lines and offered little ability to communicate classified information. It was clear that while this kind of emergency had been considered in theory, Justice was not prepared for it in practice. Eventually, the lawyers relocated to the better-equipped FBI headquarters, where they went to work uncovering the origins of the attack.

The U.S. government would bring every possible tool to bear in the Global War on Terror. The 9/11 tragedy ushered in two decades of war in Afghanistan and, later, Iraq. But it also marked the start of a new era of economic warfare. At Justice, Levey's responsibilities shifted from working on immigration policy to prosecuting facilitators of terrorism, which required tracing the funding streams of groups such as al-Qaeda and Hamas. It was Levey's first step into a much bigger world of weaponized finance. When the dust of 9/11 settled, a new battlefield had emerged, and he would find himself at the very tip of the spear.

On the morning of September 12, 2001, George W. Bush gathered with congressional leaders around a large mahogany table in the White House. Al-Qaeda's heinous acts had killed almost three thousand Americans, the deadliest foreign attack on U.S. soil in the nation's history.

"This is the beginning of war in the twenty-first century," the president told the assembled lawmakers, striking a resolute tone. "We will answer the bloodlust of the American people that is rightly at boil." A *Washington Post* column that day called the 1990s a "holiday from history," which had now come to an abrupt and painful end. After the fall of the Soviet Union, politicians and pundits had waxed optimistic about perpetual peace, guaranteed by an ever-more-connected global economy. 9/11 made clear that this was an illusion.

To confront the specter of Islamist terrorism, Bush was prepared to use force, and few in Washington had reason to doubt that the United States would succeed. In the years leading up to 9/11, the U.S. military had demonstrated that it could rapidly defeat enemies while suffering few, if any, casualties of its own. It took U.S. forces four days to win the 1991 Gulf War, eviscerating an Iraqi army that was one of the world's largest at the time. In 1995, just over two weeks of air raids by the United States and its allies pushed Serbian leader Slobodan Milošević to the negotiating table, resulting in the peace agreement that ended the four-year Bosnian War. And in 1999,

America led a seventy-eight-day air campaign that took the lives of thousands of Serbian soldiers and drove the rest of them out of Kosovo, with no U.S. troops killed in action.

Bush thus drew America's sword flush with confidence. "Our war on terror begins with al-Qaeda, but it does not end there," he declared to a joint session of Congress nine days after 9/11. "It will not end until every terrorist group of global reach has been found, stopped, and defeated." That confidence would soon falter. The wars in Afghanistan and Iraq were nothing like the short, triumphant American wars of the 1990s. After overthrowing the Taliban and Saddam Hussein with relative ease, the U.S. military was left to pick up the pieces. Both wars turned into expensive and bloody nation-building projects, with U.S. soldiers building roads and administering public services while fending off violent insurgencies. There was a Sisyphean quality to them—whenever progress was made, it was undone. In the process, military power lost its luster in Washington and the support of the American people.

As the Bush administration struggled to manage two unwinnable wars, a group of bureaucrats at the Treasury Department embarked on a different project: cutting off al-Qaeda's finances. The president himself had given them their mission, promising in the same speech to the joint session of Congress that America would "starve terrorists of funding." The 9/11 attacks cost just $500,000 to perpetrate, but the terrorists had moved this money through the U.S. financial system without incident. They had used bank accounts in their own names and openly wired funds in and out of the country. Treasury officials were determined never to allow this to happen again.

At the center of this effort was the Office of Foreign Assets Control, the Treasury agency in charge of sanctions policy and enforcement. OFAC's authority to blacklist individuals and companies from the U.S. financial system originates from a World War I–era law giving the president extraordinary powers over the economy in times of crisis. Known today as the International Emergency Economic Powers Act, or IEEPA, the law grants the president broad leeway to declare a "national emergency" that warrants punitive economic measures against the United States' enemies, including severing their access to the dollar. A Supreme Court ruling permits the president to wield this power without consulting Congress. When the president declares such a state of emergency, the job of designing the requisite economic weapons typically falls to OFAC.

Throughout most of the Cold War, OFAC was a relatively marginal force. This started to change in the 1980s, when the office began publishing the Specially Designated Nationals and Blocked Persons List, known as the SDN List for short. The list gave banks an easy way to stay up-to-date on which individuals and companies were under U.S. sanctions, and it quickly expanded the U.S. government's reach into the private sector. In the 1990s, the list became closely associated with the Clinton administration's fight against international drug trafficking. As one Latin American drug kingpin after another ended up on *"La Lista Clinton,"* even banks outside the United States began using it to screen financial transactions and steer clear of clients who might cause them legal trouble.

Then came 9/11. OFAC now added scores of suspected terrorists to the SDN List, blocking them from access to the U.S. financial system. Critically, OFAC also began sanctioning individuals and banks that it believed were funding terrorist activities. At the same time, the USA PATRIOT Act required banks and other financial institutions to perform more due diligence before accepting new clients and processing transactions. "If you do business with terrorists, if you support them or sponsor them, you will not do business with the United States of America," Bush warned in November 2001.

Through OFAC and a hodgepodge of other offices involved in checking illicit finance, the Treasury Department was taking on an important, if little-noticed, role in the War on Terror. Its legal authorities had expanded, and its influence over foreign banks and financial institutions grew. Treasury officials even struck a secret deal with SWIFT, the Brussels-based global financial messaging service, under which Treasury could subpoena certain transaction data—a significant development, given that SWIFT was one of the few pieces of critical financial infrastructure not based on U.S. soil and had successfully resisted similar American efforts in the past.

Treasury's place in the U.S. national security apparatus was changing, too. As OFAC became more prominent, the department forfeited its historic law enforcement authorities to the newly created Department of Homeland Security. Gone from Treasury were the Secret Service, the Customs Service, and the Bureau of Alcohol, Tobacco, and Firearms. In a strange twist, Treasury lost 95 percent of its national security budget and personnel just as its mission in the Global War on Terror was assuming center stage.

A small group of Treasury officials, led by a young lawyer named Juan Zarate and a veteran white-shoe attorney named David Aufhauser, stayed behind to rebuild. They worked with Congress to create a new Treasury division that would focus less on law enforcement and more on sanctions and counterterrorist financing. The new division, the Office of Terrorism and Financial Intelligence (TFI), assumed oversight of OFAC and was even given its own intelligence agency, making Treasury the only finance ministry in the world with an in-house intelligence function.

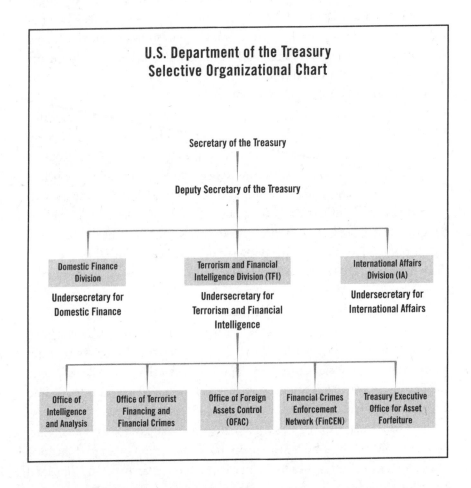

By 2004, TFI was up and running. With a few hundred employees and a budget of just over $100 million—less than half the cost of a single model of the F-35 fighter jet about to make its debut—TFI was lean. But Treasury finally had an institutional structure aligned with its new mission. Now it just needed a leader.

When Stuart Levey, who was quickly climbing the ranks at the Justice Department, heard about the creation of TFI, he was irritated. *Why won't they just go away?* he fumed silently.

The now forty-one-year-old Levey viewed Treasury as a bureaucratic rival and sometimes nuisance to Justice's own counterterrorism efforts. He was therefore surprised when he received a call in early 2004 from Dina Powell, the head of the Office of Presidential Personnel, to gauge his interest in serving as the first head of TFI. After some hesitation, he accepted the offer. Levey was a political appointee, and if George W. Bush wasn't reelected in November, he would need to look for a new job soon anyway. Why not take a flyer on a startup?

*Stuart Levey: the Treasury Department's first
undersecretary for terrorism and financial intelligence.*

Although he expected TFI to focus primarily on uprooting terrorist financing networks, Levey knew that his responsibilities would include overseeing OFAC, Treasury's sanctions office, so he tried to soak up as much academic research on sanctions as possible. Most of the papers he read explained why, in essence, sanctions didn't work. ("That's what I like: really

low expectations," he later joked.) Upon his Senate confirmation in July
2004, Levey settled into a cavernous office on the second floor of the Treasury Department, the entryway of which was the door of an old bank vault.
Joining him was one of his talented young colleagues from Justice, Adam
Szubin, who agreed to serve as Levey's aide-de-camp.

Just as Levey had previously eyed TFI with suspicion, his subordinates
did not know what to make of their new boss, whom they suspected had
been installed by the White House to keep them in check. Danny Glaser, a
career Treasury official who helped found TFI, initially viewed Levey's arrival as a "hostile takeover." A compact wrecking ball of a man, Glaser was an
anti-money-laundering expert who brooked no bullshit. Despite his initial
skepticism, he soon became one of Levey's closest allies. "I'd lie down in
front of a train for him," Glaser said.

Other parts of America's national security ecosystem, meanwhile, dismissed TFI as a collection of unwelcome upstarts. When Levey or Glaser
showed up to meetings at the White House Situation Room and took a seat
next to officials from the State Department, the Pentagon, and the CIA, they
often received puzzled stares. "Why is Treasury here?" was a common question. It didn't help that many of TFI's leaders were still in their thirties and
early forties, noticeably younger than the average top official in Washington.
But TFI's outsider status acted as a source of discipline. To be taken seriously, they had to know their stuff cold. It also fostered a nonhierarchical,
roll-up-your-sleeves culture. Juan Zarate, another TFI co-founder, described
the team as "guerrillas in gray suits."

Aside from working to bankrupt al-Qaeda, Levey's central focus at TFI
was to cut off financing to regimes that sought weapons of mass destruction—
"rogue states," in the parlance of the time, that might transfer such devastating weapons to terrorists. The countries of most concern were the three that
Bush identified in his 2002 State of the Union address as the "axis of evil":
Iraq, Iran, and North Korea.

By the time Levey arrived at TFI, the U.S. military occupied Iraq. Iran
remained worrisome, yet tensions had eased for the moment; the country's
reformist president, Mohammad Khatami, had recently struck a deal with
Britain, France, and Germany to suspend Iran's uranium enrichment program and allow more intrusive inspections of its nuclear facilities. Tensions
with North Korea, on the other hand, were ratcheting up.

7

An Economic Weapons Test

In early 2005, tensions between the United States and North Korea were boiling. Pyongyang had long experimented with nuclear technology, but that February, it formally declared that it had "manufactured nukes." Even more ominously, a top North Korean official threatened to hand over nuclear material to terrorists if "the United States drives us into a corner." Washington had to take this threat seriously, especially given recent evidence that North Korea had secretly transferred nearly two tons of uranium hexafluoride, a key ingredient in nuclear weapons, to Libya. The White House was grasping at straws for new approaches that might stop Pyongyang's nuclear activities.

North Korea was nicknamed the Hermit Kingdom for good reason. It had few links to the mainstream world economy, and none with the United States. Its sole big trading partner, China, was also its patron, providing the country with food and energy aid as well as a small amount of foreign-currency revenue in exchange for exports of textiles, coal, and other minerals. Beijing could not be counted on to rein in Kim Jong Il, North Korea's repressive dictator, who was heir to a nominally Communist regime that Beijing had propped up since the Korean War in the early 1950s. And since China had veto power on the UN Security Council, comprehensive multilateral sanctions like those imposed on Iraq in the 1990s were a nonstarter.

Stuart Levey saw the North Korea conundrum as an opportunity for TFI to prove its worth. The North Korean economy was one big criminal enterprise, running on exports of drugs, fake Marlboro cigarettes, and the world's premier counterfeit $100 bills. To profit from these illicit activities and acquire components for its nuclear program, North Korea needed access to the international financial system. And by 2005, TFI had identified a key link through which North Korea obtained that access: Banco Delta Asia, a small bank based in the Chinese coastal city of Macau. TFI officials had discovered that the North Korean regime was paying the bank a fee to utilize its financial network. Banco Delta Asia allowed Pyongyang to open accounts, wire money, and deposit large amounts of cash. Though it was not the only Chinese bank serving North Korea, it was one of the Hermit Kingdom's most important conduits to the outside world.

By the summer of 2005, Levey and Danny Glaser were pushing to designate Banco Delta Asia as a "primary money laundering concern," a classification set out in Section 311 of the PATRIOT Act. Such a designation would allow TFI to take a range of punitive steps, including shutting down the bank's connections to the U.S. financial system. Levey and Glaser hoped that the mere threat of such punishments could cause financial institutions to sever business ties with the North Korean regime.

Juan Zarate, who had since moved from Treasury to the National Security Council (NSC), advocated for the policy within the White House. Because Banco Delta Asia was tiny, the move was unlikely to have any unwelcome ripple effects in China's banking sector, much less America's own. But it could demonstrate to Pyongyang that Washington had the power to squeeze its economic lifeline.

Desperate for a policy option that did not involve military force, Bush signed off on the proposal. On September 15, 2005, Treasury designated Banco Delta Asia as a "primary money laundering concern" and signaled its intent to cut the bank off from the U.S. financial system sometime in the future. On paper, the move was little more than a shot across the bow, but it had the force of a scarlet letter. Authorities in Macau froze $25 million in North Korean assets at Banco Delta Asia and took control of the bank to stave off a run by panicked customers. Soon, banks across China and beyond began cutting ties with North Korea, fearing that they might come under scrutiny next. The speed and breadth of the response came as a surprise "even for true believers like me," Danny Glaser reflected. In the wake of 9/11, banks all over the world were skittish about violating new U.S. laws like the Patriot Act. Equally important, they dreaded the reputational consequences of being tarred as a "supporter of terrorism" or "enabler of nuclear proliferation." No executive wanted to risk getting the blood of another 9/11 on their hands.

The graybeards of America's national security establishment were stunned. Michael Hayden, an Air Force general who led both the CIA and the National Security Agency (NSA) during the Bush administration, likened the action to a "twenty-first-century precision-guided munition." Even Pyongyang couldn't deny the impact. "You . . . you Americans finally found a way to hurt us," a North Korean official admitted to an American counterpart after one too many shots of liquor.

From then on, Levey and Glaser no longer needed to justify their presence in the Situation Room. In the grand scheme of things, however, the action against Banco Delta Asia was small-time, a proof of concept. TFI had shown that it could deploy a sophisticated economic weapon, yet it had verified only that such a weapon could work against a minor target. The action resulted in the freezing of $25 million in North Korean assets—roughly the same amount of money Shaquille O'Neal made playing basketball for the Miami Heat that year. And while these frozen funds gave the United States more leverage at the negotiating table, they were not enough to move the needle on Pyongyang's nuclear calculus. There were limits to economic warfare against an adversary so isolated from the currents of globalization. But the episode hinted at the power Washington might be able to wield in a hyper-financialized, interconnected world economy.

The main proving ground for America's new economic weapons would be a country far bigger than North Korea, with much stronger ties to the international economy. That country would soon elevate a radical hard-liner to its presidency and turbocharge its nuclear program. In 2006, desperate for a solution short of war, America would place that country in its economic crosshairs, and the Age of Economic Warfare would begin.

That country was Iran.

PART TWO

==

Iran and the Bomb

8

The Technocrat

It wasn't until October 2013—after nearly a decade as a top commander in America's economic war against Iran—that Adam Szubin first came face-to-face with an Iranian official.

They had agreed to parley on neutral ground, at the Palais des Nations in Geneva, Switzerland. The Palais, a lakeside neoclassical gem with a view of the French Alps, was an upgrade for Szubin, a world apart from his usual perch in a no-frills Treasury Department annex. Then again, little about Szubin, a forty-year-old with youthful features and bookish, wire-rimmed glasses, hinted at the power he wielded, at a job that put him in charge of the world's most fearsome economic arsenal. Iran, a country of more than 80 million people, had been his hardest and highest-value target. Yet in recent years, the reams of directives coming out of his office had slowly but surely severed Iran's links to the global economy. The meeting in Geneva was the clearest sign to date that Tehran was feeling the squeeze.

U.S. sanctions were a reaction to Iran's nuclear capabilities, which had progressed at a frightening clip. Back in 2003, America had gone so far as to invade Iraq and overthrow Saddam Hussein in search of weapons of mass destruction that proved nonexistent. Iran's nuclear program, on the other hand, was all too real. The thousands of nuclear centrifuges spinning on Iranian soil were made all the more worrisome by Tehran's activities beyond its borders, where the Islamic Revolutionary Guard Corps and militant proxies like Hezbollah wreaked daily havoc. When Iranian President Mahmoud Ahmadinejad called for Israel to be "wiped off the map," his words

seemed less an empty threat than a declaration of intent. Both the United
States and Israel made clear they would not tolerate a nuclear Iran. But no
one in Washington wanted another war in the Middle East.

It fell to Szubin to design a solution short of military force. To get Iran to
abandon its nuclear program, the United States would have to inflict real
economic pain. But Iran was long subject to a U.S. trade embargo and had
possessed few meaningful ties with the American economy since the 1979
hostage crisis. U.S. officials needed a way to cut off the regime not just from
the American market but from the global economy writ large. Economic
warfare of such unprecedented scale and ambition would require forging
novel weapons and drafting up new field manuals. In the halls of power in
Washington, many initially dismissed the idea as a pipe dream. It had taken
Szubin years of work to prove the skeptics wrong.

=

In 2006, two years after joining Treasury as Stuart Levey's right-hand man,
Szubin was tapped to lead the department's Office of Foreign Assets Control.
The job at OFAC came with responsibilities not often granted to a thirtysome-
thing civil servant still early in his career. But Szubin's cool temperament
and eye for detail quickly won him allies.

Szubin grew up in Teaneck, New Jersey, in a family of religiously observant Jews. His father, Zvi, was born in 1933 in Poland and spent his childhood fleeing the Nazis. Zvi eventually made it to Palestine, where he grew up
amid the 1948 Arab-Israeli war and was ordained as a rabbi. He later moved
to the United States and became a well-respected scholar at the City College
of New York. Szubin's mother, Laurie, spent years as a stay-at-home mom
until, when Adam was a teenager, she enrolled in law school and went on to
become an administrative judge.

Zvi and Laurie's melding of religious and intellectual rigor rubbed off on
their son. After graduating from a Jewish day school in Manhattan, Szubin
spent a year in the mountains south of Jerusalem, where he attended Yeshi-
vat Har Etzion, one of the world's leading institutes of advanced Torah study.
The educational regimen was intense, with students parsing ancient texts in
the original Hebrew and Aramaic from early morning to late at night. "It
was probably the most intellectually demanding place I have ever been,"
Szubin later recalled, "and certainly the hardest I'd ever worked."

If Szubin knew firsthand the rewards of deep religious devotion, he also

Adam Szubin: director of the Treasury Department's
Office of Foreign Assets Control (OFAC).

understood its darker sides. At Harvard, where he attended college and law
school, he turned his interest to messianic movements—sects that believed
the apocalypse was nigh. He studied the Branch Davidians, whose compound in Waco, Texas, had been the target of a fifty-one-day siege by federal
agents in 1993 that left seventy-six people dead. Later, he considered becoming a public-interest lawyer. But like many law students saddled with student
loans, he soon began looking for more financially stable ways of improving
the world.

That path had led Szubin into government service, and ultimately to Geneva as a member of the U.S. delegation at the Palais des Nations. It was the
first time a U.S. Treasury official was taking part in nuclear talks with Iran.
The media interpreted Szubin's presence as significant, a sign that the Obama
administration was serious about putting its most valuable card—sanctions
relief—on the table.

Back in Washington, OFAC's offices sat empty. The federal government
was in the midst of a weeks-long shutdown, the result of efforts by Tea Party
Republicans in Congress to gut the Affordable Care Act. More than 800,000
federal employees were furloughed, including nearly everyone at OFAC.
One of Treasury's top Iran experts, Andrew Jensen, was sitting in a rocking
chair on his front porch in Fredericksburg, Virginia, bored out of his mind,
when he received a call instructing him to report to the office at once. He
and a handful of other Treasury staff worked for days without pay to support

Szubin's mission, crafting ideas for sanctions relief that could be traded for Iranian nuclear concessions.

Upon meeting Iran's top nuclear envoys, Abbas Araghchi and Hamid Baeidinejad, Szubin was struck by their command of U.S. sanctions policy. Araghchi and Baeidinejad spoke in the arcane jargon of OFAC policy wonks, all the way down to the bureaucratic acronyms. Clearly, Tehran's internal effort to study American sanctions and consider countermeasures was quite advanced. By the fall of 2013, Iranian officials had no choice but to take U.S. sanctions seriously. The previous year, Iran had suffered its first economic recession in nearly two decades, and in the opening months of 2013, its access to hard currency dried up. The government was running out of money.

For years, politicians in Tehran had denied that international pressure was harming their country's economy. But in the lead-up to the Iranian presidential election in June 2013, one candidate went off script, vowing to free Iran from the constraints of sanctions. He won in a landslide. Within days of Hassan Rouhani's inauguration in August, Tehran signaled it was ready to negotiate with Washington.

Iran Stares Down a "Toothless Tiger"

The road to Geneva was anything but straight.

It took years to build up enough pressure for Iran to concede limits to its nuclear program. The effort wound its way through America's messy and often dysfunctional policymaking process, in which Harvard-educated lawyers, smooth-talking diplomats, sharp-elbowed lobbyists, opinion-peddling think-tank scholars, and feuding members of Congress yelled over one another and hurled accusations of treason. It was a classic case of what Sigmund Freud called the "narcissism of small differences," in which factions that are fundamentally similar clash over the minutiae that divide them. Despite the contentiousness or perhaps because of it, they managed to emerge on the other side with an actionable solution to a shared goal.

Without any of these players, the pressure campaign would not have been as successful. But it was ultimately a core team at the Treasury Department—led by Stuart Levey, Adam Szubin, and David Cohen, who succeeded Levey as head of TFI—that created order from the chaos. In the process, these individuals also defined a new type of Washington official, the sanctions technocrat, who would become a mainstay of the national security ecosystem. The sanctions technocrat was to economic warfare what generals and admirals were to military conflict: they developed plans of attack, sought their leaders' approval, and commanded the troops accordingly.

It's no accident that these officials and their methods emerged from the crucible of U.S. policy toward Iran. The country is simply too big and too disruptive an adversary to ignore. Iran is the second most populous country in the Middle East after Egypt, with an educated and dynamic middle class.

In terms of landmass, it ranks second in the region after Saudi Arabia. Iran has the geographic fortune of sitting at a strategic crossroads between the Middle East and South Asia, and it is the gatekeeper of the Strait of Hormuz, a narrow waterway through which 20 percent of the world's oil supply flows. Thanks to its own massive reserves of oil (the world's third largest) and natural gas (second only to Russia's), it is an energy powerhouse.

Ever since a revolution in 1979 swept Iran's shah from power and established an Islamic republic, all these resources have been in the hands of a revolutionary Islamist regime that seeks to extend its influence across the Middle East and undermine the interests of the United States and its allies. If this regime were to acquire nuclear weapons, containing its ambitions would be harder still, perhaps impossible.

Like many of America's thorniest international challenges, Iran's nuclear pursuit is at least partly American-made. In 1957, President Dwight D. Eisenhower's administration struck a civil nuclear cooperation pact with Iran under the Atoms for Peace program, a Cold War initiative in which Washington shared scientific expertise and nuclear energy equipment with countries it was hoping to keep out of the Soviet orbit. Ten years later, the United States made good on the deal and supplied Iran with a five-megawatt research reactor, which remains in use today, and a stockpile of highly enriched uranium to fuel it. The Iranian government also sent dozens of young scientists to study at MIT and other top American universities, where they received world-class educations in nuclear engineering. They returned home to build the foundations of Iran's nuclear program.

These were the days of the deeply repressive yet staunchly pro-American reign of Shah Mohammad Reza Pahlavi. In the 1970s, Richard Nixon sought to rely on Iran, as well as Saudi Arabia, to police the Middle East and ensure the free flow of oil to world markets. To fortify the shah's regime, the Nixon administration sold Iran billions of dollars in American military hardware. Included in that massive arms haul was a fleet of F-14 Tomcat fighter jets, made famous by the 1986 blockbuster *Top Gun*, many of which are still operational in Iran today.

The 1979 revolution transformed Iran from friend to foe virtually overnight—certainly by November of that year, when a group of radical Iranian students stormed the U.S. embassy in Tehran and took fifty-two Americans hostage. President Jimmy Carter responded by turning to IEEPA, the 1977 law that gave the president extraordinary powers to weaponize the U.S. economy in times of national emergency. In the first-ever use of the law, Carter froze

$12 billion of Iranian assets and severed America's commercial and diplomatic ties with Iran.

Iran was heavily dependent on the United States, which was Iran's top trading partner and accounted for 20 percent of the country's trade with the rest of the world. As a result, the penalties hit hard. After an agonizing 444 days, Washington and Tehran reached a truce on January 19, 1981—Carter's last day in the White House. The United States unfroze the $12 billion in Iranian assets; in return, Iran freed the hostages. As one of Carter's top advisors later reflected, "It was indeed the leverage provided by the frozen assets that solidified the final deal. The fledgling Iranian regime was in desperate need of cash."

The deal, known as the Algiers Accords, rolled back most of the sanctions, but the damage was already done. By 1981, American imports from Iran were roughly 99 percent lower than they had been just before the revolution, and commercial relations between the two countries never recovered. This was due in large part to the new Iranian regime, whose disruptive acts did not end with the hostage crisis and continued to scare away American investors. Eventually, Tehran's mischief resulted in the reimposition of sanctions.

In the immediate aftermath of the revolution, Ayatollah Ruhollah Khomeini—who would soon become the Islamic Republic of Iran's first supreme leader—ordered the creation of the Islamic Revolutionary Guard Corps (IRGC), a paramilitary group charged with defending Iran's hard-line theocratic system at home and spreading its ideology abroad. In 1982, the IRGC oversaw the creation of Hezbollah, a Lebanese extremist group. In subsequent years, Hezbollah—with training and resources from the IRGC—launched a spate of violent terrorist attacks, including the devastating 1983 bombing of a U.S. Marine barracks in Beirut, which killed 241 American service members. Meanwhile, the Iranian regime resumed investment in the nuclear program through a top-secret cell called the Physics Research Center. With the aid of Vyacheslav Danilenko, a former nuclear-weapons scientist for the Soviet Union, the Physics Research Center performed critical studies into the development of a nuclear bomb. As Tehran engaged in these deadly activities, the United States gradually ratcheted up sanctions back to where they had been during the hostage crisis.

This time, however, the penalties made little difference. Iran's economy didn't even suffer much pain. After the hostage crisis, Iranian businesses had deliberately pivoted away from the United States. Now, despite American sanctions, Iran's economy was growing on pace with other emerging markets. The revolutionary regime retained a firm grip on power, and it continued supporting terrorist groups and investing in nuclear capabilities.

The futility of U.S. sanctions was brought into relief in 1995, when Conoco, a Houston-based oil company, signed a contract to develop a massive Iranian offshore oil field. It was the first energy deal between a U.S. company and Iran since the revolution, and it pushed the limits of American sanctions. (Conoco sidestepped U.S. restrictions by signing the contract through one of its foreign subsidiaries, which was legal at the time.) Under intense political pressure, President Bill Clinton issued an executive order that explicitly banned U.S. companies from participating in Iranian oil projects. Conoco swiftly withdrew from the deal, but just a few months later, the French energy giant Total announced it had signed a contract to develop the very same oil field that Conoco had abandoned. In rapid succession, Iran signed nearly a dozen additional energy deals with non-American companies. U.S. sanctions were inflicting damage, but the damage was to American businesses, not to Iran.

Outraged, the U.S. Congress sprang into action. In July 1996, the House and Senate unanimously passed a groundbreaking law known as the Iran and Libya Sanctions Act (ILSA). ILSA was unique because it aimed America's sanctions cannon not at Iran directly but rather at foreign companies doing business with Iran, many of which were headquartered in countries that were U.S. allies. The legislation threatened penalties against any firm, no matter where it was located, that made a sizable investment in Iran's energy sector—just like Total had done after Conoco backed out. If European companies invested in Iranian energy, they risked being hit by American sanctions. In effect, the law presented America's friends with an ultimatum: Get on board with our Iran policy or your companies will suffer the consequences.

ILSA marked one of the earliest attempts by the United States to wield what became known as "secondary sanctions," which reached beyond Iran to target its foreign business partners. It was an extraordinary measure, and naturally, it didn't sit well with U.S. allies in Europe. Sir Leon Brittan, the EU's trade commissioner, denounced ILSA as "extraterritorial"—an unjustified attempt by Washington to dictate decisions in which it should have no say. At Brittan's urging, the EU passed a law making it illegal for European companies to comply with ILSA or any other U.S. secondary sanctions in the future.

Congress's zeal was blowing up into a full-fledged transatlantic crisis. All the while, Iran was busy signing new business deals. In 1997, the year after ILSA was passed, Total and several other foreign companies announced major plans to develop Iran's South Pars gas field. Under the new American law, these investments should clearly have triggered U.S. sanctions, and members of Congress clamored for action. At the direction of Secretary of State Madeleine Albright, Stuart Eizenstat, a senior envoy at the State Department, and Senator Al D'Amato, one of ILSA's main sponsors, hopped on a flight to meet with Brittan. After tough negotiations, they struck a deal: In exchange for a waiver from the ILSA sanctions, the EU would tighten some of its own export restrictions on Iran. To prevent future standoffs with the EU, Albright soon expanded the deal into a general compromise: If the EU was willing to cooperate with the United States on Iran, Washington would refrain from penalizing European firms that violated ILSA.

What this EU cooperation would entail, however, was left vague. In the years to come, European energy companies continued funneling money and expertise into Iran's oil and gas sectors. In turn, the Iranian regime raked in billions in petrodollars, and its nuclear program developed apace. The secondary sanctions established by ILSA went unused, and the law's main achievement remained a breach in transatlantic relations. In 2004, years after he helped strike the compromise with the EU, Eizenstat declared ILSA an "exhausted and toothless tiger" and urged Congress to let it "die a natural death."

10

Risky Business

On September 30, 2004, at the palm-tree-lined campus of the University of Miami, President George W. Bush squared off in the first presidential debate with his Democratic challenger, Senator John Kerry. The Iraq War was not going well. Investigators had concluded that Saddam Hussein's nuclear program—the United States' purported reason for the invasion—had been shuttered more than a decade before Bush ordered troops into battle. Hours before the Miami debate, the Iraq Survey Group, a team of experts tasked with scouring Iraq for weapons of mass destruction in the wake of the invasion, issued its final report declaring there was "no evidence" the country had been pursuing such weapons.

The same could not be said of Iran.

Two years earlier, a mustachioed Iranian dissident named Alireza Jafarzadeh had held a press conference at the Willard Hotel, a short walk from the White House. Jafarzadeh, who had ties to Israeli intelligence, made a bombshell revelation: the Iranian regime was building covert nuclear facilities. On a map, he pinpointed two secret sites—an enrichment plant in the desert town of Natanz, which could supply Tehran with highly enriched uranium; and a heavy-water production plant in Arak, which could provide plutonium. Together, these sites gave Iran two distinct pathways to nuclear weapons. The facilities were light-years more advanced than anything Saddam had ever possessed. They put the Bush administration—which had just named Iran a member of the "axis of evil"—in an awkward position. If it was worth invading Iraq to stop an imaginary nuclear program, was it worth invading Iran to stop a real one?

That question hung over the debate hall in Miami like the city's thick humid air. Bush and Kerry both declared nuclear proliferation America's most serious challenge—and both singled out Iran's nuclear program as especially dangerous. But neither had a good solution. The two candidates dodged a question about whether they would order another preemptive military attack. When Kerry brought up the possibility of hitting Iran with more sanctions, Bush hunched over the podium and furrowed his brow in disbelief, like a high school debater whose opponent had just made a false claim and hoped to get away with it. "We've already sanctioned Iran!" he retorted. "We can't sanction them any more."

Bush was expressing a commonly held belief in Washington: America had tried using sanctions to stop Iran's nuclear program, and those efforts had failed. Shortly after winning reelection, Bush reiterated his view. "We've sanctioned ourselves out of influence with Iran," he said during a press conference at the White House. "We don't have much leverage with the Iranians right now." After decades of sanctions, the United States had no trade with Iran and American companies were not invested in the country. Stacking on more sanctions would be an exercise in futility.

Stuart Levey took this sense of resignation as a personal challenge. A few months before the Bush-Kerry debate in Miami, Levey had been confirmed as the Treasury Department's first undersecretary for terrorism and financial intelligence. Beneath Levey's calm, lawyerly demeanor was a fiercely competitive man with a chip on his shoulder. By agreeing to head Treasury's newly created TFI division, he had taken a professional risk. When he heard Bush's comments, Levey saw an opportunity to make his mark. He made it his mission to supply the leverage over Iran that Bush said America lacked.

The urgency of this mission grew significantly the following year. In June 2005, Iranians elected a populist hard-liner, Mahmoud Ahmadinejad, as president. Ahmadinejad was a strict adherent to a fundamentalist Shiite creed that anticipated the imminent return of the Hidden Imam, a messianic figure expected to face off against forces of evil in an apocalyptic war and ultimately usher in peace on earth. He also rattled Western audiences by frequently denying the Holocaust and threatening to destroy Israel.

Shortly after Ahmadinejad's inauguration, Tehran shrugged off a diplomatic overture from Europe and restarted uranium enrichment, which was temporarily suspended under Ahmadinejad's reformist predecessor. Iran looked poised to speed up its nuclear development. Then, in his first appearance on the world stage, Ahmadinejad unnerved the UN General Assembly in New York by concluding his speech with a prayer for the return of the Hidden Imam. "O mighty Lord," he pronounced, "I pray to you to hasten the emergence of your last repository, the promised one, that perfect and pure human being, the one that will fill this world with justice and peace."

Mahmoud Ahmadinejad: Iran's new president
addresses the UN General Assembly in September 2005.

Adam Szubin, Levey's close advisor, could be forgiven for thinking of the doomsday cults he had studied during his college days at Harvard. Back then, he'd noticed that many such sects lived totally in the present, showing little regard for the future. Since they expected the apocalypse within their own lifetimes, many followers didn't even see a need to send their kids to school. Whether Ahmadinejad's apocalyptic convictions ran so deep was unclear, but the idea of such a man at the helm of a nuclear-armed state was bloodcurdling. Could nuclear deterrence work against a leader who eagerly awaited the end of days? Neither the United States nor Israel—which felt its very existence imperiled—was willing to find out.

≡

The most obvious way to apply real economic pressure against Iran was to cut off its lucrative oil exports. But the United States didn't buy any Iranian oil, and there was no chance Washington could persuade other countries to end their own purchases. "You could go around the world and tell people you wanted them to stop buying Iranian oil, and they would just laugh at you," Levey explained. With global oil prices climbing, even the White House itself was wary of launching a frontal assault on Iranian oil. A more indirect approach would be necessary.

Levey's light-bulb moment came in January 2006 on a trip to Bahrain, just across the Persian Gulf from Iran. Flipping through a local newspaper at the breakfast table, he came across a story about a big Swiss bank that had voluntarily cut ties with Iran. "It sort of clicked for me," he later recalled. "When we say we're 'all sanctioned out,' what we mean is that it's illegal for U.S. companies to do business with Iran. It does not mean the world has stopped doing business with Iran."

It was a simple insight, not unlike the one that inspired Congress to pass ILSA a decade prior. Of course, ILSA had shown that acting on this insight through the threat of secondary sanctions was a diplomatic minefield, and Levey knew the Bush administration was not ready to go there. Upon reading about the Swiss bank, however, Levey realized he didn't need to win over foreign governments or explicitly threaten secondary sanctions. Instead, he could go directly to foreign companies—chief among them the banks that connected Iran to the world economy. From his time in private law practice, Levey was familiar with how corporate executives thought about regulatory and reputational risk. He believed he could persuade them to cut ties with Iran of their own accord, whether their home governments were on board or not.

When Levey returned to Washington, he got Szubin and the rest of the team to work. They knew that the U.S. government could use the financial sector's risk aversion to its advantage: a few months earlier, banks all over the world had ended their relationships with North Korea after Treasury declared the Macau-based Banco Delta Asia a "primary money laundering concern." To be sure, Iran was no North Korea; it was an energy giant whose commercial connections spanned the globe. But Levey and Szubin believed they could bring the same logic to bear to degrade Iran's links to the international financial system.

First, they would need buy-in from the White House. Bush had, after all, dismissed further sanctions on Iran as pointless. So in February 2006, Levey wrangled a ticket to accompany Condoleezza Rice, the secretary of state and the president's most trusted foreign policy advisor, on a trip to the Middle East. But as Rice's jet made stop after stop, Levey couldn't get a free moment to brief her. He felt like a fifth wheel. Only on the trip's final leg, the flight home to Washington, was he invited up to her cabin.

Levey made his pitch: Iran's continued business ties to Europe and Asia might seem like a strength, but America could turn them into a weakness. U.S. officials had detailed evidence showing that Iran used deceptive financial practices to fund its nuclear program at home and terrorist groups abroad. In one such tactic, known as "stripping," Iranian banks directed their counterparts to falsify financial transaction data so that all signs of Iranian involvement were removed. Because stripping is illegal in the United States—and virtually all global banks had some presence in the United States—any bank that did it risked violating American law and facing serious penalties. A few weeks prior, U.S. financial regulators had fined the Dutch bank ABN AMRO $80 million for doctoring payment instructions to Bank Melli, Iran's biggest bank. At the time, it was the largest fine ever levied for sanctions violations. Such costs far outweighed the benefits of doing business with Iran. All American officials had to do, Levey argued, was to inform banking executives of the extent of Iranian misconduct and warn them not to become the next ABN AMRO.

The campaign would be aided, Levey told Rice, by waves of American sanctions on the largest Iranian banks, penalties that would cut them off more fully from the global financial system. Iranian banks were already barred from doing business directly in the United States through an embargo in place since the mid-1990s, yet there was an important loophole: they could still use U.S. financial infrastructure to complete transactions with non-U.S. entities. When Iranian banks made payments to counterparts in Europe or Asia, their transactions often went through the U.S. financial system, making a brief pit stop at a correspondent account in New York before taking a "U-turn" to their final destination. Few bankers ever thought about this U-turn, a quirk of the invisible infrastructure of cross-border finance, but Treasury could turn it into a chokepoint.

To do so, Levey proposed using the strongest weapon Treasury had in its arsenal: "blocking sanctions," a penalty that included an asset freeze and a transaction ban, and which Washington typically wielded against terrorists and drug kingpins. Blocking sanctions would generate a twofold benefit. On a practical level, they would fully sever the targeted Iranian bank from the U.S. financial system, including from U-turn transactions. Just as valuable, however, would be the message sent to the rest of the world. The new sanctions would be *conduct-based*, meaning they would draw an explicit connection between Iranian banks and the country's nuclear program or support for terrorism. By highlighting those links, Levey would have an easier time persuading foreign financial institutions that dealing with Iran was so risky that it was best avoided entirely.

One bank at a time, Washington would condition the international financial system to reject all business with Iran—not because governments required it but because banks deemed it the right risk-based business decision. Corporate self-interest would be America's most crucial ally.

The only catch, Levey told Rice, was that the Bush administration would need to be comfortable acting alone. They could not count on UN support, which at the time remained the gold standard for impactful sanctions. Nevertheless, by declassifying intelligence and publicizing the rationale for unilateral American measures, Washington could credibly claim that it had international law on its side. The administration should still push for action at the UN, but letting the UN set the pace would be a recipe for inaction and, ultimately, failure.

Rice found the pitch compelling. She asked Levey what he needed to get started. "I need your direct support," he said, "and I need to do this in concert with the State Department." Rice agreed and shook Levey's hand. Elated, he returned to his seat at the back of the plane.

11

Stuart Levey Goes to War

In the summer of 2006, Hank Paulson left his job running Goldman Sachs and moved to Washington to become the new secretary of the treasury. The agency had been run by its fair share of Wall Street titans, but Treasury staff awaited Paulson, an affable former college football star with a hefty bald head and can-do spirit, with anticipation. He was deeply respected across global financial markets. His nomination had caused the dollar to shoot up in value.

Levey and Szubin, lawyers who had spent much of their careers in public service, were unsure of what to expect from their new boss. The last ex-Goldman executive to lead Treasury, Robert Rubin, had been wary of weaponizing America's central role in the international financial system. Since Levey's plane ride with Condoleezza Rice several months earlier, the team at TFI had intensified its investigation into the complex procurement networks Iran used to support its nuclear and missile programs. Massive charts in Levey's office mapped a dizzying network of banks, shipping firms, and front companies for the IRGC, which in addition to its military role also ruled over a vast business empire. The network crisscrossed the globe: many of the nodes were based in Iran, but just as many were located elsewhere. When Levey first met Paulson in the secretary's stately, light-drenched office on the third floor of Treasury, he lugged the charts with him.

"What do you intend to do?" Paulson asked after Levey briefed him. "Do you intend to sanction *everything* that you've just identified to me?"

Levey felt a jolt of nerves.

"No," he replied, "I intend to talk to them all."

"I love that!" Paulson intoned in his raspy voice. "I believe that if you show people what they're involved in, and they don't know it, they will act."

With endorsements from Rice and Paulson, Levey felt he had sufficient backing to go on the offensive. As the sweltering Washington summer eased into fall, Levey made a speech in which he laid out the new strategy and announced the first salvo of blocking sanctions against a major Iranian bank—in this case, Bank Saderat, which Tehran used to funnel money to Hezbollah. Treasury officials then deployed across the globe to meet with bank CEOs and compliance officers, briefing them on Iran's nuclear and missile networks. Even Paulson took part in the campaign. "There's a broad network of front companies, and these are not front companies that say 'Nuclear Acquisition Corp.' or 'Weapons Production Corp.,'" he told the press during a trip to Singapore. "These are mundane-sounding companies that do many legitimate activities, but in addition, do some of these untoward and illicit activities."

Paulson's connections in the financial sector opened doors for Levey and his team, who secured meetings with the CEOs of all the major banks in Europe, Asia, and the Middle East. Over more than a hundred of these conversations, Levey refined his pitch. On one trip, he came across a newspaper ad in which the Iranian government publicly solicited bids for the construction of nuclear power plants and a light-water reactor in Bushehr Province. The ad instructed bidders to pay a nonrefundable application fee of €15,000 to an account at Creditanstalt, an Austrian bank. Levey called Creditanstalt's CEO, who was unaware that his bank was being used as a conduit for Iranian nuclear funds. The account had originally been opened to enable Iranian diplomats in Vienna to access basic banking services. The Iranian government then employed the account to aid its nuclear procurement efforts.

Levey had his staff make thousands of copies of the ad, which he started handing out to bankers during his presentations. It was a perfect case study of Iran's deceptive financial practices—and of the risks of doing seemingly innocuous business with the country.

Creditanstalt wasn't the only firm in the dark about its entanglement with nefarious Iranian activities. When Levey met with the head of another major European bank and described Iran's practice of "stripping" its transactions of identifying markers, the executive scoffed at the notion that any reputable European financial institution could be complicit in such trickery. "We would never do something like that," he explained.

INVITATION FOR BID
Construction of Two Large-Scale Nuclear Power Plants in Iran

The Nuclear Power Production and Development Company of Iran (NPPD), (an affiliate company of the Atomic Energy Organization of Iran) as the owner invites sealed Bids from contractors/companies for the Design, Supply of Equipment, Construction and Commissioning of two large-scale (1,000-1,600 MW) third generation Nuclear Power Plants with pressurized light water reactor in Bushehr Province of Iran.

Qualified bidders who have sufficient experiences in the Construction and Commissioning of such plants are requested to obtain the respective documents upon payment of a nonrefundable fee of €15,000 (fifteen thousand Euros) transferred to the following account:
Account No. 01754283800
Name of Bank: Austria Bank – Creditanstalt
Code of Bank: 12000
IBAN: AT88 1100 0017 5428 3800
BIC: BKAUATWW
Branch: Jacquingasse 1/Rennweg 20, A1030, Austria
within 15 days from April 25, 2007 thru. AEOI's Representative Office at Heinestr, 19/1/1, A-1020 Vienna, Austria or company's Headquarters Office at No. 7, Tandis St., Africa Ave., Tehran, Islamic Republic of Iran.

All Bids must be accompanied by a Bid Bond of twenty million Euros and must be delivered to AEOI's Representative Office in Vienna by 02.08.2007 or to the company's Headquarters before 08.08.2007. The bids will be opened at the company's Headquarters' Office in Tehran on 08.08.2007 at 10:00 am in the presence of the Bidder's Representatives who wish to attend.

For further information, please contact:
Tel: (+431) 2140971, (+431) 2140972
Fax: (+431) 2140973
Contact Person: Mr. Esmaeili
E-mail: esmaeili@teleweb.at

Prop of persuasion: a newspaper ad Stuart Levey
used to illustrate Iran's deceptive financial practices.

Levey's colleagues, sitting beside him at the table, shifted in their seats and eyed their boss intently. After the meeting concluded, Levey asked to see the CEO privately. "I don't want to embarrass any of your colleagues, but you're doing this yourself," he said once they were alone. Levey then shared declassified intelligence revealing that the bank had in fact agreed to modify payment instructions to mask Iran's involvement.

Turning pale, the CEO insisted that this was news to him. "I completely believe you," Levey reassured him.

Levey's nonconfrontational style worked. Within weeks, the bank had cut off all business with Iran. Still, U.S. law enforcement agencies eventually hit the bank with a hefty fine for sanctions violations. While Treasury could shape sanctions policy, the Justice Department and other prosecutorial agencies were responsible for enforcing it. In the years ahead, as many foreign banks grew painfully familiar with this division of responsibility, their concerns about violating American sanctions rose sharply.

Levey's roadshow did not always receive a warm welcome. Many governments bristled at a foreign official conducting direct diplomacy with their countries' biggest financial institutions. And although Levey tried to appear more like a technocratic advisor than an interrogator, some bankers perceived his briefings as threatening or overbearing. After a meeting with Levey, an executive from the New York branch of the British bank Standard Chartered sent a panicked email to headquarters in London. The banker warned that continued business with Iran could cause "very serious or even catastrophic reputational damage."

The response from the bank's second-in-command captured a common sentiment across Europe: "You fucking Americans. Who are you to tell us, the rest of the world, that we're not going to deal with Iranians?" A few years later, U.S. law enforcement agencies would fine Standard Chartered hundreds of millions of dollars for violating Iran sanctions.

As Levey trotted the globe, Szubin and the team at OFAC churned out round after round of blocking sanctions that kept Iran's largest banks and companies from transacting on world markets. Treasury and State collaborated to impose penalties on Bank Melli and on Khatam al-Anbiya, a massive, IRGC-controlled engineering firm that Tehran employed for state construction projects. Near the end of Bush's second term, Treasury barred all Iranian banks from the U.S. financial system, closing off their access to the dollar even for fleeting U-turn transactions. During the same period, the UN Security Council adopted several additional resolutions demanding that Iran cease nuclear enrichment. While the resolutions did not go as far as Washington wanted—the actual trade restrictions they imposed on Iran were narrowly focused on arms and nuclear technology—they lent legitimacy to Levey's campaign. Governments might have been leery of Levey's methods, but the UN resolutions showed that his goals, at least, were shared by the international community.

Eighteen months into the campaign, nearly all the world's largest banks had stopped servicing transactions with Iran, even though neither their own governments nor the UN required it. Levey had demonstrated that the United States could wage hard-hitting economic war even when the rest of the world was reluctant to join in, disproving the age-old Washington belief that impactful sanctions needed formal buy-in from the UN.

Tehran took notice. When Ahmadinejad's finance minister was ousted in April 2008 amid rising inflation, he used his departing remarks to grumble about Levey. "We had embarked on a serious and breathtaking game of chess with America's Treasury Department," he said. "They had assigned one of their Zionist deputies to halt the Iranian economy. This person would personally travel to many countries around the world. He would use incentives and encouragement to request cooperation against Iran, and if he failed to get any results he would use threats to pursue his goal."

Levey's "whisper campaign" against Iran, as National Security Advisor Stephen Hadley dubbed it, made him a household name in U.S. foreign policy circles, too. In October 2008, the prize-winning journalist Robin Wright wrote a five-thousand-word profile for *The New York Times Magazine* titled "Stuart Levey's War." In the article, a Bush administration official compared Levey's work to the successful American effort to support the Afghan mujahideen against the Soviets that was dramatized in the film *Charlie Wilson's War*. "It's the most direct and aggressive stuff we've got going. It delivers."

This wasn't entirely true. Levey's campaign had coaxed big banks to shun Iran, but it hadn't convinced the Iranians to end their nuclear program. In fact, Iran's economy wasn't struggling nearly as much as U.S. officials anticipated. Inflation and unemployment were high, and prices were rising for staples like rice, cucumbers, and laundry detergent. Yet overall economic growth remained robust, standing at over 8 percent in 2007. Above all, the country was still awash in petrodollars. Oil prices had soared from about $60 per barrel when Levey launched his campaign in September 2006 to more than $100 in 2008, and Iran sold around 2.5 million such barrels each day. Iran's oil revenues, which amounted to over $60 billion per year, ensured that the country's elite—and its nuclear program—were comfortably sheltered from the impact of sanctions.

One problem was that Levey's method wasn't airtight. As megabanks like UBS and Deutsche Bank cut ties with Iran, enterprising Iranian bankers found new conduits to the global economy through smaller banks, many of which were eager to scoop up business that the heavyweights had forsaken. Another, even bigger issue was that it was difficult—perhaps impossible—to truly isolate a petrostate from the world economy when it continued to export oil in huge quantities and rake in untold billions in the process. And it was not just the rest of the world that wanted Iranian oil to flow. The Bush White House was petrified of taking any step that could spike oil prices further. "It was made very clear to us in the 2006 to 2008 time frame," said a senior U.S. sanctions official, "that we weren't going after oil." There was a reason Iran's central bank, which collected payments for the country's oil sales, remained free from OFAC's blocking sanctions.

The lack of progress was not lost on members of Congress, many of whom prided themselves on being tough on Iran and close friends to Israel. These Iran hawks watched in horror as the country's nuclear program charged forward, accompanied by a steady drip of vile rhetoric from Ahmadinejad. Among them was Tom Lantos, the Democratic chairman of the House Foreign Affairs Committee. Lantos, a Hungarian-born Jew and the only Holocaust survivor to have served in Congress, was convinced that so long as Iran was swimming in oil profits, its nuclear program would advance. It was time to threaten secondary sanctions against anyone supporting Iran's energy industry, including America's friends in Europe. More specifically, it was time to enforce the Iran Sanctions Act (ISA), the 1996 law formerly known as the Iran and Libya Sanctions Act or ILSA. (The legislation had been revised and renamed after Libyan leader Muammar Gaddafi agreed in 2003 to shutter his country's nuclear-weapons program.) The legal obligation in ISA to impose secondary sanctions on foreign firms that invested in Iran's energy industry remained on the books, though it was widely understood that the United States had given up on enforcing it after intense backlash from Europe had forced the Clinton administration to back down.

In 2007, Lantos introduced legislation to strengthen ISA. "The corporate barons running giant oil companies—who have cravenly turned a blind eye to Iran's development of nuclear weapons—have come to assume that the Iran Sanctions Act will never be implemented," Lantos declared. "This charade will now come to a long overdue end."

The bill passed the House but never got a vote in the Senate. It did collect a long list of co-sponsors, however, a sign that more congressional activism on Iran was forthcoming. One of the co-sponsors was a first-term senator from Illinois named Barack Obama, who would soon have to grapple with the unfinished business of Stuart Levey's war.

12

Extending a Hand

In December 2008, as Bush administration officials were cleaning out their offices, Stuart Levey received an unexpected phone call.

It was Tim Geithner—president of the New York Fed, Obama's pick for treasury secretary, and arguably one of the busiest men in America amid the swirling financial crisis. Geithner got straight to the point: Obama wanted Levey to stay on at Treasury.

Levey was caught off guard. High-level political appointees from the opposing party were rarely retained by new administrations. What's more, Obama had pledged to extend an olive branch to Iran's leaders during his campaign. Ahmadinejad had even sent the president-elect a congratulatory letter. Did Obama really want Levey, a man loathed in Tehran, on his team? Or would Levey's only purpose be to shield the new administration from the inevitable charge of being weak on Iran?

After receiving assurances that Obama planned to build on his past work, Levey accepted the offer. Other than Robert Gates, the secretary of defense, Levey was the highest-ranking Bush administration official whom Obama kept on. For the team at TFI, including Adam Szubin and Danny Glaser, the hard-charging deputy who helped spearhead the move against Banco Delta Asia, Levey's retention marked the evolution of TFI from a fledgling bureaucratic startup to a big fish in the national security ecosystem. It also meant that they, too, would keep their jobs, bringing their institutional knowledge and skill in the art of economic warfare into the new administration.

Joining their ranks would be David Cohen, TFI's new number two and an old friend of Levey's. After law school, both men had gotten their start at the same boutique litigation firm in Washington in the early 1990s. For their first assignment, they traveled together to Atlanta to represent Chabad-Lubavitch, a Hasidic Jewish movement, in a court case surrounding its quest to erect a fifteen-foot-high menorah in the rotunda of the Georgia state capitol. (Zell Miller, Georgia's governor, had opposed Chabad's effort, leading to the lawsuit, which Chabad eventually won.) Levey and Cohen had a close bond, which would serve them well at Treasury.

As the sanctions technocrats prepared for work under a new president, hawks on Capitol Hill were drawing up their own plans to attack the Iranian economy. Iran now possessed enough low-enriched uranium for a nuclear weapon, so time was running short to stop the country from crossing the point of no return. All of Washington anticipated that Obama would make a diplomatic overture to Tehran. Members of Congress on both sides of the aisle were convinced that diplomacy could succeed only if backed by a credible threat—which seemed unlikely to come from the new administration.

A few weeks before Obama's inauguration, aides to Senators Jon Kyl, a Republican, and Joe Lieberman, a former Democrat who had become an independent, arrived at a restaurant in Washington's Union Station. They were there to meet with leaders from the American Israel Public Affairs Committee (AIPAC), the powerful pro-Israel lobbying group, to craft a political strategy to advance more aggressive sanctions on Iran. Since the ILSA debacle during the Clinton administration, Congress had steered clear of the issue, with the exception of Lantos's bill from the previous year, which had looked promising but died in the Senate for want of a strong legislative champion. The lunch party agreed that Senator Evan Bayh, an influential moderate Democrat from Indiana who had been considered as a potential Obama running mate, would be the ideal torchbearer. After the meeting, Bayh, Kyl, and Lieberman formed a triad in favor of harsher Iran sanctions, and their staffs started drafting fresh legislation.

Obama, on the other hand, genuinely wanted to test out diplomacy with the Iranian regime. He did not share his predecessor's view that merely talking to foreign adversaries was a concession, instead promising America's rivals that "we will extend a hand if you are willing to unclench your fist." He also believed the United States would have much more success bringing other world powers on board with sanctions if Washington made a good-faith effort at diplomacy that Tehran rebuffed.

In his first months in office, Obama sent a series of secret letters to Ayatollah Ali Khamenei, Iran's supreme leader and ultimate decision-maker.

Obama hoped to signal that his administration would not seek regime change, which had been the preferred (if unstated) objective of many neocons in the Bush administration. He could live with the Islamic Republic if it reined in its disruptive behavior, starting with its nuclear program.

Obama drove this point home in a video message commemorating Nowruz, the Iranian new year, on March 19, 2009. "I would like to speak directly to the people and leaders of the Islamic Republic of Iran," Obama said—the first time a sitting American president had addressed Iran as the "Islamic Republic." He continued: "My administration is now committed to diplomacy that addresses the full range of issues before us, and to pursuing constructive ties among the United States, Iran, and the international community. This process will not be advanced by threats. We seek instead engagement that is honest and grounded in mutual respect."

To give the White House's diplomacy some breathing room, Levey, who had been warmly welcomed by Obama's inner circle, paused the routine of churning out new sanctions each week and feverishly warning international banks. But the Treasury team knew well that Obama's overture to Tehran carried risks for the economic pressure they had built up to date. For that pressure to hold, the private sector needed to believe that U.S. penalties on Iran would stiffen, not soften, in the future. Obama's more conciliatory stance seemed at odds with that assumption. Even some U.S. allies worried, albeit erroneously, that the Obama administration was preparing to ease the sanctions as part of a rapprochement and gearing up U.S. businesses to re-enter the Iranian market. If that narrative took hold, companies around the globe might rush back into Iran to seize commercial opportunities they'd previously deemed too risky.

To forestall that possibility, U.S. officials took pains to make clear that Obama's interest in negotiations did not mean the sanctions would end—in fact, quite the opposite. In March, Danny Glaser traveled to Brussels to deliver a classified briefing to dozens of Middle East experts from various European governments. Now, he urged, was not the time for economic reengagement with Iran. For diplomacy to work, Tehran needed to feel serious economic strain. If talks moved too slowly, Glaser suggested, Obama was ready to escalate the economic war significantly.

Back in Washington, State and Treasury officials were already working on a menu of possible sanctions that Obama could impose if his outreach faltered. Leading these preparations was Richard Nephew, a nuclear wonk turned sanctions expert. Nephew had started his government career at the

Department of Energy, where one of his jobs was briefing U.S. allies on the state of Iran's nuclear program. It was a thankless task: his audiences tended to be skeptical of America's findings, still recalling the false intelligence on Saddam Hussein's purported weapons of mass destruction that preceded the U.S. invasion of Iraq. But the role taught Nephew to master arcane details and deal with tough crowds, skills he would need in the coming years.

Now in his late twenties and working at the State Department, Nephew collaborated with Adam Szubin to assemble a series of memos laying out new ways of targeting Iran's energy, financial, and transportation industries, as well as its nuclear procurement network and arms sector. By the end of summer 2009, the Obama administration had a blueprint for a renewed sanctions push, should it become necessary.

That scenario remained a distinct possibility. In June, Iran held a presidential election riddled with irregularities. Shortly after polls closed, Iranian state TV announced that Ahmadinejad had been reelected with 62 percent of the vote, a showing so strong that many independent analysts—and many Iranian voters—suspected fraud. Protests erupted across the country, with demonstrators donning green garb, the campaign symbol of Ahmadinejad's reformist challenger, Mir-Hossein Mousavi. By the third day of what became known as the Green Revolution, more than a million people had poured into the streets of Tehran, chanting "Where is my vote?" Soon after, the government shut down the internet and let loose the IRGC's feared Basij militia, which jailed thousands of protesters, killed dozens, and placed Mousavi and his wife under permanent house arrest.

Obama's response was muted. He held off on providing rhetorical or material support to the protesters, wary of tainting them as agents of U.S. influence. He was also uncertain how much of a difference it would make if Mousavi came to power. On the nuclear file, at least, the man in charge would still be Ayatollah Khamenei. At home, Obama came under intense criticism for his restraint. The episode underscored the difficulty of pursuing diplomacy with a government as oppressive as Iran's. It was clear that the regime wasn't going anywhere, and that Obama was going to pay a political price for attempting diplomacy. But his administration was undeterred.

≡

That summer, Iran sent a letter to the International Atomic Energy Agency (IAEA), the UN's nuclear watchdog, explaining that it was running out of fuel for the Tehran Research Reactor—the five-megawatt nuclear reactor America had given it back in 1967. Iran requested the IAEA's assistance in obtaining a fresh supply of fuel. Used primarily to produce medical isotopes, the reactor wasn't inherently threatening. But the unstated implication of Iran's request was ominous: If the IAEA couldn't help Iran secure the fuel from abroad, Iran would be forced to produce its own. This would require Iran to enrich uranium domestically to a level at which it could easily be repurposed for nuclear weapons.

At the private urging of IAEA director Mohamed ElBaradei, U.S. officials came up with a creative proposal that would fulfill Iran's request while also tackling the problem of Iran's existing stockpile of enriched uranium. Under the proposal, Iran would ship much of its low-enriched uranium to Russia, which would then send back enough reactor fuel to power the Tehran Research Reactor for more than a decade. (Iran's existing stockpile of uranium could be enriched into material for nuclear weapons, whereas the Russian reactor fuel could not.) Iran would give up the lion's share of its fissile material, leaving the country far short of what it needed to produce even a single nuclear weapon. The fuel swap would, in the words of one senior White House official, "call Iran's bluff" by forcing it to uphold its repeated claim that it was pursuing only peaceful uses of nuclear energy. ElBaradei previewed the proposal with Iranian officials, who agreed to consider it.

In September, a new development gave the fuel swap proposal heightened urgency. American, British, and French intelligence discovered that Iran was building a secret nuclear enrichment site, buried deep inside a mountain in the village of Fordow, a short distance from the holy city of Qom. Its concealed location and unusual size—too small to produce the fissile material necessary for a nuclear power plant, but big enough to supply material for a handful of bombs each year—made the facility look like a smoking gun. Fordow appeared to be the site where Iran planned to produce the highly enriched uranium it needed for a nuclear weapon. If Iran hadn't already resolved on building a nuclear bomb, it was undeniably pursuing the ability to do so on short notice.

Obama publicly revealed the secret enrichment site alongside French President Nicolas Sarkozy and British Prime Minister Gordon Brown at a G20 summit in Pittsburgh. "Iran has a right to peaceful nuclear power that meets the energy needs of its people," declared Obama. "But the size and configuration of this facility is inconsistent with a peaceful program." Sarkozy was even more blunt. "We cannot let the Iranian leaders gain time

IRAN AND ITS NUCLEAR SITES

☢ NUCLEAR SITES

while the motors are running," the French president affirmed. "If by December there is not an in-depth change by the Iranian leaders, sanctions will have to be taken."

What Obama, Sarkozy, and Brown knew that most viewers didn't was that Iran had quietly come clean about Fordow to ElBaradei and the IAEA just a few days earlier—likely aware that U.S intelligence was onto them, the Iranians may have hoped to deprive Washington of a "gotcha" moment. But by going public first, Western leaders had won the PR battle. The revelation of Fordow put Iran on the back foot and unified world powers on the issue as never before. The Russians were especially irate, either because Iran had hidden the facility from them or because their own vaunted intelligence services had failed to detect it.

All eyes were now on Geneva, where America, China, France, Germany, Russia, and the United Kingdom—a negotiating bloc known as the P5+1—met with Iranian diplomats on October 1 to discuss the fuel swap proposal. On the margins of the session, Bill Burns, the number three at the State Department, sat down with Iran's chief negotiator, Saeed Jalili, a hard-nosed diplomat and veteran of the Iran-Iraq War. It was the first-ever bilateral discussion on nuclear matters between the two countries. Burns walked Jalili through the details of the fuel swap, and the Iranian indicated he could accept it.

Yet Jalili's promise soon rang hollow. In the weeks ahead, deadlines came and went, and Iranian officials dragged their feet on finalizing the terms of the agreement. It seemed that the deal was falling victim to Iranian domestic politics: the Green Revolution had badly damaged Ahmadinejad's standing, and his political rivals were not eager to give him a win by waving the deal through. Obama's diplomatic push had failed. He had extended a hand, but Tehran's fist remained clenched.

13

===

With Us or Against Us

As the fuel swap deal unraveled, U.S. officials returned to the economic warpath. Obama gave the green light to proceed with the sanctions plans that State and Treasury had drawn up over the summer, adding one condition: before the United States went ahead on its own, it should try to pass a new UN Security Council resolution.

The revelation of the secret nuclear site at Fordow, in addition to Tehran's scuttling of the fuel swap deal, had opened a window for multilateral action. With world powers indignant about Iran's behavior, a new round of UN sanctions might have a real chance. Though hardly a silver bullet, UN sanctions would offer several advantages. Walloping Iran's economy would require companies—and countries—to make hard sacrifices, which would go over better if they were not seen as a dictate from Washington. Plus, if the UN Security Council took a tough stance, it would give America's existing sanctions further international legitimacy and even spur other countries to join in. Since UN Security Council resolutions have the force of international law, all UN members would be technically obligated to comply.

So American officials fanned out once more, this time to advertise the menu of sanctions that Richard Nephew and Adam Szubin had compiled. The hope was that by sharing these ideas with close U.S. allies, they could form the basis for the new UN resolution that Obama wanted. Fortunately, there was by now more alignment on nuclear matters between Europe and America. For starters, the Europeans loved Obama, whose respect for diplomacy was such a breath of fresh air after eight years of Bush's "with us or against us" approach that the Norwegians awarded him the Nobel Peace

Prize just months into his presidency. Political changes in Europe also helped. Two years earlier, French President Jacques Chirac, who had pooh-poohed the Iranian nuclear threat, was succeeded by Nicolas Sarkozy, who was more hawkish and more willing to aid U.S. efforts to isolate Tehran. The replacement of German Chancellor Gerhard Schröder with Angela Merkel in 2005 marked a similar shift in Berlin. At EU headquarters in Brussels, the tide seemed to be turning in favor of tougher sanctions, too, especially after a renewed push led by Richard Nephew, who walked European diplomats through the American proposals in painstaking detail.

Past UN Security Council resolutions made clear that Iran's nuclear activities were squarely outside the bounds of international law. Yet the UN had been unwilling to impose broad sanctions: its existing resolutions limited the sale of nuclear technologies to Iran but did little else. They were meant to stymie Iran's nuclear procurement, not to damage its economy. The Obama administration sought to change this. In late 2009 and early 2010, the United States laid the groundwork for a far more ambitious UN resolution with comprehensive sanctions on Iranian banks, oil companies, and shipping firms.

Britain and France, the two European countries with permanent seats on the Security Council, were certain to vote yes. Even Russia, still angry about the Fordow revelation, was broadly supportive. But China, whose diplomats usually took a hands-off approach to discussions at the UN, was vehemently opposed. China was a major buyer of Iranian oil, and it didn't want to imperil domestic economic growth while the world was recovering from the global financial crisis. At one point in the negotiations, an exasperated European diplomat complained that Mao would be rolling over in his grave if he could hear his successors extolling the virtues of an unfettered world oil market. Beijing's skepticism slowed down the negotiations considerably, but America and its allies eventually got China to support a milder resolution. On June 9, 2010, UN Security Council Resolution 1929 was adopted.

Chinese opposition had eliminated the possibility of sweeping UN sanctions, but U.S. officials succeeded in getting two critical elements into the final text of the resolution. First, the resolution called on countries to require their companies to "exercise vigilance when doing business with entities incorporated in Iran," especially when they had "reasonable grounds to believe that such business could contribute to Iran's proliferation-sensitive nuclear activities." Stuart Levey's efforts to reach out directly to foreign banks and urge them to cut ties with Iran now had a clear UN imprimatur.

Second, the resolution opened the possibility of stronger penalties on Iran's energy sector. In a hat tip to Beijing, the resolution acknowledged that "access to diverse, reliable energy is critical for sustainable growth and development." But it also noted the "potential connection" between Iran's oil revenues and funding for its "proliferation-sensitive nuclear activities"— language designed to give the EU legal cover for banning European companies from investing in Iranian energy projects. (The EU was wary of taking such a step without a clear mandate from the UN.) European energy investments in Iran had drawn Washington's ire ever since Total backfilled Conoco's investment in the country in 1995. Now, between the new UN resolution and simultaneous developments on Capitol Hill, it looked like the stream of foreign investment into Iran's energy industry might finally slow to a trickle.

———

As the Obama team was hammering out the UN resolution in New York, members of Congress in Washington were champing at the bit to advance their own sanctions. Senator Evan Bayh introduced a new Iran sanctions bill in the Senate, while Representative Howard Berman pushed forward similar legislation in the House. Some skeptics on Capitol Hill wondered if sanctions alone could ever exert enough pressure. "We're asking them to give up their firstborn," said Representative Brad Sherman, referring to Tehran's nuclear program, "and we're threatening them with the possibility of paying an increase in their ATM fees." Most were unconvinced the Obama administration was ready to impose secondary sanctions on foreign companies doing business with Iran—a bridge even Bush proved unwilling to cross. Still, for the first time since the mid-1990s, Congress seemed poised to pass a major new law aimed at Iran's economy.

The law in question was the Comprehensive Iran Sanctions, Accountability, and Divestment Act, or CISADA. At the urging of the White House, the bill's sponsors had agreed to put the effort on ice until after the UN Security Council adopted its new resolution. Now that the resolution had passed, members of Congress were ironing out a final version of the bill. CISADA included a ban on shipments of gasoline to Iran, a measure backed by members of Congress who surmised that "hitting 'em at the pump" would be just as devastating to Iranians as it would be to Americans. (They were soon proven wrong.) The bill's more sensible—and much more far-reaching— provisions included robust secondary sanctions against investments in

Iran's energy sector, an attempt to give real bite to the "toothless tiger" otherwise known as ISA. CISADA would ensure that virtually any foreign investment in Iran's energy sector would trigger U.S. secondary sanctions. The bill paired these sanctions with a clever incentive for foreign oil companies to leave Iran. This measure was devised by Jim Steinberg, the number-two official at the State Department and an important ally of Levey's. Under the provision, oil companies that put together gradual exit plans from Iran in consultation with the State Department would receive sanctions waivers, which would allow them to coordinate a managed withdrawal and collect any money they were owed on their way out the door. Combined with the EU's own investment ban, this so-called "special rule" would hopefully get Europe's biggest oil and gas firms to pack up and leave Iran for good.

Most important of all, however, was a provision in the bill threatening secondary sanctions against any foreign bank that did business with Iranian financial institutions that were blacklisted by the United States—a list that included virtually all of Iran's financial sector, except for the country's central bank. As a result of Levey's campaign, the world's biggest banks already avoided Iran. But Iran still found partners among smaller banks, many of which relied on America for little more than U-turn transactions and thus judged the benefits of dealing with Iran worth the theoretical risk of getting crosswise with U.S. law enforcement. A quick perusal of the *Bankers Almanac*, a resource publication for the financial industry, revealed that Iran maintained dozens of correspondent banking relationships from the United Arab Emirates to Turkey to Armenia to Sri Lanka. It could use those links to access the euro and, ultimately, the dollar.

In the realm of international financial transactions, "there's no such thing as a small fish," recalled a member of Adam Szubin's team at OFAC. "At the end of the day, it's just zeroes and ones, and all you need is access to the U.S. dollar. You can get that however you want." Working behind the scenes, Levey and Szubin had persuaded CISADA's authors that an explicit threat of secondary sanctions might be enough to flip the smaller banks' risk-benefit calculus. The provision was added to the legislation, giving Levey and Szubin a powerful new weapon in their pressure campaign.

On June 24, 2010, CISADA passed Congress with overwhelming bipartisan support: 408–8 in the House and 99–0 in the Senate. Obama signed it into law in the White House's East Room. In his remarks, the president singled out Levey, the Bush holdover, as "outstanding." He emphasized that the law would advance the will of the international community, including the recently adopted UN Security Council Resolution 1929, which imposed the "toughest and most comprehensive multilateral sanctions that the Iranian government has ever faced." With the one-two punch of the new UN resolution and CISADA, the groundwork for a full-on economic war was laid. And against almost everyone's expectations, it was Obama who was setting it into motion.

But in his comments in the East Room, Obama neglected to mention the core of what CISADA would do in practice. As Senator John McCain, Obama's former electoral rival, put it: "Because of this legislation, we will be posing a choice to companies around the world. Do you want to do business with Iran, or do you want to do business with the United States?" The occupant of the White House had changed, but the message from Washington was again "You're either with us or against us."

14

Exodus

On the northern edge of Dubai, the UAE's sparkling financial capital, a meandering saltwater inlet opens into the Persian Gulf. Its shores are lined with old wooden dhows used by tradesmen who regularly make the seventeen-hour voyage across the Strait of Hormuz to Bandar Abbas, Iran's busiest port. From the windows of the U.S. consulate, you can see stevedores load the dhows with all manner of foreign goods destined for the Islamic Republic. You can watch sanctions evasion in real time.

The UAE and Iran are deeply linked by people, culture, and geography. Scores of Iranians fleeing the 1979 revolution settled across the water in Dubai; others stayed but moved their businesses there. Today, the UAE is home to one of the world's largest Iranian diaspora communities. As a local old saw has it, when Emiratis pray for rain, it pours in Iran.

Iran's broken links with the commercial centers of Europe were Dubai's gain. As it became harder and harder for the rest of the world to ship goods directly to Iran, the city evolved into a massive re-export hub, importing goods and shipping them onward to Iran. Nearly $10 billion in goods took this route in 2010. "Things have actually gotten busier for us now that countries aren't dealing with Iran directly," said a Dubai-based seafarer. "Everything is going through Dubai." This was true not just in trade but also in finance. Dubai was Iran's last major lifeline to the global financial system. When Obama signed CISADA in July 2010, most of Iran's biggest banks—all of them subject to U.S. sanctions—had offices in Dubai and maintained strong relationships with the city.

These connections notwithstanding, the Emirati government in Abu

Dhabi saw the Islamic Republic as its gravest foreign threat, owing to Tehran's long-standing view that the UAE was part of its sphere of influence. To keep Iran at arm's length, the Emirati government purchased billions of dollars of American military hardware and sought close relations with the Pentagon. But it avoided pressing Dubai to sever its commercial ties to Iran, wary of upsetting the delicate balance between the UAE's two most powerful emirates, Abu Dhabi (the political capital) and Dubai (the business capital). In late 2009, however, Dubai, which had been hit hard by the global financial crisis, was on course to default on its debt and was bailed out by Abu Dhabi. That settled any doubts about who was in charge. As a Western diplomat observed at the time, Mohamed bin Zayed, the crown prince of Abu Dhabi, "effectively runs Dubai now."

Since launching the economic war against Iran in 2006, Stuart Levey had made more than a dozen trips to the UAE. He had built rapport with both the crown prince and his younger brother, Foreign Minister Sheikh Abdullah bin Zayed. But he had been less successful at persuading banks in Dubai to shun Iran. Now, with Abu Dhabi ascendant and CISADA in his arsenal, Levey thought it was time for another try.

Levey and his team arrived in the UAE in September 2010. It was Ramadan, and the combination of scorching heat and scarce food and drink sapped the Americans' energy. But it didn't quell their spirits. If there was ever an opportune moment to cut the cord between the Emiratis and Iran, it was now.

Their first stop was Dubai. At a roundtable with the city's most important financial institutions, Levey and his team stressed that business with Iranian banks—most of which were blacklisted by the United States—now carried a heightened risk of secondary sanctions. Just as European oil companies could be sanctioned by the United States under CISADA, so too could Emirati banks.

Next, the delegation was scheduled to meet with Sheikh Abdullah, the foreign minister. Despite repeated efforts, they were unable to confirm the meeting. Frustrated, the team gave up and headed for the airport in Dubai, resigned to return to Washington. Only then, as they were walking through the terminal, did they receive a call from one of the sheikh's aides, who told them to wait. Minutes later, a helicopter arrived to whisk them across the desert and deposit them on the verdant lawn of Abdullah's private palace in Abu Dhabi.

The sheikh directed them to his patio, which was decked out in plush furniture. Some members of his entourage were dressed in the customary white robe and *ghutra*, the headdress favored by Emirati royals, while others wore gym clothes. The sheikh himself sported a white robe but dispensed with the *ghutra*. As he was sick and taking a break from the Ramadan fast, he nibbled on dates and sipped tea. After a long exchange of pleasantries, he got down to business.

"That was a very good presentation you gave in Dubai," he told Levey.

"Oh, have you been briefed?" asked Levey, taken by surprise. He had not expected the Emirati political leadership to pay much attention to his round-table with the bankers.

"No," Abdullah responded, "I watched it."

Abdullah's staff, as the Americans now learned, had placed a camera inside their Dubai conference room, and the sheikh had watched the meeting on video. It was a striking indication of just how seriously the Emirati government was taking CISADA. In Levey's past meetings with Abdullah, the sheikh had often spoken of his mistrust of Iran, but he had always balked at spurning it entirely. Shutting down business with Iran would not only harm the UAE's economy; it would almost definitely incite retaliation from Tehran. If the UAE was ever going to cut ties with Iran, it would need reassurances that every other major financial center was doing the same.

After a while, Abdullah asked to see Levey privately, and the two men moved to a nearby room.

"Look," Levey said, "I can't tell you honestly that everyone in the world has cut off Iran. But I've been very straight with you about the progress we've made." All the world's largest banks had ended business with Iran, and with the new threat of secondary sanctions in CISADA, the remaining stragglers were racing for the exits. "I think it's now time for the UAE to take action."

Abdullah was prepared for the ask. He posed questions and mentioned a few articles he had seen about Turkish banks still doing business with Iran.

"I'm not telling you that you're absolutely last," Levey conceded. "But we're going to keep working with the others. And the bulk of the world has gone along with this."

Finally, Abdullah gave in. Within days, the UAE's central bank cut ties with all Iranian financial institutions that were subject to American sanctions. It also circulated an advisory to banks across the UAE explaining the recent U.S. legislation, instructing them to treat Iranian counterparties as high-risk, and informing them that it would step up scrutiny of all transactions with Iran. Before long, financial relations between the two countries withered.

The Emiratis' unexpectedly swift turnabout invigorated Levey and his colleagues. It seemed their hope for CISADA—that it could complete Iran's financial isolation—might come true. Still, for the law to be taken seriously
and not disregarded the way ILSA had been in the 1990s, they would have to
be thorough. A single noncompliant bank somewhere might help Iran regain
access to the global financial system, undoing much of their work. The team
would need to walk all relevant parties through the law—from princes in the
Gulf to managers of small banks in the Caucasus and Central Asia. Additionally, the Obama administration wanted its economic war to be viewed as
justified under international law and as a natural outgrowth of UN Security
Council resolutions. America, they hoped, would be seen not as a bully but
as a good-faith partner helping others abide by their UN obligations. A consistent approach to implementation, paying as much attention to small fish
as big ones, could help this perception take hold.

Over the months that followed, Treasury officials convened every week
to identify foreign banks that retained ties with Iran. Some of this information
was drawn from intelligence, but much of it was open-source, right there for
the world to see in *Bankers Almanac*. Treasury staff then traveled to confront the banks: Stop doing business with Iran—as required by international
law—or risk being slapped with secondary sanctions and losing access to the
dollar.

Treasury officials even ventured to Dushanbe, the far-flung capital of Tajikistan, a country whose language, culture, and economy were so inextrica-
bly bound with Iran that Ahmadinejad described the two nations as "one
spirit in two bodies." After returning home, the delegation received a frantic
called from the U.S. embassy in Dushanbe. It turned out that a banker in
Tajikistan, upon learning from the Treasury officials about the risks of CIS-
ADA, had called Citibank to come clean about his bank's ties to Iranian financial institutions. In response, Citibank had closed correspondent accounts
for *all* Tajik banks. Treasury had to do back-office diplomacy with Citibank
to persuade them to reestablish business with Tajikistan.

America's economic war had put the global financial system on a hair
trigger. Gone were the days when bank executives would sneer at American
sanctions and leisurely do business that flouted U.S. policies. The costs of
such a blasé attitude had simply become too high. Fines for sanctions violations by U.S. law enforcement agencies had rocketed up—Lloyds, Credit

Suisse, and Barclays were all hit with penalties in the hundreds of millions of dollars in 2009 and 2010. With the passage of CISADA, moreover, the risks now went well beyond big fines. Doing business with Iran risked sanctions, full stop, which meant no access to the dollar and, quite probably, bankruptcy.

The other key provision in CISADA—Jim Steinberg's "special rule" granting foreign oil companies sanctions waivers in exchange for a clear roadmap for leaving Iran—was also working faster than expected. Over a period of just a few months, senior executives from the biggest foreign oil companies that remained invested in Iran, including Italy's Eni, Britain's Shell, Norway's Statoil, and France's Total, made repeated trips to the State Department to iron out their exit strategies.

In his first meeting at Foggy Bottom to discuss the new law, Leonardo Bellodi, Eni's head of government affairs, came with a fully fleshed-out plan in his pocket. A suave Italian who donned impeccable suits, Bellodi deemed it fruitless to object to the new American sanctions. For starters, neither Washington nor Brussels was in any mood to go easy on Iran. Just as important, working with the National Iranian Oil Company (NIOC) had been a nightmare for Eni. As Bellodi saw it, a win for Eni would be to recoup the money it was owed by Iran—some $3 billion in his approximation—and get out.

Bellodi's approach, which involved Eni receiving ongoing oil shipments from Iran until it recovered its investment, suited the State Department well. If all went according to plan, it would lead to Eni, one of the biggest foreign investors in Iran's energy sector, both leaving the country and withdrawing a hefty sum from Iran's coffers on its way out the door. (In the end, Bellodi's efforts were not without friction—he endured multiple threats and a mysteriously "missing" passport during a visit to Iran—but he succeeded in collecting about 90 percent of Eni's money.) While negotiations with some of the other oil giants were not as smooth, the Eni plan provided Washington with a good template. Less than three months after Obama signed CISADA, all the big European energy companies had agreed to exit Iran. Shortly thereafter, they were joined by the Japanese oil company Inpex, which abandoned a megaproject to develop Iran's Azadegan oil field.

The exodus of global banks and energy companies from Iran, so soon on the heels of CISADA, was remarkable in its speed but also because it happened without Washington ever having to deliver on the threat of secondary sanctions. Losing access to the dollar was a death sentence for any globally oriented business, so the mere threat of sanctions was enough of a deterrent.

The upheaval caused by CISADA marked a sea change in the history of American economic warfare. The last time Washington had attempted secondary sanctions—with ILSA in the 1990s—Total and the French government had tested U.S. resolve almost immediately, and the Clinton administration had backed down. The result was another decade and a half of global investment in Iran's energy industry with little fear of consequences. In the eyes of multinational oil companies, American sanctions had indeed been a "toothless tiger"—an annoyance, at most, and hardly a serious factor in their business decisions. But over a relatively short period of time, from the last two years of Bush's presidency to the first two of Obama's, the United States transformed its sanctions into a potent global force. So when U.S. officials set out to implement secondary sanctions under CISADA, the rest of the world fell into line.

At least, most of the world did. As soon as Inpex announced its departure from Iran, reports emerged that China National Petroleum Corporation, a massive oil company owned by the Chinese government, would step in to develop the Azadegan oil field. Chinese firms had remained conspicuously absent from the exodus underway. In fact, there was mounting evidence that China was backfilling commercial opportunities that Europe, Japan, and others left behind. By the first half of 2011, Iran had few surviving connections to the global economy. But those that endured—its ties to China and, above all, its steady inflow of petrodollars—would be devilishly hard to break, and perhaps impossible to sever before it no longer made a difference.

15

The Last Bastion

In February 2011, after nearly seven years in the job, Stuart Levey stepped down from his post as Treasury's undersecretary for terrorism and financial intelligence. Across two administrations—one Republican, one Democratic—Levey had built TFI, and by extension America's economic arsenal, into a powerhouse. Levey's influence was reiterated on his last day in the job, when he and Adam Szubin persuaded Obama's national security advisor, Tom Donilon, to rush through an executive order freezing a whopping $37 billion of assets belonging to Libyan dictator Muammar Gaddafi.

"When I started this job, I don't think the national security advisor would have taken my call," Levey reflected. "By the time I left, I got the president to sign an executive order within four hours of deciding it was worth doing." Thanks in no small part to Levey's personal efforts, the international financial system was now conditioned not to touch Iran with a ten-foot pole. By this measure, the strategy he had outlined for Condoleezza Rice and Hank Paulson in 2006 was a resounding success.

And yet, Iran's nuclear program had grown by leaps and bounds during Levey's tenure, and the government in Tehran seemed every bit as committed to its continuing development. A June 2011 announcement by Fereydoon Abbasi, Iran's newly appointed nuclear chief, suggested that more trouble lay ahead. Abbasi, who the previous year had narrowly survived an assassination attempt—attributed by Tehran to Israel's Mossad—unveiled plans to triple Iran's stockpile of highly enriched uranium. He also said Iran would install more advanced centrifuges, suitable to produce fuel for nuclear weapons, at the underground facility in Fordow.

Israel's government, led by Prime Minister Benjamin Netanyahu, was doing a lot more to undermine Iran's nuclear program than allegedly targeting its scientists. The Israelis were making serious plans for a military strike against Iran's enrichment facilities. Netanyahu doubted that sanctions could stop Tehran's nuclear pursuit and wanted to take more drastic action. Although Obama repeatedly assured that "all options are on the table" when it came to Iran, the White House was deeply wary of a potential Israeli military strike. Such an attack could easily spiral into a wider war that sucked America in. "We just thought this would be a catastrophe," recalled Obama national security aide Ben Rhodes. "We thought it would collapse the painstaking international house of cards we built."

The economic warriors that Levey had assembled—a deep team that would remain in place after his departure, and which included David Cohen and Adam Szubin along with dozens more—were determined to prove Netanyahu wrong. Economic pressure *could* halt Iran's nuclear program. To succeed, they would have to attack Iran's last bastion: oil exports.

America had managed to isolate Iran financially in large part thanks to a favorable cost-benefit calculus: For big banks in London, Frankfurt, or even Dubai, the costs of being blacklisted by the United States would always outweigh the benefits of maintaining ties with Iran. But oil was different. It was the lifeblood of the modern industrial economy and a scarce resource. Most countries *needed* to import oil.

As the rest of Iran's economy withered under sanctions, the importance of its energy sector only grew. Iran relied on oil and, to a lesser extent, natural gas for 65 percent of its national budget and 70 percent of its export revenues. Global oil prices had briefly dipped early in the financial crisis, but by 2011, they once again soared past $100 per barrel, propelled by voracious demand from China and instability in the Middle East, which was in the throes of the Arab Spring. Soon after Levey left Treasury, the IMF projected Tehran would collect more than $100 billion in oil proceeds in 2011, up from about $80 billion the previous year. And despite its broad reach, CISADA did nothing to stem this flood of cash. That's because one major Iranian financial institution remained free from American sanctions, and it happened to be the one at the heart of Iran's oil trade.

The Central Bank of Iran was the repository for all the money Tehran earned selling oil around the world. Dating back to the early days of Levey's economic war planning, U.S. officials had weighed sanctions against the bank. But each time, they balked at the potential ramifications. Targeting a sovereign country's central bank, some Treasury officials feared, was a line the United States should never cross. Doing so would show the world that Washington was not averse to politicizing the dollar's status as the global reserve currency, which could undermine that very status along with America's reputation as the steward of the international financial system.

More immediately, sanctions on Iran's central bank could make it difficult or impossible for importers to pay for Iranian oil, causing large amounts of that oil to disappear from world markets. The resulting spike in global oil prices would hurt American businesses and consumers. Such worries also explained why earlier American sanctions aimed at Iran's energy sector, both ILSA in 1996 and CISADA in 2010, had targeted upstream investment (exploring for oil on Iranian territory and extracting it) as opposed to current sales (buying barrels of Iranian oil). Eroding Iran's capacity to produce oil in the distant future was one thing; blocking Iran from exporting oil today was quite another. As Richard Nephew explained: "We could not figure out a way of targeting oil or Iran's central bank that we deemed feasible and that would not potentially damage international oil markets and, thereby, set back the global recovery from the Great Recession of 2008–2009."

There was a further risk—one that had even given Levey pause. What if some companies simply decided not to play ball and continued buying Iranian oil and paying the central bank? "If you sanctioned the Iranian central bank, you had to really think about whether the policy could be implemented," Levey said. "To take the step and have China and India not comply, you could see a real challenge to American power and prestige." At that point, Washington would have to choose whether to follow through on its threat and hit Chinese and Indian firms with secondary sanctions—a move that was certain to strain relations with Beijing and New Delhi without any guarantee that it would compel the firms to stop purchasing Iranian oil. If this came to pass, it would destroy the psychological power American sanctions had amassed over governments and businesses across the world since the start of Levey's tenure.

Iran hawks on Capitol Hill were undeterred. Having sat through briefing after briefing on Iran policy with AIPAC, think tanks, and Israeli officials, many members of Congress decided it was time to put up or shut up. The United States should seek to crush Iran's economy at all costs and force Tehran to relinquish its nuclear program, and if that failed, bomb Iran's nuclear facilities into oblivion. One of the most vocal hard-liners, Republican Senator Mark Kirk, had in the past lobbied for a naval quarantine of Iran, along the lines of what President John F. Kennedy ordered during the Cuban missile crisis, to starve the country of gasoline imports. Kirk had no compunction about the potential collateral damage of maximalist sanctions against Iran.

In the spring of 2011, David Cohen went to meet Kirk in his office on Capitol Hill. Cohen was there to ask the senator to support his nomination to replace Levey as the head of TFI, a role that required Senate confirmation. Kirk made clear he would not vote in favor unless Cohen committed to imposing sanctions on the Central Bank of Iran. Cohen agreed to evaluate the idea. Still, Kirk held up Cohen's confirmation, with support from his colleague Senator Bob Menendez, who had become the most influential Senate Democrat on Iran sanctions. After a lengthy standoff, Kirk lifted his opposition when Cohen privately vowed to advocate for the move within the Obama administration. Given the stakes—officials in Tehran had indicated they would view sanctions on the central bank as an act of war, and global markets would also view it as such—the decision would ultimately be Obama's to make.

Not long after Cohen was confirmed, Kirk pressed him to make good on his promise. Then, in August 2011, Kirk co-authored a letter with Democratic Senator Chuck Schumer publicly calling on Obama to sanction Iran's central bank. The letter accumulated signatures from 92 out of 100 senators, indicating overwhelming bipartisan support.

With pressure mounting from Capitol Hill, the Obama administration started analyzing how sanctions on the Central Bank of Iran might impact world markets. Leading the effort was Treasury's International Affairs division, known as IA. Within the federal bureaucracy, IA carried significant prestige, and it counted among its staff some of the country's sharpest experts on global macroeconomics. IA focused on promoting international trade and investment, not curbing it, so its economists seldom got involved in sanctions policy. In any case, U.S. sanctions had rarely run the risk of moving global markets, let alone sparking a macroeconomic shock. This time, however, there were genuine fears Washington might cause runaway oil prices and even a recession in America's own economy.

IA's conclusions did little to allay these fears. Its experts projected that sanctions on the Central Bank of Iran would send global oil prices soaring above $200 per barrel, perhaps even higher. The United States would face inflation, unemployment, and a plummeting GDP. If the sanctions shaved off just half of Iran's daily oil exports, the result would be "basically nuclear winter recession," recalled a senior Treasury official who was briefed on IA's analysis. At the same time, it was uncertain how much the move would hurt Iran, as the country would benefit from stratospheric oil prices. Tehran might even end up making more money selling less oil.

Upon learning of IA's assessment, the White House decided to vigorously oppose Congress's push for sanctions on the Central Bank of Iran. But there was a catch. If word got out that the U.S. government believed sanctions on Iran's central bank could cause a painful recession at home, it would reveal to Iran there were red lines Washington was afraid to cross. Israel, for its part, would likely conclude America was unwilling to resort to high-impact sanctions, and Netanyahu might order his military to bomb Iran's nuclear facilities.

Publicizing the results of IA's analysis would have serious drawbacks. So the White House instructed State and Treasury to oppose Congress's efforts on account of diplomatic concerns, not economic ones. Specifically, they would argue that hitting Iran's central bank would fracture the unity America had built with its closest allies. At the time, several EU countries as well as Japan and South Korea were still buying large quantities of Iranian oil—together, they accounted for more than 40 percent of Iran's oil sales. American sanctions on Iran's central bank could complicate these purchases, endangering the allies' energy security. Such an explanation, the White House judged, would be far less damaging than making public IA's nightmarish projections.

It was a fine line to walk: the Obama administration thought there needed to be limits on the economic war, but it was reluctant to acknowledge its reasons for setting these limits. With members of Congress clamoring for action, however, no better option seemed available.

16

===

100–0

In the fall of 2011, Iran engaged in a series of provocations so egregious that it became increasingly difficult for the Obama administration to resist any new sanctions, no matter the grounds for objection. In October, Attorney General Eric Holder and FBI Director Robert Mueller announced that U.S. law enforcement agents had foiled an Iranian plot to assassinate Adel al-Jubeir, the Saudi ambassador to the United States, at Cafe Milano, a popular Georgetown hangout among D.C. elites. The allegations read like a spy thriller: A member of the IRGC's Quds Force had tapped his cousin, a used-car salesman from Texas, to coordinate the attack. The cousin, in turn, paid members of a Mexican drug cartel to detonate explosives at the restaurant. When one of the Mexicans noted the risk of inflicting mass casualties among innocent bystanders, the Iranian American car salesman made clear his handlers didn't care. "They want that guy done," he allegedly said. "If the hundred go with him, fuck 'em." Unbeknownst to the Iranian American, his main contact in the drug cartel was a confidential source working for America's Drug Enforcement Administration.

News of the thwarted scheme captivated and terrified Washington. That Iran would plan such a brazen attack in the heart of America's capital was bone-chilling. It also lent credence to the view that the Iranian regime was untethered to reality and might well use a nuclear weapon—or perhaps transfer the radioactive ingredients for a "dirty bomb" to Hezbollah or another militant proxy—if its capabilities were allowed to grow. The "dirty bomb" scenario, in which Tehran might secretly help terrorists stage a catastrophic attack using a makeshift nuclear device, kept Adam Szubin up at night. Concepts like mutual assured destruction that deterred nation-states from using nuclear weapons might fail against Hezbollah, Szubin feared, because an attack by such a group would leave "no return address."

In early November, less than a month after the foiled Cafe Milano plot came to light, the IAEA issued its most damning report yet on Iran's nuclear program. The report confirmed that Iran had undertaken secret initiatives to stockpile highly enriched uranium. It also found evidence that Iran had spent years devising plans, acquiring components, and running tests in pursuit of nuclear weapons. The report was clear: Contrary to all the Iranian government's claims, Iran's nuclear program was not just for peaceful purposes.

While the news came as no surprise to the United States or Israel, it shined a spotlight on Iran's dangerous activities that no country could ignore. It thus built global support for hard-hitting sanctions against Iran that up until then had been elusive. British foreign secretary William Hague issued a call for restrictions on Iran's central bank, as did Nicolas Sarkozy, the French president, who also suggested a complete EU embargo on Iranian oil.

A little over a week later, hundreds of young members of the IRGC's Basij militia stormed the British embassy in Tehran. They broke windows, stole computers and cell phones, and tore down the Union Jack. Seven British staff members were briefly held hostage. London swiftly evacuated its diplomats from Tehran, shuttered its vandalized embassy, and expelled all Iranian diplomats from the UK. Rattled by the unrest, the EU's twenty-seven foreign ministers convened in Brussels. The EU's sanctions team began drawing up proposals for a ban on all purchases of Iranian oil.

With European powers preparing for an oil embargo and warming to sanctions against the Central Bank of Iran, the Obama administration's previous argument to Congress—that the latter action could break unity with America's closest allies, because it would complicate their ability to pay for Iranian oil—had become a tough sell. Mark Kirk and Bob Menendez, the leading Iran hawks on Capitol Hill, could smell blood in the water. The two senators filed competing amendments to the annual defense policy bill, both of which would require Obama to impose sanctions on the Iranian central bank. While the White House held firm to its opposition, sanctions officials in the administration were getting nervous. It seemed less and less likely that Obama could hold back Congress, which easily had the votes to pass the new sanctions and override a presidential veto.

So top experts at State and Treasury put their heads together to come up with a scheme that might make the sanctions workable. Straightforward blocking sanctions against the Central Bank of Iran, which would amount to ordering an immediate global cutoff of purchases of Iranian oil, would be extremely risky. For starters, Iran's biggest oil buyers—including China, India, Turkey, and even some EU countries—may well refuse to comply. They bought several hundred thousand barrels of oil from Iran each day, and such sums could not just be replaced overnight. Even if these countries could somehow take such a drastic step, it could trigger IA's nightmare scenario, in which oil prices rocketed above $200 per barrel and America was thrown into a recession.

In collaboration with energy experts at State, Adam Szubin and the technocrats at OFAC came up with a middle way: America could impose sanctions on Iran's central bank, but it could simultaneously agree to waive them for any country that significantly reduced its oil purchases from Iran over a six-month period. If successful, the policy would reduce Iran's oil exports gradually, over the span of several months or even years, rather than overnight. This would soften the economic blow to world markets. It would also allow pressure on Tehran to build progressively over time. With each passing month that Iran refused to scale back its nuclear ambitions, its economy would suffer worse and worse pain. While the idea made sense in theory, executing it successfully would require a kind of diplomatic jujitsu that could easily flop. Nevertheless, if Congress was determined to do something against Iran's central bank, this would be the most palatable option.

In late November, Cohen shared the idea with Menendez in the senator's Capitol hideaway—his secret, unmarked office near the Senate floor. The White House still opposed sanctioning the Central Bank of Iran, he explained, but if there was no other choice, an incremental approach would be preferable to a sharp cutoff. Menendez took Cohen's recommendation on board. Shortly thereafter, when Menendez and Kirk came together to file a compromise amendment to the defense bill, they included the idea for gradual reductions. They also afforded the president leeway to waive the sanctions entirely if he determined global oil markets could not weather the loss of Iranian exports. The senators had adopted Treasury's proposal, but as Cohen had warned, even this concession would not be enough to end opposition from a White House skittish about roiling oil markets.

Events came to a head on the first day of December. That morning, in a last-ditch effort to torpedo the Menendez-Kirk amendment, Treasury Secretary Tim Geithner got ready to sign a letter to the Senate making a forceful case against it. "I am writing to express the Administration's strong opposition to this amendment because, in its current form, it threatens to undermine the effective, carefully phased, and sustainable approach we have undertaken to build strong international pressure against Iran," the letter read. The White House had conceived the letter as a joint message from State and Treasury. But Secretary of State Hillary Clinton was nowhere to be found. Treasury staff tried to contact her multiple times to no avail—maybe, some speculated, because she deemed it ill-advised to put her name on the letter. Geithner was on his own.

As Geithner lifted his pen to sign the letter, he locked eyes with Danny Glaser, who was hovering nervously nearby. "You don't think I should sign this, do you?" the secretary asked.

"No, I don't," Glaser told him. As he saw it, Menendez-Kirk was certain to pass. Continued opposition would achieve nothing other than damaging the administration's credibility. Better to get on board now and try like hell to make the new sanctions work. "You know the old saying," Glaser later reflected, "'If you see a stampede, jump out in front and call it a parade.'"

Geithner signed the letter anyway.

An hour or so later, Cohen and his counterpart from State, Wendy Sherman, went up to Capitol Hill for a hearing before the Senate Foreign Relations Committee. Geithner's letter had already made the rounds, and Menendez was livid. He had fought to get Cohen's proposal for gradual reductions into the amendment, only for Geithner—Cohen's boss—to make a final stand to kill the amendment. And now Cohen and Sherman were there vouching for Geithner.

"At your request," Menendez said, glowering at Cohen, "we engaged in an effort to come to a bipartisan agreement that I think is fair and balanced. And now you come here and vitiate that very agreement." There was no evidence, he went on, that the sanctions would hurt America's economy. (The White House continued to keep a tight lid on IA's sky-is-falling analysis.) If such evidence existed, Menendez reasoned, surely Geithner would have cited it in his letter. "Nowhere does he talk about economic disruption to us, very interestingly," Menendez pointed out. "I think he would have made that case if in fact there was any such disruption."

It was highly unusual for a Democratic senator to flay officials from his own party so viciously. To add an exclamation point, Menendez took a swipe at the Obama administration's entire economic war against Iran. Any success achieved to date, he argued, should not be credited to the White House

David Cohen and Wendy Sherman:
the faces of the Obama administration's uneasy
relationship with Congress on Iran sanctions.

or Treasury but rather to Congress, which had pushed forward CISADA. "But for Congress, you would not have had the sanctions, and I have never seen this or any other administration come before the Congress and say, 'Please, give me a sanctions regime,'" Menendez unloaded. "You have rebuffed it every step of the way even though it is the sanctions law that we have given you that has allowed you to achieve some limited progress."

Cohen had barely returned to his office at Treasury when he heard the news: the amendment had passed 100–0.

That afternoon, Cohen was commiserating with Neal Wolin, Treasury's second-in-command, on the couch in Wolin's office, when Geithner unexpectedly walked in.

"You've done something that I don't think anybody thought possible," Geithner said to Cohen, his face expressionless.

"What's that?" Cohen asked.

"You have brought together Congress in a bipartisan fashion, unanimously standing behind something. Congratulations." The secretary turned around and left the room.

17

Good Cop, Bad Cop

As 2011 drew to a close, a new, more perilous phase of the economic war against Iran was dawning.

Ahmadinejad's vice president warned that if the United States and Europe slapped sanctions on the Central Bank of Iran, "not a drop of oil will pass through the Strait of Hormuz." But overwhelming congressional support left Obama with little choice but to shrug off this threat. On New Year's Eve, he signed into law the Menendez-Kirk amendment, which included sanctions on the central bank coupled with waivers for countries that gradually reduced their purchases of Iranian oil. A few days later, accelerated by developments in Washington, the EU agreed to impose an embargo on Iranian oil. It also banned European insurers from providing coverage to Iranian oil shipments, regardless of where they were headed.

In Israel, Benjamin Netanyahu and his defense minister, Ehud Barak, were convinced Iran was nearing a "zone of immunity," after which its nuclear program would be invulnerable to attack. The Israeli government was ramping up preparations for a military strike on Iran's nuclear facilities despite stern opposition from Obama, who distrusted Netanyahu as much as Netanyahu distrusted him. Israel had even begun practicing the attack, its military aircraft encroaching stealthily into Iranian airspace on several dry runs.

Inside the Obama administration, members of the sanctions team rushed back to their desks after New Year's Day to figure out how to use the new law to squeeze the Central Bank of Iran and, by extension, Iran's oil sales. They knew from experience that just passing a new sanctions law did not guarantee it would affect business decisions. And if a sanction did not affect business decisions, it could not inflict economic pain on its target. Success would require shaping the psychology of banks, companies, and governments. They had to believe that the costs of violating the newest sanctions would not be worth the benefits of continuing to buy Iran's oil.

Of course, America had long ago stopped buying Iranian oil, and the EU was gearing up to do the same. But none of Iran's other major customers—China, India, Japan, South Korea, and Turkey—were prepared to impose embargoes. For America's new policy to work, these countries would have to play ball.

Because of oil's centrality to the world economy, oil sanctions were never easy. In the 1990s, a comprehensive oil embargo against Iraq had required both full UN backing and a continuous U.S.-led naval blockade. Under Menendez-Kirk, the United States would attempt to enforce globe-spanning oil sanctions not by stopping ships from visiting Iranian ports but rather by policing payment channels to the Central Bank of Iran. In effect, it would attempt to use America's control over financial chokepoints to push the whole world into lessening its reliance on Iranian oil. Nothing like this had ever been tried before.

Fortunately, owing to David Cohen's efforts, Menendez-Kirk did not require foreign countries to quit Iranian oil cold turkey, which would be a surefire recipe for market chaos and policy failure. Instead, it allowed refineries and other oil importers to keep buying so long as their home countries "significantly reduced" their total intake of Iranian oil every six months. The law left the term "significantly reduced" vague, giving the Obama team leeway to define it.

Menendez and Kirk were aware of this and quickly moved to box in the White House. On January 12, they sent a letter to Tim Geithner arguing that "significantly reduced" should refer to "the bottom line amount of money" Iran was paid, not the quantity of oil it sold. The Obama team should push oil importers to demand price reductions from Iran of at least 18 percent. Targeting the price Iran received, rather than the quantity it sold, could reduce Tehran's revenues without depriving a tight global oil market of crucial supplies. In making this recommendation, Menendez and Kirk were guarding against the possibility that Obama might argue that it was necessary to waive the sanctions entirely to avoid spiking oil prices and damaging the U.S. economy.

The government's sanctions technocrats and energy wonks convinced the administration to take a different route. Price reductions made sense but would be hard to implement, since it was impossible to verify the actual price importers paid for any given shipment. It would be far easier to monitor volume reductions, which could be done by counting the number of tankers going in and out of Iran's ports. And as long as sales of Iranian oil slowed gradually, other producers would have time to boost their own production and fill the void, which would hopefully rebalance supply and demand and keep prices stable.

Still, pulling off this plan would require an intricate blend of diplomacy, energy market analysis and outreach, and the selective use of secondary sanctions. It would also require a fresh batch of recruits. What had started under Stuart Levey as a targeted assault on Iran's financial sector was now a multifront, combined-forces campaign, and the ranks had to swell accordingly. The energy experts exemplified this trend. None of them had entered public service expecting to work on economic warfare, but Menendez-Kirk led the administration to conscript them into the fight.

One of the latest recruits was Carlos Pascual, the head of the State Department's newly created Bureau of Energy Resources. Born in Cuba, Pascual emigrated to the United States at the age of three. After graduating from Stanford and Harvard, he spent the first dozen years of his career at the U.S. Agency for International Development (USAID), serving overseas tours in Sudan, South Africa, and Mozambique. Eventually, he rose through the ranks of the Clinton White House and became U.S. ambassador to Ukraine.

Now, Pascual took the lead on diplomacy with the biggest Iranian oil buyers, working alongside his deputy, a savvy Israeli American named Amos Hochstein. From Japan and South Korea—two of Iran's top five oil customers—Pascual and Hochstein secured commitments to cut purchases by 20 percent. Coupled with the EU embargo, which would bring Europe's imports of Iranian oil to zero within six months, the Japanese and Korean pledges would make a serious dent in Iran's oil sales.

Iran's largest oil customers, China and India, would be harder to win over. Neither Beijing nor New Delhi had imposed any sanctions on Iran beyond what was required of all UN members, and both would bristle at the notion of Washington dictating who they did or didn't buy oil from. Pascual felt that the most promising approach was to appeal cautiously to Chinese and Indian interests: Overreliance on Iranian oil for economic growth could be a vulnerability, considering not just the Obama administration's sanctions but also the zeal of Iran hawks in Congress and the threat of Israeli military action. Washington could assist Beijing and New Delhi in diversifying their oil supplies and improving their energy security.

The strategy recalled Theodore Roosevelt's maxim "Speak softly and carry a big stick." By 2012, the threat of America's economic weapons was palpable the world over. In the second week of January, the State Department had issued sanctions against three companies for supplying refined petroleum to Iran, one of which was a China-based trading firm called Zhuhai Zhenrong. Washington was clearly prepared to wield secondary sanctions to advance its Iran policy, including against Chinese businesses. Aiding the administration's diplomatic push was the fact that Menendez-Kirk had passed with a bipartisan supermajority, against the express wishes of the White House—which ironically had the effect of strengthening the Obama team's negotiating position with foreign powers, because they could point to Congress as the irrepressible bad cop forcing their hand.

Secretary of State Hillary Clinton, who visited New Delhi in the spring of 2012, agreed with Pascual that the United States should avoid coming off as pushy or prescriptive. "The more loudly we urged them to change course," Clinton reflected, "the more likely they were to dig in their heels." Pascual traveled to India a few days after Clinton left. The secretary of state's visit had drummed up attention in the Indian media surrounding Pascual's otherwise low-profile trip. When Pascual got out of his car in front of India's Ministry of External Affairs, a press gaggle was waiting for him. As journalists hurled questions, he picked up his pace and shouted, "We're not doing press today."

Moments later, as Pascual sat down with Jawed Ashraf, his Indian counterpart, an aide elbowed him and flashed her BlackBerry. Reuters had misquoted his "We're not doing press" comment as "We're *not too impressed*," and questions were pouring in as to why Washington was not impressed. A discombobulated Pascual told Ashraf what had happened. Ashraf let out a hearty laugh. What had appeared to be a gaffe turned out to be a useful icebreaker. Ashraf declined to make any commitments, but he encouraged Pascual to deliver his case against Iranian oil directly to Indian refiners.

Pascual spent the next several days shuttling between New Delhi and Mumbai meeting the owners of the country's largest refineries, including Indian Oil and ONGC. If they agreed to reduce oil purchases by roughly 20 percent, Pascual told them, the United States would help them identify alternative suppliers, such as Iraq. But failure to curtail their purchases would endanger their access to the U.S. financial system.

When Pascual returned to meet Ashraf, he handed him a list of the executives he had met with and the commitments they had made. The deal was done. The Indian government would never publicly admit that it was complying with U.S. sanctions; any reductions in India's oil purchases from Iran were to be made in the name of national energy security. But the result would be one and the same.

Pascual and Hochstein reprised this strategy with China. Once again, the stage was set with outreach by senior administration officials, including Tom Donilon and Wendy Sherman. Pascual also got an assist from Netanyahu's national security advisor, Yaakov Amidror, who warned Beijing that if Iran would not rein in its nuclear program peacefully, Israel was ready to take military action. For China, which relied on oil supplies not only from Iran but also from Saudi Arabia and other Gulf states, the prospect of another war in the Middle East that could imperil all those supplies was a grave threat.

Still, in their discussions with Pascual and other U.S. officials, the Chinese held firmly to the line that they would make their own energy decisions and would not be influenced by American sanctions. They would always object to Washington's efforts to impose what they denounced as "long-arm jurisdiction" over Chinese companies. After several rounds of discussions, however, Chinese diplomats suggested that Obama officials seek out an obscure Chinese energy journal. Buried in the middle of the journal was an announcement that the Chinese government had decided to diversify its energy sources. The announcement listed China's new mix of oil imports—and the number for Iran had gone down. This was enough for Pascual and his team. In the words of a former senior Obama official, Washington accepted the cryptic journal reference as "adherence to U.S. sanctions with Chinese characteristics."

The previous year, when Cohen had visited Menendez in his hideaway office to pitch the gradual oil reduction strategy, neither he nor anyone else in the Obama administration was confident it would work. They had come up with the idea only when it seemed probable that Menendez-Kirk would pass over the White House's objections. And yet, the strategy was operating in the wild far better than it had looked on paper. By giving the biggest customers of Iranian oil six months to reduce their purchases, the law bought time for the Obama administration to pursue intensive energy diplomacy to advance its goal. By the summer of 2012, Iran's oil exports had plunged by as much as one million barrels per day, a 40 percent decrease.

American officials were less successful in persuading other oil producers to boost output and make up for lost Iranian supplies. There had been high hopes in Washington that Saudi Arabia would fill the void. The Saudis were big supporters of America's campaign to curb Iran's nuclear ambitions. Their leader, King Abdullah, had even urged American officials to "cut off the head of the snake" and bomb Iran's nuclear facilities. Yet when oil prices soared above $120 per barrel in the spring of 2012, the Saudis increased their output only by a little.

Saudi Arabia's inaction raised the specter that IA's catastrophic forecasts might come to fruition. But in the end, a solution was found not among the Saudi oil wells but spread out across the American heartland, where the shale revolution was racing ahead at a speed few had anticipated was possible. In 2012 alone, advances in fracking and horizontal drilling caused America's domestic oil production to shoot up by nearly one million barrels per day— about the same amount that was lost in Iranian supplies. Prices soon stabilized.

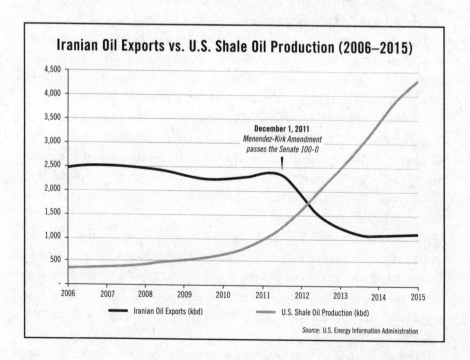

Iranian Oil Exports vs. U.S. Shale Oil Production (2006–2015)

December 1, 2011
Menendez-Kirk Amendment passes the Senate 100-0

— Iranian Oil Exports (kbd)   — U.S. Shale Oil Production (kbd)

Source: U.S. Energy Information Administration

The unanimous passage of the Menendez-Kirk amendment against the president's wishes had widely been viewed as a vote of no confidence in Obama's Iran policy. Emboldened, Iran hawks in Congress pushed for more. Starting in early 2012, Kirk advocated for sanctions against any organization that provided financial messaging services to Iranian banks. At the time, all of Iran's major banks were still using SWIFT, the Brussels-based messaging service. Whether this mattered, given Iran's lack of international banking relationships, was debatable. Yet the implication of Kirk's initiative was that if SWIFT refused to disconnect Iran, the United States might actually sanction SWIFT and its board members.

At face value, this threat was absurd. All the world's largest financial institutions relied on SWIFT. Sanctions on SWIFT, which would bar U.S. banks from using the service, would inflict serious pain on America's own financial industry. It would also undermine counterterrorism efforts, which depended on SWIFT for critical financial intelligence. Nevertheless, after Kirk suffered a stroke on January 21, Menendez and Senator Roger Wicker, along with AIPAC, took up the cause with gusto. Within two weeks, they had pushed an amendment through the Senate Banking Committee that threatened sanctions against SWIFT unless it cut off Iran's largest banks.

In a sign of just how seriously the world took Congress's initiatives on Iran, the EU leapt into action. Better to get on board with Capitol Hill's scheme, the Europeans concluded, than risk a nasty showdown with the Iran hawks in Washington. By March, all twenty-seven EU leaders agreed to institute a regulation that banned SWIFT from providing services to sanctioned Iranian banks. SWIFT's CEO called it an "extraordinary and unprecedented step" for his organization, which had always functioned as neutral wiring for the global financial system. In less than two months, a pie-in-the-sky proposal on Capitol Hill had migrated across the Atlantic and reshaped European law.

Meanwhile, the Iran hawks in Congress were still not satisfied with the Obama administration's progress in cutting Iran's oil sales. They wanted to drive sales all the way down to zero. As Congress drew up legislation that would force the White House to scrap the gradual reductions in favor of a worldwide ban, Pascual and other energy experts grew worried. A full ban was probably impossible.

Both China and India would almost definitely continue importing Iranian oil despite America's threats. Zhuhai Zhenrong, the Chinese trading firm sanctioned in early 2012, had kept buying oil from Iran long after it was hit by American sanctions. This could even become a model: China and other countries might put forward sacrificial lambs that would absorb the costs of American penalties and then continue doing business with Iran. Along the same lines, Treasury had sanctioned China-based Bank of Kunlun in July 2012 for transferring hundreds of millions of dollars on behalf of Iranian banks—yet its dealings with Iran persisted. Congress's crusade to zero out Iran's oil exports was sure to fail. Worse still, after months of intensive energy diplomacy, the administration worried that such a maximalist demand might offend Chinese and Indian officials, leading them to backtrack on the reductions they had already made.

By that point, the Obama team knew better than to simply fight Congress's efforts with blanket opposition. They couldn't stop Congress. But just as they had done with Menendez-Kirk and the gradual oil reduction strategy, they could try to steer unwanted legislation in a more productive direction.

So, in the face of Capitol Hill's renewed push to wipe out Iran's oil exports, the Treasury sanctions team gathered for a brainstorm. This time, Cohen and Szubin figured they could move the game back to the financial arena. They came up with a creative proposal: Foreign banks could continue processing payments for Iranian oil, but only if they agreed to hold the funds in restricted bank accounts in their home country. Iran could use these oil revenues to pay for non-sanctioned imports from the country in which the account was located or to buy humanitarian products like food and medicine—but it could not bring the funds back to Iran. If, say, the Chinese oil firm Sinopec bought Iranian oil, it would pay a Central Bank of Iran account *based in China*. Tehran could use those funds to buy refrigerators or vacuum cleaners from China—or food or medicine from anywhere in the world—but the money could not come home. Tehran could not, therefore, use the money to bolster its nuclear program, fund its military, prop up Hezbollah, or line the pockets of regime insiders.

In essence, the scheme would compel the creation of overseas escrow accounts, where Iran's oil wealth would accumulate instead of flowing back to the Iranian regime. Washington wouldn't drive Iran's oil sales to zero. But this strategy would afford Tehran close to zero access to its oil money.

Cohen back-channeled the idea to Brad Gordon, AIPAC's policy director, while Szubin shared it with key staffers on Capitol Hill. Before long, the

requirement to establish escrow accounts surfaced in a new piece of legislation, the Iran Threat Reduction and Syria Human Rights Act, which sailed
through Congress and was signed into law by Obama in August 2012. The
measure would go into effect early the following year, giving Cohen and
Szubin time to pursue financial diplomacy to increase its odds of success.

By the end of the summer of 2012, a pattern had emerged. There was no
sanction, no matter how severe, that Congress wouldn't thrust on Iran. And
Congress had the votes to ram through these sanctions with veto-proof majorities. This pressure forced the Obama administration to go much further
than it had ever imagined or deemed feasible. But instead of throwing up
their hands and dismissing Congress's wild ideas as impossible, Cohen,
Szubin, and the rest of the sanctions team hustled to come up with tweaks
that could make the ideas work. The gradual oil reduction strategy, embed-
ded in Menendez-Kirk, had dramatically cut Iran's oil sales; the new scheme
in the Iran Threat Reduction and Syria Human Rights Act would lock up
virtually all of Iran's oil money in overseas escrow accounts. As ever, necessity was the mother of invention.

A few months later, during the 2012 U.S. presidential campaign, Vice President Joe Biden debated Republican Representative Paul Ryan, Mitt Romney's
running mate, in Kentucky. When the subject turned to Iran, Ryan didn't
hold back: It was Congress that deserved credit for the pressure campaign
against Iran, because Congress had forced Obama's reluctant hand. "The
administration was blocking us every step of the way," he said. "Only because we had strong bipartisan support for these tough sanctions were we
able to overrule their objections and put them in in spite of the administration."

Ryan was only half right. Congress had thrown the alley-oop, but it was
the sanctions technocrats in the administration who maneuvered through
the defense, leapt into the air, and caught the ball in traffic before completing
a rim-rattling dunk.

18

Landslide

The steady drumbeat of sanctions coming out of Washington ensured that David Cohen, Adam Szubin, and others at Treasury lived on the road, shuttling between meetings with corporate executives and foreign officials to help them understand the dizzying array of restrictions on business with Iran.

In a rare moment of downtime in Brussels, Cohen hit the hotel gym. Above the treadmill, a wall-mounted TV played a CNN newscast on Iran's currency, the rial, which was in free fall. *Man*, Cohen marveled, *this is going to work*.

Over the summer of 2012, as Iran's oil sales dried up, its economy started showing signs of crisis. The Central Bank of Iran had long kept the value of the rial within a fixed range. If the rial dipped beneath the lower threshold, the central bank would step in, using its reserves of hard currency to prop the rial up. But now that both Menendez-Kirk and the EU oil embargo limited the inflow of petrodollars, the central bank was short on foreign reserves. In the first eight months of 2012, the value of the rial against the dollar—the closest thing officials in Tehran and Washington had to a scoreboard in the economic war—declined by half.

The rial's precipitous drop reverberated across Iran. The price of chicken, a staple of Iranian cuisine, tripled as imports of chicken feed became exorbitantly expensive. Half the country's chicken farms ceased production. To make matters worse, this unfolded during Ramadan, when many Iranian families fasted during the day before gathering in the evening for Iftar—a festive meal that often featured chicken prepared with saffron, plums, or pomegranates.

Most working- and middle-class families now struggled to afford chicken, and long lines outside markets brought back bad memories of the scarcity Iranians experienced in the early 1980s during the Iran-Iraq War. "There are two classes of people," an Iranian based in the city of Shiraz posted on Twitter, "below the chicken line and above the chicken line." Esmail Ahmadi-Moghaddam, the country's police chief and Ahmadinejad's brother-in-law, exhorted TV stations to stop showing films that depicted families eating chicken. "They show chicken being eaten in movies while somebody might not be able to buy it," Ahmadi-Moghaddam said. "Some people observing this class gap might say that we will take knives and take our rights from the rich."

He had a point. By September 2012, inflation was wreaking havoc everywhere in Iran, not just in the poultry aisle. The official rate of inflation stood at nearly 25 percent—a jaw-dropping figure that many economists considered an underestimate. Youth unemployment hovered around 30 percent. Conditions were ripe for social unrest.

Tragically, those hit hardest were among Iran's most vulnerable. U.S. sanctions always exempted humanitarian goods such as food, medicine, and medical devices, and Obama officials did their best to ensure these products could flow uninterrupted into Iran. But as the value of the rial plunged, all imports, including medicine and the raw materials used by pharmaceutical companies, grew scarcer and more expensive. Making matters worse, most foreign banks now refused to accept payments from Iran, regardless of their purpose. The hurt that U.S. policies inflicted on ordinary Iranians was unintentional, but that didn't lessen the pain.

Sanctions were affecting even the better-off. A thirty-two-year-old Iranian engineer bemoaned the shrinking value of his earnings. "I used to make $2,000 a month with my salary," he said, "Then it dropped to $1,000 a few weeks ago, and now my income is worth only $500." After losing two-thirds of his capital as the rial collapsed, the owner of a shoe factory was forced to lay off his longtime staff. "This means I have to expel seventy workers," he explained. "And then a long chain of people who are all connected to each other falls apart."

To try to put a lid on the brewing discontent, Ayatollah Khamenei conceded that sanctions were the cause. This seemingly obvious admission marked a major shift: Iranian officials typically scoffed at sanctions, especially in public, as a show of defiance. Now, by contrast, Khamenei acknowledged the sanctions' devastating impact, which he said was part of a U.S.

attempt at regime change. He pledged to build an "economy of resistance" that would reduce Iran's reliance on oil sales and increase its self-sufficiency.

Mohsen Rezaee, a conservative politician and former commander of the IRGC, was tapped to bring Khamenei's resistance economy to life. The aim, according to Rezaee, was to "address conditions under sanctions." If not for sanctions, he added, Tehran "would never have thought" of reducing its dependence on oil exports. "Sanctions are dragging us in that direction."

Not long before, Iran's public downplaying of sanctions had been so complete that former Iranian president Akbar Hashemi Rafsanjani pleaded with his peers in the upper echelons of power "to take the sanctions seriously and not as jokes." Now, the supreme leader himself was putting adaptation to sanctions at the top of Iran's economic agenda.

But Tehran's initial attempts to stabilize the economy only made things worse. In late September, the central bank launched a new "currency trading center" modeled after an entity created at the height of the Iran-Iraq War. The center divided Iran's economy into three tiers, each of which could access U.S. dollars at a different exchange rate. Businesses in the first tier—importers of essentials like meat, grain, and medicine—could buy dollars for the fixed official exchange rate of 12,260 rials to the dollar, less than half the rate available on the open market. The fixed rate was an attempt to ward off another fiasco like the chicken crisis. Businesses in the second tier, including in livestock, metals, and minerals, could access dollars for a small discount below the open-market rate. Everyone else—such as buyers of cars, clothes, and kitchen appliances—was on their own.

Within a week of launch, the currency trading center accomplished exactly the opposite of what it was designed to achieve. It sparked a panic as Iranians raced to convert their rials into dollars and euros, fearing their savings today would be worth even less tomorrow. On Monday, October 1, Iran's currency plummeted to 33,500 rials to the dollar on the open market. The next day, it hit 37,000 rials to the dollar. By Wednesday, it was trading at around 40,000 rials to the dollar. In just seven days, the rial lost more than a third of its value, on top of the decline it had already suffered.

As the rial plumbed new lows, protests erupted in Tehran's Grand Bazaar, the commercial heart of Iran's capital. The *bazaari* merchants were known to be solidly conservative. They had played a central role in the 1979 revolution that forged the Islamic Republic, and since then, they had reliably supported the government. But on October 3, a strike shut down most of the bazaar. The merchants hit the streets in droves, chanting anti-government slogans and calling on Ahmadinejad to resign. Among the many cheers, one stood out: "We don't want nuclear energy!" It was impossible to ignore the link between the country's economic strife and the underlying reason for the sanctions. Iranians might believe their country had a right to a nuclear program—but at what price?

Even Ahmadinejad, whose bellicose rhetoric and hard-line policies had helped build broad international support for sanctions, could not deny the gravity of the situation. The United States and its allies, Ahmadinejad said at a press conference, were waging a "hidden war, a very extensive and heavy war spread across the world" against Iran. This war had "succeeded in decreasing our oil sales" and was designed to "prevent Iran from spending or transferring its oil money, even when it can sell oil."

Tehran's attempt to stop the rial's fall through economic policy had grievously backfired. So it pivoted to what it knew best: force. Iranian police raided currency shops, confiscated their banknotes, arrested scores of traders and staff, and shut the shops down. After the crackdown, exchange rates stabilized. But the value of Iran's currency settled at around 31,000 rials to the dollar, down about 20 percent from the start of the ordeal. There was no fixing the damage already done.

═══

As Iran's economy tumbled, the rest of the world found further reasons to stay away. In December, U.S. law enforcement agencies smacked London-based HSBC, Europe's biggest bank, with a gargantuan $1.9 billion fine for sanctions violations, including a slew of deceptive dealings with Iran. It was by far the largest fine ever levied for running afoul of American sanctions. As part of the settlement, HSBC agreed to make far-reaching compliance reforms and to allow the Justice Department to install an independent monitor at the bank to keep tabs on the new policies.

To ensure airtight compliance going forward, HSBC hired Stuart Levey as its chief legal officer. Under Levey's leadership, HSBC went on to spend more than a billion dollars and bring on thousands of staff to overhaul its compliance systems. The bank created a unified set of controls that would apply across its business in every region of the world, what Levey called a "highest common denominator approach"—as he summarized, "the best way to do it anywhere is how we're going to do it everywhere."

Levey's reforms at HSBC were indicative of a broader transformation in the financial industry. Years earlier, global banks had been conscripted to fight in America's economic war. Now that they were getting a taste of the consequences of poor performance, they were beefing up to implement the latest policies concocted at Treasury. And they were doing so at the direction of people like Levey, themselves veterans of the economic war and true believers in the cause.

For the economic warriors still in the federal government, the HSBC fine came at a propitious moment. They were trying to lock up Iran's oil money in overseas escrow accounts, and the banks, spooked by the massive HSBC fine, were on high alert. Adam Szubin traveled the world to ensure governments and financial institutions understood what was expected of them. In Tokyo, meeting with officials at Japan's finance ministry, he scribbled a diagram on a sheet of paper to illustrate how Iran could and couldn't use the escrowed oil funds. The Japanese officials grasped it and vowed to comply. In Seoul, Szubin met with executives from Woori Bank and the Industrial Bank of Korea, which handled oil accounts on behalf of the Central Bank of Iran. They, too, agreed to abide by America's new restrictions.

In Beijing, Szubin had a stiff and formal meeting with Yi Gang, who oversaw foreign exchange at the People's Bank of China. Sitting awkwardly in a plush, oversized chair, Szubin laid out the new policy. Yi nodded along but gave no indication of what China would do. As was often the case when discussing sanctions with the Chinese, Szubin felt as though he was talking to himself, unsure if he was getting through. But he knew there was a powerful incentive for China to comply: forcing Tehran to keep its oil revenues in China would almost certainly boost Chinese exports to Iran.

The novel combination of the traditional stick of sanctions (losing access to the U.S. financial system) with an economic carrot (the possibility of higher exports) proved effective. After the policy went into force in early 2013, banks everywhere, including in China, fell into line. The escrow accounts were established, and Iran's petrodollars remained offshore. Tehran was blindsided by the stringency and uniformity of compliance. "They didn't see it coming," recalled Richard Nephew, who had just finished a stint coordinating Iran sanctions at the NSC. "They didn't realize that foreign banks were actually going to fulfill the terms."

As it turned out, Iran was unwilling to use its petrodollars to buy toys from China or televisions from Japan. Instead, it watched helplessly as its oil billions accumulated in the overseas escrow accounts, unable to pay for the imports it actually wanted. Factories across Iran, struggling to buy foreign components, slashed production and laid off employees in droves. "From the owner to the line worker, no one is safe," said the manager of an Iranian manufacturer of roof insulation sheets, who had been forced to terminate half his staff. "Our country is facing an economic disaster." The official inflation rate soared above 30 percent, while many economists believed it was really as high as 40 percent.

The only people managing to stay afloat were those with preferential access to scarce resources, such as regime insiders and members of the IRGC. "There is enough hard currency to import pineapples and Porsches by favorite businessmen," complained an Iranian trader who struggled to source food and medicine from abroad, "but not for wheat [imported] by a private businessman."

Tehran could come up with no solution besides subterfuge. To disguise oil shipments, the National Iranian Tanker Company repainted its fleet of oil tankers, changed their names, and registered them with new flags and home ports. Corrupt shipping magnates agreed to rendezvous their vessels with Iranian tankers on the high seas, often in the middle of the night, for so-called ship-to-ship transfers, in which the Iranian ship would surreptitiously funnel its oil to the other ship. But these cloak-and-dagger operations were the geopolitical equivalent of petty crime. Washington easily detected and squashed them.

In a more elaborate plot, the Iranian regime partnered with the gold trader Reza Zarrab, the Turkish banker Mehmet Hakan Atilla, and a motley crew of accomplices to puncture Iran's oil escrow accounts in Turkey. Zarrab and Atilla bribed Turkish officials, gained access to some of Iran's locked-up oil wealth, and exchanged it for gold bars, which they smuggled to Dubai. There, the booty was sold for cash, giving Iran a bit of hard currency that it could use freely. But U.S. officials uncovered this extravagant scheme, too. Zarrab and Atilla were both arrested while trying to fly into the United States, spending their last free moments waiting to clear passport control.

This economic chaos was the backdrop for Iran's presidential election in June 2013. Though Iranians got to vote for a president, the country was not a democracy. Ayatollah Khamenei, the unelected supreme leader, was firmly in control, and the electorate's choices for president were limited to a small group of candidates handpicked by the supreme leader and his closest advisors. This time, Khamenei would be especially careful to avoid a repeat of the previous election, in 2009, which had blown up into the abortive Green Revolution. The regime approved a slate of eight conservative candidates, all close allies of the supreme leader. The front-runner was Saeed Jalili, the arch-conservative who had managed nuclear diplomacy under Ahmadinejad. A handful of reformist contenders, including one who openly advocated for improving relations with Washington and seeking sanctions relief, were disqualified.

The lineup was designed to keep the electoral campaign uneventful. For a long time, it did. The candidates duly rejected any notion of compromise with America. Sanctions, the issue at the top of everyone's mind, were not discussed. "I love Islam, but how do we fix 100 percent inflation?" a garage owner in the holy city of Qom told a Western reporter. "I haven't seen any candidate with clear ideas for the future."

Then, all of a sudden, the candidates' tone shifted. It was Hassan Rouhani, a dark-horse candidate, who lit the spark. A week before election day, in a nationally televised debate, Rouhani attacked Jalili for his poor stewardship of the nuclear issue. "All of our problems stem from this—that we didn't make the utmost effort to prevent the nuclear dossier from going to the UN Security Council," Rouhani said. "It is good to have centrifuges running, provided people's lives and livelihoods are also running."

As soon as Rouhani dared to broach the topic, other candidates piled on. Ali Akbar Velayati, Khamenei's top foreign policy aide, went next. "What people are seeing, Mr. Jalili, is that you have not gone forward even one step [in nuclear negotiations], and the pressure of international sanctions still exists," he admonished his rival. "The art of diplomacy is to preserve our nuclear rights, not to see sanctions increase." TV viewers across Iran watched slack-jawed.

Rouhani's chutzpah to give voice to Iran's true problems catapulted him to the front of the pack. In the days ahead, he pressed his advantage. "I do not approve of the current foreign policy," he announced at a rally in northwestern Iran. "We should try to have good international interactions to gradually reduce the sanctions and finally remove them." He soon won endorsements from two former Iranian presidents.

On June 14, voters turned out en masse to cast their ballots for Rouhani, who won 51 percent of the vote; the second-place finisher garnered just

Hassan Rouhani: the politician who mobilized
Iranian voters by giving voice to their discontent.

17 percent. It was a landslide that had been unthinkable just a few weeks before. Soon there would be a president in Tehran who not only acknowledged the damage wreaked by sanctions but also had campaigned publicly for their removal.

America's economic war had brought about political change in Iran. But even optimists in Washington knew that all key decisions on the nuclear program were ultimately up to one man: Khamenei. And while the will of the Iranian people was unmistakable, the mind of the supreme leader remained a mystery.

The Freeze

Chris Backemeyer learned of the Iranian election results while shopping at a Macy's near the White House. The sandy-haired former banker and State Department sanctions expert, who a few months earlier had succeeded Richard Nephew at the NSC, received the news in a phone call from his colleague Bernadette Meehan. Rouhani had won big, Meehan said. Backemeyer had been a close observer of Iranian politics for years. Yet Rouhani's victory left him and others in Washington just as surprised as the throngs celebrating in the streets of Tehran.

Meehan told Backemeyer they needed to draft a public statement in response, but his mind was elsewhere. *How*, he silently wondered, *might this affect the U.S. government's back-channel talks with Tehran?*

The back channel was a fiercely guarded secret. It had originated in 2011, when Secretary of State Hillary Clinton and Senator John Kerry, then chairman of the Senate Foreign Relations Committee, made separate trips to Muscat, the rocky, seaside capital of Oman, to meet with the country's leader, Sultan Qaboos. The sultan, whose reign dated back to Richard Nixon's presidency, was one of the few world leaders who enjoyed warm relations with both the White House and Ayatollah Khamenei. He offered to arrange secret discussions between America and Iran to break the logjam on the nuclear issue.

Kerry, in particular, welcomed the proposal with enthusiasm. In the summer of 2012, the White House dispatched two officials, Jake Sullivan and Puneet Talwar, to Oman to test the waters with mid-level Iranian diplomats. The resulting discussion was neither substantive nor productive, but the fact that the Iranians showed up at all, with the apparent support of the supreme leader, gave the Obama administration confidence that Qaboos could deliver.

Early the next year, after Obama appointed Kerry to replace Clinton at Foggy Bottom, the new secretary of state pursued the Oman channel with indefatigable energy. His sense of urgency was well-founded. Tehran had by now amassed enough enriched uranium for eight to ten nuclear bombs, and experts assessed that it could build those weapons within just a month or two if it decided to. Netanyahu was champing at the bit for a military strike—in fact, he had been ready to attack on the eve of America's 2012 presidential election until his defense minister, Ehud Barak, turned against the idea. Meanwhile, with Iran's economy in free fall, Tehran had a strong incentive to explore a deal.

A month after being sworn in, Kerry dispatched Bill Burns, the deputy secretary of state and an esteemed career Foreign Service officer, to another secret meeting in Muscat. At the White House's instruction, Burns informed the Iranians that the United States was willing to explore a deal that allowed Iran to retain a limited, peaceful nuclear enrichment program. Obama believed that expressing this openness up front was necessary for the Iranians to negotiate seriously. While this decision would later become controversial, it no doubt laid the groundwork for more substantive talks.

In the lead-up to the 2013 Iranian election, the back channel went quiet for several months. But when Hassan Rouhani's popularity skyrocketed on the promise of improved relations with the world and a push for sanctions relief, hope blossomed in Washington that the political environment in Iran was shifting.

Now Rouhani was victorious in a landslide. When Backemeyer got off the phone with Meehan, he found his mind moving several steps ahead. If Rouhani managed to convince Khamenei to pursue a deal, what sanctions relief might America offer in return?

≡

Shortly after the election, Rouhani assembled a team of economists to thoroughly evaluate the state of Iran's economy and diagnose its ailments. Their findings were worrisome. The government's coffers were short some $200 billion. Iran was struggling to pay public workers, and the country was running dangerously low on everyday staples like wheat. The evisceration of oil revenues over the previous eighteen months, compounded by years of corrupt and incompetent management under Ahmadinejad, had created an economic disaster, the scale of which Ahmadinejad had covered up.

For Rouhani, the only way to fix the mess was to secure sanctions relief. The country direly needed access to its oil wealth, more than $100 billion of which sat frozen in overseas escrow accounts. Rouhani persuaded Khamenei of this harsh reality, telling him that even greater civil and political unrest could follow if nothing was done. Within days of Rouhani's inauguration in early August, he announced his intention to jumpstart nuclear talks with the P5+1. In parallel, the Iranians and Americans scheduled a new round of secret talks in Oman for early September.

Rouhani's most important decision was appointing Javad Zarif, a gifted career diplomat, as Iran's foreign minister. As a teenager, just before the 1979 revolution, Zarif had left Iran for America. Over nearly twenty years in the United States, Zarif completed high school and college in San Francisco, earned a doctorate in international relations from the University of Denver, and had two kids. He also spent five years in New York City as Iran's ambassador to the UN. Zarif was at home in American culture, fluent in idiomatic American English, and well connected across the U.S. foreign policy establishment. He was the ideal envoy to chase a deal with Washington.

For the Obama administration, the rise of Rouhani and Zarif was a tremendous opportunity. It felt like sanctions were finally yielding the thing they were supposed to achieve all along: a peaceful end to Iran's nuclear program. But these more congenial Iranian leaders also brought new risks. After years of piling up sanctions with little to show for it, Washington's decision to go after Iran's oil wealth had sent the Iranian economy into recession for the first time since the early 1990s, with inflation above 40 percent and ballooning public debt. Such pressure was only possible because politicians and business executives in places like China, Germany, India, and Japan had gone along with American sanctions, often reluctantly. If Rouhani and Zarif went on a charm offensive, global support for a tough policy toward Tehran might dissolve before the United States had time to extract meaningful nuclear concessions.

There was another problem: America might have already inflicted all the pain it could on Iran's economy. Since the Menendez-Kirk amendment became law, Iran's oil sales had fallen 60 percent to a meager one million barrels per day, while the number of countries buying Iranian oil had gone from twenty-one to six. Of Iran's remaining oil customers, only China and India were buying sizable amounts—and that money went straight into overseas escrow accounts anyway.

Still under nonstop pressure from Congress, the White House pressed the experts for ideas for new sanctions. In response, officials at the State Department sent a tongue-in-cheek memo to the NSC recommending that America build a time machine, go back to 1979, and prevent the Iranian revolution from happening. The few additional sanctions that remained in the hopper risked doing more harm than good. Around the time Rouhani was elected, the Obama administration hit Iran's car industry with sweeping restrictions, even though the sector had already suffered production declines of up to 80 percent and hundreds of thousands of layoffs. The new auto sanctions didn't add much, but they did anger France's government, as Renault, the French carmaker, stood to lose hundreds of millions of euros in outstanding debts in Iran. Economic warfare was showing diminishing marginal returns.

The sanctions technocrats were unanimous: Washington was either at, or close to, the point of maximum leverage. In one of his last acts at the NSC before returning to the State Department, Nephew wrote a memo to Tom Donilon arguing it was time to trade in America's chips.

These "chips" were the ability to loosen the many layers of sanctions suffocating the Iranian economy. So in the summer of 2013, Backemeyer and Nephew began quietly drawing up an exhaustive list of options for sanctions relief. As the current and former NSC directors for Iran sanctions, they were in the tiny circle of people who knew about the secret back channel with the Iranians. They were also the group's only experts on sanctions. No one at Treasury—not Adam Szubin, not David Cohen—was privy to the talks. This put Backemeyer and Nephew in the difficult position of crafting the initial ideas for sanctions relief without help from the central architects of the penalties.

Backemeyer convened a series of small-group discussions in the White House Situation Room to review the sanctions-relief menu. The secure, windowless meeting rooms, usually teeming with officials from multiple agencies and backbenchers scribbling notes, felt oddly empty. No papers were distributed beforehand, and not even the subjects of the meetings were disclosed in advance. Bill Burns, who had worked in U.S. foreign policy for decades, reflected that the secret talks with the Iranians were "the most tightly held effort" of his career, including the 2011 raid that killed Osama bin Laden.

Obama decided to keep the scope of the back-channel negotiations narrow. He was not seeking a grand bargain with Tehran but rather a technical arms control pact. America would hence offer only a *limited* reprieve from sanctions in exchange for strict controls on Iran's nuclear program. Just as U.S. officials had tied the introduction of sanctions to specific Iranian conduct (Iran's Bank Melli, for instance, was targeted for supporting the nuclear program, whereas Bank Saderat was hit for helping Tehran funnel money to Hezbollah and other terrorist proxies), Backemeyer and Nephew limited their list of relief options to sanctions whose legal justification was tied to Iran's nuclear activities.

Additionally, Burns and the White House determined that a two-phase agreement would give talks the best chance of success. The first step would be an interim deal freezing Iran's nuclear program, hopefully followed by a more comprehensive settlement. Backemeyer and Nephew thus landed on another tenet: any sanctions relief put on the table in the first phase had to be *reversible* in case the deal blew up before reaching the second phase.

The air of secrecy in the Situation Room extended beyond Washington. In late August, Richard Nephew led a delegation from State and Treasury for routine discussions on sanctions enforcement in the UAE and Oman. For most of the team, it felt like a typical work trip: they spent all day in meetings with government officials and business executives, sampled local cuisine, and even found time to go to a water park in Dubai. But only Nephew knew that their time in Muscat overlapped with a visit by Burns and a few other U.S. officials, who were at a nearby beach compound holding secret talks with the Iranians. While Nephew was out for dinner with his colleagues, his phone rang. It was a member of Burns's delegation.

"You need to be at the entrance of your hotel in two hours," he told Nephew. "You will be picked up by a woman who will take you someplace."

Nephew hung up and told his colleagues he had to return to the hotel, feigning an oncoming illness. Back in his room, he changed clothes, grabbed his notebook, and snuck out a side door to meet his driver.

Burns's team had been making headway in Muscat. On the first day of discussions, the Iranians had agreed to pursue a two-phase agreement. Burns now sought Nephew's advice on what sanctions relief to put on the table. In Nephew's view, it would be imprudent to propose specific sanctions relief until they learned what Tehran was prepared to give up on the nuclear side. Burns asked Nephew to stick around for the remainder of the talks.

Nephew fired off an email to his colleagues. His fears were confirmed, he wrote: he had a bad case of food poisoning. He would not only have to sit out the rest of their meetings but also miss their flight home to Washington. (None of his colleagues suspected anything was up.) Over the following days, Burns presented his "asks." The United States wanted Iran to stop enriching uranium, dilute whatever highly enriched uranium it already possessed, and suspend upgrades to its facilities at Natanz, Arak, and Fordow. Burns then invited the Iranians to provide their "asks" on the sanctions front. The Iranian officials, however, were vague. Since they wanted all sanctions lifted, they said, it was up to the Americans to propose a set of "gives."

Nephew suspected the Iranians didn't know what exact sanctions relief they wanted. They weren't ignorant or unprepared; it was simply hard for anyone in Tehran—or in Washington, for that matter—to predict what precise mix of sanctions relief would give Iran the economic reprieve that it desperately sought. Besides, regardless of which sanctions were suspended, Washington could not wave a magic wand and compel banks and companies to re-enter the Iranian market.

There was one tangible piece of relief that America could offer: partial access to the oil revenue trapped in overseas escrow accounts. Repatriating a portion of that money would give Rouhani's government much-needed access to hard currency. And if the cash infusions were kept small enough, Iran would get only short-term relief, which would incentivize its leaders to abide by the nuclear commitments they made in phase one and negotiate seriously toward a more comprehensive deal.

A month after the talks in Muscat, Kerry met with Zarif at the UN in New York. Cameras flashed and media swarmed: it was the highest-level encounter between American and Iranian officials since the 1979 revolution. Meanwhile, another round of secret talks was underway at the Waldorf Astoria hotel a few blocks west. As planned, Burns proposed limited cash infusions as the centerpiece of the sanctions relief package. Nephew chimed in, calling the funds "free money"—Iran would be able to move them wherever it chose. The Iranians liked the sound of that. From then on, the discussions revolved around how much of Iran's money America would agree to unfreeze.

In mid-October, the P5+1 reconvened with Iran for a formal round of negotiations in Geneva. Once again, secret talks were taking place simultaneously right around the corner. The formal U.S. delegation was led by Wendy Sherman, the number three at the State Department, and for the first time, Adam Szubin joined, too. During a break in the formal negotiations,

Nephew, who was participating in both sets of talks, met Szubin privately in a hotel room to read him into the secret negotiations that were happening in parallel. Szubin did not flinch. Ever the professional, he understood the need for secrecy and exhibited no sign of frustration, even though he had been instrumental in creating the economic pressure that had made all this diplomacy possible. Without missing a beat, the two men dove into the details of the sanctions relief package.

Szubin agreed that cash infusions were the way forward. In fact, a deal exchanging a limited amount of petrodollars for a freeze in Iran's nuclear program would be highly favorable to the United States. Iran's nuclear progress would come to a halt as its economy remained on life support. With the Iranians and the Americans aligning on the type of sanctions relief Iran should get in exchange for a nuclear freeze, negotiations progressed rapidly over the coming weeks, and the substance of the back-channel talks converged with the formal P5+1 proceedings.

On November 24, the Sunday before Thanksgiving, an interim deal was struck. Iran agreed to freeze its nuclear program for six months and dispose of its stockpile of highly enriched uranium. In return, America would unfreeze $4.2 billion, less than two months' worth of Iranian oil revenues. Washington would also suspend the sanctions on the car industry and issue a license allowing U.S. and European firms to repair Iran's rickety fleet of passenger airplanes, many of which age and lack of maintenance had turned into a disaster waiting to happen.

Richard Nephew had spent his entire career working to curb Iran's nuclear program, and for much of that time, he feared that the issue would ultimately lead to war. Shortly after the deal, which became known as the Joint Plan of Action (JPOA), was finalized, Nephew was alone in his Geneva hotel room, packing up his clothes to try to catch a flight home to Washington. A decade's worth of stress washed over him, along with a feeling of catharsis and a touch of vindication. He burst into tears.

Others were not so elated. "What was accomplished last night in Geneva is not a historic agreement; it's a historic mistake," Israeli Prime Minister Netanyahu told his cabinet hours after the JPOA was signed. "Today the world has become much more dangerous, because the most dangerous regime in the world took a meaningful step toward acquiring the most dangerous weapon in the world."

Netanyahu's words may have helped Rouhani sell the deal in Iran. They had the opposite effect in America, where they imperiled political support for the Obama administration's diplomacy, which already stood on shaky ground. In due time, however, the Israelis would learn to love the JPOA for the same reasons it appealed to sanctions technocrats like Szubin and Nephew: Iran's nuclear program was frozen, and its economy remained frozen, too.

"The World Has Avoided Another War"

For the technocrats at Treasury, the JPOA was both an end and a beginning. The deal was the culmination of the economic war against Iran. Over seven years, they had weaponized America's economic might in ways previously untried and unimaginable. The resulting economic pressure engineered a major political change inside Iran. Now, the United States had frozen Tehran's nuclear program without having fired a shot.

But the JPOA also marked the beginning of a journey into the unknown: sanctions relief. And just as rebuilding after a war is slow and difficult work, so is reconstruction in the aftermath of a prolonged sanctions campaign.

During the holiday season in 2013, as politicians in Washington either toasted the JPOA or cursed it, Treasury officials got to work figuring out how to give Iran access to the $4.2 billion in frozen oil funds promised under the deal. America had pledged to provide the money in installments of roughly $500 million as Iran took the agreed-upon steps to halt its nuclear program.

The sanctions technocrats were experts on Iran's economy, but they were relative newcomers to diplomacy. As they started holding regular meetings with the Iranians on JPOA implementation, a sanctions campaign that had sometimes felt like an academic exercise became viscerally real. So, too, did the desperation with which the Iranians wanted to regain access to their petrodollars. During a round of technical talks in Vienna shortly after the JPOA was signed, a European diplomat questioned Iran's commitment to the pact. Hamid Baeidinejad, the urbane Iranian negotiator, stood up in anger. "You have $100 billion of our money!" he snapped. "Of course we're serious."

The U.S. government could not just flip a switch and give Iran access to money from the overseas escrow accounts. A private bank would have to agree to accept the funds on behalf of the Central Bank of Iran and then allow Tehran to use the funds in a manner of its choosing. American officials looked far and wide for a bank ready to act as such a conduit. But years of massive fines and warnings from the U.S. government had taught the global financial system that the benefits of business with Iran were not worth the risks. This lesson was as good as an iron law at the world's biggest banks, which proved reluctant to budge even with Washington's seal of approval.

Only after repeated rejections did Szubin and his colleagues finally find a partner: a little-known Swiss bank called Banque de Commerce et de Placements, or BCP. With a letter from Szubin confirming that the transaction would not violate U.S. sanctions, and with support from the Swiss government, BCP agreed to help Iran get its money.

On February 3, 2014, a Japanese bank transferred the first tranche of Iran's escrowed oil funds to BCP in Switzerland, where the Central Bank of Iran had set up an account. But once the money arrived in Switzerland, Tehran struggled to withdraw it. Without proof of what Iran planned to use the money for, BCP was nervous about releasing the funds, and other banks were nervous about accepting them. Tehran had agreed to freeze its nuclear program, but it had not vowed to stop funneling cash to Hezbollah or its other militant proxies. What if it sent the funds to a terrorist group? No bank wanted to be implicated in such a transfer.

Iranian officials were enormously frustrated about the difficulty of accessing the money. At the first round of negotiations toward a comprehensive nuclear deal, held in Vienna later that February, Abbas Araghchi, Iran's chief negotiator, complained bitterly that America was not living up to its side of the deal. When Nephew outlined the technical difficulties, Araghchi got visibly upset. He glared at Nephew. "You promised this was 'free money'!" he shouted, reminding him of their conversation at the Waldorf Astoria.

The fitful start was a harbinger of things to come. In the summer of 2014, the Justice Department slapped France's BNP Paribas with a record-shattering $9 billion fine for violations of U.S. sanctions against Iran and several other countries. The astronomical penalty fully wiped out the bank's earnings for the year and elicited a stern letter of protest from French President François Hollande to Obama. The fine underscored why banks weren't eager to jump back into business with Iran: Treasury could reassure them, but it could not offer guarantees of protection from America's independent law enforcement agencies.

Politics further complicated matters. As Netanyahu raged against Obama's nuclear diplomacy, including in a controversial address to a joint session of Congress, Iran hawks on Capitol Hill ramped up pressure on the White House. For years, Republicans and Democrats in Congress had largely been united on Iran policy: both pushed hard for aggressive sanctions. But now, partisan fissures emerged, as Republicans uniformly denounced the nuclear talks while a core group of Democrats supported them.

In March 2015, Senator Tom Cotton, a young and ambitious conservative from Arkansas, got forty-six of his Republican colleagues to sign a letter to Iran's leaders, purporting to teach them a lesson in America's constitutional system. The Republican senators emphasized that Obama's nuclear deal was not necessarily binding, noting that they would "consider any agreement regarding your nuclear-weapons program that is not approved by the Congress as nothing more than an executive agreement between President Obama and Ayatollah Khamenei." Lest their message be misinterpreted, they added, "The next president could revoke such an executive agreement with the stroke of a pen and future Congresses could modify the terms of the agreement at any time." If Republicans couldn't convince Obama and other Democrats about the folly of a nuclear deal, perhaps they could convince Tehran.

This fierce opposition from Republicans added to fears across the world about resuming business with Iran. Obama officials could promise that a transaction wouldn't violate U.S. sanctions, but the president was nearing the end of his second term. How would his successor treat the firms that had cautiously re-entered the Iranian market?

Republican opposition also sharply limited the administration's options for offering sanctions relief as part of the final deal being negotiated. Forced onto the defensive, Obama officials repeatedly emphasized that they would consider lifting only "nuclear-related secondary sanctions," and that they would continue enforcing all other restrictions on Iran. Going any further might jeopardize the political survival of the deal. But the practical implications of this stance had drawbacks: it meant, in effect, that the final deal would turn back the clock on sanctions to before 2006 for the rest of the world, while the United States continued living in the present. If France's Total or Italy's Eni wanted to invest in an Iranian oil field, that would be okay; if China and India or even Germany and Spain wanted to increase their oil imports from Iran, that would be fine, too. By contrast, American companies still couldn't buy Iran's oil or invest in its energy sector. The United States had poured immense time and resources into developing the innovative economic weapons that made a nuclear deal possible. If the deal lifted secondary sanctions while the U.S. domestic embargo remained, European and Asian companies would reap all the benefits from the reopening of Iran's economy while American businesses missed out.

Keeping the full U.S. embargo in place also had strategic costs. Were Iran to cheat or backtrack on its nuclear commitments, America would have a much easier time bringing down the hammer on Iran if its economy depended on U.S. businesses for capital, critical inputs, and technical expertise. The U.S. government could tell American companies precisely what they could and could not do; it did not possess such ironclad authority over companies based abroad. Moreover, loosening the U.S. embargo might help take the wind out of the hawks' sails in the long run: if American companies re-entered Iran and found ways to make money, they would gain a stake in the long-term future of the deal. It might not be so easy for members of Congress to spurn the deal if their actions could put jobs and livelihoods in their home districts at risk.

But none of this mattered. The political situation in Washington boxed in the Obama administration and left minimal space for creativity. The lone exception was civil aviation, where the United States agreed to remove a section of the domestic embargo and allow Boeing to compete with Airbus, its European rival, to replenish Iran's decaying fleet of passenger airplanes. Aside from that, America's negotiating position was inflexible. This meant that much of the remainder of the talks ran on emotion rather than substance. The Obama administration knew that it could give the Iranians only a narrow slice of sanctions relief. The Iranians just wanted as many sanctions lifted as possible and, if they agreed to proceed, would be left to hope that the package they ultimately got would deliver the big economic boost their country needed.

In July 2015, as the P5+1 and Iran closed in on a comprehensive nuclear deal, this dynamic was on full display. Negotiations on sanctions relief descended into something resembling a fantasy sports league. The diplomats sat in a room, staring at a PowerPoint slide projected on a screen that listed dozens of the people and companies that were under sanctions. They haggled over which ones should come off the sanctions list and which should stay on, without the slightest idea of who many of these people and companies were or what the impact would be. At one point, when the Iranians pushed Chris Backemeyer, America's lead sanctions negotiator, to lift sanctions on a random Iranian, he named his price: "Yes—but for a player to be named later."

In the wee hours of the morning on July 14, Kerry, Zarif, and other envoys from the P5+1 yelled at one another at Vienna's Palais Coburg, a nineteenth-century palace turned five-star-hotel, tussling over the final details of the nuclear deal. Backemeyer was sitting with some colleagues outside the room, like a huddled mass waiting for white smoke at the Vatican. They could hear the discussion through the door. Suddenly, Kerry came storming out, his pace barely slowed by the crutches he was using as he nursed a broken leg. He was looking for Backemeyer.

"Chris! I need one more thing to give Zarif a reason to take the deal," Kerry demanded. "Let's find something that gets him over the hump without costing us."

As it happened, Backemeyer had a list of a dozen or so obscure individuals, all of whom had been penalized for helping Iran evade sanctions, and none of whom were Iranian. He had kept the names in reserve, since Iran's negotiators had never mentioned any of them during their PowerPoint sessions. Backemeyer told Kerry about the idea and rushed upstairs to print out the list. But by the time he returned, Kerry was gone and the negotiating room was empty.

Kerry had offered Zarif to remove sanctions on the list of individuals without even knowing their names, much less naming them, and Zarif had accepted it sight unseen. The deal was done. Within an hour, Kerry, Zarif, and the other members of the P5+1 announced the successful conclusion of the Joint Comprehensive Plan of Action (JCPOA). Most would just call it the Iran nuclear deal.

Under the deal, America's nuclear-related secondary sanctions would be lifted, as would virtually all sanctions imposed by the UN, the EU, and other countries. In return, Iran agreed to take major steps to roll back its nuclear program. It would dispose of 98 percent of its enriched uranium, leaving it with less than it needed for a single nuclear bomb. It would destroy the core of its heavy-water reactor at Arak, dismantle most of its centrifuges, and allow intrusive inspections and 24/7 monitoring of the key parts of its nuclear infrastructure. Before the deal, it would have taken Iran just a couple months to build a bomb. Now, that timeline was stretched to at least a full year—

John Kerry and Javad Zarif: partners—and rivals—
in negotiating the Iran nuclear deal.

giving the United States ample time to detect a decision by Iran to race ahead
and take preventive action.

Netanyahu and Iran hawks on Capitol Hill pilloried the deal, arguing
that Iran should not be allowed to conduct any nuclear activities, no matter
their scope or nature. They also took issue with the fact that the deal was
time-limited: many of the constraints it imposed on Iran would lapse in ten
or fifteen years.

Criticism aside, the deal was a remarkable feat of diplomatic endurance.
The interim deal had been extended twice; the negotiations that led to the
final agreement were a protracted, eighteen-month marathon. Many members of the U.S. negotiating team, including Szubin and Backemeyer, spent
months away from their families, missing birthdays, weddings, and anni-
versaries. Back home, government lawyers set up an industrial-scale effort to
ensure Washington could implement the sanctions relief it promised, a serious challenge given the dense thicket of legislation mandating restrictions
on Iran. Notwithstanding his broken leg, Kerry led talks for more than two
straight weeks at the Palais Coburg to clinch the deal, the longest continuous period a U.S. secretary of state had spent in an overseas negotiation in
over forty years.

Even now, the marathon was not over. As soon as the JCPOA was announced, the U.S. team's focus shifted from Vienna to Washington, where the Obama administration had to fight for the deal's survival on Capitol Hill. Earlier in the year, Congress had passed a law creating a sixty-day review period, during which legislators could study the deal before voting on it. If two-thirds of the Senate voted against the JCPOA, they would have a veto-proof majority to kill it.

For weeks, Szubin, Backemeyer, and many of the same experts who had been living in Swiss and Austrian hotels now found themselves in briefing after briefing with undecided senators, explaining the fine print of the deal and trying to persuade them to vote yes. Finally, after a trip to Vienna to meet with the IAEA officials who would be charged with monitoring Iran's compliance, Barbara Mikulski became the thirty-fourth senator to announce support for the JCPOA. With a veto-proof rejection now impossible, the agreement would go forward. In the end, just forty-two senators voted in favor of the nuclear deal—more than sufficient for the pact to survive but small enough to reveal its unsteady political foundation.

A few months later, in January 2016, the IAEA confirmed that Iran was abiding by its nuclear commitments, and Kerry signed paperwork to start removing sanctions. "As we speak," Obama boasted to Congress in his final State of the Union address, "Iran has rolled back its nuclear program, shipped out its uranium stockpile, and the world has avoided another war."

Whether the Iran nuclear deal was a "historic diplomatic breakthrough" (Obama's words) or a "historic mistake" (Netanyahu's) was in the eye of the beholder. But one thing was beyond dispute: America had won its economic war.

21

===

Black Magic

Obama and his allies touted sanctions as the critical ingredient that made the Iran deal possible. Opponents argued that sanctions were working so well that America traded them away too soon; it should have kept up the pressure, forcing Iran to permanently relinquish its entire nuclear program or, better yet, triggering the collapse of the Iranian regime. The one commonality among these competing perspectives was that sanctions worked.

This was a reversal of long-standing conventional wisdom. In a seminal 1997 article titled "Why Economic Sanctions Do Not Work," the political scientist Robert Pape found that sanctions were successful less than 5 percent of the time. Early in the George W. Bush administration, Secretary of State Colin Powell launched a public campaign for "smart sanctions" against Iraq. It was a clear rejoinder to the blunt-instrument Iraq sanctions of the 1990s, which were widely seen as having deprived innocent Iraqis of food and medicine while doing little to restrain Saddam's ambitions. But Powell's more targeted sanctions were likewise seen as a failure, paving the way for Bush's ruinous invasion of Iraq.

Most foreign policy hands in Washington saw sanctions as a symbolic gesture, not a serious alternative to war. Sanctions were a way to signal displeasure, a small step up from a strongly worded statement. Leaders used sanctions to acknowledge that something was bad without risking any blood or treasure to stop it. In an intractable crisis, sanctions allowed presidents and members of Congress to fulfill demands to "do something" without doing much of anything at all. In December 2004, when Bush bemoaned

"We've sanctioned ourselves out of influence with Iran," he was expressing a commonly held view. Only a fool or a Pollyanna would count on sanctions to coax Iran's supreme leader to curtail his country's nuclear ambitions.

But every once in a while, conventional wisdom is turned on its head. And it's often outsiders, bringing new perspectives and lacking old biases, who initiate it. This is what happened in 2006, when Stuart Levey, with help from his aide, Adam Szubin, launched the economic war against Iran. Both men were lawyers, recruited to Treasury from the Justice Department. They had no experience in foreign policy, much less sanctions. What they did have, however, was fluency in regulatory matters and an understanding of how businesses viewed risk.

These future sanctions technocrats also had chips on their shoulders. When they joined Treasury, the department was not considered a serious player in national security. Bush's public dismissal of sanctions as an effective lever against Iran only motivated them further. By the time the Iran nuclear deal was signed, their influence was undeniable. Levey was at HSBC, spearheading compliance reforms and advancing an industry-wide transformation that made banks better equipped to implement U.S. sanctions. Szubin had been promoted twice, first to head OFAC, and then, when David Cohen left to become the number two at the CIA in early 2015, to run all of TFI, the position Levey originally held. All the while, scores of others joined them, adding expertise from areas like energy, finance, and transportation.

Their efforts laid the groundwork for a diplomatic breakthrough that had eluded policymakers for years. To be sure, sanctions did not do the job alone. The United States reportedly teamed up with Israel to launch cyberattacks on Iran's nuclear infrastructure, including the Stuxnet computer virus. Multiple Iranian nuclear scientists were either killed or injured in assassination attempts allegedly perpetrated by Israel's Mossad. And of course, as the economic war went on, the United States and Israel continued to publicly threaten a military strike on Iran's nuclear facilities if Tehran raced for the bomb, which surely affected Iran's calculus.

But these were all delay tactics. They bought time, but they didn't stop Iran's nuclear development. Only sanctions, by wreaking havoc on Iran's economy, caused political change in Iran and a psychological shift among the Iranian elite. Only sanctions triggered a change in Tehran's nuclear policy.

One of the main reasons Bush and his contemporaries doubted sanctions could work against Iran was that they, like most others, viewed unilateral

sanctions as ineffective and stringent UN Security Council action as implausible. Iran's economic clout was too great, and perspectives among the
world powers too divergent, for comprehensive UN sanctions. Indeed, up
until the final stages of the sanctions campaign, the United States struggled
to get other major countries—from China to France to Brazil—to agree to
shun Iran.

Levey, Szubin, and their teammates upended this consensus with a central insight: Globalization had given America control over vital economic
chokepoints, which it could use to bend the international financial system to
its will. UN resolutions could still be helpful, as they gave Washington's exercise of this fearsome power an air of legitimacy. But they were not strictly
necessary.

Although congressional approval was not necessary, either, Congress could
play a critical role as the bad cop. When Congress passed CISADA in 2010—
which threatened secondary sanctions against any bank that did business
with Iran—it gave Levey and his colleagues ammunition to push virtually
all foreign banks to cut ties with the country. Later, when Congress ramped
up pressure on the Central Bank of Iran, it forced officials like Szubin, Cohen, and Carlos Pascual to design inventive strategies that would eventually
eviscerate Iran's oil business. It wasn't always pleasant or easy contending
with lawmakers' demands, but no one could deny that pressure from Capitol
Hill kicked the economic war into high gear.

In the end, however, congressional involvement was a double-edged sword.
Lawmakers helped make the sanctions tough enough to bring Iran to the
negotiating table, but they also made it difficult for the negotiators to explore creative options for sanctions relief and to unwind the penalties when
the time came.

As U.S. officials crafted economic weapons to wield against Iran, they
retraced networks of financial connectivity too complex to map with full
confidence. They made some surprising discoveries. Few would have expected, for instance, that Iran could be deprived of oil revenues while keeping some of its oil on the world market. But that's exactly the high-wire act
U.S. officials pulled off when they channeled more than $100 billion of Iran's
oil revenues into overseas escrow accounts. Policies like this started as pie-
in-the-sky ideas. When they actually worked, it felt a bit like black magic, a
kind of alchemy that U.S. officials had chanced upon without knowing it was
even possible. And their success emboldened them to experiment further.

A crucial breakthrough was getting the world to take seriously the threat of U.S. secondary sanctions. Congress's previous attempt to force other countries into compliance using secondary sanctions, the 1996 law known as ILSA, had ended in fierce backlash and failure: when Europe called Washington's bluff, American officials backed down and stopped enforcing the law. But over the course of the Obama administration, this changed. Officials in Washington boiled secondary sanctions down to a simple choice: foreign companies could do business with the United States or Iran, but not both. Some companies, however, did try to do both and dared America to punish them. And perversely, once they had been punished, the worst was over and there was no incentive to stop doing business with Iran.

Secondary sanctions worked like an invisible fence. There was no physical impediment to crossing them, but doing so was painful, as it entailed losing access to the dollar. Then, once you were on the other side, you could act as you pleased. China's business with Iran was a case in point. The United States sanctioned two Chinese firms, Zhuhai Zhenrong and Bank of Kunlun, for transacting with Iran. Yet after the sanctions were imposed, both absorbed the costs and increased their Iran business. What this meant for U.S. policymakers was that the threat of sanctions had to be so credible that few would dare breach the invisible fence in the first place.

As the economic war against Iran progressed, that credibility grew. The combination of intense political pressure for more sanctions, wall-to-wall implementation by the Obama administration, and increasingly harsh legal repercussions for sanctions violations tipped the scales. Business with Iran collapsed, and the country became a financial pariah. The emphasis on shaping the risk calculus of the private sector was the key to success. But ironically, when it came time to deliver sanctions relief to Iran, that strength became a weakness. Banks and companies had become so fearful of the potential ramifications of dealing with Iran that they balked at reengaging with the country even after the nuclear deal was struck. Washington was savagely effective at convincing banks and companies to end business with Iran, but it had a harder time convincing these same firms to reinvest in the country.

The Iranians hoped that once the nuclear deal was signed, companies would race to re-enter Iran to try to get ahead of competitors and snatch up newly available business opportunities. Szubin warned his counterparts that they should contain their expectations, knowing how jittery financial institutions were when it came to American sanctions. But the Iranians didn't believe him.

In the first few months of 2016, after the nuclear deal was live, Javad Zarif griped constantly to John Kerry that Iran was not reaping the economic benefits it had sought. Kerry saw this as a big problem. If the deal failed to deliver economic relief, support for the agreement in Iran could evaporate, vindicating hard-liners who argued that negotiating with the Americans was a bad idea all along. The country might even redouble its nuclear quest. The issue was so troublesome that State and Treasury embarked on a series of awkward road shows to spread a message precisely the opposite of the one Stuart Levey had preached years before: Iran was back open for business.

In May, Kerry took matters into his own hands. Accompanied by John Smith, who had just replaced Szubin as the director of OFAC, Kerry met with bank CEOs in London to try to ease their fears about resuming business with Iran. John Cryan, the head of Deutsche Bank, and António Simões, HSBC's chief, were in attendance, as were senior executives from Credit Suisse, Standard Chartered, and other megabanks. Nearly all the banks in the room had been smacked with severe penalties for violating American sanctions in just the past few years.

Kerry's soothing words fell on deaf ears. The U.S. secretary of state could not protect the banks from further penalties, and he couldn't persuade them

Words of reassurance: John Kerry, flanked by OFAC Director John Smith (right), meets with bankers in London in May 2016.

to re-enter Iran. He had no good answer to one question, in particular, from HSBC's Simões: "What happens if Donald Trump is the next president?"

The same day, the *Wall Street Journal* published an op-ed by none other than Stuart Levey, HSBC's chief legal officer. The man who had launched the economic war against Iran—and who had mentored many of the experts supporting Kerry in the London meeting—was publicly stating his opposition to Kerry's plea to re-enter Iran.

"No one has claimed that Iran has ceased to engage in much of the same conduct for which it was sanctioned, including actively supporting terrorism and building and testing ballistic missiles," Levey wrote. "But now Washington is pushing non-U.S. banks to do what it is still illegal for American banks to do. This is a very odd position for the U.S. government to be taking."

"For these reasons, HSBC has no intention of doing any new business involving Iran," Levey concluded. "Governments can lift sanctions, but the private sector is still responsible for managing its own risk and no doubt will be held accountable if it falls short." None of the banks Kerry met with that day restarted business with Iran.

The economic war against Iran had succeeded beyond imagination. But in the process, America had done more than create a new form of warfare—it had rewired the global financial system. And once that new wiring was in place, not even Washington could rip it back out.

PART THREE

=

Russia's Imperial Land Grab

22

The Diplomat

Dan Fried was a man in a hurry. In his nearly four decades in the Foreign Service, the sixty-one-year-old had developed a reputation as a tireless, happy warrior. Even so, on the morning of Monday, February 24, 2014, he zipped into the State Department headquarters in Foggy Bottom with unusual haste. Fried had a sixth sense for when a geopolitical powder keg was about to explode, and events over the weekend had sent him into high alert.

He sped up to his third-floor office, where a sign above the doorway was emblazoned with his title: COORDINATOR FOR SANCTIONS POLICY. An avid runner, he walked with an energetic limp, in long, determined strides. Aides meeting Fried for the first time occasionally offered him a hand. But they soon learned that he was much faster than they were, bum knees be damned.

On Fried's mind that morning was Ukraine, whose embattled president, Viktor Yanukovych, had just fled to Russia after months of protest and unrest. Fried was a veteran Russia hand, having served in Leningrad (today's St. Petersburg) in the early 1980s and on the State Department's Soviet desk during Mikhail Gorbachev's early years in office. He later served as U.S. ambassador to Poland as the country emerged from Communism in the 1990s and as the top official on European issues at both the NSC and State during the George W. Bush administration. The news of Yanukovych's downfall troubled Fried, not so much for what it meant for Ukraine, but for what it portended about Russia.

Yanukovych was an ally of Russian President Vladimir Putin, who would likely perceive Yanukovych's sudden abdication and flight as a direct threat

to Russian interests. Three months prior, in a major win for Putin, Yanukovych had abandoned trade talks with the EU in favor of a $15 billion loan
from Moscow. Now pro-European protesters on the Maidan, Kyiv's central
square, had run Yanukovych out of the country, turning a moment of Russian triumph into a stunning setback.

Fried's mind raced to an unsettling memory from a 2008 NATO summit, at which Putin delivered a speech casting doubt on Crimea's status as
Ukrainian territory. Like other lands at the junction of shattered empires,
Crimea was a melting pot with a tangled political history, having been ruled
by Tatar khans, Ottoman sultans, and Russian tsars before becoming part of
the Soviet Union and then modern Ukraine. At the NATO summit, Putin
had questioned Soviet leader Nikita Khrushchev's 1954 decision to bequeath
Crimea to the Ukrainian Soviet Socialist Republic, a move that mattered little
until Ukraine declared its independence decades later. Even after the collapse of the Soviet Union, Crimea remained of vital strategic importance to
Moscow. The Russian navy operated its Black Sea Fleet from a base on the
peninsula, which it leased from Ukraine's government. If Russia's presence
in Crimea was endangered—as Putin may worry was the case now, with a
nationalist, pro-European revolution underway in Kyiv—he might resort to
drastic measures.

That Monday morning, at Secretary of State John Kerry's senior staff
meeting, Fried voiced his fears. "Putin will not take this without a reaction,"
he warned. "He will move." Fried suggested Putin could hit back against the
Maidan revolutionaries by making a play for Crimea. Victoria Nuland, the
State Department's point person on Europe and Russia, agreed. Nuland, too,
had witnessed Putin's speech in 2008, and she shared Fried's concerns about
a potential escalation.

Unbeknownst to Fried and Nuland, the Russian president had already
decided to act. On Saturday, Putin had convened his top national security brass to devise a plan to exfiltrate Ukraine's disgraced president. Yanukovych would travel by car along a circuitous route down to Crimea, where
he would rendezvous with Russian operatives and continue to Russia by air.
As the meeting at the Kremlin wrapped up, around 7:00 a.m. on Sunday,
Putin added one more instruction: "We are forced to begin the work to bring
Crimea back into Russia."

Moscow had long possessed contingency plans for such an operation.
When Putin gave the order to go, his military and intelligence services knew
what to do. In the early morning hours of Thursday, February 27, a swarm of

heavily armed men, dressed in green uniforms without insignia, seized Crimea's regional parliament in Simferopol and raised a Russian flag. After the commandos blockaded the building's entrances and confiscated law-makers' cell phones, the parliament "voted" to elect as their new leader Ser-gei Aksyonov, a local pro-Russian politician with ties to organized crime.

The following day, more of the "little green men" appeared, this time taking control of Crimea's two main airports in Sevastopol and Simferopol. Putin swore the men were "local self-defense units"—just ordinary Crimeans worried about alleged threats to the peninsula's majority Russian-speaking population. But there was little doubt about the men's true origin. "We're Rus-sians," one of them plainly told a journalist. On Saturday, March 1, Aksyonov, Crimea's newly installed leader, formally requested a Russian intervention. "I call on the president of the Russian Federation, Vladimir Putin," he said, "to provide assistance in ensuring peace and tranquility on the territory."

With Ukraine's government still in disarray and the United States caught flat-footed, Russia rapidly took control of all of Crimea. Within days, the Kremlin staged a sham referendum in which Crimeans overwhelmingly "voted" to join Russia. Putin then hurriedly signed a decree formally annexing the territory, recasting it as the twenty-second republic of the Russian Federation. Sevastopol, the site of Russia's naval base, was anointed a "city of federal importance," a status shared by only Moscow and St. Petersburg.

It was the first act of territorial conquest on European soil since World War II. Fried, whose career had been defined by helping Eastern Europe es-cape the Soviet vise grip, worried that Putin's gambit threatened to push Europe, and perhaps the world at large, back into darker times. But Wash-ington was on the horns of a dilemma. On the one hand, the United States could not stand idly by as Russia gobbled up a neighbor's territory, an act of aggression not just against Ukraine but against the global order America had painstakingly built for generations. On the other hand, Russia was a nuclear superpower, so a direct military confrontation was off the table.

Faced with an unexpected crisis, people tend to reach for what they know. Just a few months earlier, on the same day that tens of thousands of pro-European protesters descended on the Maidan, the United States signed the interim nuclear deal with Iran. High on the success of economic warfare against Iran, U.S. officials started weighing a similar campaign against Rus-sia as soon as Putin's "little green men" showed up in Crimea.

Even more than Iran, Russia was an economic heavyweight deeply en-meshed in world markets and the international financial system. With the rise of China and other emerging economies having sent commodities prices into the stratosphere, the Kremlin was rolling in cash. Russia was raking in hundreds of billions of dollars each year from sales of its immense oil and gas reserves. Russia's economy, the world's eighth largest, was not just bigger than Iran's; it was bigger than all other economies under American sanctions *combined.*

Complicating matters further, some of the United States' closest allies were in a state of mutual economic dependence with Russia. The EU relied on Russia for a third of its oil and gas imports, and several European states counted Russia as their only supplier of natural gas. Without Russian energy, German factories could grind to a halt and Slovak homes might go without heat. Russia's overall trade with the EU was ten times larger than its trade with America. Iran-style sanctions on Russia could cause an economic earthquake on the continent and hand Putin his ultimate prize: a fracture in America's long-standing alliance with Europe.

This was exactly the type of diplomatic morass into which Dan Fried eagerly sallied forth. During Obama's first term, he'd served in the unenviable role of special envoy for the closure of the Guantanamo Bay prison camp. (*The New Republic* described him as "The poor schmo who has to move all the Gitmo detainees.") Fried secured the release of almost seventy detainees and garnered widespread praise for his work under impossible circumstances. His current post at State, where he now served as the first-ever coordinator for sanctions policy, had been meant as a reprieve.

Dan Fried: the State Department's first coordinator for sanctions policy.

The State Department had created the role for two reasons. First, the recurring tensions between America and its allies over Iran sanctions highlighted the need for more purposeful and consistent diplomatic engagement
on matters of economic warfare. The second reason had to do with inter-
agency maneuvering. Over the past years, technocratic dynamos like Stuart
Levey, Adam Szubin, and David Cohen had turned Treasury into a formidable
player on sanctions policy. State—America's premier foreign affairs agency—
needed a counterweight for moments when the topic came up in the Situation
Room, something that was happening with growing frequency.

For a sanctions coordinator, Fried had little experience in economic warfare. But he brought the necessary diplomatic polish, shrewd bureaucratic
instincts, and excellent connections across the European political spectrum.
Earlier in his career, he had developed close personal friendships with the
revolutionaries of 1989, many of whom were now powerful European politicians. He was on a first-name basis with figures such as Polish founding
father Lech Wałęsa and Hungarian strongman Viktor Orbán. He spoke several Slavic languages with ease and was well-versed in the region's ever-
present history. If someone could convince Europe to join an economic war
against Putin, it was him. "I came into the Foreign Service as a Soviet hand,"
Fried recalled thinking as the Ukraine crisis began. Now, in what he knew
might be his final job in government, he had come full circle.

23

———

The Fallen Bear Licks Its Wounds

Putin's conquest of Crimea took Washington by surprise, but it was hardly a bolt from the blue. Dan Fried's and Victoria Nuland's premonition "sounds like great foresight," Fried said, "but it really wasn't. It was just paying attention to what was right in front of you."

On Christmas Day 1991, in a televised speech from the Kremlin, Mikhail Gorbachev resigned as Soviet leader and handed over power to Boris Yeltsin, the first president of the Russian Federation. Moments later, officials lowered the red and gold hammer-and-sickle flags and removed them from the building. After seven decades, the Soviet Union was no more.

The Russia that was born the next morning was a shell of its former self. Its population was cut in half and its territory reduced by nearly a quarter. Imperial gains accrued over centuries, from Peter the Great to Stalin, were gone. Russia's self-perception as a great power, however, was unchanged. Unlike Gorbachev, Yeltsin actively encouraged the breakup of the Soviet Union, but neither man ever thought that Russia would lose its dominant role in its neighborhood, the so-called "near abroad."

Of the Soviet Union's fourteen non-Russian successor states, none was more important to Moscow than Ukraine. With more than 40 million inhabitants, a strategic location on the Black Sea, the world's most fertile farmland, and a military-industrial sector deeply integrated into Russia's own, Ukraine was in many ways the former crown jewel of the Soviet Union. It was also home to Sevastopol, where Russia operated its most critical warmwater naval port. "It cannot be stressed strongly enough that without Ukraine, Russia ceases to be an empire," wrote Zbigniew Brzezinski, the Polish-born former U.S. national security advisor, in 1994. An Oxbridge don put it in less delicate terms: "With the Ukraine, Russia is a USA; without, she is a Canada—mostly snow."

As early as 1993, Russia's parliament passed a resolution asserting that Sevastopol was Russian territory, and Yeltsin called on the world to grant Russia "special powers" to act as the de facto policeman in former Soviet states, including Ukraine. Russian diplomats reportedly warned their counterparts in Europe "not to bother building large embassies in Kyiv because within eighteen months they will be downgraded to consular sections." The conviction that Moscow should hold a privileged position in Ukraine—and a commanding one in Crimea—was widely shared across Russia's political spectrum.

Ukraine has always been bound to its eastern neighbor by close cultural ties. Among the 30 percent of Ukrainians who do not count Ukrainian as their first language, most claim Russian as their native tongue. Much of popular music and TV in the country is in Russian, and education is available in both languages. Yet since the breakup of the Soviet Union, Ukrainians have never wavered on the question of national belonging. In a 1991 referendum, 92 percent voted in favor of independence, including clear majorities in the predominantly Russian-speaking regions of Crimea, Sevastopol, Donetsk, and Luhansk. Even Ukraine's most ardent pro-Russian political parties, which pursued closer ties to Moscow, fiercely defended their country's independence. When Ukraine agreed to give up the massive nuclear arsenal stranded on its soil after the fall of the Soviet Union, it did so in exchange for a formal pledge by Russia to respect its territorial integrity, a deal enshrined in the 1994 Budapest Memorandum and also signed by the United States and the UK.

This fundamental tension—an uneasy truce between a former Soviet republic that moved on and a spurned ex-hegemon that didn't—never went away. What changed between 1991 and 2014 was not so much Russia's conviction that it should have the last say over questions of Ukrainian sovereignty; it was Moscow's willingness and ability to act on that conviction.

Fried's and Nuland's apprehension notwithstanding, Washington was slow to recognize this shift. American foreign policy can be like an aircraft carrier, powerful once a direction is chosen but hard to turn. Starting under President Ronald Reagan and especially after the end of the Cold War, Washington saw Russia no longer as a threat to contain but as a prize to be won— for democracy, for capitalism, for American business, and for U.S. geopolitical interests. Moscow might even be a useful sidekick in the War on Terror and other global undertakings. It was an opportunity so tantalizing that an un-broken succession of U.S. presidents actively sought warmer relations with Russia while ignoring repeated warning signs.

Bill Clinton looked the other way as Yeltsin sent troops into Chechnya, where the Russian military proceeded to level entire cities with scant regard for civilian harm, and when pressed, Clinton compared Yeltsin's actions to Abraham Lincoln's in the Civil War. George W. Bush told reporters he had looked into Putin's eyes and come away with "a sense of his soul." Seven years later, when Russia invaded neighboring Georgia and recognized two breakaway republics, the response from both Bush and his European peers barely amounted to a slap on the wrist. Barack Obama entered the White House less than six months after Russian tanks barreled within an hour's drive from Georgia's capital, but he still saw fit to "reset" relations in hopes of securing Kremlin cooperation on arms control, Afghanistan, and the Iran nuclear file. Time and again, hope triumphed over experience. And in any case, in what Washington saw as the central geopolitical dramas of the post–Cold War age—quelling violent extremism and spreading democracy and capitalism—Moscow was, at most, a supporting actor.

In 2007, Putin made his first-ever trip to the Munich Security Confer-ence, which each year brought together the who's who of Western diplomacy and national security leadership. He used the opportunity to air his griev-ances about American power. "One state and, of course, first and foremost the United States, has overstepped its national borders in every way," he said. "This is visible in the economic, political, cultural, and educational policies it imposes on other nations. Well, who likes this? Who is happy about this?"

Nuland, then serving as U.S. ambassador to NATO, sat in the fourth row and could almost feel Putin's spittle. As the Russian leader spoke, he grew more and more animated. "And of course this is extremely dangerous," he growled, as a palpable uneasiness spread across the ballroom. "It results in the fact that no one feels safe. I want to emphasize this: No one feels safe!" In Putin's grand narrative, the United States was also the main character—but it was the villain, and the central drama of the years ahead would be cutting it down to size.

Many Europeans in the audience sympathized with Putin's disdain for American unilateralism, especially against the backdrop of Bush's invasion of Iraq. His screed still left them deeply unsettled. To those from countries that had recently escaped Moscow's dominion, the speech vindicated their decision to seek membership in NATO and the EU.

Airing grievances: Vladimir Putin addresses
the Munich Security Conference in February 2007.

Putin's formative experiences—he was a KGB officer stationed in East Germany when the Berlin Wall came down—may have predisposed him to hostility against the United States and the West. He famously called the collapse of the Soviet Union "the greatest geopolitical catastrophe of the century." But he was also an enigma, a man whom Boris Yeltsin plucked from relative obscurity and appointed to the presidency on the last day of 1999 because Yeltsin believed Putin, his protégé, would protect him and his family in retirement.

As president, Putin initially flirted with the idea of closer relations with the United States. Yet he quickly came to view America as a threat, both to Russian interests and to himself personally. Putin vehemently opposed Bush's decision to invade Iraq and overthrow Saddam Hussein against the will of the UN Security Council. As Putin saw it, Iraq proved that all the talk of a rules-based international order was just window dressing for American hegemony. The Iraq War also eliminated any reservations he may have harbored about advancing Russian interests through force. If America could use its military might to get its way, why couldn't Russia?

Not long after the invasion of Iraq, a wave of democratic movements known as the "color revolutions" swept several countries in Russia's near abroad. Ukraine's 2004 Orange Revolution was a particularly searing experience for Moscow. In Ukraine's presidential election that year, Putin threw his full weight behind Viktor Yanukovych, a candidate from Russian-speaking Donetsk who favored closer ties with Moscow. Putin actively stumped for Yanukovych in Kyiv and dispatched his own political advisor, Gleb Pavlovsky, to help run Yanukovych's campaign. All told, Moscow poured tens of millions of dollars into the race. Though Yanukovych was initially declared the winner, exit polls disagreed, leading to mass protests and widespread allegations of electoral fraud. A month later, the election was rerun under international observation. In a contest deemed free and fair, the pro-Western Viktor Yushchenko prevailed by more than seven points.

It seemed Ukraine was poised to join the West and exit Russia's sphere of influence for good. The notion challenged Putin's very conception of reality. The only way Ukrainians could make such a choice, he concluded, was if guided by the hidden hand of Washington. The color revolutions could not be organic democracy movements; they must be the outgrowth of a covert American influence campaign. Putin felt viscerally threatened. Russia's gargantuan nuclear arsenal might defend him from Saddam's grim fate, but it would be of little use against American-backed street protests.

The final straw came at the end of 2011. After a four-year stint as Russia's prime minister, during which Putin ran the country from behind the scenes, he decided to return as president, relegating the hapless Dmitri Medvedev back into irrelevance. Yet there was little public enthusiasm for Putin's comeback. In November, he was booed by thousands of fans at a mixed martial arts fight in Moscow, an audience typically sympathetic to Putin, the chest-thumping, judo-practicing macho man. A poll found that just 31 percent of Russians planned to vote for him in the upcoming presidential election, scheduled for early 2012.

In December 2011, a few months before the presidential election, Putin's United Russia party performed poorly in parliamentary elections, garnering roughly 49 percent of the vote (a steep drop from 64 percent four years earlier) despite numerous unfair advantages. A week later, chants of "Putin is a thief!" and "Russia without Putin!" rang out in the streets of dozens of Russian cities as tens of thousands took part in the largest anti-Kremlin demonstrations since the twilight of the Soviet Union. Putin's worst fear seemed to be coming true: an American-led color revolution in his own country, which might end his rule just as a series of mass protests had for several Middle Eastern autocrats earlier that year. As if to drive home the point, Senator John McCain tweeted, "Dear Vlad, the Arab Spring is coming to a neighborhood near you."

Putin ultimately weathered the storm and retook the presidency a few months later, pushing through a raft of repressive laws to prevent such protests from ever happening again. In retaliation for the West's purported designs against him, he also developed his own brand of hybrid warfare. Using disinformation, media manipulation, and foreign intelligence operations, Russia would make the world safe for autocracy.

Over the following years, Putin consolidated his political control at home, just as he'd previously tightened the Kremlin's hold on Russia's centers of economic power. After ascending to the presidency at the end of 1999, Putin had sidelined the Yeltsin-era oligarchs and confiscated their most valuable assets, pushing some of them into exile and prison. Control over Russia's oil, gas, defense, construction, transportation, and financial industries went to a new elite, composed of Putin's childhood friends from St. Petersburg and former colleagues from the KGB. It was still a kleptocracy to the core, but that mattered little. Buoyed by an unprecedented commodities boom, including oil prices that shot up tenfold from 1998 to 2008, Putin repaired the state's finances, increased living standards, and modernized Russia's military.

Perversely, America aided Putin in this process. Neither Russia's invasion of Georgia nor Putin's repressive methods at home elicited any U.S. sanctions. On the contrary, American businesses shoveled more foreign investment into Russia than anyone else. In 2011, Texas-based ExxonMobil inked a far-reaching alliance with Rosneft, Russia's state-owned oil giant, to develop the next generation of Russian oil resources in the Arctic Ocean, a deal worth at least tens of billions of dollars, perhaps hundreds of billions. General Motors, which owned a large factory in the suburbs of St. Petersburg, viewed Russia as a growth market on par with China and, in 2012, pledged to invest an additional billion dollars there. Boeing, Caterpillar, General Electric, and other blue-chip American companies also made sizable investments in Russia. With unfettered access to the U.S. financial system, Russian businesses amassed more than $700 billion in external debt. The Obama administration, meanwhile, worked hard to finalize Russia's accession to the World Trade Organization, a nineteen-year process that concluded soon after Putin's return to the presidency in 2012.

Russia's economic and military power was surging, due in part to American help, even as Putin's anti-American views crystalized and fed a growing desire to take on the West. Yet there was a flip side to integration into the world economy. The same forces that made Russia rich and powerful left it exposed, and thanks to the economic war against Iran underway at the time, the United States was learning to exploit that type of vulnerability with increasing efficacy. Putin, obsessed with the threat of a color revolution, was right to fear a novel type of American warfare, only he was looking for it in the wrong places.

24

Euromaidan

U pon returning to the presidency in 2012, Putin was eager to achieve his long-held dream: restoring the power Russia once wielded beyond its borders, first through the tsarist empire and later through the Soviet Union. At least initially, he aimed to do so not by the sword but rather through the wallet.

Priority number one was to establish the Eurasian Economic Union (EEU). The EEU was modeled on the European Union, but it was heavily weighted in Russia's favor: to join meant, in essence, to hand over control of your country's economic policy to Moscow. Belarus and Kazakhstan had agreed to participate, yet they were bit players. Ukraine was the real prize. And with the Russia-friendly Viktor Yanukovych holding the reins in Kyiv—after his crooked victory was thrown out in 2004, he won the presidency fair and square in 2010—Putin could reasonably expect Ukraine to join eventually.

Yanukovych, however, was a corrupt wheeler and dealer who was happy to sell Ukraine's allegiance to the highest bidder. At the same time as he was being courted by Putin, Yanukovych pursued negotiations with the EU on an association agreement—a framework for cooperation that included a free-trade deal and was seen as a stepping stone to full EU membership. The Russo-European bidding war came to a head in the second half of 2013. In a visit to Kyiv, Putin spoke of "Ukraine's civilizational choice," indicating that, as he saw it, Yanukovych's decision was about more than dollars and cents. Meanwhile, the EU aimed to finalize its association agreement with

Ukraine in time for a summit in Vilnius, Lithuania's capital, scheduled for the end of November. Both Moscow and Brussels made clear that Kyiv faced an either-or decision: it could join the EEU or the EU, but not both.

As the clock ticked and anticipation built, Putin played hardball. First the flow of goods across Ukraine's border with Russia slowed to a trickle. Then Putin's chief economic advisor, Sergei Glazyev, explained that Moscow had imposed enhanced customs screening in case Ukraine took the "suicidal step" of signing the EU deal. Glazyev, whose aversion to understatement rivaled his anti-European sentiment, added that Ukraine's "civilizational choice was made more than a thousand years ago," and that Brussels was "pulling Ukraine, to speak in a spiritual language, into the kingdom of the antichrist."

In the long term, there was little doubt Ukraine's economy would be better off integrating with the EU than joining Russia's economic club. But Putin held a trump card. Yanukovych's venality and economic mismanagement were so egregious that Ukraine's foreign reserves could no longer pay for even three months of imports. Absent a new loan from somewhere, the country was headed for a default. Assistance from the International Monetary Fund was unpalatable, as it would require serious reforms that would neuter Yanukovych's spoils system and eviscerate social spending. The EU was willing to offer a loan of €610 million, a miserly sum compared with the $10 billion Ukraine needed. Putin, on the other hand, offered Yanukovych a $15 billion loan and a massive discount on Russian gas. On November 21, Yanukovych formally pulled out of talks with the EU.

Putin was triumphant, but his victory was short-lived. Within hours of Yanukovych's announcement, protesters gathered on the Maidan in Kyiv, waving EU flags and chanting "I want to live in Europe!" and "Ukraine is part of Europe!" Their ranks quickly swelled to 100,000. Yanukovych sent riot police into the square wielding batons and hurling stun grenades. A violent clash ensued, after which the protesters upped their demands, now calling on Yanukovych to resign.

Victoria Nuland, then serving as the State Department's assistant secretary for European and Eurasian affairs, hopped on a flight to Kyiv. Nuland was one of her generation's most respected Foreign Service officers, so undeniably talented that both Dick Cheney and Hillary Clinton—foils in almost every respect—had placed her in essential jobs and helped advance her career. She also spoke Russian like a sailor. (Literally: in her twenties, Nuland had learned the language in part by spending months on a Soviet fishing trawler.)

In addition to a blue-eyed stare that could burn a hole through anyone sitting across from her, Nuland possessed a deep-seated faith in the universal appeal of freedom and the world-changing potential of American power. Arriving in Kyiv in December 2013, she was determined to make her visit count. Her first stop was the Maidan. Accompanied by Geoff Pyatt, the U.S. ambassador to Ukraine, she toured the encampments where protesters were braving the freezing cold and repeated attempts by riot police to dislodge them with brute force. Next, she met with Yanukovych, warning him that his aggressive response to the protests was "absolutely impermissible in a European state." Ending the standoff on the Maidan would require a rapprochement with Europe and the IMF, in addition to "bringing justice and dignity" to the Ukrainian people. "The whole world is watching," she told Yanukovych.

Victoria Nuland: offering cookies to protesters on Kyiv's Maidan in December 2013.

Among those watching was Dan Fried, then a few months into his new role as sanctions coordinator. He and Nuland had been close colleagues for years, and they shared a sense of common purpose on U.S. policy in Europe. Fried was between meetings when he received a call from Nuland. "Could you all come up with sanctions options against Yanukovych and his team for their crackdown?" Nuland asked. If Yanukovych persisted in trying to suppress the protests, America needed a response.

Under normal circumstances, this might be a task for the sanctions team at Treasury, which guarded its turf vigilantly and viewed the State Department with a measure of mistrust. But Adam Szubin and his colleagues were knee-deep in the implementation of the interim nuclear deal with Iran and were happy to let Fried take the Ukraine file. "I got it," Fried said. "Wherever we go with sanctions, we're in."

Fried's low-ego leadership style was paying off. He'd never seen himself as a counterweight to Treasury, even though his role was created in part for that reason. He was honest about his lack of experience in economic warfare, and he was eager to learn. For meetings with foreign officials, Fried always invited Treasury's technocrats and readily deferred to them on nitty-gritty sanctions questions. Fried "appreciated Treasury in a way that doesn't always happen with State Department people," noted a veteran Treasury sanctions official. The result, Fried recalled, was that by the time of the Ukraine crisis, "OFAC thought I was a good guy."

Fried got to work forging a close-knit team of experts from both State and Treasury to flesh out a package of sanctions against Yanukovych and his enablers. There was a well-worn playbook for such measures, which typically included asset freezes and travel bans on politicians and security officials, more diplomatic ostracism than true economic warfare. America had issued such penalties in recent years against Syria's Bashar al-Assad and Libya's Muammar Gaddafi. The goal this time would be to bolster Nuland's efforts to broker a peaceful resolution to the standoff on the Maidan by threatening to tar Yanukovych as a pariah.

So far, Yanukovych was showing little interest in compromise. In mid-January, he pushed through a series of laws that effectively criminalized the ongoing protests. Known as the "dictatorship laws," they placed draconian restrictions on freedom of speech and assembly, and they were hurriedly passed by Yanukovych's loyalists in parliament with just a quick show of hands. Hundreds of thousands poured onto the Maidan in defiance of the new rules. More than a hundred people were injured and several killed in renewed clashes with riot police.

Putin and his advisors were egging on Yanukovych's repression. Asked whether Yanukovych should use force to put down the protests, Sergei Glazyev, Putin's economic aide and Ukraine whisperer, described the situation as a "coup attempt" that left the government in Kyiv with "no choice" but to fight back.

Nuland, meanwhile, was conducting shuttle diplomacy between Yanukovych and the opposition. The extent of her efforts was laid bare before the world in early February, when a recording of one of her phone calls with Pyatt, the U.S. ambassador, appeared on YouTube. Russian intelligence had intercepted the call and leaked it to illustrate Nuland's close involvement in the crisis. To the Kremlin, this was cold, hard evidence that what became known as the Euromaidan movement was made in America.

In reality, Washington was trying to defuse the crisis peacefully and avoid a latter-day Tiananmen Square, not oust Yanukovych. What made the call memorable, however, was not the evidence of Nuland's hands-on diplomacy but her frustration with the EU, whose two most powerful members, Germany and France, were reluctant to assist her efforts for fear of upsetting Putin. Nuland's blunt dismissal of these concerns made it onto countless news broadcasts around the world: "Fuck the EU."

It would not be the last time the United States grew tired of Europe's foot-dragging in the Ukraine crisis. Nor would it be the last time Russia stole American secrets and used them as a weapon. "A Rubicon had been crossed," Ben Rhodes, a close aide to Obama, observed. "The Russians no longer stopped at hacking information; now, triggered by the threat of Ukraine sliding out of their sphere of influence, they were willing to hack information and put it into the public domain." Such tactics would become a calling card of Russian hybrid warfare.

On February 18, Yanukovych's riot police once again ratcheted up their attacks. Over the next two days, snipers took up positions on rooftops around the Maidan and peppered the protesters with bullets, killing around a hundred and wounding scores more. In Washington, the raft of penalties that Fried's team had prepared was readied for Obama's approval.

Obama had not yet signed the executive order when, later that week, a pathway out of the crisis seemed to open. On the morning of Friday, February 21, Yanukovych reached a deal with the opposition to form a unity government and hold early elections in exchange for clearing the Maidan. But just hours later, Yanukovych suddenly went missing. After almost a full day with no word from the president, parliament voted unanimously to remove him from office.

The protesters were jubilant. For the second time in a decade, they had successfully mobilized against Yanukovych—and against his foremost backer, Putin—in pursuit of a more democratic and pro-European future. Thousands celebrated by touring the president's abandoned estate, a ludicrously garish compound on the outskirts of Kyiv with a private zoo, an eighteen-hole golf course, and an artificial lake. A full-scale replica of a Spanish galleon sat permanently moored to a riverside pier, a fitting emblem of the ex-president's plundered riches and impoverished mind.

Yet this was not the end of the crisis; it was merely the end of the beginning. On Friday, February 28, Yanukovych resurfaced in Rostov-on-Don, a provincial Russian city close to the Ukrainian border. "Russia must and has to act," Yanukovych pleaded as reporters circled. He wanted to return to Ukraine as president. But he was "categorically against any interference with the sovereign integrity of Ukraine as a state." He looked haggard.

All Yanukovych got from Russia's leader, who had fanned the flames of the Maidan standoff from the comfort of the Kremlin, was a brief phone call. As Yanukovych groveled from Rostov, Putin's "little green men" were busy taking control of Crimea. Ukraine's runaway president had outlived his usefulness. So, too, had the sanctions that Dan Fried and his team had prepared against Yanukovych, a deposed despot now poised to fade into obscurity. This was no longer just a Ukraine crisis. It was a Russia crisis.

25

===

"Aim First, Then Shoot"

As Russian troops took hold of Crimea, there was little that Ukraine, much less the United States, could do about it. Kyiv's military was outmanned and outgunned. Russia already had more than a thousand men stationed at its naval base in Sevastopol even before Putin sent in reinforcements. Moscow had also cultivated loyalists throughout Ukraine's armed forces, most of whose leaders had started their careers in the Soviet military. Some, like Sergei Yeliseyev, a top Ukrainian admiral and graduate of a Soviet naval school, defected as soon as the "little green men" showed up.

The playing field was so lopsided in Russia's favor that U.S. officials advised Ukraine's interim government against fighting back. "The White House thought they'd get slaughtered," Nuland recalled, pointing to Ukraine's lack of military equipment. "They didn't have enough stuff to win." Worse still, a half-baked attempt to defend Crimea could give Putin a pretext to expand the war deeper into Ukraine.

On Saturday, March 1, Obama spent an hour and a half on the phone with Putin in a last-ditch effort to stay the modern-day tsar's hand through his powers of persuasion. Obama appealed to international law, citing the Budapest Memorandum and the UN Charter, and expressed "deep concern over Russia's clear violation of Ukrainian sovereignty and territorial integrity." He was still trying to find a patch of common ground. But he warned that unless Putin changed course, Moscow's actions would "negatively impact Russia's standing in the international community."

Putin shrugged off the threat and issued his own. "In case of any further spread of violence to eastern Ukraine and Crimea, Russia retains the right to protect its interests and the Russian-speaking population of those areas." You didn't have to be fluent in diplospeak to catch his drift: Back off or I'll swallow even more of Ukraine's territory.

The challenge for the United States was to make sure that the costs to Russia of a wider conflict would outweigh the benefits. But what *were* these costs? They could not be military in nature, as Ukraine was ill-prepared to fight, and the United States was not ready to go to war with a fellow nuclear superpower. Words of condemnation and souring relations with the United States would mean little to Putin, who saw America as his chief adversary anyhow. Better to take the fight someplace where America held an unfair advantage: the economy.

There may have been a standard operating procedure for sanctions on a tin-pot autocrat like Yanukovych, but there was none for sanctions on Russia. Compared with the United States, Russia was an economic minnow, but it was a colossus compared with every other country America had previously sanctioned. Technocrats at OFAC and staffers on Capitol Hill could not just hit Russia with ever-more draconian sanctions from their cubicles in Washington with no thought to repercussions. If Washington were to strike Russia with the types of economic weapons it had wielded against Iran, blowback against Europe and the United States was inevitable. Concerns were so acute that powerful industry groups like the U.S. Chamber of Commerce and the National Association of Manufacturers lobbied the White House and Congress to hold back. With the recovery from the global financial crisis still fragile, all this caused serious reservations in Washington.

The Obama administration was divided. Fried, Nuland, and most of their fellow Russia hands argued for a swift and strong response. Others, including those who oversaw economic policy, urged caution; better not to rock the boat, they thought, with the economic outlook so uncertain. Obama himself tended toward restraint, as did many of his closest aides. The president was trying to engineer a "pivot" in U.S. policy toward Asia, an initiative that was already stunted by America's ongoing engagement in the Middle East, where Iran's nuclear program and Syria's civil war consumed Washington's attention. Taking on Russia on top of all this—especially when, as some of Obama's advisors believed, Moscow's cooperation was necessary to resolve the Iran and Syria issues—seemed like a bad idea. At one point, as Fried was advocating for tough sanctions, a senior White House official said to him, "You know, Dan, the United States has no serious security interests in Ukraine."

Even at Treasury, there were doubts America's sanctions arsenal could stop Putin's imperial march. First thing in the morning on Monday, March 3, OFAC held a team meeting to discuss the White House's recent request for sanctions options against Russia. The reaction among the staffers in the room was a collective eye roll. "There's no way we're sanctioning Russia," one of the attendees recalled thinking at the time. They were used to targeting little-known Iranian banks, al-Qaeda terrorists, and Latin American drug kingpins. But *Russia*? "It just seemed like bringing a pencil to a knife fight," the official said.

Fried had gotten to know OFAC well over the past year, and he sensed they were apprehensive. "This was new and scary stuff," he said. "Russia? Ukraine? They didn't know a thing about it. They didn't know the Russian economy. It was a whole other world."

Disagreements aside, the Obama administration quickly reached consensus on one principle: America should not act alone. In the economic war against Iran, unilateralism was the norm. Washington charged ahead and then dragged reluctant European leaders along—sometimes against the threat of secondary sanctions. It was a "with us or against us" approach backed by a bipartisan supermajority in Congress. The EU resented this behavior, but it didn't fundamentally endanger the transatlantic alliance. Europe's relationship with Iran was just not that important.

Russia, on the other hand, was Europe's next-door neighbor. Cultural bonds ran deep, and economic dependence ran deeper: Europe's economy and its people's quality of life were built on access to cheap Russian energy. If Washington shot first and asked questions later, trust between the United States and Europe would be shattered.

There was another, more tactical reason why unity with Europe mattered. In the 1990s, when Congress forced the Texas-based oil company Conoco to leave Iran, Conoco's European competitors promptly swooped in to take its place. Backfill like this was poison to sanctions programs. It simultaneously nullified the effectiveness of sanctions and undercut political support for them by shifting American business to other countries.

In Russia's case, the risk of backfill was extraordinarily high. Europe already had far closer economic relations with Russia than America did. If Ford and GM closed up shop in Russia, competitors like France's Renault and Germany's Volkswagen would scoop up their plants at bargain prices. If

Boeing stopped selling airplanes in Russia, it would be a bonanza for Airbus, its European rival.

The day after Obama's call with Putin, Treasury Secretary Jack Lew was already working the phones with his British and French counterparts, taking their temperature on sanctions against Russia. It was not a good time for a crisis requiring transatlantic unity. Germany, the EU's most pivotal player, was in an uproar amid allegations that the NSA had bugged Angela Merkel's phone. A measly 38 percent of Germans saw America as a "trustworthy partner," the lowest tally since the Bush years. The prospect of a united U.S.-European front seemed far-fetched.

Faced with so much uncertainty, Obama was cautious. "Aim first, then shoot," he instructed his team. They would start with a narrow set of sanctions before reaching for the big guns. In the best-case scenario, this gradual approach would give Putin more of a reason to back down, since America would still be able to up the pressure if he didn't.

Over the coming weeks, the State and Treasury sanctions teams practically lived in the West Wing, where they hashed out policy options in daily huddles in the spartan, subterranean Situation Room. After a few heated debates, they settled on targeting the assets of Putin's inner circle—the small group of friends Putin had elevated into key positions across Russia's economy. Proximity to power had won these men fabulous wealth, which they used to buy up Mediterranean villas and supersized yachts. They also safeguarded Putin's own spectacular riches, and many Kremlinologists believed these were the only people who truly had the Russian president's ear.

Victoria Nuland pushed hard for going after the cronies. "The theory of the case was that they would go to Vova and say it wasn't worth it," she said, using a nickname for Putin. "We definitely thought they were a circle of influence around him, that Ukraine didn't matter to them, but money did."

Ordinarily, identifying the members of this circle would be a job for the CIA and other intelligence agencies. But American capabilities and expertise on Russia had atrophied in the years after 9/11 as priorities shifted to tracking jihadist networks in the Middle East and beyond. Absent a strong voice from the intel community, Russia experts at State like Nuland and Fried filled the void. With help from staff at the U.S. embassy in Moscow, Fried started working on a list of Putin cronies and potential targets.

At the same time, the White House was putting together its own list, this one compiled by Rory MacFarquhar, the senior director for international economics at the NSC. A cerebral, stone-faced economist with a wry sense of humor and close-cropped, salt-and-pepper hair, MacFarquhar had spent nearly a decade working for Goldman Sachs in Moscow. He knew Russia's business elite as well as anyone in Washington. He had sipped vodka and nibbled on blinis with many of them.

In meeting after meeting in the Situation Room, MacFarquhar emphasized that there was a distinction between plain old oligarchs and Putin's dyed-in-the-wool cronies. The oligarchs, MacFarquhar contended, had "made their money before Putin was on the stage" and "would happily plunge a knife in his back if they had the opportunity." Going after them was not a smart move. They held no real influence over the Kremlin, and asset freezes and travel bans would simply force them into Putin's corner. (They'd be all the more grateful for his annexation of Crimea, which might not be the French Riviera but still offered warm and sunny summers by the sea.) By contrast, a surgical strike on the true cronies would not only give them an incentive to lobby Putin to stand down in Ukraine; it would give the oligarchs an incentive to distance themselves from the Kremlin so as not to risk coming under sanctions personally.

Some of the cronies were relatively easy targets. They were either Kremlin officials or the CEOs of state-owned companies, so an executive order that froze the assets of Russian government officials would do the trick. But many of those closest to Putin did not hold official government positions; instead, they did his bidding from the outside. They were men like Arkady Rotenberg, who befriended Putin at age twelve when they both began practicing *sambo*, a judo-like martial art developed by the Soviet Red Army. Arkady and his brother Boris managed construction projects for Putin, from $7 billion worth of contracts to stage the 2014 Winter Olympics in Sochi to $1 billion to build Putin's own gargantuan palazzo on the Black Sea coast. The Rotenbergs were not Kremlin officials, but they were the ultimate regime insiders.

There was a useful policy precedent for sanctions against cronies like the Rotenbergs: Treasury's efforts to stem the flow of cash to terrorists and drug lords. OFAC often sanctioned a given terrorist leader or narcotrafficker and subsequently sanctioned their henchmen and funders for providing "material support" to them. The result was a network of restrictions, starting at the top before spreading down to the enablers.

From a technical perspective, this approach was a perfect fit for Putin's inner circle, but it would require imposing sanctions on Putin himself, since he was the figurative terrorist boss or drug kingpin in this scenario. The United States wasn't ready for such a step, not because it would bankrupt Putin (that was impossible) but because it would symbolize a complete break in U.S.-Russian relations. Instead, TFI chief David Cohen and a handful of OFAC staffers settled on a formulation that would freeze the assets of individuals who provided support to a nameless "senior Russian government official." Anyone could deduce who that anonymous official was, but it would allow the U.S. government to pursue sanctions against Putin's cronies without targeting him directly.

Crimea was by now firmly under Russian control, but there was still a smidgen of hope that Putin might refrain from formally annexing the territory. Secretary of State John Kerry was in constant contact with Sergei Lavrov, his gruff Russian counterpart, pressing for a resolution that would give Crimea more autonomy within Ukraine instead of absorbing it into Russia. Everyone knew that annexation was a one-way street. Once Putin took that route, there was no going back. Obama opted to hold Fried's and MacFarquhar's lists of cronies in reserve until Putin made a final decision.

As a warning shot, however, Obama signed an executive order on March 16, the same day the Kremlin staged its sham referendum in Crimea. In it, he authorized sanctions against any Russian government official as well as individuals who provided material support to a "senior Russian government official," as Treasury had recommended. He also issued the first tranche of asset freezes against a handful of Putin's most hawkish aides and facilitators of the Crimea operation. Among them were Sergei Glazyev, the Kremlin advisor who had urged Yanukovych to shoot at protesters, and Sergei Aksyonov, the self-proclaimed "prime minister of Crimea" who had requested a Russian intervention. The EU followed suit with a similar list the next day.

Two days after Obama's executive order, Putin gathered an audience of political and economic power brokers at the Grand Kremlin Palace, an ornate estate that was once the Moscow home of the tsars. Flanked by gilded chandeliers and a row of enormous Russian tricolor flags, he signed a treaty formally annexing Crimea and Sevastopol into Russia, then rose to deliver an emotional speech.

"In people's hearts and minds, Crimea has always been an inseparable part of Russia," he declared, launching into a lengthy historical disquisition.

Sanctions were a small price to pay, he argued, for being a great power instead of a lackey to the West. "They are constantly trying to sweep us into a corner because we have an independent position, because we maintain it and because we call things like they are and do not engage in hypocrisy. But there is a limit to everything. And with Ukraine, our Western partners have crossed the line." Pushing Russia into a corner, Putin warned, would always carry consequences. "If you compress the spring all the way to its limit, it will snap back hard. You must always remember this."

As Putin gave his impassioned address, David Cohen was in New York for the premiere of the fourth season of *Game of Thrones*, the hit HBO series created by his brother-in-law, David Benioff. He knew that the annexation was the nail in the coffin of Kerry's diplomacy and the trigger for a major raft of new sanctions. Cohen raced back to Washington for a full meeting of the NSC, chaired by Obama. (This meant Cohen would miss the premiere, but he made up for it a few seasons later with a cameo as a ragged resident of Winterfell waiting in a soup line.) Cohen's boss, Treasury Secretary Jack Lew, had been hospitalized with an emergency prostate issue during an official visit to Mexico. But the meeting with Obama looked to be decisive, so Lew, still in excruciating pain, headed back to Washington.

At the meeting, Obama approved the first round of asset freezes against members of Putin's innermost circle. The Rotenbergs made the list, as did Vladimir Yakunin, the chairman of Russian Railways and a Putin confidant since the two men worked together in St. Petersburg in the 1990s. Gennady Timchenko, another old friend of Putin's, made the cut, too. Timchenko was a co-founder of Gunvor, a lucrative commodities trading firm that earned billions buying and reselling Russian oil.

To draw attention to Putin's own ill-gotten wealth, Obama gave Treasury the green light to publicize his suspicious links to Gunvor. ("Putin has investments in Gunvor and may have access to Gunvor funds," a later press release stated.) The final marquee name was Yuri Kovalchuk, whom U.S. officials described as one of Putin's "cashiers." Kovalchuk owned Bank Rossiya, a midsize Russian bank that provided white-glove services to Putin's cronies. Obama also agreed to sanction Bank Rossiya directly, a move that would cut it off from the U.S. financial system. The White House was comfortable taking this step because the bank was not big enough to risk stirring up trouble in financial markets outside Russia.

Toward the end of the NSC meeting, the conversation shifted to the question of broader sanctions against entire sectors of the Russian economy.

The United States wasn't ready for this yet, and Europe was nowhere close to ready. But perhaps an executive order threatening such "sectoral sanctions" could deter Putin from making any further moves against Ukraine.

Obama liked the idea, so David Cohen drafted the executive order in an all-night session with a group of lawyers from Treasury and the White House. They were still adding final edits in pencil by morning, rushing to finish before Obama left for an event in Orlando, Florida. Marine One, the president's helicopter, sat waiting on the South Lawn of the White House, and it was decided that the aircraft, a gleaming emblem of American power, would make a fitting backdrop for Obama to publicly threaten broad economic sanctions against Russia. Susan Rice, Obama's national security advisor, approved the text just in time for Obama's scheduled departure, and the president made his way out to the lawn.

"I signed a new executive order today that gives us the authority to impose sanctions not just on individuals but on key sectors of the Russian economy," he said. "This is not our preferred outcome. These sanctions would not only have a significant impact on the Russian economy, but could also be disruptive to the global economy. However, Russia must know that further escalation will only isolate it further from the international community."

The order threatened sanctions against *any* company in Russia, calling out specifically those operating in financial services, energy, metals, mining, engineering, and defense—in other words, all the major sectors of Russia's economy. But it stopped short of imposing any actual penalties.

Obama was drawing a line in the sand, still hopeful that the threat alone would suffice.

26

The Contact Group

I need to get on the road.

When Dan Fried felt frustrated, his mind invariably turned to travel. He had a diplomat's conviction in the value of consistent, face-to-face interaction—"tending the garden," as former Secretary of State George Shultz called it. This was especially true in moments like the current one, when the policy process in Washington was stuck.

It was April 2014, a few weeks after Putin had redrawn the map of Europe at the point of a gun. America had frozen the assets of a handful of Putin's cronies, so far to no avail. Gennady Timchenko had even magically sold his shares in Gunvor, the commodities trading firm, hours before he was targeted. Being close to Putin had its perks.

Obama had also threatened sanctions on the commanding heights of Russia's economy. But his administration remained deeply divided on whether to make good on it, much less what the sanctions would actually look like. This was a problem, as Putin's appetite in Ukraine was not sated with his devouring of Crimea. On the contrary, his success there appeared to have left him wanting more.

Earlier that month, "little green men" started popping up across Ukraine's eastern provinces, seizing government buildings in Donetsk, Luhansk, and Kharkiv. These were major industrial centers and some of the largest cities in the country. Ukrainian forces quickly regained control of Kharkiv, but the shadowy militias held firm in Donetsk and Luhansk, a region collectively known as the Donbas. Under the leadership of Russian intelligence officers, they hastily declared independence from Ukraine and called for referenda.

Putin was rerunning the Crimea playbook, this time in Ukraine's industrial heartland.

Putin made no bones about his grandiose ambitions. His propagandists were touting the formation of *Novorossiya*, or "New Russia," a broad swath of territory encompassing eastern Ukraine and the country's southern coastline on the Black Sea. "It's New Russia. Kharkiv, Luhansk, Donetsk, Odessa were not part of Ukraine in tsarist times; they were transferred in 1920. Why? God knows," Putin said during a four-hour question-and-answer marathon on national television. "Then, for various reasons, these areas were gone, and the people stayed there. We need to encourage them to find a solution."

Still at odds over what to do about Putin's efforts to "encourage" a "solution" in eastern Ukraine, White House officials came up with a compromise. They would seek hard-hitting sanctions, but only at a pace the Europeans would support. This was acceptable to the more cautious camp, as they assumed the EU would recoil from poking the Russian bear or, at best, move at a plodding speed. Unity with Europe was important for substantive reasons, too, but the requirement to move in lockstep with the EU was meant in part as a check against officials like Fried and Nuland, who were pushing for a tougher line. Rory MacFarquhar, the NSC economist and one of the voices urging restraint, called it a "Dan Fried containment strategy."

MacFarquhar and his like-minded colleagues feared unintended spillovers into the world economy and were wary of blowing up U.S.-Russian relations over Ukraine. The compromise, MacFarquhar confessed, would act as a constraint on those officials who "just wanted to do more, more, more, and more regardless of the consequences for the global economy and for financial stability." Fried knew what the White House was up to, but he didn't mind. "Anything that isn't a brick wall provides openings," he said.

In fact, Fried considered the White House's instructions a diplomat's dream. They gave him and his team license to negotiate handshake deals with the Europeans and then bring them back to Washington for action. "If our instructions are 'Go at a pace the Europeans will accept,'" he explained, then "whatever we can get the Europeans to agree to is something we can agree to."

Fried credited Tony Blinken, the influential number two at the NSC, with empowering him to take the case for more aggressive sanctions to Europe. The two men had known each other since their days in the Clinton

White House, and they tended to see eye to eye. "He was giving me a nego-tiating mandate," Fried said of Blinken. "Instead of an elaborate one, he was giving me a simple one."

In late March, the leaders of the G7—a democratic bloc composed of the United States, the EU, Germany, France, Italy, the United Kingdom, Can-ada, and Japan—met in the Dutch city of The Hague. (The group was known as the G8 until Russia was kicked out following Putin's annexation of Crimea.) Echoing Obama's executive order, the G7 leaders warned in a joint statement that they would "intensify actions including coordinated sectoral sanctions . . . if Russia continues to escalate this situation." These were just words—no one even knew what the term "sectoral sanctions" meant, other than that it would be something stronger than the current approach of targeting mostly individuals. But the statement was enough to give Fried's diplomacy the seal of authority.

Soon thereafter, Fried created a Russia sanctions contact group, consist-ing of the members of the G7 plus a few other interested parties, including the Poles, the Norwegians, and the Australians. Its purpose would be to gen-erate ideas for sanctions, share concerns, and analyze the potential impact of different options. It would not have the power to make decisions, but it would strive to achieve enough alignment that, when G7 leaders decided it was time to ramp up sanctions, their governments could quickly act in uni-son. The contact group would operate under the radar but not in secret—outside the media spotlight yet well within range of Russia's intelligence services, to whom its existence would hopefully prove that the West's threat of harsher penalties wasn't empty talk.

The Europeans jumped at the idea. On Iran sanctions, they'd seldom been consulted ahead of time; instead, they'd been informed of American decisions and left to choose whether to follow along or risk seeing European firms shunned from the U.S. financial system. Now Fried was giving them the chance to act rather than just react. Not that they'd have needed much convincing anyway: Every time the EU made a foreign policy decision, it needed to corral unanimous support from all twenty-eight member states. One could not survive long as a European diplomat without relishing con-sultations and process.

The group's first meeting was held at an annex to the U.S. Mission to the EU, a stripped-down flex space with small breakout rooms and a sparsely stocked kitchenette. It looked more like the office of a fledgling startup than the diplomatic conference hall of a global superpower. But the informal setting suited Fried, as it made his European counterparts lower their guard somewhat.

Before the session started, Fried sat down with Germany's representative to go over the ground rules. As was often the case, Germany was the key player—if Berlin wasn't on board, Brussels wouldn't move—so alignment was critical, and Berlin was even more divided on the question of Russia sanctions than Washington was.

"You're not going to insist on a formal agreement or agreed minutes?" the German diplomat asked.

"Of course not," Fried said. "That's fatal. If I do that, it's all we'll discuss. This will all be an exercise in producing a piece of paper."

"Well, thank God!" the German said, visibly relieved.

"Zero formality, maximum flexibility," Fried assured him.

Fried repeated that message to the dozens of representatives at the meeting. Most of the time, multilateral diplomacy is a highly formal affair, with delegates reciting canned talking points as others doze off. Fried was creating something different—a place for free-flowing discussion, more university seminar than UN snoozefest.

From then on, Fried and his colleagues took a red-eye to Europe every second or third week. No one was allowed to check a bag, and all had to be ready to dive right into meetings upon getting off the plane. They almost always visited Brussels, where the flex space became the unofficial headquarters of the contact group, and often stopped in Berlin, London, and Paris. They became regulars at a handful of local restaurants, whose maître d's greeted them like neighbors.

On some occasions, they visited sanctions skeptics in Hungary and Slovakia and hawks in Lithuania and Poland. In Kyiv, they sat down with Ukraine's new prime minister, Arseniy Yatsenyuk, a balding, bespectacled economist who was overseeing political reforms in the messy aftermath of Yanukovych's departure. Each night, they'd groggily return to the local U.S. embassy to fire off an email to Washington summing up the day's discussions. These emails, in turn, shaped the policy debate in the Situation Room. On account of his wall-to-wall diplomacy, Fried was serving as something more than America's sanctions coordinator; he was serving as the de facto quarterback of the West's sanctions campaign against Putin.

In the process, he cultivated several crucial allies. He particularly valued his rapport with Henrik Hololei, a jovial Estonian and high-ranking member of the European Commission, the executive branch of the EU. The Commission's policy staff, sometimes referred to as Eurocrats, were said to be drab and dull. (It was up for debate whether Hololei, a transportation aficionado, helped disabuse people of that notion by adorning his office in the Commission's modern, light-filled Brussels headquarters with scores of toy airplanes and trains.) Hololei had grown up under the Soviet yoke and needed no lessons on the threat of Russian imperialism. Most important, his staff knew the inner workings of Russia's economy like a crack auto mechanic knows an engine.

Fried had a knack for identifying officials like Hololei and his teammates: the people responsible for "writing the memo," as he put it, the ones that shaped decisions upstream of the decision-makers. Many were relatively unknown figures, but their ranks or titles belied the considerable influence they wielded behind the scenes. In short order, Fried's network of memo-writers spanned Brussels, London, Berlin, and Warsaw. The British, who had not yet voted to leave the EU, were particularly helpful. Like Fried, they favored aggressive sanctions against Russia, and they had their fingers on the pulse in Brussels and could advise him on what would pass muster in the EU.

While it wasn't clear at first, Fried's diplomacy was laying the groundwork for a new model of economic war planning. As Russia and China migrated further away from the West, it became untenable to rely on the UN Security Council as the main negotiating forum for multilateral sanctions. During its economic war against Iran, the United States realized that the UN would never go far enough to give nuclear diplomacy a real chance, so it took matters into its own hands. Now, with an economic war against Russia looming, America looked to its allies in the G7—most important of all, the EU—to forge a "coalition of the willing" for multilateral sanctions. The UN Security Council was fading into irrelevance, and the G7 was slowly emerging as a replacement. If the G7, a group of like-minded democracies that together contributed nearly half of global economic output, could wage economic war as a bloc, it would be a force to be reckoned with.

Yet in the spring of 2014, as Putin drove toward his *Novorossiya* fantasy, hesitation still racked Western leaders. A leaked EU report warned that Iran-style sanctions on Russia, including an oil and gas embargo, could cost Germany almost a full percentage point of GDP. With the eurozone still reeling from the financial crisis, it was apparent that any "sectoral sanctions" on Russia would, by necessity, be less sweeping than the penalties that were imposed on Iran. But thanks to Fried's work—his success in forming a traveling team of U.S. officials who left their respective bureaucratic allegiances at home, his push for a united transatlantic front—future sanctions stood a real chance of garnering full support from both America and Europe. Now all that was needed were creative ideas.

27

The Scalpel

As Dan Fried pounded the pavement in Europe, the economic policy team in Washington was growing worried. Putin was shrugging off the threat of broad economic sanctions—that much had always been a distinct risk. But financial markets didn't seem to care much, either. Initially, jittery investors reacted to Russia's incursion into Crimea by pulling capital out of the country, causing Russia's main stock market to fall by 10 percent. But after the United States imposed the first round of sanctions and markets digested the limited scope of the penalties, Russia's economy stabilized.

In late March, Barack Obama had stood in front of Marine One and warned Putin that further escalation would result in sanctions against "key sectors of the Russian economy." Unfazed, Putin promptly escalated further, sending his "little green men" into the Donbas. Obama had drawn a line in the sand, and Putin was breezing past it. Even so, Wall Street doubted Washington was ready to bring down the hammer.

In April, the IMF and World Bank held their spring meetings in Washington, a yearly confab for high-flying policymakers, economists, and financiers. Rory MacFarquhar, the NSC economist, was in attendance and found himself discussing the Ukraine crisis with a group of investors. To his astonishment, his interlocutors ridiculed him to his face. One was particularly blunt: "You guys, you're going to do nothing."

At the same gathering, Treasury Secretary Jack Lew sat down with his Russian counterpart, Anton Siluanov, to reiterate the threat of harsher sanctions. But given the prevailing mood in the conference hall, Siluanov could be excused for taking Lew's warning with a grain of salt.

Ever since 2006, when Hank Paulson helped Stuart Levey launch the economic war against Iran, Treasury secretaries had largely stayed out of sanctions policy. Paulson's last two years in office were spent fighting a global financial crisis, as was more or less the entire tenure of his successor, Tim Geithner. After Lew took over in early 2013, however, he took a keen interest in sanctions policy. Now, as he reviewed his department's proposals for "sectoral sanctions" against Russia, he understood why the private sector wasn't too spooked by Obama's threats.

Treasury's proposed plan of attack, drawn up by David Cohen and the team at TFI, borrowed from the Iran playbook and started with blocking sanctions against major Russian banks. But these Russian banks were closely connected with big European banks, which were in turn connected to big American banks. If sanctions caused one of the major Russian banks to fail, the potential for financial contagion to spread westward was real. Such a systemic threat to financial stability had never been a serious concern with Iran sanctions, because Iranian banks lacked the global connections of their Russian peers. For these reasons, the risks of Iran-style sanctions against Russia were simply too high, and it was implausible that the instinctively cautious Obama would ever approve them.

Lew—a lanky Orthodox Jew who wore round glasses and faithfully observed Shabbat despite his high-powered job—had an understated air, yet he was one of a small handful of people in American history to have held three different cabinet posts. Prior to heading Treasury, he'd served as White House chief of staff and twice as the director of the Office of Management and Budget. He had also been a top official at the State Department, and his mix of political, economic, and diplomatic experience gave him confidence in handling sanctions issues.

"We have people here who actually know the wiring of U.S. banks and the wiring of European banks as well as anybody," Lew told his senior staff. "We have to think this through as a team." In particular, Lew was thinking of Treasury's International Affairs division. IA had been marginally involved in the Iran campaign; the division's most notable appearance came when its macroeconomic experts helped forecast the potential global ripple effects of sanctions on Iran's central bank. This time, instead of only modeling the impact of sanctions, IA would be brought on board to help design the penalties themselves.

Not all IA officials were excited to work on economic warfare. One who jumped at the chance was Daleep Singh. Then IA's chief for Europe, Singh

Jack Lew: U.S. secretary of the treasury, 2013–2017.

had spent eight years as a trader at Goldman Sachs before joining Treasury, including a stint in London focused on foreign exchange and emerging markets. He had long hoped to work in public service, but he didn't know how to get started. One day, his Moscow-based Goldman colleague, Rory MacFarquhar, told him he was joining the Obama administration. Singh let MacFarquhar know about his aspirations and a year later got an opportunity to help Tim Geithner set up Treasury's new Markets Room, an in-house group that prepared daily financial briefings for Treasury leadership.

Singh possessed not only native fluency in finance but also an uncanny ability to explain things in plain English. That skill won him many friends in Washington, a town chronically short on financial literacy. Singh had traveled to Kyiv to try to iron out an IMF loan days after Yanukovych fled, and the smell of burning tires was still fresh in his memory. A few weeks later, before a meeting on Ukraine in the Situation Room, he shared an epiphany with Adam Szubin: "I can take everything I've learned about how markets work well and turn it upside down."

That was exactly what Lew thought Treasury needed: OFAC's mastery of the nuts and bolts of sanctions married with IA's financial expertise. Singh and a few others at IA started crunching numbers. Which Russian banks and companies were most exposed to Europe and the United States? What did their external debt portfolios look like? Their work resembled intelligence analysis, but instead of relying on spy reports and intercepts, they used Bloomberg terminals, corporate filings, and financial statements. U.S.

foreign policy was typically hashed out through elegantly written memos; Singh and his team preferred Excel spreadsheets. It wasn't long before officials at OFAC realized how helpful these IA newcomers could be. "They're smarter," conceded an OFAC official who was working on Russia sanctions. "They put numbers together, they do graphs, they do spreadsheets, all the stuff we didn't do at OFAC."

The Russian economy was big but not all that complicated. At the top was the state, which owned the only sectors that were globally competitive: natural resource extraction first and foremost and, to a lesser extent, weapons and nuclear equipment (the product of decades of massive Soviet investment in the military-industrial complex). The country's vast landmass, covering eleven time zones, was rich in all manner of natural resources, but none rivaled the abundance of fossil fuels. The oil and gas industries, controlled by the state through Rosneft and Gazprom, respectively, were the cash cows of Russia's economy. They alone accounted for *half* of Russia's federal budget and *two-thirds* of its export revenues. They made Russia into the world's largest exporter of fossil fuels—by far.

Moscow took the colossal rents it generated selling oil and gas and redistributed them to pensioners and to industries that were not globally competitive but employed large numbers of people, such as auto manufacturing. It also used these rents to finance Putin's military buildup, which was costing Russia 25 percent of its total federal budget by the time the "little green men" descended on Crimea. All this meant that Russia was completely dependent on foreign trade—more so than the United States, more than Japan, more than even China. But that dependency cut both ways, and it was clear that Europe would never agree to anything amounting to an oil or gas embargo.

Russia's financial sector was likewise dominated by a few state-owned behemoths. Sberbank, or "savings bank," which was founded during the nineteenth-century reign of Tsar Nicholas I, was the biggest of them all. Because Russia's domestic financial industry was primitive and its base of customer deposits shallow, Russian companies were forced to look abroad for credit. By 2014, they had piled up well over $700 billion in external debt, denominated in dollars and euros and owed to U.S. and European financial institutions.

This financial exposure was a double-edged sword, too. On the one hand, it made Russia even more vulnerable to outside pressure than it already was on account of its exports. At the stroke of a pen, Obama could cut Russian firms off from the U.S. financial system and freeze their assets. On the other hand, Lew's concerns about financial contagion were well-founded: what happened in Russia might not stay in Russia.

If Rosneft and Sberbank were too big to sanction, America could wield the cudgel of blocking sanctions against smaller players. Obama had already approved such penalties on Bank Rossiya, the midsize bank that served many of Putin's cronies, and SMP Bank, an even smaller institution owned by the Rotenberg brothers. Nearly $600 million of Bank Rossiya's assets and more than $60 million of SMP's were frozen. Visa and MasterCard shut down service to the banks entirely. But hitting these institutions was "like the Death Star blowing up Tatooine," said Singh, referring to a sparsely inhabited planet in the Star Wars universe. It might annoy Putin and his pals but wouldn't rock Russia's economy.

Blocking sanctions, which cut off their targets fully from the U.S. financial system, had been the United States' weapon of choice against Iran. But deploying them against Russia's biggest companies carried too much risk of collateral damage outside Russia, and taking aim at smaller targets wouldn't cause all that much damage. As Singh saw it, the best solution was to develop newer, more precise weapons. His Treasury colleague, the brainy economist Brad Setser, agreed. With such an approach, "you wouldn't have to go after the small, insignificant sectors of the Russian economy," Setser said, "you would go right for the jugular"—hopefully without slicing your own hand in the process.

Singh's idea was to bar Russia's biggest banks and energy companies from American capital markets. Unlike Iranian banks, Russian firms would not have their assets frozen, and they would still have access to the U.S. financial system for basic services like payments. They would not, therefore, be at risk of failure owing to an incapacity to perform essential functions, lowering the threat of contagion. But they would lose the ability to raise new debt and equity through U.S. markets. This meant they'd have a much harder time refinancing their existing debt, which they surely expected to be able to do when they accumulated hundreds of billions of dollars' worth of foreign obligations.

It was a narrow but elegant restriction. Firms like Rosneft and Sberbank had huge dollar-denominated debts that they needed to roll over every few months. A sudden stop in capital flows would increase the yield on their debt, reduce their creditworthiness, and force them to pay down existing debt rather than refinance it. Given the size of the debt, cash from their balance sheets wouldn't suffice, so the Russian government would probably have to bail them out. The result would be large capital outflows and a weakening ruble. At that point, Moscow would be left with just a few options. It could spend down its reserves to try to stabilize the ruble. It could impose capital controls, which would terrify foreign investors. It could hike up interest rates, which would hurt the domestic economy. Or it could do some combination of these options, all of which were bad.

In effect, the United States would use Russia's reliance on U.S. capital markets as a chokepoint—one that would allow America to tighten the squeeze in a palpable yet controlled manner. Its subtlety may even be a strength: it would grant multinational companies some leeway to decide their risk tolerance for business with Russia, which in turn might give Putin a reason for restraint. "I really started to like the idea, because the velocity of the negative feedback loop is determined by millions and millions of market participants who are looking at how Putin responds," Singh explained. If Putin escalated in Ukraine, the negative feedback loop would accelerate, shocking Russia's economy. If he backed down, pressure might ease. It was an idea only a trader could come up with.

The concept was novel, and it took several extended discussions with Singh for OFAC and the rest of TFI to buy in. But by late spring, the Obama administration had finally figured out how to define "sectoral sanctions."

In May, Victoria Nuland teased the idea at a public hearing on Capitol Hill. When asked what sectoral sanctions would look like, Nuland explained they would be a "scalpel" rather than a "sledgehammer," focusing on areas "where Russia needs us far more than we need Russia."

Now it was time to sell Singh's idea to the Europeans. Fried and his team found them to be amenable—the image of a scalpel and the precision it implied allayed their fears of overreach. In their endless horse-trading sessions on the issue, held in the dimly lit rooms of the brutalist Justus Lipsius building in Brussels, the representatives of the twenty-eight EU member states often agreed on only one thing: whatever pain Russia sanctions caused at home should be shared. If French cheesemakers took a hit, so too should Italian fashion houses and German industrial plants. The capital markets sanctions were agreeable to most of them, however, as it seemed that America and Britain, home to the financial centers of New York and London, would bear the brunt while the rest of the EU would get off relatively easy.

Above all, the Europeans were relieved the Americans weren't pushing for restrictions on energy sales—which had been the coup de grâce against Iran's economy. Fried and his team stressed that sanctions should try to constrain Russia's prospects for growth in the future, not to create an immediate economic shock. The EU also liked that principle. In addition to the capital markets restrictions, Fried and his European counterparts began discussing whether similar forward-looking penalties could be applied to Russia's oil industry.

Russia was a massive oil producer, but the lion's share of its output came from aging Soviet fields that were being depleted. To retain its status as an energy superpower, it needed to develop a new generation of oil projects, most of them in remote offshore deposits beneath the Arctic Ocean and in relatively inaccessible shale formations. Tapping into these reservoirs required world-class technology and know-how, which Putin had secured through deals with Western oil companies like Exxon and Shell. He didn't have any other choice: Russia relied on U.S. and European firms for at least 80 percent of the equipment and software it needed to develop offshore oil fields.

The experts Fried had cultivated at the Departments of Commerce and Energy proposed banning sales of this cutting-edge oil equipment to Russia. Perhaps the West could exploit its dominance in oil-field technology as another chokepoint. As it turned out, the EU was amenable to this idea as well. The penalties would allow Europe to continue buying oil and gas from Russia to its heart's content. Within a decade or so, they would deal a serious blow to Russia's oil production. But by then, the Europeans hoped, they would all be driving electric cars anyway.

By June, America and Europe had aligned on the nature and scale of sectoral sanctions. They would not cut off Russia's biggest companies from the global financial system in one fell swoop, as Washington had done with Iran, but they'd carefully sever their access to Western capital markets and technology, dramatically narrowing Russia's economic horizons. Even Angela Merkel—who was deeply reluctant to curb economic ties with Russia— had come around. The existing proposal, crucially, focused on capital markets and oil extraction, and Germany was neither a banking powerhouse nor home to an oil major. German industrial giants such as Siemens and BASF and carmakers like Volkswagen and BMW would not be affected.

The process had taken months, but it was culminating as Ukraine was finally getting back on its feet. Ukrainians had just elected Petro Poroshenko, a billionaire chocolate magnate and supporter of the Euromaidan, as their new president. On the seventieth anniversary of the D-Day landings, Poroshenko joined Obama, Putin, Merkel, and French president François Hollande in Normandy for a commemorative ceremony. The mood was icy, but there were some shoots of hope. On the sidelines of the event, Merkel and Hollande brought Putin and Poroshenko together for brief talks. (Deferring to Merkel and Hollande, Obama stayed out.) The four leaders discussed a potential ceasefire, and Ukraine's new president announced that he would soon unveil a comprehensive peace plan. From that day onward, Germany, France, Ukraine, and Russia formed a negotiating group known as the Normandy Format.

On the eve of summer, with Ukraine's onion-domed cityscapes drenched in sunlight, Poroshenko released his fifteen-point peace plan. The plan suggested a trade: the Russian-backed militias in the Donbas would disarm and return control over the region to Kyiv; in exchange, the Ukrainian government would commit to more decentralization of power in the country. Ukraine's military was performing ably in the Donbas, making slow but steady gains, so Russia had good reason to consider Poroshenko's proposal. And if diplomacy proved to be a dead end, the West now had another plan in its back pocket.

28

The Opening Salvo

Summer dawned with a rush of activity. Phone lines between Washington, Berlin, and Paris buzzed while Dan Fried and company continued touring various European capitals to negotiate the fine print on the recently agreed sanctions proposal. In Ukraine, President Poroshenko prepared to sign an association agreement with the EU, reversing the turn toward Moscow that had been his predecessor's undoing. A fragile ceasefire between Ukraine's military and the Kremlin-backed militias in the Donbas was called yet often broken. Russia massed regular army troops along Ukraine's eastern border, ominously close to the fighting.

It was late June 2014. Several days had passed since the publication of Poroshenko's peace plan, but there was still no word from the Kremlin. Western leaders awaited Putin's reaction with growing frustration. "Progress has not been as clear as I would wish," Angela Merkel told the press before an EU summit on June 27, at which Ukraine was scheduled to sign the association agreement. If the situation remained stuck, Merkel warned, "we will have to talk about how we need to go further with sanctions."

Several smaller EU members—such as Austria, Greece, and Hungary—still opposed sanctions, as did Italy's new prime minister, Matteo Renzi, whose country was facing its worst economic crisis since World War II. Renzi feared the potential repercussions sanctions would have on Italy's ailing economy, especially on Eni and UniCredit, two Italian heavyweights in the oil and banking industries, respectively.

These holdouts notwithstanding, European leaders at the summit agreed to issue a public ultimatum. They demanded that Russia return several checkpoints along Ukraine's eastern border to Kyiv's control and agree to "substantial negotiations" based on Poroshenko's peace plan. If Russia failed to meet these conditions by June 30, which was only three days away, it would suffer "significant" sanctions. Poroshenko unilaterally extended the ceasefire in the Donbas to match Brussels's deadline.

In Washington, Rory MacFarquhar and other White House officials had spent the spring worrying that the private sector wasn't taking their threats against Russia seriously. Now it was the private sector's turn to worry. Western governments were looking increasingly united on the sanctions front. Bits and pieces of their plan for sectoral sanctions were already leaking to the press.

Industry lobbyists sprang into action. The U.S. Chamber of Commerce and the National Association of Manufacturers banded together and bought full-page ads in *The New York Times*, *The Wall Street Journal*, and *The Washington Post* warning about the risks of sanctions. "The most effective long-term solution to increase America's global influence is to strengthen our ability to provide goods and services to the world through pro-trade policies and multilateral diplomacy," the ad stated. Sanctions on Russia were not a "pro-trade" policy.

The newspaper ads were an extraordinary step. These were two of the country's largest and most influential lobbying groups, but even they almost never spoke out publicly against U.S. policy on matters of national security. Their stance revealed just how different an economic war against Russia would be from the one against Iran. During the Iran campaign, all of the external lobbying was *in favor* of sanctions, not against them. No one scored political points by going easy on the Islamic Republic. For American politicians, advocating harsher sanctions against Iran was virtually cost-free; no U.S. jobs stood to be lost and no retirement portfolios were likely to suffer because of Iranian economic hardship. Draconian Iran sanctions bills regularly passed Congress with unanimous support. But an economic war with Russia would be a whole new ballgame—American businesses had a lot to lose. There was a reason Congress had mostly stayed silent on the matter.

June 30, the deadline set by European leaders, came and went. Poroshenko ordered Ukraine's troops to resume military operations in the Donbas. Would America and Europe make good on their threats? Or had they been bluffing, as Putin evidently assumed?

Early signs were not promising. Instead of convening an emergency summit, EU leaders chose to wait for their prescheduled meeting on July 16 to render a decision. In the meantime, hundreds of Russian navy sailors arrived in France to train on two Mistral warships, which Paris had agreed to sell to Moscow for more than a billion euros.

Obama had committed to move in lockstep with Europe, but his patience was wearing thin. At the White House's request, Fried started sounding out his contacts in Europe. How would they feel if the United States jumped out in front and fired an opening salvo, perhaps by imposing an initial tranche of capital markets sanctions on July 16, irrespective of how the EU summit played out? Fried was a Russia hawk, and he thought serious sanctions were past due. But he was also a true believer in the transatlantic alliance and felt that sanctions weren't worth blowing up unity with Europe. His conversations, thankfully, left him feeling sanguine. "I thought the system would bear this kind of leadership," he said.

The Obama administration readied a sanctions package for July 16. It settled on two banks, Gazprombank and VEB, and two energy companies, Rosneft and Novatek. This target selection covered the right sectors (finance and fossil fuels) and would signal the necessary resolve, since Rosneft was the world's biggest oil company by output. Crucially, Rosneft held that distinction only because of its purchase, the previous year, of one of its rivals, a deal for which Rosneft borrowed a whopping $40 billion, primarily from Western banks. Capital markets sanctions would prevent the company from refinancing these loans. That would likely be the case even if the United States acted without Europe. "Because of the dominance of the dollar and the preeminence of U.S. institutions in global financial markets," Singh reasoned, "even if we moved unilaterally, we could have substantial impact, maybe close to equal impact as if the Europeans joined us, at least initially."

As the EU summit got underway in Brussels, the United States pulled the trigger. Some perceived America's unilateral foray as a pressure tactic aimed at the reluctant Europeans. Still, the EU remained hopelessly stuck, and its member states failed to reach the necessary unanimity on the sanctions package. In the end, they refrained from penalizing any Russian companies and approved a paltry set of sanctions that came nowhere near the extent of the American action.

The New York Times assessed that these "disparate moves" signaled "a widening gulf in the response to the crisis in Ukraine" and predicted that divisions between Washington and Brussels might "dilute the impact of the American actions." The Associated Press reported that Washington's decision to move ahead on its own marked "a shift in strategy that reflects the

Obama administration's frustration with Europe's reluctance to take tougher action against Moscow."

The phones at the White House and Treasury rang off the hook as Wall Street executives registered their anger. Just a few years earlier, Morgan Stanley had helped take Rosneft public. Three consecutive Rosneft CFOs were recruited from the iconic New York bank, and the former CEO of Morgan Stanley, John Mack, had served on Rosneft's board. The well-known head of another Wall Street bank called the White House, furious at the administration for acting on its own and weaponizing the U.S. financial system. Policies like this, the executive warned, would endanger America's financial leadership and cause business to migrate to rival hubs such as London and Frankfurt.

But the controversy died down almost as soon as it began. Less than twenty-four hours after Washington announced the first round of sectoral sanctions, headlines focused instead on reports from a patch of farmland in the Donbas. There, in the afternoon of July 17, a dense cloud of black smoke had been spotted rising near the village of Hrabove, and below it, amid a jumble of carry-on bags and stray passports, a sea of bodies and the smoldering wreckage of a Boeing 777 passenger jet.

29

MH17

"I'm getting reports that an aircraft has just crashed in eastern Ukraine." It was Vladimir Putin who broke the news to Barack Obama, in a phone call the Russian leader had originally requested in reaction to the first round of U.S. sectoral sanctions. Dan Fried heard about the crash when a White House staffer interrupted his meeting in the Situation Room. "There are reports of bodies and suitcases falling from the sky," the staffer said.

The wreckage, it quickly emerged, belonged to Malaysia Airlines Flight 17 (MH17), a commercial airliner en route from Amsterdam to Kuala Lumpur. The site of the disaster was in territory held by the Kremlin-backed militias, right on the boundary between the breakaway provinces of Donetsk and Luhansk and about an hour's drive from the Russian border. The plane appeared to have been shot down. All 298 passengers and crew were dead.

One of the first reporters on the scene was Sabrina Tavernise, a *New York Times* journalist who had previously served as the paper's Moscow correspondent. Tavernise found the bodies of victims still wrapped in seat belts, lying motionless beside a scattering of playing cards, children's books, and parking tickets. "It was like the end of the world," she recalled. Tavernise happened to be married to Rory MacFarquhar, and her private reports to her husband were the best source of ground-level information the White House had that day.

The U.S. intel community determined that MH17 had fallen victim to a Buk, a Russian-made surface-to-air missile system. While the Ukrainian army possessed Buks, it did not have them deployed in eastern Ukraine

The crash site of Malaysia Airlines Flight 17 (MH17)
in eastern Ukraine on July 17, 2014.

at the time of the incident. By contrast, Russia was smuggling military equipment across the border to its separatist proxies in the vicinity of Hrabove in the hours before the crash. Deleted social media posts and intercepted phone calls revealed initial jubilation among the Kremlin-backed militiamen in thinking they had downed a Ukrainian military jet and subsequent shock upon realizing it was a commercial airliner. Video footage depicted separatist forces arriving at the crash site, first surprised at what they found ("It's a civilian!" shouted their commander), and then rummaging through the debris in search of wallets, cell phones, and jewelry. With such a mountain of evidence, it did not take Washington long to ascertain what investigators later formally concluded: Russian-backed separatists fired the Buk that downed MH17, and they obtained the weapon directly from their patron.

Victoria Nuland worked tirelessly to get this information declassified so it could be shared with the public. She succeeded, and within seventy-two hours, John Kerry was on *Meet the Press* explaining that a Buk was spotted in separatist-held territory in eastern Ukraine right before the tragedy. Russia was caught red-handed.

If Russia's culpability in the slaughter, which claimed the lives of more than two hundred Europeans, wasn't enough to galvanize the EU to act, nothing would. "This certainly will be a wake-up call for Europe and the world that there are consequences to an escalating conflict in eastern Ukraine," Obama said.

For days, the Kremlin-backed militias blocked rescue workers and investigators from accessing the crash site. They also looted the ghastly rubble, stripping the corpses and their tattered luggage of valuables. Among the dead were 196 Dutch nationals. Frans Timmermans, the Dutch foreign minister, had known some of them personally. "To my dying day I will not understand that it took so much time for the rescue workers to be allowed to do their difficult job, and that human remains should be used in a political game," Timmermans told the UN Security Council shortly after the shootdown.

Next, Timmermans met with his twenty-seven EU counterparts, some of whom had stood firm against sanctions only days prior. He spoke uninterrupted for half an hour, letting loose his grief and anger. Several in the audience started crying. "The Dutch are normally very level-headed and over-rational, and here he was emotional," Radek Sikorski, Poland's foreign minister, said of Timmerman's speech that day. "He carried the room."

Timmermans asked his colleagues to give the green light to sectoral sanctions. "No one found it possible to speak against that," another EU diplomat recalled. The dam had broken.

Dan Fried and his European colleagues called an emergency meeting of the contact group. Berlin's representative showed up with a proposal that was even tougher than America's actions of July 16. It would ban *all* of Russia's state-owned financial institutions, including the behemoths Sberbank and VTB, from raising new debt or equity on Western capital markets, and it would prohibit sales to Russia of the technologies the country needed to exploit its next generation of oil resources. This was serious stuff. Fried and his team liked it. They saw no reason to quarrel with Germany's proposal, so instead of putting their own ideas on the table, they simply endorsed it. Just like that, Washington and Brussels agreed on a plan for a joint strike on Russia's economy.

An EU memo detailing the proposal promptly leaked to the press. "Restricting access to capital markets for Russian state-owned financial institutions would increase their cost of raising funds and constrain their ability to finance the Russian economy, unless the Russian public authorities provide them with substitute financing," the document read. "It would also foster a climate of market uncertainty that is likely to affect the business environment in Russia and accelerate capital outflows."

The oil sanctions would bite, too. "Russia needs EU technologies to develop some of the most competitive and export-oriented sectors of its economy, including energy," the memo explained. "The possibility for Russia to substitute such products and technologies originating from the EU or U.S. is low in view of the likely unavailability of similar products."

The White House welcomed the proposal, but it decided to stop short of matching the EU and exempted Sberbank. Sanctioning Sberbank, MacFarquhar argued, was like "sanctioning the Russian people." Roughly one in two Russians held an account there, and even after MH17, strong voices in the White House were not yet ready to deem Russia a clear-cut adversary. The sanctions were intended to change Putin's calculus—to convince him that a larger invasion of Ukraine was not worth the costs, and to coax him into peace negotiations with Poroshenko. If these goals were met, the logic went, everyone could return to business as usual.

The first round of unilateral American sanctions had already left their mark, both on the targeted companies and on the broader Russian economy. But the disruptive effect of the new, joint U.S.-European strike, launched on July 29, was even more immediate—including for Western banks.

Days after the new sanctions went into effect, OFAC held a question-and-answer session in London with the British Bankers' Association, a trade group for the financial industry. "They were, to put it mildly, flummoxed by the new restrictions," one of the OFAC officials recalled. Some banks had chosen to simply stop all transactions with Russia for fear of running afoul of the new regulations. Others had taken the extraordinary step of reviewing all their transactions with Russia by hand, which meant asking staff to scour thousands of payment records each day.

The British bankers' wariness was reasonable given the potential repercussions of messing up: Earlier that summer, U.S. law enforcement agencies had fined BNP Paribas an astonishing $9 billion for sanctions violations. But too much of a chilling effect would end up harming Western economic and political interests. Massive American pension funds like CalPERS and asset managers like BlackRock had significant exposure to Russia. Half of Sberbank's openly traded shares were owned by American and British investors. Confusion and excessive risk aversion could therefore dent retirement portfolios on both sides of the Atlantic.

To avoid that outcome, OFAC released reams of public guidance and FAQs. The agency clarified that the restrictions applied only to *new* debt and equity; securities issued before the sanctions went into effect could still be traded. Derivatives, whose value could be linked to the debt of blacklisted Russian firms like Rosneft, were exempt from the restrictions. With a lot of help and hordes of new hires, the banks eventually figured out how to comply. OFAC, the odd duck at Treasury focused more on economic damage than growth, could even boast that the new sanctions were a kind of stimulus package for bank compliance divisions.

It had taken an unspeakable tragedy, but finally, five months after Putin's "little green men" turned up in Crimea, the West's economic war against Russia had begun. And in the wake of the protracted sanctions campaign against Iran, the world's biggest banks were primed to play their part on the front line. If anything, for the penalties against Russia to perform more like a scalpel than a sledgehammer, Washington would need to nudge the banks to ease up.

Escalation

"Thrust in the bayonet; when you hit fat, keep pushing; when you hit steel, pull back." Dan Fried had a habit of quoting Lenin to describe Putin's strategy. For the first time that year, Putin was hitting steel. Western economic sanctions were in full effect. Ukraine's military was making progress against the Kremlin-backed militias in the Donbas, and it seemed that Kyiv might even recapture its territory, dealing a humiliating blow to Putin's vision of *Novorossiya*.

In early August, Putin attempted to strike back by banning Western food imports. This would hurt European farmers who counted Russia as a major export market, but it would be even worse for Putin's own people: Russia was the world's fifth-largest food importer and ran a sizable agricultural trade deficit. Sure enough, Russians quickly found ways to smuggle in their favorite products, and Putin eventually ordered all illegally imported food to be seized and destroyed. On Russian TV, propaganda reels showed bulldozers pulping heaps of peaches and tomatoes, meats set ablaze in front of supermarkets, and heads of French cheese being squashed by tractors. It was all fun and games until Russian diners tasted Russky Parmesan or mozzarella di Bryansk. "There will still be pizza on the menu," said an Italian chef working in Russia, but "it will be a different kind of pizza."

Ukraine's armed forces continued their advance in August and were soon on the verge of a strategic victory. They recaptured the town of Ilovaisk, a critical node without which Russia would struggle to resupply its proxy forces. Yet Putin still doubted the strength of the steel in his path. Rather than pulling back, he ordered regular army forces to cross over into Ukrainian territory. Russian tanks and heavy weapons encircled the Ukrainians in Ilovaisk and routed them in a bloodbath that left hundreds of Ukrainian troops dead and scores in Russian captivity. Putin called José Manuel Barroso, the president of the European Commission, and reveled in his victory. "If I want," he boasted, "I'll take Kyiv in two weeks."

Analysts now reported thousands of Russian troops in the Donbas. In public, however, Putin still denied their presence. This suited the narrative sold to the Russian people: Ukraine was an artificial nation, created by the West to weaken Russia. Ukrainians spoke Russian, ate the same foods as Russians, and practiced the same religion as Russians. They were, in a word, Russians. The violence in eastern Ukraine was not Putin's attempt to subjugate and break up a neighboring state by force; it was a homegrown insurrection seeking reunification with the motherland.

The spotlight was back on the West. Dalia Grybauskaitė, the hard-nosed president of Lithuania, declared that Putin was "at war with Europe." British Prime Minister David Cameron warned against a policy of appeasement, calling on Europe to avoid "repeating the mistakes made in Munich in 1938." The West's choice, in the words of U.S. Vice President Joe Biden, was between "paying now or paying double later." Prominent American politicians called on Obama to start sending weapons to Ukraine. "For God's sake," pleaded Senator John McCain on *Face the Nation*, "can't we help these people defend themselves?"

Ultimately, however, both Obama and Merkel shot down the idea of providing arms, which they feared would only exacerbate the conflict. Nonlethal supplies like night-vision goggles and blankets were okay; bullets and artillery were not. Ukrainians appreciated whatever they could get, even if, as Petro Poroshenko reminded the U.S. Congress a few weeks later, "one cannot win the war with blankets."

Instead of sending weapons, the West's response would be to further escalate its economic war. The obvious first step was to tighten the capital markets sanctions. Washington could match the EU and hit Sberbank, while Brussels could match the United States and hit Rosneft. Both could also expand the restrictions to cover Russian defense conglomerates like Rostec. But such penalties, promising as they were, would not develop their full force for another few months, when large debt payments by several major Russian companies came due. In the meantime, high global oil prices ensured that all was hunky-dory in Moscow.

Worse yet, the other component of the Western sanctions—export controls on technology for offshore oil drilling and fracking—looked like a bust. Two days after the shoot-down of MH17, a drilling rig operated by ExxonMobil set sail from Norway headed for the Kara Sea, a remote body of water in the Russian Arctic. It was the kickoff of a joint venture between Exxon and Rosneft that some believed could be worth hundreds of billions of dollars. Putin deemed the partnership essential to the future of Russia's oil industry. During the halcyon days of the "reset," he had told Obama that the deal was the most significant achievement of U.S.-Russian relations in decades. The "reset" was long over, but the Exxon-Rosneft partnership was still going strong. After moving the oil rig into the Arctic, the two companies would soon start drilling an exploratory well.

This was precisely the type of project the Western export controls were supposed to frustrate. Yet Exxon charged on, confident that it could make do with whatever technology it already had in Russia. Exxon, and oil giants more generally, were not like the banks that fretted in the face of American sanctions. Rex Tillerson, Exxon's CEO and one of the world's most powerful oil executives, was used to doing business in geopolitical hotspots. Russia, in particular, was familiar turf. During his rise at Exxon, Tillerson had at one point overseen his company's business in Russia and earned accolades for his management of Sakhalin-1, a complex oil and gas project in the Russian Far East that involved drilling a well that extended more than seven miles below the seafloor. There was more reputational risk for Exxon in fleeing the country at the first sign of danger than in sticking around after more circumspect firms had rushed for the exit.

Putin loved the Texas oilman with the charcoal eyebrows, whose macho vibe fit right in at the Kremlin. Just nine months before he seized Crimea, Putin had personally awarded Tillerson the Order of Friendship, one of Russia's highest honors. With billions of dollars and a critical relationship on the line, Tillerson took a stance against sanctions on Russia, which he aired publicly and privately with top Obama officials.

All the while, Exxon was pushing forward with its big Russia plans. Its executives even signed multiple contracts with Igor Sechin, Rosneft's CEO, after he had been personally sanctioned. (Exxon was later fined for doing this but then sued OFAC, claiming the agency had not given Exxon fair notice that the signatures were illegal, and won.) The sight of Exxon drilling for oil in the Russian Arctic as Putin's tanks wreaked havoc in Ukraine was not sending the right message to the Kremlin.

In addition to expanding the capital markets sanctions, the Obama ad-

*The oilman and the tsar: Rex Tillerson and Vladimir Putin
smile during the signing ceremony for a strategic
partnership between Exxon and Rosneft.*

ministration decided to tighten the restrictions on Russia's next generation
of oil projects. It would not just ban technology exports; it would prohibit
the provision of *all* services to such ventures, a move that would make a
continuation of Exxon's operations in the Kara Sea clearly illegal. It would
draw a line so bright that even the swaggering bigwigs of the oil industry
wouldn't dare cross it.

As Washington and Brussels finalized their sanctions packages, Poroshenko played his trump card. In recent months, Ukrainian troops had
amassed hundreds of dog tags from Russian soldiers killed or captured in
the Donbas. Poroshenko warned Putin that if he didn't accept a ceasefire,
Kyiv would post photos of the dog tags on the internet and call the Russian
soldiers' wives and mothers to reveal where their loved ones really were. Such
a move would cast doubt on Putin's assertion Russia was not fighting in
Ukraine, and it could rattle his domestic support. Within days, Ukrainian and
Russian representatives had signed a ceasefire deal in the Belarusian capital
of Minsk. Drawn from Poroshenko's peace plan, which envisioned trading
more local autonomy in Donetsk and Luhansk for the withdrawal of the
Russian-backed militias from the provinces, it became known as the Minsk
agreement.

A week later, America and Europe launched their new sectoral sanctions. Now all Russia's state-owned banks, including Sberbank, were barred from both U.S. and European capital markets. The same was true of Rosneft and Rostec. France announced it would not deliver the Mistral warships to Russia, canceling what was set to be the largest-ever sale of Western military hardware to Moscow. Exxon and other oil companies were given two weeks to shutter their projects in the Russian Arctic.

Tillerson had fought hard against the sanctions, but he knew when a battle was lost. He flew to Washington to meet with top officials including Jack Lew and Jeff Zients, the director of the White House's National Economic Council. He did not ask them to reconsider American policy. He just asked for a little more time for Exxon to wind down its operations in the Russian Arctic. This was needed, Tillerson explained, so Exxon could stop drilling without risking an oil spill in the Kara Sea.

Exxon was granted a short extension. Yet it dutifully complied with the new sanctions and suspended its joint venture with Rosneft. As Exxon closed up shop, Rosneft announced that the two companies had found some 930 million barrels of oil beneath the icy waters, one of the biggest new oil discoveries in years. So long as the new sanctions remained in place, those barrels might well stay underground forever.

For the moment, the war in the Donbas was frozen. But the effects of the economic war on Russia were heating up.

31

"Economy in Tatters"

In fashioning himself as a twenty-first-century tsar, Vladimir Putin layered Russia's power centers with loyalists. He stacked influential government posts and the C-suites of big businesses with cronies, whose qualifications often boiled down to practicing judo with Putin, hunting with him in Siberian forests, or owning property in his lakeside dacha cooperative outside St. Petersburg.

There was one notable exception, a section of the elite in which meritocracy reigned: the managers of the country's economic policy. The gold-plated résumé of a Putin confidante like Elvira Nabiullina, chair of the Central Bank of Russia, could easily pass muster at the IMF or the U.S. Federal Reserve: a PhD in economics from Moscow State University, the most prestigious institute of higher education in Russia; a stint as a World Fellow at Yale; jobs of growing responsibility in the Russian government, including five years as minister of economic development; and an appearance in *Forbes* as one of the "Most Powerful Women in Politics," a list that also included Angela Merkel and Michelle Obama.

Nabiullina took the wheel of Russia's central bank less than a year before the "little green men" raised the Russian flag in Sevastopol. Putin's Crimea gambit set off an initial rush of capital flight by jumpy foreign investors. But the macroeconomic situation soon stabilized. Oil prices were above $100 per barrel and showed no sign of falling, buoyed in part by the geopolitical uncertainty caused by Putin's war of aggression. Western sanctions came slowly and even when they hit, they were focused on the long run—and in the long run, another famous economist once said, we are all dead.

*Elvira Nabiullina: the highly credentialed technocrat
at the helm of Russia's central bank.*

Nonetheless, Russia's economic technocrats spent the spring of 2014 planning for the possibility of choppy waters ahead. As Jack Lew was corralling Treasury's wonks to develop ideas for sectoral sanctions, experts in the Kremlin held their own study sessions in which they examined America's economic war against Iran and drew lessons for what might await their own country. In a strange mirror image of what was transpiring in Washington, they quickly spotted Russia's core economic vulnerabilities, including its dependence on Western capital markets and technology for offshore oil drilling. They concluded that if the West got its act together on sanctions, Russia would be left with no other choice than to go hat in hand to China.

In May, Putin traveled to Shanghai to meet with Chinese leader Xi Jinping. The two men agreed to a massive, thirty-year deal in which Russia would supply China with natural gas through a new pipeline called "Power of Siberia." Valued at $400 billion, the deal entailed up to 38 billion cubic meters in annual gas shipments to China. This was a lot of gas but a drop in the bucket compared with the 150 billion cubic meters Gazprom sold to Europe annually. Still, the deal oozed with strategic significance. Shunned by the West, Putin was turning east. He even agreed to cover the full cost of the pipeline, a price tag north of $55 billion, much of which would line the pockets of his cronies.

Also in May, Igor Shuvalov, Russia's deputy prime minister, made a separate trip to China to discuss options to mitigate the two countries' reliance on the Western financial system. Within a few months, the overture bore fruit: Nabiullina's Central Bank of Russia closed a deal with the People's Bank of China to create a $25 billion currency swap line. This would allow Russia and China to settle some of their bilateral trade in rubles and renminbi, reducing their need to use dollars and euros.

The pivot to China was one part of a multifaceted strategy to reduce Russia's vulnerability to economic warfare. Another was Nabiullina's launch of SPFS, a Russian alternative to SWIFT, the Brussels-based financial messaging service. Under intense pressure from Washington, SWIFT had disconnected Iranian banks in 2012, a move that left Iran further isolated from the global financial system. The sanctions on Russia in 2014 were nowhere near as far-reaching, but Nabiullina and her colleagues at the central bank wanted to get in front of the problem.

Moscow also passed a regulation forcing Visa and MasterCard to process all domestic payments through a center based in Russia. The step was retaliation for the companies' decision to cut off Bank Rossiya when it was sanctioned in March. But it carried wider significance, as it would ensure Russians' credit cards would keep working inside the country regardless of the West's decisions on sanctions. To further bolster Russia's financial self-reliance, Nabiullina sped up the creation of Mir, a card payment system owned by the central bank, which would provide payment rails for domestic transactions and eventually issue its own branded credit cards. "Your card is free from external factors," Mir assured in its ads.

Even Putin's ban on food imports from the West, crass as it was, could be justified as a tactic to protect Russia's economy from sanctions. (Never mind that American law requires *all* U.S. sanctions programs to include exemptions for food, medicine, and other humanitarian products.) Sure, the ban hurt everyday Russians, who had to pay higher prices for staples at the grocery store and no longer had access to items like authentic Parmigiano Reggiano. But at least Russia would no longer depend on food from the West, and more Russians might even find employment as cheesemakers.

None of these defensive measures, however, addressed the fundamental weakness of Russia's economy: its sensitivity to world oil prices. As went the price of oil, so went Russia—and Moscow had little sway over the direction of oil prices. Putin's policies to centralize state control over the economy and quash the development of a thriving private sector had left his country with limited economic sovereignty. All this constrained Russia's options in a crisis and tied the fate of its economy to the whims of the global oil market.

In the fall of 2014, a crisis came. A few weeks after the signing of the Minsk agreement, as Exxon was preparing to leave the Russian Arctic, the price of oil started to fall. The main driver was a surge in supply, as U.S. shale producers kept on setting new production records. By the end of September, oil was trading at about $90 per barrel, the lowest level since 2012. The price was down 10 percent from the beginning of the month, 20 percent since a peak in June.

Russia's corporate titans were getting nervous. Igor Sechin, the boss of Rosneft, was confronting the grim reality of sliding oil prices, an abrupt suspension of the megadeal with Exxon, and exclusion from Western capital markets just as Rosneft faced some $20 billion in debt repayments over the coming months. Sechin was more than a friend to the Kremlin. His company's oil pumps were the heartbeat of Russia's economy.

Sechin had long sought to acquire one of his rivals, the smaller Russian oil company Bashneft. Now, with Exxon's departure from the Arctic putting Rosneft's future oil output at risk, Sechin was keener than ever to go ahead with the acquisition. Yet the owner of Bashneft, Vladimir Yevtushenkov, refused to sell. In September, Russian investigators placed Yevtushenkov under house arrest. The government nationalized Bashneft and eventually transferred a controlling stake to Rosneft.

This cloak-and-dagger spooked foreign investors. There were rumors of more expropriations and even capital controls. On the last day of September, Russia's exchange rate fell to a record low of nearly 40 rubles to the dollar. (It had opened the year at around 33 rubles to the dollar.) Putin sought to reassure investors, promising at an annual finance summit in Moscow that there would be "no capital controls whatsoever." Putin insisted he'd have no difficulty inviting investment back to Russia. "All I have to do is smile and show the devil is not as frightening as he seems," he said.

In truth, Russia's troubles were just beginning. Putin embarked on the Ukraine operation with a full war chest, including more than $500 billion in foreign exchange reserves. As the ruble slumped, these reserves gave Nabiullina ample ammunition to deploy. In the first ten days of October, she spent some $6 billion to prop up the ruble. Yet it did little to turn the tide.

On October 29, U.S. Federal Reserve chair Janet Yellen announced the end of quantitative easing, a post-2008 policy in which the Fed had bought up tens of billions of dollars' worth of assets each month. The move tightened credit conditions around the globe, weakening oil demand at the same time as supply was booming, further depressing oil prices. Additionally, market expectations that the Fed would raise interest rates led to a surging dollar. In 2014, for the first time since the turn of the century, the dollar appreciated against all other major currencies. As oil is priced in dollars, the dollar upswing made oil more expensive to buyers. This put even more downward pressure on oil prices.

By the start of November, oil was down to $80 per barrel, and the ruble continued to drop apace. The scale of the crisis was coming into full view. Rosneft owed Western lenders some $10 billion before the end of the year. Other Russian banks and corporations were on the hook for $32 billion in debt repayments in December. These debts were mostly denominated in dollars, not rubles, and with each passing day, the ruble was worth less in dollar terms.

As the ruble tumbled and inflows of petrodollars shrunk, it was unclear how all this debt would be repaid. Russian businesses were desperate for dollars. Rosneft alone appealed to the state for a $50 billion bailout. Russian firms slashed investment to conserve cash for debt repayments, and demand for safety-deposit boxes shot up as ordinary Russians hoarded foreign currency.

Putin's popularity had skyrocketed in the wake of the Crimea annexation. His approval rating hit an all-time high of 88 percent. But it was doubtful Russians would remain so supportive if their economy went into free fall. Plummeting living standards would be a high price to pay for new classroom maps that shaded Crimea in the same color as Russia.

Putin charged Elvira Nabiullina with navigating the storm. On November 5, Nabiullina hiked interest rates to 9.5 percent. The central bank stood ready "at any moment," she declared, to deploy far more of its hard currency reserves to support the ruble. She did not downplay the stakes: Russia was on the brink of a full-fledged financial crisis.

Yet the storm got worse. At the end of November, market watchers held their breath as OPEC, the Saudi-led oil cartel, met to weigh production cuts.

With oil prices falling, many expected a sizable cut. Several OPEC members were clamoring for one. But Saudi Arabia was opposed. The oil kingdom could endure a period of low prices, but it refused to cede market share to upstarts like America's shale producers. So OPEC decided to keep production flat, betting that plunging prices would kill the business model of U.S. shale and drive it out of the market.

This was bad news for Moscow. The price of oil had been sliced in half since the summer. At $60 per barrel, it now stood at the lowest level since the depths of the 2008 financial crisis. Scores of Russians canceled holiday travel plans amid the ruble's tumble. Nabiullina came under fire. A member of Russia's parliament called for a criminal investigation of the Central Bank of Russia, tarring it as an "enemy of the nation" and accusing Nabiullina of seeking to inflict "maximum evil." But as the crisis entered a decisive phase, Putin stood by his captain.

On Thursday, December 11, Nabiullina raised interest rates again, this time to 10.5 percent. Later that day, she turned to Rosneft. The oil giant faced a $7 billion loan repayment in just ten days. Unable to raise this money on Western capital markets, Rosneft issued 625 billion rubles worth of bonds, the equivalent of around $10 billion. With backing from Nabiullina, Rosneft sold the bonds at yields below those on comparable Russian government securities. On Monday, December 15, the Russian central bank accepted the Rosneft bonds as collateral in exchange for rubles. The complex scheme amounted, in effect, to a bailout of Rosneft by the Central Bank of Russia.

Markets were not impressed. Even though oil prices stood pat on Monday, the ruble fell by 10 percent against the dollar—the worst single-day rout since Russia defaulted on its domestic debt in 1998. The reasons were something of a mystery, but the most plausible explanation is that Rosneft sold rubles en masse for the dollars it needed to repay its debt. Later in the day, Nabiullina deployed billions of dollars of the central bank's reserves to try to catch the ruble's fall. It was all for naught.

Putin called an emergency meeting. He deliberated with Nabiullina and a small circle of advisors late into the night about what to do next. At 1:00 a.m., they rendered their decision. Nabiullina announced that the central bank had lifted its benchmark interest rate to 17 percent. The massive, 650-basis-point rate hike was meant to finally provide a floor to the ruble's descent. It was interpreted, however, as a sign of panic. In what became known as "Black Tuesday," the ruble nosedived. At one point, it plunged all the way down to 80 rubles to the dollar before closing at around 70. All told, the ruble had lost half its value in just a few months.

Russians lined up at banks, anxiously waiting to convert their rubles into dollars and euros as they watched their savings slip away on flashing currency-exchange signs. Others dashed to appliance stores to scoop up washing machines, televisions, and refrigerators. All these widgets seemed a safer bet than a pile of rubles. Volvo stopped selling cars at its dealerships in Russia, and Apple suspended sales of iPhones in the country.

The next day, a million Sberbank customers received anonymous text messages warning that withdrawals were about to be blocked. The messages were fake, perhaps the work of independent cyber trolls or foreign agents, but in the climate of panic, they seemed plausible. Snaking queues formed at Sberbank ATMs, and within a week, customers withdrew 1.3 trillion rubles, equal to more than $20 billion. It was a bank run of epic proportions.

Nabiullina had charted a familiar course: raising interest rates and spending down reserves. It hadn't worked. Putin's security council inserted a handful of Kremlin insiders into key posts at the Central Bank of Russia. Nabiullina was allowed to stay, but her orthodox methods had to go. It was time for strong-arm tactics.

Moscow quickly imposed a set of informal capital controls. These forced Russia's biggest exporters—the only segment of the economy that retained access to hard currency—to convert their dollars into rubles. Putin also offered amnesty to wealthy Russians who would bring their cash back to the motherland, no questions asked. The government stepped in to rescue Trust Bank, a high-street lender, and UTair, the country's third-largest airline, both of which had gone insolvent. And it recapitalized Russia's largest state-owned banks, furnishing them with nearly a trillion and a half rubles to weather the storm.

The extraordinary measures stabilized the ruble, but the price tag was hefty. By the end of 2014, Russia's foreign exchange reserves had fallen below $390 billion—a decline of some $120 billion from just before Putin's seizure of Crimea. Investors had siphoned more than $150 billion of capital out of Russia, making 2014 by far the worst year of capital flight in the country's history. To kick off the new year, S&P downgraded Russia's credit rating to junk status, a blemish not seen since the early years of Putin's rule. The cost of credit default swaps on Russian debt exceeded that of similar insurance on the debt of Pakistan and Lebanon. Russia's economy was headed for a stifling recession.

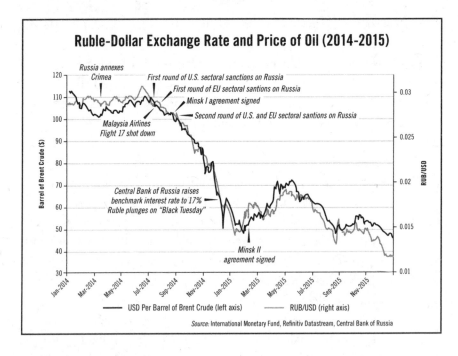

For everyday Russians, the ordeal of December 2014 and its aftermath were a lot more painful than the 2008 financial crisis. Real incomes were down by roughly 10 percent for much of the following year, the steepest drop since the late 1990s—before Putin's ascent to the presidency. Putin had consolidated power on a wave of rising oil prices and living standards. Now, that legacy was in danger.

Western sanctions were finally having an effect. Daleep Singh, the man who first suggested cutting off Russian access to capital markets, had been right: the sanctions had triggered a negative feedback loop, which the collapse of oil prices was now accelerating. Even Putin conceded that sanctions were responsible for at least 25 percent of the ruble's decline. Alexei Kudrin, another respected economist in the Russian president's orbit, thought it was closer to 40 percent.

On January 20, Obama stood before a packed house at the U.S. Capitol to deliver his State of the Union address. When he got to foreign policy, he looked as poised as ever. "Last year, as we were doing the hard work of imposing sanctions along with our allies," he said, "Mr. Putin's aggression, it was suggested, was a masterful display of strategy and strength. That's what I heard from some folks." Obama flashed a slight grin. "Well, today, it is America that stands strong and united with our allies, while Russia is isolated with its economy in tatters."

America's economic weapons could throw even a big power like Russia off balance. Sanctions had not, however, changed facts on the ground in Ukraine. Russian flags still fluttered over Crimea, and Kremlin-backed militias still ruled swaths of the Donbas. And as Obama's speech beamed to TV screens around the world, Putin's fighters were readying a new offensive.

32

Back from the Edge

January in Moscow was cold, dark, and snowy. As Russians gathered for Orthodox Christmas amid a severe, barely contained economic slump, a creeping doubt clouded their celebrations. It was impossible not to wonder, if only in the inner sanctum of their minds, whether the Kremlin had overreached in Ukraine.

Vladimir Putin was a gambler, but he could adapt when his fortunes changed. On New Year's Day, the first prime minister of the self-proclaimed Donetsk People's Republic conceded that the *Novorossiya* project was a "false start" and "a dream that was not brought to life." Soon thereafter, the leaders of both Russian-backed, breakaway statelets in the Donbas formally suspended their plans to build *Novorossiya*, the imaginary nation encompassing some 40 percent of Ukraine's territory. (By comparison, the separatists currently occupied less than 5 percent of Ukraine.) Putin and his imperial dreams were humbled. The Kremlin threw out maps of *Novorossiya*—or perhaps stowed them in a filing cabinet to revisit at a later date.

In Washington, the mood was more sanguine, if also tinged with uncertainty. In December, as the Russian economy teetered on the brink, Daleep Singh delivered a message to Jack Lew. "We have the capacity to deliver a full-fledged knockout blow financially, if we want to," Singh said. He provided this information out of a sense of duty, not because he thought it was the right thing to do. In fact, it was an explicit objective of U.S. policy to *prevent* Russia from spiraling into an uncontrolled financial crisis. The risk of contagion was too high.

"There were pretty substantial collateral risks in Europe in particular,"

Lew explained. "And we had spent a lot of time between 2011 and 2014 worrying about whether a European economic collapse would lead to another round of recession in the United States." Besides, it was not at all clear that wrecking the Russian economy would encourage a retreat from Ukraine any more than the existing sanctions would. Russians were a tough lot. "One of the things they would say is, 'We survived Leningrad, we could survive this,'" Lew said. "Their definition of what they were willing to tolerate was well beyond the realm of what we would consider tolerable."

Instead, in late December, Washington and Brussels unveiled new sanctions targeted narrowly at Russian-occupied Crimea. The restrictions made it illegal for Western companies to invest in or trade with any part of Crimea's economy. The goal, in Dan Fried's words, was "to turn Putin's war prize into a liability." All of the peninsula's basic infrastructure, from electricity to water, still depended on Ukraine. Crimea was not even connected to Russia by land; they were divided by the Kerch Strait, a waterway several miles wide. None of this was tenable if Putin wanted to make the annexation real and lasting, meaning he would have to spend billions of dollars to incorporate the territory into Russia. Building the necessary infrastructure would be especially hard without help from the West. As Victoria Nuland put it, "If you bite off a piece of another country, it will dry up in your mouth."

The approach to Crimea recalled the West's reaction after the Soviet Union occupied Estonia, Latvia, and Lithuania in 1940. For half a century, Western leaders refused to recognize Moscow's claims over the Baltic states. By the time the three countries regained their independence in 1991, they had retained their national identities and were ready to thrive as independent states within Europe. The Crimea sanctions were a more aggressive reprisal of this policy: in word and deed, the West would do its best to stall the peninsula's assimilation into Russia.

By creating standalone penalties on Crimea, moreover, America and Europe were signaling that all other sanctions on Russia were fair game at the negotiating table. They assessed that while Putin would never reverse the annexation of Crimea, he might be willing to pull out of the Donbas, so that was the place to play their cards. The upshot for Putin was that if he ended the war in Ukraine's east, he could free Russia from the hardest-hitting sanctions. Exxon could return to drill in the Arctic, and Rosneft and Sberbank could once again borrow from Western banks to their hearts' content. Except for in Crimea, Russia and the West would reestablish normal economic ties.

Whether Putin was open to such a deal was unclear. The Minsk agreement was by now barely worth the paper it was written on. Poroshenko took preliminary steps to give Donetsk and Luhansk more autonomy, but the Kremlin-backed militias did not leave the provinces. The fighting eased yet never stopped. Then, in January, the militias made a push to capture Donetsk International Airport, setting off the worst hostilities in months. Relentless shelling turned the place into a disaster zone, a shadow of the airport that had served more than a million passengers back in 2013. Still, the site carried symbolic weight, and it had been held by a handful of gutsy Ukrainian paratroopers for months. After a bloody battle, Putin's fighters took the airport in late January. The Minsk agreement was dead.

U.S. officials feared that Russia's next move would be to make a play for Mariupol, an industrial port on Ukraine's southeastern coast. Mariupol was sandwiched between Crimea and the Russian-occupied parts of the Donbas. If Putin snatched it, he would secure a land bridge to the annexed territory. In anticipation of a potential attack, Ukraine fortified Mariupol's defenses, while Western governments readied another round of sanctions, including a so-called "reject program" that would apply to a few big Russian banks and companies. The penalties would go beyond the capital markets restrictions and ban all payments in dollars and euros; if the targeted Russian firms tried to pay a Western bank, their funds would simply bounce back. It would pack much of the punch of Iran-style blocking sanctions without the disruption of a full asset freeze. The threat of this reject program, coupled with Ukraine's hardening defenses around the city, was intended to protect Mariupol with both an economic and a military tripwire.

Instead of attacking Mariupol, however, Russian-backed fighters launched an offensive to take Debaltseve, a small, little-known town that was the site of a critical highway crossing and rail junction. Debaltseve was a hub for transporting the Donbas's rich industrial output, including coal, iron, and steel. It also connected Donetsk and Luhansk, the two Donbas provinces that Russia was trying to peel away from Ukraine.

As the fighting around Debaltseve intensified, the Obama administration reopened debate on lethal military aid. Ukraine's army was pleading for Javelins—portable, American-made anti-tank missiles that would help fend off the invading columns of Russian armored vehicles. Most of the players in the Situation Room, including officials from the Pentagon and State, supported sending Javelins to Ukraine. So did Vice President Joe Biden. But Obama remained unconvinced.

Cautious by nature, Obama was also influenced by Angela Merkel, who was firmly against arming the Ukrainians. Since the collapse of the Minsk agreement, she and François Hollande had revived the Normandy Format and were vigorously pushing for a new peace deal. The German and French leaders held regular calls with Putin and Poroshenko, and they flew to Kyiv and Moscow to meet with them in person. Both were spooked by the rapid deterioration of Russia's economy, which threatened to spill over into their own countries. They hadn't expected the sanctions, supposedly scalpel-like in their precision, to inflict such a gaping wound.

Merkel, whose Christian Democratic Union governed Germany in a coalition with the Moscow-friendly Social Democrats, was under domestic political pressure to ease up on Russia. Her foreign minister, the Social Democrat Frank-Walter Steinmeier, counseled against "turning the screw" any further, while Sigmar Gabriel, the Social Democrat economy minister, warned that more sanctions would "risk a conflagration" and that the West should not "force Russia to its knees."

France, for its part, was reeling from a horrific terrorist attack in Paris, in which Islamist extremists gunned down a dozen people in an assault on the satirical newspaper *Charlie Hebdo*. Hollande considered terrorism a far bigger threat than Russia, which might even act as an ally in the global fight against jihadism. The French president said publicly that he hoped sanctions on Russia could be lifted if the Normandy Format made progress, and he was inclined to believe Putin had no interest in the Donbas. "Putin doesn't want to annex eastern Ukraine," Hollande affirmed. "He told me that."

Merkel and Hollande both wanted the Ukraine conflict to just go away. On February 8, they held a conference call with Putin and Poroshenko to discuss a successor to the failed Minsk agreement. After the call, Merkel jetted to Washington for an Oval Office meeting with Obama. She knew that the White House was close to a decision on sending Javelins to Ukraine. She wanted to tell Obama personally that such a move would threaten her diplomacy with Putin.

Most of America's political and foreign policy establishments favored arming the Ukrainians. On the day of Merkel's arrival, Senator John McCain sent a message to the chancellor on German public radio. "How many people have to die in Ukraine before we help them defend themselves?" McCain asked.

But Obama cared more about Merkel's perspective than McCain's. From a low point after the NSA spying scandal, German-American relations were warming again, thanks in no small part to close cooperation between Washington and Berlin on the Ukraine crisis. In addition, Merkel had previously stiffened the EU's spine for tough sanctions. Obama didn't take that for granted. He decided against the Javelin shipments. Days later, Merkel and Hollande spent sixteen straight hours in negotiations with Putin and Poroshenko in Minsk. They emerged from the marathon talks with a new deal bearing the inelegant and inauspicious name "Minsk II."

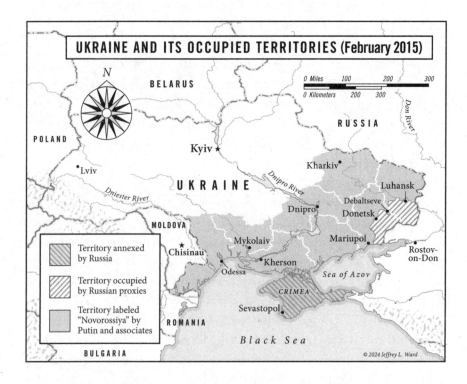

Merkel and Hollande's diplomacy not only swayed Washington against arming the Ukrainians; it also undercut momentum for further sanctions. Their red line was painted in front of Mariupol, not Debaltseve, and there was no consensus in the EU on kicking Russia's economy when it was down.

Minsk II was more detailed than its predecessor, but its basic contours were the same. Ukraine would afford more autonomy to Russian-speaking regions like Donetsk and Luhansk in exchange for control over these eastern provinces. If Putin was serious about implementing it, the deal could provide a path out of the conflict.

The early signs did not inspire confidence. Putin's fighters around Debaltseve paid no heed to Minsk II. The deal didn't say who should control the town, so they rained down shells on it with reckless abandon. Hundreds were killed and injured, and on February 18, Ukrainian forces withdrew. "There's no city left," said a Ukrainian soldier, nursing his wounds after a bitter defeat.

Putin's *Novorossiya* fantasy was on hold. But Ukrainians could not have their country back. If the Russian president couldn't claim the Donbas for himself, he would turn the region into a festering hellhole that drained Ukraine of blood and treasure and prevented it from moving toward the West. While this was not the triumph Putin had imagined, it was still a kind of victory.

Putin had ended 2014 on his back foot. Yet less than two months into 2015, he had his mojo back. He'd always seen the West as decadent and weak, and its sanctions policy appeared to have proved him right: America and Europe pushed the Russian economy to the edge but then backed down. Putin could rightly feel vindicated. His next step would be to rid Russia of sanctions altogether. And he would do it not by leaving Ukraine, but rather by sabotaging the West from within.

33

From Russia with Bribes

Vladimir Putin did not doubt the impact of sanctions on Russia. He just doubted the West's resolve to stick to them.

In Russia, the Kremlin held corporate titans in a vise; if they crossed Putin, they'd lose their livelihoods or even their lives. But in the West, Putin believed, the situation was reversed. The private sectors in America and Europe would never sit idly by as they missed out on business opportunities. No government in Berlin could survive if it stiffed German industrialists. Obama might be fine with squeezing Exxon's profits, but he wouldn't be president much longer. Besides, the EU had twenty-eight members, which had to unanimously agree to keep the sanctions in place every six months. Surely a Hungary or a Cyprus could be bought.

Putin set out to find and exploit the weak links in the West's sanctions coalition. In addition to easing the pressure on Russia's economy, undermining sanctions would have the geopolitical benefit of sowing division among Western allies. If Hungary vetoed the continuation of sanctions, imagine how anti-Russian hard-liners in the Polish and Lithuanian governments would react. Would they grin and bear it? Much more likely was an internal crisis that could very well tear the EU apart.

In late 2014, at a summit of world leaders in Brisbane, Australia, Jean-Claude Juncker, a Luxembourgish politician who was serving as president of the European Commission, had warned Putin that trying to split the transatlantic alliance was a fool's errand. Putin's response was self-assured: "I won't fail."

Putin's first target was Greece. In January 2015, Greek voters elected a government led by Syriza, an anti-establishment party of the radical left. The country was in the throes of a vicious, years-long economic crisis, with nearly 27 percent unemployment and one in six people going hungry on a daily basis. Alexis Tsipras, the new prime minister, vowed to fight the austerity measures imposed on his country by the troika, a group consisting of the European Commission, the European Central Bank, and the IMF. With so many problems at home, Greece's willingness to make sacrifices on behalf of Ukraine was limited.

Almost immediately, Putin associates began cultivating members of the new government in Athens. They found a receptive audience. "Greece has no interest in imposing sanctions on Russia," said the country's new energy minister, days after Syriza took power. "We have no differences with Russia and the Russian people."

The EU's sectoral sanctions were due to expire in July. Now, in the wake of Russia's victory in Debaltseve, European leaders debated whether to extend them until the end of the year. Doing so would harmonize the sanctions with the timeline of Minsk II, which required Moscow to restore Kyiv's control over its eastern border by the end of 2015.

With the sanctions extension hanging in the balance, Putin invited Tsipras to Moscow for a tête-à-tête in April. Tsipras was at odds with Brussels over debt negotiations. Putin was at odds with Brussels over sanctions. Perhaps they could strike an alliance of convenience—a Greek veto on sanctions in exchange for Russian help in reducing Greece's mountain of debt.

Tsipras's visit to Moscow "could not have come at a better time," Putin said. Standing beside Putin at the Kremlin, Tsipras underscored his opposition to sanctions. "We have repeatedly declared our disagreement," he affirmed. "This is our point of view that we constantly express to our colleagues in the EU. We don't think that this is a fruitful decision. It's practically an economic war."

Tsipras left the Kremlin with the promise of a potential pipeline deal that would bring Russian gas to Europe via Greece, plus €5 billion in advance funds from Moscow linked to future profits. Upon returning home, Tsipras was ebullient. He told his finance minister, Yanis Varoufakis, that he had secured a commitment from Putin for the €5 billion. Two weeks later, Gazprom CEO Alexey Miller flew to Athens to continue talks on the pipeline with Tsipras and his energy minister.

By June, Greece was nearing a default to the IMF, and Tsipras was eager to turn his flirtation with Putin into a committed relationship. That month, he returned to Russia for the St. Petersburg International Economic Forum, a glitzy business conference. Tsipras's mere attendance at the event, which all other Western leaders were boycotting to protest Russia's war in Ukraine, was a sign of his determination. But Putin spurned him. The pipeline deal he'd promised Tsipras two months earlier might be lucrative for Greece in the long term, but the looming debt default meant that Tsipras needed tens of billions of euros *now*, and Russia did not have that kind of money. Only Germany—the most influential player in the troika—could solve Tsipras's problems. "You must strike a deal with the Germans," Putin told Tsipras.

Anton Siluanov, Russia's finance minister, followed up with a phone call to Varoufakis to explain Putin's decision. As Varoufakis recalled, Siluanov told him that "international sanctions were depleting Moscow's coffers and unfortunately he did not have the capacity to help us." The predicament was ironic. Russia was trying to bribe its way out of sanctions, but those same sanctions pinched the cash it had available to pay bribes.

Russia's attempt to win over the Greeks had faltered. Shortly after Tsipras returned from St. Petersburg, he and other EU leaders agreed to extend sectoral sanctions on Russia for another six months. Later in the summer, Tsipras accepted an €86 billion bailout from the EU.

Putin tried his luck with other small EU members. He dangled a sweetheart loan in front of Cypriot President Nicos Anastasiades. He offered Hungarian strongman Viktor Orbán two Russian-made nuclear reactors plus financing to pay for them. He plied Slovakia's Prime Minister Robert Fico and several other European leaders with cheap gas.

Each time, Dan Fried and his team traveled to Europe and reminded the sanctions skeptics that America cared about their positions just as much as Russia did. In Hungary and Slovakia, whose ruling parties displayed antidemocratic tendencies that irked Washington, Fried was the highest-level U.S. government visitor in years. "This is policy, this isn't purity," he explained. "I'll talk to just about anybody in pursuit of a sanctions policy that helps constrain Putin and his war against Ukraine." In Hungary, Fried met with Péter Szijjártó, Orbán's foreign minister, and in Slovakia, he met with Fico himself. During both visits, he made a point not to scold his interlocutors but rather to listen to their concerns in earnest. In the end, both governments stuck to the EU consensus on sanctions.

If Putin couldn't buy off the weakest states in the sanctions coalition, perhaps he could win over the strongest. At the same St. Petersburg conference at which Putin rebuffed Tsipras, Gazprom agreed to build a new pipeline across the Baltic Sea to Germany. Known as Nord Stream 2, it would supply Europe with 55 billion cubic meters of natural gas per year, substantially reducing the EU's reliance on gas pipelines that crossed Ukraine. In the process, Nord Stream 2 would also deal a major strategic blow to Ukraine by depriving Kyiv of critical gas transit fees and enabling Russia to shut off Ukraine's gas supplies without affecting its European customers. Gazprom would pay for half of the project, while the remainder would come from a consortium of European energy companies, including Britain's Shell, Austria's OMV, and Germany's Wintershall, a subsidiary of chemical giant BASF.

Merkel maintained that Nord Stream 2 was a purely commercial venture. Aside from Gazprom, none of the major shareholders was a state-owned company. Berlin was not using any taxpayer money to finance the project, and nothing about the pipeline violated sanctions. America and Europe had explicitly agreed that their economic war against Russia would not touch its gas industry. The commitment was so strong that they refused to cut off Gazprom from Western capital markets, a penalty they had readily applied to Rosneft. Washington didn't even impose any personal sanctions on Gazprom's boss, Alexey Miller, making him the most prominent Putin crony to avoid that fate.

Despite all this, Nord Stream 2 angered many of Merkel's European colleagues. How could she insist on EU unity on sanctions when Germany was inking new megadeals with Russia? It smacked of hypocrisy. Poland and Lithuania opposed the pipeline—as was to be expected—but so, too, did Italy and Slovakia. Matteo Renzi, Italy's prime minister, was incensed. Many small Italian firms had given up good business in Russia. Now German industrialists were reaching out their hands.

By December, Ukraine still did not control its eastern provinces. Another six-month renewal of EU sanctions looked like a no-brainer. But Renzi was so mad about Nord Stream 2 that he held up the decision in order to force a debate over the pipeline. The EU eventually renewed the sanctions, but Putin's efforts to sow discord in the EU were clearly having an effect.

Putin was right: German leaders were not prepared to take on big business at home. In addition to defending Nord Stream 2, Merkel's government buried its head in the sand when the German industrial powerhouse Siemens sold seven gas turbines to Russia. Like the pipeline project, this deal did not technically run afoul of sanctions. But there was strong evidence that Moscow intended to use the turbines in Crimea, despite Russian claims to the contrary, and that they were a central part of Putin's efforts to build new infrastructure on the peninsula. Transferring the turbines to Crimea would be a clear violation of sanctions.

It did not take a sleuth to uncover Moscow's intentions. Two new power plants under construction in Crimea were compatible only with Siemens turbines. Fried and other U.S. officials warned Siemens that the turbines were almost certainly destined for Crimea. Reuters even published a news story revealing Russia's plans. But Siemens CEO Joe Kaeser had made his priorities plain on a trip to Moscow right after the annexation of Crimea. "Siemens has been present in Russia since 1853—a presence that has survived many highs and lows," he said. "We want to maintain the conversation even in today's politically difficult times." Siemens delivered the turbines and pleaded ignorance when Russia promptly transferred them to Crimea. The German government stood by the company throughout the whole ordeal.

Putin's wooing of German industry did not end the sanctions that were already in place. But it sapped Germany's—and by extension the EU's—enthusiasm for additional measures. Even as the Kremlin dragged its feet on implementing Minsk II and kept on supporting militias in the Donbas, the EU took no further action. That standstill was in itself a win for Putin, as it gave Russia's economy time to recover. And hopefully, eventually, the fighting in the Donbas would congeal into a frozen and forgotten conflict, the West would move on, and the sanctions would crumble.

34

"Dark Thought"

On September 30, 2015, at 9:00 a.m., a three-star Russian general unexpectedly turned up at the U.S. embassy in Baghdad. His message was curt. Russian warplanes would soon conduct airstrikes in Syria, and the United States should vacate the skies immediately. "If you have forces in the area we request they leave," he said.

U.S. officials did not honor his request. Russian bombs smashed targets across Syria an hour later.

Russia's new air campaign in Syria was a dramatic escalation of its military's involvement in the country. The Kremlin's public line was that the strikes targeted ISIS, a terrorist group that had taken control of large swaths of Syria and neighboring Iraq, but in reality, they were aimed at the various opponents of brutal Syrian dictator and stalwart Putin ally Bashar al-Assad.

The air campaign began just two days after Putin met with Obama on the sidelines of the UN General Assembly in New York, their first bilateral meeting since the start of the Ukraine crisis. Obama had agreed to the sit-down because of Russia's military buildup in Syria. America was already leading a global coalition to uproot ISIS, and Putin was eager to gain a seat at the table.

Putin's principal aims in Syria were to shore up Assad's rule and secure a foothold for Russia in the Middle East as America attempted, however fitfully, to shift its geopolitical focus elsewhere. But there was another, less obvious element to the gambit. By the fall of 2015, Syria's brutal civil war and the concomitant rise of ISIS in the region had sent millions of refugees fleeing into neighboring countries. Many eventually made their way to Europe, where over a million people sought asylum in 2015, the largest number since World War II. Addressing the root cause of this crisis—the Syrian civil war—was now the top foreign policy priority for America and the EU's most powerful members. Putin knew that if he dangled cooperation in the fight against ISIS in front of Western leaders, they might set aside their concerns about Ukraine.

This strategy had worked well for Russia before. Early in their presidencies, both George W. Bush and Barack Obama had excused Moscow's past misdeeds in hopes of securing cooperation on what they perceived as the most pressing issues of the day. America was inclined to view Russia as a swing state in other policy areas—from Afghanistan to Iran to counterterrorism—as opposed to a country worthy of a policy itself. The rise of ISIS presented Putin with a fresh opportunity to exploit this tendency.

Many European leaders were ready for a reset, too. In November 2015, Jean-Claude Juncker, the president of the European Commission, sent Putin a letter asking for closer ties between the EU and Russia, "which to my regret have not been able to develop over the past year." He went so far as to propose a trade pact between the EU and Putin's pet project, the Eurasian Economic Union. That same month, a gruesome Islamist terror attack shook Paris, with ISIS assailants killing 130 people in several coordinated shootings and suicide bombings across the city. Two weeks after the attack, François Hollande flew to Moscow and called for a "broad coalition" to fight ISIS in Syria.

Some European governments were now pushing for a "partial lifting" of sanctions in exchange for "partial implementation" of Minsk II, the peace agreement negotiated with French and German assistance more than nine months prior. By now, it seemed clear that Putin wouldn't allow Ukraine to control its eastern border, contrary to what he had pledged under the agreement. But if he gave up some political prisoners or ordered his militias in the Donbas to stop firing at Ukrainian positions, maybe that was enough for the EU to remove some of the sanctions.

The EU members that felt most threatened by Russia—Poland, the Baltics, and the Nordics—were nervous. Lithuania's foreign minister, Linas Linkevičius, expressed surprise that Juncker's letter to Putin hadn't mentioned Russian aggression in Ukraine or Western sanctions. As he saw it, Ukraine was "the litmus test of Russian behavior"—and the signals from Moscow on that front were not good. "We do not see either a clear or a constructive change in policy," Linkevičius said. And yet, there were signs that other Western leaders were weighing some sort of compromise with Russia on counterter-rorism that might, in effect, leave Ukraine to its own devices.

Speaking alongside Linkevičius on a panel in Brussels in early December 2015, Dan Fried acknowledged that the Lithuanian diplomat could be forgiven "if the dark thought crossed his mind about that kind of trade-off." But Fried assured him, "We are not interested in that kind of trade-off."

Two weeks later, John Kerry traveled to Moscow for a three-hour meeting with Putin in the Kremlin focused on Syria. Afterward, Kerry said that he and Putin found some "common ground." But he quashed the idea of a "partial lifting" of sanctions. "Russia has a simple choice: fully implement Minsk or continue to face economically damaging sanctions," Kerry declared at the Munich Security Conference in February 2016. "Put plainly, Russia can prove by its actions that it will respect Ukraine's sovereignty, just as it insists on respect for its own."

Coming from America's secretary of state, who was publicly seeking closer cooperation with Russia on Syria, these words carried weight. Washington would stand firm behind sanctions until Ukraine regained control over the Donbas, no matter how long it took, and no matter how many shiny objects Putin waved in the air.

The West's economic clash with Russia settled into a predictable rhythm. Anxieties over a European veto of sanctions had calmed, and the United States had rejected the possibility of another reset with Putin over Syria. Every six months, Brussels dutifully renewed its sanctions while Washington performed "sanctions maintenance," which consisted of updating sanctions lists to close loopholes and check evasion schemes. The economic war cooled into an uneasy stalemate. There was still the occasional skirmish but little movement on the front lines.

Putin had tried to kill the sanctions using a variety of methods, from bribing Greece and Hungary to forging pipeline deals with German industrialists and casting himself as an indispensable partner in the fight against ISIS. None of them worked, at least not fully. But he did secure a freeze, a partial victory.

His next target would not be a politician or business tycoon. It would be the minds of American voters.

35

A Way Out via Golden Escalator

With the Obama administration in its last year, the president and his cabinet were thinking about their legacy. Treasury Secretary Jack Lew was one of the few officials who joined at the very beginning and never left. He had worked on countless issues of consequence, but he deemed the administration's approach to sanctions novel and important enough to merit a farewell address. The date was set for March 30, 2016, and he chose the Carnegie Endowment for International Peace, a Washington think tank, as the venue.

"Economic sanctions have become a powerful force in service of clear and coordinated foreign policy objectives—smart power for situations where diplomacy alone is insufficient, but military force is not the right response," Lew said. He hailed the dramatic success of the economic war against Iran, which led to a deal that rolled back the country's nuclear program.

He also applauded the fine line America walked to impose sanctions on Russia. "While some called for the United States to respond with everything in our sanctions arsenal, President Obama directed us to develop a coordinated response in concert with our allies, that would deliver strong but measured pressure, and which could preserve our options and be ratcheted up or down over time depending on Russia's behavior," Lew explained. The United States "sought out asymmetries—particular areas where the Russian government relied upon European and U.S. technology and financing, but where sanctions would have the smallest possible spillover effects on us, our allies, and the Russian people."

He concluded his speech with a warning. "Sanctions should not be used lightly. They can strain diplomatic relationships, introduce instability into the global economy, and impose real costs on companies here and abroad," Lew said. The biggest risk was "overuse," which "could threaten the central role of the U.S. financial system globally, not to mention the effectiveness of our sanctions in the future." Unless Washington was careful, "overuse of sanctions could undermine our leadership position within the global economy."

It was remarkable that Lew, who had led Treasury through the Iran deal and the Ukraine crisis, would sound such a cautionary note. But it was indicative of just how integral economic warfare had become to U.S. foreign policy. The Obama administration, Lew believed, had used sanctions wisely, but this wisdom was hard-earned, and successors may not be so judicious. To guard against that risk, he was trying to lay out some best practices. And in his telling, the campaigns against Iran and Russia were both examples of best practice, even though the latter did not produce a clear-cut victory like the former did.

It was hard to argue with Lew's verdict on Iran. But the Russia case was more ambiguous. Putin's war against Ukraine had taken the White House by surprise. Suddenly confronted with an act of aggression by a fellow nuclear superpower, many in the Obama administration saw sanctions as the least bad option. Wary of rattling Russia's economy, the United States limited the first round of penalties to personal sanctions on Putin's cronies. The measures crimped the cronies' lifestyles. Italian authorities seized several villas in Sardinia and a hotel in Rome owned by Arkady Rotenberg, Putin's judo partner. Gennady Timchenko liquidated his shares in Gunvor, the lucrative oil trading firm he founded.

But Putin compensated each of these men handsomely for their troubles. Rotenberg was handed a multibillion-dollar deal to build a twelve-mile bridge, the longest in Europe, which would run across the Kerch Strait and connect Crimea to the Russian mainland. Both Timchenko and Rotenberg were given juicy, no-bid contracts to construct parts of the Power of Siberia gas pipeline to China. They partied less on the Mediterranean, but they kept their wealth and stayed close to Putin. There was no evidence these sanctions affected Russian foreign policy at all.

The sectoral sanctions were more significant. It took months to design economic weapons tough enough to change Putin's calculus without splintering the transatlantic alliance or threatening the health of the global economy. With diplomats like Dan Fried logging thousands of airline miles and financial whizzes like Daleep Singh designing "scalpel-like" sanctions, Washington eventually found the balance.

In strictly economic terms, the sanctions worked beyond anyone's imagination. Accelerated by the collapse of global oil prices, they sent Russia's economy into a tailspin. In 2015, Russia was one of the world's worst-performing economies, ranking alongside war-torn Libya and South Sudan. The value of the ruble against the dollar was chopped in half and never recovered. Inflation spiked to more than 15 percent. Russia's foreign exchange reserves dipped below $400 billion for the first time since 2009. It would take years to build them back up.

Most importantly, sanctions put a lid on Russia's economy that would be stubbornly hard to remove. According to the IMF, Russia's economic growth "virtually stopped when sanctions and lower oil prices hit." Lacking full access to Western capital markets, Russia missed out on hundreds of billions of dollars in investment. These funds would have fueled economic growth, enabling Putin to pour even more money into his military machine.

All this proved that the West could, in fact, impose devastating economic pressure not just on a midsize economy like Iran but on a large one that was deeply integrated into world markets. It provided further evidence of how globalization itself could be fashioned into a weapon. Russia's steep economic decline in the face of modest sanctions underlined that the more globalized an economy was, the more vulnerable it would be to economic warfare.

Remarkably, the blowback for America and Europe was negligible. Early in the Ukraine crisis, Jack Lew and other top Obama officials worried that an economic war with Russia could cause a meltdown in the EU. As it happened, the combination of Western sanctions and Russia's food ban didn't even cause a blip in Europe's economic performance. The sole exceptions were the three Baltic states, which sent 40 percent of their exports to Russia before the crisis. But although they suffered a lot worse than everyone else in the EU, they remained the most ardent supporters of sanctions. With the loss of the Russian market, Lithuania's dairy industry teetered on the brink of bankruptcy. When a team of State and Treasury officials met with a Lithuanian dairy farmer outside Vilnius in 2015, they expected her to express frustration. She did, but it wasn't about her declining business. "You should be hitting Russia harder," she said.

Dan Fried and his colleagues had created a new kind of economic warfare. The campaign against Iran aimed to shock and awe, confronting the

Islamic Republic with the full brunt of America's economic arsenal. With a strong push from Congress, officials such as Stuart Levey and Adam Szubin expelled Iran from the global financial system, cratered its oil revenues, and threatened companies the world over with losing access to the dollar unless they shunned Iran. By contrast, the campaign against Russia was a series of surgical strikes. In full partnership with the EU, the United States curtailed Russia's access to capital and technology. The vast majority of business with Russia remained untouched. Sanctions inflicted major damage on Russia's economy, but they left behind a relatively small blast radius.

Yet just as with Iran, economic damage was never the end goal. It was supposed to be a means to an end: changing Putin's policy on Ukraine. And on that score, the campaign against Russia was much less impressive.

To be sure, it's possible sanctions served as a deterrent. Russia's swirling economic crisis likely influenced Putin's decision to shelve plans for *Novorossiya*. But ultimately, the sanctions failed. They did not restore Ukraine's control over its territory, and they left Russia with enough breathing room to stabilize its economy and continue building up its military.

Like Jack Lew, Dan Fried and his team were proud of their work. They had helped turn the aircraft carrier of U.S. policy on Russia while keeping the West united. Yet they couldn't help but wonder whether the administration had been wrong to err on the side of caution. Washington prioritized avoiding unintended economic consequences over inflicting pain on Moscow. It also put a premium on diplomatic alignment with Europe, even though doing so further watered down the penalties.

These two factors, in turn, pushed the United States toward incrementalism. Instead of unleashing the full force of their economic arsenal immediately after Russia annexed Crimea, American officials spent months crunching numbers and negotiating with allies before settling on sanctions a fraction as potent as those they had wielded against Iran. These decisions reflected fear and uncertainty in the Obama administration about launching an economic war against Russia. The world economy was still recovering from the 2008 financial crisis, and Europe remained especially fragile. Under these circumstances, driving Russia off an economic cliff seemed too risky. There was also political risk in sanctioning Russia: American businesses had real skin in the game, and Congress wasn't nearly as enthusiastic about isolating Russia as it had been about Iran. And of course, European support for sanctions was always a question mark. Heavily dependent on Russian energy, the

EU had a lot to lose from a protracted economic struggle with its eastern neighbor. The zeal for sanctions in Europe after the MH17 tragedy was an exception, not the norm.

In the end, the West's caution proved a costly error. It allowed Russia to absorb the initial shock of sanctions and then carry on much as it had before. It gave Putin the chance to partially rehabilitate his country without doing anything to reverse the damage he had inflicted upon Ukraine. And it ultimately reinforced Putin's view that the West was weak and unwilling to bear the burden of a high-intensity economic standoff. All this would have ripple effects well beyond the current crisis.

There was a crucial difference between the economic war against Iran and the one against Russia. In the Iran campaign, merely *freezing* the country's nuclear activities—as opposed to fully reversing them—favored the United States, even if it required a partial lifting of sanctions. An unfinished nuclear program was not the same as a stockpile of nuclear weapons, and Iran was so iced out of the global economy that easing some of the sanctions would hardly permit a flowering of business in the country. Under a freeze, Iran would still not possess nuclear weapons, and its economy would still be reeling.

In the Russia campaign, the situation was reversed: freezing the Ukraine conflict favored Moscow, so long as sanctions didn't intensify. Putin's occupation of Ukraine was incomplete, but it was still an occupation, and with each passing day Russian control over Ukraine's territory ossified. Moreover, the West's "scalpel-like" sanctions weren't so daunting as to keep Russia off balance indefinitely. By the end of 2015, Russia's economy was stable enough that *Euromoney* magazine named Elvira Nabiullina the "Central Bank Governor of the Year." Her policies stopped Russia from tipping into the abyss.

A freeze would also give Putin more time to insulate his economy against American economic warfare. In the years after the sanctions were imposed, Moscow steadily reduced its dependence on the dollar. It diversified its foreign exchange reserves away from dollars; built up the Mir card payment system and SPFS, its alternative to SWIFT; and settled more of its foreign trade in euros, renminbi, and other non-dollar currencies. It also deepened its alliance with China, which eagerly gobbled up Russia's natural resources and funded Russian energy projects that were spurned by Western banks. Hence Lew's concern that excessive reliance on sanctions could undermine American leadership in the global economy.

There was one more reason a freeze favored Putin. If it lasted long enough, a new U.S. administration could come to power that wanted to make nice with Russia. Such seesawing was a recurring theme of American policy toward Moscow throughout the post–Cold War era. And in June 2015, when Donald Trump descended a golden escalator in New York's Trump Tower and announced he was running for president, that possibility crystallized like never before.

—

Trump stood apart from his Republican primary opponents in almost every way. On foreign policy, perhaps the starkest difference was on Russia. Trump often spoke of his admiration for Russia's leader. The annexation of Crimea was "so smart." Putin had "done an amazing job of taking the mantle." While other Republicans criticized Obama and his anointed successor, Hillary Clinton, for being too soft on Moscow, Trump promised that, if he were elected, "we're going to have a great relationship with Putin and Russia."

As Trump moved closer toward securing the Republican nomination, he hired several aides with close links to the Kremlin. Paul Manafort, whose most recent job was advising the ousted Ukrainian president and Putin stooge Viktor Yanukovych, was brought on as a convention strategist and eventually as chairman of the whole Trump campaign.

It's scarcely surprising Putin assessed that a Trump victory would be good for him. Putin also despised Trump's Democratic opponent: Hillary Clinton had served as secretary of state until 2013, and Putin blamed her personally for the wave of protests that erupted after he decided to return to the Russian presidency in 2011.

Sure enough, around the same time Jack Lew gave his speech at the Carnegie Endowment, FBI agents showed up unannounced at Clinton's campaign headquarters in Brooklyn. The Clinton campaign was the target of a sophisticated cyberattack, the agents said. What they did not say—but already suspected—was that Russia was behind the attack as well as a separate intrusion by hackers into the computer systems of the Democratic National Committee, or DNC. None of them knew that just a few days earlier, John Podesta, the Clinton campaign's chairman, had personally fallen victim to a spearfishing attack that handed over his emails to the Russians.

At first, the Obama administration was not all that worried. The Russian cyber-incursions seemed like run-of-the-mill espionage. But then, on June 15, the day after news of the Russian hacking first broke, a batch of DNC emails was posted online. The next month, on the eve of the Democratic National Convention in Philadelphia, a much larger trove of emails was released. The leaks were explosive—showing that the DNC had favored Clinton over her primary challenger, Bernie Sanders. DNC chair Debbie Wasserman Schultz was forced to resign hours before the start of the convention.

Collecting intelligence was one thing; turning it into a weapon of information warfare was quite another. It felt like a rerun of the leak of Victoria Nuland's "Fuck the EU" call, only on a larger scale and with much more serious repercussions.

In August, CIA Director John Brennan told Obama that Putin himself had ordered the interference in America's election. This was a big deal. Brennan called his Russian counterpart, FSB chief Alexander Bortnikov, and told him to knock it off. As Obama departed for a two-week vacation on Martha's Vineyard, Brennan and the rest of the president's senior national security team began working on a response.

They held a series of secretive discussions in the Situation Room. No memos were distributed beforehand. Officials were invited to the meetings without even being told of their subject. The participants concluded that retaliating with cyberattacks would not be wise. The United States could "end up on the losing end" of a "tit-for-tat escalatory cycle with Russia in the cyber domain," explained Tony Blinken, then serving as the number two at State. It would be better to strike back where America held its biggest advantage: economic warfare. Once more, Treasury put together a menu of sanctions options.

As this work progressed, the intelligence community dropped a bombshell: Russian hackers had so thoroughly penetrated state election systems that they could alter actual vote tallies. Suddenly, the hack-and-leak operation seemed small-time. Clinton was far ahead of Trump in the polls, and Russian email leaks were unlikely to change that. If Russia had the ability to falsify vote counts, however, it could shatter public confidence in the election and perhaps even corrupt the entire process.

By the time Obama returned from New England, the president and his team resolved on a cautious approach. They would not hit Russia with sanctions or other serious penalties before the election. Doing so could be perceived as too partisan; worse yet, it might provoke Putin to sow chaos on Election Day. And sowing chaos on Election Day, Victoria Nuland explained, was what Obama and his closest aides were really worried about. By contrast, the White House was "not focused at all on what we knew had been very effective elsewhere: the influence campaign, changing public opinion," Nuland recalled.

In early September, on the sidelines of a G20 summit in Hangzhou, China, Obama and Putin met for an hour and a half, accompanied only by interpreters. As Obama later summarized his message, he issued a private warning, telling the Russian leader to "cut it out" or face "serious consequences." A U.S. official briefed on the meeting described Obama's threat more colorfully: "You fuck with us over the election and we'll crash your economy."

Nuland and other Russia hands in the administration were disappointed. They had been advocating for a tough response for months. "All of my Soviet and Russia training told me we had to deter with a strong set of measures up front and have them calculate the costs of continuing to attack us, particularly with a player like Putin," Nuland said.

It was doubtful the Obama team, with so little time left in office, could get the Europeans on board with aggressive new sanctions. If America was going to act, it would have to act alone. Even so, Dan Fried favored charging ahead. "We should have dropped the hammer on them," Fried said. "Maybe the Germans and French didn't want this. They wanted to play out Minsk. But we should have elevated it."

To confront Russia's interference in the 2016 election, Obama settled for a policy a lot like the one he had opted for in the Ukraine crisis. He would not throw the book at Russia to try to undo the gains it had already made. (The Kremlin would leak John Podesta's emails, kept on the shelf since March, in the weeks leading up to Election Day.) Obama would accept a level of Russian interference in the U.S. election, just as he accepted a partial Russian occupation of Ukraine. He would hold his toughest weapons in reserve for the sake of deterrence against further transgressions, whether that was altering votes on Election Day or driving deeper into Ukraine's territory.

On November 8, 2016, just 77,000 votes in Michigan, Pennsylvania, and Wisconsin delivered the presidency to Trump. The Obama team was in shock. One of the main reasons they had held back on punishing Putin for his interference in the election was their belief that Clinton would win. What should they do?

Again, caution prevailed. Heavy sanctions could spark a crisis that President-elect Trump was ill-equipped to deal with—and in any case, he could rescind such sanctions with the stroke of a pen. On December 29,

Obama imposed sanctions on two Russian intelligence agencies, the FSB and the GRU; four intelligence officers; and three obscure companies that aided Russian intelligence services. None of these targets likely held any assets in the United States. In addition, the State Department expelled thirty-five Russian diplomats and closed Kremlin-owned compounds in Maryland and New York.

The "serious consequences" that Obama had privately threatened against Putin turned out to be a slap on the wrist. Needless to say, they would not "crash" Russia's economy.

The same day Obama rolled out the sanctions, Michael Flynn, Trump's pick for national security advisor, called Sergei Kislyak, Russia's ambassador to the United States. Flynn urged Moscow to limit its retaliation. Relations would be better when Trump was in the White House, so it would be best for "cool heads to prevail."

Putin got the message. The next day, he announced Russia would not respond to Obama's actions at all. He would wait and see how the incoming Trump administration approached relations with Moscow. Trump was pleased. "Great move on delay (by V. Putin)—I always knew he was very smart!" Trump tweeted.

Throughout the Ukraine crisis, Putin had consistently underestimated the West. He thought he could conquer Crimea and build *Novorossiya* with little pushback. Instead, America and Europe jointly imposed sanctions that battered Russia's economy. He thought he could use money or pipeline deals or promises to end the war in Syria to remove the sanctions. Instead, America and Europe had vowed to keep the penalties in place until Russia left the Donbas.

Now, as Donald Trump got ready to move into the White House, it looked like the West had underestimated Putin.

PART FOUR

China's Bid for
Technological Mastery

≡≡≡

The Interpreter

The news hit the White House with a deafening thud: the United Kingdom would allow Huawei, the Chinese tech giant, to build the backbone of its next-generation telecommunications network. Known as 5G, the network was expected to be up to a hundred times faster than its predecessor, ushering in a new era of connectivity that would enmesh everything from refrigerators and dialysis pumps to factory robots and autonomous weapons in a so-called Internet of Things. The Trump administration believed that if this new era were built on a foundation of Huawei technology, China would gain an enormous advantage in its deepening geopolitical standoff with the United States.

It was April 24, 2019. Springtime in Washington was in its full glory. Yet Matt Pottinger, the top China expert at the Trump NSC, was in a dark mood. Over the past two years, he had painstakingly engineered a major shift in U.S. policy toward China—a pivot that was slowly but surely taking hold in the national security bureaucracy. Washington had finally accepted that Beijing's "peaceful rise" was not so peaceful after all. China was an adversary, and the United States was reorienting its foreign policy to confront the threat.

Britain's decision to hitch its digital future to Huawei imperiled all that. Officially, Huawei was a private Chinese tech company, but it also served as a de facto arm of the Chinese government and as an executor of Beijing's geopolitical agenda. Any sensitive data traversing Huawei's 5G equipment—its base stations, antennas, and switches—was well within the reach of China's massive surveillance apparatus. Worse, U.S. officials feared that the global

spread of Huawei equipment could one day enable Beijing to disrupt its enemies' economies and military operations from afar. After much of the world
became dependent on Huawei to run its cities, industrial plants, and even
militaries, the Chinese Communist Party (CCP) could paralyze whole societies to impose its will.

Britain was the United States' closest ally, so its embrace of Huawei over
strong objections from the White House was bad news. Other Western countries looking to build 5G infrastructure would now feel encouraged to follow
suit, attracted by Huawei's technological expertise and relative affordability.
"If we couldn't persuade the Brits," recalled John Bolton, Trump's national
security advisor, "we weren't going to persuade anybody else in Europe."
And if Huawei equipment formed the spine of the world's 5G networks, CCP
would obtain a geopolitical asset matched only by the U.S. dollar—an economic and political kill switch of global reach. London's decision, in other
words, stacked the deck against the new, more confrontational China strategy that Pottinger had marshaled.

Pottinger, a former journalist with short blond hair, was an odd fit in a
Trump White House dominated by bullheaded businessmen, brusque generals, and pugnacious media personalities. Characterized by a colleague as a
"Boy Scout," the forty-six-year-old impressed people both in and out of government as earnest, hardworking, and knowledgeable. Pottinger started taking Chinese classes in high school, majored in Chinese at UMass Amherst, and
studied abroad in Beijing and Taiwan. He spent years working as a reporter
for Reuters and *The Wall Street Journal* in China, perfecting his Mandarin in
the process. He also got a taste of life as a journalist under CCP rule, as when
he was arrested and forced to flush his notes down a toilet, or when a Chinese government thug sucker punched him in a Beijing Starbucks.

In 2004, while back in the United States, Pottinger came across an online
video of the jihadist Abu Musab al-Zarqawi beheading an American hostage
in Iraq. Two days later, he sought out a recruiter for the Marine Corps and
left with an application in hand. He then returned to China, still unsure
whether he would fill it out. Later that year, he covered the aftermath of a
devastating tsunami in Thailand and watched in awe as U.S. Marines swooped
in to deliver food, water, and medicine. He picked up the application that
still lay on his desk. After passing the Marines' grueling fitness test and re-

Matt Pottinger: senior director for Asia at the Trump NSC.

ceiving an age waiver—he was already in his early thirties—he was commis-
sioned as a second lieutenant in December 2005.

While serving in the Marines, Pottinger deployed to both Iraq and
Afghanistan and earned a Bronze Star. He also caught the eye of an Army
intelligence officer named Michael Flynn. Years after both men had retired
from the military, when Pottinger was running a small consultancy in New
York that helped American investors navigate the Chinese economy, President-
elect Donald Trump named Flynn his national security advisor. Flynn lasted
just twenty-four days in the post, resigning after it came to light that he had
secretly communicated with Sergei Kislyak, the Russian ambassador, during
the presidential transition. But he left behind at least one legacy: Pottinger,
whom Flynn had picked to serve as the NSC's top China official.

Overseeing the Trump administration's China policy was not a job for
the faint of heart. China had been a constant theme of Trump's campaign,
but now that he was in office, his cabinet was bitterly divided on what to do
about the country. Longtime China hawks like Robert Lighthizer, the hard-
nosed U.S. trade representative, and Peter Navarro, the White House's resident gadfly on trade issues, pushed for a dramatic break in economic relations,
eager to smash the narrative that cooperation with China was necessary or

beneficial. On the other side were Wall Street mainstreamers like Treasury Secretary Steven Mnuchin and Gary Cohn, director of the National Economic Council. Both were Goldman Sachs veterans who still believed in free markets, unfettered global capital, and the limitless potential of the Chinese market for U.S. companies. Trump's encouragement of a chaotic policy process ensured that, for much of his presidency, these camps remained at odds.

Pottinger navigated this landscape with the resourcefulness of a reporter and the discipline of a Marine. Not many members of Washington's foreign policy establishment, and far fewer still in the Trump White House, had the fluency or patience to parse Xi Jinping's speeches and the reams of strategy documents issued by the CCP, a task that a prominent sinologist likened to "swallowing sawdust by the bucketful." Pottinger was an exception, leading him to assume the role of an interpreter who could help Trump and his inner circle understand what Beijing's words and deeds really meant.

Pottinger also tried to translate Trump's views on China to key constituencies outside the White House. The president's rhetoric on China vacillated between hostility and obsequiousness, which could leave even his closest advisors with whiplash. Pottinger, by contrast, impressed upon anyone who would listen that the United States was adopting a more competitive posture toward China and that the president stood firmly behind it.

For months leading up to the UK's announcement, Pottinger and other Trump officials had been urging their British counterparts to keep Huawei out of the country's 5G network, even warning that the United States might stop sharing intelligence with them if they went forward. Nevertheless, on April 23, Prime Minister Theresa May greenlit Huawei's involvement during a meeting with her national security council. The news leaked to the *Daily Telegraph* before anyone in London had given Washington the courtesy of a heads-up. This was not the way the "special relationship" was supposed to work.

Pottinger's dismay deepened when, two days later, he learned of a shockingly pro-China speech delivered by Philip Hammond, the UK's chancellor of the exchequer. Hammond was speaking in Beijing at a conference on the Belt and Road Initiative (BRI), China's landmark plan to develop massive infrastructure projects across the globe, including a Digital Silk Road that would have Huawei and other Chinese tech firms rewire the world. Washington considered BRI a fig leaf for Chinese economic imperialism, but as Hammond's speech made plain, London was far less worried.

Touting BRI's "extraordinary, ambitious vision," Hammond predicted the dawn of a "golden era" in British-Chinese relations, with London playing the trusty sidekick to the rising Chinese superpower. "Our offer," he declared, "is to bring the best of Chinese manufacturing, engineering, and construction with the best of British project design and legal, technical, and financial services expertise."

May's Huawei decision and Hammond's speech signaled to the White House that Britain was drifting dangerously close to China's orbit. Within hours, Pottinger and two colleagues were on a flight to London to implore the British government once again not to use Chinese-made 5G infrastructure. The Americans saw the British as confident to the point of smugness that they could contain any potential security threats from Huawei. The British saw the Americans as stubborn and overbearing. An official from GCHQ, the UK's signals intelligence agency, later leaked to the press that "Pottinger just shouted and was entirely uninterested in the UK's analysis. The message was, 'We don't want you to do this, you have no idea how evil China is.'"

Pottinger denied he ever raised his voice. But it was clear the gulf between the two allies was wide and the atmosphere tense. In a meeting with British Treasury officials, one of Pottinger's colleagues, Josh Cartin, reached into a large black portfolio and took out a poster on which he'd pasted blown-up quotes from Hammond's fawning speech in Beijing—"just so you know that we're paying attention to what you guys say."

Pottinger's meetings in London convinced him that, contrary to what UK officials were claiming, the decision to welcome Huawei was based not on technical risk analysis but rather on a simple political calculation: post-Brexit, Britain needed new partners, and it had decided to cozy up to China. "The UK was in the frame of mind that if you can't beat 'em, join 'em," Pottinger recalled. He left London feeling deflated.

Turning the tide against Huawei would take more than persuasion and vague threats. The United States would need to revamp the economic weapons that it had wielded against Iran and Russia to use against an even bigger target. And to do so, Washington would have to learn how to manipulate another chokepoint of the world economy—not Wall Street and the U.S. dollar but Silicon Valley and cutting-edge American technology.

≡≡

Irresponsible Stakeholder

Trump officials saw their economic war against China as a defensive campaign aimed at righting past wrongs and leveling a woefully uneven playing field. Their efforts were rooted not just in fear of a rising rival superpower but also in feelings of betrayal and regret about how China had attained that status—feelings that had been building for years before Trump arrived in Washington. U.S. officials felt that China had cheated them by reaping the benefits of integration into the global economy without playing by the rules of the system. And they regretted that America had aided China's rise and hadn't acted sooner to reverse course.

According to this narrative, Beijing had been waging an economic assault on the United States for decades: stealing American intellectual property, closing off the domestic Chinese market to U.S. companies, suppressing the value of the renminbi, and pumping domestic firms with subsidies so rich that foreign companies couldn't hope to compete. America just hadn't fought back. "We were already at war," explained Robert Lighthizer, who led U.S.-China trade talks and devised a series of escalating tariffs on Chinese imports during the Trump years, "and we were losing."

The Trump administration's economic pressure campaign against China progressed in fits and starts, marred by persistent bureaucratic sniping and friendly fire amid the general chaos of the Trump presidency. The campaign's objectives weren't always clear or consistent. Trump, for one, seemed less interested in technological competition than in closing the U.S. trade deficit with China by boosting sales of American soybeans and other farm goods—an obsession he maintained throughout his time in office. His resurrection of tariffs, a tool that had fallen out of fashion in the 1930s, and the resulting U.S.-China trade war captured the headlines. But the most enduring aspect of Trump's China policy was the effort to stop China from seizing global leadership of a handful of critical technologies, most notably 5G telecommunications infrastructure and the semiconductors that underpin the entire digital economy. This technological confrontation will remain at the heart of U.S. policy toward China for the foreseeable future.

Huawei and its quest to dominate the world's 5G networks became a symbol of what the United States had gotten wrong about China. And it would provide Washington with its first major opportunity to turn things around.

Huawei's origins were humble: $5,000 in seed money, with which Ren Zhengfei, a former officer in the People's Liberation Army (PLA) and card-carrying member of the CCP, founded the company in 1987. Originally, Huawei imported and resold foreign-made telephone switches. But by the early 2010s, it had become the world's largest manufacturer of telecommunications equipment. Two factors were instrumental in this transformation: support from the Chinese government and expertise from abroad.

In 1994, shortly after Huawei started making its own switches and won its first contract to sell them to the PLA, Ren met with Chinese leader Jiang Zemin. Ren told Jiang that the kind of telecom gear Huawei was producing was a technology critical to China's national security. In a more and more connected world, Ren argued, a nation without its own switching equipment was like one without a military. Jiang agreed, and in the coming years, Beijing provided Huawei with a raft of grants, credit facilities, and tax breaks to the tune of $75 billion, which the company used to bolster its in-house manufacturing capabilities. At the same time, the Chinese government imposed tariffs and other protectionist measures to insulate Huawei from foreign competition.

With its position at home secured, the company set its sights on worldwide expansion. Thanks to the government's largesse, Huawei had no difficulty undercutting competitors such as Sweden's Ericsson and Canada's Nortel on price, often by 30 percent or more. To match these global telecom leaders in quality, however, Huawei needed expertise that Chinese companies didn't possess.

Ren created a team dedicated to copying foreign technologies—typically through legal means like setting up joint ventures that required technology transfers—and spent lavishly on American management consultants. An

Ren Zhengfei: founder and CEO of Huawei.

army of advisors from IBM helped Huawei win its first big overseas contract, with UK-based telecom company BT, in 2005.

But Huawei also resorted to shadier tactics. It illegally copied code from Cisco to use in one of its routers, and it benefited from a massive theft of Nortel's confidential information by state-backed Chinese hackers. General Keith Alexander, a longtime head of the NSA, called China's cybertheft of intellectual property and trade secrets "the greatest transfer of wealth in history." Huawei was one of the biggest beneficiaries.

By the time the UK and other countries started building out their 5G networks in the late 2010s, Huawei was an international juggernaut. It had only two viable competitors left in the telecom equipment market, Ericsson and the Finnish firm Nokia. All other players had either been bought up or killed off. "Huawei drove every single American, Canadian, and European competitor out of business through their theft of IP and their subsidies," Pottinger lamented. Nortel had filed for bankruptcy in 2009, after which Huawei hired scores of its former employees.

Huawei also created new business lines and conquered adjacent markets. It began selling its own phones, overtaking Apple to become the world's second-largest manufacturer of smartphones and trailing closely behind South Korea's Samsung. Its chip design unit, HiSilicon, rose to become the second-largest customer of TSMC, the world's leading chip foundry. By lavishing Huawei with subsidies and other unfair advantages, Beijing was not playing by the rules of the international trading system, yet the United

States and other countries refrained from imposing any penalties. Given the lack of response, it's hard to blame Beijing or Huawei for their choices.

=

Huawei's ascent was part of the larger story of China's rise—a story in which the United States played a pivotal role, though many Americans would come to regret it. In the waning days of the Cold War and over the decades of American hegemony that followed, the United States made several of the same errors in China as it made in Russia, only the errors were even less justifiable. In Europe, 1989 was a year of revolution and renewal, marked by the fall of the Berlin Wall and the triumph of a pro-democracy movement that would bring down the Soviet Union. In China, 1989 was a year of bloodshed and dashed hopes that saw the brutal crushing of pro-democracy protests at Tiananmen Square. Post-Soviet Russia may not have been a true democracy, but it explicitly aimed to become one. The Chinese state that emerged from the carnage of Tiananmen wanted no such thing. Still, American leaders hoped that ushering China into the global economy would put the country on the road to democracy. Once the Chinese people had a taste of economic empowerment, they would eventually demand political freedom, too. It was only a matter of time.

But while Washington reveled in what it thought was the end of history, Beijing chafed at American dominance. From 1989 to 1991, Chinese officials experienced what the scholar Rush Doshi dubbed a "traumatic trifecta." First there were the Tiananmen Square protests, which showed the CCP how Western liberal ideology could lead to unrest at home. Then came the Gulf War, which demonstrated America's vast and increasingly unrivaled military might. Finally, the dissolution of the Soviet Union removed the main counterweight to American power and underscored the existential threat the United States posed to Communist regimes.

To leaders in Beijing, these three events cemented America's status as China's chief adversary. But they also laid bare the risks of confronting that adversary head-on. To displace the United States as the world's leading power, China would need to proceed slowly and methodically, avoiding confrontation until it had amassed preponderant strength. China would, in keeping with Deng Xiaoping's famous dictum, hide its strength and bide its time.

Economic competition, undertaken by hook or by crook, was central to this strategy. Through a wide range of methods, from seemingly innocuous academic collaboration to outright espionage, Beijing gained access to foreign industrial secrets for its own economic and military modernization. It took advantage of the openness of American society, planting CCP agents in U.S. research labs. It exploited the short-term profit incentives of American companies, requiring them to share crown-jewel technologies and intellectual property with Chinese firms as a precondition to accessing the vast Chinese market. And it benefited from American hubris, flouting international economic rules by showering favored Chinese companies with subsidies and protecting them from foreign competition—all with no fear of retaliation.

In fact, far from checking Beijing's ambitions, Washington helped realize them. After intense lobbying from Boeing, General Electric, and other American multinational corporations, Bill Clinton joined ranks with congressional Republicans in 2000 to grant China permanent normal trading privileges with the United States. He also paved the way for China's accession to the World Trade Organization the following year, a milestone that would supercharge the country's economic growth.

U.S. policymakers' confidence that China would evolve into a democracy and U.S. firms' hunger for new markets reinforced each other. America's political and corporate classes were comfortable in the belief that they could do well and do good at the same time. The overwhelming consensus that China's integration into the global economy would eventually encourage democratic change proved that there is at least one thing as powerful as an idea whose time has come: an idea that serves the interests of deep-pocketed elites.

"By joining the WTO, China is not simply agreeing to import more of our products; it is agreeing to import one of democracy's most cherished values: economic freedom," Clinton declared in a March 2000 speech. "The more China liberalizes its economy, the more fully it will liberate the potential of its people." Clinton mocked Beijing's attempts to control the Chinese people's access to the internet, a technology still in its infancy. "Now there's no question China has been trying to crack down on the internet," Clinton said. "Good luck! That's sort of like trying to nail Jell-O to the wall." The audience erupted in laughter.

It did not take long after China joined the WTO for some American officials to question Clinton's optimistic predictions. While China's exports were booming as it benefited from the open trading system afforded to WTO members, the country routinely violated the spirit—and often the letter—of

WTO rules by subsidizing domestic firms, erecting barriers to market access, and trampling on intellectual property rights. Beijing treated the WTO as a system to be gamed, daring other members, all of which were gorging on cheap Chinese imports, to do something about it. Meanwhile, the WTO's dispute settlement mechanism proved incapable of stopping China's economic malfeasance.

As for the U.S. government, the rapid growth of China's economy and its increasingly deep integration with America's own provided a strong incentive not to act. Between the 1989 Tiananmen Square massacre and the 2000 normalization of U.S.-China economic relations, trade between the two countries leapt from around $15 billion annually to almost $120 billion. Five years later, that number approached $300 billion. China surged to become the United States' second-largest trading partner. Behind that distinction were countless American jobs and cheap products that U.S. consumers eagerly gobbled up. Consequently, as the Chinese economy skyrocketed, American officials felt powerless to do anything that might stifle its rise. This might have been fine if China's political system was evolving as U.S. officials expected. But it wasn't, and that fact was becoming hard to deny.

In 2005, Robert Zoellick, the number two in George W. Bush's State Department, cautioned that the rich rewards China was reaping from the international system were difficult to square with the country's "rampant theft of intellectual property and counterfeiting, both of which strike at the heart of America's knowledge economy." Yet Zoellick's solution still reflected optimism that China could one day become a defender of the norms and institutions at the center of the post–World War II international order. "It is time to take our policy beyond opening doors to China's membership into the international system," Zoellick said. "We need to urge China to become a responsible stakeholder in that system." As Zoellick saw it, the United States had focused too narrowly on bringing China into the WTO and other international structures without requiring Beijing to follow the rules of the road.

The Chinese government, however, had little incentive to follow those rules. It already enjoyed the fruits of integration into the global economy, and it had no reason to fear losing them. With each passing day, China's economy was becoming more and more integral to the system, making the costs of kicking it out increasingly unpalatable. The logical course of action for China was to wait—to keep on hiding its strength and biding its time.

Furthermore, while China's unsavory tactics were undermining parts of the American economy, there were more urgent issues to address. Much like it did with Russia, the United States viewed China less as a foreign policy problem in and of itself than as a swing player in bigger global problems, from the campaign against a nuclear Iran to the race to curb global carbon emissions. Taking on China over its economic policies wouldn't just anger influential U.S. businesses; it would jeopardize cooperation on these cross-cutting global challenges.

As in the case of Russia, hope triumphed over experience. The United States kept the faith that China would evolve, no matter how long it took. Ultimately, China didn't change—only the balance of power did, and not in America's favor.

38

The Awakening

Hank Paulson made his career doing business in China. In 1997, as president of Goldman Sachs, he helped launch the IPO of China Telecom, which became the first major Chinese state-owned enterprise to be listed on the New York Stock Exchange. In 2004, Paulson helped Goldman secure approval from Beijing to establish a joint venture in China, enabling the firm to provide investment banking services to mainland Chinese clients for the first time. When he was named treasury secretary in 2006, Paulson had already visited China some seventy times.

Key to Paulson's success was his ability to befriend the right people—people like Wang Qishan, a fellow banker-cum-bureaucrat who served first as governor of the enormous China Construction Bank, then as mayor of Beijing, and eventually as China's vice premier. Paulson lauded Wang as a "born leader." So when the two men met in Beijing in 2008, at the height of the global financial crisis, Wang's words of reproach cut deep. "You were my teacher, but now here I am in my teacher's domain, and look at your system, Hank," Wang said. "We aren't sure we should be learning from you anymore." As Paulson later recalled, "The crisis was a humbling experience, and this was one of its most humbling moments."

The 2008 financial crisis dealt a major blow to perceptions of the United States and its place atop the geopolitical pecking order. As America and its closest allies wallowed in recession, China charged forward, aided by a gargantuan stimulus package three times the size of the United States' own. That stimulus didn't just sustain China's robust economic growth; it also buoyed growth across Asia and helped stabilize the reeling global economy.

China emerged from the crisis with newfound confidence, eager to claim its place in the sun. Speaking in 2009, Chinese leader Hu Jintao said a "major change in the balance of international power" had occurred. This called for a move away from the longtime strategy of hiding one's strength and biding one's time. Hu's directive that China should now "actively accomplish something" was vague, but it was the first-ever revision to Deng's old dictum, which had guided CCP leaders for almost two decades. China now had enough power to assert itself.

A year later, on the morning of September 7, 2010, a Chinese fishing trawler rammed two Japanese coast guard ships near the disputed Senkaku Islands, which are administered by Japan but claimed by both Japan and China. Japanese authorities detained the Chinese skipper, leading to a diplomatic row in which Beijing cut off exports of rare-earth minerals to Japan. At the time, China accounted for some 97 percent of global production of rare earths, which are critical ingredients in all manner of high-tech products, such as smartphones, wind turbines, and automobiles—the type of products that Japanese companies excel at making.

Beijing never publicly announced it was banning sales of rare earths to Japan. Shipments just stopped. Even after Japanese authorities released the Chinese skipper, the embargo lasted for another two months. Tokyo would go on to invest hundreds of millions of dollars to secure supplies of rare earths from domestic sources and countries other than China. The world was on notice. Beijing might object to what it called the "long-arm jurisdiction" of American sanctions, but it was hardly averse to waging economic war itself—even if, for the time being, it did so informally and behind a veil of deniability.

When Xi Jinping succeeded Hu Jintao as paramount leader in 2012, some Western observers expected Beijing to change tack. Xi was widely viewed as a political and economic reformer. But the new leader soon revealed himself a dyed-in-the-wool party man, bent on tightening the CCP's authoritarian control at home and expanding its influence abroad.

Xi grew up the privileged son of Xi Zhongxun, a comrade of Mao's and CCP grandee who became China's vice premier in the late 1950s. The younger Xi attended an elite preparatory school and regularly visited his father at Zhongnanhai, the expansive leadership compound in Beijing where top CCP officials live and work. His life was turned upside down in his teens, when Mao purged his father from the Party. Xi was detained, forced to denounce his father, and banished to a poor village in the Chinese countryside. His sister died, reportedly driven to suicide by the Red Guards.

The ordeal didn't cause Xi to sour on the Party; on the contrary, he embraced it. He formally joined the CCP in 1974 and steadily climbed the ranks, determined to become, as the China scholar Richard McGregor put it, "the Reddest leader of his generation."

Shortly after Xi took over in 2012, CCP leadership disseminated an internal directive that would become a canonical text of Xi's rule. Known as Document No. 9, it spelled out in sweeping terms the existential threat that the West posed to the Party's control over China. The text urged Party members to "clearly see the ideological situation as a complicated, intense struggle," and dismissed the principles of constitutional democracy, civil society, and press freedom as "false ideological trends." The document warned that "Western anti-China" forces would use the pretext of liberal reforms to foment revolution in China and even try to break the country up.

This was hardly the language of a reformer. And it didn't augur well for China's status as a "responsible stakeholder" in the international order. Instead, Xi set out to build a twenty-first-century economic empire, one that would rival America's global network of economic dominance and ultimately serve as a launchpad for China to achieve "national rejuvenation"—shorthand for replacing the United States as the world's preeminent superpower.

Digital technology became a core area of focus. Xi kept out American tech firms like Google and sidelined Chinese entrepreneurs such as Jack Ma in a bid to strengthen the Party's grip on China's burgeoning tech industry. He also built a vast, Orwellian surveillance apparatus that could suppress domestic dissent before it had a chance to reverberate across society.

Xi used this brand of techno-authoritarianism to particularly appalling effect in his crackdown on the Uyghurs, a predominantly Muslim ethnic group in the northwestern region of Xinjiang. Starting in the mid-2010s, state authorities in Xinjiang conducted the largest mass internment of an ethnic minority group since World War II, detaining more than a million Uyghurs in concentration camps. Huawei and other Chinese tech companies helped enable these gross human rights abuses by providing the facial recognition technology, location monitoring tools, and mobile traffic analysis the state used to round up its targets.

These new technologies also pushed forward China's economic imperialism. Xi courted foreign autocrats with offers to export his techno-authoritarian toolkit. By providing these homegrown technologies on the cheap to countries looking to upgrade their telecom and security infrastructure, the CCP would gain eyes and ears everywhere, giving it serious leverage over foreign governments.

In 2013, Xi launched the Belt and Road Initiative, a grand vision to connect the world through Chinese-financed infrastructure. Sri Lanka received a gleaming new container terminal, bridges linked islands in the Maldives, and Huawei data centers and surveillance systems were installed in Serbia and Zambia—all made possible by Chinese money. That these projects would never turn a profit, let alone provide real development benefits, was irrelevant; they gave Beijing influence over the infrastructure that makes modern societies function.

The megaprojects also came with strings attached. They were built with Chinese materials by Chinese companies that employed Chinese laborers, allowing Beijing to export some of the excess labor capacity created by its colossal 2008 stimulus package. More troublingly, recipients of Chinese largesse soon found themselves drowning in debt and interest payments, as BRI loans carried interest rates several times higher than typical infrastructure loans. When countries struggled to repay, Beijing simply seized the infrastructure that it built. This is how China secured a ninety-nine-year lease on Sri Lanka's Hambantota port in 2017. The practice became known as "debt-trap diplomacy."

The same year Xi kicked off BRI, he launched the Asian Infrastructure Investment Bank (AIIB), a China-dominated multilateral development bank designed to rival the Washington-based World Bank. Although the AIIB provided only a small portion of funding for BRI projects, it offered them a stamp of legitimacy, recasting Chinese economic imperialism as disinterested development assistance.

———

Ernest Hemingway described going bankrupt as a process that happens in two steps: gradually, then suddenly. The same was true of Washington's awakening to the scope and implications of Xi's geopolitical ambitions. The realizations began coming quickly in early 2015, when Beijing was lobbying countries all over the world to join the AIIB. By then, China's charm offensive wasn't targeting just small fish like the Maldives and Sri Lanka, but also large Western countries, including America's closest allies.

The United Kingdom was the first to break ranks. In March, George Osborne, the chancellor of the exchequer, announced that the UK would become "the first major Western country to seek to join the AIIB." An Obama administration official railed against London's "constant accommodation of China" in an interview with the *Financial Times*, but to no avail: within days of London's announcement, Australia, France, Germany, and Italy all followed the UK's lead and opted to join China's new bank.

The AIIB fiasco filled Washington with "real concern and insecurity about America's leadership position in the world," another senior Obama official said. Alliances were America's biggest advantage over rivals and its strongest claim to global leadership. Now China's power had grown so great that it was beginning to loosen those bonds.

Unease was also spreading inside the Pentagon. China's economic imperialism—plus its more assertive military activities, especially the construction of artificial militarized islands in the South China Sea—did not just endanger America's alliances; it imperiled U.S. military dominance. China's population was more than four times the size of America's, and its economy was projected to become the world's largest in a matter of years. In military contests, such quantity had a quality all its own.

Secretary of Defense Ash Carter and his deputy, Bob Work, argued that the United States needed to gain a decisive technological edge over China to offset the country's numerical advantages. But most of the technological innovations that would underpin the future of military competition were being produced by the U.S. private sector—which, in a free market, meant that China had access to those innovations, too. Matt Turpin, who served under Pottinger on Trump's NSC, described this as an "inherent contradiction" of U.S.-China competition at the time: the Pentagon's job was to deter military challengers, but its capabilities depended on "our civilian economy, a globalized research and development infrastructure, and a technology industry in which our principal competitor was sitting at the center." The technological gap between Washington and Beijing was narrowing rapidly. In frontier technologies like artificial intelligence and quantum computing, it was no longer even clear who held the lead.

The Pentagon now recognized China as America's most fearsome military adversary. U.S. economic agencies like Treasury and Commerce, however, still clung to the notion that cooperation, as opposed to competition or outright confrontation, would yield greater benefits, including a virtuous cycle of political and economic liberalization in China. But such liberalization remained conspicuously absent. If anything, Xi's methodical concentration of power had pushed his country in the opposite direction.

The China policies being advanced by American economic officials were increasingly working at cross purposes with those of their colleagues at the Pentagon. The problem was that there was no clean way to separate U.S.-China economic relations from the realm of military competition. For one thing, Silicon Valley was becoming more and more important to both America's and China's military-industrial complexes. Complicating matters further was the Chinese government's relationship to its country's private sector: under an approach known as "military-civil fusion," Beijing broke down barriers between the military and commercial domains. Just as intellectual property theft and forced technology transfer helped Chinese companies conquer world markets, they also accelerated China's military modernization. Even private Chinese firms were legally bound to gather intelligence for the CCP and expected to collaborate with the military.

In May 2015, Xi Jinping unveiled a new initiative that laid bare the growing indivisibility of China's economic power, military might, and geopolitical ambitions. "Made in China 2025" was a wide-ranging strategy for China to achieve self-sufficiency in critical technologies. Chinese firms would seek to obtain a 40 percent domestic market share in several high-tech products by 2020 and a 70 percent share by 2025. Xi frequently recited talking points promoting "win-win cooperation" between China and the United States. But this quest for market share was nakedly zero-sum, since it could succeed only at the expense of Western companies.

"Made in China 2025" spurred American businesses to start changing their tune on China. Since the days of Bill Clinton's push for China to join the WTO, big business had been Beijing's crucial ally in Washington. Now, China's stated goal was to undercut these companies' market share.

Nowhere was that goal more apparent than in China's plan to end its reliance on foreign-made computer chips. Chips, or semiconductors, are the foundational component of the digital economy. China spent more on semiconductors than it did on oil. In 2015, China imported some 85 percent of its semiconductors. "Made in China 2025" sought to bring that figure down to 30 percent. To drive toward this target, China launched an investment vehicle known as the Big Fund, which would pour tens if not hundreds of billions of dollars into domestic chipmakers.

The U.S. semiconductor industry was a crown jewel of the American economy. Its mastery of a certain metalloid put the "Silicon" in Silicon Valley. But it was also a fiercely competitive market, subject to unforgiving economies of scale. If Beijing started pumping hundreds of billions of dollars into homegrown chipmakers, the West's chip industry might soon go the way of the telecom equipment sector and the erstwhile rivals of Huawei.

News of the Chinese plan sent American chipmakers into a panic. When the board of the Semiconductor Industry Association, the sector's main lobbying group, met in late 2015, chair Brian Krzanich entered the room with "fear in his eyes," according to a participant. "Made in China 2025," Krzanich warned, was an existential threat to America's technological supremacy. Joining the meeting that day was Bruce Andrews, a top-ranking Commerce Department official. "If you don't do something," Krzanich told Andrews, "this is going to be the end of the U.S. industry."

Andrews agreed and passed on the warning to his boss, Secretary of Commerce Penny Pritzker. He drew an analogy to the American steel industry, large parts of which had been decimated in recent decades by Chinese competitors despite belated efforts by the U.S. government to stop the bleed. "In ten years, we don't want to be having the same conversation about the semiconductor industry that we're having about the steel industry today," Andrews told Pritzker.

On November 2, 2016, Pritzker spoke about the U.S.-China competition in chipmaking at the Center for Strategic and International Studies, a Washington think tank. "We cannot afford to cede our leadership," Pritzker declared. "We will not allow any nation to dominate this industry and impede innovation through unfair trade practices and massive, non-market-based state intervention." But a White House report published two months later was pessimistic about the U.S. government's ability to stop China from using unfair practices to catch up to the United States in semiconductor technology. "The United States will only succeed in mitigating the dangers posed by Chinese industrial policy if it innovates faster," the report claimed. "Policy can, in principle, slow the diffusion of technology, but it cannot stop the spread."

A major reason the White House advocated for trying to out-innovate China, rather than fighting the CCP's economic malfeasance, was that a successful counterpunch would require support from other countries. The report expressed doubt that this would be possible, and acting alone would not be worth it. "Unilateral action is increasingly ineffective in a world where the semiconductor industry is globalized," the report stated.

Yet everything the United States had learned about economic warfare over the past decade suggested that globalization actually *increased* the power of America's economic weapons, even when used unilaterally. To be sure, an economic clash with China would be unlike anything the United States had ever attempted. China's economy wasn't just big; it was thoroughly enmeshed in the global financial system and supply chains, far more so than Russia's or Iran's ever was. Its links with the U.S. economy ran extraordinarily deep and spanned virtually every industry. Those links would make any economic conflict with China fraught with risk—but they were also precisely what gave America's economic arsenal its power.

39

Let a Hundred China Policies Bloom

A t noon on January 20, 2017, Donald Trump approached the podium to deliver his inaugural address from the steps of the U.S. Capitol. The sky was gray, and rain fell as America's new president took to the microphone.

"For many decades, we've enriched foreign industry at the expense of American industry," Trump intoned, squinting at his teleprompter. "We've made other countries rich while the wealth, strength, and confidence of our country has dissipated over the horizon. One by one, the factories shuttered and left our shores, with not even a thought about the millions and millions of American workers that were left behind."

Bleak as it was, this was mild fare by Trump's standards. "We can't continue to allow China to rape our country," he'd snarled on the campaign trail. "And that's what they're doing. It's the greatest theft in the history of the world." In the end, he'd won 89 of the 100 counties whose local industries were estimated to have suffered the most from economic competition with China.

Days before Trump declared "America first" as his governing ideology in his inaugural address, Xi Jinping had appeared at the World Economic Forum in Davos, Switzerland. The Chinese leader painted a very different picture of the world and of his role in it. If Trump pledged to be a disrupter, Xi presented himself as a defender of the status quo—a status quo that had made many of the people in the Davos audience rich.

"Economic globalization was once viewed as the treasure cave found by Ali Baba in *The Arabian Nights*, but it has now become the Pandora's box in the eyes of many," Xi said in his Davos speech. This trend, exemplified by Trump's protectionist leanings, was a mistake. "The point I want to make is that many of the problems troubling the world are not caused by economic globalization," Xi professed. Even if they were, it was no use trying to swim against the tide. "Like it or not, the global economy is the big ocean that you cannot escape from," Xi stated, as his listeners nodded along in agreement. Regardless of the rumblings in Washington, Beijing sought "a model of open and win-win cooperation," because "no one will emerge as a winner in a trade war."

The contrast between Xi's remarks at Davos and Trump's inaugural address was stark. That the rising power, China, seemed more comfortable with the current state of the world than the incumbent, the United States, revealed just how much had changed since China entered the WTO in 2001. That year, the Chinese economy was just 10 percent the size of America's; it had ballooned to 70 percent by the time Trump took the oath of office. No challenger had come so close to equaling America's economic might in more than a century.

Despite Trump's aspiration to disrupt, his foreign policy was beset by false starts. On Russia, candidate Trump had promised to "get along very well with Vladimir Putin." Michael Flynn and Steve Bannon, Trump's chief strategist, fantasized about pulling off a "reverse Nixon" by joining forces with Russia to take on China. Flynn was out as national security advisor in three weeks and Bannon was shown the door in seven months, but they were around long enough that some officials at the Trump White House explored lifting sanctions on Russia unconditionally. A worried Dan Fried, who remained in his post as coordinator for sanctions policy until his retirement from the State Department in late February 2017, informed members of Congress, who were so alarmed that they drew up legislation to give themselves the power to reject any presidential decision to remove the sanctions. The law, known as the Countering America's Adversaries Through Sanctions Act (CAATSA), sailed through the House and Senate with commanding bipartisan majorities. As Congress had the votes to override a presidential veto, Trump reluctantly signed the bill, adding a statement bemoaning the measure as "significantly flawed."

Trump also had big plans to upend U.S. foreign policy on Iran, starting by axing the nuclear deal (in his words: a "disastrous deal" and quite possibly "the worst deal ever negotiated"). But even Trump's own national security team—now led by Flynn's replacement as national security advisor,

H. R. McMaster—thought this was a bad idea. Iran was complying with its nuclear obligations, and America's allies strongly supported the agreement. A withdrawal would leave the United States isolated internationally. McMaster and Rex Tillerson, who had left Exxon to become Trump's improbable first secretary of state, persuaded the president to stick to the deal for the time being. Better to press Iran and the other parties to strengthen the agreement rather than simply abandon it.

Even on China, Trump initially set off fewer fireworks than expected. At first, he followed the path of previous administrations and let relations with Beijing be subsumed under a different, seemingly more pressing issue: North Korea's nuclear program. Upon leaving office, Obama had warned Trump that North Korea would be the most urgent national security matter on his plate, and since China accounted for up to 90 percent of North Korea's foreign trade, Beijing had massive leverage over Pyongyang. On Tillerson's first trip to Beijing as secretary of state in March 2017, he gave no hint of a hardening in U.S. policy toward China. Instead, he struck a conciliatory tone and asked for assistance in curbing North Korea's nuclear program. Matt Pottinger, who joined Tillerson on the trip, winced as America's top diplomat stressed the need for "win-win solutions," a phrase borrowed straight from Xi's talking points.

The captains of Trump's economic team, Treasury Secretary Steven Mnuchin and National Economic Council Director Gary Cohn, had no interest in pursuing a hard line, either. They preferred to follow the path of Hank Paulson, their former boss at Goldman Sachs, and tighten the embrace between the U.S. and Chinese economies. As two of the wealthiest members of Trump's cabinet, Mnuchin and Cohn carried significant clout and social cachet in the opening months of an administration run by a man who prided himself on being "really rich." By contrast, when Trump first met Xi at his Mar-a-Lago resort, his most hawkish China advisor, Peter Navarro, was originally left off the manifest and only made it to the meeting thanks to Steve Bannon, who sneaked him on the plane to Palm Beach at the last minute.

The atmosphere at the Trump-Xi summit at Mar-a-Lago was positive. Ivanka Trump and Jared Kushner's young children performed a Chinese folk song, the Chinese government approved a slew of trademarks for Ivanka to sell jewelry and handbags in China, and Trump treated the Chinese president to "the most beautiful piece of chocolate cake that you've ever seen." Trump also told Xi that Washington could forgive Chinese economic

*Donald Trump and Xi Jinping: bonding over
chocolate cake at Mar-a-Lago in April 2017.*

misconduct—and even Trump's bugbear, the U.S. trade deficit with China—
if Beijing reined in Pyongyang. "You want to make a great deal?" Trump
proposed. "Solve the problem in North Korea. That's worth having deficits."

Still, Trump did use the summit to try to tackle the deficit issue, with the
two sides agreeing to devote the next hundred days to finding ways to boost
U.S. exports to China. This marked the start of Trump's quest for a trade
deal that could eliminate America's enormous deficit with China in one fell
swoop—a white whale that preoccupied him above anything else in U.S.-
China relations. Trump hated the fact that Americans bought more from
China than Chinese bought from the United States, seeing this as proof that
America had "lost" to China. Yet he did not seem to grasp that the deficit also
reflected that the average American consumed more than the average Chinese
and enjoyed a far higher standard of living. He also did not seem to appreciate
that ending the deficit by increasing U.S. exports to China would require
an unfathomable increase in exports. The year before Trump entered office,
the U.S. trade deficit with China stood at a whopping $350 billion, three times
the total value of American exports to the country. Closing a gap this wide
would be impossible by simply inking a trade deal that promised to grow
U.S. exports, but Trump charged on anyway.

As Trump's economic team pursued this elusive objective, his national security team was crafting a wholly different approach. Matt Pottinger wrote an internal white paper taking stock of the various ways the CCP was engaging in "economic aggression," as the memo's title put it, against the United States. The document highlighted China's plans to dominate the digital economy by stealing critical technologies from the West and propping up its own firms through generous subsidies. It argued that America should use its own economic arsenal in response, including export controls and investment restrictions focused on the technologies Beijing was seeking to master. Pottinger and H. R. McMaster briefed the memo to Trump in October 2017. The president signed it, making it the Trump administration's first official China strategy, at least on paper.

Meanwhile, U.S. Trade Representative Robert Lighthizer was preparing for a trade war. The Trump administration was flush with former businessmen—such as Steven Mnuchin, Gary Cohn, and Commerce Secretary Wilbur Ross—who believed their financial success made them experts on trade and jockeyed for control of Trump's China policy. Lighthizer was rich, too, but he'd made his millions as a lawyer suing China and other countries for unfair trade practices. He had also done a stint as deputy U.S. trade representative in the

Vying for the boss's ear: Robert Lighthizer and Steven
Mnuchin (right) sit before Donald Trump in the Oval Office.

Reagan administration. He'd forgotten more about trade policy than his ex-financier cabinet colleagues ever knew.

A tall and unyielding man who joined the Trump administration just shy of his seventieth birthday, Lighthizer had been a lonely voice against the free-trade consensus of the 1990s, arguing publicly against China's accession to the WTO. "China wants to join the WTO to achieve a dominant position in world trade," he cautioned in a 1997 *New York Times* op-ed. "If China is allowed to join the WTO on the lenient terms that it has long been demanding, virtually no manufacturing job in this country will be safe." Now, feeling vindicated, Lighthizer started to lay the groundwork for a flood of tariffs on Chinese products. "Tariffs were the only way we could start decoupling," Lighthizer explained, "and stop sending hundreds of billions of dollars each year to a mortal enemy." As he saw it, tariffs would help close the U.S. trade deficit not by boosting American exports (as Trump hoped) but by cutting *imports* from China—the endless array of Chinese-made electronics, toys, furniture, and clothing that Americans bought from places like Walmart and Amazon. It was a more practical approach, but also one that would be costly to U.S. consumers and businesses accustomed to buying these cheap products.

Lighthizer had been around the block enough times to know that any policy that disrupted U.S.-China commercial ties would be challenged in court. This was especially true for old-fashioned tariffs, which would levy taxes on American firms that imported Chinese products, meaning that U.S. companies had plenty of money at stake.

To guard against future legal threats to the tariffs he envisioned, Lighthizer turned to Section 301 of the Trade Act of 1974. This was a provision that allowed the U.S. government to impose tariffs and other trade sanctions on foreign states that engaged in "unjustifiable" acts that burden or restrict U.S. commerce. Washington had rarely used these authorities since the creation of the WTO in 1995, but the law remained on the books. If the United States demonstrated that China's theft of intellectual property and forced technology transfers met the criteria of Section 301, Lighthizer reasoned, the administration would be on strong legal footing to hit China with retaliatory tariffs. As soon as it became clear that Mnuchin and Ross had nothing to show for their hundred days of trade talks with the Chinese, Lighthizer persuaded Trump to approve a 301 investigation into China's trade practices.

A conclusive 301 investigation would protect U.S. tariffs from being struck down in court, and it was also politically astute. Big business and labor rarely saw eye to eye on China, but everyone agreed that Chinese firms should stop stealing American business secrets. By focusing the investigation on "Chinese laws, policies, and practices which may be harming American intellectual property rights, innovation, or technology development," as Lighthizer said upon initiating the probe in August, he was laying the foundation for a politically unimpeachable case.

In November 2017, with Pottinger's internal strategy document on countering Chinese economic aggression approved and Lighthizer's 301 investigation plowing ahead, Trump traveled to Beijing for a state visit. The Chinese had prepared an itinerary with a heavy dose of grandeur. Xi and his wife, the famous folk singer Peng Liyuan, awaited Donald and Melania Trump at the entrance to the Forbidden City, the opulent palace complex that housed Chinese emperors for more than five hundred years. As they got started on a tour intended to introduce Trump to the sweep of Chinese history, H. R. McMaster realized that Matt Pottinger was nowhere to be found. Pottinger had been denied entry at the gate to the Forbidden City. McMaster suspected it was because Xi preferred to give Trump his version of history free from the scrutiny of a knowledgeable interpreter.

The next day, Trump and his advisors met Xi's second-in-command, Premier Li Keqiang. Li treated them to a history lesson of his own, the conclusion of which was that China's modernization was now complete and that the country no longer needed the United States for technological innovation. Moving forward, America's role would be to supply China with food, oil, and other commodities.

Trump may have wanted to help U.S. farmers sell more soybeans, but he still couldn't stomach Li's depiction of the United States as a hinterland of the Chinese economic empire. After Li finished speaking, Trump stood up and abruptly ended the meeting. "If anyone in our party, including President Trump, had any doubts about China's view of its relationship with the United States, Premier Li's long monologue should have removed those doubts," McMaster later wrote. If only it had been so simple.

40

The Clue: ZTE

On March 22, 2018, Robert Lighthizer released a 215-page report detailing the findings of his Section 301 investigation into China's trade practices. In it, he made the case that China was seeking to build an economic empire using technology and intellectual property stolen from the United States.

Lighthizer's review was thorough. He had convened a series of hearings in which business leaders, union representatives, and legal scholars testified that China had a playbook for stealing American technology. He also collected comments from more than seventy petitioners, mostly trade associations. Even the U.S.-China Business Council, once a fierce lobbyist for China's WTO membership, contributed. In a scathing eighteen-page letter, the council detailed how the "requirement to transfer technology as a condition to gain market access in China is an acute concern of American companies in key sectors, who often must make difficult choices about managing the trade-off of technology sharing and access to the world's second-largest economy."

The complaints against Chinese economic policy were too many to count. Subsidies and unequal trade barriers threatened everyone from Detroit automakers and Pennsylvania steel manufacturers to Georgia chicken farmers and North Carolina furniture craftsmen. But one area stood out: technology.

The Chinese government "seeks to attain domestic dominance and global leadership in a wide range of technologies for economic and national security reasons," Lighthizer's 301 report stated. Technological mastery would allow China to leapfrog America economically, militarily, and, over time, diplomatically. If America lost its technological leadership, little else would matter.

But it was far from clear what an effective technological counteroffensive would look like. Lighthizer's favored tool, tariffs, would lower demand for Chinese technology in the U.S. domestic market, but they would not reduce the appeal of Chinese products anywhere else, and thus they would do little to impede Chinese firms from taking global market share from American businesses. Washington could increase subsidies for U.S. tech companies, but it would never match the massive cash infusions the CCP gave to state-affiliated firms. And even if this were possible, it would not stop those firms from stealing and copying American innovations.

The Trump administration's earliest effort to stymie Huawei's 5G dominance was a case study in these difficulties. Led by Robert Spalding, the NSC's senior director for strategic planning, the campaign aimed to insulate America's own 5G networks from Huawei tech. But even this relatively modest project ran into obstacles almost immediately.

At the time, major U.S. telecom companies such as AT&T and Verizon were in the process of building and testing their 5G capabilities. For years, these U.S. carriers had largely shunned equipment made by Huawei and ZTE, China's number-one and number-two telecom equipment makers. In 2012, a report by the House Intelligence Committee concluded that "Huawei and ZTE cannot be trusted to be free of foreign state influence," and that "the risks associated with Huawei's and ZTE's provision of equipment to U.S. critical infrastructure could undermine core U.S. national-security interests." Though they were not legally bound to do so, the big U.S. telecoms heeded the warning and stopped procuring base stations from Huawei and ZTE. (Several smaller, rural carriers kept on using Huawei equipment, as it was substantially cheaper than the alternatives.)

Yet executives at the major carriers couldn't ignore their fiduciary responsibility to maximize shareholder value. By 2017, Huawei's 5G equipment was considered best-in-class. It was also priced 30 percent below comparable equipment made by Ericsson and Nokia, and often came with generous financing terms. The carriers' decision to boycott Chinese manufacturers based on nothing but a gentlemen's agreement with Congress was becoming a hard sell. Absent stronger government action, America's own 5G networks might be built with Huawei equipment because it made economic sense.

Spalding's proposed solution was for Washington to play a much larger role in building the country's 5G networks. The federal government could procure all the necessary equipment itself, ensuring that it was free of Chinese-made components, and rent it out to carriers like AT&T, Sprint, Verizon, and T-Mobile. Another option was for the government to organize the major carriers into a consortium that would jointly finance and build a nationwide network.

With Spalding's ideas still in the early stages of development, on January 28, 2018, Axios published a story under the headline "Scoop: Trump team considers nationalizing 5G network." Based on a leaked PowerPoint deck and a memo, both authored by Spalding, the article reported that "Trump national security officials are considering an unprecedented federal takeover of a portion of the nation's mobile network to guard against China."

The carriers, fearing that the Trump administration was planning to nationalize their industry, quickly mobilized to kill Spalding's ideas. The White House raced to control the damage, and the chair of the Federal Communications Commission promised that "the market, not government, is best positioned to drive innovation and investment." Within seventy-two hours, Spalding was instructed to pack his bags. "There was no 'Hey, thank you for your service,'" Spalding later reflected. "It was just 'Get out. Don't let the door hit your butt.'"

Spalding was gone, but Matt Pottinger and his team of China experts at the NSC kept sounding the alarm on Huawei. Much of the rest of the U.S. government questioned whether anything could be done to prevent the company from owning the whole 5G market. "Everybody, including the intelligence community, was like, 'You're a bunch of crazy people at the NSC, because this is a lost cause,'" recalled Ivan Kanapathy, a former Marine fighter pilot who worked for Pottinger. "It was like, 'You've lost. You can't stop Huawei.'"

In April, a new development in a years-long legal dispute involving ZTE provided a clue as to how they might prove the naysayers wrong. The case traced its origins to an incident during Obama's second term, when U.S. authorities seized a laptop from ZTE's chief financial officer as he passed through security at Boston's Logan Airport. The laptop was found to contain a "treasure trove" of documents illustrating an elaborate plot by ZTE to buy U.S. technology and resell it to Iran. ZTE was caught red-handed violating American sanctions and export control laws.

In response, the Obama Commerce Department issued an order restricting U.S. companies from selling to ZTE. Since ZTE relied heavily on imports from the United States, including software from Google and chips from Intel and Qualcomm, it rushed to the negotiating table. Talks dragged into the new administration, and a week after Wilbur Ross took up his post as Trump's commerce secretary, the two sides reached a settlement. ZTE pleaded guilty to criminal charges and agreed to overhaul its management and pay a $1.2 billion fine, the largest ever levied by the U.S. government in an export control case. Over the previous decade, big global firms had come to worry incessantly about running afoul of U.S. financial sanctions. Now, they had another thing to worry about: export controls, which blocked foreign companies not from accessing the U.S. financial system but rather from buying certain American products.

Ross had had little to do with the settlement, which was all but signed by the time he arrived at Commerce, but it was still his first major public action as secretary. When Ross learned in early 2018 that ZTE was violating the terms of the settlement—the company had even awarded juicy bonuses to executives it had promised to reprimand—he was furious. On April 16, Ross approved a "denial order" on ZTE, a rarely used, draconian export control that barred the Chinese company from buying *all* U.S.-made products. American sanctions got their power from the indispensability of the dollar and the U.S. financial system. The denial order on ZTE got its power from the indispensability of American technology.

The impact was swift and devastating. The day after Commerce imposed the penalty, ZTE suspended trading of its shares on the Hong Kong and Shenzhen exchanges as it assessed the "full range of implications." Three weeks later, the company made a stunning announcement: "As a result of the denial order, the major operating activities of the company have ceased." ZTE had effectively shut down. By weaponizing America's central role in high-end technology, Washington was on the cusp of destroying China's second-largest telecom equipment maker. And it all happened in less than a month.

Xi Jinping could not sit idly by as a major Chinese tech company imploded. On May 8, he placed an emergency phone call to Trump. Xi pleaded with Trump to give ZTE a reprieve as a personal favor. He cited the tens of thousands of Chinese workers who stood to lose their jobs (an appeal that would have been more compelling coming from a democratic leader than the head of a one-party dictatorship who didn't answer to voters). Still, Trump agreed, assuming that Xi would owe him one down the road.

A few days later, Trump revealed the abrupt reversal in what one advisor called "the most off-brand tweet that the president ever made." It read:

President Xi of China, and I, are working together to give massive Chinese
phone company, ZTE, a way to get back into business, fast. Too many jobs
in China lost. Commerce Department has been instructed to get it done!

Why Trump suddenly cared about Chinese jobs was anyone's guess. The
next day, he clarified in another tweet that American businesses also had a
stake in ZTE's future:

ZTE, the large Chinese phone company, buys a big percentage of individual parts from U.S. companies. This is also reflective of the larger trade
deal we are negotiating with China and my personal relationship with
President Xi.

Trump was giving ZTE a new lease on life. His motivations were also becoming clearer: He was willing to set aside national security concerns and
undercut a decision by his own commerce secretary if it might help him get
the China trade deal that he coveted. This was now obvious both to his own
administration and to the rest of the world, and Xi would use this knowledge to his advantage in the years to come.

Congress tried but failed to reverse Trump's concession on ZTE through
legislation. The Commerce Department hurriedly resumed negotiations
with ZTE, and in June, Ross dutifully announced another settlement in
which the Chinese firm agreed to pay an additional $1 billion fine—a pen-
alty that was, inexplicably, smaller than the first one. Paying up was a much
better deal for ZTE than going out of business. Before long, the company
resumed operations and its stock rebounded.

ZTE had been spared, but for Chinese leaders, the episode was a wake-up
call to the vulnerability of their technology champions. Beijing could not
always rely on the goodwill of U.S. presidents. Shortly after the original
denial order, Xi implored his countrymen to "acutely grasp the historical
opportunity" to achieve homegrown technological breakthroughs. He
proceeded to launch several new initiatives seeking to end China's dependence on foreign-made hardware and software. Over the next few months, a
newspaper run by China's Ministry of Science and Technology published a
series of thirty-five articles titled "What Are Our Chokepoints?" The "heavy

fist" of the denial order on ZTE had driven home to China the urgent need to break reliance on a variety of U.S.-controlled "chokepoints," including high-end computer chips.

The ZTE fracas was a wake-up call for Washington, too. It was conventional wisdom that the United States would struggle to wield economic leverage over China the way it had over Russia and Iran, especially if it acted unilaterally. Yet here was Wilbur Ross, dispatching and then resuscitating a leading Chinese tech company at the stroke of a pen.

Two additional developments around the same time further reinforced that America's economic weapons could have far-reaching impact even without help from other countries. A few weeks earlier, a former Russian double agent named Sergei Skripal and his daughter Yulia were found unconscious on a park bench in the British town of Salisbury. They had been poisoned with Novichok, a lethal nerve agent originally developed by the Soviet Union. The British government quickly shared with its allies conclusive intelligence linking the attack to Moscow.

Russia had deployed a chemical weapon on NATO territory, an act so brazen even Trump conceded it demanded a response. First, the State Department expelled sixty Russian officials from the United States and closed the Russian consulate in Seattle. A few weeks later, Treasury issued the first major sanctions against Russia since 2014. Among the targets were the oligarch Oleg Deripaska and his aluminum company, Rusal. Unlike Obama's "scalpel-like" sanctions, which barred Russian targets only from U.S. capital markets, Rusal was hit with blocking sanctions that cut the company off from the U.S. financial system entirely. This was hardly trivial, considering that Rusal was the world's second-largest aluminum company, responsible for some 7 percent of global aluminum production.

As with the denial order on ZTE, the sanctions on Rusal were unilateral. No one from the Trump administration had bothered consulting America's allies beforehand. The move sent shock waves across world markets regardless. Rusal's stock was slashed in half. The London Metal Exchange refused to accept trades in Russian aluminum unless buyers could prove that the metal was not made by Rusal. Aluminum prices skyrocketed by 30 percent, affecting everything from Boeing's production of airplanes to Ford's manufacture of the F-150 pickup truck. After days of nonstop lobbying from U.S. executives and foreign diplomats, Treasury waived the sanctions on Rusal and eventually lifted them as part of a deal with Deripaska struck later in the year.

The same day Xi called Trump to ask for leniency on behalf of ZTE, Trump announced that the United States was leaving the Iran nuclear deal. He had fired Rex Tillerson from his post as secretary of state and H. R. Mc-Master from his role as national security advisor, replacing them respectively with Mike Pompeo and John Bolton, two men with no qualms about torching the JCPOA. Trump then resurrected sanctions against Iran in an approach he dubbed "maximum pressure," which amounted to reinstating all the Obama-era sanctions and enforcing them aggressively. The sanctions lacked support from any other major country. They would upend Iran's economy all the same.

In the span of just a few weeks, the Trump administration had demonstrated that America's economic weapons could wreak havoc with staggering speed even when the United States acted alone. This was an unsettling revelation not just for U.S. rivals such as China, Russia, and Iran—each of which had been targeted directly—but for allies like Germany and Japan. Trump had also shown that he was much less risk-averse than his predecessor had been. Obama officials had agonized over the potential economic blowback of sanctions and spent countless hours coordinating with U.S. allies. The Trump administration shot from the hip and without warning, collateral damage be damned.

If nothing else, foreign adversaries could take comfort in the fickleness and fecklessness on display in Trump's treatment of ZTE and Rusal. The U.S. president was quick to anger and quicker to submit when either of his favored constituencies, American CEOs and foreign autocrats, complained. Faced with pushback from these quarters, Trump would reverse course even if he got nothing in return and regardless of the criticism he was sure to face from hawks on Capitol Hill and in his own administration.

To Matt Pottinger, however, Trump's reversal mattered less than the lesson taught by the strike on ZTE: Washington could exploit technology as a chokepoint, much like it did with the U.S. dollar. In fact, American technology was so essential that cutting off access to it—a measure that Pottinger had already recommended in his strategy paper—could send a major Chinese tech company into a death spiral. As new instances of Chinese economic malfeasance came to light in the months ahead, Pottinger and his colleagues would keep that lesson in mind.

41

The Validation: Fujian Jinhua

On Saturday, September 29, 2018, dignitaries and diplomats assembled at the Chinese embassy in Washington, a limestone edifice of Lego-like shapes designed by the renowned Chinese American architect I. M. Pei. They had come in honor of China's National Day, a holiday commemorating the proclamation of the People's Republic of China by Mao Zedong in 1949.

Their host, the Chinese ambassador Cui Tiankai, delivered a boilerplate diplomat's speech about the need for "mutual respect and win-win cooperation." Matt Pottinger, also in attendance, skipped the niceties and addressed the crowd with unusual candor. "In the United States, competition is not a four-letter word," he said. "We at the Trump administration have updated our China policy to bring the concept of competition to the forefront. It's right there at the top of the president's national security strategy."

Pottinger exhorted the audience not to beat around the bush about the state of U.S.-China relations. Breaking into Mandarin, he recited a passage from Confucius's *Analects*: "If names cannot be correct, then language is not in accordance with the truth of things; and if language is not in accordance with the truth of things, affairs cannot be carried on to success."

Pottinger's remarks gave voice to what everyone could already see. Over the summer, as a follow-on to Robert Lighthizer's 301 investigation, Trump had launched his much-anticipated trade war, slapping China with a slew of tariffs. The White House Council of Economic Advisers created an algorithm to select categories of goods where tariffs were more likely to hurt

Chinese exporters than American importers. The algorithm recommended a list of high-tech goods and industrial products.

Beijing swiftly retaliated, kicking off a cycle of tit-for-tat escalation. By the time Pottinger spoke at the Chinese embassy, Lighthizer's office had imposed tariffs on roughly half of the $500 billion-plus of annual U.S. imports from China. As the standoff intensified, the Dow Jones Industrial Average shed some 1,000 points. Hank Paulson, now a semi-retired wise man and philanthropist living in small-town Illinois, warned that an "economic Iron Curtain" risked fracturing the global economy.

Though it was the trade war making headlines, the administration and Congress simultaneously pushed through a raft of less-noticed measures that would be just as consequential. In August, Trump signed a law that bolstered the authority of the Committee on Foreign Investment in the United States (CFIUS), the body tasked with blocking attempts by foreign firms to acquire U.S. companies if the acquisition poses national security concerns. The new law required that any foreign investment involving critical technology first obtain approval from CFIUS, and it empowered the committee to block even minority investments.

The law did not mention China by name. But as Senator John Cornyn, one of its main proponents, testified, "The context for this legislation is important and relatively straightforward, and it's China." Gone were the days when Beijing-backed firms could snatch up stakes in Silicon Valley tech start-ups as if they were just like any other VC fund on Sand Hill Road.

In the months that followed, Trump also signed laws that strengthened export control authorities and created the U.S. International Development Finance Corporation, a new institution intended to enable the United States to make overseas investments in competition with China's Belt and Road Initiative. In Congress, a bipartisan group of senators introduced legislation that would not only prohibit all federal agencies from buying Huawei and ZTE products but also bar them from dealing with companies that did. American firms that used Huawei and ZTE kit would be cut off from doing business with the U.S. government, which in practice amounted to a near-total ban on buying either company's equipment. The amendment passed into law as part of the Pentagon's annual budget bill. Consensus was growing in Washington that China had to be kept at arm's length from the U.S. tech sector—and the policy levers were emerging to make it happen.

Still absent, however, was any clear strategy to prevent China from chipping away at the load-bearing pillar of U.S. technological primacy: the semiconductor industry. In the final days of the Obama administration, lobbyists for the U.S. chip sector had raised a red flag about Beijing's persistent efforts to supplant American companies' leading role in the market, but their warnings had not produced any meaningful change.

The case of Micron was instructive. Headquartered in Boise, Idaho, Micron was America's largest manufacturer of memory chips, a brutally competitive segment of the semiconductor industry. The world market for these chips was dominated by just three companies: Micron and its South Korean rivals, Samsung and SK Hynix. Producing memory chips at scale required sophisticated technical know-how and billions of dollars of investment. Clearing these hurdles as a newcomer was next to impossible—unless, of course, that newcomer had the patronage of the CCP.

Sure enough, in 2016, the Chinese central government partnered with authorities in Fujian, a coastal province in the country's southeast, to set up a homegrown memory chip company. With more than $5 billion in government capital, the new venture, known as Fujian Jinhua, would advance the marquee goal of "Made in China 2025": increasing China's self-sufficiency in semiconductors.

What happened next was a textbook case of Chinese intellectual property theft. Fujian Province sat just a hundred miles across the sea from Taiwan, where Micron operated factories in which thousands of skilled engineers produced its proprietary memory chips. Using a Taiwanese semiconductor foundry called UMC as its proxy, Fujian Jinhua poached the president of Micron's Taiwanese subsidiary, Stephen Chen, and several other high-level Micron employees in Taiwan. From his new role as a senior vice president at UMC, Chen negotiated a deal to transfer memory chip technology to Fujian Jinhua and recruited a number of his former Micron colleagues to join him. One of those individuals, Kenny Wang, brought nine hundred confidential files with him, containing valuable trade secrets belonging to Micron. Fujian Jinhua and UMC used this stolen information to file for patents in China.

In late 2017, Micron sued Fujian Jinhua in California; the following year, Fujian Jinhua countersued Micron on its home turf, Fujian Province. To say that the deck was stacked against Micron would be an understatement. The Fujian provincial government was a partial owner of Fujian Jinhua, and the company Micron was suing had been created to advance one of the CCP's top strategic objectives. The Fujian court swiftly ruled in favor of Fujian Jinhua, concluding that Micron was violating its rival's patents. The ruling was outrageous. But Micron was nervous about taking a stand that could risk its access to the Chinese market, where it earned more than half of its $30 billion in annual revenue. It needed support from Washington.

In the summer of 2018, Sanjay Mehrotra, Micron's CEO, turned to the Trump administration for help. He first tried to get Treasury to impose blocking sanctions on Fujian Jinhua, but ran into immediate opposition from Steven Mnuchin, who remained leery of putting pretty much any economic pressure on Beijing. Mehrotra had more luck with Wilbur Ross. Unlike Mnuchin, Ross could not play gatekeeper to the almighty U.S. dollar. But he was more of a China hawk, and as commerce secretary he could block foreign companies from buying critical American technology. Ross's strike against ZTE a few months prior had shown that such penalties could have devastating effects.

Export controls on a Chinese semiconductor company could be just as damaging as they had been to a Chinese telecom firm. The reason was that U.S. companies had almost exclusive control of the high-end machinery needed to manufacture advanced chips. Three Silicon Valley companies— Applied Materials, Lam Research, and KLA—dominated this vital part of the supply chain, with just a few viable competitors in Japan. Without machinery from these U.S. or Japanese firms, it was impossible to produce advanced chips. Fujian Jinhua was months away from full-scale production of memory chips, but all of the company's gains would be undone if it lost access to the machinery and spare parts that powered its factory.

Until now, Commerce had used its toughest export controls only in circumstances that fit a narrow definition of America's national security interests—typically, when firms were caught supporting rogue regimes or terrorist groups. ZTE, for instance, had violated U.S. sanctions by reexporting American-made technology to Iran. Ross, however, was coming to favor a more expansive view of national security, one that included Chinese intellectual property theft.

On October 29, Commerce announced that it was adding Fujian Jinhua to the Entity List, meaning that no U.S. company could sell anything to the Chinese firm without first obtaining a license. This was not quite as harsh as a denial order, but since licenses were almost never granted, the practical effect was similar. Three days later, the Justice Department filed criminal charges against Fujian Jinhua for stealing Micron's trade secrets. NSC officials secured a commitment from Tokyo that Japanese firms would cease doing business with Fujian Jinhua, too. In short order, Fujian Jinhua was forced to halt production.

For the second time in a matter of months, Ross had cut down a Chinese tech champion. Just as Treasury had done a decade earlier, Commerce was showing the underappreciated power of its economic arsenal. Restricting access to American technology, it appeared, could be just as damaging as cutting off access to the U.S. dollar. Commerce, an agency whose hodge-podge of responsibilities included forecasting the weather and conducting the census, was taking a seat at the high table of U.S. national security policy.

42

The First Shot at Huawei

In December 2018, Donald Trump and Xi Jinping were in Buenos Aires for a G20 summit. Amid the worsening economic standoff between their governments, the two men sat down one night at the Park Hyatt Hotel to break bread (and steaks, onions, and ricotta).

Trump again asked for Xi's help boosting Chinese purchases of American farm goods and reining in North Korea's nuclear program. He also pressed him to curb trafficking of fentanyl into the United States. Xi seemed receptive. As a goodwill gesture, Trump agreed to delay the next round of U.S. tariffs, which had been scheduled to take effect on New Year's Day. The conversation was cordial, even friendly.

Trump and Xi also pledged to renew the push for a U.S.-China trade deal. The Chinese side would be led by Liu He, a savvy economist and childhood friend of Xi. Leading the American side was Robert Lighthizer, whom Trump elevated above Steven Mnuchin as the top U.S. negotiator with China at the urging of Matt Pottinger and Jared Kushner.

But the biggest news in U.S.-China relations that night came not out of Buenos Aires but from an arrival gate at Vancouver International Airport. Around the time Trump and Xi sat down for dinner, Meng Wanzhou, Huawei's CFO and the daughter of the company's founder, Ren Zhengfei, was arrested by Canadian authorities as she got off a plane from Hong Kong.

The arrest was made at the request of U.S. law enforcement, which sought Meng's extradition to stand trial in the United States. American authorities suspected that several years earlier, Huawei had used a subsidiary called

Skycom to transfer telecom equipment to Iran—in violation of U.S. sanctions—and collect more than $100 million in payments.

Meng, who had previously served on the board of Skycom, denied that the company had any relationship with Huawei. One of Huawei's banks, HSBC, was not so sure. In 2012, HSBC was fined $1.9 billion for violating U.S. sanctions, an experience it was eager not to repeat. The bank agreed to install an independent monitor and hired Stuart Levey, a founding father of American financial warfare, as chief legal officer. When HSBC concluded that Meng's assurances were fishy and that Huawei may have evaded American sanctions, the bank informed federal prosecutors in Brooklyn.

The evidence against Huawei went much further than HSBC's suspicions. In 2014, when U.S. authorities seized the laptop of ZTE's CFO at Boston's Logan Airport, they had found evidence of ZTE's sanctions violations. But the laptop also contained a document outlining how ZTE's larger rival—identified by the code name "F7"—had developed even more sophisticated methods to dodge American sanctions. The document explained that F7 used "cut-off companies" to sign and execute deals on its behalf in countries like Iran. "This cut-off company's capital credit and capability are relatively strong compared to our company," ZTE lamented. "It can cut off risks more effectively." The details left little doubt that F7 was in fact Huawei.

The wheels of justice turned slowly, but in August 2018, after three years of investigation, U.S. prosecutors filed sealed charges against Meng and Huawei, and a federal judge in Brooklyn issued a warrant for Meng's arrest—all of it unbeknownst to Trump and his national security team.

Four months later, Meng's layover in Vancouver—she was traveling en route to Mexico—gave Canadian law enforcement the chance to make the arrest at the behest of their American counterparts. National Security Advisor John Bolton learned of the impending arrest some twenty-four hours before, but he decided not to inform Trump, whom Bolton feared would slip up and tip off Xi over dinner in Buenos Aires. Trump and Xi didn't find out about Meng's arrest until after they had bid each other farewell.

The heir apparent of China's largest private company now awaited extradition proceedings in a Canadian jail. (She would later be moved to house arrest in her multimillion-dollar Vancouver mansion.) True to form, Trump grumbled about the arrest, telling his top aides that Meng was "the Ivanka Trump of China." Chinese officials denounced the United States and Canada for having "seriously harmed" Meng's human rights. Soon thereafter, in a barely disguised act of hostage diplomacy, Chinese authorities arrested two Canadian nationals, the former diplomat Michael Kovrig and the businessman Michael Spavor, on phony charges.

Meng's arrest also rattled the corporate world. The charges against Huawei resembled the ones U.S. law enforcement had levied against ZTE. It stood to reason that Huawei, therefore, could soon become the target of powerful export controls as well. At minimum, this would mean a huge hit for American companies that sold billions of dollars of parts to Huawei each year. If the penalties destabilized Huawei itself, the fallout would be global. Huawei was larger and more resilient than ZTE, but it still depended heavily on U.S. technology. The company sold personal computers powered by Intel processors; its smartphones used American-made memory chips and radio frequency components. Even its vaunted 5G equipment couldn't function without American semiconductors and other microelectronics. As for Huawei's in-house chip design unit, HiSilicon, it had outsourced production to TSMC, a Taiwanese company whose foundries ran on American software and machine tools. A senior telecom executive told the *Financial Times* that a ZTE-style denial order on Huawei would have the effect of a "small nuclear weapon" on the global telecom industry.

Indeed, the blast radius would extend well beyond Huawei and be felt in sectors outside of telecom. In 2018, Huawei spent some $11 billion buying components and services from American companies. This was a sizable chunk of the $120 billion of total U.S. exports to China that year, and it pointed to a broader dilemma: Trump could ban certain U.S. exports to China, or he could boost those exports in an effort to close the trade deficit, but he could not do both.

Beijing faced a similar problem. It was telling that the only two major U.S. imports that China had so far exempted from its retaliatory tariffs were American semiconductors and commercial aircraft. Beijing needed these products and had few viable substitutes, despite its efforts under "Made in China 2025." In fact, when trade talks resumed after the Trump-Xi dinner in Buenos Aires, Chinese negotiators offered to buy hundreds of billions of dollars' worth of American chips over the coming years.

Ren Zhengfei projected confidence that Huawei could weather the storm unleashed by the U.S. criminal charges and Meng's arrest. For a time, it looked as if he might be right. Toward the end of 2018, Huawei closed a major new 5G deal in Portugal. The company now held more than twenty commercial 5G contracts around the world, cementing its status as the market leader. Pottinger and his colleagues were pushing the UK, Germany, and others to ban Huawei from their forthcoming 5G networks. But besides Australia, Japan, and New Zealand, which had each implemented official or de facto bans, progress was scant. "Actions speak louder than words," crowed one of Huawei's board members. Huawei's low prices, generous financing terms, and reliable customer service were drowning out Washington's warnings.

The charges against Huawei had opened the door for export controls, but the Trump administration was divided on how to proceed. While Matt Pottinger and his team at the NSC wanted to come down hard on Huawei, they left it to other parts of the government to recommend a specific course of action. At the State Department, Christopher Ford, the assistant secretary for international security and nonproliferation, pushed for export controls on Huawei and proposed adding the company to the Entity List—the same penalty that had just undone Fujian Jinhua. Top officials at Treasury, chief among them Steven Mnuchin, vehemently opposed the plan.

Commerce Secretary Wilbur Ross, for his part, was of two minds. Ross was a China hawk, and Commerce officials were pleased to have a say in matters of national security. But their main constituency was U.S. industry, which had plenty to lose in any sanctions or export controls on Huawei. Ross remained undecided, but the Commerce officials responsible for export controls actively resisted Ford's proposal.

That was, at least, until Nazak Nikakhtar showed up. An Iranian-born trade lawyer in her mid-forties, Nikakhtar had spent much of her career representing U.S. companies in business disputes before joining the Commerce Department in 2018. Initially, she worked on trade issues. In early 2019, however, Ross asked her to temporarily head up the Commerce bureau that oversees export controls until he could find a permanent leader. This put her at the center of the Huawei debate at a critical moment.

Like Robert Lighthizer, Nikakhtar was shaped by her time representing companies that suffered unfair treatment at the hands of Chinese rivals. "Once we allowed China to join the WTO, that's when we really started to see the onslaught of China's predatory economic tactics beginning to hollow out our industries," she maintained. China's playbook, in Nikakhtar's telling, was to capture industries from the bottom up. First Chinese firms took over low-margin businesses that U.S. companies readily let go. The Chinese firms would then recycle their revenues into R&D and gradually move up the value chain. All the while, they benefited from massive subsidies, stolen intellectual property, and other unfair advantages, allowing them to skip costly stages of technological development and undercut their competitors' prices. Eventually, they came to own the entire industry. Huawei's rise in the global telecom equipment market fit this strategy to a tee.

Meanwhile, Washington's tools to counter these practices—for instance, filing disputes at the WTO—were woefully deficient. They were not designed to thwart economic misconduct committed under a veil of deniability, which was Beijing's way. "We've been witnessing this assault on our industries," Nikakhtar explained, "and our laws have not been updated to adequately fight against it."

If Nikakhtar had her druthers, the Treasury Department would hit Huawei with blocking sanctions. Since this was a nonstarter under Mnuchin's leadership, she settled for supporting State's proposal to add Huawei to the Entity List. Yes, some American companies would lose a big customer, which made many of her colleagues at Commerce nervous. But the alternative was giving Huawei a free pass to continue endangering U.S. national security.

With this reasoning, Nikakhtar managed to win over Ross and overrule her skeptical colleagues. There was now consensus among the agencies that managed export controls—State, Commerce, Defense, and Energy—to add Huawei to the Entity List. While Treasury remained opposed, it did not have a seat on the committee.

Given the major economic and diplomatic ramifications of imposing export controls on Huawei, the final decision rested with Trump. But getting the president's approval would be its own problem. Trump was chasing a trade deal with China that he envisioned as the crowning achievement of his presidency. Lighthizer and Liu He, China's chief negotiator, seemed to be making progress. They were working on a 150-page agreement that—at least in draft form—would commit Beijing to revise its laws and regulations to better protect intellectual property and put an end to forced technology transfers. Lighthizer had come to respect Liu and trusted that he was serious about making a deal. Bringing down the hammer on Huawei would endanger that progress.

It didn't help that Trump was notoriously receptive to flattery—and Huawei, pulling out all the stops to avoid being slapped with export controls, wasn't afraid to use it. Ren Zhengfei had recently embarked on a charm offensive, giving a rare public interview in which he applauded Trump's tax cuts and lauded him as "a great president." This was an uncharacteristic move for the septuagenarian CEO, who instilled a "wolf culture" at Huawei that encouraged daring, aggressiveness, and grueling work hours. He had a reputation in China as an intrepid entrepreneur and uncompromising visionary in the mold of Steve Jobs. But with his daughter now under house arrest in Canada and his business staring down the barrel of U.S. penalties, Ren opted for a conciliatory tone. "I love my country. I support the Communist Party," he told his interviewer. "But I will never do anything to harm any country in the world." In the following weeks, Huawei went on a global media blitz. "Don't believe everything you hear. Come and see us," implored a full-page ad that Huawei ran in the *Wall Street Journal* in February 2019.

The Chinese government also did its part to lower the temperature in Washington. In March, Chinese premier Li Keqiang opened the annual session of China's rubber-stamp legislature with an almost two-hour-long address on the economy. Speaking from the rostrum at the Great Hall of the People, Li discussed tax cuts and initiatives to curb pollution but made no mention of "Made in China 2025," which had featured prominently in his addresses the previous several years—and which Lighthizer cited at length in his 301 report.

Despite China's effort to soften its tone and the positive progress on the trade talks, U.S. national security officials remained wary. Beijing often dangled the prospect of improved economic relations to try to fend off unwanted action by Washington. And China's drive for global economic domination hadn't slowed down. On March 12, the European Union released a public strategy labeling China a "systemic rival"—a first, and a departure from the EU's usual emphasis on partnership and cooperation with Beijing. Yet just over a week later, Italian Prime Minister Giuseppe Conte welcomed Xi to Rome and announced that Italy would be the first major democracy to join the Belt and Road Initiative. Soon thereafter, Germany revealed that it would not ban Huawei from its future 5G infrastructure, despite American pressure. The following month, the United Kingdom followed suit, and Phillip Hammond, the chancellor of the exchequer, jetted to Beijing to offer Britain's hand in advancing the Belt and Road Initiative.

Any American hopes of an economic reset with Beijing were dashed on Friday, May 3. That day, Lighthizer's team of trade negotiators received an unexpected email from their Chinese counterparts with a Microsoft Word version of the draft trade agreement, including edits from the Chinese side in Track Changes. Crossed out in red were all of Beijing's key concessions on issues like intellectual property and forced technology transfers. Apparently, Xi had weighed in and deemed the proposed concessions a bridge too far.

An apoplectic Trump took to Twitter over the weekend, warning that he would raise tariffs on China within days. "The Trade Deal with China continues, but too slowly, as they attempt to renegotiate. No!" Trump fumed. The new tariffs went into effect a week later.

Now, an angry Trump was finally ready to consider hitting Huawei with export controls. Around 3:30 p.m. on Wednesday, May 15, Trump and his top aides gathered in the Oval Office to discuss the idea. Steven Mnuchin once again tried to throw cold water on the plan, citing the spillover effects on U.S. industry and the risk of fully torpedoing the trade talks with Beijing. Bolton and Ross argued the other side. Trump opted to move forward.

In a last-ditch effort, Mnuchin complained that the wording of Ross's draft press release was too extreme. Couldn't they at least tone it down? Ross read the statement aloud. "It's a fucking great statement," Trump gushed. "It's beautiful. Add 'with the approval of the President.'"

43

≡

A False Start

Jiangxi, a landlocked province in southeastern China, is known for its rolling mountains and dense forests. It's where Mao Zedong and his followers hid out and established the country's first Communist government. Jiangxi was also the starting point of the Long March, the Communists' brutal, yearlong, six-thousand-mile-trek across the country, which would become a founding myth of the People's Republic of China.

On May 20, 2019, five days after the Trump administration slapped export controls on Huawei, Xi Jinping traveled to Jiangxi with his chief trade negotiator and childhood friend Liu He to lay a wreath at the site where the Long March began. "We are here at the starting point of the Long March to remember the time when the Red Army began its journey," Xi proclaimed before a cheering crowd. "We are now embarking on a new Long March, and we must start all over again!" With the recent shock of the U.S. action against Huawei, Xi was sounding a note of defiance.

Jiangxi wasn't significant only because of its history. The region is also home to many immense rare-earth processing facilities, one of which Xi toured on his visit. (China boasts the world's largest known reserves of rare earths, and Chinese firms dominate the step in the production chain in which the minerals are processed into essential industrial materials.) China's commanding position in the rare-earths trade gave it significant geopolitical leverage. Beijing had demonstrated that leverage in 2010 when it cut off exports of these minerals to Japan. Just as Huawei depended on chips and software from America, Lockheed Martin depended on rare earths from China. "The Middle East has oil," Deng Xiaoping once said, "China has rare earths."

China's trump card: Xi Jinping tours a rare-earth
processing facility in Jiangxi in May 2019.

"Will rare earths become China's counter-weapon against the U.S.'s unwarranted suppression?" mused an online bulletin by China's economic planning agency a few days after Xi's visit to Jiangxi. The *People's Daily*, the official newspaper of the CCP, published an ominous line that also appeared in the paper before China's 1962 war against India and its 1979 attack on Vietnam: "Don't say you were not warned."

For Beijing, the export controls against Huawei were a turning point. Until then, most Chinese officials believed that Trump didn't want the kind of protracted economic war that Matt Pottinger and other hawks at the NSC advocated. He wanted to appear tough on China and deliver a quick economic "win"—after he declared victory in the trade war, U.S.-China relations would go back to normal. The Huawei decision challenged this conviction. "This was a watershed moment in how China views the trade war," a Chinese official said. "It's crystal clear that the U.S.'s motive isn't just trade. It's both political and strategic. They want to keep China from becoming stronger."

At the end of May, China's commerce ministry announced that it would create its own "Unreliable Entity List" to match the U.S. Commerce Department's Entity List. Details were sparse, but Chinese officials indicated that they planned to blacklist foreign firms suspected of "damaging the legitimate rights and interest of Chinese companies and jeopardizing China's national security and interests." Beijing also resorted to its traditional, more informal methods of economic warfare, summoning executives from Microsoft, Dell, Samsung, and other foreign companies and warning of dire consequences if they complied with U.S. export controls on Huawei.

Nonetheless, several companies did comply, severing their ties to Huawei within days. One of the biggest firms to cut Huawei loose was Google. Most of the smartphones Huawei sold outside China relied on a proprietary version of Google's Android operating system, which Huawei now had to abandon. Future Huawei smartphone users would lose access to the Google Play Store—one of the leading mobile app marketplaces—and to Google products such as Gmail and YouTube. Existing users would eventually stop receiving software updates.

Huawei's smartphones were cheap and in high demand, but it would be hard to persuade consumers outside China to buy them if the phones lacked some of the world's most basic and popular apps. (Google had long been banned inside China, so its decision to jettison Huawei wouldn't affect Huawei's domestic sales.) Huawei's international smartphone revenues plummeted by 40 percent in May alone. Even the ever-confident Ren Zhengfei was taken aback. "We didn't think that the U.S. would attack Huawei with such great strategy and determination," Ren said. He estimated that his company would need to reduce smartphone production by $30 billion.

By contrast, the export controls seemed to barely dent Huawei's 5G business. As the company's chief strategy architect noted, Ren "always argued that our business should be ready to prepare a Plan B," and so it had. After the U.S. government's denial order against ZTE the previous year, Huawei had begun stockpiling semiconductors and other key components. It now had a year's worth of the chips needed to build 5G base stations, meaning the division's work could proceed unimpeded for at least a while despite being cut off from U.S. suppliers. In the two months after Huawei was added to the Entity List, it racked up another eleven contracts for 5G networks.

America's chipmakers, on the other hand, could feel the ripple effects of the move against Huawei. Shares in Qualcomm, which earned 5 percent of its revenue from Huawei, swooned, as did those of other U.S. semiconductor firms. Micron, the U.S. chipmaker that previously pushed for export controls against Fujian Jinhua, was hit hard, too. Huawei was Micron's single biggest customer, with annual sales to the Chinese firm in the billions of dollars. More than 10 percent of Micron's annual revenue was on the line.

Soon, Sanjay Mehrotra, Micron's CEO, was back in Washington, except this time he was arguing against, not for, export controls. When Mehrotra had pushed the United States to sanction Fujian Jinhua, Steven Mnuchin had stonewalled him. Now, the treasury secretary was an ally. Mnuchin accompanied Mehrotra and other executives from the board of the Semiconductor Industry Association on a visit to Wilbur Ross at the Commerce Department. In a presentation that one Commerce official described as "hostile," Mnuchin and the chip executives laid out their case that American firms stood to lose massive revenues because of the Huawei restrictions, perhaps to the point of industry collapse. They argued that Ross should remove Huawei from the Entity List or, failing that, water down the penalties so that U.S. business with Huawei could carry on largely as before.

Ross held firm, but as a longtime businessman, he understood the executives' concerns. Their companies did so much business with Huawei because it was both lucrative and legal; indeed, until recently, Washington had cheered them on. Their ties with Huawei were the manifestation of the type of economic interdependence that was supposed to encourage China to adopt democratic reforms and sustain good relations between Beijing and Washington.

To the worried executives, the strike on Huawei seemed like the beginning of a bigger economic war. If selling components to Huawei undermined American national security, what did that mean for selling to other Chinese tech companies? These concerns were heightened by Commerce's decision, a month after adding Huawei to the Entity List, to impose export controls on a Chinese supercomputer manufacturer, Sugon, which also had close links to U.S. companies. The logical endpoint of the administration's approach, it seemed, was a much broader technological decoupling between the United States and China. Decades of U.S.-China business ties in the tech sector could unravel.

In June, Xi placed another call to Trump. Just as he had done to win relief for ZTE, Xi implored Trump to cut Huawei a break. This time, his entreaty was laced with a threat: If Washington didn't back down on Huawei, the overall U.S.-China relationship would suffer. Trump, whose top priority remained securing a trade deal, took this seriously and suggested that lifting restrictions on Huawei could be on the table as part of the trade negotiations.

Ten days later, on the sidelines of another G20 summit, Trump and Xi met face-to-face at the Imperial Hotel in Osaka, Japan. Again, Xi pressed for relief on Huawei. Eager to restart the trade talks, Trump was ready to throw Xi a bone. At a press conference the next day, Trump indicated he would soften restrictions on Huawei. "U.S. companies can sell their equipment to Huawei," the president affirmed. "We're talking about equipment where there's no great national security problem with it." In justifying his about-face, Trump explained that American companies "were not exactly happy that they couldn't sell" to Huawei.

The precise nature and extent of Trump's concession remained unclear. But Huawei rejoiced anyway, while Bolton, Pottinger, and other national security officials were furious. It seemed like the ZTE reversal all over again but on a much bigger scale and with more serious implications. Wilbur Ross, the official ultimately on the hook to implement Trump's policy, raced to get out in front of it. Shortly after Trump's press conference, Ross explained that Huawei would remain on the Entity List, but that Commerce would consider granting licenses for specific sales to Huawei, on a case-by-case basis, "where there is no threat to U.S. national security." He stressed that Commerce would review license applications with a "presumption of denial."

In the coming months, Commerce received hundreds of license applications from American companies seeking to sell to Huawei, which piled up as agency officials struggled to devise coherent criteria for evaluating them. As they waited, U.S. semiconductor firms found legal ways to get around the export controls. There were plenty of loopholes, partially because, unlike Treasury, the Commerce Department had not spent the previous decade on the forefront of economic warfare. U.S. companies that manufactured their chips outside the United States, for instance, could still sell the chips to Huawei with no license required. They could also continue selling chips to Huawei subsidiaries that were not explicitly named on the Entity List.

Once the semiconductor companies caught on, they took full advantage. Micron resumed sales of memory chips to Huawei, causing Micron's stock to rally. Arm, a leading British chip designer, initially suspended business with Huawei because it relied on American intellectual property. But the company soon reversed course and determined that its sales to Huawei were "UK-origin technologies."

Notwithstanding the pain it inflicted, the economic weapon fired at Huawei was starting to look like a dud. It had managed to wipe out Huawei's smartphone sales outside China, but the company compensated for these losses by boosting sales domestically. Critically, Huawei's 5G business survived unscathed; in fact, it continued to dominate, amassing more than sixty commercial contracts. Through the end of the third quarter of 2019, Huawei's total revenues hit $86 billion—nearly 25 percent higher than the same period the previous year. It helped that Huawei had hoarded 5G components in preparation for this sort of contingency. But the most important reason for the company's resilience was that the U.S. export controls simply weren't potent enough to move most global companies to shun such a big customer.

Meanwhile, even though American firms had avoided the worst, they still bristled at the distortions caused by the Huawei restrictions. U.S. chipmakers that had invested in the United States were discriminated against, as the semiconductors they produced domestically could no longer be sold to Huawei, whereas competitors that had moved manufacturing abroad thrived. This created a perverse incentive to shift even more production overseas.

To make matters worse, rivals in places like Japan, South Korea, and Taiwan faced no restrictions whatsoever on selling to Huawei, enabling them to supply the Chinese giant with products it could no longer source from the United States. If American companies spurned Huawei, a massive customer, only for foreign rivals to scoop up their business, Huawei would be unharmed while U.S. firms suffered. A policy that drove such outcomes was illogical, and it left no one on the American side—from national security officials like Pottinger to economic officials like Mnuchin to the companies themselves—satisfied.

By the end of summer 2019, it was clear that U.S. export controls were not nearly as damaging to Huawei as they had been to ZTE or Fujian Jinhua. They had done nothing to stop Huawei's conquest of the global 5G market, and to add insult to injury, they had prompted Beijing to develop a new class of economic weapons and infuriated American industry. The Commerce Department had become a key command center in the economic war, but suddenly, its arsenal didn't look so formidable.

More than a decade earlier, Stuart Levey realized that to impose serious pressure on the Iranian economy, it was not enough for American companies to stop doing business with Iran—companies all over the world had to leave the market, and Washington could compel them to do it. To thwart Huawei, it turned out, the same logic would apply.

44

―――

"Backdoors" and "Betrayal"

By year three of Trump's presidency, Matt Pottinger had distinguished himself as a survivor. He had outlasted three national security advisors, Michael Flynn, H. R. McMaster, and John Bolton. He now served as deputy to the fourth, Robert O'Brien. He also began assuming a more visible role as a face of the China policies he'd helped shape.

On September 19, 2019, Pottinger met with members of the Semiconductor Industry Association at the Hay-Adams Hotel, a short walk from the White House. He was there to listen to the industry's concerns but also to persuade. Ever since the Commerce Department had imposed export controls on Huawei, American chipmakers had been seeking ways to circumvent them. Pottinger hoped to convince the assembled executives that reducing sales to Huawei would be the wiser long-term strategy.

Pottinger explained that Huawei operated, in part, as a surveillance branch of the CCP. Chinese espionage in Africa was a case in point. The African Union's headquarters, a futuristic complex in the Ethiopian capital of Addis Ababa, was built with generous funding from the Chinese government and state-of-the-art network equipment from Huawei. After construction finished in 2012, Chinese intelligence used that Huawei equipment as a "backdoor" to siphon data from the building's servers every single night for five straight years. (What Pottinger could not mention explicitly—because it was still classified at the time—was that the United States had intelligence indicating that Huawei could use similar "backdoors" hidden in its equipment to secretly access telecom networks around the world.) Spying was not the only concern. Huawei's 5G gear could also function as a kill switch that Beijing might one day use to shut down power plants, water systems, and other critical infrastructure. Hence the CCP's dogged support of Huawei in its quest for global 5G leadership.

As Pottinger concluded his presentation, he surveyed the room. "The conscience of everyone sitting around this table should be shocked," he said. The American semiconductor industry sold critical components to Huawei and thus was indirectly enabling its ascent. To continue with business as usual, he argued, would be like letting the KGB build U.S. telecommunications systems at the height of the Cold War simply because the Soviets were offering a discount.

Although the executives were sympathetic to Pottinger's message, most doubted Washington could do much about the problems he described. For one thing, European telecom networks, which were closely linked to America's, were already heavily dependent on Huawei for legacy offerings. More than 50 percent of sites in Germany's 4G network used Huawei technology, and the country was hardly an outlier on the continent. It appeared Europe's reliance on Huawei would only deepen as it upgraded to 5G, as Huawei's edge in this newest technology was even more pronounced than it was for the previous generation, and European governments were rebuffing Washington's entreaties to blacklist Huawei. The executives responded to Pottinger's presentation with a simple and frustrating message: If the U.S. government wanted to avoid all the risks posed by Huawei's dominance, it would not be enough for American companies to cut ties with Huawei; European companies would have to do so, too.

Even in Trump's own administration, not everyone had internalized that China should be viewed more as a rival than as an economic partner. Officials' lack of access to Trump, and the president's vague and off-the-cuff directives—the last thing he'd said on the matter was that "U.S. companies can sell their equipment to Huawei" as long as "there's no great national security problem with it"—did little to clear things up. Commerce officials were neck-deep in license applications by U.S. companies seeking exemptions from the export controls on Huawei, and they were unsure what to do.

Pottinger told his Commerce colleagues that Trump was pursuing a two-pronged strategy. On the one hand, the president was seeking to preserve his personal relationship with Xi Jinping and the appearance of pursuing warmer ties. But as for officials in the bureaucracy, Trump "wants us punching as hard as we can." In effect, Pottinger was telling the Commerce officials to take Trump seriously, not literally—to tune out the verbal concessions that Trump made in public and maintain a default position of being "tough" on China.

This left the issue of getting U.S. allies in Europe and Asia on board with the Huawei restrictions. The United States and its allies had used a similar model during the Cold War, when they formed the Coordinating Committee for Multilateral Export Controls, better known as CoCom, to choke off the Soviet Union's access to certain critical technologies. Resurrecting this strategy would both maximize pressure on Huawei and protect the competitive interests of U.S. industry.

Trump, however, was notoriously wary of cooperating with allies and seemed to take pleasure in taunting them. When French president Emmanuel Macron suggested working together on China during a 2018 meeting at the White House, Trump accused the EU of being "worse than China" and went on a tirade about German car exports. By the fall of 2019, most European countries planned to allow Huawei to help build their own 5G networks. It would make no sense for them to join America's crusade to cut Huawei's access to critical technologies at the same time as they hitched their digital future to the very same company.

With allied cooperation looking unlikely, Commerce officials and lobbyists from the U.S. semiconductor industry—who were eager to level the playing field with foreign competitors—floated a more aggressive approach: pressuring Huawei's business partners around the world. Their first idea was to revise the "de minimis rule," which held that foreign-produced items that used more than 25 percent American content were subject to U.S. export controls. Lowering this threshold would make it harder for chipmakers anywhere to sell to Huawei, so long as their products contained some U.S. components.

The problem was that the de minimis rule applied only to physical components, so it would further incentivize companies to move manufacturing overseas and substitute American components with foreign ones. It would neither crush Huawei nor create a more equitable business landscape for U.S. companies; in fact, it might even make these problems worse.

Owing to these concerns, the lobbyists and Commerce officials moved on to a second option: dusting off a little-known 1959 policy called the Foreign Direct Product Rule, or FDPR, and modifying it to use against Huawei. The original FDPR stated that if foreign factories produced missile components or other sensitive items using U.S. technology, those items were subject to U.S. export controls. A new, Huawei-focused FDPR could ban chip sales to Huawei from *anywhere in the world* so long as the chips were *made using U.S. technology,* as opposed to containing some percentage of American-made content. Virtually all advanced semiconductors relied on intellectual property, design software, and machine tools produced by American firms. While chips were often fabricated overseas, U.S. industry contributed 39 percent of the total value across the semiconductor supply chain, compared with just 6 percent for Chinese firms. No other country came close to America's share.

The new FDPR would function much like secondary sanctions. During the Obama administration, U.S. secondary sanctions presented companies around the world with a stark choice: you can do business with America or Iran, but not both. This cudgel had proven devastatingly effective, slashing Iran's oil sales and severing Iranian banks from the global financial system. After leaving the Iran nuclear deal, the Trump administration had reimposed these secondary sanctions against Iran. And even though other countries objected to them, businesses all over the world fell into line.

The practical implications of a new FDPR would be similar. The Taiwanese tech giant TSMC, the world's largest semiconductor foundry, counted Huawei as its second-biggest customer, right after Apple. Huawei accounted for upward of 15 percent of TSMC's revenue. But TSMC also needed a variety of American software and machine tools to power its foundries. The new FDPR would present TSMC and other chip companies around the world with a choice: you can sell to Huawei or you can buy U.S. technology, but you can't do both.

While the FDPR was being developed and debated, the Trump administration continued its diplomatic push to get allies to shun Huawei. In late 2019, it presented what it considered its strongest piece of evidence: the intelligence revealing that, for more than a decade, Huawei had been embedding secret "backdoors" in its equipment that gave the company access to telecom networks all over the world.

On a December trip to Berlin, Pottinger shared this intelligence with German officials. Afterward, the German Foreign Office produced a memo stating that he had indeed provided a "smoking gun" about the serious espionage threat emanating from Huawei. A lawmaker from Chancellor Angela Merkel's party went so far as to say that allowing Huawei to build Germany's 5G network "would be a maximal loss of control and sovereignty."

Yet Germany was in a tough spot: all three of its top telecom operators were heavily dependent on Huawei. Deutsche Telekom, the market leader, had already begun installing 5G base stations containing Huawei equipment. Banning Huawei would be exorbitantly expensive and could delay the rollout of the country's 5G network, which was supposed to help sustain Germany's industrial prowess into the future.

Germany's leading automakers, for their part, bought components from Huawei and partnered with the Chinese firm on R&D. They also earned massive amounts of money in China: Volkswagen banked almost half of its revenue in the country. Those revenues might now be on the line. Wu Ken, China's ambassador to Germany, warned of "consequences" if Germany were to exclude Huawei from its market, hinting that German automakers would face punishment. Volkswagen CEO Herbert Diess cautioned that losing access to China would destroy tens of thousands of German jobs.

Beijing's threats could not be written off as idle. In fall 2019, amid large-scale street protests in Hong Kong against the CCP's creeping takeover of the territory, Daryl Morey, the general manager of the NBA's Houston Rockets, tweeted a photo that read: "Fight for Freedom. Stand with Hong Kong." For this affront, Beijing canceled the broadcast of NBA games on state-run television, and the Rockets lost a slew of sponsorships in China. Morey's tweet ended up costing the NBA hundreds of millions of dollars. If Germany blacklisted Huawei, who knew how far Beijing would go?

Pottinger traveled to London in January 2020 to share the same intelligence he'd disclosed to German officials. But as in the past, his warnings fell on deaf ears. The UK was in a bind similar to Germany's. Boris Johnson, the new prime minister, was more closely aligned with the Trump administration than his predecessor Theresa May had been. Yet he had also made big promises to deliver a mammoth infrastructure package at home, which would ensure that "fantastic full-fiber broadband" would be "sprouting in every household." British telecom executives warned Johnson that this promise would be impossible to keep if Huawei were banned from the network.

In a last-ditch attempt to get London to reverse course, three Republican senators sent a letter to the British national security council making "a genuine plea from one ally to another" to ban Huawei and warning that they did not want "to have to review U.S.-UK intelligence sharing." A Republican congressman introduced a bill that would explicitly halt U.S. intelligence sharing with any country that used Huawei in its 5G infrastructure. On January 24, 2020, Trump placed a call to Johnson, a kindred spirit whom he'd hailed as "Britain Trump." Johnson still wouldn't budge. A seething Trump accused Johnson of "betrayal" and slammed down the phone.

A few days later, London officially announced that it would allow Huawei into its 5G network. In a token concession to the United States, it capped the amount of equipment British telecom operators could procure from Huawei at 35 percent.

In their conversations with Pottinger, British intelligence officials had continued to express confidence that they could contain any threat from Huawei. But it was also clear that national security considerations were not guiding London's decision. The paramount factor was no longer even solic-iting Beijing's affection. Huawei was providing the UK with cheap broad-band, plain and simple. It was the kind of decision that Trump, king of deals, should have understood better than anybody else.

=====

The Second Shot at Huawei

On February 14, 2020, Nancy Pelosi, the Speaker of the U.S. House of Representatives, took the stage at the Munich Security Conference. The ballroom of the Hotel Bayerischer Hof, filled with a who's who of diplomacy, was the same place where, in 2007, Vladimir Putin had vowed to knock America off its pedestal.

For the Europeans in the room, Pelosi's presence was a breath of fresh air. Less than two months earlier, Pelosi had overseen Trump's impeachment on charges of abuse of power and obstruction of Congress. She was Trump's toughest opponent in Washington—and unlike the president, a powerful advocate of America's alliances.

Yet in Pelosi's remarks, she made clear that at least on one issue, she and Trump saw eye to eye. "I'm going to say something that may not be agreeable to many of you here, because you invited candor," Pelosi said, "and that is the subject of 5G and cybersecurity." She went on:

> China is seeking to export its digital autocracy through its telecommunication giant, Huawei, threatening economic retaliation against those who do not adopt their technologies. The United States has recognized Huawei as a national security threat, by putting it on our Entity List, restricting engagement with U.S. companies. Nations cannot cede our telecommunication infrastructure to China for financial expediency. Such an ill-conceived concession will only embolden Xi as he undermines democratic values, human rights, economic independence, and national security.

If European countries persisted in their plans to let Huawei build their 5G networks, Pelosi affirmed, they would be doing nothing short of choosing "autocracy over democracy."

Pelosi's harsh tone stunned many in the ballroom. After she concluded her remarks, a member of the audience asked: "Does it mean that you agree in substance with the China policy of President Trump?"

"We have agreement in that regard," Pelosi responded. "I don't know why it's not self-evident to everyone that you do not want to give that power to an entity created by the People's Liberation Army," Pelosi said, referring to Ren Zhengfei's careerlong ties to the Chinese military. "This is the most insidious form of aggression," she continued, "to have that line of communication, 5G, dominated by an autocratic government that does not share our values."

America was just ten months away from a presidential election. On many of Trump's pet issues, world leaders hoped they could simply wait him out. Pelosi had made clear that Huawei was not one of those issues.

In their remarks at Munich the following day, Secretary of State Mike Pompeo and Secretary of Defense Mark Esper echoed Pelosi's message. "Huawei and other Chinese state-backed tech companies are Trojan horses for Chinese intelligence," Pompeo warned. "In the long run," Esper counseled, "developing our own secure 5G networks will far outweigh any perceived gains from partnering with heavily subsidized Chinese providers that ultimately answer to Party leadership."

Europeans had heard these arguments before. They still weren't convinced. Toomas Hendrik Ilves, a former Estonian president, gave voice to the frustration of many in the audience.

"Many of us in Europe agree that there are significant dangers with Huawei, and the U.S. for at least a year has been telling us: 'Do not use Huawei,'" Ilves said, as Pompeo and Esper fielded questions from the stage. "Are you offering an alternative? Are you going to subsidize Nokia and Ericsson? I mean, what do we get? What is it that we should do other than not use Huawei?"

Ilves had a point. Huawei benefited from Beijing's unfair economic practices, but it did not become the world's leading telecom equipment maker by selling its products at the point of a gun. It achieved that dominance by beating competitors from capitalist countries at their own game: winning business with reliable products, good customer service, and the lowest prices in the market. And now that the UK, America's closest ally, had officially given

Huawei its stamp of approval, the floodgates were open. A few days after the Munich Security Conference, Ryan Ding, the president of Huawei's carrier business, announced that the company had signed ninety-one commercial 5G contracts, including forty-seven in Europe alone. Ding boasted that Huawei remained "eighteen months ahead of our competitors in 5G technology."

With the wind at its back, Huawei went on the offensive. On February 26, Guo Ping, Huawei's rotating chairman, spoke at the Mobile World Congress, a marquee trade show for the telecom industry, in Barcelona. His message was simple: Instead of talking a big game on security, the Americans should look in the mirror. "Prism, prism on the wall. Who's the most trustworthy of them all?" Guo asked, as if reciting an incantation. "If you don't understand this question, go ask Edward Snowden." Guo was referring to PRISM, an American program that collected online data from foreigners, whose existence had been leaked by a former NSA contractor. Washington's warnings about Huawei were hypocritical and untrustworthy. If anything, Guo argued, Huawei was the safer option.

Keith Krach, the State Department's undersecretary for economic affairs, watched in frustration. Krach had an atypical résumé for an official on the ornamented seventh floor of State's Foggy Bottom headquarters. Growing up on the outskirts of Cleveland, Ohio, Krach worked as a welder in his father's machine shop. After graduating from Purdue University and Harvard Business School, he rapidly climbed the corporate ladder at General Motors. Eventually, he moved to Silicon Valley, where he founded and sold an e-commerce startup and served as the CEO of DocuSign, the electronic-signature company. Krach had no diplomatic experience, but everything he had learned as a business executive made him question the U.S. government's approach to countering Huawei.

In his second week at the State Department, Krach was invited to a dinner at the Italian embassy in Washington. The event would include face time with Italy's economy minister, who was visiting from Rome. Krach huddled with his staff to go over his talking points.

"Give him the 5G talk," an advisor recommended.

Krach was confused. "What's the 5G talk?" he asked.

"Tell him, 'Don't buy Huawei,'" the advisor explained.

Krach looked at his staff in disbelief. "That's the stupidest thing I've ever heard in my life," he said. "If I'm the CEO, and somebody came in and said, 'Don't buy Huawei,' I would lean over to my chief of staff and say, 'Check out Huawei. They must have some really good stuff.'"

In essence, Krach agreed with Ilves, the Estonian politician who'd challenged Pompeo and Esper: To beat Huawei, America needed to offer a better alternative. It couldn't conjure one out of thin air, but as a start, Krach suggested coming up with a set of principles that would serve as an industry standard for secure 5G. The principles would not discriminate against specific countries or companies, but they would be structured in such a way as to exclude Huawei. Krach would then collect signatories to these "Clean Network" principles among governments, civil society organizations, and telecom companies. Over time, Krach suggested, Washington could dole out financial assistance for new overseas telecom projects, and it could make such funding conditional on signing up for the Clean Network.

Years earlier, in commanding America's economic war against Iran, Stuart Levey found that speaking directly to foreign bankers about the legal and reputational risks of dealing with Iran was often more effective than engaging with foreign government officials. Krach envisioned a similar approach. Even if governments refused to ban Huawei outright, perhaps Washington could coax the telecom carriers to shun the Chinese company of their own initiative. Signing up for the Clean Network could even become something that telecom companies advertised to their customers.

Sensible as it was, Krach's strategy highlighted the biggest weakness in American economic warfare: Washington was better at shutting off economic activity than turning it on. This problem could not be solved overnight. It might be solved in time for 6G. But with each passing day, Huawei was spreading its influence in the world's 5G networks.

Another danger of entirely different origin was also spreading with alarming speed. During his days as a journalist in China, Matt Pottinger had covered the 2003 SARS outbreak, which killed hundreds as Chinese authorities hid behind a wall of lies. Now, with reports of a new, mysterious viral outbreak coming out of the city of Wuhan, Pottinger tapped his old network of contacts among Chinese doctors and parsed Chinese social media feeds to try to grasp what was going on. He soon concluded that the situation was far worse than Beijing portrayed. His findings were instrumental in Trump's decision to ban travelers from China from entering the United States at the end of January 2020.

Once Trump was confronted with the enormity of the crisis that became known as the COVID-19 pandemic, his instinctive response was denial. It soothed his ears when, in a February phone call, Xi Jinping reassured him that China was sparing no effort to contain the outbreak. Even in late March, when it was clear a once-in-a-century pandemic was underway, Trump remained hopeful. "Fifteen days to slow the spread," the tagline of the administration's campaign to prevent contagion, kept alive the delusion that maybe it would all be over in a matter of weeks. Meanwhile, faced with a critical mask shortage—China produced 85 percent of the world's medical masks and had curbed exports to preserve domestic supplies—U.S. public health officials broadcast the confusing and false message that the general public would not benefit from masks, but that healthcare workers desperately needed them.

Through a series of draconian lockdowns, China initially controlled its own COVID outbreak with ruthless efficiency. By the time daily cases in China had dwindled to a handful, the United States was registering tens of thousands, its hospitals and morgues overflowing. Among many CCP functionaries, the pandemic was soon thought of in much the same terms as the 2008 financial crisis: yet another testament to the superiority of the Chinese system.

Beijing's messages to Washington reflected that perception, their tone gradually shifting from reassuring to threatening. Chinese diplomats told Trump officials that if they kept using terms like "Wuhan virus," Beijing might cut off exports of medical supplies to the United States. Chinese state media warned that America risked its access to Chinese-made masks unless it softened its stance on Huawei. When Australia pushed for an independent investigation into the origins of COVID, China imposed sweeping sanctions on the country, blocking imports of Australian beef, wine, and barley. When Swedish media covered stories that offended the CCP, China's ambassador to Sweden declared in a public interview, "For our friends, we have fine wine, but for our enemies, we have shotguns." Gone were the days of hiding one's strength and biding one's time. China was now pursuing what it called "Wolf Warrior diplomacy."

Trump and his team soon moved from denial to anger. Anger that Beijing's obfuscation had ignited the worst pandemic in a century, killing thousands of Americans and paralyzing the world economy. Anger that Xi was flexing China's muscles and kicking the United States when it was down.

And anger that Trump's own economic war had failed to achieve its objectives. Tariffs had not plugged the trade deficit, and export controls had not stopped Huawei. China's drive for an economic empire had not abated; it had advanced.

In May 2020, Trump chaired a meeting of the National Security Council to discuss the proposal for the revamped economic weapon that his administration had been developing since the previous fall. The Foreign Direct Product Rule, or FDPR, would ban companies all over the world from selling chips to Huawei that were made using U.S. technology. To comply, manufacturers could either stop selling to Huawei or rip out all the American software and machine tools that powered their factories. Much like secondary sanctions, the FDPR would effectively force companies to choose between the United States and Huawei.

Deploying this new weapon carried significant risk. When the choice was between the United States and a much smaller adversary like Iran, the answer for most firms was a no-brainer. But the same might not be true when it came to cutting ties with a global heavyweight like Huawei. Another issue was that the FDPR would pose this choice not to financial institutions but to industrial juggernauts such as TSMC and Samsung. These powerful corporations were less habituated to complying with U.S. sanctions and held more political clout in their home countries than the big banks. Even if the FDPR successfully cajoled these industrial giants to ditch Huawei, Beijing could retaliate viciously. China's embrace of Wolf Warrior diplomacy was strong evidence that blowback was probable, if not inevitable.

When Trump's national security team gathered in the Situation Room, the most forceful advocate for the FDPR was Bill Barr, the attorney general. The FBI, which Barr oversaw, had recently briefed the White House on the findings of a secret investigation into Huawei. Among its conclusions was that Huawei equipment in cell towers in the American Midwest, located near sensitive military installations, could intercept and even disrupt communications related to U.S. nuclear weapons. It was possible that in a crisis, Beijing would be able to use this Huawei equipment as a kill switch to stifle the United States' command and control over its nuclear arsenal. If Huawei succeeded in becoming the backbone of the next generation of the internet, Barr concluded, "the power the United States has today to use economic sanctions would pale by comparison to the unprecedented economic leverage we would be surrendering into the hands of China."

Barr's argument carried the day. On May 15, the Commerce Department unleashed the FDPR, an upgraded yet untested economic weapon, at China's 5G king. For now, the FDPR was just a press release and some regulatory jargon, posted on the Commerce Department's website. But its disruptive potential was far-reaching.

The world braced for impact.

The Dominoes Fall

At stake in the FDPR were hundreds of billions of dollars of business—for both Huawei and the scores of companies that supplied it with semiconductors. So it didn't take corporate lawyers long to find loopholes. The FDPR extended export controls to non-U.S. firms, but it applied only to items destined directly for Huawei and its affiliates. Companies could still sell chips to subcontractors that assembled base stations and smartphones on Huawei's behalf. This was a serious oversight, and technocrats at the Commerce Department scrambled to write an updated version of the policy.

Among the companies whose actions would determine the FDPR's success or failure, none carried more weight than Taiwan-based TSMC, the world's largest semiconductor foundry. TSMC's close ties to both Huawei and American companies exemplified the dilemma that the FDPR posed to businesses around the world. Huawei was TSMC's second-biggest customer, yet TSMC also relied on American technologies to run its foundries, and the company produced the processors that ran every Apple iPhone and the Nvidia chips that powered most advanced AI algorithms.

Ultimately, TSMC decided that its U.S. connections mattered more. A few weeks after Commerce issued the FDPR, TSMC's chairman announced that the company would not exploit the loopholes but rather cut ties with Huawei. TSMC also revealed plans to invest $12 billion in a new chip factory in Arizona, a deal brokered in part by Keith Krach and backed by generous federal and state subsidies.

Others took notice. Within days of the U.S. announcement, the UK government launched an emergency review of Huawei's role in Britain's 5G network. London had persevered through intense pressure from Washington to ban Huawei. Boris Johnson had rebuffed a personal entreaty from Donald Trump, a man he admired and often praised. Now, one post on the Commerce Department's website had done more to shake London's confidence in Huawei than years of cajoling and threats.

The FDPR would have "very, very serious" ramifications for Huawei's role in Britain's 5G network, according to UK government officials. For starters, the loss of TSMC and other suppliers would force Huawei to overhaul its list of components, which meant British intelligence could no longer plausibly claim to understand the inner workings of Huawei's systems. "Our long-standing understanding of how the supply chain works just disappears," lamented a British official. Moreover, the FDPR had imperiled Huawei's commercial future. Did the UK really want to build its digital economy around a company with such uncertain prospects? British telecom executives, who had long advocated for permission to buy from Huawei, were getting cold feet, too. Huawei admitted it would be "months" before the company could provide reassurance to British customers on how the new U.S. regulation would affect its deliveries.

Indeed, Huawei did not sugarcoat the ramifications for its business. "This decision was arbitrary and pernicious, and threatens to undermine the entire industry worldwide," the company protested in a blistering statement. "This new rule will impact the expansion, maintenance, and continuous operations of networks worth hundreds of billions of dollars that we have rolled out in more than 170 countries." At Huawei's annual conference with analysts, held just seventy-two hours after the FDPR was announced, rotating chairman Guo Ping struck a somber tone. "We will now work hard to figure out how to survive," he said. "Survival is the keyword for us now."

In its economic wars against Iran and Russia, the United States had weaponized its financial clout to devastating effect. Cut off from the dollar, Iran resorted to barter. Russia built a homegrown alternative to SWIFT and forged a $25 billion currency swap line with China. Both countries stockpiled gold. Chinese leaders looked on in apprehension, suspecting they might one day share the same fate. In 2015, a year after Russia annexed Crimea, Beijing launched its own alternative to SWIFT, the Cross-Border Interbank Payment System (CIPS). The project was part of a broader strategy to internationalize the renminbi—China's currency—and reduce the country's vulnerability to America's financial weapons.

Now, Beijing's fears of an American economic attack had come true, except the attack didn't rely on U.S. financial power. Instead, the United States was weaponizing its leadership in cutting-edge technology. A public statement by Huawei hit the nail on the head: "The U.S. is leveraging its own technological strengths to crush companies outside its own borders."

With Huawei under siege, the company became a source of immense national pride for many Chinese, an emblem of America's refusal to accept their country's rise. Washington might think it was checking Beijing's economic imperialism, but from China's perspective, the United States already possessed an economic empire, and it was using its privileged position to keep China down. Chinese social media users expressed their support for Huawei and pledged to buy its products. Meng Wanzhou, the Huawei CFO under house arrest in Vancouver, was treated like an A-list celebrity by Chinese media, which dubbed her the "princess of Huawei" and published glitzy photos of her going about town in fashionable dresses with a tracking device cuffing her ankle.

Both Huawei and the Chinese public expected a response from Beijing. "The Chinese government will not just stand by and watch Huawei be slaughtered on the chopping board," a Huawei executive predicted. Before

Meng Wanzhou: Huawei CFO—and patriotic symbol—
outside her Vancouver mansion.

long, Xi Jinping unveiled a new economic strategy to turbocharge the country's quest for technological self-sufficiency. To back up the new strategy, which was given the anodyne name "dual circulation," Beijing pledged to invest nearly $1.5 trillion in the coming years, much of which would flow to homegrown tech giants such as Huawei.

Beijing also doubled down on its warning that those who spurned Huawei would have hell to pay. One of the best illustrations of how well the FDPR was working was the emergency review of Huawei underway in one of the most reluctant countries: the UK. The Chinese government wanted the British to know that it would not look kindly upon an about-face. "We want to be your friend. We want to be your partner," Liu Xiaoming, China's ambassador to the UK, told reporters. "But if you want to make China a hostile country, you will have to bear the consequences."

After Brexit, British politicians had looked to China as the future. Having exited its failed marriage to continental Europe, the country was ready for a golden era in UK-China relations. Now that vision hung in the balance. "The China business community are all watching how you handle Huawei," Liu emphasized. There would be costs to succumbing to Washington's pressure. "If you dance to the tune of other countries, how can you call yourself Great Britain?"

Already, UK telecom operators were grudgingly acknowledging that the lure of Huawei's low prices might no longer be enough. Without access to high-end chips, there was no telling how well Huawei's products would function or whether the company could maintain its equipment over time. Before the UK had even concluded its emergency review, Telefónica, the parent company of Britain's largest mobile carrier, agreed to sign on to Keith Krach's Clean Network.

For a little while longer, the British government wavered. In the end, China's domineering behavior on the other side of the globe made a tough decision more palatable. At 11:00 p.m. on June 30, Xi Jinping rammed through a new national security law for Hong Kong. The law granted Beijing sweeping powers over the city, which had operated semi-autonomously under a policy called "one country, two systems" since the UK handed Hong Kong over to China in 1997. The law was clearly aimed at crushing the pro-democracy protests that had roiled the city for the past year. For the UK, the destruction of Hong Kong's freedoms hit close to home. Many British had family, friends, and colleagues who lived in the former colony. If this was the future China was building, they wanted no part of it.

Two weeks later, Boris Johnson rendered his judgment: Huawei would be barred completely from Britain's 5G network. Telecom operators would have until the end of the year to stop buying equipment from Huawei and until 2027 to remove Huawei gear from their older systems. The move would cost the United Kingdom some £2 billion and set back its rollout of 5G by up to three years. But London saw no other viable course of action.

In August, the Commerce Department published a revised FDPR that closed the loopholes in the original version. "We believe this step to significantly (almost completely) curtail Huawei's ability to source any semiconductor from anyone," Credit Suisse assessed in a research note. Within weeks, a slew of Asian chipmaking powerhouses announced plans to sever ties with Huawei, including Taiwan's MediaTek and South Korea's Samsung and SK Hynix.

Ren Zhengfei had spent decades cultivating a "wolf culture" at Huawei. His staff had won accolades for their grit and can-do spirit. Now, executives were quitting, orders were drying up, work hours were decreasing. "Our company has been urging us to get used to this state of war," said an employee in Huawei's R&D department. "But we're still worried. Will our benefits be sacrificed, will the layoffs finally land on me?" On a company message board, another employee asked, "What products can we still make?"

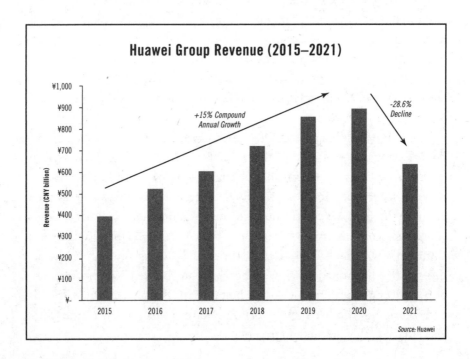

Dan Wang, a well-known analyst of China's technology sector, took a stab at an answer. In a report titled "A Death Sentence for Huawei," Wang prognosticated that the company "is probably finished as a maker of 5G network equipment and smartphones once its inventories run out early next year." During the months that followed, Huawei's growth ground to a halt. Then, in the first half of 2021, its revenue plummeted by almost 30 percent. Even Huawei's output for the Chinese market languished. The company delayed the production of its flagship smartphone, and the rollout of China's own 5G network was set back. Executives frantically tried to pivot to new business lines.

American officials had feared that London's initial approval of Huawei would cause a domino effect: other countries would follow suit, just as they had lined up to join the AIIB after the UK embraced the Chinese bank years earlier. Now London's decision to ban Huawei pushed the dominoes in the opposite direction. As Huawei floundered, more and more countries decided to ban it from their 5G networks. Telecom carriers that had already signed 5G contracts with Huawei rushed to terminate them. Even Matt Pottinger was surprised at how fast the tide had turned.

47

Iron Curtain

On October 23, 2020, less than two weeks before Donald Trump and Joe Biden would square off in the U.S. presidential election, Matt Pottinger stared into a camera from a book-lined corner of the White House. He was there to lay out the Trump administration's legacy on China policy. His speech, delivered in Mandarin and broadcast online, would be "a conversation about China's relationship with the rest of the world."

The failures of U.S. policy toward China following the Cold War were rooted in the false belief that ushering China into the global economy would propel it toward democratic change. Integration into the global economy, the theory went, would encourage China to become a "responsible stakeholder" in the system. Entrenched business interests and plain old inertia ensured that U.S. policy stuck to this assumption long after it was proven wrong. The Trump administration had finally changed course.

As Pottinger saw it, confronting Beijing required following two simple principles: reciprocity and candor. "Reciprocity is the straightforward idea that when a country injures your interests, you return the favor," he said. "It's an inherently defensive approach, rooted in notions of fair play and deterrence." While China had been waging an economic assault against the United States for decades, the U.S. government had largely opted to grin and bear it. Under the Trump administration, America fought back. It started with crude tools like tariffs but eventually found its way to innovative economic weapons, which derived their power from America's central position in the world's technology ecosystem.

The principle of candor, as Pottinger described it, was "the idea that democracies are safest when we speak honestly and publicly about and to our friends, our adversaries, and ourselves." Glossing over problems—or minimizing them in an attempt at de-escalation—only gave Washington an excuse for inaction and Beijing an invitation to push the envelope.

To be sure, the Trump administration had acted on these insights with varying consistency. Trump's priority, for much of his time in office, was to reset U.S.-China economic ties through the "biggest trade deal ever"—a deal that came together, in greatly diminished form, in early 2020, just in time for U.S.-China relations to unravel amid the outbreak of COVID. To no one's surprise, Beijing failed to honor its commitments in even this marginal "Phase One" trade deal, which did nothing to close America's deficit with China.

Trump's pursuit of his elusive goal led him to make major concessions, none of which China reciprocated. He repeatedly walked back his own administration's policies, first on ZTE and later on Huawei. (After Trump softened the initial Huawei restrictions, Commerce licenses allowed American companies to sell Huawei tens of billions of dollars of equipment.) Steven Mnuchin's Treasury Department never got on board with a tougher policy toward Beijing. In the economic war against China, the agency that had pioneered much of the strategy in prior campaigns stayed on the sidelines.

Nevertheless, by the fourth year of Trump's presidency, Washington's China policy mostly aligned with Pottinger's precepts. U.S. officials no longer refrained from calling out Beijing for its economic malfeasance—candor had replaced timidity. More important, Washington was pushing back against Beijing's quest to seize the commanding heights of the digital economy. Chinese tech firms had already made substantial progress, aided by Beijing's vast subsidies, intellectual property theft, and prohibitions on American competition. But now, the United States was returning the favor by choking off China's access to the foundational technologies that it desperately needed, could only get from abroad, and could not yet produce itself. And by the final months of Trump's term, the administration had seemingly lost all inhibitions about pursuing this kind of economic war.

Indeed, with China's failure to contain COVID and its stifling of freedoms in Hong Kong, Washington was ready to settle scores. Not long after releasing the FDPR, the Trump administration began toying with the idea of banning TikTok. The Chinese video-sharing app had surged in record time to become the most popular social media platform among American teenagers. While TikTok's parent company, ByteDance, was privately held and counted well-known American investors among its largest shareholders, U.S. officials worried that the company had no choice but to comply with Chinese laws that required cooperation with Beijing's intelligence services.

Was it really a good idea to allow tens of millions of Americans to hand over intimate data such as biometric identifiers, geolocation, and browsing history to a company beholden to the CCP? The Trump administration believed it wasn't, and it began swinging wildly at TikTok. First it tried to force the company to divest its American assets. Then it tried to broker a sale of the app to Oracle, whose CEO, Safra Catz, was a close White House confidante. When that effort failed, the White House tried to ban TikTok outright, using its authority under the International Emergency Economic Powers Act (IEEPA)—the same law that gives the president wide latitude to impose sanctions. In late September, just hours before the ban was set to take effect, a federal judge blocked it. A 1988 amendment to IEEPA barred the president from sanctioning "informational materials." As a social media platform, TikTok was thus protected.

Next up on Washington's hit list was Semiconductor Manufacturing International Corporation, or SMIC. Founded in 2000 by an ex-TSMC employee named Richard Chang, SMIC was supposed to be China's answer to the world-class Taiwanese chip foundry. It had never quite caught up but was making meaningful progress. Now, with Xi's drive for self-sufficiency, SMIC was riding high. After delisting from the New York Stock Exchange, SMIC listed its shares in Shanghai in July 2020. Buoyed by expectations of massive support from Beijing, SMIC raised nearly $8 billion in its Shanghai debut, the biggest haul of any mainland Chinese offering in a decade. As Beijing plotted to break what it would come to call America's "technology blockade," SMIC was the homegrown chip champion at the center of its plan.

SMIC's ascent raised eyebrows at the White House. If Huawei and its suppliers should be blocked from accessing American technology, then so should SMIC. Like other foreign chipmakers, SMIC was already barred from using U.S. technology to make chips for Huawei, but as a partially state-owned enterprise that benefited from the largesse of the Chinese government, SMIC could hardly be counted on to comply with American regulations. Moreover, given Beijing's policy of "military-civil fusion," Washington had to assume that SMIC's chips would also find their way into Chinese military technology.

A widely circulated report by a Virginia-based defense contractor, pub-

lished in August 2020, illustrated SMIC's ties to China's military in considerable detail. A few weeks later, the Commerce Department warned that
exports to SMIC carried an "unacceptable risk" of being diverted for military purposes. Two American makers of semiconductor manufacturing
tools, Applied Materials and Lam Research, were among SMIC's most critical suppliers. In just the past year, SMIC had signed orders with the companies for more than $2 billion of equipment. Commerce directed both firms
to suspend sales to SMIC.

Among Washington's biggest concerns was that SMIC could gain access
to an ultra-complex chipmaking machine made by the Dutch company
ASML. Known as extreme ultraviolet lithography (EUV), it was the most
expensive mass-produced machine tool in history. No other company made
anything like it, and it was essential to produce the most advanced chips.

ASML had agreed to sell the machine to SMIC for roughly $150 million.
Under pressure from the Trump administration, the Dutch government
dragged its feet on approving the necessary export license. But Washington
could not expect diplomatic pressure to work indefinitely. ASML was by far
the most valuable company in the Netherlands, and its executives held a lot
of sway with the Dutch government. China was an enormous market, so ASML
stood to miss out on a lot of money if it couldn't sell its machines there.

The White House was set on halting the sale come hell or high water. The
prevailing mood, according to an NSC official, was that the president should
send the U.S. Navy after the shipment if necessary. In December, just over a
month after Biden defeated Trump in the presidential election, the Commerce Department added SMIC to the Entity List. Commerce also drafted a
new FDPR that would apply to the company. The rule was never issued, but
its mere existence gave Trump officials the leverage they needed to secure
a gentlemen's agreement from the Dutch government to continue blocking
the sale.

The move was one of a flurry of similar actions in the lame-duck period
between the election and Biden's inauguration. Additional export controls
targeted DJI, the world's largest maker of commercial drones, and dozens of
other Chinese tech companies. Under a new rule, Americans were banned
from investing in the stocks of more than thirty firms connected to the Chinese military, including video surveillance company Hikvision and telecom
operator China Mobile. A bevy of restrictions targeted China National Offshore Oil Corporation (CNOOC), a giant Chinese oil company. In his last
days in the White House, Pottinger took part in internal debates about

banning investments in China's largest tech companies, including e-commerce behemoth Alibaba, social media conglomerate Tencent, and search engine giant Baidu. (Shortly thereafter, Pottinger resigned in protest of Trump's role in inciting the insurrection at the U.S. Capitol on January 6, 2021.) The plan was ultimately dropped, but it showed how broad the scope of Trump's economic war against China had become.

A decade earlier, U.S. officials had recoiled at the prospect of imposing sanctions on the Central Bank of Iran for fear of upsetting global markets. Similar concerns had led the Obama administration to design its Russia sanctions with "scalpel-like" precision. Given the risk of collateral damage, the United States needed to use its economic arsenal judiciously. Best not to aim the most heavy-hitting weapons at an economy whose collapse would drag everybody else down with it.

To say that China fit this description would be a colossal understatement. It was the world's second-largest economy, a key link in virtually every supply chain, and the number-one trading partner of more than 120 countries. For these reasons, before Trump entered the White House, it was unthinkable that the United States would ever impose aggressive economic penalties on China. The Chinese economy was too big, too important, and too intertwined with America's to try to pressure it. An economic war against China was guaranteed to cause fallout so extensive that the global economy would spiral into recession.

Trump turned this consensus on its head. "Everyone said the sky was going to fall," Pottinger reflected. "But it didn't. We had psyched ourselves out." The blowback from the economic war against China was surprisingly limited. The U.S. economy hummed along during the Trump years until COVID struck. Xi's threats proved more bark than bite. Beijing even balked at adding American companies to its Unreliable Entity List. It stuck to symbolic actions, such as slapping individual sanctions on Pottinger, Krach, and other Trump officials on the president's final day in the White House. "We've actually got massive leverage," Pottinger said. "And we need to use the leverage while we've still got it."

The Trump administration brought about a sea change in U.S. policy toward China. It did the same for American economic warfare more broadly. Until the Commerce Department's denial order on ZTE in 2018, the financial system had served as the primary combat theater, the dollar as the weapon of choice. Financial sanctions crushed Iran's economy and brought Russia's to the brink of collapse. But the denial order on ZTE—which, in an ironic twist, originated from the company's violation of Iran sanctions— showed that the tech sector was as promising an arena, that access to U.S. technology could prove as vital as access to the dollar, and that removing such access could be just as lethal. There were some precedents, most notably the Obama administration's decision in 2014 to sever Russia's access to offshore oil drilling technology. But the Trump administration's campaign against Chinese tech companies elevated the approach into a systematic policy.

Even when they failed to inflict as much damage, technology restrictions could still serve as a valuable complement to the existing financial arsenal. And if a financial offensive wasn't possible—owing, for instance, to the opposition of a treasury secretary, as with Steven Mnuchin—technology restrictions enabled another agency, the Commerce Department, to fill the void. Indeed, just as the Iran campaign had done for Treasury, the high-tech siege against China boosted Commerce's profile. While the department historically opposed policies that could stifle business—"economic growth" was its official mission—Commerce gradually came to serve as one more command center for economic war.

The Iran campaign had made Stuart Levey, Adam Szubin, and David Cohen into archetypes of the sanctions technocrat and spawned a network of think tanks and advocacy groups that scoured the global financial system for traces of Iranian money. Now, universities and think tanks founded research programs and opened new divisions to study the global semiconductor supply chain and track Chinese investments in artificial intelligence. Aspiring foreign policy wonks used to learn Arabic and study counterterrorism; now they learned Chinese and parsed the fine print of the FDPR.

The Trump administration also redefined the aims America considered appropriate for an economic war. For the Obama administration, economic pressure was always a means to an end—curbing the Iranian nuclear program, getting Russian troops to pull out of Ukrainian territory. Economic damage was meant to change an adversary's behavior. Washington was careful to emphasize that the sanctions were neither punitive nor permanent. They would be lifted as soon as Tehran and Moscow revised their policies.

There was no such behaviorist calculus in the minds of Trump officials. Xi Jinping would not reverse course and abandon his imperial ambitions in the face of American resistance. He believed that supplanting the United States as the world's preeminent superpower was China's destiny. The Trump administration thus made little effort to build off-ramps. Washington had declared Chinese domination of global 5G networks as a threat, and it would seek to weaken the companies at the forefront of that threat. The expectation was for this to be a permanent effort, even if no one said so out loud. The penalties were not designed to change behavior but to downsize China's role in the world economy. Over time, inflicting economic damage on China became an end in and of itself.

In the last year of the Obama administration, Treasury Secretary Jack Lew had voiced his fear that U.S. sanctions threatened to unwind economic globalization. Lew took this to be an evident downside, a wholly unintended consequence of U.S. policies. Not so the Trump administration, for which partially reversing globalization was in line with U.S. interests and thus an active, explicit goal. Huawei operated in more than 170 countries. In some ways it was a poster child of globalization. But for the Trump administration, Huawei's role in the global economy was a problem that needed fixing.

If this was true of Huawei, what about its peers? Chinese companies featured prominently in just about every major industrial and technological supply chain. The implication, perhaps even the logical end point, of Trump's policy was a much broader economic decoupling between the United States and China than anyone talked about openly. In private, some Trump officials welcomed this prospect. "The only fair way to do this is just to cut off all trade," admitted a senior administration official. "If you look at all the bad things that are going on with China, the answer is to stop trading with them, or you're just going to continue to fuel their rise and our demise." That China was America's number-one trading partner in 2020, accounting for more than half a trillion dollars' worth of exports and imports, was no matter.

Following the economic war against China to its natural conclusion would create a world splintered into rival blocs, far removed from the hyperglobalization of the 1990s and 2000s. It was tempting to picture a neat split down the middle—one camp headed by China, the other by the United States—in a mirror image of the Cold War standoff between East and West. But with Trump in power, it seemed just as likely that there would be at least three, with Europe forming its own. Trump had called the EU "worse than China" and paid little heed to its preferences. His administration bludgeoned Huawei with export controls in large part because it failed to win support from the UK and other European countries to ban the Chinese firm. This was a world apart from Dan Fried's international contact group and his tireless efforts to secure EU buy-in for sanctions against Russia. This, too, was no accident. When Fried retired from the Foreign Service in February 2017, the Trump administration didn't look for a successor to fill the role of the State Department's coordinator for sanctions policy. It eliminated the office.

Trump's withdrawal from the Iran nuclear deal so angered the UK, France, and Germany that they spent the following years actively seeking to weaken some of the economic ties that bound them to the United States. "It is indispensable that we strengthen European autonomy by creating payment channels that are independent of the United States," declared Heiko Maas, Germany's foreign minister. Bruno Le Maire, the French finance minister, agreed. "I want Europe to be a sovereign continent, not a vassal," he said, "and that means having totally independent financing instruments." London, Paris, and Berlin joined forces to create the Instrument in Support of Trade Exchanges, or INSTEX, a channel for European companies to bypass American sanctions and do business with Iran. INSTEX struggled to get off the ground—it was foiled, ironically, by participants' fears that they would be hit with U.S. secondary sanctions. But the attempt alone, an explicit effort to circumvent Washington's economic restrictions, was remarkable.

When the United States intensified its siege of the Chinese tech sector during Trump's final months in office, the EU did not join in. On the contrary, European officials were at that moment finalizing a landmark investment deal with China. Despite firm opposition from Washington, German Chancellor Angela Merkel made it a top priority to conclude the agreement, which would more deeply entwine the European and Chinese economies.

Jake Sullivan, Joe Biden's pick for national security advisor, grew concerned about the EU-China talks. Why was the EU racing to cut a deal with China when America's soon-to-be president was poised to mend transatlantic relations? "The Biden-Harris administration would welcome early consultations with our European partners on our common concerns about China's economic practices," Sullivan tweeted in late December.

EU leaders ignored this plea. Days later, Merkel joined a video call with French President Emmanuel Macron, European Commission President Ursula von der Leyen, and Xi Jinping to close the deal. The EU touted it as "the most ambitious agreement that China has ever concluded." China celebrated it as a crowning achievement for Xi as the Chinese Communist Party approached its one hundredth anniversary.

America was finally fighting back against China's economic aggression. Huawei's 5G business lay in shambles. But the victory had its costs. As a new economic Iron Curtain descended across the globe, the United States risked ending up alone behind a wall.

PART FIVE

===

Russia's Invasion of Ukraine

48

———

The Practitioner

On the last Friday in February 2022, Daleep Singh huddled with his team in the Eisenhower Executive Office Building. The imposing complex, built in the French Second Empire style, sits across a narrow walkway from the West Wing and is home to officials who work around the clock to translate the president's vision into policies. That day, Singh and his staff were even wearier than normal. They were grasping for a way to use American economic power to stop the Russian troops headed for Kyiv.

Russia's full-scale invasion of Ukraine was barely a day old. Within that time, the United States and its allies had announced sanctions on a handful of Russian banks, but the penalties didn't meet the moment. As Russian tanks, armored vehicles, and paratroopers converged on the Ukrainian capital, Singh was pushing for the White House to show more resolve.

Others were urging caution. The Treasury Department, led by the venerated academic economist and former Fed chair Janet Yellen, warned that Russia's economy was a sanctions minefield. One misstep could have dire collateral consequences for the West and the world economy at large.

Singh put less stock than others in these warnings. Perhaps this was simply his low aversion to risk. Before government, Singh cut his teeth in Goldman Sachs's trading division, where he helped run an in-house hedge fund whose core activities, though very lucrative, carried so much danger for the broader banking system that they were mostly banned following the 2008 financial crisis. Yet Singh was also drawing on the lessons of his last economic war. During his own stint at Treasury eight years earlier, he'd helped design sanctions in the wake of Russia's annexation of Crimea. Like Yellen, he'd worried back then about the potential for worldwide financial contagion. In the end, sanctions had sent Russia's economy into a tailspin while global markets did just fine.

Singh lacked Yellen's academic pedigree, but his résumé traced a march through the institutions of American financial power both public and private: Goldman, Treasury, the New York Fed. A colleague described him as "*The Economist* personified." Now in his mid-forties, with a few streaks of gray in his shiny black hair, Singh served as the Biden White House's top official on international economics. In 2021, when he moved into his new office—spacious by White House standards, with high ceilings, ornate fixtures, and aging furniture—he made just two changes. One was to replace a Civil War–era painting of Robert E. Lee and Ulysses S. Grant with a photo of Muhammad Ali. The other was to install a Bloomberg terminal so he could monitor markets in real time.

That Friday, as Russian tanks were rolling into Ukraine, Singh's staff felt dejected. Neither the long shadow of the post-2014 sanctions nor the White House's repeated warnings during Russia's months-long troop buildup on the Ukrainian border had convinced Vladimir Putin to back down. The previous day's sanctions had likewise fallen flat. The team looked to Singh for guidance.

Singh stared back at them intently. He had barely slept in weeks, and his warm brown eyes were bleary with exhaustion. "Let's do something about the central bank," he said.

===

With more than $630 billion in assets, Russia's central bank was massive. It was worth more than Iran's *entire* GDP at any point in the past several decades. Its teeming coffers were Putin's attempt to "sanctions-proof" his economy. Yet well over half of the bank's reserves were in dollars, euros, pounds, and yen, which in practice left them exposed to Western sanctions.

That Putin had allowed for such exposure suggested he did not expect the West to ever go after the central bank. Surprising though this was for a man as suspicious and guarded as the Russian president, it was in line with his view that the West was ultimately weak and feckless. Putin and his aides were so sure of the diffidence of European leaders, in particular, that Elvira Nabiullina, the longtime head of the central bank, made the unusual choice of holding most of Russia's foreign exchange reserves in euros instead of dollars.

Daleep Singh: deputy national security advisor for
international economics at the Biden White House.

In Putin's defense, the Central Bank of Russia would be the largest sanctions target in modern history. Hitting it seemed far-fetched even to Washington's foreign policy establishment. If any entity was too big to sanction, this was it.

The trouble, as Daleep Singh argued to his staff, was that the central bank could use its foreign exchange reserves to prop up the ruble and rescue the Russian financial sector in case of a crisis, as it had done in 2014 when Nabiullina spent over $100 billion of reserves to cushion the blow of sanctions. As long as the central bank was secure, it could blunt pretty much any other U.S. attack on the Russian economy. On the flip side, if Putin was not expecting them to target the central bank, they could catch him off guard the same way he had repeatedly done to the West.

Sanctioning the Central Bank of Russia was such an extreme option that it had never received thorough advance vetting—neither by OFAC, the office at the heart of Treasury's sanctions apparatus, nor by Janet Yellen or any other experts who were in a position to assess its economic implications. Even more problematic, the idea had never been seriously discussed with the EU. And Singh knew that Joe Biden's first question would be whether the Europeans would back it.

"Who do I call if I want to call Europe?" For Singh, the answer to this famous quip credited to Henry Kissinger was a German bureaucrat by the name of Bjoern Seibert. Seibert served as a top advisor to Ursula von der

Leyen, who as president of the European Commission headed the EU's de facto executive branch. In Brussels, Seibert had carved out an informal role similar to Singh's in Washington: chief strategist of the economic war against Russia. Singh's frequent phone calls with Seibert over the previous months, as a Russian invasion looked more and more inevitable, had been pivotal to the West's preparations for sanctions.

After meeting with his staff in the Eisenhower Executive Office Building, Singh snatched his cell phone from a lockbox and darted outside in search of reception. Seibert was expecting the call. He relayed his impression that a momentous political shift was underway, with street protests against the Russian invasion drawing out people in the hundreds of thousands all across Europe. Measures which had seemed too extreme earlier that week were now in play. "We've been rolling this boulder up the mountain for months," Seibert told Singh. "Now it's starting to roll downhill."

49

The Best-Laid Plans

In December 2020, when future National Security Advisor Jake Sullivan asked Daleep Singh if he was interested in serving as the incoming administration's "sherpa"—the official in charge of preparing the president's agenda for big-ticket summits such as the G7 and G20—neither man expected the job to focus on economic warfare. Singh's task would be to spearhead the foreign policy elements of Biden's broader economic program. Beyond tackling the damage wrought by the pandemic, that program envisioned a paradigm shift: abandoning decades of neoliberal dogma and welcoming more forceful government intervention in pursuit of the national interest, be it supporting American workers, fueling the clean-energy transition, or outcompeting China.

The new administration's ambitions in economic warfare were modest by comparison, despite a collection of high-level officials with deep experience in the field. Sullivan and his deputy, Jon Finer, were veterans of the campaign that led to the Iran nuclear deal. So were Wendy Sherman, now the number two at the State Department, CIA Director Bill Burns, and Burns's deputy, David Cohen. Victoria Nuland, a central figure in the 2014 Ukraine crisis, returned to State. With that experience came an appreciation for what economic weapons could accomplish but also, as Finer explained, "some humility about their use."

Sanctions policy during the Trump years offered a cautionary tale, too. No previous administration in U.S. history had been as trigger-happy in its use of economic penalties. During Trump's single term in office, OFAC imposed sanctions on more individuals and companies than it did during

George W. Bush's two terms combined, and nearly as many as during Obama's eight years in office. Trump's sanctions turned out to be highly destructive even when imposed unilaterally, without backing or help from allies. But they rarely compelled their targets to bend to Washington's will. Trump's aggressive, go-it-alone approach also encouraged many countries, including America's allies, to seek greater independence by moving their economic activities away from U.S.-controlled chokepoints.

Iran offered a grim example of this dynamic. Trump tore up the 2015 nuclear deal and reintroduced aggressive sanctions that lacked international support but stifled Iran's economy nonetheless, triggering a recession almost as bad as the one that preceded Hassan Rouhani's election as president in 2013. Unlike the Obama administration, Trump officials never offered the Iranian regime a viable off-ramp through earnest negotiations. Tehran responded by restarting its nuclear program, and the time it would need to build a nuclear bomb was slashed from a full year to mere weeks. Meanwhile, three of America's closest allies—Britain, France, and Germany—joined forces to create a financial channel to bypass Trump's sanctions on Iran. In 2021, Iranians elected an ultraconservative hard-liner to succeed Rouhani, whose championing of nuclear diplomacy had been discredited. Years of hard work by both sides had come undone.

The Trump administration also used sanctions to try to overthrow the autocratic president of Venezuela, Nicolás Maduro. The sanctions, coupled with Maduro's corruption and gross policy mismanagement, tipped the Venezuelan economy into free fall. In the end, the Trump administration failed to topple Maduro, who held on to power in part thanks to economic assistance from Russia and China. It did, however, contribute to a severe humanitarian crisis reminiscent of the one Iraq faced under the UN embargo in the 1990s.

The Trump administration went as far as sanctioning Fatou Bensouda, the prosecutor of the International Criminal Court, and one of her colleagues after they opened an investigation into potential war crimes committed in Afghanistan. Trump's move was seen as so extreme in some quarters of Washington that several influential voices pushed to amend IEEPA, the law that gives the president the authority to impose sanctions, to limit this power.

In light of such overreach—and in hopes of restoring America's badly damaged image abroad—the new administration aimed to be more circumspect in matters of economic warfare, and it announced plans for a top-to-bottom review of U.S. sanctions policy. In a sign of the changing political winds, the review would be led by Wally Adeyemo, a protégé of Jack Lew, the Obama-era official who in his farewell address had cautioned against the "overuse of sanctions."

The one area in which Biden did not look to turn the page from Trump was China. In fact, his administration intended to strengthen the export controls that Trump had imposed on Huawei and began planning to restrict China's access to frontier technologies more comprehensively.

The new president was also a certified Russia hawk. As vice president in 2014, Biden had urged Obama to make Putin "pay in blood and money" for his conquest of Crimea and advocated sending weapons to Ukraine. Since then, Russia had racked up a long list of further misdeeds, including interfering in America's 2016 election, poisoning the opposition leader Alexei Navalny, hacking the U.S. government by inserting malicious code into software made by the company SolarWinds, and allegedly offering bounties to Afghan militants to kill American soldiers. These had largely gone unanswered— Trump shied away from taking actions that might anger the Kremlin. On the 2020 campaign trail, Biden lambasted Trump as "Putin's puppy" and touted his own experience going "head-to-head" with Russia's dictator.

Still, Biden's focus on competition with China, combined with the challenges of governing during a pandemic, meant that Russia did not figure prominently in his foreign policy priorities. His primary objective was to reestablish a measure of deterrence in U.S.-Russian relations to ensure "a stable and predictable relationship." This did not entail turning back the clock on Ukraine. Moscow had now been ruling Crimea for the better part of a decade, and its proxies still occupied a chunk of the Donbas. The front lines in eastern Ukraine hadn't shifted much over the past four years, nor had there been any diplomatic breakthrough since 2015, the year of the still-unimplemented Minsk II agreement. The Biden team was skeptical it could do much to alter this status quo. The Russo-Ukrainian war, it seemed, had become another frozen conflict.

Biden signed an executive order in April 2021 levying a flurry of new sanctions on Russia, the harshest of which barred U.S. banks from lending money directly to the Russian government. This signaled a change of tone from the Trump era, but the immediate impact was negligible. "We didn't want to be so heavy-hitting early on that it looked like we were escalating," recalled Peter Harrell, a sanctions expert who worked as a deputy to Singh.

Yet storm clouds were on the horizon. Around the same time Biden issued the new sanctions, Russia amassed some 100,000 troops along its border with Ukraine. It was Putin's largest military buildup since he'd conquered Crimea and invaded the Donbas seven years earlier. The buildup worried U.S. intelligence agencies. Putin was "clearly considering military action on some level," said Avril Haines, the director of national intelligence. To try to defuse the situation, Biden called Putin, urged him to stand down, and offered to meet him face-to-face in the coming months. "The United States is not looking to kick off a cycle of escalation and conflict with Russia," Biden said in remarks at the White House after the call. A few days later, Russian troops pulled back from Ukraine's border and returned to their bases. A time and place were set for Biden's promised summit with Putin: June 16 in that perennial capital of diplomacy, Geneva.

"America Is Back"

Biden arrived in Geneva brimming with confidence. He'd just attended a G7 meeting in the United Kingdom, his first as president, and he was feeling optimistic about the prospect of revitalizing America's global alliances. The president brought this confidence to his tête-à-tête with Putin. The Russian military had by now pulled back from Ukraine's border, so Biden focused on issues closer to home, including recent cyberattacks by Russian hackers on U.S. government systems and on a major American petroleum pipeline. There was no love lost between the two men, but neither seemed raring for a fight, either. "I think the last thing he wants now is a Cold War," Biden said of his Russian counterpart. "'There is no happiness in life—there are only glimmers of it,'" said Putin, quoting Tolstoy. True friendship between Washington and Moscow was impossible, "but I think we've seen some glimmers."

Soon after Biden returned home, he sent another conciliatory signal to both Russia and Europe. U.S. relations with Germany had come under strain in recent years over Nord Stream 2, the pipeline that was to deliver Russian natural gas across the depths of the Baltic Sea directly to Germany. (Its predecessor, Nord Stream 1, had been open since 2011; Nord Stream 2 would double the capacity of the existing pipeline, enabling the system to handle the majority of Russian gas exports to Europe.) Ever since the new project was announced in 2015, it had been a bête noire of the more hawkish members of the transatlantic alliance, such as Poland and the Baltic states. They worried that the pipeline, by allowing Russian gas to reach Germany and the rest of Western Europe without first crossing Eastern Europe, would empower Moscow to bully its former imperial subjects with impunity. Nord Stream 2 had also drawn the ire of the U.S. Congress, whose members objected to Germany's deepening economic ties with Russia and would rather use American liquefied natural gas (LNG) to satisfy European energy needs.

The Biden administration now negotiated a truce with Berlin. It agreed to refrain from imposing sanctions on Nord Stream 2, as both Trump and Biden had threatened but never implemented. In exchange, Berlin committed to back tougher penalties against Russia if it committed "further aggressive acts against Ukraine."

In his first foreign policy speech, Biden proclaimed, "America is back." He was now turning those words into action. He was undoing some of the damage wrought by Trump's "America first" bravado. He was breathing new life into critical alliances and injecting a measure of stability into U.S.-Russian relations, freeing up time and resources to take on the biggest challenges of the day: COVID, climate change, and China. But the foreign policy visions of U.S. presidents rarely withstand contact with the vagaries of history. Less than a month after Biden's meeting with Putin in Geneva, the Russian president published a rambling, five-thousand-word manifesto declaring that the Ukrainian nation-state was a fiction and remained "an inalienable part of Russia." He asserted that "Russia was robbed" of territory after the collapse of the Soviet Union and hinted that he might annex the Donbas. A Russian newspaper called the essay Putin's "final ultimatum to Ukraine." Although barely covered by the American press, the manifesto raised antennae in the White House.

Biden's foreign policy honeymoon officially ended in August amid the shambolic withdrawal of U.S. troops from Afghanistan. Biden had pledged to "end America's longest war," but he hadn't meant to turn the whole country over to the Taliban, revealing the futility of twenty years of U.S. effort and trillions of dollars of investment. Kabul airport descended into chaos as desperate Afghans flooded the runway, trying to board any plane to get out of the country. At one point, a suicide bomber detonated his vest in the crowd near the airport gate, killing more than 180 people.

The swift collapse of Afghanistan's U.S.-backed government and the fall of Kabul were a national embarrassment. Even after two decades of war and occupation, American officials had failed to anticipate how quickly and totally their proxies would falter when confronted by the Taliban's advance. Jake Sullivan, the national security advisor, faced calls to resign. The forty-four-year-old had long been a rising star in America's foreign policy establishment, with admirers on both sides of the aisle. Biden touted him as a "once-in-a-generation intellect." Now Sullivan's reputation was at risk of crumbling almost as fast as the final slivers of resistance to the Taliban.

By the start of September, the last American soldier was out of Afghanistan. Around the same time, thousands of miles away from Kabul, Russia was preparing for a military exercise known as *Zapad*, the Russian word for "west." Moscow had conducted similar exercises along its western border in the past. But as the U.S. military reviewed the incoming intelligence, they noticed that this year's *Zapad* exercise was much bigger than those before it.

51

Standing Athwart History, Yelling Stop

For American officials, Russia's second, full-scale invasion of Ukraine felt like a meteor careening toward Earth: they saw it coming from thousands of miles away, yet that didn't make it any less terrifying. By early fall, U.S. intelligence agencies concluded that Putin was moving troops and tanks into position for battle, and that the centerpiece of his plan would be a dash straight toward Kyiv. They were confident in their assessment not just because of the size of the Russian military buildup near Ukraine's border—which numbered roughly 100,000 soldiers—but also on account of what else it included: logistical resources and ammunition stocks that would not be necessary for an ordinary exercise. What's more, U.S. officials believed they had enough information to piece together Putin's intentions. The Russian president's end goal, they predicted, was total victory over a country of some 40 million people and a landmass almost twice the size of Germany. Briefing this bleak assessment to Biden in the Oval Office, General Mark Milley, the chairman of the Joint Chiefs of Staff, warned of the bloodshed to come: "This is going to be the most horrific combat operations since the end of World War II."

In many of the biggest national security crises in American history—think Pearl Harbor or 9/11—intelligence agencies failed to connect the dots until it was too late. Officials were forced to catch up to events instead of shaping them. Such lack of foresight and preparation can be especially inimical to economic warfare. By the time numbers are crunched and diplomacy is complete, the crisis is well underway, making it much harder to reverse or resolve. When the United States figured out how to throttle Iran's economy, the country's nuclear program was already advanced. When the Obama administration imposed sanctions on Russia in 2014, troops had already created facts on the ground in Crimea and the Donbas. And Washington's full-court press against Huawei got started when the Chinese firm already dominated the global telecom market.

As Putin was plotting to seize Kyiv, by contrast, Washington caught him dead to rights. There was ample time to prepare a counterpunch. And if the West acted more quickly and resolutely than it had in 2014, perhaps the mere threat of harsh economic reprisals might yank the Russian president out of his imperial fantasies and prevent the invasion before it began.

The Afghanistan debacle had badly damaged Biden's reputation as a statesman, carefully cultivated during his time as vice president and as chair of the Senate Foreign Relations Committee. U.S. intelligence had led him astray, assessing that the Taliban were much further from taking Kabul than they proved to be. Now, with evidence suggesting that an even bigger crisis was in the offing, the White House was determined to get out in front of the problem. According to U.S. intelligence, Putin expected the costs of war, including any Western sanctions, to be manageable. Russia would absorb plenty of criticism, yet any real economic pain would be short-lived, just as it had been following the annexation of Crimea. If war was to be averted, the West would need to act fast and disabuse the Kremlin of that notion.

Jake Sullivan set the pace with daily meetings in his West Wing corner office. His staff knew they needed to avoid a direct confrontation between American and Russian troops at all costs. The Russian military had demonstrated its power in Georgia, Crimea, and Syria. It had since executed an expensive, multiyear modernization program. Even if nuclear escalation could be averted, the Russian military would be a formidable opponent, probably the fiercest the United States had faced since Nazi Germany.

Economic war would keep the United States off the conventional battlefield. It would also play to its greatest strength. "We have a significant comparative military advantage over Russia, but not as decisive as our comparative economic advantage," said Jon Finer, Sullivan's deputy. By throwing its economic weight around, the United States could "inflict more pain on Russia than it would cause us."

As in 2014, securing the EU's buy-in would be paramount. Unfortunately, the bloc had done little to wean itself off Russian oil and gas since the annexation of Crimea; in fact, European reliance on Russian energy had only increased. The Nord Stream 2 pipeline, expected to come online imminently, would further deepen that dependence. Overall, Russia remained the EU's fifth-largest trading partner in 2021. (By comparison, Russia did not even crack the top 20 for the United States, and America imported only small quantities of Russian oil.) If push came to shove, Biden could perhaps coerce the Europeans to change course with the threat of secondary sanctions. Yet doing so would hardly help his goal of restoring U.S. alliances in the post-Trump era.

To get the EU to take the Russian troop buildup seriously, the White House decided to share any pertinent intelligence well in advance. Given their economic ties to Russia, European countries could not afford aggressive sanctions without thorough prior vetting. At the same time, they would balk at the necessary preparatory work unless they actually believed an invasion was likely. The best way to ensure this was to reveal the overwhelming U.S. intelligence pointing to that conclusion.

A G20 summit in Rome at the end of October offered an opportunity to communicate the urgency of the situation. As Daleep Singh consulted with Bjoern Seibert and Jonathan Black, his counterparts from the European Commission and the UK prime minister's office, respectively, he realized that none of the other sherpas—and few of their bosses—had been in office during the 2014 sanctions against Russia. Back then, Singh and his colleagues had fretted about the risk of contagion for the global economy, but their fears had proved exaggerated. Singh now worried that less experienced officials at home and abroad would fall into the same trap.

This time, moreover, Western governments would not have the time to ratchet up sanctions incrementally. U.S. intelligence suggested Putin was preparing a blitzkrieg and expecting his battalions to hoist the Russian flag over Kyiv within forty-eight hours of the first combat operations. "Unlike in 2014, we can't afford to think about a gradual escalation ladder," Singh warned his international colleagues in Rome. "We need to start at the very top." They did, however, have the luxury of advance warning and could use it to Putin's disadvantage. Singh invited his foreign counterparts to join the U.S. government in "very public messaging that signals our readiness to impose the most severe sanctions in our arsenal."

His colleagues listened, but many still suspected a bluff. Putin might pressure Volodymyr Zelensky, the Ukrainian president, into making certain concessions and then order his troops back to their bases, just as he had done a few months prior. Even Putin's own staff doubted a war was on the horizon. When Singh sat down with Svetlana Lukash, the Russian sherpa, she seemed genuinely incredulous upon hearing that the United States was bracing for a large-scale invasion of Ukraine. Putin was a chess player, a gambler, not a maniac.

Skepticism and reluctance also prevailed among the geopolitical swing states at the G20 summit. Countries such as Brazil, India, and Turkey wanted nothing to do with a major land war in Europe, not even by way of sanctions. They were determined to stay on the sidelines. Even with ample time to prepare, Biden still had his work cut out for him.

52

Panic at the Pump

In early November, Bill Burns was back in the city he once called home: Moscow. The sixty-five-year-old former U.S. ambassador to Russia, whose gray mustache and soft-spoken eloquence were the stuff of diplomatic legend, was there to meet with Putin and discuss the tensions over Russia's military buildup on the Ukrainian border. Upon arriving, however, Burns learned that Putin was not in town. The Russian president had retreated to his residence by the Black Sea, a thousand miles to the south, hoping to dodge a new wave of COVID infections. So Burns was escorted into a Kremlin office and connected to the Russian leader by phone.

The unexpected change of protocol undercut the psychological heft of Burns's visit. The CIA director carried a letter from Biden, which he'd hoped to hand-deliver to the Russian leader. Instead, Burns made do with issuing a direct threat over the phone: If Russia invaded Ukraine, Putin would face severe and immediate economic consequences that went well beyond what he confronted in 2014. The costs would be so high that he would not simply be able to absorb them, wait until everyone moved on, and return to business as usual.

Burns's words had been carefully scripted and revised several times over by officials in Washington. His threat was deliberately left vague. It didn't specify any penalties or targets. This was partly because U.S. officials didn't want to tip Putin off to their exact plans. But there was also a more practical reason: the White House had not yet decided what it was going to do.

The task of compiling a menu of sanctions options fell to Daleep Singh at the White House and Wally Adeyemo at Treasury. Complicating their work were tectonic shifts in the global economic landscape. By the second half of 2021, demand for oil was bouncing back fast from a lull during the pandemic. Oil producers, who had drastically cut output in 2020, struggled to keep up. The resulting supply crunch led oil prices to reach their highest point in seven years. Americans were feeling the pinch both at the pump and in their everyday shopping, as soaring energy costs contributed to rising prices for all manner of products. By November, inflation was at levels unseen in four decades.

These trends struck terror in the White House. 1970s-style inflation was a surefire way to unravel any presidency. Every day at around 3:30 a.m., when Ron Klain, Biden's chief of staff, woke up, he reached for his phone and anxiously checked the average national gasoline price.

The timing for a renewed sanctions campaign against Russia could not have been worse. The Russian economy did not offer many high-value sanctions targets that weren't in some way connected to oil and gas. Even compared with classic petrostates such as Saudi Arabia and Bahrain, Russia's economy lacked diversification. The Kremlin was staggeringly dependent on sales of fossil fuels, which paid for almost half of its federal budget. Yet hitting the Russian energy industry could drive up oil prices—and inflation—even further.

U.S. officials hoped their biggest petrostate ally, Saudi Arabia, would boost oil production enough to offset any losses in Russian supply. But their pleas to the Saudis fell on deaf ears. The U.S.-Saudi relationship was in a bad place, and besides, Riyadh jealously guarded decisions on oil production from external pressure. (In 2012, the Saudis even resisted American entreaties to increase oil output to allow for harsher sanctions against Iran, a goal that was very much aligned with Riyadh's interests.) The upshot for the White House was that any new U.S. sanctions would need to steer clear of Russia's most vital industry lest they potentially supercharge a brewing economic crisis in the West. "Make sure that whatever sanctions you do, carve out energy," was how one of the American economic war planners described the order from the top.

Sticking to this directive while still inflicting a steep cost on Russia—in keeping with Biden's threat to Putin—would be a difficult needle to thread. Working in parallel, both Singh's team at the NSC and Adeyemo's at Treasury converged on the same proposal: a strike on Russia's largest banks. In 2014, the Obama administration had identified Russia's reliance on Western financing as a core vulnerability. Along with the EU, it had barred the country's

biggest banks, energy companies, and defense firms from raising funds on
U.S. and European capital markets. Singh and Adeyemo recommended reprising this strategy on a larger scale: Instead of focusing only on capital
markets, the United States could impose blocking sanctions that cut the
banks off from the dollar entirely. (America had used blocking sanctions
against a major Russian firm just once before—in 2018, against the aluminum giant Rusal—but the collateral damage was so extensive that the Trump
administration immediately backpedaled.)

It was uncertain whether penalties against the financial sector alone
would suffice at a time of rising oil prices, which guaranteed Russia would
enjoy a steady stream of petrodollars. But this was the best the Biden team
could do for the time being, and U.S. financial sanctions had proven their
considerable power in the past.

As the planning progressed, Jake Sullivan suggested a second axis of attack. Since the beginning of the Biden administration, he'd been overseeing
a project to strengthen and expand Trump's tech-related export controls on
China. Why not impose similar restrictions on Russia? Like China, Russia
was highly dependent on chips and other Western technology. Sweeping export controls, perhaps in the form of a scaled-up version of the FDPR that
had been imposed on Huawei, would both hurt Russia's economy and disrupt its military-industrial complex.

The outlines of a strategy were emerging. Finance and technology would
be the central sanctions targets. Energy would be excluded for now. Limiting
as it was, the directive to avoid oil and gas at least had the benefit of aligning
America's interests with those of the EU, which deemed energy sanctions a
total nonstarter.

Most European governments still doubted a large-scale invasion would
come to pass, but they agreed it was better to prepare for the worst. They also
took some relief in Biden's openness to continued diplomacy with Moscow.
Biden spoke to Putin by phone on December 7, offering a path out of the
standoff that included addressing Russia's concerns about European security. A day later, Olaf Scholz succeeded Angela Merkel as Germany's chancellor, ending her sixteen-year tenure. Where Scholz stood on Russia was a
little unclear, but it was helpful not to have the EU's most important country
run by a lame-duck government. In a formal statement shortly thereafter, all
twenty-seven EU leaders echoed Biden's warning to Putin: "Any further military aggression against Ukraine will have massive consequences and severe
cost in response." The West's faint red line was becoming clearer.

=====

"An Invasion Is an Invasion"

O n the thirteenth floor of the Berlaymont building, the European Commission's hulking, X-shaped headquarters in Brussels, Bjoern Seibert occupied the type of office one might envision for a Eurocrat: sparse with a conference table, a pile of papers, and a lonely houseplant. Seibert was both a policy wonk and a political operator. Tall and bespectacled, he had a protean nature about him, an ability to adapt his talking points to best appeal to whomever he was addressing while still advocating the same point. This was a handy skill in Brussels, where the trick was not just developing a good idea but also making representatives from twenty-seven different countries each think they had come up with it.

Seibert's office was down the hall from that of his boss, Ursula von der Leyen, the Commission's president. Von der Leyen, a commanding presence with swept-back blond hair, charted a winding path to the EU's top job. The daughter of a high-level Eurocrat much like Seibert, von der Leyen had grown up between Brussels and the German city of Hanover. She started her career as a physician, raised seven children, and spent time as a housewife on the sun-drenched campus of Stanford University, where her husband was a professor. Having entered Angela Merkel's government as minister of family affairs in 2005, at age forty-seven, she eventually rose to the position of defense minister and for a time was viewed as Merkel's heir apparent. Instead, von der Leyen was elected president of the European Commission in 2019, making her the first woman to hold the post. To signal the intensity she planned to bring to the job, von der Leyen made her home in Brussels a roughly 250-square-foot quarters next to her office.

Like his boss, Seibert had spent time in the United States, working as a

*Powerful Eurocrats: Ursula von der Leyen
and her chief of staff, Bjoern Seibert (left).*

researcher at Harvard and the U.S. Army War College. His background in defense strategy made him an unusual presence at the Commission, which did not play a big role in European military matters. Yet Seibert's expertise suited the present crisis, with its prospect of a colossal land war right on the EU's doorstep. By January 2022, Seibert and Daleep Singh were speaking multiple times per day. When they weren't on the phone, they traded texts on WhatsApp. Twice weekly, their teams held secure videoconferences to go over potential sanctions options. Seibert's team quickly got on board with the U.S. proposal to focus on finance and technology, two sectors in which the West possessed asymmetric leverage over Russia.

Seibert got to work building support for the idea around Brussels. To prevent politically damaging leaks, he put nothing down on paper and held only small-group meetings with disparate configurations of countries, always including representatives from the EU's eastern flank to sway the discussion in a more hawkish direction. He avoided convening representatives from all twenty-seven member states at the same time, which would be a recipe for deadlock. Slowly but surely, the sanctions proposal spread, behind the scenes and without Seibert's or Singh's fingerprints on it.

It helped that the plan centered on two industries of greater importance to America than Europe. Wall Street and Silicon Valley, crown jewels of the U.S. economy, world capitals of finance and technology: they would be the front lines of the economic war, meaning that big U.S. companies would have to sacrifice profitable business lines. Most important of all, Washington was pledging to weaponize two of the most vital sectors of the American economy. It was risking the international reputation of the U.S. dollar and possibly accelerating the fragmentation of the world into parallel technology ecosystems. The United States was putting a lot of skin in the game, without asking the EU to give up its critical energy imports from Russia. This made the plan much easier for the Europeans to swallow.

=

Just before the new year, the White House had conducted a series of elaborate tabletop exercises that simulated a Russian invasion of Ukraine and required U.S. officials to devise a response. The project, spearheaded by NSC director for strategic planning Alex Bick, was inspired by the calamitous U.S. withdrawal from Afghanistan, when officials had wrongly assumed that American personnel would be leaving the country while Kabul was still in friendly hands. Under Bick's direction, the NSC convened representatives from all relevant government agencies to game out a variety of scenarios for how and where Putin might strike.

The exercises revealed that officials disagreed on how to respond if the Russian attack fell short of a full-scale invasion. As during some other sanctions debates, Treasury officials urged restraint: If Russia's territorial ambitions were limited to the Donbas, for instance, was it really worth imposing sweeping sanctions and putting the global financial system under stress? The world economy was in a delicate state as it was, with rising inflation and the rapid spread of a new, hyper-contagious variant of COVID known as Omicron. But there was a problem with Treasury's caution: Once Russian tanks crossed into Ukrainian territory, there was no telling where they'd go next, and the most crucial time for deterrence would have passed. It would be very hard to distinguish between a large-scale invasion, a smaller incursion, and some sort of feint, and the last thing the West could afford was to debate what did or didn't count as an "invasion" in the middle of a Russian attack.

By late January, the United States and its allies agreed on a common line:

If just one Russian tank crossed the border, that would be enough to trigger sanctions. As the Biden administration put it: "An invasion is an invasion," period. They would not prepare different sanctions options for each potential contingency. They would prepare only one big package, known as the Day Zero sanctions. The West would "start high, stay high," as Singh liked to say.

Over the course of January, the prospects for a diplomatic resolution to the crisis dimmed. Russia's military presence near Ukraine kept growing, and ominously, blood supplies and equipment for field hospitals were being moved to the border. Efforts by Wendy Sherman, one of Washington's most experienced negotiators, to hammer out a deal with Russian deputy foreign minister Sergei Ryabkov went nowhere. Ryabkov's demands were maximalist: Russia wanted a permanent end to NATO expansion and the withdrawal of all NATO troops and weapons from countries that joined the alliance after 1997, such as Poland and the Baltic states. Sherman came away from the meeting convinced that Moscow was merely going through the motions of diplomacy with its mind set on war. A subsequent meeting in Geneva between Secretary of State Tony Blinken and his Russian counterpart, Sergei Lavrov, also ended in disappointment.

If diplomacy was a dead end, Washington's next best bet was deterrence. Putin had to grasp how painful an invasion would be for Russia both economically and militarily, and he had to be denied a pretext for escalation. Some members of Congress were calling for U.S. sanctions to go into effect right away. But a preemptive strike might in fact *increase* Putin's incentive to invade. "The purpose of the sanctions, in the first instance, is to try to deter Russia from going to war," Blinken explained. "As soon as you trigger them, that deterrent is gone."

Instead, the Biden administration publicly warned that an invasion was looming and forcefully argued that Russia was the aggressor. In the process, it was building a case for a unified global response. It was also justifying its own actions, including sending weapons to Ukraine—Biden had recently approved a shipment of shoulder-fired Javelin missiles—and threatening tough sanctions. "If Russia is sincere about addressing our respective security concerns through dialogue, the United States and our allies and partners will continue to engage in good faith," Biden said in a statement from the White House on January 31. "If instead Russia chooses to walk away from diplomacy and attack Ukraine, Russia will bear the responsibility, and it will face swift and severe consequences." The precise meaning behind this

No limits: Vladimir Putin and Xi Jinping declare a new Sino-Russian partnership during the 2022 Winter Olympics in Beijing.

last phrase—"swift and severe consequences"—would take on immense importance over the following weeks.

For his part, Putin seemed attentive to the opinion of one man above all: Xi Jinping. On February 4, the opening day of the Winter Olympics in Beijing, Putin met with the Chinese president to announce an extensive new Sino-Russian partnership. "Friendship between the two States has no limits," proclaimed the five-thousand-plus-word joint statement released as part of the announcement. "There are no 'forbidden' areas of cooperation." Western intelligence reports alleged that Xi asked Putin to delay any invasion until after the Olympics—a worrying sign, if true, that Russia's planned war of imperial conquest had Beijing's tacit consent. The closing ceremony of the Olympics was scheduled for February 20. That meant Western officials had all of two weeks to finish their preparations.

≡

Deterrence requires a combination of capability and will. There was no doubt the West possessed the capability to throttle Russia's economy. The question was whether it also had the will. The intensive coordination between bureaucrats in Washington, Brussels, and other G7 capitals—a scaled-up version of the transatlantic diplomacy Dan Fried had led years earlier, and the most intensive collaboration between America and its allies in decades— was encouraging. But ultimately, the decision to act was in the hands of elected leaders, not all of whom were eager for a standoff with Putin.

Olaf Scholz, the new German chancellor, was an understated politician who showed little interest in foreign policy. His party, the Social Democrats, traditionally favored warmer relations with Moscow. Prominent members of the party had been publicly critical of sanctions on Russia. Scholz's own views remained murky, and since coming to power in December, he had been mum on the situation on Ukraine's border. He had avoided direct diplomacy with Moscow and refused to send weapons to Kyiv. His reticence was rapidly eroding Germany's reputation as a reliable partner in Washington. "Berlin, we have a problem," wrote Emily Haber, Germany's ambassador to the United States, in a cable sent home in late January.

Some belated progress was made when Scholz visited the White House in early February. In a joint press conference with Biden, the German chancellor assured his support for "severe sanctions" in case of a Russian attack. One reporter asked about Nord Stream 2, long a point of contention between

The new chancellor: Olaf Scholz (left) speaks next to Joe Biden at the White House on February 7, 2022.

Berlin and Washington. "If Russia invades," Biden said, "there will no longer be a Nord Stream 2. We will bring an end to it." Scholz did not confirm Biden's threat, but he did not deny it, either.

Behind the scenes, officials worked feverishly to identify targets for the Day Zero sanctions, the package of financial and technology penalties that would go into effect as soon as any Russian troops crossed into Ukraine. On the financial front, the choice of targets was clear-cut. The top two Russian banks, Sberbank and VTB, accounted for almost 60 percent of household deposits in Russia, and more than half of all wages in the country were paid through Sberbank. Russia's third-largest bank, Gazprombank, had significantly less market share but handled payments for Russian energy sales. For the financial sanctions to leave a mark, they would need to hit at least one of these banks, if not all three. Tech-focused export controls were a more contentious matter, but after several weeks of protracted negotiations, American and European officials agreed that the Day Zero package would restrict exports of semiconductors to Russia, which was heavily reliant on foreign chips. (The United States would do so by issuing an FDPR, while the EU would release its own equivalent restrictions.)

As these negotiations were underway, Daleep Singh and one of his deputies, Peter Harrell, called leading U.S. executives, urging them to prepare for the possibility of major sanctions. Many of the executives rapidly directed their companies to devise contingency plans to exit the Russian market, from liquidating assets to evacuating personnel. Regardless of whether the new sanctions would require them to close up shop in Russia, they might need to get out anyway depending on how the Kremlin retaliated. Singh and Harrell assumed that the calls, which took place on open phone lines, were being listened in on by Russian intelligence, a prospect they welcomed. Perhaps these discussions would help clarify for Moscow the tangible costs of invading Ukraine.

Singh also began taking on a more visible role in the administration's aggressive public messaging campaign. On February 18, he joined White House press secretary Jen Psaki to reveal to reporters more detail about what Biden's threat of "swift and severe consequences" would entail. "If Russia invades Ukraine, it would become a pariah to the international community, it would become isolated from global financial markets, and it would be deprived of the most sophisticated technological inputs," he said. The West had the power to do this because it controlled critical chokepoints in the world economy. "Both financial sanctions and export controls deny something to

Russia that it needs and can't get from anywhere other than the United States or our allies and partners," Singh added. The West understood its strengths and was prepared to use them.

At noon on Sunday, February 20, Biden convened an emergency meeting of the National Security Council. Jake Sullivan, Tony Blinken, Janet Yellen, Bill Burns, Daleep Singh, and other top officials, all donning medical masks, gathered in the Situation Room. In Beijing, fireworks lit up the night sky, marking the end of the Winter Olympics. Russian tanks could start rolling toward Kyiv at any moment.

The financial sanctions package was in good shape, Yellen said. Its cornerstone would be sanctions on Sberbank and VTB, Russia's two largest banks. But there was a catch. Because Sberbank and VTB had subsidiaries in Vienna and Frankfurt, blocking sanctions risked spilling over into the European banking system. It would be wisest to bar Sberbank and VTB from banking services on U.S. soil without freezing all their assets. To compensate, Treasury would impose blocking sanctions on a handful of smaller Russian banks.

Singh thought these measures didn't go far enough, but he felt it would be fruitless to argue further while discussions were happening in the abstract. As Seibert often told Singh, the best they could do was come to an understanding among policy wonks and have options ready for their bosses when the moment came. The leaders themselves would most likely hedge until confronted with the inescapable, grim spectacle of war: tanks rolling, missiles falling, buildings burning.

54

The Scholz Jolt

On Monday, February 21, Vladimir Putin sat behind a small desk in an expansive Kremlin ballroom. Surrounded by soaring white columns, bronze statues, and gilded moldings, Putin surveyed the members of his security council, who were seated so far away that they could barely have heard him were he not speaking into a microphone.

Officially, they had gathered to discuss recognizing the independence of the Donetsk People's Republic and the Luhansk People's Republic, the two self-proclaimed statelets in the Donbas under the rule of Russian-backed warlords since 2014. But the true purpose of the televised meeting was to broadcast that the war on which Putin was about to embark enjoyed full support from his top brass.

In a performance reminiscent of a Stalinist show trial, Putin grilled the assembled officials about their views on the Donbas, glowering at them as they shifted in their seats and mumbled their way through tepid responses. "Speak directly!" he barked at Sergei Naryshkin, the head of the foreign intelligence service, who struggled to get his words out. A visibly flustered Naryshkin said he supported annexing Donetsk and Luhansk into Russia. Putin reminded him that they were there to discuss recognizing the regions' independence, not making them part of Russia.

After the meeting, Putin signed a decree recognizing the two breakaway republics and ordered Russian troops, more than 150,000 of whom had by now set up camp at various points along the Ukrainian border, to help "keep the peace" in the Donbas. The decree had the unanimous support of the security council. Not that this consensus mattered: As Foreign Minister Sergei

Holding court: Vladimir Putin chairs a televised meeting with his security council in the Kremlin on February 21, 2022.

Lavrov is said to have told a Russian oligarch around this time, Putin's only real advisors were Ivan the Terrible, Peter the Great, and Catherine the Great.

Later that day, the first eyewitness reports trickled in from the Donbas: Russian armored vehicles were plowing through the region. Biden wanted a response, yet some European governments remained unwilling to roll out the Day Zero sanctions, holding out hope that Putin's real plan was a campaign to consolidate control over Donetsk and Luhansk instead of invading all of Ukraine. As a result, the White House hurriedly prepared a raft of alternative penalties. On Monday afternoon, Biden signed an executive order imposing a trade embargo on Donetsk and Luhansk, a mirror image of the sanctions Obama had levied on Crimea in 2014. It was a sensible but toothless move. Reporters peppered Biden officials with questions: Was this an "invasion"? And if it was, why were the consequences so small? "An invasion is an invasion," Jon Finer clarified the next morning, "and that is what is underway." Shortly thereafter, the United States announced blocking sanctions on VEB, a Russian state-owned development bank, and tighter restrictions on Russian sovereign debt.

A second shot across the bow came from an unexpected place: Berlin. On Tuesday, Olaf Scholz announced that he had rescinded the German government's certification of the Nord Stream 2 pipeline, turning $11 billion worth of undersea infrastructure into a useless heap of metal. Coming after weeks of conspicuous silence, Scholz's surprise announcement marked a turning point not just for Germany but for the whole EU. The bloc's debates on Russia fit a familiar pattern, with eastern states such as Poland and Lithuania pushing for tougher policies while Greece, Hungary, and a smattering of others urged caution. Invariably, Germany's position tipped the balance in one direction or the other. Scholz's decision to cancel Nord Stream 2 signified that Germany now stood on the side of action. In short order, the EU agreed to match the U.S. sanctions on VEB and the embargo on Donetsk and Luhansk. Japan and the rest of the G7 followed suit.

Scholz's foray also had the effect of rousing other European leaders, if only out of political envy. Boris Johnson, the flamboyant British prime minister, saw in the Ukraine crisis an opportunity to burnish his image as a latter-day Churchill and attain a loftier distinction than his dubious legacy as an architect of Brexit. He would certainly not let himself be upstaged by a soft-spoken bore like Scholz. At the crack of dawn on Wednesday, February 23, Johnson held an emergency meeting with his cabinet to discuss possible sanctions. The prime minister was in a hawkish frame of mind, and he was ready to push for more aggressive measures, including kicking Russian banks out of SWIFT—a penalty that had hitherto been considered too extreme for the Day Zero sanctions, which themselves had not yet been issued. Later in the day, Johnson spoke to executives from Barclays, Goldman Sachs, HSBC, and Lloyd's of London, warning that the next round of sanctions would "really bite." Jonathan Black, the British sherpa, took to WhatsApp to alert his G7 colleagues that his government was ready to go much further on sanctions than the group had previously contemplated. The replies indicated that the winds were shifting in other capitals, too.

Western governments had prepared for months for this moment—both to enable quick action and to signal to Putin that an invasion would carry dire costs. Yet now that the moment had arrived, their plans seemed insufficient.

55

<hr/>

Banks vs. Tanks

On Thursday, February 24, in the wee hours before 5:00 a.m. in Moscow, Vladimir Putin returned to Russian TV screens. Sitting at the same table he spoke from following the security council session on Monday, Putin announced that he had ordered a "special military operation" for the "demilitarization and de-Nazification of Ukraine." Moments later, missiles rained down on airports and cities across Ukraine, from Kharkiv to Kyiv to Odessa. In their magnitude and precision, the strikes were a ruthless demonstration of military might unseen since America's 2003 invasion of Iraq.

Even in these early hours, however, there were signs Putin was in over his head. In his twenty-plus years at the helm of the Russian state, he'd cultivated an image as a master tactician always two steps ahead of his adversaries. Yet here he was, sticking to the exact script that U.S. officials had previewed weeks ago: building up troops while denying plans to invade, cooking up a pretext about the supposed persecution of Russian-speakers in the Donbas, and casting the subsequent invasion as a necessary act to defend that population from their "Nazi" oppressors in Kyiv. He was also getting sloppy. In his Thursday morning statement announcing the invasion, Putin was clad in the same black blazer and maroon tie he wore during the security council meeting on Monday. Even by the conservative sartorial standards of modern politics, such monotony was odd. The reason, as revealed by metadata from the Kremlin website, was that Putin had pre-recorded the war speech three days in advance, shortly after he had recognized the two statelets in the Donbas.

None of this changed the grim reality that Ukraine was under full-fledged assault by one of the world's most powerful militaries. Russian tanks rolled across the border from the east and from the north, where they used Belarus as a staging ground. Kyiv and its three million inhabitants stood just 140 miles away from the Belarusian border, a distance that a Russian blitzkrieg should be able to cover in a day or two. Western officials expected Russian forces to push straight toward the capital in an attempt to "decapitate" Ukraine's government. It was doubtful Ukrainian forces could withstand for long. Russian soldiers packed parade uniforms in anticipation of a victory march through the streets of Kyiv.

Daleep Singh had just returned to his home on a leafy Washington street in the vain hope of getting an hour of sleep when he heard the news. He stuffed his backpack with espresso pods, jumped into his car, and drove along the Potomac River back to the White House. The full-scale invasion was now underway, which meant it was time to trigger the Day Zero sanctions that Singh and his G7 counterparts had been preparing for months. At the center of the Day Zero plan would be penalties on Russia's two largest banks, Sberbank and VTB, which would hinder their ability to transact in dollars; and high-tech export controls on the entire Russian economy. All that was needed was final signoff from Biden.

It would take a few hours for the president and his National Security Council to assemble in the Situation Room, and Singh hoped to use that time to advocate for an even tougher response. From his discussions with the other G7 sherpas, he was confident America's allies would follow its lead. There was no longer any need to restrain the use of financial weapons on account of concerns about Europe. Within the White House, Singh pushed to bump up the penalty on VTB to blocking sanctions, which would both cut the bank off from the dollar and freeze all its assets. His team was also prepared to use this cudgel against Sberbank, but they didn't want to risk alienating their more cautious colleagues at Treasury.

Soon after Biden kicked off the meeting, the discussion turned to VTB. Should Washington hit Russia's second-largest bank with its most devastating economic weapon? Janet Yellen expressed reservations. VTB held 20 percent of all assets in Russia's banking sector. It would be one of the biggest financial institutions Treasury had ever blocked. But her main concern was Germany, where VTB owned a subsidiary. Berlin was not ready to sanction VTB, and a unilateral American strike on the bank could break transatlantic unity.

As he listened to Yellen, Singh scribbled a note and passed it to Sullivan.

He did not share the treasury secretary's opinion. Singh was in close contact with Jörg Kukies, Olaf Scholz's sherpa and the former co-head of Goldman Sachs in Germany. Scholz tended to defer to Kukies on matters of economic warfare, and Singh felt certain Kukies would have no problem with hitting VTB. As time was short, Sullivan and Singh stepped out and hurried to the national security advisor's office. With Sullivan by his side, Singh called Kukies on his cell phone and asked how Berlin would react if Washington imposed blocking sanctions on VTB. "We can live with it," said Kukies. The two men raced back to the Situation Room to share the news.

Biden approved the package. In addition to the blocking sanctions on VTB, Washington would require U.S. financial institutions to close all of Sberbank's correspondent accounts within thirty days, a move that would disrupt its ability to process dollar payments. VTB, Sberbank, and other Russian financial institutions processed almost $40 billion every single day in dollar transactions. This flow would now largely come to a halt. Treasury would also impose blocking sanctions on several smaller Russian banks and expand individual asset freezes beyond the people in Putin's inner circle, most of whom had been under sanctions since 2014, to include their family members and scores of other Russian oligarchs. At the same time, Commerce issued its FDPR on Russia, cutting the country off from semiconductors and other high-tech gear from both American firms and companies abroad that used U.S. equipment or software. Shortly after this announcement, TSMC and other big chipmakers all over the world terminated sales to Russia, just as they had done to Huawei two years earlier. Other G7 states soon pledged to match the latest U.S. sanctions with equivalent penalties of their own.

In the weeks before the invasion, Russian financial markets had whipsawed up and down as traders placed bets on whether Biden's threat of "swift and severe consequences" was bark or bite. On February 24, they went into free fall. Russia's main stock market lost a third of its value in a single day. The ruble plunged to a record low against the dollar.

Whatever temporary relief this caused Western leaders faded in the face of Russia's continued advance on the battlefield. Hundreds of thousands of Ukrainians fled their homes. Explosions wrecked residential buildings and killed untold numbers of civilians. Zelensky declared martial law and ordered a general mobilization, banning all Ukrainian men between the ages of eighteen and sixty from leaving the country.

Compared with all this, the sanctions felt inadequate. In relation to their principal goal—preventing a Russian invasion in the first place—they were a resounding failure. Months of preparations, threats, and red lines had made no apparent impression on Putin. America and its friends "will always find an excuse to introduce more sanctions regardless of the situation in Ukraine," Putin told the Russian people earlier that week. "The only goal they have is to contain the development of Russia." Whether Putin truly believed in the inevitability of sanctions was unknown. Either way, nothing about the preceding years, in which the pain of the 2014 penalties subsided and Russia faced minimal consequences for its further incendiary acts, gave him reason for concern that a new wave of sanctions would be insurmountable. Despite all the warnings from Biden and other Western leaders, Putin clearly did not expect the economic costs of an invasion to be daunting enough to make him reconsider.

Now with the Day Zero sanctions unveiled, a PDF bearing the unassuming title General License 8 seemed to support Putin's conclusion. Published as part of the reams of documents and information that OFAC released about the new penalties, it exempted all energy-related transactions—such as payments for Russian oil, natural gas, and coal—from the financial sanctions. Biden specifically highlighted the exemption in his speech announcing the penalties, reassuring the public that he was "taking active steps to bring down the costs" that the measures would impose on Americans, which is why they were "specifically designed to allow energy payments to continue."

Scholars, financial analysts, and lawyers scrutinizing the Day Zero sanctions were quick to point out that the decision to leave Russia's energy sector untouched amounted to a major gap. In the twenty-four hours after Putin had initiated his grisly plan with the televised security council meeting, the United States and its European allies paid Russia some $350 million for oil and another $250 million for natural gas. So long as General License 8 remained in effect, these sums looked poised to increase: on February 24, oil prices topped $100 per barrel for the first time since 2014.

That evening, as the leaders of all twenty-seven EU states gathered in Brussels for an emergency meeting, it was impossible not to feel that the Day Zero sanctions, even in their latest iteration, still fell short. A horrific imperialist war was unfolding a short drive away from towns and villages that were safely ensconced within the EU and NATO. The assembled leaders spoke by video link to Volodymyr Zelensky, who was holed up in a bunker somewhere in Kyiv and sporting green military fatigues. "This may be the last time you see me alive," Zelensky warned. Ukrainians were dying in pursuit of European values, he said, and if there was ever a time for the EU to step up, it was now. Several of the European leaders, dressed in business attire and comfortably seated in a Brussels conference room, broke down in tears.

56

Pandora's Box

As Daleep Singh walked to his office on the morning of Friday, February 25, he passed a throng of protesters in Lafayette Square. They were demonstrating against the Russian invasion, now in its second day. In a show of how prominent America's economic weapons had become, some of them waved signs reading BAN RUSSIA FROM SWIFT!

In his call with EU leaders, Volodymyr Zelensky had made the same demand. The idea quickly took hold, and protesters across major European cities started clamoring for it, too. Soon, Singh's phone was buzzing with messages from his European colleagues asking about the possibility of sanctions that would kick Russian banks out of SWIFT.

Singh was not averse to such a move, but he worried about the outsize expectations attached to it. The idea of a SWIFT ban attracted attention because journalists and lawmakers gave it undue credit for isolating Iran back in 2012, and because the Kremlin had warned years earlier that it would retaliate harshly against any effort to do the same to Russian banks. To be sure, access to SWIFT was valuable. More than eleven thousand banks used the service to send more than 40 million messages each day, making it the lingua franca of cross-border payments. But it was not indispensable. Other similar systems existed, including Russia's own SPFS, which it created following the annexation of Crimea and resulting sanctions in 2014. Iran, for its part, was shunned from the global financial system not because of the SWIFT ban but rather because *all* the country's major banks were hit with American blocking sanctions. There was a long way to go before Russia's financial sector was as isolated as Iran's, and severing its access to SWIFT would not suffice. More promising, Singh believed, would be a strike at the heart of Russia's financial system: the country's central bank.

In late 2014, the one-two punch of Western capital markets sanctions and collapsing oil prices sent the ruble into a nosedive. The Russian economy was saved from worse by Elvira Nabiullina, the central bank's governor, who quickly hiked interest rates and spent down the country's foreign exchange reserves, stabilizing the ruble in the process. Among other things, the episode taught Moscow that it needed to beef up its holdings of foreign exchange. In the years since, the central bank had amassed a war chest of more than $630 billion in hard currency. The funds could be used to defend the ruble, buy imports, and finance combat operations.

Now, to try to prop up a ruble that was again plunging in the face of sanctions, Nabiullina would reprise her old strategy and deploy Russian foreign reserves to buy rubles. Her counterparties in these transactions would be other central banks and global financial institutions. Yet since most of Russia's foreign-cash pile consisted of dollars, euros, and other G7 currencies, Russia's financial counterparties would by necessity be institutions that fell under the jurisdiction of the United States, the EU, and other allied governments. If they wanted, therefore, the United States and its allies could render Russia's giant foreign reserves useless. And this was exactly what Singh thought they should do: impose sanctions on the Central Bank of Russia that thwarted its ability to spend its hoard of hard currency.

The United States had sanctioned other central banks in the past. Most notably, under pressure from Congress, the Obama administration targeted the Central Bank of Iran in 2012, a move that served as the foundation for the critical oil sanctions that cratered the country's economy and pushed Tehran to the nuclear negotiating table. But Russia's central bank was more than six times larger than Iran's had been, and vastly more integrated into the global financial system. In the months leading up to Russia's invasion, the G7 had not prepared for sanctions against the Central Bank of Russia. The only other top official to have pushed for it was Chrystia Freeland, the Canadian finance minister, who in a previous career was the *Financial Times*'s Moscow bureau chief. But her advocacy had not gotten very far. To the extent people were thinking about tougher sanctions, they were fixated on SWIFT, SWIFT, and SWIFT.

Early that Friday afternoon, Singh pitched Bjoern Seibert and Jonathan Black on the central bank idea. Both intuitively grasped its merits, but they cautioned that their leaders had never seriously considered it, so they would

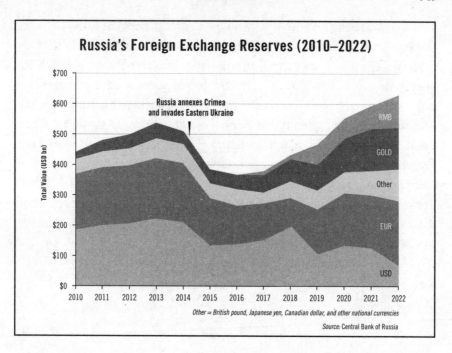

Russia's Foreign Exchange Reserves (2010–2022)

Russia annexes Crimea
and invades Eastern Ukraine

RMB

GOLD

Other

EUR

USD

Other = British pound, Japanese yen, Canadian dollar, and other national currencies

Source: Central Bank of Russia

need time to take their temperature. They agreed it was worth convening a conference call of the G7 sherpas that evening to discuss next steps on sanctions, including both SWIFT and the central bank proposal.

At the start of the call, the sherpas quickly agreed to ban a handful of Russian banks from SWIFT. Only then did Singh turn to the subject at the top of his mind—the central bank. He was frank about the enormity of the step: by stopping Russia's central bank from using its foreign exchange reserves, which it had methodically accumulated over decades, the United States would be jeopardizing the dollar's future. The dollar was the world's reserve currency: roughly 60 percent of global foreign exchange reserves were held in dollars. Like many others, Singh considered the dollar a national treasure that underwrote American prosperity and enabled the U.S. government to function. If the United States weaponized its currency in this manner, other central banks might no longer feel so secure holding dollars. But Singh believed it was worth taking this risk.

The other sherpas recognized the weight of Singh's words. After a brief silence, Singh got a boost from the country that was historically the most reluctant G7 member on sanctions: Italy. Like Singh, Italian prime minister Mario Draghi had at one point worked for Goldman Sachs, and the two men had known each other for more than a decade. Draghi had gone on to head

Italy's central bank and eventually served as president of the European Central Bank, where, in the throes of the eurozone crisis, he famously declared that the ECB would do "whatever it takes" to preserve the euro. Singh had also built a warm relationship with Draghi's diplomatic advisor, Luigi Mattiolo. On the G7 conference call, after Singh concluded his presentation, Mattiolo piped up and said that he believed Draghi could support the proposal. Black then added that Boris Johnson could support it, and Seibert said the same of Ursula von der Leyen. Canada was in favor, too, and neither Germany nor France expressed opposition. (It was the middle of the night in Tokyo, so Hiroshi Suzuki, Japan's sherpa, missed the call.) By the end of the discussion, the G7 sherpas had reached verbal agreement to take some sort of action against Russia's central bank.

Within just a few hours, Singh had sold the other G7 sherpas on his big idea. But he had not yet sold his own government.

"Big nations don't bluff"—this mantra, which Biden was fond of reciting, rang in Singh's ears as he paced around his office early the next morning. Sanctions on the Central Bank of Russia, he believed, would put Biden's credo into action and prove to Putin that the president had been serious when he warned of "swift and severe consequences."

While Singh's advocacy over the past twenty-four hours had built significant momentum behind the proposal, he took nothing for granted. Getting the blocking sanctions against VTB across the finish line had been an uphill battle, and that measure was a fraction as severe as the one now on the table. Singh and his team knew they would need to be deliberate about how they marketed the idea.

To soothe voices of caution, they devised a plan. Singh would not advocate for sanctions on the Central Bank of Russia explicitly. Instead, he would advocate a policy that would prevent the central bank from "deploying its international reserves in ways that undermine the impact of our sanctions." This was a rhetorical sleight of hand—but it was conjured precisely to win over leaders wrestling with competing impulses to hit Russia hard and contain fallout in the global economy. Russia's central bank assets would not be "frozen," they would be "immobilized," which was a distinction without a difference. Singh and his team drafted a statement for G7 leaders that would commit their governments to take such an action and then sent it to Bjoern Seibert to provide comments and coordinate it with others in the EU.

As Singh saw it, world leaders had already invested significant political capital in sanctions against Russia. If Putin could simply use his central bank's riches to buoy the Russian economy, it would offset the impact of those sanctions. Closing off this possibility would require barring the Central Bank of Russia from transactions with Western banks. The logic was unassailable, and when Seibert and the other sherpas presented the plan to their bosses, who were watching in horror as Russian bombs pummeled Ukraine's onion-domed cities, they were ready to go for it.

That left the United States as the decisive vote. Singh had kept Jake Sullivan updated on where the proposal stood with others in the G7, and Sullivan saw fit to arrange a conversation with Biden to ensure they had his approval. The president was in Wilmington that day for the memorial service of a family member, so Sullivan gathered Biden's top advisors in his office for a conference call with the boss. Singh huddled around Sullivan's table with Jon Finer, Ron Klain, and fellow senior Biden aide Steve Ricchetti; on the line were Biden, Tony Blinken, and Janet Yellen. After Sullivan provided a situational update, he turned to Singh to brief the president on the state of the next sanctions package. Singh laid out his rationale for immobilizing Russia's central bank reserves. It would prevent Moscow from undermining the potency of all the other sanctions, and best of all, Putin wasn't expecting it. This was their chance to take the Kremlin by surprise.

When Singh finished speaking, Biden asked Yellen for her perspective. She was hesitant. As a former Fed chair, Yellen recoiled at the idea of weaponizing the dollar's role as the world's reserve currency. She wanted more time for her team to analyze a proposal that might endanger this central pillar of American economic leadership. They were opening Pandora's box, and the potential consequences might be felt for generations.

Singh was sympathetic to Yellen's perspective. He viewed the dollar's global status as an exorbitant privilege that enabled America to absorb economic shocks and fund the government, households, and businesses far more cheaply than would otherwise be possible. He also admired Yellen, an economist-turned-policymaker thirty years his senior whose career he dreamed of emulating. But he feared the window of opportunity for a move like this would not last forever. Besides, no amount of analysis would sweep away every speck of doubt. Yellen was right that the action would subordinate

Janet Yellen: U.S. secretary of the treasury
during the Biden administration.

America's economic interests to the higher purpose of national security. But Washington would be moving in tandem with the issuers of the world's other reserve currencies—the euro, pound, and yen—and it would be doing so to try to thwart a blatant violation of the UN Charter. Time was short: the first financial markets would open on Sunday night, and Russian tanks were bearing down on Kyiv.

Yellen was unmoved. She needed time to mull it over and to discuss it with the other G7 finance ministers. Biden was not prepared to go forward with a course of action that his treasury secretary opposed, so the meeting ended with no decision.

Upon leaving Sullivan's office, Singh got on the phone with Seibert and Black. He cut to the chase: "I know you guys are ready to go, and I know I pushed for this, but I don't have Yellen." They decided to urge Mario Draghi, the Italian prime minister, to call Yellen personally and attempt to sway her. It was unusual for a foreign leader to place a direct call to the U.S. treasury secretary. But Yellen and Draghi had a close relationship dating back years; they worked side-by-side when Yellen was Fed chair and Draghi led the ECB. Seibert persuaded von der Leyen to call Draghi, and von der Leyen persuaded Draghi to speak to Yellen.

At around 1:00 p.m., Singh received a call from his daughter. A strange man was loitering outside their house. Singh alerted the Secret Service, sprinted to his car, and raced home to protect his family. By the time he arrived, the man had left. He had neither stolen anything nor approached Singh's daughter. Perhaps someone was trying to intimidate Singh, who had recently entered the spotlight as America's chief economic war plan-ner. Unnerved but relieved at the same time, he returned to the White House around 3:00 p.m. By the time he got back to his office, Draghi had already spoken to Yellen. She was now on board, and Biden had signed off on the proposal.

The White House press team was ready to go live with the G7 statement when it dawned on Singh that he had not yet spoken to Hiroshi Suzuki, the Japanese sherpa who'd missed the G7 conference call. In the rush of activity over the preceding hours, it had slipped Singh's mind. Japan was a critical member of the G7 and the issuer of a key reserve currency, so this was a se-rious oversight.

Singh called Suzuki and apologized profusely. Everyone at the White House was locked and loaded for a big press rollout. Could Japan support the proposal? Ever the diplomat, Suzuki betrayed no hard feelings. He said he would do his best to get Japan's prime minister, Fumio Kishida, to sign off. Singh and the White House press team waited for an hour or so and then Suzuki called back. It was the wee hours of the morning in Tokyo, and he could not get Kishida briefed in time. But there was no need to wait; he was confident the prime minister would okay it when he returned to the office.

Around 5:30 p.m. in Washington, the members of the G7, minus Japan, issued a statement committing themselves to target Russia's central bank. The statement was scarce on detail and lacked the force of law. It merely represented a pledge to act in the future. Yet it still amounted to an act of economic warfare without precedent, one that was sure to rattle financial markets and forever change their perception of Russia.

"You heard about Fortress Russia—the war chest of $630 billion of foreign reserves," Singh told reporters in a background briefing that ac-companied the announcement. "It's impressive, but it's only impressive if Russia can use those reserves." Singh let out a flash of confidence: "This will show that Russia's supposed sanctions-proofing of its economy is a myth."

At the very least, he was right about one thing: Russia was blindsided. "Nobody saw that coming," Sergei Lavrov later said of the move against the central bank. "It was just theft."

Monetary Policy at the Point of a Gun

O n Sunday evening, just over twenty-four hours after the G7 announcement, a tense Daleep Singh stared at his Bloomberg terminal as the first quotes on the ruble were coming in. Russia's currency—which had started the year at a value of 75 rubles to the dollar, a level it retained until it slid to around 80 a few days prior—was trading for well below 100 rubles to the dollar. A ruble was now worth less than a single U.S. cent.

Earlier that day, Jake Sullivan had asked Singh whether he was worried about the reaction to the strike on the central bank, which would officially take effect the following morning. Both men understood that this was uncharted territory, entered without much advance planning. "I don't worry about having enough impact," Singh confessed. "I worry about the impact getting out of our ability to control." They did not want to trigger a global financial crisis, and they did not want to be viewed as reckless stewards of the international financial system. As the first data trickled in, Singh worried they might have achieved this kind of catastrophic success.

The immobilization of Russia's central bank reserves reverberated from the financial districts of New York and London to the streets of Moscow and St. Petersburg. Russians rushed to withdraw cash in any foreign currency they could get their hands on, and lines formed outside banks and ATM machines, sometimes snaking around entire blocks. It was a giant bank run, unfolding on a nationwide scale across the country's eleven time zones. As bank branches everywhere were drained of dollars, some people took to chasing cash trucks around the city in hopes of catching them as they unloaded their cargoes.

On Sunday night, Putin got back on state television. Owing to "the unfriendly measures against our country in the economic dimension," he ordered Russia's nuclear forces to go on high alert. Russia may lack the means to match the West blow-for-blow in the economic sphere, but it did have other weapons at its disposal. Google searches in Russia for the word "emigration" spiked by a factor of five.

The fallout went beyond Russia. The ECB issued a warning that Sberbank's subsidiaries in Europe were about to fail as liquidity dried up. This was happening even though the U.S. penalties on Sberbank would not take effect for several more weeks and even though the EU had not included Sberbank as one of the seven Russian banks it had barred from SWIFT. It was a sign of possible financial contagion, just what Janet Yellen feared.

A month before Russia's assault on Kyiv, Putin convened a secret meeting with Russia's leading economic minds at his residence outside Moscow. During the session, Elvira Nabiullina, along with Herman Gref, the chief executive of Sberbank, and several others warned of the economic ramifications of further escalation in Ukraine. A new wave of Western sanctions risked sending the economy into a death spiral. Putin asked how they could soften the blow. While the answer was plain to see—he could simply back off Ukraine—no one had the guts to say it.

Nabiullina had held on to her position as chair of the central bank despite the efforts of hard-liners in the Russian government to replace her with Sergei Glazyev, the Putin advisor and ardent nationalist who once accused the EU of tempting Ukraine into the "kingdom of the antichrist." Now, the task of mitigating the damage wrought by Putin's foreign adventurism once again fell into her hands.

During her ascent to become one of the world's most respected central bankers, Nabiullina developed a sartorial trademark. When communicating her views on the economy and monetary policy, she donned a brooch to symbolize her outlook. A pigeon brooch signified she would ease interest rates, a hawk brooch that she would raise them. But when Nabiullina met with Putin at the Kremlin on Monday, February 28, at the height of the bank run caused by the latest sanctions, she wore no brooch on her lapel. It seemed like a tacit admission: the West's strike against the central bank had caught her off guard and without a plan.

Like virtually everyone else in Moscow, Nabiullina had first learned of the invasion on television. And like other members of Russia's financial elite, she was stuck between a rock and a hard place. She could resign and make way for a more pliable and less competent successor while risking political persecution for having dared to signal opposition to the war. Or she could remain and help Putin fight an unjust war while suffering Western condemnation and, most likely, personal sanctions that would make it hard to ever leave her native land. Nabiullina chose the latter.

Ordinarily, Nabiullina would have reached for her foreign exchange reserves to slow the ruble's fall. By using the central bank's dollars and euros to buy rubles in bulk, she would have boosted demand for rubles and, in turn, increased their price. Since doing so was no longer possible, she turned to more drastic methods. That Monday, she more than doubled interest rates to an eye-popping 20 percent and shut down trading on Moscow's stock exchange.

Nabiullina quickly identified the weak spot in the sanctions regime: the West's unwillingness to do anything that might stop the flow of Russian fossil fuels to world markets. While the central bank lost access to hard currency, Rosneft and Gazprom, the country's oil and gas giants, were together raking in more than a billion dollars every single day. So the Kremlin ordered Russian businesses to exchange 80 percent of all the money they earned overseas, dating back to the start of the year, into rubles. In essence, Moscow was using the country's big exporters as a de facto central bank. As long as the West recoiled from targeting Russia's energy sales, there was little it could do to stop this maneuver.

Following the G7 statement, scores of multinationals announced plans to divest from Russia. BP, the London-based oil company, declared that it would abandon its roughly 20 percent stake in Rosneft, booking a loss of some $25 billion. To stave off a frenzy of capital flight, the Kremlin banned foreigners from selling their Russian assets. It introduced harsh currency controls on everyday Russians to stem the nationwide bank run. By decree, Russians could no longer transfer money abroad, withdraw more than $10,000 in foreign currency, or travel outside the country with that same amount in cash. The Kremlin also ordered the closure of cash-based exchanges in which Russians could convert rubles into dollars and euros.

The domestic reaction to these draconian measures was muted. Nabiullina, who'd told her friends that she would rather resign than oversee currency controls, remained in her post. There were no mass protests or violent tumult outside banks. As a notable Russian economist was quick to point out, "The central bank is backed by riot police."

Brick by brick, Nabiullina was dismantling the work that had cemented Russia into the global financial system and had made her career. The West's sanctions were pushing Russia toward isolation, and Nabiullina's emergency measures were compounding the effect.

Surveying the wreckage, analysts projected that Russia's economy would contract by 10 to 15 percent in 2022, wiping out two full decades of economic growth. These forecasts were staggering. Before the sanctions were announced, analysts expected Russia's economy to grow by 3 percent or more. Now it looked poised for a slump far worse than even Iran had suffered at the height of the economic war against that country.

Back in 1991, when America led an international coalition to drive Saddam Hussein's forces out of Kuwait, the world had watched in awe as the U.S. military used its technological superiority to crush the Iraqi army in all of 100 hours. It seemed like a new age was dawning: America was a hyperpower that could destroy its enemies with terrifying efficiency. In the weeks after the G7 launched its strike on the Central Bank of Russia, the world seemed to be witnessing a different kind of hyperpower—one that relied not on precision-guided missiles but rather on economic chokepoints, invisible yet all-powerful.

In his State of the Union address on March 1, Biden could not help but gloat. Putin "thought he could roll into Ukraine and the world would roll over," but he had "badly miscalculated," Biden said. The United States and its allies had stayed united: They had stood by Ukraine in its darkest hour, and they had hit Russia with "powerful economic sanctions" that rendered "Putin's $630 billion war fund worthless." And this was all just the beginning. Putin "has no idea what's coming."

The House chamber erupted in applause, a rare moment of unity between Republicans and Democrats in a Washington riven by bitter partisanship.

58

A Potemkin Currency

On Thursday, March 3, a German-flagged oil tanker entered the mouth of the River Mersey in northwest England. It sailed past Liverpool and was granted permission to dock at Tranmere Oil Terminal, where it was scheduled to deliver a shipment of Russian crude.

Nothing about the tanker or its cargo ran afoul of Western sanctions, but dockworkers at the terminal refused to process the shipment. Sharon Graham, head of the British trade union Unite, declared that her workers would "under no circumstances unload any Russian oil." Union bosses and dockworkers at other major European ports made similar vows. "There is blood on this oil, blood on this coal, and blood on this gas," said a spokesperson for the main Dutch dockworkers union, whose members ran Europe's largest port in Rotterdam.

U.S. and European officials had deliberately exempted Russian oil and gas sales from sanctions. This was the sole economic sector where Russia, the world's largest exporter of fossil fuels, arguably held the advantage over the West and not the other way around. Cutting off its oil and gas exports would push global energy prices to historic highs and possibly plunge parts of Europe into literal darkness. But as the dockworkers of Liverpool and Rotterdam were showing, economic wars lacked the rigid command-and-control structures of conventional military conflicts. Their outcomes depended, in part, on the millions of private actors whose decisions shaped global markets at any given moment, whether they aligned with the wishes of their governments or not.

Adding to this dynamic was the surprising resilience of Ukrainian forces on the battlefield, which made it harder for those watching the war from afar to resign themselves to inaction. Within a week of the initial invasion, it was apparent that military analysts had been far too pessimistic about Ukraine's ability to defend itself—and far too taken in by Russia's military prowess. In the opening days of the war, Ukrainian forces fended off elite Russian paratroopers from rapidly seizing Antonov Airport, northwest of Kyiv, which Russia had intended to use as a launchpad for its assault on Ukraine's capital. The Russians eventually captured the airport, but it took longer than planned, and the runway was so badly damaged that it was no longer usable. The Ukrainians also deprived Russia of air superiority by shooting down dozens of planes and helicopters. A thirty-five-mile convoy of Russian tanks and military vehicles stalled before it could reach Kyiv. Putin's plan for a blitzkrieg was failing, and the prospects for achieving his original war aims of overthrowing the Ukrainian government and installing a pro-Russian puppet regime were dimming rapidly. Some began to wonder whether the Ukrainians might even end up trouncing their colossal neighbor.

Ukraine's stunning battlefield success won it a flood of international support. The United States agreed to send Ukraine billions of dollars of weapons. The EU followed suit, marking the first time the bloc had ever financed "the purchase and delivery of weapons and other equipment to a country that is under attack," as Ursula von der Leyen noted. Speaking before the Bundestag, Olaf Scholz declared a *Zeitenwende*, a historic turning point, and pledged to modernize his country's second-rate armed forces into a world-class military, starting with an emergency infusion of €100 billion into the defense budget. Even traditionally neutral Switzerland got off the fence, matching the G7 restrictions on Russia's central bank.

Apple, Coca-Cola, McDonald's, and hundreds of other multinational companies announced their exits from Russia, less out of legal necessity than to avoid the stigma of any association with the war. A new Justice Department task force, KleptoCapture, began hunting and seizing Russian assets in the United States; European law enforcement agencies did the same on their turf. Though most Russian oligarchs believed themselves beyond the reach of the law, their superyachts were not. The mining magnate Alisher Usmanov was forced to part with all five hundred feet of the *Dilbar*, including her supersized indoor swimming pool, now in the hands of German authorities. The *Crescent*, a 443-foot pleasure vessel belonging to Rosneft CEO Igor Sechin, met the same fate in Spain. Roman Abramovich bid farewell to the fans of the vaunted Chelsea soccer club, hoping that he could "visit Stamford Bridge one last time to say goodbye to all of you in person." British authorities were forcing him to sell the team and donate the proceeds to victims of the war in Ukraine. It seemed that Russia was turning not just into an economic pariah but into a political and cultural one, too.

None of this kept the Kremlin from flexing its own muscles and passing on the costs of the Western economic war whenever the opportunity presented itself. Russia and Ukraine together accounted for almost a third of global wheat exports, and within days of the war's outbreak, wheat prices soared to record highs as traders braced for disruptions and shortages. Hoping to push the states of the Global South to advocate for an end to the war on terms favorable to Russia, Putin ordered a naval blockade of Ukraine's ports, stopping grain shipments via the Black Sea, despite warnings from the UN that large parts of Africa and the Middle East could suffer famine as a result.

On March 22, a storm damaged parts of the Caspian Pipeline Consortium, which carries crude oil from wells in Kazakhstan to Russia's Novorossiysk port on the Black Sea. Using the incident as a pretext and deliberately overstating the extent of the damage, Russian officials halted the flow of more than one million barrels of Kazakh oil each day. The ploy worked: oil prices leapt to over $120 per barrel, edging closer to the all-time high of around $147, set in 2008.

These manufactured shortages did not sway Western public opinion in Russia's favor. Polls found that nearly 80 percent of Americans supported an embargo on Russian oil even if it meant higher gasoline prices. Media reports about Shell's purchase of a heavily discounted cargo of Russian crude caused a fierce political backlash, prompting the company to apologize and announce plans to cease all operations in Russia. Even Exxon, notoriously immune to political pressure, decided to withdraw from Russia and leave behind some $4 billion of assets in the country. White House officials worked the phones, reminding energy and financial executives that they were, in fact, allowed to keep trading Russian oil. "Popular opinion turned against Russian energy much more quickly than policy opinion," explained Peter Harrell, who led many of those calls from the White House.

Less than a week into the war, Canada unilaterally banned oil imports from Russia. Under pressure from Congress, the Biden administration soon did the same. Neither country was sacrificing much, as they did not rely on Russian fossil fuels. (Although America bought a small amount of oil from Russia, the White House rightly assumed that purchases from elsewhere would make up for any shortfall.) Soon thereafter, the UK and Australia joined the embargo.

Pressure was now mounting on the EU to follow suit. Yet European countries bought more than four million barrels of crude oil and other petroleum products from Russia each day—roughly 30 percent of the continent's total oil imports. Zeroing out these purchases overnight was not a viable option. Weaning off Russian natural gas, a resource with fewer substitutes, would be harder still.

By the end of March, Russian troops were in retreat from their positions around Kyiv. The Ukrainians had successfully defended their capital, forcing the Russians to focus their firepower elsewhere. By contrast, the situation on the economic battlefield looked better for Russia than it had a few weeks prior, owing partly to a decision made in Washington. Without consulting the White House and contrary to the expectations of most market participants, the Treasury Department had allowed the Russian government to continue servicing its debt instead of letting sanctions push Moscow into default.

Treasury officials reasoned there was no harm in siphoning funds from the Russian government to pay foreign bondholders, but the decision had the unintended consequence of boosting investor confidence in Russia. Moscow's own actions also brought a measure of relief. A payment system created in the wake of the 2014 sanctions ensured that Russian credit cards kept working even after Visa and MasterCard exited the country in early March. Emergency measures by the central bank stabilized the ruble, which by the end of the month bounced back to its pre-war dollar exchange rate. Admittedly, much of this recovery was artificial, fueled not by market dynamics but by Moscow's strategy of forcing exporters to buy the ruble and blocking most avenues for selling it. Yet even with the ruble now a "Potemkin currency," it was undeniable that the swirl of crisis had subsided.

All the while, Russia was growing more brazen in its attempts to retaliate against the West in kind. On the last day of March, Putin signed a decree mandating that buyers of Russian natural gas from "unfriendly" countries, including the members of the EU, make payments to Russia in rubles into an account at Gazprombank, the biggest Russian bank that remained free from blocking sanctions. Any country that failed to comply, he warned, could lose access to Russian gas altogether.

The biggest reason for Putin's confidence—and for the relative calm that now pervaded the Russian economy—was an inconvenient truth: despite

Russia's loss of some Western oil customers, sky-high prices were enabling the country to reap windfall profits from its energy exports. In effect, Russia was collecting a massive premium on the war. Its trade surplus rose to the highest level in more than a decade. The cracks in the West's economic war plan were starting to show. There would be no way to make Putin pay for his aggression without doing something about oil.

≡

Supply and Demand

Stretching across three hundred miles of America's Gulf Coast, from Freeport, Texas, to Baton Rouge, Louisiana, is a network of subterranean salt caverns. Acquired by the U.S. government following the devastating Arab oil embargo of 1973, the caverns have taken on a key role in American economic security: they are the site of the Strategic Petroleum Reserve, or SPR, a massive government-run oil cache with a total capacity of more than 700 million barrels.

The reserve was originally intended as a buffer against supply shocks caused by war and natural disasters. Presidents had ordered emergency drawdowns on just three occasions: in 1991, amid the Gulf War; in 2005, when Hurricane Katrina caused 25 percent of U.S. domestic production to be shut in; and in 2011, during the war in Libya.

In late 2021, after trying and failing to persuade Saudi Arabia to pump more oil, Daleep Singh and several colleagues secured a release of 50 million barrels of oil from the SPR. They coordinated the move with other major oil-consuming countries, including China, India, Japan, and South Korea, all of which agreed to release oil from their own strategic stocks. It was an unorthodox use of the reserve, made not in reaction to a supply disruption but rather as an attempt to tame prices and coax the Saudis to open their taps.

By March 2022, with oil prices continually rising, the White House was contemplating a second, even bigger drawdown. Singh hoped that a significant release of oil reserves would signal the government's resolve to keep the market well supplied and thus lower prices. This, in turn, would create leeway for more aggressive energy-related sanctions on Russia. Brian Deese, the director of the National Economic Council, recommended a release of one million barrels per day over six months, for a total of 180 million barrels. This was a huge amount of crude oil, equivalent to more than a full month's worth of Russian exports.

The plan met immediate resistance. Officials from the Department of Energy warned that the SPR was not built for such frequent releases. To tap the reserve, engineers needed to push oil to the surface by injecting freshwater into the bottom of the caverns. When carried out too often, this procedure could alter the shape of the caverns, reducing their structural integrity and requiring expensive maintenance. Government lawyers questioned whether the president had the legal authority for a withdrawal of such massive proportions, given that the global oil supply was not yet in a state of acute shortage. Oil industry executives and lobbyists also disliked the idea and called on the administration to instead remove regulatory barriers to domestic fossil fuel investment. (This was a somewhat disingenuous ask: thanks to soaring oil prices, U.S. producers were flush with cash and had ample capacity for investments and expanded production as it was, only they preferred funneling their profits to shareholders.)

None of these objections swayed the White House, and by the end of March, plans for the giant SPR release were finalized. Once again, the United States coordinated the move with allies. The EU would support the U.S. release by selling off some 30 million barrels of its own strategic stocks. In return, the Biden administration pledged to do all it could to surge supplies of LNG to Europe and help reduce the EU's dependence on Russian gas.

"Putin's war is imposing a cost on America and our allies and democracies around the world," Biden said in a speech announcing the release—by far the largest-ever in U.S. history—on March 31. Because American companies weren't acting fast enough to offset that cost, the government was taking matters into its own hands.

Emptying the salt caverns could help overcome one big hurdle to choking off Putin's oil money: ensuring the market had enough supply. But another hurdle came from demand. The growing Western effort to boycott Russian oil would be nullified if other countries increased their purchases at the same time. This, unfortunately, was already happening. As the Anglosphere outlawed Russian oil outright and EU countries reduced imports for fear of political backlash, Russia swiftly redirected its cargoes to China, Turkey, and, above all, India.

In the first month of the war, India's purchases of Russian oil shot up more than sixfold compared to the previous year's average, and they showed no sign of slowing. The Indian government refrained from picking a side in the Russo-Ukrainian conflict, and public opinion in the country was divided, so Indian refineries saw no reason to avoid scooping up more and more Russian crude, which was selling at a discount for want of other buyers. To make matters worse, India's central bank was in talks with Moscow on a new rupee-ruble mechanism that would allow the two countries to conduct trade while skirting Western financial sanctions. Although India continued to assert its neutrality, these actions amounted to an economic lifeline for Russia.

The apparent rapprochement between India and Russia came as a surprise to the White House. New Delhi and Moscow had long enjoyed warm relations and close military ties. Yet the Western response to the war in Ukraine had dramatically increased Russia's economic and political dependence on China, India's chief strategic rival. As a result, U.S. officials assumed the war would push India further into their own geopolitical camp. Somehow, the opposite was occurring.

Since Western sanctions explicitly carved out the energy trade, there was nothing illegal about India's oil imports. But their sheer scale was troublesome, as it signaled to the rest of the Global South that Russia remained open for business, and that there would be no stigma in ramping up trade with Russia as the West backed away. While the position of U.S. officials was something of a contradiction—they wanted Russian oil to keep flowing, but they didn't like where it was going—that didn't lessen their frustration.

Owing to these concerns, the White House decided to send an envoy to India. The task fell to Singh, who had close personal ties to the country. (He was the son of Indian immigrants and a relative of Dalip Singh Saund, an Indian-born politician who was the first Asian American to serve in the U.S. Congress.) "I think of India as part of my extended family," Singh told P. K. Mishra, principal secretary to Prime Minister Narendra Modi, upon his arrival in New Delhi in late March, "and with family, you tell the truth—even the hard truths." Singh acknowledged that America had been on the "wrong side of history many times," and that he had come to "urge India, my ancestral home, not to be on the wrong side now." He offered Washington's support in replacing the arms and energy that India bought from Russia. He also argued that Indian oil purchases, though legal, were so substantial as to undermine the impact of sanctions, and he warned that the proposed rupee-ruble channel risked furnishing Russia with an all-purpose sanctions workaround. Mishra made no promises, but the discussion was warm and friendly.

Singh shared similar messages with the Indian press, at one point warning that "there are consequences to countries that actively attempt to circumvent or backfill these sanctions." The media took much less kindly to his words than government officials had. In their eyes, it took a lot of gall for the White House to send an Indian American to try to strongarm India—a major power in its own right—into abandoning a longtime partner such as Russia. "Singh may be a whiz kid, but he is clearly a bad diplomat," jeered one outlet.

Deflated, Singh packed his suitcase at the Imperial Hotel and headed for the airport. The past six months of his life had been a whirlwind of sleep deprivation and time spent away from loved ones. His efforts had been essential to imposing some of the strongest sanctions in modern history, yet every day brought reports of new horrors in Ukraine. Now he was facing a media storm in his parents' native country. He began to consider stepping away from the White House.

As Singh departed New Delhi, Sergei Lavrov touched down for his own slate of meetings. He came bearing a different message. Russia and India had been loyal friends for "many decades," he said. "We will be ready to supply to India any goods which it wants to buy from us." As for the rupee-ruble mechanism, India was looking out for its own interests, and rightfully so. "India must not be dependent on systems whose masters can steal your money overnight."

60

≡

The Rubik's Cube

O n April 1, Ukrainian forces advanced into towns surrounding Kyiv that were recently abandoned by retreating Russian troops. As they made their way into a leafy suburb northwest of the capital, an area popular among middle-class families, they were confronted with a stomach-churning sight. Littering the streets were scores of bodies. Many of them were civilians, shot at point-blank range and left to rot where they'd fallen, victims of a weeks-long orgy of violence unleashed by Russian soldiers. Some had been tortured and others raped in what were evidently deliberate war crimes.

News of the massacre in Bucha spread as Daleep Singh returned to Washington from New Delhi. He and his staff began drawing up retaliatory sanctions, this time with little input from the Treasury Department. Janet Yellen and her team had kept a foot on the brake throughout the preceding months, warning of potential negative spillovers and the risk of long-term reputational damage to the dollar and America's global financial stewardship. Frustrated with this excess of caution—and still bristling at Treasury's decision to allow Russia to continue servicing its debt—Singh and his colleagues now sought to keep the department's involvement to a minimum.

In response to the atrocities in Bucha, the United States tightened penalties on Sberbank; imposed blocking sanctions on Alfa-Bank, the largest privately-held Russian bank; and banned all new investment by American firms in Russia. The White House also overturned Treasury's decision on Russian debt repayments, putting the country on an inexorable path to its first default on its foreign obligations since 1918, in the wake of the Bolshevik

Revolution. (The Russian government had most recently defaulted on its domestic debt in 1998.) As Singh saw it, a default to foreign creditors would enshrine Russia's status as a financial pariah and ensure that investors viewed the country with suspicion indefinitely. It was an indelible stain that time alone could not wash away.

U.S. financial sanctions on Russia were now almost as tight as they could be. Export controls against Russia's tech sector were in place but would take time to bite. This left the question of what to do about the Russian energy industry. Despite the emergency release of U.S. and European oil reserves, oil prices remained above $100 a barrel. The Kremlin's oil revenues had surged by 50 percent from the previous year, with oil and gas sales generating around $1 billion every single day. Indian imports of Russian oil kept climbing even after Singh's trip to New Delhi. By spring, India's purchases of Russian oil for the year already surpassed the total for all of 2021.

A decade earlier, a series of innovative U.S. sanctions had slashed Iran's oil sales and locked up more than $100 billion of its money in overseas escrow accounts. The Biden administration included a number of veterans of this campaign. At the White House, there was Peter Harrell, the senior director for international economics. A politically astute lawyer from Atlanta, Harrell worked at State during the Obama years, where he played a behind-the-scenes role implementing the oil sanctions against Iran. At Treasury, there was Andrea Gacki, the director of OFAC, who had served in various leadership roles at the agency over more than a decade, and Elizabeth Rosenberg, the assistant secretary at TFI, who started her career as an oil and gas reporter before joining the Obama Treasury as an advisor to David Cohen when he spearheaded the oil sanctions against Iran. Finally, at State, there was Amos Hochstein, a trusted Biden confidant who in 2012 helped coax refineries in China and India to reduce their purchases of Iranian oil.

The pivotal sanctions on Iranian oil had worked from two different angles. First, they cut the *volume* of Iranian sales. At the behest of Congress, the Obama administration threatened to impose secondary sanctions on any company that bought Iranian oil while offering waivers to countries that significantly reduced their total purchases every six months. Countries thus had an incentive to gradually reduce their imports over time, which they did: Iran's oil sales plummeted by 60 percent within eighteen months of the policy going into effect. Second, the sanctions limited how Tehran could *use* its oil money. They did so by requiring banks to keep Iran's oil wealth in overseas escrow accounts. Tehran was allowed access to these funds only to buy food, medicine, and other non-sanctioned goods. Banks that failed to comply would face secondary sanctions.

Despite this model's success, Biden officials were wary of applying it to Russia. With oil prices already near record highs, no one in the administration was comfortable advocating a policy that would take Russian barrels off the market, which could push prices higher still. Part of the problem was the sheer size of Russia's exports. Russia sold five million barrels of crude oil each day—twice as much as Iran did at the start of 2012—plus three million barrels of diesel and other petroleum products. The domestic political context was different, too. In 2012, Congress forced the Obama White House to target Iran's oil sales by passing legislation with a veto-proof majority, whereas in 2022, Capitol Hill largely deferred to Biden on Russia policy. Torpedoing Russia's economy was a riskier bet politically than doing the same to Iran's, and there were nowhere near as many lobbyists and interest groups in Washington urging such a course of action.

Even if the Biden administration decided against seeking reductions in the volume of Russian oil exports and only pushed for the creation of escrow accounts, Putin might retaliate by refusing to sell any oil. Economists in the administration doubted he could do this without causing catastrophic damage to his own economy and federal budget, but some Russia watchers thought he might be crazy enough to do it anyway. Put simply, the United States needed a new strategy.

The first idea to gain traction was a tariff: U.S. allies that continued importing Russian oil could levy taxes on their purchases. Economists loved the concept, believing it would force buyers to demand lower prices from Russia to compensate for the duties they had to pay their governments, thus reducing Russian oil revenues. Allied governments could then use the resulting tax proceeds to support Ukraine financially. But this approach had major shortcomings, too. The first was political: voters in allied countries might blame the tariff for steep prices at the pump. The second was diplomatic: for the tariff to work as intended, all big buyers of Russian oil would have to join in, including China, India, and Turkey. Yet the latter countries were almost guaranteed to oppose such openly punitive measures against Russia.

The Biden administration needed to cut Russia's oil revenues without reducing the volume of its sales, and the strategy needed to work even without

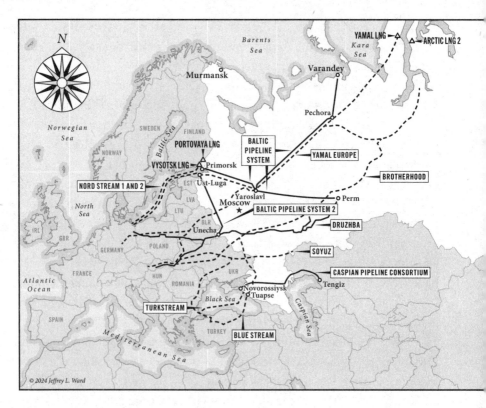

formal backing from Russia's biggest non-Western customers. It felt like a political and economic Rubik's Cube, where any move to align the colors on one pane would scramble them elsewhere.

Finally, Andrea Gacki and Peter Harrell struck upon an idea. Since early in the war, Italian prime minister Mario Draghi had been pushing the EU to impose a cap on the price that European companies paid for Russian natural gas. What if they repurposed Draghi's proposal and applied it to Russia's oil sales? Specifically, Washington could threaten some kind of punitive action—perhaps even secondary sanctions—against any buyer of Russian oil *unless* the oil was sold for below a specific price. Meanwhile, Western countries that still bought oil from Russia, including several EU members, could refuse to pay anything above that same price. The U.S. government could also pressure the insurers and shipping companies that facilitated Russian oil exports to deny service to any cargoes sold for above this "price cap." Effectively, the West could use all the economic chokepoints at its disposal to impose a cap on the price Russia earned for each barrel of oil. The aim was to "use sanctions to make oil cheaper," as Gacki put it, a notion that sounded

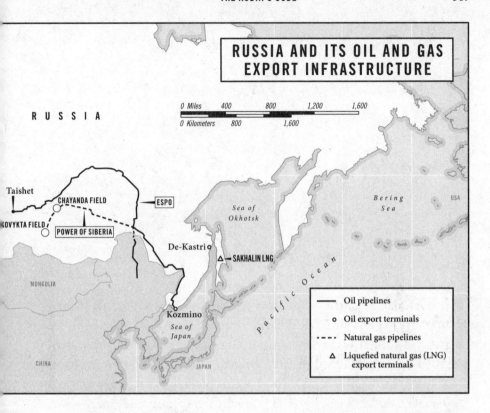

RUSSIA AND ITS OIL AND GAS EXPORT INFRASTRUCTURE

too good to be true. But nothing in Gacki or Harrell's long experience with sanctions told them it was impossible. Gacki also knew that Yellen respected Draghi, so she felt confident the concept could secure buy-in from the treasury secretary.

There was another reason Gacki and Harrell saw merit in the idea. "We didn't need the importing countries—China and India and Turkey—to publicly go along with it," Harrell said. Biden officials could talk directly to the refiners and traders that bought Russian oil, explaining the upside of complying with the price cap and the risks of violating it. At the same time, they could consult quietly with the governments in Beijing, New Delhi, and Ankara, all of which would benefit handsomely from the policy in the form of lower oil import bills without having to take a public stance against Moscow. If all went according to plan, Russia would keep on exporting large quantities of oil, but it would make far less money on each barrel.

There was a long way to go to gain confidence in this untested idea, much less actually deploy it. But the U.S. government finally had a potential solution to the Rubik's Cube.

61

"What Other Option Do We Have?"

I n Washington, where policy ideas are a dime a dozen, it's rare for any initiative to get by on intellectual merit alone. More often, it takes a complex network of backers—politicians, businesspeople, thought leaders, and voters, each with divergent priorities and interests—for anything to get done. Peter Harrell, who'd once covered that process as a reporter for *Congressional Quarterly*, knew it would be no different for his and Andrea Gacki's idea for a price cap on Russian oil. So he set about releasing it into the ecosystem, working through his Rolodex of energy executives, oil traders, and fellow sanctions experts.

The feedback he received was a collective and resounding "no." How could the U.S. government—let alone the multitude of banks, insurance companies, refineries, and shipping firms involved in the global oil trade—verify the exact price paid for any given cargo of Russian oil? Even if this were possible, how would the level of the price cap be set? The market for crude oil was vast, accounting for almost 5 percent of all global trade, and some stretches of it were a Wild West of opportunity and lawlessness. The allure of big, quick profits attracted a fair share of shady actors. It was a landscape too expansive and rugged for Washington bureaucrats to control.

A concept similar to the price cap had also been considered during the Obama administration's economic war against Iran. The idea was attractive then for the same reasons it was now—it would reduce the adversary's flow of petrodollars without depriving a tight oil market of crucial supplies. But the idea was ultimately deemed too hard to implement. It would be easier to seek to reduce the *volume* of Iran's oil sales, because monitoring compliance would simply require counting the tankers going in and out of Iranian ports.

None of these downsides had gone away in the intervening decade. A price cap was also a tortuously complex mechanism, one that would be hard to explain publicly. It was, as some of Daleep Singh's White House colleagues complained, just not very "sexy." But for lack of a better plan, he directed Treasury to conduct an in-depth evaluation of the price cap proposal.

The review was led by Catherine Wolfram, a senior Treasury official and former colleague of Janet Yellen's in the economics department at UC Berkeley. Wolfram's conclusions were encouraging. She found that Russia was unlikely to ever weaponize its oil sales by strategically cutting them off—the revenues were too important to sacrifice. Wolfram also suspected that Russia would continue selling more or less the same amount of oil even if faced with a drastic price cap. "Russia's supply is essentially 100 percent inelastic," she explained. "They have very low marginal costs. So as long as the price is above $10, they're going to export as much as they can." Recent experience showed as much: even when prices for Russian oil plunged below $15 per barrel during the first months of the pandemic, the country kept on pumping oil in large quantities.

Meanwhile, evidence of Russian war crimes in Bucha and other Ukrainian towns continued to mount. So did the scale of the atrocities. In Mariupol, home to 480,000 Ukrainians before the war, Russian bombs killed tens of thousands of civilians and leveled much of the city. In the EU, public outrage and renewed calls for a full-scale oil embargo grew loud enough for Yellen to publicly urge caution. "Medium-term, Europe clearly needs to reduce its dependence on Russia with respect to energy, but we need to be careful when we think about a complete European ban on say, oil imports," she said. An EU embargo would "clearly raise global oil prices" and "have a damaging impact on Europe and other parts of the world," and it might even help the Kremlin. The West would be better served by finding some way to allow both oil and gas sales to proceed while reducing Russia's energy windfall—a clear, albeit indirect, reference to the possibility of a price cap.

Soon thereafter, Wolfram and other Treasury officials put together a slide deck on the price cap idea, which they sent to Bjoern Seibert in hopes of nudging Brussels away from an embargo. But the effort came too late to turn the political tide in the EU, which had shifted decisively in favor of a full-scale ban. The price cap was dead on arrival.

Though the economic war was far from over, Singh decided that he would step down from his post at the White House in May. The nonstop demands of the campaign had taken a personal toll, and he was ready to spend more time with his family.

———

On May 4, 2022, Ursula von der Leyen gave an impassioned speech on the war in Ukraine before the European Parliament in the French city of Strasbourg. The Ukrainians were "fighting to reaffirm basic ideas" about the sanctity of international law, and as a result, "the future of the European Union" was being "written in Ukraine." Considering these existential stakes, the time had come for the EU to end its dependence on Russian oil. Von der Leyen proposed that the bloc phase out its oil imports from Russia by the end of the year.

Even though von der Leyen's announcement was expected, it was a big deal. The world's largest buyer of Russian oil was gearing up to quit in a matter of months. This was sure to reshape the global oil market in fundamental ways. Brussels was taking a leap into the unknown.

Later that day, when the full details of von der Leyen's proposal became public, it emerged that the EU was also planning to ban European companies from providing shipping, brokerage, insurance, and financing services to transactions involving Russian oil, regardless of where the oil was headed. If Russia wanted to keep selling oil to India, for example, it would have to find a way to do so without any services from EU-based firms—a major logistical challenge. News of this "services ban" came as an unwelcome surprise to officials in Washington. Under a simple embargo, trade routes and customer relationships would reshuffle, while total oil supplies from Russia would remain constant. But with a services ban added on top, there was a risk that some portion of Russian oil would come off the market entirely, because Russia might struggle to find adequate insurance coverage or enough tankers to ship it all. This would almost certainly spike prices, the outcome the Biden administration was trying hard to avoid. Indeed, as traders and energy analysts parsed the proposal and assessed its implications, oil prices started to climb.

Within the EU, however, the services ban was seen as a logical step, and it was one the EU had taken previously against Iran. If European refineries and traders were prohibited from buying Russian oil, why should European banks, shipping firms, and insurance companies be allowed to assist others in procuring it? The measure also provided a way for the burden of the oil sanctions to be shared more equitably across the EU. To implement the embargo, some EU members would have to reduce their purchases of Russian oil more than others; adding the services ban could help even out the impact across the twenty-seven member states.

As Wolfram and her Treasury colleagues digested the new EU proposal, their hearts began to race. If it were implemented, their models suggested oil prices could rise above $180 per barrel, well above the all-time high. The commodities desk of a Wall Street bank told Treasury officials that its model projected an even steeper increase, potentially all the way up to $300. Either of these scenarios would thrust the world economy into a painful recession.

These forecasts jolted Biden officials. Depending on how high the EU services ban pushed up prices, it could even lead to a perverse outcome in which the Kremlin earned *more* money selling *less* oil. Yet when Treasury officials shared these concerns with their European counterparts, they were met with a shrug. The services ban, it seemed, was a done deal. American officials would have to move to Plan B: finding a way to bore a hole in the EU services ban that would allow Russian oil to continue to flow. The best way to do this, they concluded, was to resurrect the price cap idea and tweak it to serve as a kind of relief valve.

U.S. officials reasoned that a price cap could be built around an exemption to the EU services ban. Specifically, if Russian oil was sold for a price *above* the cap, the services ban would apply; but if Russian oil was sold for a price *below* the cap, the services ban would be waived. If Russia were to sell an oil cargo to India, for instance, European firms could provide the insurance coverage and tankers so long as the Indian buyer paid a price below the cap. Assuming the West could make such an arrangement stick, it could alleviate any potential supply crunch and accomplish the twin goals of maintaining global oil supplies while reducing Russian revenues.

Of course, there was no guarantee that the Europeans would go for such a scheme, much less that it would work. But in the face of chilling forecasts about the future trajectory of oil prices—and for want of other viable ideas— even skeptics within the Biden administration began to see this version of the price cap as a necessity. "Shit, if Russian oil just comes off the market, that'll be catastrophic," one senior White House official recalled thinking. "What other option do we have?" What began as a proposal for cutting Russian oil revenues thus evolved into something even more urgent: a plan to stave off a global economic disaster.

With their concerns falling on deaf ears in the EU, American officials shifted their focus across the English Channel. Perhaps London could serve as an ally in concocting an alternative proposal to the services ban that they could eventually sell to Brussels. At the very least, U.S. Treasury officials wanted to discourage the British government from issuing its own services ban, modeled on the EU's. The UK was the global hub for maritime insurance, so a British services ban would compound the harmful economic effects of the EU measure. To try to persuade the British to take a different approach, Wally Adeyemo and Elizabeth Rosenberg worked the phones, calling UK officials and warning them of the potential dire consequences of the services ban. Wolfram briefed the UK on her analysis alongside her boss, Ben Harris, Treasury's chief economist. Their outreach produced the intended effect: London agreed to refrain from following Brussels's lead on the services ban, and it pledged to work with Washington on a price cap mechanism that could alleviate the looming market disruption.

While America and the UK agreed to collaborate, both understood that for the price cap to work, they would ultimately need to win support from their allies, too. The International Group of P&I Clubs, the umbrella organization that insured the vast majority of the global tanker fleet, was based in London, yet its membership consisted of clubs based in the EU, Japan, and elsewhere. Officials at the organization said that if the EU implemented its services ban, all member clubs would immediately stop insuring ships that carried Russian oil. As a result, U.S. and UK officials knew they had to craft the price cap proposal in such a way that the EU could get behind it.

On May 31, the twenty-seven EU leaders formally signed on to von der Leyen's sanctions proposal. A few items were watered down in the final negotiations. Instead of a complete embargo, the EU agreed to phase out roughly 90 percent of its oil purchases from Russia within six months. It also agreed to implement the services ban along the same timeline, with one key exception: the Greeks and the Maltese won a carve-out for shipping, so the ban would apply only to insurance and finance. Nevertheless, these were the "toughest sanctions yet on Russia," *The Wall Street Journal* reported.

Both the embargo and services ban would not take effect until December 5. But officials in the Biden administration were already bracing for impact. When the EU sanctions were finalized, oil prices rocketed up to $120 per barrel, the highest level since the early weeks of the war.

62

The Service Providers' Cartel

On an unseasonably hot June day, a delegation of American officials sat in a conference room at Bercy, the sprawling modernist head-quarters of the French finance ministry in Paris. At the center of the table was a trio from the U.S. Treasury Department: Elizabeth Rosenberg, Ben Harris, and Catherine Wolfram. Following the EU's decision to go forward with the oil services ban, Janet Yellen made it a top priority to turn the price cap into a reality. She entrusted Rosenberg, Harris, and Wolfram to get the job done.

The trio was in Paris to warn of the dramatic consequences of the EU's latest sanctions. They were confident that, if the EU moved ahead with its proposed ban on oil-related services, oil prices would spike, and the world economy would sink into recession. The price cap may not be a perfect option, but it was the best chance they had to avoid this cruel fate.

The room inside Bercy was packed, the windows were shut, and there was no air conditioning. As the Treasury team waited for their host to arrive, they sweated profusely. When the head of the French delegation finally walked in, one of her colleagues asked how she was doing. "Well, it's five-thirty, how do you think I'm doing?" she shot back in French, loud enough for one of the Americans to hear.

The remark set the tone for the rest of the meeting. The French politely listened to the Americans' analysis and then proceeded to tell them why they were wrong and that France would never agree to revise the EU oil sanctions. It had been a hard slog in Brussels to get those sanctions done, and it was certainly not worth reopening the debate based on U.S. alarmism.

Besides, even if the Americans were right, the price cap was doomed to fail. Not even a hyperpower like the United States could dictate the price of oil. As the head French official put it, "The Russians will eat grass before they let Janet Yellen tell them what price they get for their oil." After more than an hour, the meeting ended with no progress made. The French opened the windows to let in some fresh air as the Americans left the room.

This was just one stop on a three-day trip in which the U.S. delegation also visited Berlin, Brussels, and London. The Germans were less hostile than the French, but they too were unconvinced. EU officials in Brussels told their American visitors that oil markets had already built in a reaction to the European sanctions, so there was little risk that prices would shoot up further. In London, the conversation was friendlier. Wally Adeyemo joined the American delegation for that discussion, and while the UK officials did not believe oil prices would spike as high as the Americans feared, they agreed to assist U.S. efforts by advocating for the price cap at the G7, which would hold its annual summit at the end of the month.

Since the start of the economic war, Washington had relied on the G7's political authority to push through its most ambitious ideas for new sanctions. In February, Daleep Singh had quickly coordinated a strike on Russia's central bank by using his connections with the other G7 sherpas and securing their buy-in. The Biden administration assessed that its best chance of getting the price cap done was once again to win a commitment from the G7 and announce the measure publicly at the group's upcoming summit in Bavaria, Germany.

Singh's successor as the White House's sherpa was Mike Pyle, a former Treasury official and chief investment strategist at BlackRock, the world's largest asset manager. Pyle was as experienced in the global economic arena as Singh, but he was new to the dark arts of economic warfare, and he was joining the sanctions campaign in medias res. Thankfully, there was continuity among other officials, and Peter Harrell took the lead on drafting text on the price cap for the G7 communiqué.

Harrell's aim was to insert language into the communiqué that explicitly instructed G7 governments to develop a price cap. Yet it quickly became apparent that the French would not stand for this. The Japanese were also resistant; they relied on LNG from the Sakhalin-2 project in the Russian Far East, and they were nervous that the Kremlin would cut off these critical supplies if Tokyo supported the price cap. As the host of the upcoming summit, the Germans held the pen. They proposed compromise language in which the G7 would "consider a range of approaches" that could cut Russia's energy revenues while stabilizing world markets, including a price cap. This fell short of what the White House wanted, but it would still provide Treasury officials such as Rosenberg, Harris, and Wolfram with a political mandate to develop the concept with U.S. allies. With final pushes from Pyle and ultimately Joe Biden himself as he met with the other leaders at a castle in the Bavarian Alps, the G7 included this language in its communiqué on June 28.

With the imprimatur of the G7, Treasury officials had the top cover they needed to roll up their sleeves and start building their new economic weapon. In July, UK officials spent multiple days in Washington hashing out how the price cap might work in practice. The list of items to resolve was long. Would the price cap apply at the point of sale (a Russian export terminal) or at the point of delivery (say, an Indian port)? Would the cap come with an expiration date, or would the G7 commit to suppressing the price of Russian oil indefinitely?

One question loomed the largest: In addition to implementing the policy through an exemption to the services ban, would the G7 enforce the price cap with the threat of secondary sanctions? Would it wield that cudgel against any noncompliant actor anywhere in the world, be it a Swiss oil trading firm or a Chinese refinery? That threat had been critical to the success of oil sanctions against Iran, but it was highly controversial. On the one hand, secondary sanctions would give the price cap real teeth, and it was not clear the policy could work without them. Moreover, the stick of secondary sanctions would be paired with a juicy carrot, since complying with the price cap meant paying Russia *less* for its oil—and surely no one could complain about paying *less* for oil. On the other hand, at a moment when the G7 was trying to rally the world in support of Ukraine—and making little progress in the Global South—the inclusion of secondary sanctions made some American and British officials uncomfortable.

There was another, even bigger obstacle. The EU had long denounced secondary sanctions as illegal and even passed a law banning European companies from complying with them. (European companies tended to abide by them anyway, and the law was rarely enforced.) "The Europeans were totally allergic to secondary sanctions and were never going to embrace that," Rosenberg explained.

All this suggested that secondary sanctions were a less-than-ideal enforcement tool. As an alternative, American and British officials envisioned creating a cartel of sorts: G7 member states would allow their companies to provide services for Russian oil shipments only if the underlying sale complied with the price cap. In effect, the whole G7 would match the EU services ban, strengthen it by including shipping, and then jointly agree to waive it for any sale of Russian oil for a price below a cap set by the bloc. If Russia sold a cargo of oil to India, for instance, it could use British insurance or Greek tankers—but only if the oil was sold for a price lower than the G7 cap.

Oil-consuming countries had long aspired to gain pricing leverage over petrostates. As early as 1973, while the U.S. economy writhed under an Arab oil embargo, Henry Kissinger floated the idea of establishing a buyers' cartel as a counterweight to OPEC, but he did not get very far. What Washington now envisioned was not quite a *buyers'* cartel, since all G7 members had either stopped importing Russian oil or made plans to do so. It was a *service providers'* cartel, and the aim was similar: to control the price that Russia, one of the world's largest oil exporters, was paid for its wares.

The strategy rested on two assumptions. The first was that Russia would find it impossible to sell much of its oil without access to G7 services—specifically, British insurance, European shipping, and American finance. Of these three logistical components, British insurance was a particularly important chokepoint: the London-based International Group of P&I Clubs insured roughly 95 percent of the global tanker fleet, making Britain *the* global hub for maritime insurance.

The second assumption was that buyers of Russian oil would utilize the price cap to negotiate lower prices with Russian sellers. This, however, was hardly guaranteed: Buyers might be hesitant to ask for lower prices for fear of antagonizing Moscow. And of course, Russia could refuse to sell oil for prices below the cap.

To test the waters, U.S. Treasury officials quietly reached out to large buyers of Russian oil. What they heard was encouraging. Officials from India and Turkey declined to publicly support the price cap but said they would not stop their companies from driving a hard bargain with Russian oil suppliers. In August, Rosenberg and Wolfram traveled to Jakarta, where Indonesian officials told them that the mere possibility of a future price cap was already giving buyers of Russian oil leverage in price negotiations. Shortly after Rosenberg and Wolfram returned home, an Indonesian minister went public with this information, posting on Instagram that Russia had offered to sell his country oil "at a price that's 30 percent lower than the international market price."

Another important piece of evidence came later in August, when Adeyemo and Wolfram traveled together to Mumbai. Executives at Indian refineries explained that they would be reluctant to buy oil that wasn't covered by G7 maritime insurance, even if Russia provided an alternative. If there was a crash or some other incident as their oil cargoes made the long journey from Russian ports in the Baltic Sea to India, they worried the Russians would not follow through with a payout. Russia was not exactly known for the rule of law, and between Putin's enormous war expenditures and the ongoing burden of Western sanctions, the country was hardly in a reassuring financial position.

The discussions seemed to confirm the Biden administration's sense that a cartel of service providers would have the necessary power to enforce a price cap, even without the threat of secondary sanctions. The threat of withholding essential logistical services, especially maritime insurance, would likely be enough to get private companies around the world to comply. U.S. officials did not rule out the possibility of secondary sanctions, but only as a last resort.

On September 2, the G7 finance ministers formally pledged to implement the price cap policy by December 5, the date on which the EU planned to drastically reduce its imports of Russian oil. The decision was welcomed by Ukrainian officials, one of whom praised the price cap as "exactly what we needed." Indeed, Ukraine could use all the help it could get: Having repulsed the Russians from Kyiv and borne the brunt of the initial invasion, the Ukrainians were gearing up for a counteroffensive.

63

An Economic War of Attrition

When the West began planning a sanctions campaign in the lead-up to Russia's invasion of Ukraine, the goal was deterrence. Perhaps the mere threat of painful economic blowback would compel Putin to relinquish his imperial fantasies. When that effort failed, the goal shifted. Some in the West now viewed sanctions as a potential source of leverage for Ukraine in future peace negotiations. Yet this was improbable. As early as eight months into the war, estimates of the cost of rebuilding Ukraine already ranged from $500 billion to over $1 trillion. It was unthinkable that sanctions would be lifted absent Russia paying Ukraine enormous reparations, which was also unthinkable. More likely, the West would eventually move to seize Russian assets, including the $300 billion-plus of its central bank reserves that were immobilized, to finance Ukraine's reconstruction.

What was clear was that the sanctions no longer aimed to change Russian behavior. They aimed at something simpler: to damage Russia's economy and, in turn, make it harder for Putin to achieve his dreams of conquest. They had become a tool of attrition, a means of gnawing away at Russian power until it no longer posed such a grave threat to Ukraine or anyone else. Just as the Trump administration had identified China as a geopolitical adversary and used economic warfare to undo aspects of globalization that benefited its rival, the Biden administration now took the same position against Russia. The days in which Putin could use the rewards of globalization to propel his country's reemergence as a great power were over. In remarks that stirred controversy for their bluntness, U.S. Secretary of Defense Lloyd

Austin outlined this emerging consensus following a visit to Kyiv in April: "We want to see Russia weakened to the degree that it can't do the kinds of things that it has done in invading Ukraine."

Sanctions were only one pillar of this strategy. As the conflict progressed, Washington significantly ramped up military aid to Ukraine, providing tens of billions of dollars' worth of advanced weaponry. By summer, its shipments included HIMARS, a truck-mounted weapons system that could fire precision-guided rockets at a range of around fifty miles. The HIMARS were more sophisticated than their Russian equivalent, giving Ukraine a qualitative edge on the battlefield. Coupled with the superior morale and tactics of Ukrainian troops, the HIMARS helped turn the tide of the war. In the south, Ukrainian forces used their new weapons to pummel Russian supply lines to devastating effect. By early fall, a Ukrainian counteroffensive was making substantial progress. It was starting to look plausible that Kyiv could recapture large swaths of its territory.

U.S. and allied military assistance was essential to help Ukraine expel the invaders. But economic warfare could play a supporting role by degrading Russia's military capabilities and undermining morale at home. This was already apparent in the difficulties Russia faced in replacing some of its

Wartime bonds: Volodymyr Zelensky and
Jake Sullivan (right) shake hands in Kyiv.

weapons stocks. Despite a gargantuan military-industrial complex, Russia relied on imports of Western-made computer chips to produce its most advanced weapons. The FDPR and other export controls had severed Russia's access to these components. The Russian military was left to dust off Soviet-era munitions, which were no match for the high-tech kit Ukraine was receiving from the West.

The chip shortage cascaded across the Russian economy. Authorities resorted to stripping imported refrigerators and dishwashers for chips, leaving everyday citizens without the kind of consumer goods they were accustomed to. Even more problematic, the lack of chips devastated the country's car, truck, and locomotive industries. Auto manufacturing and its offshoots, which together employed over three million Russians, were hit especially hard: the sector's output was down 80 percent in September 2022 compared with the same month the prior year. Millions of workers were furloughed or put on other forms of unpaid leave.

Shortages went well beyond semiconductors. Most major Russian industries relied on imports for 50 percent or more of their inputs. There were shortages of chicks for broiler hens and tires for tractors. Those lucky enough to remain in business saw the quality of their products collapse. Moscow eased safety standards for passenger vehicles to accommodate the crunch of foreign components. AvtoVAZ, Russia's largest automaker, began selling vehicles without airbags and anti-lock brakes. Putin had built his domestic support by improving the lot of everyday Russians; now the state of the economy brought back memories of Soviet times. "There will be more paper in the sausage," grumbled a sanctioned Russian oligarch.

At the same time, Russia found workarounds. Along fourteen thousand miles of land borders, there were plenty of back roads for doing business beyond the reach of sanctions and export controls. Russian firms set up front companies in neighboring states such as Armenia and Kazakhstan, then imported goods and smuggled them across the Russian border. It was hard for America and its allies to curtail these practices, particularly when the contraband was as small as computer chips. Like Iran before it, Russia would inevitably come up with innovative methods of sanctions evasion over time. Washington and other G7 capitals could try to stay one step ahead, yet the result would be a never-ending game of cat and mouse.

If there was any surefire way to keep up the pressure, it was to deprive the Russian economy of cash. Smuggling routes would be of little use if there was no money to buy anything. The same was true of the country's war machine. Whether the military used smart bombs or old Soviet-era leftovers, it needed soldiers whose training, equipment, and deployment cost a whole lot of money, especially when maintained in large numbers over a long period of time.

On September 21, in a desperate attempt to regain momentum on the battlefield, Putin imposed a draft, unveiling plans to conscript some 300,000 civilians into military service. Tens of thousands of Russians fled the country to avoid being sent to fight in Ukraine, and scores of brave protesters took to the streets despite certain arrest. Shortly thereafter, Putin formally annexed the Ukrainian regions of Donetsk, Luhansk, Kherson, and Zaporizhzhia—large parts of which were not even under Russian control—and vowed to use "all the means" at Moscow's disposal to ensure they remained part of Russia "forever."

The conscription push and annexations were a serious military and political escalation. But they also heightened the regime's acute need for cash. Oil exports remained Russia's most vital source of cash, and their importance was only growing as the rest of the economy withered. It was imperative for the West to finally cut the spigot of oil money to the Kremlin. It was imperative, in other words, for the price cap to work.

64

A Partitioned Market

Within the global energy industry, most people saw the price cap as a harebrained scheme cooked up by know-nothing Washington bureaucrats. "My friends and I have agreed to impose a price cap on our local pub's beer," the *Bloomberg* columnist Javier Blas taunted in a viral tweet about the policy. "Mind we actually do not plan to drink any beer there. The pub's owner says he won't sell beer to anyone observing the cap, so other patrons, who drink a lot there, say they aren't joining the cap. Success."

The jibe so frustrated the Treasury Department that Ben Harris, the agency's chief economist, saw fit to respond from his official Twitter account. Because "the G7 dominates necessary financial & other services for global oil trade," it could "restrict trade above a certain price," Harris retorted. "The global energy trade is a bit more complicated than the local pub." From commodities analysts to academics, few bought Harris's argument. "I was called an idiot by so many people," he recalled.

Yet even as the price cap was publicly pilloried, Harris and Elizabeth Rosenberg were engaging in productive talks with those who would implement it: banks, insurance companies, commodities trading houses, refineries, shipowners, and flagging authorities. Many of their interlocutors usually stayed as far off Treasury's radar as possible. (Oil traders, in particular, were better known for skirting sanctions than engaging transparently with the U.S. government.) But Treasury needed to seek dialogue. The worst-case scenario would be for companies to conclude that the price cap was impossible to abide by and that they had better stay away from Russian oil entirely. Such overcompliance was the norm with U.S. sanctions. The refusal of major European firms to re-enter Iran after the 2015 nuclear deal was a case in point. In the present circumstances, Treasury feared that overcompliance would cause Russian oil to come off the market, which would spike global oil prices—the exact outcome the price cap was designed to prevent.

Harris and Rosenberg spent countless hours convincing cagey executives that the United States was not playing a "gotcha game." The price cap, they argued, offered Treasury and private companies a win-win: by giving their input, the executives would help ensure that the policy was workable, and Treasury would get the executives' implicit assurance that their firms would comply. Banks and companies had long served as the front-line infantry in economic warfare; now they were given a chance to advise the generals, too.

Arab petrostates watched this process unfold with growing unease. Saudi Arabia, the kingpin of the world oil market, was used to calling the shots on prices, a privilege it had held since the 1970s and maintained through its leadership of OPEC+. (In 2016, OPEC invited Russia and nine other countries to coordinate production levels, creating OPEC+.) The price cap threatened the cartel's price-setting power. If the G7 succeeded in suppressing the price of Russian oil, it would prove that the West could exert leverage over the oil market by controlling access to the services that enabled the market to function. And an economic weapon fired on Russia today could be aimed at another oil exporter tomorrow. Ministers from OPEC+ countries were set to meet in Vienna on October 5, and anticipation mounted over what they would do.

U.S. officials knew they would need Saudi Arabia on their side. A few months earlier, Joe Biden even traveled to Jeddah to meet personally with Saudi Crown Prince Mohammed bin Salman, better known as MBS. This was a major diplomatic about-face for the president, who had previously vowed to make Saudi Arabia "pay the price" for the 2018 murder of *Washington Post* journalist Jamal Khashoggi. Biden walked away from the meeting with a loose commitment from the Saudis to increase oil output to help relieve pressure on prices. In the lead-up to the OPEC+ meeting in October, Amos Hochstein and other U.S. officials returned to Jeddah to remind MBS of this commitment, and they received assurances that Saudi Arabia at the very least would not support any production cuts.

When the moment of decision came, however, Riyadh sided with Moscow. At the Vienna meeting, OPEC+ ministers agreed to slash oil production by two million barrels per day. This was a direct shot at the price cap: the G7 could try to lower the price of Russian oil, but these efforts would be for naught if OPEC+ jointly cut output and sent prices soaring.

The White House was furious, denouncing the decision as "shortsighted" and pledging to work with Congress "to reduce OPEC's control over energy prices." Just before the OPEC+ decision, the Treasury Department was touting that the price cap would save the Global South billions by pushing down energy costs. These promises now seemed premature.

Speaking from Vienna, Alexander Novak, Russia's representative to OPEC+, declared that Moscow stood ready to make further cuts if the price cap was introduced. This threat could not be taken lightly. Catherine Wolfram had previously assessed that oil money was too valuable for the Kremlin to seriously consider withholding exports. But perhaps Putin would go there nonetheless, driving oil prices even higher in hopes of dealing Biden a political blow in the upcoming U.S. midterm elections.

Russia had already shown itself willing to weaponize energy exports when it came to gas. In September, Gazprom indefinitely shut down all Europe-bound gas supplies through the Nord Stream 1 pipeline that connected Russia to Germany via the Baltic Sea. A few weeks later, the pipes were damaged in a mysterious act of sabotage. Overall, Russian deliveries of natural gas to EU countries had dropped by more than 80 percent since the start of the war. Russia would have much more trouble sacrificing oil revenues—its leading source of export income—than gas earnings, but the situation was still dicey.

Ultimately, these fears proved unwarranted. Russia did not cut off oil exports, and the Democrats performed better than expected in the midterms. In mid-October, the Biden administration sold another 15 million barrels of oil from the U.S. government's strategic reserves, completing the emergency release the president had ordered in March. Meanwhile, changing economic conditions in the United States (where persistent inflation pushed the Fed to hike interest rates) and China (where a massive wave of COVID infections strained the economy) exerted downward pressure on global oil prices. As the December 5 start date for the price cap neared, conditions in the oil market were surprisingly favorable. All the G7 had left to do was agree on a price.

≡

The Treasury Department fell in love with the price cap based on economic forecasts—complex mathematical models produced by an army of academic economists and reviewed by a treasury secretary who was herself an elite economist and former Fed chair. When it came time to set the actual price, however, the process was more art than science.

As the Biden team saw it, the price cap should be lower than the current market price but high enough for Russia to keep selling oil. This was a wide range, and opinions diverged over how to calculate its limits. One potential yardstick was Russia's marginal cost of production—the minimum threshold above which Russia made a profit and therefore still had an incentive to sell. The problem was that not all Russian oil wells had the same production costs: some were cheap and efficient, others less so. Exact numbers were hard to come by: Treasury officials estimated the marginal cost of production to lie somewhere between $25 and $35 per barrel; most independent analysts estimated it was significantly lower, perhaps even under $10 per barrel. Yet whether it made economic sense or not, a cap of $10 per barrel would be so humiliatingly low as to almost guarantee that Moscow would stop selling.

Another reference point was Russia's government budget. In recent years, the budget envisioned an oil price of around $45 per barrel. At any price above that threshold, Russia's budget was projected to be in surplus. With military expenditures now surging and sanctions tightening, Russia's budgetary reliance on oil revenues increased dramatically. The breakeven point had risen to at least $70. So long as the price cap was set below this threshold, it could be expected to tip the Russian government into a deficit.

A third method for setting the price was to calculate how much, roughly, the Russian invasion of Ukraine had pushed up oil prices compared with previous years. You could then subtract the increase from current oil prices, and the result would be a rough approximation of where prices would stand without a war premium. This method yielded numbers between $55 and $65 per barrel—enough for Russia to have a clear incentive to maintain its exports—while also carrying the benefit of being easy to justify politically.

In the end, the most valuable input came from consultations with buyers of Russian oil such as India and Turkey. If the price cap were set too low, it would not give these buyers credible leverage in negotiations with Russia. For instance, if the price cap were set at $30 when prevailing market prices were closer to $90, the Indians could only demand Russian oil for $30 if they were obviously abiding by the cap—a stance that the Kremlin warned would prompt Russia to cut off sales. And the top priority for Washington was to motivate Russia to *continue to sell oil*. The better approach, therefore, was to set a conservative cap, one that gave Russia a clear incentive to keep selling while also providing India, Turkey, and other buyers with credible leverage to haggle for steep discounts.

Two weeks before the December 5 deadline, a price still hadn't been set. While the G7 was the backer of the price cap, all twenty-seven EU member states also had to agree on the final price, and the differences within the EU were much sharper than those among the G7. Within the EU, Poland and the Baltic states, urged on by Volodymyr Zelensky, were pushing for a cap of $30, which they thought would thrust Russia into a bitter fiscal crisis at a moment when Ukraine's forces were advancing. (The Ukrainians had just liberated Kherson, the largest city that the Russians had conquered.) Meanwhile, the EU countries with the biggest stake in shipping Russian oil— Greece, Cyprus, and Malta—sought a cap north of $70, essentially the same price Russia was receiving at that point. "It's a total nightmare," Bjoern Seibert reported to his G7 colleagues. To avoid further gridlock, Washington and other G7 capitals gave Seibert the green light to take a range of $65 to $70 to the EU member states, allowing for the final price to be set through internal EU horse-trading.

The Poles held firm at $30. They were ready to play a game of chicken, refusing to give in as the deadline got closer and closer. Finally, after calls from senior U.S. officials including Janet Yellen and Tony Blinken, Warsaw agreed to relent if the price cap was lowered to $60. This felt reasonable, and so the final price was set just over forty-eight hours before the policy was scheduled to take effect. Biden officials were relieved. They had fought hard for more than six months to get to this point. They had been called idiots and worse. Now their experimental economic weapon would be tested by the only judge that really mattered: the market.

The early evidence was alarming. After the clock struck midnight on December 5, a traffic jam formed at the mouth of the Bosphorus, the narrow strait that flows through the center of Istanbul. Turkish maritime authorities were refusing to allow oil tankers to transit the chokepoint unless they could demonstrate that their cargoes complied with the price cap. As proof, the officials demanded a written letter from a member of the International Group of P&I Clubs confirming that insurance coverage would "remain in place under any circumstances throughout the duration of the transit or the time the ship is in Turkish waters." The London P&I Club, the leading member of the international insurance group, complained that this requirement went "well beyond" the norm, but the Turkish government was unmoved. An incident involving an oil tanker in the Bosphorus would "cause catastrophic consequences for our country," said Turkey's maritime director-general, and with the price cap now in effect, "it is absolutely required for us to confirm in some way that their P&I insurance cover is still valid and comprehensive." Turkey was clearly taking the price cap seriously, but its behavior smacked of overcompliance and threatened to trigger a supply crunch in oil markets. Perhaps the price cap was indeed too clever by half.

For several nerve-wracking days, U.S. and European officials and executives from the major P&I clubs engaged with counterparts in Turkey in search of a solution. About a week after the price cap entered into force, Turkish authorities finally allowed the tankers to proceed. The impasse was broken.

As the tankers sailed freely through the Bosphorus, global oil prices fell below $80 per barrel, the lowest level of the year. The price of Russian oil fell even further, dropping below $50 per barrel, comfortably under the $60 cap. Before the invasion, Russian oil had sold for essentially the same price as Brent, the international benchmark. It now came with discounts of $30 or more. Partly, this reflected the changing geography of the Russian oil trade. The journey from Russia's oil ports on the Baltic Sea to Rotterdam and other EU import terminals took less than a week; the journey to India, now the main maritime transit route for Russian oil, took more than a month. Higher shipping costs to India meant lower revenues for Russian oil producers.

But the discounts also reflected that the price cap was working. Oil prices had not spiked; in fact, they had fallen dramatically, benefiting consumers all over the world. And the steep discounts for Russian oil were eroding the Kremlin's profits. In the first half of 2023, Russia's oil revenues were down by nearly 50 percent from the previous year, and Moscow was running a sizable budget deficit. To fund the war, the Kremlin would need to squeeze more and more money out of Russian oil companies, which were already starved of investment and shut out of major export markets due to sanctions. The International Energy Agency projected that Russia would lose over $1 trillion in oil and gas revenues by 2030—a hole that the petrostate would struggle to fill by other means. The hit might not come fast enough to tilt the war in Ukraine's favor. Yet over time, these trendlines were dire for Putin and his imperial ambitions.

The transformation of the Russian oil business represented something bigger, too: the end of an era. The oil market was an emblem of globalization, with ships crisscrossing the sea and selling their wares using common standards and services. Those days were over. At the molecular level, Russian oil may be similar to petroleum from the North Sea or Saudi Arabia, but for the foreseeable future, it would rely on a parallel supply chain and sell for a lower price.

Daniel Yergin, an eminent historian of the oil industry, was initially skeptical of the price cap, deeming it a "very difficult" undertaking. But shortly after it took effect, he saw its potential world-historical importance. The price cap and the EU embargo mark "the end of the global oil market," Yergin wrote in late December. "In its place is a partitioned market whose borders are shaped by not only economics and logistics but also geopolitical strategy."

Over the previous fifteen years, economic warfare had rewired the global financial system. Now, as the West sought to defang Putin's Russia, it was doing the same to the world oil market.

PART SIX

The World Economic Rupture

65

"Small Yard and High Fence"

In late November 2022, Chinese customs officials arrested a woman trying to enter the country while sporting a fake pregnancy bump. Hidden inside her bulging midsection was a hefty stash of computer chips. The ploy was part of a bigger story unfolding across China. Companies were racing to stockpile as many foreign-made semiconductors and chipmaking tools as they could, filling warehouses with billions of dollars in equipment. Before long, a thriving black market emerged to meet skyrocketing demand.

The impetus for the buying frenzy was a wave of new export controls on China, announced by the U.S. Commerce Department on October 7. The sweeping rules included three new FDPRs, which aimed to cut off China's access to advanced semiconductors and supercomputers. The new regulations applied both to U.S. companies and to firms all over the world that used American technology. They were issued without comment from the White House or State Department. The only publicity to speak of was a boilerplate press release by Commerce's Bureau of Industry and Security. The muted PR was a deliberate attempt to avoid provoking Beijing, but it did not lessen the weight of the measures, which were, in the words of a senior White House official, "a big fucking deal."

The oil market was just one part of the world economy that was fracturing. In the tech industry, too, economic warfare was disrupting transnational supply chains, the beating heart of globalization.

The export controls driving this process were a long time in the making, and their creation spanned successive U.S. administrations. Joe Biden, whose ascent to the presidency was in many ways a repudiation of his predecessor's record, did not walk back Donald Trump's most aggressive penalties on China's tech sector; he doubled down. Like the previous administration, Biden's team viewed supremacy in frontier technologies as a central pillar of geopolitical power, particularly in the intensifying rivalry between the United States and China. As soon as he entered the White House, Biden and his staff made plans to extend Trump-era export controls on Huawei to cover the entire Chinese tech industry.

Tarun Chhabra, who held the newly created position of NSC senior director for technology and national security, was tapped to lead this effort. Chhabra joined the White House from Georgetown's Center for Security and Emerging Technology, a think tank founded in 2019 with funding from Silicon Valley. In just a few years, CSET had become Washington's go-to resource on issues at the intersection of technology and national security. Chhabra staffed up the new NSC directorate with other experts from CSET, building a team primed to fix everything they thought was wrong with U.S. policy in the tech competition with China.

There was much Washington could do to fortify Trump's export controls, which, for all their impact, were mainly focused on a single Chinese tech giant. Trump had added several Chinese tech firms to the Commerce Department's Entity List, cutting them off from direct U.S. exports, but the far broader FDPR applied only to Huawei. Nevertheless, the Biden administration resolved not to rush things. U.S.-China trade still clocked in at a whopping $615 billion in 2020, and notwithstanding Trump's trade war and the supply-chain disruptions caused by the pandemic, China was America's number-one trading partner in goods. The sheer depth of these ties—and the millions of American jobs and livelihoods that depended on them—meant that the Biden administration could not simply fire untested economic weapons at China and expect little blowback. They had to do their homework.

Unlike the Trump administration, the Biden team also hoped to act in concert with allies. Securing support from the EU and fellow democracies in the Indo-Pacific, such as Japan, South Korea, and Australia, would undoubtedly slow down the campaign, but it would likely yield a stronger result. This was especially true when it came to export controls, since China's tech sector relied on critical inputs not only from Silicon Valley but also from the Netherlands and Japan, which provided machine tools and software whose level of sophistication China's indigenous semiconductor industry couldn't match.

EUV technology—essential for manufacturing high-end chips—was a case in point. The market leader in the field, the Dutch company ASML, sold EUV machines of otherworldly complexity, consisting of 100,000 parts and requiring extensive training by ASML personnel to operate. The machines, which were the size of a bus and sold for $150 million apiece, were unlike anything on offer elsewhere, making them a critical chokepoint. Early in his tenure as Biden's national security advisor, Jake Sullivan brought up the matter with his counterpart in the Netherlands. The Dutch government promised to continue withholding the license that ASML needed to export its EUV machines to China. But winning over the Dutch for full-fledged export controls proved a much taller order. Beijing had been exerting considerable pressure on the Dutch government over the delay of the license. ASML, for its part, warned that export controls could backfire. China was the world's biggest buyer of semiconductor manufacturing equipment, accounting for almost 30 percent of the global market. Shunning China would require ASML to forego substantial revenues that would otherwise flow into R&D and enable the company to stay on the bleeding edge.

Despite extensive efforts by U.S. officials, the Dutch were hesitant to act. The same was true of Japan, whose semiconductor industry formed another valuable chokepoint. Too much money hung in the balance, and the Japanese were wary of disadvantaging their own companies.

As Biden officials pondered their next step, the recently imposed FDPR against Russia showed what semiconductor-focused export controls could achieve when targeted at an entire economy. That FDPR, coupled with similar restrictions issued by almost forty other governments, wreaked havoc on Russia's military-industrial complex, yet one could not help but wonder whether it was too little, too late. Russian troops already occupied large parts of Ukraine, and Putin vowed to use any means necessary to defend those conquests. In any case, Russia didn't need access to high-tech weapons to level Ukrainian towns and critical infrastructure; it could do that with Soviet-era dumb bombs.

This bleak assessment—that export controls on Russia were working, but that they should have been imposed years earlier—convinced the White House that tougher tech restrictions on China were overdue. Henceforth, the United States would aim to maintain "as large of a lead as possible" in semiconductor technology, Jake Sullivan explained. Washington would no longer fall prey to the illusion that all economic relations with Beijing were win-win, as it had during the heyday of globalization, when "our competitors and adversaries took advantage of our complacency and inherent openness." Sullivan's words could easily have been uttered by a Trump official.

In early August 2022, Speaker of the House Nancy Pelosi traveled to Taiwan, making her the highest-level U.S. government official to visit in twenty-five years. Beijing's reaction was instant and severe, and it offered further evidence of the very real prospect that China would invade the island sooner or later. Chinese forces embarked on several days of elaborate military exercises that looked like a dry run for an amphibious assault, with missiles fired over Taiwanese cities and naval maneuvers on every side of the island. The exercises were so extensive that commercial ships evacuated the waters around Taiwan. Beijing also banned imports from more than a hundred Taiwanese brands and arrested a businessman for allegedly supporting Taiwan's formal independence from China. Like the Russian leader with whom he had forged a "no limits" partnership, Xi might decide that a war of aggression was worth the costs. If the United States was prepared to use export controls to degrade China's military capacity, it had better act soon.

Given this sense of urgency, the Biden administration decided to move unilaterally. It would issue its own set of tightened export controls and focus on locking in support from the Netherlands, Japan, and other countries afterward. As a first step, in late August, the Commerce Department ordered Nvidia to stop selling its marquee graphics processing units—which provide the computing power necessary to run AI algorithms—to two Chinese tech giants, Alibaba and Tencent. That month, Biden also signed the CHIPS and Science Act, which included investments of more than $50 billion in America's own chip industry. (As things stood, over 90 percent of the world's most advanced chips were made by TSMC in Taiwan, a dependence that would prove disastrous if China invaded the island.) Finally, on October 7, the Commerce Department announced the three new FDPRs against the Chinese tech sector. A Commerce official described them as a "down payment" intended to give U.S. allies the confidence to follow suit.

These unilateral measures had an immediate impact. Applied Materials, Lam Research, and KLA, three heavy hitters in the U.S. semiconductor industry, suspended business with China and started pulling staff from the country who helped Chinese chipmakers operate their equipment. ASML, the Dutch EUV manufacturer, instructed all employees who were U.S. citizens, green card holders, or foreign nationals living in the United States to halt dealings with Chinese customers at once. On the first day of trading after the new export controls were unveiled, Chinese chip stocks lost almost $10 billion in value.

The measures also had the desired effect on U.S. allies. In March 2023, the Netherlands and Japan agreed to impose their own export controls, barring firms such as ASML and Tokyo Electron from selling critical chipmaking equipment to China. A new model for American economic warfare was emerging. The United States would lead from the front while working shoulder-to-shoulder with allies. It would act before a crisis started instead of scrambling to play catch-up. And it would pair the use of economic weapons with proactive domestic investments, boosting America's defenses against future shocks.

In a speech at Washington's Brookings Institution in April 2023, Jake Sullivan articulated a vision for a "new Washington consensus" in international economic policy. The era of free-market fundamentalism was over. In its stead, America would embrace an aggressive industrial policy, including massive subsidies, to lure jobs to the United States and preserve the country's leadership in sectors such as semiconductors, biotech, and clean energy. (As it was doing for the semiconductor industry, the Biden administration was pouring billions into the domestic clean-energy sector through the Inflation Reduction Act.) Export controls would play a central role in this strategy, but with a narrow focus on "technology that could tilt the military balance." Echoing a phrase coined by Ursula von der Leyen, Sullivan declared that America was "for de-risking and diversifying, not decoupling," and that its "tailored measures" did not amount to a "technology blockade" (as Beijing called it). The goal, Sullivan professed, wasn't to wall off the entire U.S. economy but rather to protect a "small yard" of foundational technologies with a "high fence." Economic warfare did not have to reverse globalization in its entirety. Sectors deemed too critical for any degree of interdependence could be cordoned off while transnational links in other areas remained as tight as ever.

U.S. export controls undoubtedly represented a "high fence." Whether they would enclose only a "small yard," as Sullivan asserted, was up for debate. Sullivan had identified computing-related technologies, biotech, and clean energy as three technological "families" that "will be of particular importance over the coming decade," making American leadership in each of them "a national security imperative." These were not small industries. They were some of the fastest-growing sectors of the U.S. economy. Moreover, China was bound to retaliate against any U.S. export controls, which could trigger a tit-for-tat economic war that gradually engulfed other sectors. Sure enough, a few months after Sullivan's speech at Brookings, Beijing announced that it was restricting exports of gallium and germanium, critical minerals essential for manufacturing chips, solar panels, and fiber optics.

———

As the Biden administration put the finishing touches on the new export controls against China, a Russian military aircraft touched down in Tehran. On board was a cache of American and British military equipment that had fallen into Russian hands in Ukraine. The Iranians wanted to study the weapons in hopes of reverse-engineering them. Also on board was €140 million in cash—given the thicket of sanctions on both Russia and Iran, there was no other foolproof way to transfer money between the two countries. In return, Iran gave Russia more than a hundred of its domestically produced Shahed drones. These "suicide drones" were designed to fly directly into their targets (in this case, critical infrastructure in Ukraine) and explode on impact, a remote-controlled version of the Japanese kamikaze pilots who slammed their aircraft into enemy warships during World War II.

"We are openly and avowedly trying to do harm to the Russian economy," said a top White House official. "We are *not* openly and avowedly trying to do harm to the Chinese economy." But such distinctions mattered little to Russian, Chinese, and Iranian officials, all of whom saw themselves as targets of a unified and coordinated Western attack. As a result, all three states doubled down on efforts to deepen their commercial ties and build detours around the West's economic chokepoints. Russia and Iran were becoming close military partners. Sino-Russian trade flourished, and Chinese firms furnished Russia with industrial components, bulletproof vests, and various other equipment with battlefield applications. China ramped up its imports of Iranian oil and brokered an agreement between Iran and Saudi Arabia that helped break Tehran's diplomatic isolation.

The consolidation of this authoritarian axis signaled a new phase for the world economy, one that would be fundamentally different from the era of globalization that preceded it. The default state of the world was no longer one in which capital and trade flowed freely. Economic war was now the norm, a necessary feature in a world that proved much less peaceful than Americans once hoped.

"Thanks to globalization," Alan Greenspan said in 2007, shortly after retiring as Fed chair, "policy decisions in the U.S. have been largely replaced by global market forces." But as the years that followed showed, global market forces were no match for the states that controlled critical economic chokepoints. The era of unfettered free markets was over, collateral damage of a world at economic war.

The Scramble for Economic Security

"Every night I ask myself why all countries have to base their trade on the dollar."

It was a perfect spring day in April 2023, and Luiz Inácio Lula da Silva was in Shanghai for a meeting of the BRICS, a club of emerging-market countries that included Brazil, Russia, India, China, and South Africa. In an impassioned speech, Lula, now in his second stint as Brazil's president, wondered aloud about the dollar's role at the center of the world economy. "Why can't we do trade based on our own currencies?" he asked. "Who was it that decided that the dollar was the currency after the disappearance of the gold standard?"

In truth, no one required companies around the world to use the dollar for cross-border transactions; they did so because of its convenience and reliability, and because there was no good alternative. Yet the United States had taken active steps to propel the dollar to its lofty status, starting with the creation of the post–World War II Bretton Woods system and the Marshall Plan. Deals to price oil in dollars, negotiated with Saudi Arabia in the 1970s, further solidified the currency's hegemony, as did Western policies to deregulate finance in subsequent decades. More recently, the Fed's massive interventions to contain global financial crises, first in 2008 and again during the 2020 COVID shock, had a similar effect. Chinese officials also helped sustain the dollar's role, albeit inadvertently, by prioritizing the CCP's authoritarian control rather than reforms that might enable the renminbi to compete with the dollar internationally.

Since its formation more than a decade earlier, the BRICS had been a

*Wall of BRICS: leaders from the BRICS countries
unite during the Russo-Ukrainian war.*

loose coalition whose internal rivalries overshadowed any recognition of mutual interests. The quintet was once hyped by Wall Street as the next engine of global economic growth—its name had been coined by a Goldman Sachs economist—but in practice it was a talk shop with no serious geopolitical purpose. If anything, growing tensions between two of its members, India and China, had cast further doubt on the group's potential in recent years. But amid the bloodshed in Ukraine, its members were finding at least one common purpose: shielding one another from the West's economic weapons. Even though Brazil, India, and South Africa were not themselves under sanctions, each felt caught in the crossfire of the G7 price cap on Russian oil and the West's export controls on Russia and China. And they could not help but feel rattled as the G7 jettisoned the largest Russian banks from the international financial system and locked up more than $300 billion of Moscow's sovereign reserves. If the West could use these weapons against great powers such as Russia and China, it could use them against anybody.

The BRICS backlash was part of a global trend: a scramble for economic security, in which governments were racing to patch up vulnerabilities that their rivals could exploit. A highly interdependent world economy, it turned out, did not mix well with intensifying geopolitical competition. Supply-chain professionals had long advocated for more redundancies and resilience in the face of unforeseen crises and natural disasters. Their wishes largely went unanswered: the benefits were too small and the costs too high in a business environment marked by fierce competition to slash prices. The COVID pandemic and the attendant supply-chain disruptions led some to reconsider this equation. But it was the West's economic wars against Russia and China that decisively tipped the scales, prompting a growing number of states and companies to diversify their supply chains and financial relationships. Overseeing this shift were some of the same executives who'd once championed the breaking down of borders and barriers.

As the BRICS states prepared to protect themselves from the West's economic weapons, the West did the same in reverse. Beijing and Moscow had long waged economic wars of their own, sometimes behind a veil of deniability but increasingly out in the open. As Chinese and Russian tactics grew more aggressive, the United States and its allies began focusing on defense. When the Trump administration fought to curtail Huawei's 5G ambitions, for instance, it did so in large part because it worried about the far-reaching economic power Beijing would amass otherwise. U.S. export controls against Huawei were a *preventive strike* on China's future economic warfare capabilities. A broader desire to preempt potential attacks was now central to the West's international economic policy. "This version of globalization that we are living in has not taken us to a place where we feel more secure," explained Katherine Tai, the U.S. trade representative, in March 2022. "We are feeling increasing senses of insecurity in terms of our supply chains and our reliance on partners who we aren't comfortable relying on."

The answer, as Janet Yellen put it, was "friendshoring"—instead of striving for the unattainable goal of total self-sufficiency, America should pursue economic integration with "the countries we know we can count on" while lessening dependence on China, Russia, and other adversaries. "We cannot allow countries to use their market position in key raw materials, technologies, or products to have the power to disrupt our economy or exercise unwanted geopolitical leverage," Yellen said. The watchword in Washington was no longer "free trade" but rather "secure trade."

At a summit in Hiroshima in May 2023, the leaders of the G7 issued a sweeping statement pledging to transform the bloc into an economic security alliance. The G7 would henceforth take collective action to defend itself against "economic coercion," a necessity considering the "disturbing rise" of attempts by governments to "exploit economic vulnerabilities and dependencies." (Left unsaid was that the United States, the leading member of the G7, was the world's most capable practitioner of the art.) Japan, the summit's host, had already overhauled its domestic laws to protect itself from foreign economic coercion and appointed a cabinet-level minister for economic security. A month after the Hiroshima summit, the EU released its first-ever Economic Security Strategy.

The trouble with all this, as suggested by the BRICS backlash, is that defensive measures may not seem so defensive from the outside. The world economy is experiencing what scholars call a "security dilemma": as one state builds up its economic arsenal to improve its security, others feel less secure and build up their own arsenals in turn. The resulting economic arms race will likely intensify in the years ahead. And as soon as government or business leaders come to view an economic dependency as a vulnerability, they cannot unsee it. Even if a new U.S. administration vowed to restrain the use of sanctions, Chinese leaders would still not feel comfortable relying so heavily on the dollar. Likewise, no amount of reassurance from Beijing would placate American concerns about depending on China for pharmaceuticals or critical minerals. Trust, once lost, is not easily regained. Now that the scramble for economic security is underway, there's little chance everyone will return to the starting line.

67

Breaking the Chokepoints

S tuart Levey has been the Zelig of the Age of Economic Warfare: present for all the pivotal moments, moving fluidly between Washington, Wall Street, and Silicon Valley. Levey served as the first undersecretary for terrorism and financial intelligence at the Treasury Department and hatched the strategy that ostracized Iran from the international financial system. As chief legal officer of HSBC, he oversaw mass-scale compliance reforms that turned the bank and others like it into highly effective infantry in America's economic wars. Levey's team at HSBC was also instrumental in uncovering the sanctions evasion scheme orchestrated by Meng Wanzhou, the daughter of the founder of Huawei, which precipitated the Trump administration's campaign to cut the Chinese tech giant down to size.

By the time of Russia's full-scale invasion of Ukraine, Levey was CEO of a Facebook-led consortium known as the Diem Association. Originally called Libra, Diem planned to launch a digital currency, or cryptocurrency, that its creators hoped would one day replace the dollar as the backbone of the financial system. It would do so by making it much easier to move money around the globe without passing through the intermediary infrastructure that such transactions traditionally required. Yet those intermediaries—correspondent banks, clearinghouses, and messaging services such as SWIFT—were the very chokepoints the West relied on to conduct financial warfare. Because of this, and because Facebook's official motto was once "move fast and break things," politicians and regulators in Washington eyed Diem's crypto project with deep suspicion.

When he was offered the CEO job, Levey was skeptical, too. "I thought crypto was a threat to the type of tools we used at Treasury," he said. "It seemed like a very dangerous thing." But by taking the helm of Diem, he could perhaps build a cryptocurrency that was fully compatible with Washington's national security interests. Facebook and other members of Diem hoped that Levey could win over regulators in Washington; Levey joined them because he wanted to ensure digital currencies would not undermine American financial power.

Cryptocurrencies represent but one of many potential threats to the dollar's continued global dominance. Russia and China, among others, have likewise sought to undermine the U.S. currency's hegemonic position. Their initial efforts centered on the creation of alternative intermediaries, which allow cross-border payments without relying on the services of SWIFT and the U.S.-based clearinghouse CHIPS. But these initiatives have struggled to gain traction abroad. Even if successful, they alone would not decrease the power of American financial sanctions: so long as using the dollar is necessary for participation in the world economy, Washington's ability to deny access to it will remain a fearsome economic weapon—no matter which messaging service or settlement mechanism is used.

At present, there are few signs that the dollar's role is in real jeopardy. Many predicted that the 2008 financial crisis would knock the currency off its pedestal, and Beijing spent the immediate aftermath trying to advance the renminbi as a replacement. Yet the dollar has only become more essential in the years since, in large part owing to American monetary policy. As the world teetered on the brink of a financial meltdown in 2008, the U.S. Federal Reserve came to the rescue by extending swap lines to other major central banks, fashioning itself as the global lender of last resort. When the world economy came to a screeching halt in the early stages of the COVID pandemic in 2020, the Fed again used swap lines to distribute dollar funding wherever it was needed. The Fed's aggressive interventions did far more to shore up faith in the dollar than U.S. sanctions have ever done to shake it.

By contrast, China's attempts to internationalize the renminbi have fallen flat. In August 2015, in a bid to boost slowing economic growth, Beijing devalued its currency. The ensuing capital flight so frightened Chinese leaders that they tightened capital controls. Confidence in the renminbi plummeted. The share of China's foreign trade settled in renminbi, which had peaked at almost 30 percent that year, fell by more than half. If there is a single point that best illustrates the dollar's dominance, perhaps it is this: China is the world's leading exporter by far, but to this day less than 30 percent of its trade is settled in China's own currency. The remainder is overwhelmingly settled in U.S. dollars. Put simply, although China sells the most stuff, it struggles to get buyers to pay in anything other than dollars.

China's most ambitious effort to dethrone the dollar has taken the form of a digital currency issued by its central bank. A pilot version of this digital renminbi, also known as the e-CNY, launched in 2020. Since then, the Chinese government has facilitated the e-CNY's adoption by hundreds of millions of citizens, making it the world's most widely used state-backed digital currency. Just as mobile payments in the United States lag behind China, where today virtually every transaction can be completed with mobile apps such as Alipay and WeChat, Beijing could soon become the global leader and standard setter in digital currencies. The implications for its financial power are clear, as is the trouble this would spell for America's economic arsenal. The e-CNY is a direct liability on the balance sheet of China's central bank—effectively the digital equivalent of cash. This means it can change hands without the use of any intermediaries. From the perspective of U.S. financial power, the e-CNY has all the downsides of crypto plus another: Beijing can monitor all transactions.

If the e-CNY finds international success, the dollar could indeed face a serious threat. But even in that scenario, the U.S. currency wouldn't automatically lose its privileged status. The truth is that many countries shudder at the strength of America's economic arsenal, but they would be even more alarmed if China possessed the same capabilities. For all the fear in foreign capitals about U.S. sanctions, America's approach to economic warfare has been less capricious than that of its chief superpower rival. It is one thing to freeze Russia's central bank reserves after it launched a war of conquest in clear violation of international law; it is quite another to slap a trade embargo on Australia for merely proposing a probe into the origins of COVID, or to impose harsh economic penalties on Lithuania for allowing Taiwan to open a representative office in Vilnius, both of which China has done in recent years.

Then there is the widespread concern about Chinese state surveillance. The case of China's leading mobile payment apps, Alipay and WeChat, is instructive. Despite their success in China and the global spending power of Chinese tourists, both apps have struggled to win market share abroad, in large part because other governments worry about leaving their citizens vulnerable to Chinese snooping. After a deadly skirmish between Chinese and

Indian soldiers on the Sino-Indian border in June 2020, India banned dozens of popular Chinese mobile apps, including Alipay and WeChat, citing concerns that China was stealing users' personal data. Now as then, India's most popular mobile app is not of Chinese origin; it is WhatsApp, the messaging platform owned by Facebook. The digital renminbi will struggle to achieve global dominance for the same reasons Alipay and WeChat have made little headway abroad.

The United States still has the chance to outpace China in the realm of digital currencies. Stuart Levey failed to convince the U.S. government to back Facebook's crypto project—Diem folded in 2022 after it received pushback from Janet Yellen and other U.S. officials. Slowly but surely, however, the Fed has gotten into the game. In late 2022, the New York Fed announced that it would pilot a digital dollar in cooperation with several heavyweights of the U.S. financial industry, including Citibank, MasterCard, and Wells Fargo. It also ran an experiment demonstrating that a digital dollar can dramatically speed up cross-border payments, cutting a two-day process down to a few seconds. The Fed has every reason to expand these efforts and eventually launch its own digital currency, which would enable Washington, not Beijing, to set standards for the sector.

The renminbi has a long way to go until it can match the dollar in terms of the depth and liquidity of U.S. capital markets and the ease of moving across borders. But its biggest impediment may be the character of the Chinese state: increasingly authoritarian and unconstrained by the rule of law. Currencies ideally function as a kind of everyday infrastructure that one uses without having to do much thinking, like a road for a driver. The less the average company needs to worry about the currency it uses, the better. The dollar may give some companies pause because of its association with U.S. sanctions, but the renminbi remains a far riskier alternative. And when deals go sideways, most executives would rather find themselves in an American courtroom than a Chinese one.

In the years ahead, China may well build deeper capital markets or even loosen capital controls, but it cannot match the fundamental advantages of the dollar unless it revamps its entire political system for the better or America's is remade for the worse. As a result, the greatest threat to the dollar's supremacy and, in turn, the U.S. economic arsenal may emanate not from China but from America's own political system. If a future U.S. administration politicizes the Fed and ends its monetary policy independence—

or worse, if the justice system is debased and the rule of law called into question—the advantages of the dollar over the renminbi would begin to fade.

Not all chokepoints are created equal. The others under U.S. control are less formidable than the dollar—yet breaking them will be neither cheap nor easy.

Russia is already well on its way to standing up its own end-to-end supply chain for oil and gas exports. Overland pipelines to China protect Russia's most vital energy flows from sanctions. At sea, Russia has successfully found ways to export oil to places such as India without relying on Western shipping and insurance, amassing a "shadow fleet" of over a hundred aging oil tankers that flout maritime safety rules and sail covertly with their transponders switched off. It could one day fulfill all its shipping needs by buying up hundreds more of these tankers, even if doing so is an expensive proposition that Russia's sanctions-burdened, wartime economy can ill afford. Replacing Western maritime insurers will be a taller order. Still, Russia could eventually get there with the help of sovereign guarantees, as Iran did after the imposition of oil sanctions in 2012. Oil is such an important commodity that, over time, buyers will find ways to acquire Russian oil even if they have to use a patchwork of sketchy services. The chokepoints that the United States exploited for the price cap have fractured the world oil market and taken a chunk out of Moscow's revenues, but they won't restrain trade forever.

Saudi Arabia and other major oil producers, meanwhile, could one day decide to accept payments for oil in a currency other than the dollar. China is already settling some of its energy bills in its own currency, and Xi Jinping has called for oil to be traded in renminbi more broadly. But that prospect is far-fetched. For starters, petrostates need a place to invest all the oil money that flows into their coffers, and U.S. capital markets provide far more depth and liquidity than Chinese alternatives. Most Middle Eastern currencies, including the Saudi riyal and UAE dirham, are pegged to the dollar, so these countries require a steady influx of dollars to maintain their exchange rates. And if Riyadh allowed China to pay for oil in renminbi, other big customers such as India, Japan, and South Korea could demand similar arrangements for their own currencies, making it difficult for oil-producing governments to manage their finances. The path of least resistance is to stick to the petrodollar, a system that has worked reasonably well for half a century.

What of the Western efforts to constrain China's access to cutting-edge technology? Only time will tell, but breaking the West's chokepoints in the semiconductor industry will require not only large amounts of money but also extraordinary technical ingenuity. China seems intent on marshaling both. Beijing is pouring tens of billions of additional dollars into its domestic chip sector, and it has put Huawei in charge of a coordinated, state-backed plan to erect a self-sufficient semiconductor design and production network. These efforts are already bearing fruit. In August 2023, Huawei stunned the world by releasing a new 5G smartphone whose cellular speeds matched the latest iPhone. Known as the Mate 60 Pro, the new model boasted an advanced chip designed by Huawei's HiSilicon unit and manufactured by SMIC. It was precisely the type of technology U.S. export controls were supposed to stop China from producing.

To drive home the point, a top CCP official prevailed upon Huawei to move up the release date of the Mate 60 Pro to coincide with a trip to Beijing by U.S. Commerce Secretary Gina Raimondo, who oversaw American export controls. "Extreme suppression by the U.S. has failed," gloated a state-run Chinese media outlet. The fact that Huawei and SMIC could produce an advanced chip at the scale required for a mass-market smartphone surprised even U.S. officials. It turned out the Chinese companies achieved this feat by using less advanced ASML lithography machines, pirated American software, and a huge repository of Western equipment and spare parts they had hoarded before the latest export controls kicked in. The manufacturing process was much slower and costlier than TSMC's for making comparable chips; it wasn't even clear it could be done profitably. But that didn't matter for the Chinese government, which was happy to cover any losses.

Nevertheless, for all their efforts and impressive product launches, Chinese firms remain at least five years behind cutting-edge chip manufacturers such as TSMC, and even further behind equipment makers such as Applied Materials, ASML, and Tokyo Electron. Huawei and SMIC still rely heavily on Western technology, and they've retained access to it through their stockpiles, a booming underground market, and loopholes in the export controls. But the stockpiles will eventually run out, and the challenges posed by the underground market and loopholes are fixable if the United States and its allies tighten restrictions. It would be devilishly hard—if not impossible—for China to build a vertically integrated domestic industry that could produce chips equal to those made with best-in-class technology from the United States, Europe, Japan, South Korea, and Taiwan. That won't stop China from trying, however, and it seems probable that Beijing will spend untold sums striving to catch up to the West on semiconductors without ever getting there.

A more plausible way for China to level the technological playing field is to solidify control over emerging chokepoints rather than existing ones. The most important of these is clean-energy technology, an industry that relies on a supply chain of critical minerals that China dominates. China produces some two-thirds of the world's supply of lithium and cobalt, both of which are essential for building electric cars. It is a massive producer of other ingredients for the clean-energy transition, such as aluminum, graphite, and nickel, and it controls nearly *all* the world's supply of some rarer and lesser-known critical minerals, such as gallium. The most vivid demonstration of China's proficiency in clean-energy technology is the meteoric rise of its auto sector. Largely on the back of electric vehicles, China became the world's top car exporter in 2023, with sales growing at an astonishing clip of more than 50 percent year-over-year.

These eye-popping statistics notwithstanding, China's control of clean-energy chokepoints could prove short-lived. Its dominance of the market for critical minerals, for instance, stems less from its natural-resource bounty than its expertise in *processing* minerals. While it retains a sizable lead in that area, the technical challenges of mineral processing are not so complex as to keep others from catching up over time, especially when boosted by generous state subsidies for clean tech such as those included in the U.S. Inflation Reduction Act.

At least for several years to come, however, the clean-energy industry will offer chokepoints that China can exploit for economic warfare. Among other things, Beijing could use this advantage to deter the West from tightening the "technology blockade." China's export controls on gallium and germanium, announced in July 2023, were followed by high-level outreach from U.S. officials and public reassurances that America sought only "narrow de-risking," after which the two countries could "begin consequential diplomacy"—a sign that China's shot across the bow had accomplished the desired effect. But there's also a risk that China's weaponization of critical minerals will lead to a spiraling economic war that destroys every last shred of the U.S.-China economic relationship. The hard reality is that, in the coming years, the scramble for economic security is likelier to break the global economy than it is to break just the chokepoints.

68

Strategy and Sacrifice

I s any of this worth it? Sanctions against Iran paved the way for the 2015 nuclear deal, which constrained the country's nuclear program. But the deal eventually fell victim to American domestic politics, and after Donald Trump abrogated the accord in 2018, Iran revived its nuclear program and edged closer to building a bomb than it had before the deal was signed. Export controls against Huawei stifled the company's quest to dominate global 5G networks and slashed its revenue, but they neither put an end to Chinese economic aggression nor created a new stable equilibrium in U.S.-China relations. Most tragically of all, the barrage of economic weapons fired at Russia failed to stop the invasion of Ukraine. With such a mixed track record, it's reasonable to ask whether the benefits of economic warfare are worth the costs.

Politics, according to Otto von Bismarck's dictum, is the art of the possible. Sanctions, export controls, and other economic weapons are not magic bullets—but no instrument of statecraft is. It's no accident that the rise of economic warfare in U.S. foreign policy in the mid-2000s came on the heels of two costly and ultimately failed American-led wars in Afghanistan and Iraq. Washington's heightened interest in sanctions was driven as much by confidence in their efficacy as by disillusionment with the main alternative, military force.

The 2022 sanctions against Russia did not prevent its invasion of Ukraine. They also did not degrade its military capacity quickly or comprehensively enough to facilitate a decisive Ukrainian victory on the battlefield. But the lasting damage they inflicted on Russia's economy will prevent the country from regaining its pre-war economic or military power anytime soon. In this sense, they corrected a fatal flaw in globalization: the ability of a revisionist state like Putin's Russia to profit from the U.S.-led world order at the same time as it strove to upend it.

When judging economic warfare on its own merits, moreover, it's important to consider counterfactuals. What would the world look like had the West refrained from striking Russia with hard-hitting economic weapons in 2022? Europe would still be reliant on Russian energy. The Russian economy and war machine would continue growing on the back of Western financing and technology. The lesson for the rest of the world would be that you can keep on reaping the benefits of the global economy no matter what you do. China would see fewer obstacles to seizing Taiwan by force, as would other would-be aggressors salivating over their neighbors' territory.

Even if one doubts the signaling effect of sanctions, it's hard to argue the United States and its allies would be better off having maintained economic interdependence with Russia. Those ties outlived their purpose long ago—at least since Russia annexed Crimea in 2014, if not since it invaded Georgia in 2008—and it's a pity it took such a heinous act of Russian aggression for the West to finally cut them. Still, sanctions are now undermining the economic model on which Putin built his imperialist foreign policy, blunting his capacity to do more harm.

Back in 2014, when Dan Fried helped refashion the G7 into an economic war coalition against Russia, his diplomacy entailed a major trade-off: because not all allies were willing to impose sanctions as harsh as those favored by the United States, Western unity came at the expense of tougher measures against Moscow. To the Obama administration, this was an acceptable compromise. What good were tough sanctions if they caused a rift in the transatlantic alliance, which would hand Putin an even bigger prize than Crimea? When such considerations fell by the wayside during the Trump administration, the United States paid a heavy price. Trump's unilateral economic warfare caused a lot of damage in places like China, Iran, and Venezuela, yet it also sowed deep distrust among America's closest friends. Washington won support for its campaign against Huawei not through diplomacy but rather through the threat of economic pain: the FDPR, like secondary sanctions, forced the world to choose between America and Huawei.

When Russia launched its full-scale invasion of Ukraine, the Biden administration managed to do both: impose potent sanctions *and* maintain allied unity. Partly, this was owed to the brutality of the war, the courage of the Ukrainians, and a groundswell of popular support for harsh sanctions across Europe. But it was also thanks to months of tireless diplomacy between Washington, Brussels, and the other G7 capitals. The trust built between Joe Biden and Ursula von der Leyen, Daleep Singh and Bjoern Seibert, and countless other officials down the line proved essential in the moment of crisis.

Together, the economies of the G7 account for almost half of global GDP, and their dominance in the most important sectors of the world economy is greater still. The bloc's unity in imposing sanctions against Russia made the penalties much stronger than they would have been otherwise. By acting in concert with allies, the United States also kept the sanctions campaign from turning into a global referendum on American economic leadership. Russia's decision, starting in 2018, to shift its foreign exchange reserves *away* from the dollar and *toward* the euro was based on its expectation of just this kind of referendum: Russian leaders believed that when the United States would one day go on the economic offensive against them, the EU wouldn't join in. Had this assumption proved correct, other states would have drawn similar conclusions. For instance, had the United States targeted Russia's central bank while the EU refused to follow suit, the likely result would have been a mass exodus from the dollar toward the euro by countries the world over. Instead, Russia was caught flat-footed, and more than half of its war chest was immobilized. As it happened, the dollar's usage in global payments has shot up to record highs in the aftermath of the Russia sanctions, gaining much more than the renminbi or any other currency. In effect, by acting in unison with the issuers of the world's other reserve currencies, the United States was able to weaponize its leadership of the global financial system without forfeiting that leadership. It's not for nothing Jake Sullivan celebrated the G7 as the "steering committee of the free world."

Friendships also paid dividends for Putin. The willingness of India, China, Turkey, the UAE, and other countries outside the G7 to continue doing business with Russia cushioned the blow of sanctions. When Russia lost its biggest market for oil—the EU—it swiftly found a new one in India, which went from buying very little Russian oil to buying two million barrels per day. By 2023, Russia had become India's largest source of foreign oil. China massively ramped up trade with Russia, too, filling the void left behind by departing Western firms. Turkey boosted imports of Russian oil and started selling Russia many of the products it used to get from the EU.

The UAE emerged as an all-purpose hub for sanctions evasion, reprising the tricks it learned during years of restrictions against Iran. Dubai is now a haven for sanctioned Russian oligarchs and home to many traders of Russian oil.

Thanks in part to this cushion, the immediate impact of sanctions on Russia was not as devastating as analysts initially projected. The country's economy contracted by just over 2 percent in 2022. While that was a significant decrease—absent sanctions, Russia was poised for growth—it was a far cry from the dire forecasts thrown around in the early days of the sanctions campaign, which predicted Russian GDP would shrink by 10 or even 15 percent. The following year, Russia's economy returned to modest growth, fueled by a surge in military spending and domestic arms production that masked deeper economic dysfunction. Because large swaths of the Global South have been unwilling to go along with the sanctions, Russia's economy is experiencing a gradual decline instead of a rapid demise. The decline is inexorable all the same.

As the G7 has emerged as the "steering committee of the free world" on matters of economic warfare, the BRICS has been coalescing into a counterweight. In August 2023, the bloc invited in six new members—Argentina, Egypt, Ethiopia, Iran, Saudi Arabia, and the UAE. The inclusion of Iran was particularly noteworthy. During the Obama years, China, India, and Russia grudgingly went along with sanctions against Iran in support of America's nuclear diplomacy. The UAE, too, eventually severed economic ties with Iran. The Saudi king urged U.S. officials to "cut off the head of the snake" and bomb Iran's nuclear facilities. Now these same states were facilitating Iran's diplomatic rehabilitation.

Two months later, Hamas launched a spate of gruesome attacks against Israel, inciting a war in Gaza that threatened to engulf the entire Middle East. Suddenly, pressuring Iran—Hamas's patron—became a top priority again in Washington. But this time, the United States would have to make do with less international support. It would also have to bear the risks of sanctioning two big oil producers, Russia and Iran, at the same time. The specter of rising oil prices had haunted the Biden administration since the start of the Russo-Ukrainian war; it was the main reason the White House recoiled from hitting Russia with the full range of America's economic arsenal, particularly when it came to Russian oil exports. A two-front economic war against Russia and Iran was sure to compound these fears.

With Iran in the fold, the expanded BRICS was even less coherent from a geopolitical or ideological perspective. Yet it reinforced that the bloc's unifying purpose was to blunt the West's economic weapons. The BRICS states might not manage to unseat the dollar or conjure alternatives to the most advanced Western technologies, but they could support one another whenever they came under attack. For China, the BRICS could provide a bulwark against the wave of economic penalties it would surely face if it invaded Taiwan.

American officials were pleased with the damage sanctions were doing to Russia's military-industrial base and proud of their efforts to maintain unity among the G7. But they also had to grapple with the inescapable fact that deterrence had failed. The Biden administration had hoped that the threat of massive sanctions would keep Putin from invading Ukraine in the first place. This was the intent behind its repeated public warnings of "swift and severe consequences" in the months leading up to the war. It didn't work. By the time Putin ordered the tanks to roll, sanctions had already failed in their paramount objective.

It is possible deterrence was always bound to fail—that Putin was hellbent on his imperialistic project, come what may. Perhaps the threat of *economic* pain just wasn't enough; successful deterrence may have required a credible threat of military force, a threat the United States was never prepared to make. The truth is unknowable, but it's worth asking what, if anything, the United States and its allies could have done better.

A potential clue lies in the sanctions against Russia's central bank. Sergei Lavrov, the Russian foreign minister, later admitted that "nobody" in Moscow expected the G7 to target the central bank, and Elvira Nabiullina came under internal pressure to resign for her failure to anticipate it. On the one hand, the surprise of Russian officials was a good thing: had they expected the move, they would not have left more than half of the central bank's reserves exposed to sanctions, and the G7 would not have been able to lock up so much of Russia's war chest within days of the invasion. On the other hand, the episode suggests that the Russian government *underestimated* the severity of the sanctions it would face. And deterrence can't work if your adversary underestimates your ability or willingness to act.

This underscores an important point: while the G7 spent countless hours preparing possible sanctions options long before the invasion began, it never managed to reach consensus on a fleshed-out response ahead of time. As Bjoern Seibert often emphasized, European leaders needed to see the "visuals" of the war before committing to a course of action. In Washington, Daleep Singh pushed for tough measures, but on the eve of the invasion, the Biden administration remained divided on how hard to hit Russia. The best evidence that no one in Moscow expected sanctions on Russia's central bank is that no one in Washington or Brussels did, either. Behind the public threats of "swift and severe consequences" was a G7 coalition that had not yet determined what those words meant. The West left it up to Putin's imagination, and Putin concluded, as he often did, that the West would prove weak. If the United States and the rest of the G7 could do things over again, they would be better served by clearly articulating the costs Russia would face and stiffening their spines for economic war before Russian missiles began raining down on Ukrainian cities.

There's another trade-off of sanctions that Washington must consider as it draws lessons from the Russo-Ukrainian war. While holding economic weapons in reserve can be helpful from a deterrence perspective, it does little good if deterrence is not a viable goal. Put differently, if it's true that sanctions could never have deterred Putin, the West would have been better served by weakening Russia's economy as much as possible before the invasion. The G7's costliest error was to defer serious discussion of oil sanctions until after the war began, at which point it took nearly ten months to implement the price cap and the EU oil embargo. As a result, Russia raked in a whopping $220 billion from oil exports in 2022, contributing to the highest single-year energy revenues the Kremlin has ever collected.

The implications for Western policy toward China are uncomfortable. If officials conclude that Xi Jinping is determined to try to conquer Taiwan at some point, the most logical course of action is to take more aggressive steps *now* to degrade Chinese power. To be sure, this would involve significant economic costs for the West. But it would be better to bear these costs now than to wait until after war has broken out. Economic attrition takes time, and the current approach, built around the idea of a "small yard and high fence," could prove too limited to make a serious dent in Chinese military capabilities.

In many ways, the United States and its allies got lucky this time around. They enjoyed the luxury of early warning in the lead-up to Russia's invasion of Ukraine, which gave their leaders almost five months to prepare a response. The West cannot count on this advantage in the future. If China decides to invade Taiwan, the move could easily take the G7 by surprise, just as the Russian annexation of Crimea did in 2014. It doesn't matter if the goal of Western economic warfare against China is deterrence or attrition—either way, the time to get ready is now.

These preparations should center on policy and diplomacy: creating options for sanctions and export controls, coordinating them with allies, and embedding them into a coherent strategy. But they must also be informed by politics. Years of war in Afghanistan and Iraq soured Americans on the use of military force because it appeared both costly and futile. Economic warfare seemed preferable by comparison, particularly after sanctions led to the Iran nuclear deal at virtually no cost to the U.S. economy. But as the United States has turned its economic arsenal against Russia and China, it has become clear that effective sanctions against other great powers are possible only if America is willing to accept real economic risks. The immediate impact of the 2022 Russia sanctions fell short of expectations because the Biden administration worried about the domestic political consequences of cutting Russian oil sales and increasing gasoline prices. A major escalation of sanctions against China would carry even starker risks—blowback against the U.S. economy would be guaranteed. It's thus imperative for U.S. officials who are strategizing for a potential Taiwan conflict to heed political realities, devise proactive steps to mitigate harm, and prepare the American people for the costs they may have to endure.

If there's a central lesson of the economic war against Russia, it is that deferring hard choices does America no good. Sanctions and export controls involve sacrifice, especially when levied against other big economies. They also require intensive preparation to succeed. Should the United States continue relying on these weapons as much as it has in the past two decades, it needs to be clear-eyed about their costs and more intentional in their use. Only then can it ensure the sacrifice is not in vain.

CONCLUSION

===

Impossible Trinity

The Age of Economic Warfare began innocuously enough: with Stuart Levey, then a little-known official at the helm of a brand-new division of the Treasury Department, trying to prove the president wrong. As Iran's nuclear program raced forward, George W. Bush lamented that America had "sanctioned ourselves out of influence" with the country. The only options, it seemed, were to go to war or let Iran join the ranks of nuclear-armed states. Levey set out to show there was another way.

Over the coming years, Levey and his colleagues overhauled U.S. sanctions policy. Using their legal expertise and their understanding of the financial sector's risk calculus, they conscripted multinational banks into a campaign to isolate Iran from the world economy. Prodded by Congress, they tested the limits of their new economic weapons—they even found a way to freeze more than $100 billion of Iran's oil money in overseas escrow accounts. Over time, this economic pressure triggered political change in Iran and opened a path to the 2015 nuclear deal. The United States had managed to put Iran's nuclear aspirations on hold, and as Barack Obama boasted in a speech the following year, it did so "without firing a shot."

As the Iran nuclear deal was being negotiated, Vladimir Putin shocked the world by sending "little green men" into Crimea and swiftly annexing the territory. Determined to punish Russia for this flagrant imperial land grab but unwilling to risk war with a fellow nuclear power, U.S. officials again reached into their economic arsenal. Russia was a trickier target than Iran: it was much bigger and more integral to the world economy. European countries depended on Russian oil and gas. If sanctions wreaked too much havoc on Russia, the fallout would quickly reach Europe. From there, it might spread to the United States itself. As a result, any sanctions imposed on Russia needed to be limited in scope and "scalpel-like" in their precision. They also required the support of European allies lest they might fracture the transatlantic relationship.

Enter Dan Fried, a veteran American diplomat serving his last tour after nearly four decades in the Foreign Service. Fried stitched together a sanctions coalition with the EU and the rest of the G7, creating an economic version of the NATO alliance in embryo. The sanctions imposed by this alliance, surgical though they were, quickly sent Russia's economy spiraling. The unexpected severity of the damage frightened Western leaders, who backed off and prayed the Russo-Ukrainian conflict would simmer down. After Donald Trump entered the White House in 2017, the sanctions gradually atrophied.

Toward almost every country besides Russia, Trump was as sanctions-happy a president as America ever had. This approach often did more harm than good. His administration ripped up the Iran nuclear deal and tried to bludgeon Tehran with "maximum pressure" sanctions, which achieved nothing of value while removing the shackles on Iran's nuclear program. Meanwhile, other countries grew increasingly wary of the power and arbitrariness of U.S. economic warfare and intensified their efforts to shield themselves from it. The Russian central bank traded most of its dollars for euros and gold. China sought new ways to promote its own currency internationally by launching a digital version of the renminbi and creating a homegrown financial messaging and settlement platform. Even the EU tried to establish workarounds to U.S. sanctions.

On one issue, at least, the Trump administration left behind a more constructive legacy. Under the patient guidance of Matt Pottinger, Washington came to see Beijing's economic policies as a concerted effort to challenge U.S. technological leadership and seize the commanding heights of the digital economy. The long-standing misconduct of Chinese authorities and companies in their dealings with the West, ranging from intellectual property theft to forced technology transfer to unfair trade practices, was not motivated by a simple desire for economic gain; it was integral to China's strategy to replace the United States atop the geopolitical pecking order. Huawei was at the forefront of this strategy—it was nominally the largest private company in China, but it was actually the tip of the spear of the CCP's grand designs.

To thwart Beijing's plans, U.S. officials turned to a different class of economic weapons. Instead of trying to cut China off from the international financial system, the United States set about choking off Huawei and other Chinese companies from cutting-edge technology. These companies could retain access to Wall Street, but they would be pushed out of Silicon Valley. It took Trump officials several years and multiple false starts to arrive at this approach, but by Trump's final year in office, U.S. export controls were sending Huawei into a tailspin. Eventually, the Biden administration expanded the high-tech siege to all Chinese companies and declared an explicit policy of maintaining "as large of a lead as possible" over China in critical technologies. The win-win logic of globalization that had defined U.S.-China relations for decades gave way to the zero-sum reality of a technological confrontation between rival superpowers.

In each of these three campaigns—against Iran from the mid-aughts to the 2015 nuclear deal, against Russia after its 2014 annexation of Crimea, and against China from the mid-2010s to the present—U.S. officials found themselves playing catch-up to address long-festering problems or unforeseen crises. Not so in the latest iteration of U.S. economic warfare following Russia's 2022 full-scale invasion of Ukraine: U.S. officials knew months ahead of time that Russia was gearing up to invade. They thus had the opportunity to use sanctions to *deter* Russian aggression rather than reverse or punish it after the fact. But Joe Biden's warning that any renewed Russian attack on Ukraine would incur the "most severe sanctions that have ever been imposed"—a threat echoed by multiple European leaders—failed to sway Putin. Russia went to war anyway, and the West was left to make good on its threat.

Now seeking to undermine Putin's war effort and permanently weaken the Russian economy, the United States and its allies turned to measures used previously against Iran and China: financial sanctions, including on Russia's central bank and two largest commercial banks; and high-tech export controls. Fearing a spike in energy prices, however, the West initially avoided taking steps to reduce Russia's oil revenues, the lifeblood of the country's economy. Only after nine months did America and its allies institute a price cap, a mechanism much milder than the restrictions that successfully dried up Iran's oil money. So far, the impact of the latest Russia sanctions has been significant and disappointing at the same time: Russia has been sidelined from major parts of the world economy, and its status as a world power has diminished a great deal in the process, but the war in Ukraine grinds on. Economic weapons have not stopped Putin's battalions.

What's more, the dramatic scale of the penalties, coming on the heels of Trump's Iran sanctions and the U.S. siege of China's tech sector, kicked off a broader scramble for economic security. Today, governments around the world are trying to unwind aspects of globalization that leave them susceptible to external pressure. The chokepoints that made the Age of Economic Warfare possible have become such glaring vulnerabilities that they threaten the interdependent global economy that has flourished since the end of the Cold War.

Part of the reason is that the United States has consistently grown bolder in its use of economic weapons. "On Iran, we were using machetes to cut down the path step by step," Stuart Levey reflected, "but now people are able to go down it very quickly." Despite the frequency with which it uses sanctions and export controls, America has hardly perfected the art of economic war. On the contrary, the U.S. government continues to rely on an ad hoc process and a rudimentary policy apparatus. Compared with the way the Pentagon prepares for conventional war—including recruiting and training professional troops, devising plans, and rehearsing them repeatedly—the U.S. agencies responsible for economic war are still playing in the minor leagues.

To up its game, America should start by investing in people. Successful economic warfare requires an interdisciplinary toolkit: the legal acumen of an Adam Szubin, the diplomatic skill of a Dan Fried, the regional expertise of a Matt Pottinger, and the economic creativity of a Daleep Singh. It's hard for any one person to master all these areas, but the U.S. government should cultivate teams that do. Moreover, every member of these teams should possess enough fluency in each of the disciplines to understand their colleagues' perspectives.

A good way to do this is to create a permanent economic war council within the U.S. government. The council would consist of officials on temporary assignment from State, Treasury, Commerce, the CIA, and other relevant agencies, all of whom would serve for at least a year or two. Before joining, officials would go through a training program on economic warfare with coursework that covers all the bases. The council should also pull in talent from the private sector, creating a pipeline for industry experts to serve their country in high-impact tours of duty. Universities have a role to play, too. Academic programs in public policy and international relations should include required courses on economic warfare, which should be treated as a subject of equal importance to military affairs.

The council would fill a pressing need: planning for the economic wars of tomorrow. Typically, U.S. officials respond to a crisis by rushing to the Situation Room and cobbling together options for new sanctions. Government economists then forecast the impact under intense time pressure, which tends to lead to excessive caution. There's a reason the U.S. government *overestimated* the negative spillover effects of new economic weapons in every episode recounted in this book. The council could rectify this problem by developing ideas for new sanctions and vetting them thoroughly *before* crises start.

Sanctions are like antibiotics: they work well when used correctly but cause a host of problems when used excessively or inappropriately. In some cases, they're simply the wrong approach: when Washington seeks regime change—as the Trump administration did in Iran and Venezuela—it's a fool's errand to expect sanctions to get the job done. In other cases, sanctions have the potential to work, but only if they're administered in strong enough doses over a long enough period to avoid resistance. This is the problem both Obama and Biden faced in confronting Russia: they ratcheted up sanctions incrementally, giving Russia time to adapt and build up resistance along the way. As a result, neither president delivered a knockout blow to Russia's economy, which, at least in Biden's case, was the goal. Sometimes it's best to go big or go home.

Following that mantra would be easier if the United States were more resilient to the ripple effects of economic war. Investing in American industrial capacity and fortifying supply chains through "friendshoring" are crucial steps, but more is needed. Beyond the environmental benefits, reducing domestic oil consumption would insulate U.S. households and businesses from oil price shocks—putting the country on much firmer footing for future economic conflicts. America would have wider latitude to craft effective sanctions if White House officials were not constantly fixated on gasoline prices.

The United States should also explore novel uses for sanctions and export controls. Some of humanity's biggest challenges today, including climate change and the risk of unconstrained artificial intelligence, are transnational collective-action problems—not usually the province of economic warfare. But just as Washington can bar companies from dealing with Iran or Russia, it could bar them from participating in carbon-intensive energy projects anywhere in the world. Since those projects often require substantial financing and technology, such restrictions would have real bite. Sophisticated artificial intelligence, meanwhile, relies on hardware that largely comes from American firms. A single Silicon Valley–based company, Nvidia, designs more than 70 percent of the AI chips sold worldwide. To cajole foreign governments and businesses into embracing standards for the responsible use of AI, Washington could ban Nvidia and other U.S. tech firms from transacting with anyone that refuses to adopt these standards.

Such uses of the U.S. economic arsenal would not be as unorthodox as they seem. In truth, they would rely on the same logic as recent U.S. economic measures against China and Russia: to reverse or permanently scale back aspects of globalization that risk doing more harm than good in the long run. For much of the past three decades, China and Russia used their extensive economic ties with the United States to modernize their militaries and erect extensive surveillance states. U.S. officials went along with and often encouraged this process. Unfettered trade and investment were understood to be natural and ultimately benevolent, especially when American businesses were making money. Washington is now using economic weapons to change course, and it could do the same to check carbon-intensive megaprojects and dangerous applications of AI.

In addition to improving its own economic warfare capabilities, the United States should deepen its capacity to work alongside allies. The G7 has already declared its aspiration to become an economic security alliance. In the years ahead, Washington should invest in this vision by teaming up with like-minded democracies for regular sanctions-planning dialogues. Just as America would be well served by developing and vetting ideas for new economic weapons ahead of time, it would benefit from early alignment with allies so that diplomacy is not a bottleneck in moments of crisis. Diplomats shouldn't have to build international coalitions from scratch for each new economic offensive.

The biggest weakness in American economic statecraft today, however, is not a lack of sticks but rather a shortage of carrots. For every White House, a major temptation of sanctions and export controls is that U.S. law makes them easy to deploy: all the president needs to do is sign an executive order and—voilà!—they take effect. It's not so simple for large-scale foreign investments and international economic agreements, which tend to require backing from Congress. But imagine how much more effective U.S. policy could be if Washington had a big sovereign wealth fund, a strategic stockpile of critical minerals and other commodities extending beyond crude oil, or the leeway to direct capital abroad at the scale of China's Belt and Road Initiative. Unfortunately, political dysfunction has deprived the United States of economic assets that several other countries possess.

In the years to come, fighting and winning economic wars will only get harder, especially as China and other countries strengthen both their offensive capabilities and their defensive fortifications. The United States cannot afford to rest on its laurels. It must continuously improve its economic arsenal and make domestic investments that solidify its global lead in finance and technology, which, after all, are the foundation of American power.

=

Every age contains within it the seeds of its own destruction. The post–World War II system established at Bretton Woods was founded on the premise that restraining international finance through capital controls and fixed exchange rates was essential for economic recovery and political stability. For almost three decades, the system worked: from the rubble of war emerged a world economy more dynamic and productive than ever before. Countries torn apart under the stress of years of combat, dictatorship, and military occupation blossomed into prosperous welfare states. The French fondly remember this era as *les trente glorieuses*, or the glorious thirty. But the core features that once made Bretton Woods successful eventually caused friction. Fixed exchange rates, originally considered a guarantor of stability, became a source of distrust and resentment. Multinational corporations found ways to dodge capital controls, and their efforts gradually won backing from a few self-interested governments. When Bretton Woods met its demise in the early 1970s, it collapsed under the weight of its own design.

Unlike Bretton Woods, the era of economic globalization that surged to prominence in the 1990s and persisted well into the twenty-first century lacked a distinct founding moment. Yet it was nonetheless built on a foundational premise: that economic interdependence would make the world richer and more secure. For a while, it also worked: parts of the global economy that did not partake in *les trente glorieuses*—including China, the former Soviet bloc, and other developing countries—experienced their own economic miracles, while the United States and its industrialized peers enjoyed another season of prosperity.

Economic interdependence indeed made the world richer. But it never proved that it could make the world more secure. It's hard to remember now, in a time of war and rising geopolitical tensions, but the win-win logic of integrated markets and supply chains was once supposed to make conflict between states obsolete. To the extent interstate competition would persist, it would move into the realm of "soft power." The World Cup and the Eurovision Song Contest would replace the geopolitical machinations of old. LeBron James and Yao Ming would take the place of Kennedy and Khrushchev.

Missing from that optimistic narrative, however, was the recognition that hyperglobalization became possible only with the end of the Cold War. World-scale economic integration was a consequence of the end of the Cold War, not its cause. As the historian John Lewis Gaddis wrote, stark divisions between the U.S. and Soviet economies resulted in a relationship characterized by "mutual *in*dependence" rather than interdependence. What we have today is a world economy still built for the benign geopolitical environment of the 1990s as opposed to the more dangerous one that currently exists.

Globalization's triumphant march first slowed during the 2008 financial crisis and the ensuing political backlash across industrialized economies, which saw an explosion of populist anger over decades of worsening domestic inequality and the steady decline of manufacturing. But its retreat set in for good only after governments began viewing economic interdependence as a liability rather than an asset: because the economies of all the great powers were linked to one another, governments could exploit chokepoints to pressure rivals. In a world in which the specter of nuclear annihilation made a hot war between great powers almost unthinkable, globalization gave states a more viable way to fight. This was the context in which the United States built its economic arsenal—the context that birthed the Age of Economic Warfare.

We don't yet know when the Age of Economic Warfare will end, but we can envision how. The trade-offs facing policymakers in Washington, Beijing, Brussels, and Moscow can be thought of as an impossible trinity consisting of *economic interdependence, economic security,* and *geopolitical competition.* Any two of these can coexist but not all three.

During the Cold War, geopolitical competition reigned supreme. Each bloc enjoyed a degree of economic security because it renounced interdependence with the enemy. But when the Cold War ended, this calculus shifted. The West's triumph rendered the notion of geopolitical competition almost meaningless. With American military, economic, and cultural power at its apogee, what was there left to compete for? In those halcyon days, the United States viewed China and Russia more as budding friends than ominous rivals. America was thus free to embrace interdependence without losing its sense of economic security.

Today, another shift is looming. Russian imperialism and China's bid for world mastery have brought geopolitical competition back with a vengeance. Yet economic interdependence persists. The result is that none of the great powers—neither the United States, nor China, nor Europe, nor Russia—feels economically secure. Something has to give.

One way to restore a sense of security would be to rein in competition. But conflicting interests and pent-up grievances among today's great powers make this implausible. The more likely outcome is that economic interdependence will continue to unravel. Right now, in its relations with China, the United States is trying to exchange a little interdependence for a lot of security. That is a difficult trade to execute, and over time, attempts to scale back interdependence will probably grow more aggressive and comprehensive.

The Age of Economic Warfare will likely end when the chokepoints upon which it depends no longer squeeze so tight. It could happen a decade from now, or two, or even more than that. Today's chokepoints will be no easier to break than they were to build. Even as some fade over time, the emergence of new industries will create fresh chokepoints elsewhere. But eventually, the great powers will find ways to erode them to the point that they cease to pose an acute threat. The biggest question is whether this will happen gradually—through "friendshoring" and long-term investments in self-sufficiency—or suddenly, through the outbreak of a catastrophic great-power war in Taiwan or another hotspot.

Some will surely cheer the closing of the Age of Economic Warfare. And maybe, there will be reason for applause: If the great powers no longer fear one another's economic weapons, a new stability could take hold. The world will lose the efficiency and low prices enabled by economic interdependence, but it will gain a sense of security. Supply chains will return home, and employment opportunities will multiply. The world will be divided into economic blocs, yet it will be at peace.

There is also a bleaker scenario. Throughout most of history, great-power rivalry has been a stubborn fact of life. It will likely remain so even after today's economic weapons have lost their edge. Without the ability to channel geopolitical conflict into the economic arena, great powers could once again find themselves fighting on the actual battlefield. The dream of economic war, for all its downsides, is that it can be an *alternative* to a more violent kind of war. Someday, the Age of Economic Warfare will end, but we might miss it when it's gone.

Acknowledgments

This book is the product of decades of learning and experience. Over those years, I've been blessed with the support of family, friends, teachers, and colleagues. Collectively, they made this book possible.

My parents, Jill and Mark Fishman, have provided love and support beyond measure. My mom inspired me to follow my dreams, nurtured my curiosity, and instilled an appreciation for reading and writing. Her unconditional love has been a foundation of strength and her values an unfailing guide. My dad is my hero: the wisest, most dependable person I know. He taught me self-discipline and the importance of keeping my priorities straight. Both my parents imparted on me that relationships matter above all else. Any success I've had is as much a credit to them as it is to me.

My life has also been shaped by great teachers. At Gladwyne Elementary, Thelma Williams taught me to hold myself to a high standard in the classroom. At Welsh Valley Middle School, Janet Chung and Charlie Flaster showed me the joys of academic rigor. At Harriton High School, Paul Kinney stoked my interest in world affairs; Susan Gross, in foreign cultures; Brian Gauvin, in scientific inquiry; and Chris Santa Maria, in history. I'm thankful to all my wonderful teachers over twelve years of public school education.

My time at Yale laid the foundation for my subsequent work in foreign policy and as a writer. Donald Kagan was the best teacher I've ever had. Across four semesters of classes and a summer research fellowship, he taught me how to evaluate historical decisions and craft a sound argument. So much of this book bears his influence, starting with its adherence to chronology. John Gaddis, Charlie Hill, Paul Kennedy, and Walter Russell Mead—instructors in Studies in Grand Strategy and authors of exceptional books on international affairs—sharpened my writing and helped me bridge my historical studies with contemporary foreign policy. They also provided advice and support long after graduation. Adam Tooze sparked an interest in global economics and supervised my senior essay on British policy toward the newly unified Germany in the 1870s. He pushed me to expand my intellectual range. Joanne Freeman, Robert Greenberg, John Harris, Giuseppe Mazzotta, Sean McMeekin, Stephen Roach, Tim Snyder, Charles Walton, and the instructors in Directed Studies also had an enduring influence on my thinking.

At Cambridge, Brendan Simms expertly supervised my dissertation on U.S. foreign policy in the early 1990s—a project that was, to some extent, a precursor to this book. Amrita Narlikar deepened my understanding of international political economy. Her influence is evident in this book's early chapters on the rise and fall of Bretton Woods. At Stanford, Ed Batista, Rob Chess, Peter DeMarzo, David Dodson, Keith Hennessey, Josh Rauh, Condoleezza Rice, Amit Seru, Rob Siegel, Russ Siegelman, and their colleagues taught me a great deal not only about business and public affairs, but also about managing life and professional challenges.

My time in the U.S. government was formative. I'm grateful to David Cohen for giving me my first opportunity in public service at the Treasury Department, as well as Jen Fowler and Liz Rosenberg for helping me figure out how to navigate a federal agency. At the State Department, I drank from a firehose and had some of the most fulfilling years of my career. I'm grateful to Jon Finer, Dan Fried, Peter Harrell, John Hughes, Andrew Keller, David McKean, Siddharth Mohandas, and many others for trusting me and putting me in the position to make a difference. I'm also grateful to my colleagues at the Policy Planning Staff and the Office of Economic Sanctions Policy and Implementation for their friendship and collaboration on work worth doing. Brian O'Toole, Adam Smith, and others at OFAC were first-rate travel companions and helped me learn the nitty-gritty of how sanctions work. At the Pentagon, I was lucky to work alongside military officers and defense professionals who welcomed me with open arms, never mind that I was from the State Department. My colleagues at General Martin Dempsey's CAG will always hold a special place in my heart.

Outside of government, my colleagues at Via, *Foreign Affairs*, Zoox, CNAS, and the Atlantic Council helped me learn and grow in important ways. I'm particularly thankful to the people who've offered wisdom and support at important professional and life junctures, including Michèle Flournoy, Gideon Rose, Matt Olsen, Jeffrey Goldstein, Jon Foster, Cariann Chan, and Brad Hirschfield.

There is a long list of people without whom this book would literally not exist. Right at the top are Gail Ross, my incomparable agent, and Noah Schwartzberg, my editor at Portfolio. Both immediately grasped my vision for the project and provided incalculable support. Gail guided me through the byzantine process of pitching and selling a book proposal, and she helped me find the perfect partners in Noah and Adrian Zackheim at Portfolio. Noah has been more than an editor; he has been a coach, trusting me to execute my plan for the book, caring deeply about getting everything right, and providing guidance and encouragement at critical moments. Every author should be so lucky as to have an editor like Noah. Adrian's enthusiasm from the start gave me confidence as a first-time author. I'm also thankful to Niki Papadopoulos for her support for the project; Leila Sandlin for helping turn my manuscript into a real book; Carolyn Foley for conducting a careful legal review; Ryan Boyle for overseeing the production process; Ritsuko Okumura for working to bring the book to readers around the world; and Kirstin Berndt, Lindsay Prevette, Savana Bishop, Catherine Morrissette, Rachel Baldauf, and Taylor Williams for managing publicity and marketing. I am fortunate to be part of the Portfolio team.

The Center on Global Energy Policy at Columbia University provided the ideal intellectual environment to pursue a project of this scale. Jason Bordoff, CGEP's founding director, saw merit in the book back when it was just the germ of an idea and generously offered me an institutional home. He gave me the greatest gift someone can give to a person who's working on a book: the time and space to read, think, and write. Melissa Lott and Robert Johnston, CGEP's research directors, likewise put their confidence in me to bring this project to completion. My colleagues at CGEP, meanwhile, provided a sounding board whenever I needed it. I'm also grateful to Natalie Volk, CGEP's former associate director for communications, for aiding this project at its earliest stages.

Columbia's School of International and Public Affairs, where I've taught for the past several years, played a central role in this project: my class, Economic and Financial Statecraft, inspired the book, and the syllabus formed the initial outline. I'm grateful to Andrea Bubula and Richard Robb for sponsoring my course and recommending it to so many excellent students. The ideas and arguments in these pages bear the influence of all the dedicated students who've taken my class.

In addition to helping me organize my thoughts and sparking new ones, teaching at SIPA introduced me to several students who ultimately played hands-on roles in the creation of this book. Kevin Brunelli and Kiran Kaul, two of the best students in the first iteration of my class, joined the project as part-time research associates shortly after I started it. (Kevin also worked full time at CGEP after graduation, which involved helping me see this project to completion.) Without Kevin and Kiran's assistance, this book would be far from what it is. Kevin doggedly tracked down news reports, testimonies, speeches, and other primary sources. His sharp eye for detail, thorough understanding of politics and energy policy, and intellectual curiosity substantially improved the final product. Kiran's meticulous research and analytical skills were instrumental in helping me understand the economic impact of the sanctions described in this book. She scoured economic data and the financial press, and she served as a thought partner in making sense of it all. I feel tremendously lucky to have had Kevin and Kiran on my team—and we're all lucky that they both have now gone on to their own careers in public service.

Zach Krivine and Rachel Cifu joined the project as part-time research assistants in the final stages, and both made invaluable contributions. Zach gathered data for the charts, created mockups, and improved them over time. Rachel formatted and organized the endnotes, provided research support on the last few chapters, and helped assemble the Cast of Characters and the Glossary. Both Zach and Rachel read the entire manuscript and offered good suggestions.

I'm deeply grateful to the more than one hundred individuals whom I interviewed for this book. Many of them spent multiple hours sharing their recollections, confirming facts, and digging up evidence on my behalf. Their stories form the book's texture, and I'm thankful to them for trusting me to be a fair and accurate narrator. A partial list of interviewees, including only those who agreed to be mentioned, appears in A Note on Sources.

A handful of editors, fact checkers, and artists enriched this book in too many ways to count. I owe a great deal of gratitude to Victor Brechenmacher, a fellow former editor at *Foreign Affairs*, whose keen editorial judgment improved every page. He helped me trim extraneous details, streamline the narrative, and clarify my core arguments. He is one of the finest editors I've ever worked with. Usha Sahay, another brilliant editor, helped me polish the manuscript in a two-week sprint between important speechwriting jobs. She saved me from slip-ups and consistently pushed me to simplify. I'm grateful she took the time to work with me during a period she might otherwise have spent on vacation. Mark Hitz helped me think through Part One and offered valuable suggestions to tighten my prose. I'm thankful to Mark for ensuring the book gets off to a strong start. Katia Zoritch and Corinne Leong painstakingly checked every fact in this book, preventing numerous mistakes. I appreciate their thoroughness and professionalism. Henry Nuhn created a cover that is both striking and conceptually clever, and Alissa Theodor designed the book's beautiful interior layout. Jeff Ward drew the maps and charts (and tolerated my repeated requests for tweaks), and Edie Weinberg collected the photos. Both were a pleasure to work with. This is my first book, and when I started it, my biggest concern was that it would be a solitary process. The individuals named above made this project much more of a team effort—and much more fun—than I ever anticipated.

After I finished writing, a number of friends, colleagues, and family members generously read the entire manuscript. I'm grateful to Harrison Avart, Jason Bordoff, Sam Breidbart, Richard Danzig, Adam Deutsch, Mark Fishman, Krishna Jha, Chris Miller, Siddharth Mohandas, Stuart Reid, Edoardo Saravalle, and Adam Verhasselt for reading early drafts and providing feedback that significantly enhanced the final product. Ben Alter reviewed my book proposal and always answered my calls for input. Wes Mitchell shared valuable suggestions on the charts and the cover. Louise Knight and Al Song gave early encouragement to consider writing a book. Hannah Zornow Alter, Max Barbakow, Meryl Breidbart, Jay Dockendorf, Dani Isaacsohn, Lee Isaacsohn, Willie Kalema, Sam Kleiner, and Jordan Schneider provided tips on everything from the creative process and source materials to cover design and interior layout. Linda Kinstler, Lev Menand, Chris Miller, Aaron O'Connell, Stuart Reid, Tatiana Schlossberg, Alex Ward, and Ali Wyne—all of whom had either recently finished their own books or were in the process of writing them—offered useful advice at the outset of the project and helped me make key decisions. I'm especially grateful to Stuart, who initially encouraged me to write for a general audience and whose wise counsel I relied on repeatedly.

All these people made this book much better. Any shortcomings, of course, are my responsibility alone.

My friends have supported me unconditionally in all my endeavors, and this book was no exception. My friends from childhood, college, and graduate school are like family to me. They have been unfailingly loyal and stood by my side through ups and downs. I'm endlessly grateful to them for enriching my life in so many ways.

My grandparents set an example and left an indelible influence on my life. I would not be the person I am today without their love and hard work. I am thankful that my grandmother, Annabelle, and my grandmother-in-law, Gayatri, can share in celebrating the publication of this book. Their love and support mean the world to me.

My siblings, Samantha and Josh, and siblings-in-law, Rahul, Lissa, Steven, and Sydney, have always cheered me on. I love them more than they know. My in-laws, Bandana and Krishna Jha, have provided love, encouragement, and support for more than a decade. I'm so blessed to have them as a second set of parents.

I first started thinking about this book a couple months after the birth of my daughter, Ibha, and I finished it a few months after the birth of my son, Ayan. The two of them light up my life. I know of no greater joy than watching them grow, laugh, and learn. Whenever Ibha darted into the room when I was writing, I felt remarkably fortunate to be working on a project that allowed me to be so present in their lives. I love them both to the moon and back.

My deepest gratitude goes to my wife, Lepi—my partner in all things and the love of my life. As she has done time and again when I've presented her with new ideas, Lepi encouraged me to write this book and gave me the confidence that I could pull it off. She advised me through every single step of the process, fielding my requests for guidance on the most granular matters and suggesting dozens of incisive edits. She consistently stepped up during times when I was heads-down trying to meet a deadline. And she has steadfastly supported me through the vicissitudes of life: highs and lows, triumphs and setbacks. This book is dedicated to her.

A Note on Sources

Writing this book would not have been possible without the candid reflections of more than one hundred current and former U.S. officials, foreign officials, and business executives who agreed to be interviewed. Many of these individuals generously spoke to me for several hours over multiple conversations, and many devoted additional time to helping me confirm facts.

Owing to the sensitivities of internal policy discussions and diplomatic meetings, most of my interview subjects were comfortable sharing their unvarnished recollections only on a not-for-attribution basis. As a result, when using interviews to reconstruct events or reproduce dialogue, I do not attribute them to specific individuals. The only instances in which I cite my own interviews are when I directly quote an individual's on-the-record analysis or interpretation of past events.

The reader should not assume that any individual mentioned in this book was the primary source for the dialogue or scenes in which they appear. These reconstructions are based on a combination of sources, including accounts from advisors, colleagues, notetakers, and other eyewitnesses.

In the vast majority of cases, I was able to confirm the events described in this book with multiple sources. Whenever possible, I also corroborated details and timelines with documentary evidence that many of my sources dug up on my behalf: emails, text messages, personal calendars, passport stamps, and ticket receipts. I'm grateful to these individuals for their assistance in the service of accuracy and precision. Any material in this book that is not explicitly cited in the endnotes was drawn from my interviews and evidence provided by my sources.

I directly participated in some of the events described in this book, particularly those recounted in Parts Two and Three. I served at the Treasury Department in 2011 and at the State Department and Pentagon from 2013 to 2017. Since leaving government, I have regularly consulted with U.S. officials on sanctions policy. Without this experience and the relationships I built along the way, I could not have written this book. My personal experiences certainly contributed to my analysis, and they also helped me identify the right people to talk to and gauge whose version of events to trust. But I did not rely on my own memories as the sole source for any of the stories, dialogue, or facts that appear in these pages.

In addition to my interviews, I relied on a wealth of publicly available sources, including books, newspaper articles, speeches, testimonies, economic data, academic articles, and government documents and press releases, all of which are cited in the endnotes. I am grateful to the scholars, journalists, and other individuals who produced these materials. To avoid confusion, when quoting from these sources, I have taken the liberty of standardizing spellings (such as substituting "Kyiv" for "Kiev") and fixing typos.

This book is a first draft of history. Future scholars will no doubt add to its account and its conclusions, especially as further documentary evidence becomes available. My hope is that it inspires more people to try to make sense of the Age of Economic Warfare, which—despite the degree to which it has shaped the history of the past two decades—remains underexplored.

LIST OF INTERVIEWEES

The following individuals, along with others who preferred to remain anonymous, graciously granted me interviews and contributed invaluable insights: Bruce Andrews, Rich Ashooh, Chris Backemeyer, Esfandyar Batmanghelidj, Leonardo Bellodi, Alex Bick, Jonathan Black, Josh Black, John Bolton, Jason Bordoff, Matt Borman, Erik Britton, Jonathan Burke, Josh Cartin, Tarun Chhabra, Christy Clark, David Cohen, Earl Comstock, Adam Deutsch, Mark Dubowitz, Robert Einhorn, David Feith, Jon Finer, Eytan Fisch, Christopher Ford, Dan Fried, Andrea Gacki, Anthony Gardner, Danny Glaser, Richard Goldberg, Zach Goldman, Brad Gordon, Alexander Gray, Eric Green, Peter Harrell, Ben Harris, Meghan Harris, Doug Hengel, Henrik Hololei, John Hughes, Cordell Hull, Andrew Jensen, Avi Jorisch, Ivan Kanapathy, Sean Kane, Andrew Keller, Emily Kilcrease, Keith Krach, Thomas Krueger, Jörg Kukies, Charles Kupchan, Stuart Levey, Jack Lew, Robert Lighthizer, Eric Lorber,

Stephen Lovegrove, Rory MacFarquhar, Colin McGinnis, H. R. McMaster, Tim Morrison, David Mortlock, Nicholas Mulder, Richard Nephew, Tyler Nielsen, Nazak Nikakhtar, Victoria Nuland, Brian O'Toole, Peter Orszag, Carlos Pascual, Michael Pedroni, Matt Pottinger, Jason Prince, Elizabeth Rosenberg, Robert Rubin, Josh Rudolph, Vance Serchuk, Brad Setser, Radek Sikorski, Daniel Silverberg, Daleep Singh, Adam Smith, John Smith, Colleen Stack, James Steinberg, Josh Steinman, David Stilwell, Adam Szubin, David Tessler, Liza Tobin, Matt Turpin, Howie Wachtel, Clete Willems, Kevin Wolf, Catherine Wolfram, Tom Wyler, Juan Zarate, Josh Zoffer, and Matt Zweig.

Notes

INTRODUCTION: WIN WITHOUT FIGHTING

1 **Ships loaded grain:** Donald Kagan, *The Outbreak of the Peloponnesian War* (Ithaca: Cornell University Press, 1989), 179–80.

1 **came to an end:** Donald Kagan, *The Fall of the Athenian Empire* (Ithaca: Cornell University Press, 1987), 396–97.

1 **capital of the eastern branch:** Norman Stone, *Turkey: A Short History* (London: Thames & Hudson, 2017), 29–39.

3 **its new capital:** Stone, *Turkey*, 30–39.

3 **coveted the strait:** Ahmed Sükrü Esmer, "The Straits: Crux of World Politics," *Foreign Affairs*, January 1947, www.foreignaffairs.com/articles/turkey/1947-01-01/straits-crux-world-politics.

3 **maritime traffic jam:** Tom Wilson, "How the G7's Oil Price Cap Blocked the Bosphorus," *Financial Times*, December 6, 2022, www.ft.com/content/dc40a88f-7d20-4a17-a37c-332f35b65942; America Hernandez, Hanne Cokelaere, and Charlie Cooper, "Tanker Pile-up at the Exit of the Black Sea," *Politico*, December 7, 2022, www.politico.eu/article/tanker-pile-up-at-the-exit-of-the-black-sea.

3 **sharp bends and fierce currents:** Kareem Fahim and Zeynep Karatas, "A Devil's Current, a Hairpin Turn: Aboard a Tanker in the Risky Bosporus Strait," *The Washington Post*, January 9, 2022, www.washingtonpost.com/world/2022/01/09/bosporus-strait-canal-istanbul-erdogan; Lejla Villar and Mason Hamilton, "The Danish and Turkish Straits are Critical to Europe's Crude Oil and Petroleum Trade," U.S. Energy Information Administration, August 18, 2017, www.eia.gov/todayinenergy/detail.php?id=32552.

3 **were new regulations:** "Price Cap on Crude Oil of Russian Federation Origin," Office of Foreign Assets Control, U.S. Department of the Treasury, December 5, 2022, ofac.treasury.gov/media/929776/download?inline.

3 **institutions was next to impossible:** Robert Perkins, "Fuel for Thought: G7 Price Cap on Russian Oil Hangs on Asia's Ability to Squeeze Russia," S&P Global, September 13, 2022, www.spglobal.com/commodityinsights/en/market-insights/blogs/oil/091322-fft-g7-price-cap-russia-oil; Summer Said and Stephen Kalin, "Saudi Arabia Considers Accepting Yuan Instead of Dollars for Chinese Oil Sales," *The Wall Street Journal*, March 15, 2022, www.wsj.com/articles/saudi-arabia-considers-accepting-yuan-instead-of-dollars-for-chinese-oil-sales-11647351541.

4 **demanding extra proof:** Wilson, "Price Cap."

4 **paragraphs of regulatory jargon:** "Russian Harmful Foreign Activities Sanctions," Office of Foreign Assets Control, U.S. Department of the Treasury, December 5, 2022, ofac.treasury.gov/sanctions-programs-and-country-information/russian-harmful-foreign-activities-sanctions.

4 **This is economic warfare:** This book uses Thomas Schelling's definition of economic warfare: "economic means by which damage is imposed on other countries or the threat of damage used to bring pressure on them." I have used Schelling's term "economic warfare" instead of the related term "economic statecraft," coined by David Baldwin, because Baldwin's term includes both positive and negative instruments, whereas the focus of this book is on economic weapons, not economic inducements. See Thomas Schelling, *International Economics* (Ann Arbor: Allyn & Bacon, 1958), 487; David Baldwin, *Economic Statecraft* (Princeton: Princeton University Press, 2022), 28–50.

5 **In 1958, Thomas Schelling:** William Grimes, "Thomas C. Schelling, Master Theorist of Nuclear Strategy, Dies at 95," *The New York Times*, December 13, 2016, www.nytimes.com/2016/12/13/business/economy/thomas-schelling-dead-nobel-laureate.html.

5 **as "*economic* means":** Thomas Schelling, *International Economics*, 487.

5 **"governed by market forces":** Quoted in Adam Tooze, "Beyond the Crash," *The Guardian*, July 29, 2018, www.theguardian.com/commentisfree/2018/jul/29/city-of-london-desperate-gamble-china-vulnerable-economy.

5 **"global electronic infrastructure":** Walter B. Wriston, "Technology and Sovereignty," *Foreign Affairs*, Winter 1988–89, www.foreignaffairs.com/articles/1988-12-01/technology-and-sovereignty.

5 **top CEO on Wall Street:** Henry Farrell and Abraham Newman, *Underground Empire: How America Weaponized the World Economy* (New York: Henry Holt and Company, 2023), 17; Patricia Sullivan, "Walter B. Wriston, 85; Chairman of Citicorp," *The Washington Post*, January 21, 2005, www.washingtonpost.com/wp-dyn/articles/A25323-2005Jan20.html; "Walter Wriston," *The Wall Street Journal*, January 24, 2005, www.wsj.com/articles/SB110651946402433460.

6 **"As these alliances grow":** Walter Wriston, *The Twilight of Sovereignty: How the Information Revolution is Transforming Our World* (New York: Charles Scribner's Sons, 1992), 11.

6 **beyond the reach of traditional state institutions:** See Quinn Slobodian, *Globalists: The End of Empire and the Birth of Neoliberalism* (Cambridge: Harvard University Press, 2018), for an account of how globalization came to be seen as a force that was impervious to politics.

6 **centralized financial network:** Farrell and Newman, *Underground Empire*, 20. As the authors write, "The irony was that [Wriston] and other business leaders were centralizers by their nature: they sought to dominate markets, so that other businesses would have to use their systems and pay tribute to them. They built world-spanning networks that centered on a few key choke points."

6 **And these chokepoints:** Henry Farrell and Abraham L. Newman, "Weaponized Interdependence: How Global Economic Networks Shape State Coercion," *International Security* 44, no. 1 (2019), 42–79, direct.mit.edu/isec/article/44/1/42/12237/Weaponized-Interdependence-How-Global-Economic. Farrell and Newman use the term "chokepoint effect" to refer to situations in which states "limit or penalize [the] use of hubs" such as the SWIFT payment system as a means of coercion.

7 **"subdue the enemy without fighting":** Sun Tzu, *The Art of War*, trans. Samuel B. Griffith (New York: Oxford University Press, 1963), 3.3, p. 77.

7 **one-fifth of the world's oil supply:** Samuel Granados, "Tensions Rise in the World's Most Strategic Oil Chokepoint," Reuters, July 19, 2019, www.reuters.com/graphics/MIDEAST-ATTACKS-HORMUZ/0100B0B50N3/index.html.

8 **the "swing states":** Daniel M. Kliman and Richard Fontaine, "Global Swing States: Brazil, India, Indonesia, Turkey and the Future of International Order," German Marshall Fund, November 1, 2012, www.gmfus.org/news/global-swing-states-brazil-india-indonesia-turkey-and-future-international-order; Jared Cohen, "The Rise of Geopolitical Swing States," Goldman Sachs, May 15, 2023, www.goldmansachs.com/intelligence/pages/the-rise-of-geopolitical-swing-states.html.

8 **warned that the "overuse of sanctions":** Jacob J. Lew, "The Evolution of Sanctions and Lessons for the Future" (speech, Washington, D.C., March 30, 2016), Carnegie Endowment for International Peace, carnegieendowment.org/events/2016/03/us-treasury-secretary-jacob-j-lew-on-the-evolution-of-sanctions-and-lessons-for-the-future.

CHAPTER 1: THE OLD WAY

13 **The Megarian Decree barred:** Donald Kagan, *The Outbreak of the Peloponnesian War* (Ithaca: Cornell University Press, 1989), 251–72, provides the best available account and analysis of the Megarian Decree.

13 **Megarians "slowly starving":** Quoted in Kagan, *Peloponnesian War*, 255.

13 **Historians disagree about Pericles's intentions:** David Baldwin, *Economic Statecraft* (Princeton: Princeton University Press, 2022), 155–59.

13 **making an example:** Kagan, *Peloponnesian War*, 265–66.

13 **"demonstration of what sea power really meant":** Alfred Zimmern, *The Greek Commonwealth*, 4th ed. (Oxford: Clarendon Press, 1924), 426.

14 **accelerated the descent:** Kagan, *Peloponnesian War*, 269.

14 **known as the Continental System:** Bruce W. Jentleson, *Sanctions: What Everyone Needs to Know* (New York: Oxford University Press, 2022), 47–50.

14 **"To keep the English away":** Quoted in Eli F. Heckscher, *The Continental System: An Economic Interpretation* (Oxford: Clarendon Press, 1922), 367.

14 **fateful decision to invade Russia:** Jentleson, *Sanctions*, 50.

15 **"something more tremendous than war":** Quoted in Nicholas Mulder, *The Economic Weapon: The Rise of Sanctions as a Tool of Modern War* (New Haven: Yale University Press, 2022), 1. Mulder's book provides a comprehensive history of the dream and reality of sanctions as a peacekeeping tool during the interwar period.

15 **"economic, peaceful, silent, deadly remedy":** Woodrow Wilson, "Address at the Coliseum at the State Fair

Grounds in Indianapolis, Indiana" (speech, September 4, 1919), The American Presidency Project, www
.presidency.ucsb.edu/documents/address-the-coliseum-the-state-fair-grounds-indianapolis-indiana.

15 **Congress voted down America's entry:** Henry Cabot Lodge, *The Senate and the League of Nations* (New York: Charles Scribner's Sons, 1925); "Senate Rejects the Treaty of Versailles," United States Senate, November 19, 1919, www.senate.gov/about/powers-procedures/treaties/senate-rejects-treaty-of-versailles .htm.

15 **promptly lifted sanctions:** Jentleson, *Sanctions*, 50–54.

15 **well beyond Ethiopia:** Mulder, *Economic Weapon*, 202–258.

15–16 **emboldened Adolf Hitler:** Baldwin, *Economic Statecraft*, 162–63; Mulder, *Economic Weapon*, 222; for a prominent critique of the League of Nations, see Edward Hallett Carr, *The Twenty Years' Crisis, 1919–1939*, reissued with a new preface by Michael Cox (London: Palgrave Macmillan, 2016).

16 **an invasion of Kuwait:** Michael Wines, "Hints of Hussein's Strategy in an Iraqi Map," *The New York Times*, October 24, 1990, www.nytimes.com/1990/10/24/world/mideast-tensions-hints-of-hussein-s -strategy-in-an-iraqi-map.html.

16 **a "blatant violation":** David Remnick, "Gorbachev Cautious about Gulf," *The Washington Post*, August 18, 1990, www.washingtonpost.com/archive/politics/1990/08/18/gorbachev-cautious-about-gulf /d6e479a7-ae5a-42fd-8de4-02699aec1e58.

16 **banning all trade with Iraq:** UN Security Council, Resolution 661, August 6, 1990, S/RES/661, digitallibrary.un.org/record/94221.

16 **condition for lifting sanctions:** UN Security Council, Resolution 661.

17 **implemented the policy by force:** Patrick E. Tyler and Al Kamen, "American Blockade Is Criticized at U.N.," *The Washington Post*, August 14, 1990, www.washingtonpost.com/archive/politics/1990/08/14 /american-blockade-is-criticized-at-un/ed8e8999-3b0b-44ce-8505-09ceb084578f.

17 **60 percent of its GDP:** Jentleson, *Sanctions*, 177–78.

17 **"performs as envisioned":** George H. W. Bush, "Address Before a Joint Session of the Congress on the Persian Gulf Crisis and the Federal Budget Deficit" (speech, Washington, D.C., September 11, 1990), George H. W. Bush Presidential Library and Museum, bush41library.tamu.edu/archives/public -papers/2217.

17 **took just 100 hours:** "Operation Desert Storm," U.S. Army Center of Military History, January 2021, history.army.mil/html/bookshelves/resmat/desert-storm/index.html.

17 **Until inspectors could verify:** UN Security Council, Resolution 687, April 3, 1991, S/RES/687, digitallibrary.un.org/record/110709.

17 **continuous deployment of naval forces:** Robert J. Schneller Jr., *Anchor of Resolve: A History of U.S. Naval Forces Central Command/Fifth Fleet* (Washington: Naval Historical Center, 2007), 63–69.

17 **The Oil-for-Food program:** UN Security Council, Resolution 986, April 14, 1995, S/RES/986, digitallibrary.un.org/record/176622.

17 **sending out oil samples for laboratory testing:** Schneller Jr., *Anchor of Resolve*, 66.

18 **Swashbuckling oil traders:** Javier Blas and Jack Farchy, *The World for Sale: Money, Power, and the Traders Who Barter the Earth's Resources* (New York: Oxford University Press, 2021), 222–32. The authors describe in detail how commodities traders viewed the Oil-for-Food program and other sanctions regimes as arbitrage opportunities.

18 **Saddam demanded kickbacks:** Sharon Otterman, "Iraq: Oil for Food Scandal," Council on Foreign Relations, October 28, 2005, www.cfr.org/backgrounder/iraq-oil-food-scandal.

18 **$11 billion from oil smuggling:** Otterman, "Oil for Food Scandal."

18 **Hunger and infant mortality:** John Mueller and Karl Mueller, "Sanctions of Mass Destruction," *Foreign Affairs*, May/June 1999, www.foreignaffairs.com/articles/iraq/1999-05-01/sanctions-mass-destruction; Schneller Jr., *Anchor of Resolve*, 65.

18 **embargo was universally reviled:** George A. Lopez and David Cortright, "Containing Iraq: Sanctions Worked," *Foreign Affairs*, July 1, 2004, www.foreignaffairs.com/articles/iraq/2004-07-01/containing -iraq-sanctions-worked.

18 **disastrous decision to invade Iraq:** On January 30, 2001, during a discussion about Iraq policy at the very first meeting of George W. Bush's National Security Council, Secretary of Defense Donald Rumsfeld asked rhetorically, "Why are we even bothering with sanctions?" See Peter Baker, *Days of Fire: Bush and Cheney in the White House* (New York: Knopf Doubleday Publishing Group, 2013), 91.

18 **embargo achieved its main objective:** Lopez and Cortright, "Containing Iraq."

18 **"succeeded in disarming Iraq":** Hans Blix, *Disarming Iraq* (New York: Pantheon Books, 2004), 259.

18 **$1 billion per year:** Mueller and Mueller, "Sanctions of Mass Destruction."

CHAPTER 2: INVISIBLE INFRASTRUCTURE

20 **an "invisible hand":** Adam Smith, *The Wealth of Nations* (New York: Modern Library, 2000), 485.

20 **60 percent of all foreign exchange reserves:** "Currency Composition of Official Foreign Exchange Reserves," International Monetary Fund, June 2023, data.imf.org/?sk=e6a5f467-c14b-4aa8-9f6d -5a09ec4e62a4.

20 **boast market capitalizations:** "Largest Stock Exchange Operators Worldwide as of September 2023, by Market Capitalization of Listed Companies (in Trillion U.S. Dollars)," chart, Statista, accessed October 15, 2023, www.statista.com/statistics/270126/largest-stock-exchange-operators-by-market-capitalization-of-listed-companies.

20 **Valued at over $50 trillion:** "Summary of Debt Securities Outstanding," table, Data Portal, Bank for International Settlements, April 2023, https://data.bis.org/topics/DSS/tables-and-dashboards/BIS,SEC_C1,1.0; Dorothy Neufeld, "Ranked: The Largest Bond Markets in the World," *Visual Capitalist*, April 12, 2023, www.visualcapitalist.com/ranked-the-largest-bond-markets-in-the-world.

21 **70 percent of foreign-currency debt:** Carol Bertaut, Bastian von Beschwitz, and Stephanie Curcuru, "The International Role of the U.S. Dollar: Post-COVID Edition," Board of Governors of the Federal Reserve System, June 23, 2023, www.federalreserve.gov/econres/notes/feds-notes/the-international-role-of-the-us-dollar-post-covid-edition-20230623.html.

21 **90 percent of foreign exchange transactions:** Bafundi Maronoti, "Revisiting the International Role of the US Dollar," Bank for International Settlements, *Quarterly Review*, December 2022, www.bis.org/publ/qtrpdf/r_qt2212x.htm.

21 **most common currency pairings:** In 2022, the lone exception in the top ten most common currency pairings was number ten on the list, the euro and the British pound. "Triennial Central Bank Survey: OTC Foreign Exchange Turnover in April 2022," Monetary and Economic Department, Bank of International Settlements, October 27, 2022, www.bis.org/statistics/rpfx22_fx.pdf.

22 **huge penalties for violating U.S. sanctions:** Pierre-Hugues Verdier, *Global Banks on Trial: U.S. Prosecutions and the Remaking of International Finance* (New York: Oxford University Press, 2020), 109–46.

22 **conscripting firms outside the financial sector:** David J. Lynch, Simon Denyer, and Heather Long, "U.S. Reaches Deal with China's ZTE That Includes $1 Billion Fine, Commerce Secretary Says," *The Washington Post*, June 7, 2018, www.washingtonpost.com/business/economy/us-reaches-deal-with-chinas-zte-that-includes-1-billion-fine-commerce-secretary-says/2018/06/07/ccffa4b0-6a52-11e8-9e38-24e693b38637_story.html; "OFAC Cites the Use of U.S.-Origin Software and U.S. Network Infrastructure in Reaching a Nearly $8 Million Settlement with a Swiss Commercial Aviation Services Company," Paul, Weiss, Rifkind, Wharton & Garrison, March 16, 2020, www.paulweiss.com/practices/litigation/economic-sanctions-aml/publications/ofac-cites-the-use-of-us-origin-software-and-us-network-infrastructure?id=30879; Paul Mozur and Cecilia Kang, "U.S. Fines ZTE of China $1.19 Billion for Breaching Sanctions," *The New York Times*, March 7, 2017, www.nytimes.com/2017/03/07/technology/zte-china-fine.html.

CHAPTER 3: FINANCE UNCHAINED

24 **a French warship:** Benn Steil, *The Battle of Bretton Woods: John Maynard Keynes, Harry Dexter White, and the Making of a New World Order* (Princeton: Princeton University Press, 2013), 337; Helen Thompson, *Disorder: Hard Times in the 21st Century* (Oxford: Oxford University Press, 2022), 108; Michael J. Graetz and Olivia Briffault, "A 'Barbarous Relic': The French, Gold, and the Demise of Bretton Woods," in *The Bretton Woods Agreements, Together with Scholarly Commentaries and Essential Historical Documents*, Naomi Lamoreaux and Ian Shapiro (eds.), Yale University Press, 2019; Yale Law & Economics Research Paper No. 558; Columbia Law & Economics Working Paper No. 560, August 19, 2016, Scholarship Archive, Columbia Law School, scholarship.law.columbia.edu/cgi/viewcontent.cgi?article=3545&context=faculty_scholarship.

24 **backstop all British holdings:** Graetz and Briffault, "A 'Barbarous Relic.'"

25 **unraveling of the gold standard:** International Monetary Fund, "Conflict and Cooperation (1871–1944)," in "Money Matters: An IMF Exhibit—The Importance of Global Cooperation," www.imf.org/external/np/exr/center/mm/eng/mm_cc_01.htm.

25 **heart of Bretton Woods:** "The IMF and Bretton Woods Conference," UK Government National Web Archive, webarchive.nationalarchives.gov.uk/ukgwa/20091003173312/http://nationalarchives.gov.uk/cabinetpapers/themes/bretton-woods-conference.htm.

25 **walling off a key route through which financial instability had spread:** Barry Eichengreen, *Globalizing Capital: A History of the International Monetary System*, 3rd ed. (Princeton: Princeton University Press, 2019), 41–85.

25 **a principal architect of Bretton Woods:** An article in the quarterly journal of the International Monetary Fund called John Maynard Keynes and Harry Dexter White the two "founding fathers of the Bretton Woods institutions." See James M. Boughton, "Harry Dexter White and the International Monetary Fund," *Finance & Development*, September 1998, vol. 35, no. 3, www.imf.org/external/pubs/ft/fandd/1998/09/boughton.htm.

25 **barriers to cross-border capital movements:** Niall Ferguson, *The Ascent of Money: A Financial History of the World* (New York: The Penguin Press, 2008), 280–81.

26 **"right to control all capital movements":** Quoted in Eric Helleiner, *States and the Reemergence of Global Finance: From Bretton Woods to the 1990s* (Ithaca: Cornell University Press, 1994), 25.

26 **"drive the usurious moneylenders":** Quoted in James M. Boughton and K. Sarwar Lateef, *Fifty Years After Bretton Woods: The Future of the IMF and the World Bank* (Washington: International Monetary Fund, 1995), 66.

26 **Charles de Gaulle:** Graetz and Briffault, "A 'Barbarous Relic'"; "Money: De Gaulle v. the Dollar," *Time*, February 12, 1965, content.time.com/time/subscriber/article/0,33009,840572,00.html.

26 **America's "exorbitant privilege":** Barry Eichengreen, *Exorbitant Privilege: The Rise and Fall of the Dollar* (Oxford: Oxford University Press, 2011), 4.

26 **the so-called Eurodollar market:** Milton Friedman, "The Euro-Dollar Market: Some First Principles," *Morgan Guaranty Survey*, Morgan Guaranty Trust Company, October 1969, www.chicagobooth.edu /~/media/44CEE6C8A25B4FF2A48925163DAA2F85.pdf.

26 **preserve the City of London's role:** Helleiner, *Reemergence of Global Finance*, 14, 84.

26 **appeal of dollar holdings:** Helleiner, *Reemergence of Global Finance*, 90.

26 **foreigners to finance American deficits:** Edwin L. Dale Jr., "What Vietnam Did to the American Economy," *The New York Times*, January 28, 1973, www.nytimes.com/1973/01/28/archives/what-vietnam -did-to-the-american-economy-worsening-payments-deficit.html; "Foreign Relations of the United States, 1969–1976, Volume III, Foreign Economic Policy, International Monetary Policy, 1969–1972," document 76, eds. Daniel J. Lawler and Erin R. Mahan (Washington: Washington National Records Center, U.S. Department of the Treasury, Office of International Monetary Affairs, 1971), history.state .gov/historicaldocuments/frus1969-76v03/d76; Thompson, *Disorder*, 104.

27 **"game was indeed over":** Paul A. Volcker and Toyoo Gyohten, *Changing Fortunes: The World's Money and the Threat to American Leadership* (New York: Times Books, 1992), 77.

27 **"all-out war on the American dollar":** Richard Nixon, "Address to the Nation Outlining a New Economic Policy: 'The Challenge of Peace'" (speech, August 15, 1971), The American Presidency Project, www.presidency.ucsb.edu/node/240602; Jeffrey Garten, *Three Days at Camp David: How a Secret Meeting in 1971 Transformed the Global Economy* (New York: HarperCollins, 2021), 227.

27 **share of global GDP:** Govind Bhutada, "The U.S. Share of the Global Economy over Time," *Visual Capitalist*, January 14, 2021, www.visualcapitalist.com/u-s-share-of-global-economy-over-time; Mike Patton, "U.S. Role in Global Economy Declines Nearly 50%," *Forbes*, February 29, 2016, www.forbes .com/sites/mikepatton/2016/02/29/u-s-role-in-global-economy-declines-nearly-50/?sh=74d9e7405e9e.

CHAPTER 4: THE DEAL IN THE DESERT

28 **dollar to plunge:** David E. Spiro, *The Hidden Hand of American Hegemony: Petrodollar Recycling and International Markets* (Ithaca: Cornell University Press, 1999), 23.

28 **heavy spending on the Vietnam War:** Art Pine, "War in Vietnam Started 13-Year Spiral of Prices," *The Washington Post*, October 25, 1978, www.washingtonpost.com/archive/politics/1978/10/25/war -in-vietnam-started-13-year-spiral-of-prices/eb322c1f-d1a2-4e40-bfbd-bccae51a9efc; Jeffrey Garten, *Three Days at Camp David: How a Secret Meeting in 1971 Transformed the Global Economy* (New York: HarperCollins, 2021), 23–24.

28 **Inflation soared to heights:** Cecilia Rouse, Jeffery Zhang, and Ernie Tedeschi, "Historical Parallels to Today's Inflationary Episode," Council of Economic Advisers, White House, July 6, 2021, www .whitehouse.gov/cea/written-materials/2021/07/06/historical-parallels-to-todays-inflationary -episode; Phil Gramm and Mike Solon, "Lessons from the Great Inflation of 1973–81," *The Wall Street Journal*, August 2, 2022, www.wsj.com/articles/lessons-from-the-great-inflation-of-1973-81-volcker -reagan-guns-and-butter-bracket-creep-tax-revenue-spending-monetary-policy-11659448515.

28 **declining as an energy superpower:** Daniel Yergin, "The 1973 Energy Crisis: The Oil Embargo and the New Age of Energy" (speech, New York, October 11, 2023), School of International and Public Affairs, Columbia University, www.energypolicy.columbia.edu/events/the-1973-energy-crisis-the-oil-embargo -and-the-new-age-of-energy.

28 **peaked in 1970:** Helen Thompson, *Disorder: Hard Times in the 21st Century* (Oxford: Oxford University Press, 2022), 52.

28 **dependent on oil imports:** Daniel Yergin, *The Prize: The Epic Quest for Oil, Money & Power* (New York: Free Press, 2008), 570–71.

28 **imposed an oil embargo:** Michael Corbett, "Oil Shock of 1973–74," Federal Reserve History, Federal Reserve Bank of Boston, November 22, 2013, www.federalreservehistory.org/essays/oil-shock-of -1973-74.

28 **10 percent of worldwide production:** Yergin, *The Prize*, 596.

28 **"a vicious cycle":** "Excerpts from the Opening Address by Secretary Kissinger at the International Oil Meeting in Washington," *The New York Times*, February 12, 1974, www.nytimes.com/1974/02/12/archives /excerpts-from-the-opening-address-by-secretary-kissinger-at-the.html.

29 **"right of Genghis Khan":** Quoted in Eric Helleiner, *States and the Reemergence of Global Finance: From Bretton Woods to the 1990s* (Ithaca: Cornell University Press, 1994), 115.

29 **career as a bond trader:** Gary Gerstle, *The Rise and Fall of the Neoliberal Order* (New York: Oxford University Press, 2022), 111–12.

29 **factories over motorists:** Richard W. Stevenson, "William E. Simon, Ex-Treasury Secretary and High-Profile Investor, Is Dead at 72," *The New York Times*, June 5, 2000, www.nytimes.com/2000/06/05/us/william-e-simon-ex-treasury-secretary-and-high-profile-investor-is-dead-at-72.html.

29 **"the guy that caused the lines":** Stevenson, "William E. Simon."

29 **surged by 40 percent:** Yergin, *The Prize*, 598–99.

29 **oil prices did not fall:** Corbett, "Oil Shock of 1973–74."

29 **increase of more than 2,000 percent:** Spiro, *Hidden Hand*, 1.

29 **boarded a plane:** Andrea Wong, "The Untold Story Behind Saudi Arabia's 41-Year U.S. Debt Secret," *Bloomberg*, May 30, 2016, www.bloomberg.com/news/features/2016-05-30/the-untold-story-behind-saudi-arabia-s-41-year-u-s-debt-secret.

29 **he was noticeably drunk:** Spiro, *Hidden Hand*, ix.

29 **desert kingdom with a deal:** Spiro, *Hidden Hand*, 107–9; Andrea Wong, "Untold Story."

30 **fresh deal with Riyadh:** Spiro, *Hidden Hand*, 105, 121–24.

CHAPTER 5: OUR CURRENCY, YOUR PROBLEM

31 **power of the free market:** William E. Simon, *A Time for Truth*: (McGraw-Hill: Reader's Digest Press, 1978). See David Harvey, *A Brief History of Neoliberalism* (New York: Oxford University Press, 2005) and Gary Gerstle, *The Rise and Fall of the Neoliberal Order* (New York: Oxford University Press, 2022) for accounts of neoliberalism and its impact on America and the world.

31 **destroy official files:** Eric Helleiner, *States and the Reemergence of Global Finance: From Bretton Woods to the 1990s* (Ithaca: Cornell University Press, 1994), 150.

31 **deregulated vast parts:** Paul Krugman, "Reagan Did It," *The New York Times*, May 31, 2009, www.nytimes.com/2009/06/01/opinion/01krugman.html; Helleiner, *Reemergence of Global Finance*, 147.

32 **"Government cannot solve our problems":** Jimmy Carter, "The State of the Union Address" (speech, January 19, 1978), The American Presidency Project, www.presidency.ucsb.edu/documents/the-state-the-union-address-delivered-before-joint-session-the-congress-1; Gerstle, *Neoliberal Order*, 67.

32 **earthquake struck: the end of the Cold War:** For more on the consequences of the fact that the Cold War ended when neoliberalism was ascendant, see Edward Fishman, "The Death and Rebirth of American Internationalism," *Boston Review*, August 12, 2020, www.bostonreview.net/articles/death-rebirth-american-internationalism/.

32 **"his ideas validated":** George H. W. Bush, "Remarks on Presenting the Presidential Medal of Freedom Awards" (speech, Washington, D.C., November 18, 1991), George H. W. Bush Presidential Library & Museum, bush41library.tamu.edu/archives/public-papers/3642.

32 **turning "globalization" from an abstract concept:** Paul James and Manfred B. Steger, "A Genealogy of 'Globalization': The Career of a Concept," *Globalizations* 11, no. 4 (2014): 417–34, www.tandfonline.com/doi/full/10.1080/14747731.2014.951186.

32 **preached the "Washington Consensus":** Michael Kimmage, *The Abandonment of the West: The History of an Idea in American Foreign Policy* (New York: Basic Books, 2020), 254–58; Gerstle, *Neoliberal Order*, 145, 156, 177.

32 **"all Friedmanites now":** Lawrence Summers, "A Fond Farewell: Milton Friedman," *Time*, December 25, 2006, content.time.com/time/specials/packages/article/0,28804,2019341_2017103_2016956,00.html.

32 **more globalized than ever:** Helen Thompson, *Disorder: Hard Times in the 21st Century* (Oxford: Oxford University Press, 2022), 131.

32 **repealed the Glass-Steagall Act:** Gerstle, *Neoliberal Order*, 173–76.

32 **stretched into a second decade:** Richard W. Stevenson, "Greenspan Named to a Fourth Term as Fed Chairman," *The New York Times*, January 5, 2000, www.nytimes.com/2000/01/05/business/greenspan-named-to-a-fourth-term-as-fed-chairman.html.

33 **finance, including CHIPS:** "About CHIPS," The Clearing House, www.theclearinghouse.org/payment-systems/chips.

33 **a lingua franca:** Henry Farrell and Abraham Newman, *Underground Empire: How America Weaponized the World Economy* (New York: Henry Holt and Company, 2023), 26–28.

33 **of the standardized shipping container:** Marc Levinson, *The Box: How the Shipping Container Made the World Smaller and the World Economy Bigger* (Princeton: Princeton University Press, 2006), 355–56.

33 **world's largest single market:** "From 6 to 27 Members," European Commission, February 1, 2020, neighbourhood-enlargement.ec.europa.eu/enlargement-policy/6-27-members_en; "Towards Open and Fair World-wide Trade," European Union, european-union.europa.eu/priorities-and-actions/actions-topic/trade_en.

33 **powered the digital revolution:** Chris Miller, *Chip War: The Fight for the World's Most Critical Technology* (New York: Scribner, 2022).

33 **a trillion dollars' worth of U.S. debt:** "Major Foreign Holders of U.S. Treasury Securities," U.S. Department of the Treasury, ticdata.treasury.gov/resource-center/data-chart-center/tic/Documents/mfhhis01.txt. The accumulation of U.S. government debt during the late 1990s and early 2000s was not just a Chinese phenomenon. Following the Asian financial crisis of 1997, governments across the

world began hoarding dollar-denominated assets to insulate themselves from similar currency crises. As Klein and Pettis point out, in 1997, governments owned $970 billion in dollar-denominated reserve assets; by 2008, that number had grown to more than $5 trillion. See Matthew C. Klein and Michael Pettis, *Trade Wars Are Class Wars: How Rising Inequality Distorts the Global Economy and Threatens International Peace* (New Haven: Yale University Press, 2020), 199–200.

33 **the ascent of "Chimerica":** Niall Ferguson, *The Ascent of Money: A Financial History of the World* (New York: The Penguin Press, 2008), 304–12; David Barboza, "China's Treasury Holdings Make U.S. Woes Its Own," *The New York Times*, July 18, 2011, www.nytimes.com/2011/07/19/business/china-largest-holder-of-us-debt-remains-tied-to-treasuries.html.

33 **$1 trillion *per day*:** Helleiner, *Reemergence of Global Finance*, 1.

33 **foreign exchange trading eclipses:** Bafundi Maronoti, "Revisiting the International Role of the US Dollar," Bank for International Settlements, *Quarterly Review*, December 5, 2022, www.bis.org/publ/qtrpdf/r_qt2212x.htm; "Global Trade Set to Hit Record $32 Trillion in 2022, but Outlook Increasingly Gloomy for 2023," United Nations Conference on Trade and Development, December 13, 2022, unctad.org/news/global-trade-set-hit-record-32-trillion-2022-outlook-increasingly-gloomy-2023; Bank of International Settlements, "Triennial Central Bank Survey: OTC Foreign Exchange Turnover in April 2022," October 27, 2022, www.bis.org/statistics/rpfx22_fx.pdf; "Global Trade Outlook and Statistics," World Trade Organization, April 5, 2023, www.wto.org/english/res_e/booksp_e/trade_outlook23_e.pdf.

34 **"dollar is our currency, but it's your problem":** Kevin Hebner, "The Dollar Is Our Currency, but It's Your Problem," *Investments and Pensions Europe*, October 2007, www.ipe.com/the-dollar-is-our-currency-but-its-your-problem/25599.article#:~:text=At%20the%20G%2D10%20Rome,20%25%20depreciation%20of%20the%20dollar.

34 **Robert Rubin, the powerful:** As treasury secretary, Robert Rubin prioritized keeping the dollar strong and often repeated the mantra "A strong dollar is in the U.S. interest." Paul Blustein, "Rubin Signals Shift to Curb Dollar's Rise," February 8, 1997, www.washingtonpost.com/wp-srv/politics/govt/admin/stories/rubin020897.htm; Saleha Mohsin, *Paper Soldiers: How the Weaponization of the Dollar Changed the World Order* (New York: Portfolio/Penguin, 2024), 38–55.

34 **"undermine the role of the dollar":** Author interview with Robert Rubin, 2024.

35 **"Once you do it once":** Author interview with Robert Rubin, 2024.

35 **Clinton's weapons of choice:** Derek H. Chollet and James Goldgeier, *America Between the Wars: From 11/9 to 9/11* (New York: PublicAffairs, 2008), 73; John Hillen and Michael P. Noonan, "The Coming Transformation of the U.S. Military?" *Foreign Policy Research Institute*, February 4, 2002, www.fpri.org/article/2002/02/the-coming-transformation-of-the-u-s-military.

CHAPTER 6: "GUERRILLAS IN GRAY SUITS"

36 **"read into the threat stream":** Author interview with Stuart Levey, 2023.

37 **deadliest foreign attack:** "9/11 in Pennsylvania," Pentagon Memorial Fund, 2021, pentagonmemorial.org/events-of-9-11/9-11-in-pennsylvania; Alfred Goldberg, "9/11 Attack," Historical Office, Department of Defense, history.defense.gov/DOD-History/Pentagon/9-11-Attack.

37 **"bloodlust of the American people":** Peter Baker, *Days of Fire: Bush and Cheney in the White House* (New York: Knopf Doubleday Publishing Group, 2013), 134.

37 **"holiday from history":** George F. Will, "The End of Our Holiday from History," *The Washington Post*, September 12, 2001, www.washingtonpost.com/archive/opinions/2001/09/12/the-end-of-our-holiday-from-history/9da607fd-8fdc-4f33-b7c9-e6cda00453bb.

37 **prepared to use force:** See Andrew J. Bacevich, *The New American Militarism: How Americans Are Seduced by War*, 2nd ed. (New York: Oxford University Press, 2013).

37 **eviscerating an Iraqi army:** "Iraq and the World's Biggest Armies," *Los Angeles Times*, March 6, 1991, www.latimes.com/archives/la-xpm-1991-03-06-mn-359-story.html; "Operation Desert Storm," U.S. Army Center of Military History.

37 **two weeks of air raids:** James T. Patterson, *Restless Giant: The United States from Watergate to Bush v. Gore* (New York: Oxford University Press, 2005), 370–71; Robert C. Owen, *Deliberate Force: A Case Study in Effective Air Campaigning* (Montgomery: Air University Press, 2000).

38 **seventy-eight-day air campaign:** Patterson, *Restless Giant*, 400–401.

38 **"war on terror begins":** George W. Bush, "Address to a Joint Session of Congress and the American People" (speech, Washington, D.C., September 20, 2001), The White House, georgewbush-whitehouse.archives.gov/news/releases/2001/09/20010920-8.html.

38 **military power lost its luster:** The unpopularity of the American wars in Iraq and Afghanistan ultimately cost the Republican Party both houses of Congress in 2006. See John M. Broder, "Democrats Gain Senate and New Influence," *The New York Times*, November 10, 2006, www.nytimes.com/2006/11/10/us/politics/10elect.html.

38 **"starve terrorists of funding":** George W. Bush, "Address to a Joint Session of Congress and the American People" (speech, Washington, D.C., September 20, 2001), The White House, georgewbush-whitehouse.archives.gov/news/releases/2001/09/20010920-8.html.

38 **$500,000 to perpetrate:** According to a monograph produced by the staff of the 9/11 Commission, "The plot cost al Qaeda somewhere in the range of $400,000–500,000, of which approximately $300,000 passed through the hijackers' bank accounts in the United States." John Roth, Douglas Greenburg, and Serena Wille, "Monograph on Terrorist Financing," National Commission on Terrorist Attacks upon the United States, Staff Report to the Commission, p. 3, govinfo.library.unt.edu/911/staff_statements /911_TerrFin_Monograph.pdf.

38 **in their own names:** Juan Zarate, *Treasury's War: The Unleashing of a New Era of Financial Warfare* (New York: PublicAffairs, 2013), 20.

38 **as the International Emergency Economic Powers Act:** Andrew Boyle and Tim Lau, "The President's Extraordinary Sanctions Powers," The Brennan Center for Justice, July 20, 2021, www.brennancenter .org/our-work/research-reports/presidents-extraordinary-sanctions-powers; Christopher A. Casey, Dianne E. Rennack, and Jennifer K. Elsea, "The International Emergency Economic Powers Act: Origins, Evolution, and Use," R45618, September 28, 2023, Congressional Research Service, U.S. Library of Congress, sgp.fas.org/crs/natsec/R45618.pdf.

38 **permits the president to wield this power:** Boyle and Lau, "Sanctions Powers."

39 **relatively marginal force:** Bruce Jentleson, *Sanctions: What Everyone Needs to Know* (New York: Oxford University Press, 2022), 2–3.

39 **"La Lista Clinton":** Zarate, *Treasury's War*, 24–25.

39 **scores of suspected terrorists:** Executive Order 13224, signed by George W. Bush on September 23, 2001, gave the State Department and the Treasury Department joint authority to impose sanctions on suspected terrorists and their financial enablers. "Executive Order 13224," September 23, 2001, Bureau of Counterterrorism, U.S. Department of State, www.state.gov/executive-order-13224.

39 **USA Patriot Act:** Zarate, *Treasury's War*, 30, 47, 147; "USA PATRIOT Act," Financial Crimes Enforcement Network, U.S. Department of the Treasury, www.fincen.gov/resources/statutes-regulations/usa -patriot-act.

39 **"you will not do business with the United States of America":** George W. Bush, "President Announces Crackdown on Terrorist Financial Network" (speech, Vienna, Virginia, November 7, 2001), The White House, georgewbush-whitehouse.archives.gov/news/releases/2001/11/20011107-4.html.

39 **secret deal with SWIFT:** Zarate, *Treasury's War*, 49–58. Most notably, SWIFT rejected an overture in the late 1980s by then–Justice Department attorney and future FBI Director Robert Mueller. But soon after 9/11, SWIFT's CEO Leonard Schrank, who was an American, relented. The agreement between Treasury and SWIFT, known as the Terrorist Finance Tracking Program (TFTP), was deemed so vital to the Global War on Terror that the Bush administration rolled out the red carpet for Schrank on multiple occasions. Juan Zarate details how Schrank was afforded audiences with Federal Reserve chair Alan Greenspan and National Security Advisor Condoleezza Rice and stayed at Vice President Dick Cheney's private residence.

39 **forfeited its historic law enforcement authorities:** "Information on the Office of Enforcement's Operations," GAO-01-305, U.S. General Accounting Office, Department of the Treasury, March 2001, www.gao.gov/assets/gao-01-305.pdf.

39 **Treasury lost 95 percent of its national security budget:** Zarate, *Treasury's War*, 138.

40 **in-house intelligence function:** Consolidated Appropriations Act, 2005, Public Law 108-447, 118 Stat. 2809 (December 8, 2004), www.govinfo.gov/content/pkg/PLAW-108publ447/pdf/PLAW-108publ447.pdf; "Fact Sheet: Combating the Financing of Terrorism, Disrupting Terrorism at Its Core," U.S. Department of the Treasury, September 8, 2011, home.treasury.gov/news/press-releases/tg1291.

40 **just over $100 million:** "Combating Illicit Financing: Treasury's Office of Terrorism and Financial Intelligence Could Manage More Effectively to Achieve Its Mission," GAO-09-794, U.S. Government Accountability Office, October 26, 2009, www.gao.gov/assets/a295926.html; Valerie Insinna, "Inside America's Dysfunctional Trillion-Dollar Fighter-Jet Program," *The New York Times*, August 21, 2019, www.nytimes.com/2019/08/21/magazine/f35-joint-strike-fighter-program.html.

41–42 **"really low expectations":** Author interview with Stuart Levey, 2022.

42 **a cavernous office:** Levey eventually moved to a similarly spacious office on the fourth floor of the Treasury building, which remains the office of the undersecretary for terrorism and financial intelligence.

42 **a "hostile takeover":** Author interview with Danny Glaser, 2022.

42 **"lie down in front of a train for him":** Author interview with Danny Glaser, 2022.

42 **"guerrillas in gray suits":** Zarate, *Treasury's War*, xi.

42 **regimes that sought weapons of mass destruction:** George W. Bush, "2002 Graduation Speech at West Point" (speech, West Point, New York, June 1, 2002), The White House, georgewbush-whitehouse.archives .gov/news/releases/2002/06/20020601-3.html; President George W. Bush, "V: Prevent Our Enemies from Threatening Us, Our Allies, and Our Friends with Weapons of Mass Destruction," in "The National Security Strategy," The White House, September 2002: georgewbush-whitehouse.archives.gov/nsc /nss/2002/nss5.html.

42 **as the "axis of evil":** George W. Bush, "The State of the Union Address" (speech, Washington, D.C., January 29, 2002), The White House, georgewbush-whitehouse.archives.gov/news/releases/2002/01 /20020129-11.html.

42 **suspend Iran's uranium enrichment program:** "Iran Agrees to Nuclear Demands," Carnegie Endowment for International Peace, October 21, 2003, archived at web.archive.org/web/20201217071715

/carnegieendowment.org/2003/10/21/iran-agrees-to-nuclear-demands-pub-14521; Semira N. Nikou, "Timeline of Iran's Nuclear Activities," The Iran Primer, The United States Institute of Peace, August 17, 2021, iranprimer.usip.org/resource/timeline-irans-nuclear-activities.

CHAPTER 7: AN ECONOMIC WEAPONS TEST

43 **it had "manufactured nukes":** "Transcript of North Korea's Statement on Nuclear Arms," The Wall Street Journal, February 10, 2005, www.wsj.com/articles/SB110806551783751592; James Brooke and David E. Sanger, "North Koreans Say They Hold Nuclear Arms," The New York Times, February 11, 2005, www.nytimes.com/2005/02/11/world/asia/north-koreans-say-they-hold-nuclear-arms.html.

43 **"United States drives us into a corner":** Sonni Efron, "U.S. Looks to China to Rein in North Korea," Los Angeles Times, April 23, 2005, www.latimes.com/archives/la-xpm-2005-apr-23-fg-norkor23-story .html; Victor Cha, The Impossible State: North Korea, Past and Future (New York: HarperCollins, 2018), 255–56; Kelsey Davenport, "Chronology of U.S.–North Korean Nuclear and Missile Diplomacy, 1985–2022," Arms Control Association, April 2022, www.armscontrol.org/factsheets/dprkchron.

43 **North Korea had secretly transferred:** David E. Sanger and William J. Broad, "Evidence Is Cited Linking Koreans to Libya Uranium," The New York Times, May 23, 2004, www.nytimes.com/2004/05 /23/world/evidence-is-cited-linking-koreans-to-libya-uranium.html.

43 **sole big trading partner:** Cha, Impossible State, 220.

43 **food and energy aid:** Daniel Wertz, "China–North Korea Relations," The National Committee on North Korea, November 2019, www.ncnk.org/resources/briefing-papers/all-briefing-papers/china-north -korea-relations; Jim Yardley, "Sanctions Don't Dent N. Korea–China Trade," The New York Times, October 27, 2006, www.nytimes.com/2006/10/27/world/asia/27border.html.

43 **world's premier counterfeit $100 bills:** Juan Zarate, Treasury's War: The Unleashing of a New Era of Financial Warfare (New York: PublicAffairs, 2013), 219–21. North Korea's counterfeit $100 bill was known as the "supernote" as most bank tellers at the time could not tell the difference between it and the real thing.

44 **Banco Delta Asia allowed Pyongyang:** Zarate, Treasury's War, 226.

44 **"primary money laundering concern," a classification:** U.S. Department of the Treasury, "311 Actions," home.treasury.gov/policy-issues/terrorism-and-illicit-finance/311-actions.

44 **shutting down the bank's connections:** David L. Asher, Victor D. Comras, and Patrick M. Cronin, "Pressure: Coercive Economic Statecraft and U.S. National Security," Center for a New American Security, January 2011, www.jstor.org/stable/resrep06338.

44 **Desperate for a policy option:** Zarate, Treasury's War, 232.

44 **Treasury designated Banco Delta Asia:** U.S. Department of the Treasury, "Treasury Designates Banco Delta Asia as Primary Money Laundering Concern under USA PATRIOT Act," September 15, 2005, home.treasury.gov/news/press-releases/js2720.

44 **Macau froze $25 million:** Asher, Comras, and Cronin, "Pressure."

44 **cutting ties with North Korea:** For a full description of the fallout from the Section 311 action against Banco Delta Asia, see Zarate, Treasury's War, 239–47.

44 **"even for true believers like me":** Author interview with Danny Glaser, 2022.

45 **"twenty-first-century precision-guided munition":** Zarate, Treasury's War, 244.

45 **"finally found a way to hurt us":** Cha, Impossible State, 266.

45 **money Shaquille O'Neal made:** Marc Stein, "Heat Take Big Gambles with Shaq Savings," ESPN, August 3, 2005, www.espn.com/nba/columns/story?columnist=stein_marc&id=2123211; "Shaquille O'Neal NBA Salary," HoopsHype, hoopshype.com/player/shaquille-oneal/salary.

45 **move the needle:** See Zarate, Treasury's War, 249–67, and Davenport, "Chronology." In 2007, the United States agreed to facilitate the return of the $25 million to North Korea in exchange for restarting diplomatic talks over the country's nuclear program.

CHAPTER 8: THE TECHNOCRAT

49 **thousands of nuclear centrifuges:** Michael R. Gordon and Thomas Erdbrink, "In New Nuclear Talks, Technological Gains by Iran Pose Challenges to the West," The New York Times, October 14, 2013, www. nytimes.com/2013/10/15/world/middleeast/us-iran-sanctions.html.

49 **"wiped off the map":** Nazila Fathi, "Wipe Israel 'Off the Map' Iranian Says," The New York Times, October 27, 2005, www.nytimes.com/2005/10/27/world/africa/wipe-israel-off-the-map-iranian-says.html.

50 **family of religiously observant Jews:** Adam J. Szubin, "Statement by Adam J. Szubin, Nominee for Under Secretary for Terrorism and Financial Crimes, Before the Senate Committee on Banking, Housing, and Urban Affairs" (speech, Washington, D.C., September 17, 2015), U.S. Department of the Treasury, home.treasury.gov/news/press-releases/jl0165; Joanne Palmer, "Remembering Dr. Zvi Szubin," Jewish Standard, blogs.timesofisrael.com/remembering-dr-zvi-szubin.

50 **"hardest I'd ever worked":** Joanne Palmer, "Who Was That with Cory Booker?" Jewish Standard, October 15, 2015, jewishstandard.timesofisrael.com/who-was-that-with-cory-booker.

51 **interpreted Szubin's presence as significant:** "Iran Nuclear Talks Get Off to 'Positive' Start in Geneva,"

Al Jazeera America, October 15, 2013, http://america.aljazeera.com/articles/2013/10/14/u-s-and-eu -nationsmeetingenevaforirannucleartalks.html; "World Powers Meet Iran for Nuclear Talks in Geneva," *France 24*, October 15, 2013, www.france24.com/en/20131015-geneva-iran-usa-uk-france-israel -nuclear-talks-rouhani-obama-united-nations.

51 **OFAC's offices sat empty:** Brad Plumer, "Absolutely Everything You Need to Know About How the Government Shutdown Will Work," *The Washington Post*, September 30, 2013, www.washingtonpost .com/news/wonk/wp/2013/09/30/absolutely-everything-you-need-to-know-about-how-the -government-shutdown-will-work.

CHAPTER 9: IRAN STARES DOWN A "TOOTHLESS TIGER"

53 **"narcissism of small differences":** Sigmund Freud, *Civilization and Its Discontents*, trans. James Strachey (New York: W.W. Norton & Company, 2010), 68–69.

53 **dynamic middle class:** Djavad Salehi Isfahani, "Iran's Middle Class and the Nuclear Deal," The Brookings Institution, April 8, 2021, www.brookings.edu/articles/irans-middle-class-and-the-nuclear-deal.

54 **20 percent of the world's oil supply:** Karl Russell, Denise Lu, and Anjali Singhvi, "Why This Narrow Strait Next to Iran Is So Critical to the World's Oil Supply," *The New York Times*, July 11, 2019, www .nytimes.com/interactive/2019/07/07/business/economy/iran-strait-of-hormuz-tankers.html.

54 **an energy powerhouse:** "International Data: Annual Crude and Lease Condensate Reserves," U.S. Energy Information Administration, accessed June 27, 2024, www.eia.gov/international/data/world /petroleum-and-other-liquids/annual-crude-and-lease-condensate-reserves; "International Data: Dry Natural Gas Reserves," U.S. Energy Information Administration, accessed June 27, 2024, www.eia .gov/international/data/world/natural-gas/dry-natural-gas-reserves; Central Intelligence Agency, "Crude Oil: Proved Reserves," www.cia.gov/the-world-factbook/about/archives/2021/field/crude-oil-proved -reserves/country-comparison; Central Intelligence Agency, "Natural Gas: Proved Reserves," www .cia.gov/the-world-factbook/about/archives/2021/field/natural-gas-proved-reserves/country-comparison.

54 **at least partly American-made:** Matthew Fuhrmann, "Spreading Temptation: Proliferation and Peaceful Nuclear Cooperation Agreements," *International Security* 34, no. 1 (May 2009), papers.ssrn.com /sol3/papers.cfm?abstract_id=1356091.

54 **Atoms for Peace program:** Ariana Rowberry, "Sixty Years of 'Atoms for Peace' and Iran's Nuclear Program," The Brookings Institution, December 18, 2013, www.brookings.edu/articles/sixty-years-of -atoms-for-peace-and-irans-nuclear-program; Semira N. Nikou, "Timeline of Iran's Nuclear Activities," The Iran Primer, August 17, 2021, iranprimer.usip.org/resource/timeline-irans-nuclear-activities.

54 **five-megawatt research reactor:** Rowberry, "Sixty Years."

54 **young scientists to study at MIT:** Abbas Milani, "The Shah's Atomic Dreams," *Foreign Policy*, December 29, 2010, foreignpolicy.com/2010/12/29/the-shahs-atomic-dreams.

54 **F-14 Tomcat fighter jets:** Harrison Kass, "The F-14 Tomcat: A 'Top Gun' Legend and Iran's Best Fighter Jet," *Business Insider*, June 10, 2022, www.businessinsider.com/f14-tomcat-fighter-top-gun -legend-and-iran-best-jet-2022-6.

54 **first-ever use of the law:** Hooman Estelami, "A Study of Iran's Responses to U.S. Economic Sanctions," *Middle East Review of International Affairs* 3, no. 3 (September 1999), ciaotest.cc.columbia.edu/olj /meria/meria99_esh01.html; "The International Emergency Economic Powers Act: Origins, Evolution, and Use," R45618, Congressional Research Service, U.S. Library of Congress, September 28, 2023, sgp.fas.org/crs/natsec/R45618.pdf.

55 **Iran's top trading partner:** Estelami, "Iran's Responses."

55 **"leverage provided by the frozen assets":** Stuart E. Eizenstat, "Do Economic Sanctions Work? Lessons from ILSA & Other US Sanctions Regimes," The Atlantic Council, February 2004, www.atlanticcouncil .org/wp-content/uploads/2004/02/2004-02-Economic_Sanctions.pdf.

55 **Physics Research Center performed:** Jay Solomon, *The Iran Wars: Spy Games, Bank Battles, and the Secret Deals that Reshaped the Middle East* (New York: Penguin Random House, 2016), 119–26.

55 **penalties made little difference:** Bryan R. Early, *Busted Sanctions: Explaining Why Economic Sanctions Fail* (Stanford: Stanford University Press, 2015), 94.

56 **first energy deal:** Agis Salpukas, "Iran Signs Oil Deal with Conoco; First Since 1980 Break with U.S.," *The New York Times*, March 7, 1995, www.nytimes.com/1995/03/07/world/iran-signs-oil-deal-with -conoco-first-since-1980-break-with-us.html.

56 **Clinton issued an executive order:** "Executive Order 12957—Prohibiting Certain Transactions with Respect to the Development of Iranian Petroleum Resources," C.F.R. titles 3 and 50, March 15, 1995, 424–25, www.govinfo.gov/content/pkg/WCPD-1995-03-20/pdf/WCPD-1995-03-20-Pg424.pdf.

56 **Conoco swiftly withdrew:** Douglas Jehl, "Oil Concern Ends a Deal with Iran as President Acts," *The New York Times*, March 15, 1995, www.nytimes.com/1995/03/15/us/oil-concern-ends-a-deal-with-iran -as-president-acts.html.

56 **French energy giant Total announced:** Max Berley, "U.S. Senator Cites Total's Business with Iran: French Warned of Sanctions," *The New York Times*, June 3, 1996, www.nytimes.com/1996/06/03/business /worldbusiness/IHT-us-senator-cites-totals-business-with-iran-french.html.

56 **energy deals with non-American companies:** Rex J. Zedalis, "The Total S.A. Case: Meaning of 'In-

vestment' under the ILSA," *The American Journal of International Law* 92, no. 3 (July 1998): 539–48, www.jstor.org/stable/2997928.

56 **denounced ILSA as "extraterritorial":** Eizenstat, "Do Economic Sanctions Work?"

56 **illegal for European companies to comply:** "Extraterritoriality (Blocking Statute)," European Commission, July 2021, finance.ec.europa.eu/eu-and-world/open-strategic-autonomy/extraterritoriality -blocking-statute_en.

57 **into a general compromise:** This account of the deal struck by the United States and the EU to end the standoff over ILSA is largely drawn from Eizenstat, "Do Economic Sanctions Work?"

57 **"exhausted and toothless tiger":** Eizenstat, "Do Economic Sanctions Work?"

CHAPTER 10: RISKY BUSINESS

58 **there was "no evidence":** "Comprehensive Report of the Special Advisor to the DCI on Iraq's WMD, with Addendums (Duelfer Report)," Central Intelligence Agency, April 25, 2005, www.govinfo.gov /app/details/GPO-DUELFERREPORT.

58 **covert nuclear facilities:** Jay Solomon, *The Iran Wars: Spy Games, Bank Battles, and the Secret Deals that Reshaped the Middle East* (New York: Penguin Random House, 2016), 116.

58 **two secret sites:** Connie Bruck, "Exiles," *The New Yorker*, March 6, 2006, p. 48, www.newyorker.com /magazine/2006/03/06/exiles-6.

58 **of the "axis of evil":** George W. Bush, "2002 State of the Union Address" (speech, Washington, D.C., January 29, 2002), *The Washington Post*, www.washingtonpost.com/wp-srv/onpolitics/transcripts /sou012902.htm.

59 **"We've already sanctioned Iran!":** George W. Bush and John Kerry, "Remarks by President Bush and Senator Kerry in First 2004 Presidential Debate" (speech, Miami, October 1, 2004), georgewbush -whitehouse.archives.gov/news/releases/2004/10/20041001.html.

59 **"We've sanctioned ourselves out of influence":** George W. Bush, "President Holds Press Conference" (speech, Washington, D.C., December 20, 2004), georgewbush-whitehouse.archives.gov/news/releases /2004/12/20041220-3.html.

59 **Ahmadinejad was a strict adherent:** Scott Peterson, "Waiting for the Rapture in Iran," *The Christian Science Monitor*, December 21, 2005, www.csmonitor.com/2005/1221/p01s04-wome.html.

59 **restarted uranium enrichment:** "Iran Agrees to Nuclear Demands," Carnegie Endowment for International Peace, October 21, 2003, carnegieendowment.org/2003/10/21/iran-agrees-to-nuclear-demands -pub-14521; Rosalind Ryan, "Iran Resumes Uranium Enrichment," *The Guardian*, August 8, 2005, www .theguardian.com/environment/2005/aug/08/energy.iran.

60 **"hasten the emergence of your last repository":** Mahmood Ahmadinejad, "Address by H. E. Dr. Mahmood Ahmadinejad, President of the Islamic Republic of Iran, before the Sixtieth Session of the United Nations General Assembly" (speech, New York, NY, September 17, 2005), www.un.org/webcast/ga/60 /statements/iran050917eng.pdf.

60 **lived totally in the present:** Joanne Palmer, "Who Was That with Cory Booker?" *Jewish Standard*, October 15, 2015, jewishstandard.timesofisrael.com/who-was-that-with-cory-booker.

61 **"they would just laugh at you":** Author interview with Stuart Levey, 2022.

61 **"does not mean the world has stopped":** Author interview with Stuart Levey, 2022.

62 **fined the Dutch bank ABN AMRO:** "Joint Press Release," The Federal Reserve Board, December 19, 2005, www.federalreserve.gov/boarddocs/press/enforcement/2005/20051219/default.htm.

62 **it was the largest fine ever levied:** Barnaby J. Feder, "ABN to Pay $80 Million for Violations," *The New York Times*, December 20, 2005, www.nytimes.com/2005/12/20/business/worldbusiness/abn-to-pay -80-million-for-violations.html; "Joint Press Release," *Federal Reserve Board*, December 19, 2005.

63 **"I need your direct support":** In addition to interviews conducted by the author, this account of Stuart Levey's conversation with Condoleezza Rice draws from reporting by Juan Zarate and Robin Wright. See Juan Zarate, *Treasury's War: The Unleashing of a New Era of Financial Warfare* (New York: PublicAffairs, 2013), 291–295; Robin Wright, "Stuart Levey's War," *The New York Times Magazine*, October 31, 2008, www.nytimes.com/2008/11/02/magazine/02IRAN-t.html.

CHAPTER 11: STUART LEVEY GOES TO WAR

64 **shoot up in value:** David Wessel and Henry Paulson, Jr., hosted by Steve Inskeep, "Treasury Secretary Resigns, Bush Announces Nominee," *Morning Edition* (podcast), NPR, May 30, 2006, www.npr.org /templates/story/story.php?storyId=5438948.

65 **Levey made a speech:** Stuart Levey, "Prepared Remarks by Stuart Levey Before the American Enterprise Institute for Public Policy Research" (speech, Washington, D.C., September 8, 2006), home.treasury .gov/news/press-releases/hp86; U.S. Department of the Treasury Office of Foreign Assets Control, "Treasury Cuts Iran's Bank Saderat Off from U.S. Financial System," September 8, 2006, ofac.treasury .gov/recent-actions/20060908a.

65 **"broad network of front companies":** Peter S. Goodman, "Treasury Warns G-7 about Iran: Paulson Describes Financial Network to Help Nuclear Drive," *The Washington Post*, September 17, 2006, www

.washingtonpost.com/archive/politics/2006/09/17/treasury-warns-g-7-about-iran-span-classbank headpaulson-describes-financial-network-to-help-nuclear-drivespan/c95859f8-0a62-40b5-b55f -d961a99b60e6.

67 **"You fucking Americans"**: "In the Matter of Standard Chartered Bank, New York Branch," Order Pursuant to Banking Law § 39 (New York State Department of Financial Services, August 6, 2012); Tom Bawden, "Standard Chartered Fights Back," *The Independent*, August 8, 2012, www.independent .co.uk/news/business/news/standard-chartered-fights-back-8022616.html.

67 **fine Standard Chartered:** "Federal Reserve Board Issues Consent Cease and Desist Order, and Assesses Civil Money Penalty against Standard Chartered PLC and Standard Chartered Bank," Board of Governors of the Federal Reserve System, December 10, 2012, www.federalreserve.gov/newsevents /pressreleases/enforcement20121210a.htm; "Standard Chartered Bank Agrees to Forfeit $227 Million for Illegal Transactions with Iran, Sudan, Libya, and Burma," Office of Public Affairs, U.S. Department of Justice, December 10, 2012, www.justice.gov/opa/pr/standard-chartered-bank-agrees-forfeit -227-million-illegal-transactions-iran-sudan-libya-and.

67 **Treasury and State collaborated:** "Designation of Iranian Entities and Individuals for Proliferation Activities and Support for Terrorism," U.S. Department of State, October 25, 2007, 2001-2009.state .gov/r/pa/prs/ps/2007/oct/94193.htm.

67 **Treasury barred all Iranian banks:** U.S. Department of the Treasury, "Treasury Revokes Iran's U-Turn License," November 6, 2008, home.treasury.gov/news/press-releases/200811611403711686.

67 **several additional resolutions:** UN Security Council, Resolution 1696, July 31, 2006, S/RES/1696, digitallibrary.un.org/record/580191; UN Security Council, Resolution 1737, December 23, 2006, S/ RES/1737, digitallibrary.un.org/record/589783; UN Security Council, Resolution 1747, March 24, 2007, S/RES/1747, digitallibrary.un.org/record/595373; UN Security Council, Resolution 1803, March 3, 2008, S/RES/1803, digitallibrary.un.org/record/621380.

68 **"breathtaking game of chess"**: Robin Wright, "Stuart Levey's War," *The New York Times Magazine*, October 31, 2008, www.nytimes.com/2008/11/02/magazine/02IRAN-t.html; Zahra Hosseinian and Fredrik Dahl, "Outgoing Iran Finance Minister Fires Parting Shot," Reuters, April 23, 2008, www.reuters .com/article/uk-iran-economy-minister/outgoing-iran-finance-minister-fires-parting-shot-idUKDAH 32038320080423.

68 **"Stuart Levey's War"**: Wright, "Stuart Levey's War."

68 **Inflation and unemployment were high:** Anna Fifield, "Iran's Elite Paper Over the Economic Cracks," *Financial Times*, March 13, 2008, www.ft.com/content/30364c64-f150-11dc-a91a-0000779fd2ac; Najmeh Bozorgmehr, "Iranians Focus on Inflation Woes," *Financial Times*, March 12, 2008, www.ft.com /content/6be16510-f050-11dc-ba7c-0000779fd2ac.

68 **over 8 percent in 2007:** World Bank, "GDP Growth (Annual %): Iran, Islamic Rep," 2020, data.worldbank .org/indicator/NY.GDP.MKTP.KD.ZG?end=2020&locations=IR&start=1960&view=chart.

68 **awash in petrodollars:** "Iran Plans 2009–10 Budget on $55–60 Oil Price: Report," Reuters, October 15, 2008, www.reuters.com/article/us-iran-oil-budget/iran-plans-2009-10-budget-on-55-60-oil-price-report -idUSTRE49E3W920081015; "IMF Country Report No. 10/74: Islamic Republic of Iran," International Monetary Fund, March 2010, www.imf.org/external/pubs/ft/scr/2010/cr1074.pdf; "IMF Country Report No. 11/241: Islamic Republic of Iran," International Monetary Fund, August 2011, www.imf.org/external /pubs/ft/scr/2011/cr11241.pdf.

68 **Iranian bankers found new conduits:** Glenn R. Simpson and John R. Wilke, "Sanction Threat Prompts Big Firms to Cut Iran Ties," *The Wall Street Journal*, January 31, 2006, www.wsj.com/articles /SB113867909286660722.

69 **Muammar Gaddafi agreed:** Libya, the "L" in ILSA, was removed from the law after its leader, Muammar Gaddafi, agreed to give up his weapons of mass destruction, in 2003. The law was subsequently renamed the Iran Sanctions Act, or ISA.

69 **"cravenly turned a blind eye":** Tom Lantos, "The Iranian Challenge" (speech, Washington, D.C., March 6, 2007), Committee on Foreign Affairs, U.S. House of Representatives, democrats-foreignaffairs.house .gov/2007/3/advisory-tue-03062007-1200am.

CHAPTER 12: EXTENDING A HAND

70 **Obama's pick for treasury:** Jackie Calmes, "Fed Official Is Said to Be Choice for Treasury," *The New York Times*, November 21, 2006, www.nytimes.com/2008/11/22/us/politics/22policy.html.

70 **olive branch to Iran's leaders:** Zbigniew Brzezinksi, hosted by Ted Koppel, "Obama's Approach to U.S. Relations with Iran," *Talk of the Nation* (podcast), NPR, November 25, 2008, www.npr.org/2008 /11/25/97464073/obamas-approach-to-u-s-relations-with-iran.

71 **fifteen-foot high menorah:** *Chabad-Lubavitch of Georgia v. Miller*, 976 F.2d 1386 (11th Cir. 1992).

71 **enough low-enriched uranium for a nuclear weapon:** "Iran Allows Nuclear Inspections," *CBS News*, August 20, 2009, www.cbsnews.com/news/iran-allows-nuclear-inspections.

71 **"willing to unclench your fist":** Barack Obama, "Inaugural Address" (speech, Washington, D.C., January 21, 2009), The White House, obamawhitehouse.archives.gov/blog/2009/01/21/president-Barack -obamas-inaugural-address.

71 **series of secret letters:** Jay Solomon, *The Iran Wars: Spy Games, Bank Battles, and the Secret Deals that Reshaped the Middle East* (New York: Penguin Random House, 2016), 168–70.

72 **"pursuing constructive ties":** Barack Obama, "In Celebration of Nowruz" (video speech, Washington, D.C., March 20, 2009), *The Wall Street Journal*, www.wsj.com/articles/SB123752091165792573.

72 **Danny Glaser traveled to Brussels:** David E. Sanger, James Glanz, and Jo Becker, "Around the World, Distress over Iran," *The New York Times*, November 28, 2010, www.nytimes.com/2010/11/29/world/middleeast/29iran.html.

73 **blueprint for a renewed sanctions push:** Richard Nephew, *The Art of Sanctions: A View from the Field* (New York: Columbia University Press, 2018), 71–72.

73 **62 percent of the vote:** Daniel Berman and Thomas Rintoul, "Preliminary Analysis of the Voting Figures in Iran's 2009 Presidential Election," Chatham House, June 21, 2009, www.chathamhouse.org/sites/default/files/public/Research/Middle%20East/iranelection0609.pdf; Ian Black and Saeed Kamali Dehghan, "Riots Erupt in Tehran over 'Stolen' Election,'" *The Guardian*, June 13, 2009, www.theguardian.com/world/2009/jun/13/iran-mahmoud-ahmadinejad-riots-tehran-election.

73 **"Where is my vote?":** Solomon, *Iran Wars*, 184; Ulrike Putz, "Iranian Demonstrators Put the Regime on the Defensive," *Spiegel International*, December 28, 2009, www.spiegel.de/international/world/violence-in-tehran-iranian-demonstrators-put-the-regime-on-the-defensive-a-669317.html.

74 **far short of what it needed:** Daniel Poneman and Sahar Nowrouzzadeh, "The Deal That Got Away: The 2009 Nuclear Fuel Swap with Iran," Belfer Center, Harvard Kennedy School, January 2021, www.belfercenter.org/publication/deal-got-away-2009-nuclear-fuel-swap-iran.

74 **"call Iran's bluff":** Poneman and Nowrouzzadeh, "Deal That Got Away."

74 **"inconsistent with a peaceful program":** Barack Obama, Nicolas Sarkozy, Gordon Brown, "Statements by President Obama, French President Sarkozy, and British Prime Minister Brown on Iranian Nuclear Facility" (speeches, Pittsburgh, PA, September 25, 2009), The White House, obamawhitehouse.archives.gov/the-press-office/2009/09/25/statements-president-obama-french-president-sarkozy-and-british-prime-mi.

76 **quietly come clean:** William J. Burns, *The Back Channel: A Memoir of American Diplomacy and the Case for its Renewal* (New York: Penguin Random House, 2019), 350–51.

76 **first-ever bilateral discussion:** Burns, *Back Channel*, 352.

76 **dragged their feet:** Poneman and Nowrouzzadeh, "Deal That Got Away."

76 **badly damaged Ahmadinejad's standing:** Poneman and Nowrouzzadeh, "Deal That Got Away."

CHAPTER 13: WITH US OR AGAINST US

77 **Bush's "with us or against us":** As George W. Bush famously said in a speech after 9/11, "Every nation, in every region, now has a decision to make. Either you are with us, or you are with the terrorists." He later put it more simply, stating, "You're either with us or against us in the fight against terror." See George W. Bush, "Address to a Joint Session of Congress and the American People" (speech, Washington, D.C., September 20, 2001), The White House, georgewbush-whitehouse.archives.gov/news/releases/2001/09/20010920-8.html and "'You Are Either with Us or Against Us,'" CNN, November 6, 2001, edition.cnn.com/2001/US/11/06/gen.attack.on.terror. For Obama's Nobel Prize, see "The Nobel Peace Prize 2009 Press Release," The Nobel Prize, October 9, 2009, www.nobelprize.org/prizes/peace/2009/press-release and Steven Erlander and Sheryl Gay Stolberg, "Surprise Nobel for Obama Stirs Praise and Doubts," *The New York Times*, October 9, 2009, www.nytimes.com/2009/10/10/world/10nobel.html.

78 **succeeded by Nicolas Sarkozy:** On Chirac, see Elaine Sciolino and Katrin Bennhold, "Chirac Strays from Assailing a Nuclear Iran," *The New York Times*, February 1, 2007, www.nytimes.com/2007/02/01/world/europe/01france.html. On Sarkozy, see "Is Sarkozy a Neo-con?" *The Economist*, October 16, 2007, www.economist.com/certain-ideas-of-europe/2007/10/16/is-sarkozy-a-neo-con.

78 **China was a major buyer:** Marybeth Davis et al., "China-Iran: A Limited Partnership," U.S.–China Economic and Security Review Commission, updated April 2013, www.uscc.gov/sites/default/files/Research/China-Iran--A%20Limited%20Partnership.pdf.

78 **UN Security Council Resolution 1929 was adopted:** "Security Council Imposes Additional Sanctions on Iran, Voting 12 in Favour to 2 Against, with 1 Abstention," UN Security Council, June 9, 2010, press.un.org/en/2010/sc9948.doc.htm.

78 **to "exercise vigilance":** UN Security Council, Resolution 1929, June 9, 2010, S/RES/1929, digitallibrary.un.org/record/683939.

79 **the "potential connection":** UN Security Council, Resolution 1929.

79 **"give up their firstborn":** Michael Hirsh, "Obama Prepares to Get Tough on Iran," *Newsweek*, December 11, 2009, www.newsweek.com/obama-prepares-get-tough-iran-75581.

79 **soon proven wrong:** Richard Nephew, *The Art of Sanctions: A View from the Field* (New York: Columbia University Press, 2018), 86.

80 **trigger U.S. secondary sanctions:** "Fact Sheet: Comprehensive Iran Sanctions, Accountability, and Divestment Act (CISADA)," U.S. Department of State, May 23, 2011, 2009-2017.state.gov/e/eb/esc/iransanctions/docs/160710.htm.

80 **gradual exit plans:** Jonathan Allen and Amie Parnes, *HRC: State Secrets and the Rebirth of Hillary Clinton* (New York: Broadway Books, 2014), 186–91.

80 **CISADA passed Congress:** Susan Cornwell, "US Congress OKs Sanctions on Iran's Energy, Banks," Reuters, June 24, 2010, www.reuters.com/article/idUSN2414825120100624.

80 **Obama signed it:** Peter Baker, "Obama Signs into Law Tighter Sanctions on Iran," *The New York Times*, July 1, 2010, www.nytimes.com/2010/07/02/world/middleeast/02sanctions.html.

81 **"most comprehensive multilateral sanctions":** Barack Obama, "Remarks by the President at Signing of the Iran Sanctions Act" (speech, Washington, D.C., July 1, 2010), The White House, obamawhitehouse .archives.gov/the-press-office/remarks-president-signing-iran-sanctions-act.

81 **"posing a choice to companies around the world":** John McCain, speech in the U.S. Senate, *Congressional Record* 156, part 8 (June 24, 2010): 11596; Cornwell, "US Congress OKs Sanctions."

CHAPTER 14: EXODUS

82 **the seventeen-hour voyage:** John Dennehy, "Dubai's Historic Dhow Trade to Iran Feels Pressure from US Sanctions," *The National*, July 13, 2019, www.thenationalnews.com/uae/government/dubai-s-historic -dhow-trade-to-iran-feels-pressure-from-us-sanctions-1.885424.

82 **pray for rain:** Karim Sadjadpour, "The Battle of Dubai: The United Arab Emirates and the U.S.-Iran Cold War," Carnegie Endowment for International Peace, July 2011, 5, carnegieendowment.org/files /dubai_iran.pdf.

82 **Nearly $10 billion:** Sadjadpour, "Battle of Dubai," 5.

82 **"Everything is going through Dubai":** Sadjadpour, "Battle of Dubai," 21.

82 **offices in Dubai:** Avi Jorisch, *Iran's Dirty Banking: How the Islamic Republic Skirts International Financial Sanctions* (Arlington: Red Cell Intelligence Group, 2010), 27–28.

83 **bailed out by Abu Dhabi:** John Hudson, "Why Did Abu Dhabi Bail Out Dubai World?" *The Atlantic*, December 14, 2009, www.theatlantic.com/business/archive/2009/12/why-did-abu-dhabi-bail-out-dubai -world/347262.

83 **"runs Dubai now":** Sadjadpour, "Battle of Dubai," 10.

84 **UAE's central bank cut ties:** Chip Cummins and Jay Solomon, "U.A.E. Cuts Off Ties to Iran Banks," *The Wall Street Journal*, October 6, 2010, www.wsj.com/articles/SB1000142405274870329850457553340 41013995702.

85 **"one spirit in two bodies":** James Brooke, "Iran Extends Influence in Central Asia's Tajikistan," *VOA News*, November 1, 2011, www.voanews.com/a/article--iran-extends-influence-in-central-asias-tajikistan -133111348/168606.html.

86 **hit with penalties:** Orde F. Kittrie, *Lawfare: Law as a Weapon of War* (New York: Oxford University Press, 2016), 141–42.

86 **agreed to exit Iran:** James B. Steinberg, "Briefing on Iran Sanctions Act Implementation" (speech, Washington, D.C., September 30, 2010), U.S. Department of State, 2009-2017.state.gov/s/d/former /steinberg/remarks/2010/169315.htm.

86 **the Japanese oil company Inpex:** "Japan's Inpex Quits Iran Azadegan Oilfield Project," Reuters, October 15, 2010, www.reuters.com/article/japan-iran-inpex/update-2-japans-inpex-quits-iran-azadegan -oilfield-project-idUSTOE69E04E20101015.

87 **develop the Azadegan oil field:** Josh Rogin, "Will the Obama Administration Sanction Chinese Companies Doing Business in Iran?" *Foreign Policy*, October 5, 2010, foreignpolicy.com/2010/10/05/will -the-obama-administration-sanction-chinese-companies-doing-business-in-iran.

CHAPTER 15: THE LAST BASTION

88 **freezing a whopping $37 billion:** Cheyenne Hopkins, "Libya's $37 Billion Stays Frozen over Legal Issues, U.S. Says," *Bloomberg*, August 22, 2011, www.bloomberg.com/news/articles/2011-08-22/libya-s -37-billion-stays-frozen-over-legal-issues-u-s-treasury-says; Barack Obama, "Executive Order 13566, Blocking Property and Prohibiting Certain Transactions Related to Libya," February 25, 2011, The White House, obamawhitehouse.archives.gov/the-press-office/2011/02/25/executive-order-13566-libya; Zarate, *Treasury's War*, 343–47.

88 **"got the president to sign":** Author interview with Stuart Levey, 2022.

88 **survived an assassination attempt:** "Is the Mossad Targeting Iran's Nuclear Scientists?" *Time*, November 30, 2010, content.time.com/time/world/article/0,8599,2033725,00.html; Ronen Bergman, "When Israel Hatched a Secret Plan to Assassinate Iranian Scientists," *Politico*, March 5, 2018, www.politico .com/magazine/story/2018/03/05/israel-assassination-iranian-scientists-217223.

88 **triple Iran's stockpile:** "Iran: Advanced Centrifuges to Be Set Up Soon at Qom Nuclear Site," *Haaretz*, June 8, 2011, www.haaretz.com/2011-06-08/ty-article/iran-advanced-centrifuges-to-be-set-up-soon-at -qom-nuclear-site/0000017f-dc25-db22-a17f-fcb5c6280000; David E. Sanger and William J. Broad, "Survivor of Attack Leads Nuclear Effort in Tehran," *The New York Times*, July 22, 2021, www.nytimes .com/2011/07/23/world/middleeast/23iran.html; "Is the Mossad Targeting Iran's Nuclear Scientists?" *Time*.

89 **plans for a military strike:** Ronen Bergman and Mark Mazzetti, "The Secret History of the Push to Strike Iran," *The New York Times*, September 4, 2019, www.nytimes.com/2019/09/04/magazine/iran-strike-israel-america.html.

89 **"all options are on the table":** Jeffrey Goldberg, "Obama to Iran and Israel: 'As President of the United States, I Don't Bluff,'" *The Atlantic*, March 2, 2012, www.theatlantic.com/international/archive/2012/03/obama-to-iran-and-israel-as-president-of-the-united-states-i-dont-bluff/253875.

89 **"would be a catastrophe":** Solomon, *Iran Wars*, 24.

89 **65 percent of its national budget:** Antoine Heuty, "A Ticking Bomb? Iran's Oil and Gas Management," Revenue Watch Institute, February 2012, resourcegovernance.org/sites/default/files/rwi_bp_iran2.pdf.

89 **past $ 100 per barrel:** "2011 Brief: Brent Crude Oil Averages over $100 per Barrel in 2011," January 12, 2012, U.S. Energy Information Administration, www.eia.gov/todayinenergy/detail.php?id=4550.

89 **$100 billion in oil proceeds:** "IMF Country Report No. 11/241: Islamic Republic of Iran."

90 **"We could not figure out a way":** Nephew, *Art of Sanctions*, 107.

90 **"real challenge to American power":** Solomon, *Iran Wars*, 194.

90 **naval quarantine of Iran:** Mark Kirk and Norm Coleman, "Congressional Roundtable on Iran" (discussion, Washington, D.C., May 2007), Jewish Policy Center, www.jewishpolicycenter.org/2007/05/31/congressional-roundtable-sen-norm-coleman-and-rep.

91 **an act of war and global markets:** Jay Solomon, "Senators Press Obama on Iran's Central Bank," *The Wall Street Journal*, August 8, 2011, www.wsj.com/articles/SB10001424053111904480904576494463569720404#U502700941592OSH.

91 **publicly calling on Obama:** "Congress & the Middle East: Senate Letter Urging President Obama to Sanction Iranian Central Bank," Jewish Virtual Library, August 9, 2011, www.jewishvirtuallibrary.org/senate-letter-urging-president-obama-to-sanction-iranian-central-bank-august-2011.

92 **40 percent of Iran's oil sales:** "Iran Oil Exports: Where Do They Go?" *The Guardian*, June 2011, www.theguardian.com/news/datablog/2012/feb/06/iran-oil-exports-destination.

CHAPTER 16: 100–0

93 **"They want that guy done":** "Two Men Charged in Alleged Plot to Assassinate Saudi Arabian Ambassador to the United States," Federal Bureau of Investigation, October 11, 2011, archives.fbi.gov/archives/newyork/press-releases/2011/two-men-charged-in-alleged-plot-to-assassinate-saudi-arabian-ambassador-to-the-united-states.

93 **captivated and terrified Washington:** Benjamin Weiser, "Man Sentenced in Plot to Kill Saudi Ambassador," *The New York Times*, May 30, 2013, www.nytimes.com/2013/05/31/nyregion/mansour-arbabsiar-sentenced-for-plot-to-kill-saudi-ambassador.html.

94 **"no return address":** Author interview with Adam Szubin, 2023.

94 **undertaken secret initiatives:** Michael Adler, "What's New in the U.N. Nuclear Report?" U.S. Institute for Peace, November 8, 2011, iranprimer.usip.org/blog/2011/nov/08/what%E2%80%99s-new-un-nuclear-report.

94 **call for restrictions:** Chris McGreal and Julian Borger, "Iran Faces New Wave of Sanctions over Nuclear Programme," *The Guardian*, November 21, 2011, www.theguardian.com/world/2011/nov/21/iran-wave-sanctions-nuclear-programme.

94 **complete EU embargo:** Ian Katz and Gonzalo Vina, "U.K., France Increase Pressure on Iran as U.S. Plans Measures," *Bloomberg*, November 21, 2011, www.bloomberg.com/news/articles/2011-11-21/u-k-france-increase-pressure-on-iran-as-u-s-plans-measures.

94 **stormed the British embassy in Tehran:** Robert F. Worth and Rick Gladstone, "Iranian Protesters Attack British Embassy," *The New York Times*, November 29, 2011, www.nytimes.com/2011/11/30/world/middleeast/tehran-protesters-storm-british-embassy.html; Adrian Croft, "UK Envoy Tells of Fear as Mob Rampage in Iran Embassy," Reuters, December 2, 2011, www.reuters.com/article/idUSTRE7B1288.

94 **expelled all Iranian diplomats:** John F. Burns, "As Britain Closes Embassies, Iran's Isolation Could Complicate Nuclear Issue," *The New York Times*, November 30, 2011, www.nytimes.com/2011/12/01/world/middleeast/british-embassy-iran-diplomats-evacuated.html.

96 **"Administration's strong opposition":** Tim Geithner, "U.S. Strategic Objectives Towards Iran: Hearing Before the Senate Committee on Foreign Relations," 112th Cong., 1st sess., December 1, 2011, www.govinfo.gov/content/pkg/CHRG-112shrg73918/html/CHRG-112shrg73918.htm.

96 **"call it a parade'":** Author interview with Danny Glaser, 2022.

96 **"vitiate that very agreement":** Robert Menendez, "U.S. Strategic Objectives Towards Iran: Hearing Before the Senate Committee on Foreign Relations," 112th Cong., 1st sess., December 1, 2011, www.govinfo.gov/content/pkg/CHRG-112shrg73918/html/CHRG-112shrg73918.htm.

97 **"But for Congress":** Menendez, "U.S. Strategic Objectives."

97 **had passed 100–0:** "Menendez, Kirk Amendment for Stronger Sanctions Against Iran Passes Unanimously in the Senate," Office of Senator Menendez, December 1, 2011, www.menendez.senate.gov/newsroom/press/menendez-kirk-amendment-for-stronger-sanctions-against-iran-passes-unanimously-in-the-senate.

CHAPTER 17: GOOD COP, BAD COP

98 **"not a drop of oil":** "Iran Threatens to Block Strait of Hormuz Oil Route," *BBC News*, December 28, 2011, www.bbc.com/news/world-middle-east-16344102.

98 **included sanctions on the central bank:** "Section 1245 of the National Defense Authorization Act for Fiscal Year 2012," Bureau of Economic and Business Affairs, U.S. Department of State, November 8, 2012, 2009-2017.state.gov/e/eb/tfs/spi/iran/fs/200286.htm.

98 **an embargo on Iranian oil:** Justyna Pawlak and Parisa Hafzei, "EU Agrees Embargo on Iranian Crude," Reuters, January 4, 2012, www.reuters.com/article/iran-eu/eu-agrees-embargo-on-iranian-crude-idIND EE8030D720120104.

98 **banned European insurers:** Javier Blas, "Insurance Ban Hits Iranian Oil Sales," *Financial Times*, June 18, 2012, www.ft.com/content/662d2994-b95d-11e1-a470-00144feabdc0.

98 **"zone of immunity":** Mark Landler and David E. Sanger, "U.S. and Israel Split on Speed of Iran Threat," *The New York Times*, February 8, 2012, www.nytimes.com/2012/02/09/world/middleeast/us -and-israel-split-over-how-to-deter-iran.html; Shashank Joshi, "What Is the Zone of Immunity? Iran, Israel, and the IAEA's New Report," The Royal United Services Institute for Defence and Security Studies, September 3, 2012, rusi.org/explore-our-research/publications/commentary/what-zone-immunity -iran-israel-and-iaeas-new-report.

98 **practicing the attack:** Adam Entous, "Spy vs. Spy: Inside the Fraying U.S.-Israel Ties," *The Wall Street Journal*, October 22, 2015, www.wsj.com/articles/spy-vs-spy-inside-the-fraying-u-s-israel-ties-1445562074; Solomon, *Iran Wars*, 198.

99 **"bottom line amount of money":** Edward J. Krauland and Meredith Rathbone, "Examining OFAC Guidance on NDAA Iran Sanctions," Steptoe, March 5, 2012, www.steptoe.com/en/news-publications /examining-ofac-guidance-on-ndaa-iran-sanctions.html.

100 **Carlos Pascual, the head:** "Pascual, Carlos," The Cuban Studies Institute, cubansinamerica.us/prominent -cuban-americans/law-politics/carlos-pascual.

100 **cut purchases by 20 percent:** "Iran Oil Exports: Where Do They Go?" *The Guardian*, June 2011, www .theguardian.com/news/datablog/2012/feb/06/iran-oil-exports-destination.

100 **Chinese and Indian interests:** Carlos Pascual, "The New Geopolitics of Energy," Center on Global Energy Policy, Columbia University, September 15, 2015, www.energypolicy.columbia.edu/publications /new-geopolitics-energy.

101 **sanctions against three companies:** "Three Companies Sanctioned under the Amended Iran Sanc- tions Act," U.S. Department of State, January 12, 2012, 2009-2017.state.gov/r/pa/prs/ps/2012/01/180552 .htm.

101 **"dig in their heels":** Hillary Rodham Clinton, *Hard Choices* (New York: Simon & Schuster, 2014), 440.

101 **"We're *not too impressed*":** "US 'Not Impressed' with India's Efforts to Cut Iran Oil," *The Jerusalem Post*, May 15, 2012, www.jpost.com/Breaking-News/US-not-impressed-with-Indias-efforts-to-cut-Iran -oil; "US 'Unhappy' with India's Efforts to Cut Iran Oil Buys," *Hindustan Times*, May 15, 2012, www .hindustantimes.com/business/us-unhappy-with-india-s-efforts-to-cut-iran-oil-buys/story-YPPuYm 3ATZTzoMRL2rG5jK.html.

103 **40 percent decrease:** "Fact Sheet: Sanctions Related to Iran," The White House, July 31, 2012, obamawhite house.archives.gov/the-press-office/2012/07/31/fact-sheet-sanctions-related-iran.

103 **American officials to "cut off the head of the snake":** "'Cut Off Head of Snake' Saudis Told U.S. on Iran," Reuters, November 29, 2010, www.reuters.com/article/us-wikileaks-iran-saudis/cut-off-head-of -snake-saudis-told-u-s-on-iran-idUSTRE6AS02B20101129.

103 **America's domestic oil production:** Pascual, "New Geopolitics of Energy"; "U.S. Field Production of Crude Oil," U.S. Energy Information Administration, www.eia.gov/dnav/pet/hist/LeafHandler.ashx?n =PET&s=MCRFPUS2&f=M.

104 **vote of no confidence:** Jennifer Rubin, "Senate Passes Iran Sanctions 100–0; Obama Objects (Really)," *The Washington Post*, December 2, 2011, www.washingtonpost.com/blogs/right-turn/post/senate-passes -iran-sanctions-100-0-obama-objects-really/2011/12/02/gIQA7yELKO_blog.html.

104 **pushed an amendment through:** "Menendez Hails Banking Committee Passage of Iran Sanctions Legislation," Office of Senator Menendez, February 2, 2012, www.menendez.senate.gov/newsroom/press /menendez-hails-banking-committee-passage-of-iran-sanctions-legislation.

104 **"extraordinary and unprecedented step":** "Swift Instructed to Disconnect Sanctioned Iranian Banks Following EU Council Decision," Swift, March 15, 2012, www.swift.com/insights/press-releases/swift -instructed-to-disconnect-sanctioned-iranian-banks-following-eu-council-decision.

105 **China-based Bank of Kunlun:** U.S. Department of the Treasury, "Treasury Sanctions Kunlun Bank in China and Elaf Bank in Iraq for Business with Designated Iranian Banks," July 31, 2012, home.treasury .gov/news/press-releases/tg1661.

105 **of overseas escrow accounts:** The idea was inspired by an approach South Korea's government had taken in 2010, when, in an effort to keep trading with Iran without running afoul of international sanctions, it appointed two state-owned banks to collect all payments for Iranian oil on behalf of the Central

Bank of Iran. See Christian Oliver, Song Jung-a, Anna Fifield, "Seoul Finds New Way to Finance Iran Trade," *Financial Times*, October 7, 2010, www.ft.com/content/ae807f44-d1ff-11df-965c-00144feabdc0.

106 **Iran Threat Reduction and Syria Human Rights Act, which sailed:** "Iran Sanctions Contained in the Iran Threat Reduction and Syria Human Rights Act," U.S. Department of State, September 28, 2012, 2009-2017.state.gov/e/eb/rls/fs/2012/198393.htm.

106 **"overrule their objections":** Joseph R. Biden and Paul Ryan, "Vice Presidential Debate" (debate, Danville, KY, October 11, 2012), NPR, www.npr.org/2012/10/11/162754053/transcript-biden-ryan-vice-presidential-debate.

CHAPTER 18: LANDSLIDE

107 **declined by half:** Najmeh Bozorgmehr, "Iran Struggles to Curb Currency Crisis," *Financial Times*, September 27, 2012, www.ft.com/content/f1b5e5ba-0894-11e2-b57f-00144feabdc0.

107 **The price of chicken:** Marcus George and Yeganeh Torbati, "Iran's 'Chicken Crisis' Is Simmering Political Issue," Reuters, July 22, 2012, www.reuters.com/article/us-iran-economy-chicken/irans-chicken-crisis-is-simmering-political-issue-idUKBRE86L08E20120722.

107 **unfolded during Ramadan:** Saeed Jamali Dehghan, "Long Queues for Chicken as Ramadan Comes to Sanction-hit Iran," *The Guardian*, July 17, 2012, www.theguardian.com/world/iran-blog/2012/jul/17/long-queues-chicken-ramadan-iran.

108 **"below the chicken line":** George and Torbati, "Iran's 'Chicken Crisis.'"

108 **"chicken being eaten in movies":** Robert Tait, "Chickens Facing Censorship in Iran," *The Telegraph*, July 15, 2012, www.telegraph.co.uk/news/worldnews/middleeast/iran/9401491/Chickens-facing-censorship-in-Iran.html.

108 **inflation was wreaking havoc:** Najmeh Bozorgmehr, "Iran Develops 'Economy of Resistance,'" *Financial Times*, September 10, 2012, www.ft.com/content/27ec70a6-f911-11e1-8d92-00144feabdc0.

108 **hurt that U.S. policies inflicted:** Najmeh Bozorgmehr, "Sanctions Take Toll on Iran's Sick," *Financial Times*, September 4, 2012, www.ft.com/content/43abcb36-f5cc-11e1-a6bb-00144feabdc0.

108 **"worth only $500":** Farnaz Fassihi, "Iran Blames Currency's Fall on Rogue Traders, Sanctions," *The Wall Street Journal*, October 2, 2012, www.wsj.com/articles/SB10000872396390444138104578032860972093062.

108 **"expel seventy workers":** Najmeh Bozorgmehr, "Rial's Plunge Sparks Tehran Clashes," *Financial Times*, October 3, 2012, www.ft.com/content/86fc0ee8-0d67-11e2-97a1-00144feabdc0.

109 **"economy of resistance":** Bozorgmehr, "'Economy of Resistance.'"

109 **"address conditions under sanctions":** Bozorgmehr, "'Economy of Resistance.'"

109 **"take the sanctions seriously":** D. Parvaz, "Iran Sanctions: All Pain, No Gain," *Al Jazeera*, November 13, 2010, www.aljazeera.com/features/2010/11/13/iran-sanctions-all-pain-no-gain.

109 **"currency trading center":** Bozorgmehr, "Iran Struggles to Curb Currency Crisis."

109 **33,500 rials to the dollar:** Benoît Faucon and Katie Martin, "Pressures Drive Iran's Currency to New Low," *The Wall Street Journal*, October 1, 2012, www.wsj.com/articles/SB1000087239639044459240457802981011726875.

109 **37,000 rials to the dollar:** Benoît Faucon and Katie Martin, "Iran Currency Slides Further," *The Wall Street Journal*, October 2, 2012, www.wsj.com/articles/SB10000872396390444138104578031913596553342.

109 **40,000 rials to the dollar:** Farnaz Fassihi, "Iran Currency Woes Spark Rare Strike," *The Wall Street Journal*, October 3, 2012, www.wsj.com/articles/SB10000872396390443768804578034402848509458.

110 **"We don't want nuclear energy":** Fassihi, "Rare Strike."

110 **waging a "hidden war":** Najmeh Bozorgmehr, "Ahmadi-Nejad Admits Sanctions Hurt Iran," *Financial Times*, October 2, 2012, www.ft.com/content/db368004-0ca1-11e2-a73c-00144feabdc0.

110 **police raided currency shops:** Najmeh Bozorgmehr, "Iran Uses Force to Strengthen Rial," *Financial Times*, October 7, 2012, www.ft.com/content/a5f1e336-1087-11e2-a5f7-00144feabdc0.

110 **31,000 rials to the dollar:** Najmeh Bozorghmehr, "Iran's Currency Traders Forced Underground," *Financial Times*, October 26, 2012, www.ft.com/content/d3396c9c-1c4e-11e2-a63b-00144feabdc0.

110 **$1.9 billion fine:** Carrick Mollenkamp, "HSBC Became Bank to Drug Cartels, Pays Big for Lapses," Reuters, December 11, 2012, www.reuters.com/article/us-hsbc-probe/hsbc-to-pay-1-9-billion-u-s-fine-in-money-laundering-case-idUSBRE8BA05M20121211.

110 **far-reaching compliance reforms:** Kittrie, *Lawfare*, 144–45.

110 **"highest common denominator approach":** Author interview with Stuart Levey, 2022.

111 **"didn't see it coming":** Author interview with Richard Nephew, 2022.

112 **"no one is safe":** Farnaz Fassihi and Jay Solomon, "In Iran's Factories and Shops, Tighter Sanctions Exact Toll," *The Wall Street Journal*, January 3, 2013, www.wsj.com/articles/SB10001424127887324595904578120250597512768.

112 **above 30 percent:** Bijan Khajehpour, "Inflation Takes Its Toll on Iran," *Al-Monitor*, May 8, 2013, www.al-monitor.com/originals/2013/05/iran-inflation-economy-outlook.html.

112 **"by "favorite businessmen":** Najmeh Bozorghmehr, "Sanctions Benefit Iran's Rich and Powerful," *Financial Times*, March 8, 2013, www.ft.com/content/ae8c8308-80d9-11e2-9fae-00144feabdc0.

112 **disguise oil shipments:** Javier Blas, "Iran Disguises Tankers in Sanctions Game," *Financial Times*, June 28, 2012, www.ft.com/content/db49c9ba-c13e-11e1-8eca-00144feabdc0.

112 **so-called ship-to-ship transfers:** "Treasury Targets Iranian Attempts to Evade Sanctions," U.S. Department of the Treasury, May 9, 2013, home.treasury.gov/news/press-releases/jl1933.

112 **more elaborate plot:** "Special Report: Golden Loophole: How an Alleged Turkish Crime Ring Helped Iran," Reuters, April 29, 2014, www.reuters.com/article/us-iran-turkey-special-report/special-report-golden-loophole-how-an-alleged-turkish-crime-ring-helped-iran-idUSBREA3S07120140429.

112 **U.S. officials uncovered:** Isobel Finkel and Christian Berthelsen, "U.S. Arrests Top Turkish Banker in Iran Sanctions Probe," *Bloomberg*, March 28, 2017, www.bloomberg.com/news/articles/2017-03-28/halkbank-deputy-g-m-arrested-in-u-s-in-iran-financing-probe; Patricia Hurtado, "Turkish Trader Says U.S. Agents Illegally Searched iPhone," *Bloomberg*, July 18, 2016, www.bloomberg.com/news/articles/2016-07-18/turkish-gold-dealer-wants-statements-to-u-s-suppressed.

113 **slate of eight conservative candidates:** "Latest on the Race: Economy Top Election Issue," The Iran Primer, May 1, 2013, iranprimer.usip.org/blog/2013/may/01/latest-race-economy-top-election-issue.

113 **were not discussed:** Thomas Erdbrink, "In Iran Race, All 8 Candidates Toe Hard Line on Nuclear Might," *The New York Times*, June 9, 2013, www.nytimes.com/2013/06/10/world/middleeast/iran-candidates-toe-hard-line-for-nuclear-bid.html.

113 **"how do we fix 100 percent inflation?":** Thomas Erdbrink, "A Spiritual Center of Power Is a Required Stop on Iran's Campaign Trail," *The New York Times*, June 5, 2013, www.nytimes.com/2013/06/06/world/middleeast/in-iran-qum-is-a-required-campaign-stop.html.

113 **"prevent the nuclear dossier":** Saeed Kamali Dehghan, "Iran Elections: Former Presidents Endorse Moderate Hassan Rouhani," *The Guardian*, June 11, 2013, www.theguardian.com/world/2013/jun/11/iran-elections-presidents-endorse-rouhani.

113 **"preserve our nuclear rights":** Dehghan, "Former Presidents Endorse Moderate."

113 **"gradually reduce the sanctions":** Dehghan, "Former Presidents Endorse Moderate."

113 **51 percent of the vote:** "Hassan Rouhani Wins Iran Presidential Election," *BBC News*, June 15, 2013, www.bbc.com/news/world-middle-east-22916174; Thomas Erdbrink, "Iran Moderate Wins Presidency by a Large Margin," *The New York Times*, June 15, 2013, www.nytimes.com/2013/06/16/world/middleeast/iran-election.html.

CHAPTER 19: THE FREEZE

115 **separate trips to Muscat:** John Kerry, *Every Day is Extra* (New York: Simon & Schuster, 2018), 489–91; Burns, *Back Channel*, 356–59.

116 **enough enriched uranium:** Kerry, *Every Day is Extra*, 485.

116 **ready to attack:** Bergman and Mazzetti, "Push to Strike Iran."

116 **willing to explore a deal:** Burns, *Back Channel*, 361–62.

116 **short some $200 billion:** Solomon, *Iran Wars*, 204.

116 **running dangerously low:** Kevan Harris, "Rouhani's Next Test: Empty Coffers," The Iran Primer, December 5, 2013, iranprimer.usip.org/discussion/2013/dec/05/rouhani%E2%80%99s-next-test-empty-coffers.

117 **created an economic disaster:** Thomas Erdbrink and Rick Gladstone, "Iran's Next President Faults Ahmadinejad on Economy," *The New York Times*, July 15, 2013, www.nytimes.com/2013/07/16/world/middleeast/irans-president-elect-describes-a-bleak-economy.html.

117 **Rouhani persuaded Khamenei:** Burns, *Back Channel*, 368–69; Solomon, *Iran Wars*, 205.

117 **appointing Javad Zarif:** Don Melvin, "6 Lesser-known Facts About Iran's Foreign Minister Javad Zarif," CNN, April 3, 2015, www.cnn.com/2015/04/03/middleeast/irans-foreign-minister-six-things-to-know.

117 **into recession for the first time:** World Bank, "GDP Growth (Annual %): Iran, Islamic Rep" 2020, data.worldbank.org/indicator/NY.GDP.MKTP.KD.ZG?end=2020&locations=IR&start=1960&view=chart; Fassihi and Solomon, "Iran's Factories"; Harris, "Rouhani's Next Test."

117 **fallen 60 percent:** Matthew Philips and Golnar Motevalli, "Iran Gets Ready to Sell to the World," *Bloomberg*, September 10, 2015, www.bloomberg.com/news/articles/2015-09-10/iran-gets-ready-to-sell-oil-to-the-world; "Under Sanctions, Iran's Crude Oil Exports Have Nearly Halved in Three Years," U.S. Energy Information Administration, June 24, 2015, www.eia.gov/todayinenergy/detail.php?id=21792.

118 **hit Iran's car industry:** Fassihi and Solomon, "Iran's Factories."

118 **lose hundreds of millions of euros:** David Pearson, "Iran Provision Hits Renault Earnings," *The Wall Street Journal*, July 26, 2013, www.wsj.com/articles/SB10001424127887324110404578629104294270488.

118 **"most tightly held effort":** Burns, *Back Channel*, 359.

119 **specific Iranian conduct:** "Designation of Iranian Entities and Individuals for Proliferation Activities and Support for Terrorism," U.S. Department of State, October 25, 2007, 2001-2009.state.gov/r/pa/prs/ps/2007/oct/94193.htm; U.S. Department of the Treasury Office of Foreign Assets Control, "Treasury Cuts Iran's Bank Saderat Off from U.S. Financial System," September 8, 2006, ofac.treasury.gov/recent-actions/20060908a.

119 **a two-phase agreement:** Burns, *Back Channel*, 371.
120 **Kerry met with Zarif:** Elise Labott, Michael Pearson, and Joe Sterling, "Kerry, Iranian Minister Hail 'Constructive' First Meeting," CNN, September 6, 2013, www.cnn.com/2013/09/26/politics/us-iran/index.html; Solomon, *Iran Wars*, 7.
121 **interim deal was struck:** "Joint Plan of Action on Iran's Nuclear Program," *The New York Times*, November 24, 2013, archive.nytimes.com/www.nytimes.com/interactive/2013/11/25/world/middleeast/iran-nuclear-deal-document.html.
121 **unfreeze $4.2 billion:** "Background Briefing on the Implementation Plan of the P5+1 and Iran's First Step Nuclear Agreement" (teleconference, Washington, D.C., January 13, 2014), U.S. Department of State, 2009-2017.state.gov/r/pa/prs/ps/2014/01/219571.htm.
121 **"a historic mistake":** Lazar Berman, "Iran Nuclear Agreement a 'Historic Mistake,' Netanyahu Says," *The Times of Israel*, November 24, 2013, www.timesofisrael.com/iran-nuclear-agreement-a-historic-mistake-prime-minister-says.

CHAPTER 20: "THE WORLD HAS AVOIDED ANOTHER WAR"

123 **installments of roughly $500 million:** Laurence Norman, Nour Malas, and Benoît Faucon, "Iran Can't Withdraw Much Oil Revenue under Interim Nuclear Deal," *The Wall Street Journal*, April 6, 2014, www.wsj.com/articles/SB10001424052702304819004579485231513658774.
124 **Banque de Commerce et de Placements, or BCP:** Norman, Malas, and Faucon, "Iran Can't Withdraw Much."
124 **Japanese bank transferred the first tranche:** Norman, Malas, and Faucon, "Iran Can't Withdraw Much."
124 **$9 billion fine:** "BNP Paribas Agrees to Plead Guilty and to Pay $8.9 Billion for Illegally Processing Financial Transactions for Countries Subject to U.S. Economic Sanctions," U.S. Department of Justice, June 30, 2014, www.justice.gov/opa/pr/bnp-paribas-agrees-plead-guilty-and-pay-89-billion-illegally-processing-financial.
124 **stern letter of protest:** "2014 Annual Report: New Dynamics," BNP Paribas, 2014, invest.bnpparibas/en/document/annual-report-2014; "BNP's Post-fine Woes," *Deutsche Welle*, July 31, 2014, www.dw.com/en/bnp-paribas-logs-huge-quarterly-loss-after-us-fine/a-17823333; "Hollande Tells Obama Mooted BNP Fine Disproportionate: French Official," Reuters, June 4, 2014, www.reuters.com/article/bnpparibas-france-hollande/hollande-tells-obama-mooted-bnp-fine-disproportionate-french-official-idUSWEB00O1E20140604; Noémie Bisserbe, "Hollande Backs BNP Paribas in Letter to Obama," *The Wall Street Journal*, June 4, 2014, www.wsj.com/articles/hollande-backs-bnp-paribas-in-letter-to-obama-1401885257.
125 **address to a joint session of Congress:** Krishnadev Calamur, "In Speech to Congress, Netanyahu Blasts 'A Very Bad Deal' with Iran," NPR, March 3, 2015, www.npr.org/sections/thetwo-way/2015/03/03/390250986/netanyahu-to-outline-iran-threats-in-much-anticipated-speech-to-congress.
125 **"next president could revoke":** "Cotton and 46 Fellow Senators to Send Open Letter to the Leaders of the Islamic Republic of Iran," Office of Senator Cotton, March 9, 2015, www.cotton.senate.gov/news/press-releases/cotton-and-46-fellow-senators-to-send-open-letter-to-the-leaders-of-the-islamic-republic-of-iran.
127 **"gets him over the hump":** Kerry, *Every Day is Extra*, 516.
127 **The deal was done:** Carol Morello and Karen DeYoung, "Historic Deal Reached with Iran to Limit Nuclear Program," *The Washington Post*, July 14, 2015, www.washingtonpost.com/world/historic-nuclear-deal-with-iran-expected-to-be-announced/2015/07/14/5f8dddb2-29ea-11e5-a5ea-cf74396e59ec_story.html.
127 **the Joint Comprehensive Plan of Action (JCPOA):** "Joint Comprehensive Plan of Action," U.S. Department of State, July 14, 2015, 2009-2017.state.gov/documents/organization/245317.pdf.
127 **at least a full year:** The White House, "The Historic Deal That Will Prevent Iran from Acquiring a Nuclear Weapon," January 16, 2016, obamawhitehouse.archives.gov/issues/foreign-policy/iran-deal.
128 **the deal was time-limited:** "Joint Comprehensive Plan of Action," U.S. Department of State.
128 **longest continuous period:** "Kissinger Setting Records with Long Vienna Stay," *VOA News*, July 10, 2015, www.voanews.com/a/kerry-setting-records-with-long-vienna-stay-/2856393.html.
129 **thirty-fourth senator to announce:** Kerry, *Every Day is Extra*, 517.
129 **forty-two senators voted:** Seung Min Kim and Burgess Everett, "Senate Dems Block GOP Measure to Kill Iran Deal," *Politico*, September 10, 2015, www.politico.com/story/2015/09/iran-deal-senate-dems-block-gop-measure-to-kill-213506.
129 **the IAEA confirmed:** "IAEA and Iran: Chronology of Key Events," International Atomic Energy Agency, November 2022, www.iaea.org/newscenter/focus/iran/chronology-of-key-events.
129 **"avoided another war":** Barack Obama, "State of the Union" (speech, Washington, D.C., January 13, 2016), The White House, obamawhitehouse.archives.gov/the-press-office/2016/01/12/remarks-president-barack-obama-%E2%80%93-prepared-delivery-state-union-address.
129 **"historic diplomatic breakthrough":** Barack Obama, "Remarks by the President on the Iran Nuclear Deal" (speech, Washington, D.C., August 5, 2015), obamawhitehouse.archives.gov/the-press-office/2015/08/05/remarks-president-iran-nuclear-deal; Joshua Mitnick, "Netanyahu Calls Iran Deal 'Historic

Mistake,'" *The Wall Street Journal*, July 14, 2015, www.wsj.com/articles/netanyahu-calls-iran-deal-historic-mistake-1436866617.

CHAPTER 21: BLACK MAGIC

130 **successful less than 5 percent:** Robert Pape, "Why Economic Sanctions Do Not Work," *International Security* 22, No. 2 (1997): 90–136, doi.org/10.2307/2539368.

130 **"smart sanctions" against Iraq:** Neil King Jr., "Powell's Plan for New Sanctions on Iraq Runs Aground at U.N.," *The Wall Street Journal*, July 3, 2001, www.wsj.com/articles/SB99409531596545089; Peter Slevin, "Revised Sanctions on Iraq Backed," *The Washington Post*, May 8, 2002, www.washingtonpost.com/archive/politics/2002/05/08/revised-sanctions-on-iraq-backed/fbc3d951-7346-4644-ac20-006a2fd41eb7.

131 **Stuxnet computer virus:** David E. Sanger, "Obama Order Sped Up Wave of Cyberattacks Against Iran," *The New York Times*, June 1, 2012, www.nytimes.com/2012/06/01/world/middleeast/obama-ordered-wave-of-cyberattacks-against-iran.html.

131 **injured in assassination attempts:** Danielle Pletka, "Why Does Israel Keep Assassinating Iranian Officials? Because It Works," *Foreign Policy*, June 29, 2022, foreignpolicy.com/2022/06/29/iran-irgc-assassinations-israel-targeted-killing-nuclear.

134 **series of awkward road shows:** Felicia Schwartz, "Kerry Tries to Drum Up Some Business in Europe for Iran," *The Wall Street Journal*, May 10, 2016, www.wsj.com/articles/kerry-tries-to-drum-up-some-business-in-europe-for-iran-1462902185.

134 **Kerry met with bank CEOs in London:** Felicia Schwartz and Margot Patrick, "U.S. Secretary of State John Kerry Meets with European Bankers in Iran-Business Push," *The Wall Street Journal*, May 12, 2016, www.wsj.com/articles/kerry-meets-with-european-bankers-in-iran-business-push-1463045793.

135 **op-ed by none other than Stuart Levey:** Stuart Levey, "Kerry's Peculiar Message about Iran for European Banks," *The Wall Street Journal*, May 12, 2016, www.wsj.com/articles/kerrys-peculiar-message-about-iran-for-european-banks-1463093348.

CHAPTER 22: THE DIPLOMAT

139 **Dan Fried was a man:** U.S. Department of State, "Daniel Fried," 2009-2017.state.gov/r/pa/ei/biog/46525.htm.

140 **$15 billion loan from Moscow:** Michael McFaul, *From Cold War to Hot Peace: An American Ambassador in Putin's Russia* (Boston: Houghton Mifflin Harcourt, 2018), 396.

140 **tangled political history:** "A Brief History of Crimea," *VOA News*, February 27, 2014, www.voanews.com/a/the-history-of-crimea---in-brief-/1860431.html.

140 **Putin had questioned:** Vladimir Putin, "Speech at NATO Summit" (speech, Bucharest, Romania, April 2, 2008), *UNIAN*, www.unian.info/world/111033-text-of-putin-s-speech-at-nato-summit-bucharest-april-2-2008.html.

140 **exfiltrate Ukraine's disgraced president:** Paul D'Anieri, *Ukraine and Russia: From Civilized Divorce to Uncivil War* (Cambridge: Cambridge University Press, 2019), 221–22.

140 **"bring Crimea back":** Quoted in "Putin Reveals Secrets of Russia's Crimea Takeover Plot," *BBC News*, March 9, 2015, www.bbc.com/news/world-europe-31796226.

140 **possessed contingency plans:** Tor Bukkvoll, "Russian Special Operations Forces in Crimea and Donbas," *Parameters* 46, no. 2 (Summer 2016), article 4, press.armywarcollege.edu/cgi/viewcontent.cgi?article=2917&context=parameters.

141 **seized Crimea's regional parliament:** D'Anieri, *Ukraine and Russia*, 226–27.

141 **"We're Russians," one of them:** Carl Schreck, "From 'Not Us' to 'Why Hide It?': How Russia Denied Its Crimea Invasion, Then Admitted It," *Radio Free Europe/Radio Liberty*, February 26, 2019, www.rferl.org/a/from-not-us-to-why-hide-it-how-russia-denied-its-crimea-invasion-then-admitted-it/29791806.html.

141 **"I call on the president":** Quoted in D'Anieri, *Ukraine and Russia*, 227.

141 **thousands of pro-European protesters:** Frank Hofmann, "The Maidan Movement," *Deutsche Welle*, November 22, 2015, www.dw.com/en/the-maidan-movement-and-the-period-that-followed/a-18867029; D'Anieri, *Ukraine and Russia*, 211.

142 **mutual economic dependence:** Adam Tooze, *Crashed: How a Decade of Financial Crises Changed the World* (New York: Viking, 2018), 499.

142 **a third of its oil and gas imports:** "European Energy Security Strategy," European Commission, COM(2014) 330 final, May 28, 2014, eur-lex.europa.eu/legal-content/EN/TXT/PDF/?uri=CELEX:52014DC0330&from=EN.

142 **"The poor schmo":** Michael Crowley, "Prisoners Dilemma," *The New Republic*, June 17, 2009, newrepublic.com/article/64253/prisoners-dilemma.

142 **almost seventy detainees:** Michelle Shephard, "Gitmo's Fallen Czar," *Foreign Policy*, May 23, 2013, foreignpolicy.com/2013/05/23/gitmo-fallen-czar.

143 **"a Soviet hand":** Author interview with Dan Fried, 2022.

CHAPTER 23: THE FALLEN BEAR LICKS ITS WOUNDS

144 **"right in front of you":** Author interview with Dan Fried, 2022.

144 **resigned as Soviet leader:** Greg Myre, "How the Soviet Union's Collapse Explains the Current Russia-Ukraine Tension," *Morning Edition* (podcast), NPR, December 24, 2021, www.npr.org/2021/12/24/1066861022/how-the-soviet-unions-collapse-explains-the-current-russia-ukraine-tension.

144 **"Russia ceases to be an empire":** Zbigniew Brzezinksi, "The Premature Partnership," *Foreign Affairs*, March–April 1994, www.foreignaffairs.com/articles/russian-federation/1994-03-01/premature-partnership.

145 **"With the Ukraine, Russia is a USA":** Norman Stone, *World War One: A Short History* (New York: Basic Books, 2009), 6.

145 **"special powers" to act:** Paul D'Anieri, *Ukraine and Russia: From Civilized Divorce to Uncivil War* (Cambridge: Cambridge University Press, 2019), 28, 53–54.

145 **"downgraded to consular sections":** Chrystia Freeland, "Russia 'Trying to Isolate Ukraine': Campaign Suspected to Bring Kiev Back under Moscow's Hegemony," *Financial Times*, March 17, 1993.

145 **Russian as their native tongue:** "The National Composition of the Population of Ukraine and Its Linguistic Features," State Statistics Committee of Ukraine, 2001.ukrcensus.gov.ua/results/general/language.

145 **available in both languages:** D'Anieri, *Ukraine and Russia*, 185.

145 **92 percent voted in favor:** D'Anieri, *Ukraine and Russia*, 34.

145 **defended their country's independence:** D'Anieri, *Ukraine and Russia*, 83.

145 **1994 Budapest Memorandum:** Michael McFaul, *From Cold War to Hot Peace: An American Ambassador in Putin's Russia* (Boston: Houghton Mifflin Harcourt, 2018), 402–3.

146 **Lincoln's in the Civil War:** David Hoffman and John F. Harris, "Clinton, Yeltsin Gloss over Chechen War," *The Washington Post*, April 22, 1996, www.washingtonpost.com/archive/politics/1996/04/22/clinton-yeltsin-gloss-over-chechen-war/6c51c44b-34b8-4443-b7ba-8d2cee6d0249.

146 **"a sense of his soul":** George W. Bush and Vladimir Putin, "Press Conference by President Bush and Russian Federation President Putin" (press conference, Brdo Pri Kranju, Slovenia, June 16, 2001), The White House, georgewbush-whitehouse.archives.gov/news/releases/2001/06/20010618.html.

146 **amounted to a slap on the wrist:** Daniel Fried, interview by Vazha Tavberidze, Radio Free Europe/Radio Liberty, August 14, 2022, www.rferl.org/a/georgia-russia-war-fried/31987472.html.

146 **to "reset" relations:** McFaul, *Cold War*, 87.

146 **"overstepped its national borders":** Vladimir Putin, "Speech and the Following Discussion at the Munich Conference on Security Policy" (speech, Munich, Germany, February 10, 2007), The Kremlin, http://en.kremlin.ru/events/president/transcripts/copy/24034.

146 **feel Putin's spittle:** Victoria Nuland, interview by Michael Kirk, *Frontline*, PBS, June 14, 2017, www.pbs.org/wgbh/frontline/interview/victoria-nuland.

146 **"No one feels safe!":** Vladimir Putin, "Speech and the Following Discussion," February 10, 2007.

146 **left them deeply unsettled:** Daniel Fried and Kurt Volker, "The Speech in Which Putin Told Us Who He Was," *Politico*, February 18, 2022, www.politico.com/news/magazine/2022/02/18/putin-speech-wake-up-call-post-cold-war-order-liberal-2007-00009918.

146 **vindicated their decision:** Helena Spongenberg, "Putin's Speech Raises Alarms in EU," *Bloomberg*, February 12, 2007, www.bloomberg.com/news/articles/2007-02-12/putin-speech-raises-alarms-in-eubusinessweek-business-news-stock-market-and-financial-advice.

147 **"greatest geopolitical catastrophe":** "Putin: Soviet Collapse a 'Genuine Tragedy,'" *NBC News*, April 25, 2005, www.nbcnews.com/id/wbna7632057; Masha Gessen, "How the Fall of the Berlin Wall Radicalized Putin," *The Daily Beast*, November 9, 2014, www.thedailybeast.com/how-the-fall-of-the-berlin-wall-radicalized-vladimir-putin.

147 **Putin, his protégé:** McFaul, *Cold War*, 59.

147 **eliminated any reservations:** D'Anieri, *Ukraine and Russia*, 124–26.

148 **stumped for Yanukovych:** D'Anieri, *Ukraine and Russia*, 129.

148 **poured tens of millions:** McFaul, *Cold War*, 69.

148 **Viktor Yushchenko prevailed:** C. J. Chivers, "Yushchenko Wins 52% of Vote; Rival Vows a Challenge," *The New York Times*, December 28, 2004, www.nytimes.com/2004/12/28/world/europe/yushchenko-wins-52-of-vote-rival-vows-a-challenge.html.

148 **booed by thousands:** "Moscow's Martial Arts Fans Boo Putin as He Steps into the Ring," *The Guardian*, November 20, 2011, www.theguardian.com/world/2011/nov/20/putin-booed-moscow-martial-arts-fans.

148 **31 percent of Russians:** "So Far, Only 31% of Russians Are Ready to Vote for Putin," Levada Center, November 28, 2011, www.levada.ru/2011/11/28/poka-tolko-31-rossiyan-gotov-progolosovat-za-putina; McFaul, *Cold War*, 243.

148 **"Russia without Putin!":** Ellen Barry, "Rally Defying Putin's Party Draws Tens of Thousands," *The New York Times*, December 10, 2011, www.nytimes.com/2011/12/11/world/europe/thousands-protest-in-moscow-russia-in-defiance-of-putin.html.

148 **dozens of Russian cities:** Steve Gutterman, "Protests across Russia to Test Putin and Opponents," Reuters, December 10, 2011, www.reuters.com/article/us-russia-idUSTRE7B610S20111209.

148 **"Dear Vlad, the Arab Spring":** Tim Mak, "Putin: McCain Has Blood on His Hands," *Politico*, December 15, 2011, www.politico.com/story/2011/12/putin-mccain-has-blood-on-his-hands-070488.

149 **own brand of hybrid warfare:** Mark Galeotti, "The Mythical 'Gerasimov Doctrine' and the Language of Threat," *Critical Studies on Security* 7, no. 2 (2019), 157–61, www.tandfonline.com/doi/abs/10.1080 /21624887.2018.1441623.

149 **repaired the state's finances:** Adam Tooze, *Crashed: How a Decade of Financial Crises Changed the World* (New York: Viking, 2018), 128–29.

149 **more foreign investment:** Mike Dorning, "Business at Odds with Obama over Russia Sanctions Threat," *Bloomberg*, June 25, 2014, www.bloomberg.com/news/articles/2014-06-25/business-at-odds -with-obama-over-russia-sanctions-threat.

149 **far-reaching alliance with Rosneft:** Andrew E. Kramer, "Exxon Reaches Arctic Oil Deal with Russians," *The New York Times*, August 30, 2011, www.nytimes.com/2011/08/31/business/global/exxon-and -rosneft-partner-in-russian-oil-deal.html.

149 **invest an additional billion:** Andrew E. Kramer, "Russia's Desire for Cars Grows, and Foreign Makers Take Notice," *The New York Times*, December 25, 2012, www.nytimes.com/2012/12/26/business /global/foreign-automakers-see-potential-in-russian-market.html.

149 **sizable investments in Russia:** Dorning, "Business at Odds."

149 **more than $700 billion in external debt:** Tooze, *Crashed*, 499.

149 **Russia's accession to the World Trade Organization:** Catherine Belton, "Russia Joins WTO after 19 years of Talks," *Financial Times*, August 22, 2012, www.ft.com/content/113bd1be-ec6c-11e1-81f4-00144feab49a; Pascal Lamy, "WTO Accession Puts Russia in a Better Position to Address its Domestic Challenges" (speech, January 18, 2013), World Trade Organization, www.wto.org/english/news_e/sppl_e/sppl263_e .htm.

CHAPTER 24: EUROMAIDAN

151 **Eurasian Economic Union (EEU):** Michael McFaul, *From Cold War to Hot Peace: An American Ambassador in Putin's Russia* (Boston: Houghton Mifflin Harcourt, 2018), 393.

151 **weighted in Russia's favor:** Paul D'Anieri, *Ukraine and Russia: From Civilized Divorce to Uncivil War* (Cambridge: Cambridge University Press, 2019), 192.

152 **the "suicidal step":** Stephen Blank, "Russia Leans on Its Neighbors," *The New York Times*, August 28, 2013, www.nytimes.com/2013/08/29/opinion/global/russia-leans-on-its-neighbors.html.

152 **"into the kingdom of the antichrist":** Sergei Glazyev, "Искусственно созданное наваждение" ["Artificially Created Obsession"], *Izborsky Club*, November 7, 2013, izborsk-club.ru/2121; D'Anieri, *Ukraine and Russia*, 201.

152 **integrating with the EU:** Veronika Movchan and Ricardo Giucci, "Quantitative Assessment of Ukraine's Regional Integration Options: DCFTA with European Union vs. Customs Union with Russia, Belarus, and Kazakhstan," German Advisory Group, Institute for Economic Research and Policy Consulting, November 2011, www.case-research.eu/sites/default/files/Movchan_0.pdf.

152 **three months of imports:** D'Anieri, *Ukraine and Russia*, 200–201.

152 **loan of €610 million:** Adam Tooze, *Crashed, How a Decade of Financial Crises Changed the World* (New York: Viking, 2018), 493–96; D'Anieri, *Ukraine and Russia*, 202.

152 **$15 billion loan and a massive discount:** Tooze, *Crashed*, 495; McFaul, *Cold War*, 393; D'Anieri, *Ukraine and Russia*, 215.

152 **"Ukraine is part of Europe":** "Huge Ukraine Rally over EU Agreement Delay," *BBC News*, November 24, 2013, www.bbc.com/news/world-europe-25078952.

152 **Soviet fishing trawler:** John Hudson, "The Undiplomatic Diplomat," *Foreign Policy*, June 18, 2015, foreignpolicy.com/2015/06/18/the-undiplomatic-diplomat.

153 **toured the encampments:** Keith Gessen, "The Quiet Americans Behind the U.S.-Russia Imbroglio," *The New York Times*, May 8, 2018, www.nytimes.com/2018/05/08/magazine/the-quiet-americans-behind -the-us-russia-imbroglio.html.

153 **"world is watching":** Mark Memmott, "'World is Watching,' U.S. Diplomat Tells Ukraine," NPR, December 11, 2013, www.npr.org/sections/thetwo-way/2013/12/11/250215712/world-is-watching-u-s -diplomat-tells-ukraine; Laura Smith-Spark, Diana Magnay, Victoria Butenko, "Ukraine Protesters Rebuild Barricades after Crackdown," CNN, December 11, 2013, www.cnn.com/2013/12/11/world /europe/ukraine-protests/index.html.

154 **"OFAC thought I was a good guy":** Author interview with Dan Fried, 2022.

154 **the "dictatorship laws":** "Ukraine's President Signs Anti-protest Bill into Law," *BBC News*, January 17, 2014, www.bbc.com/news/world-europe-25771595; Will Englund and Kathy Lally, "In Ukraine, Protesters Appear to Be Preparing for Battle," *The Washington Post*, January 20, 2014, www.washingtonpost .com/world/in-ukraine-protesters-appear-to-be-preparing-for-battle/2014/01/20/904cdc72-81bd-11e3 -9dd4-e7278db80d86_story.html.

155 **a "coup attempt":** "Ukraine Crisis: Putin Adviser Accuses US of Meddling," *BBC News*, February 6, 2014, www.bbc.com/news/world-europe-26068994.

155 **world: "Fuck the EU":** "Ukraine Crisis: Transcript of Leaked Nuland-Pyatt call," *BBC News*, February 7, 2014, www.bbc.com/news/world-europe-26079957.

155 **"A Rubicon had been crossed":** Ben Rhodes, *The World as It Is: A Memoir of the Obama White House* (New York: Random House, 2018), 268.

155 **killing around a hundred:** "A Timeline of the Euromaidan Revolution," *Euromaidan Press*, February 19, 2016, euromaidanpress.com/2016/02/19/a-timeline-of-the-euromaidan-revolution.

155 **deal with the opposition:** Sabine Siebold, "Ukraine's President, Opposition Sign Deal to End Crisis," Reuters, February 21, 2014, www.reuters.com/article/uk-ukraine-crisis-signing/ukraines-president-opposition-sign-deal-to-end-crisis-idUKBREA1K1AA20140221.

155 **remove him from office:** William Booth, "Ukraine's Parliament Votes to Oust President; Former Prime Minister Is Freed from Prison," February 22, 2014, www.washingtonpost.com/world/europe/ukraines-yanukovych-missing-as-protesters-take-control-of-presidential-residence-in-kiev/2014/02/22/802f7c6c-9bd2-11e3-ad71-e03637a299c0_story.html; "Parliament Votes 328–0 to Impeach Yanukovych on Feb. 22; Sets May 25 for New Election; Tymoshenko Free," *Kyiv Post*, February 23, 2014, www.kyivpost.com/post/7028.

156 **the president's abandoned estate:** "In Pictures: Luxury Ukraine Presidential Home Revealed," *BBC News*, February 23, 2014, www.bbc.com/news/world-europe-26307745; Oliver Poole, "Ukraine Uprising: The Private Zoo, the Galleon Moored on a Private Lake, the Fleet of Vintage Cars: Ukrainians Left Open-mouthed at the Opulence of Yanukovych's Country Estate," *The Independent*, February 23, 2014, www.independent.co.uk/news/world/europe/ukraine-uprising-the-private-zoo-the-galleon-moored-on-a-private-lake-the-fleet-of-vintage-cars-ukrainians-left-openmouthed-at-the-opulence-of-yanukovych-s-country-estate-9146886.html.

156 **"Russia must and has to act":** Tom Watkins, "From Russia, No Love for Yanukovych," CNN, February 28, 2014, www.cnn.com/2014/02/28/world/europe/russia-ukraine-yanukovych-speech/index.html.

CHAPTER 25: "AIM FIRST, THEN SHOOT"

157 **Sergei Yeliseyev, a top Ukrainian admiral:** Pavel Polityuk and Anton Zverev, "Why Ukrainian Forces Gave Up Crimea without a Fight: And NATO Is Alert," Reuters, July 24, 2017, news.yahoo.com/news/why-ukrainian-forces-gave-crimea-without-fight-nato-061847289.html.

157 **against fighting back:** Josh Rogin and Eli Lake, "U.S. Told Ukraine to Stand Down as Putin Invaded," *Bloomberg*, August 21, 2015, www.bloomberg.com/view/articles/2015-08-21/u-s-told-ukraine-to-stand-down-as-putin-invaded.

157 **"they'd get slaughtered":** Author interview with Victoria Nuland, 2022.

157 **"impact Russia's standing":** "Readout of President Obama's Call with President Putin," The White House, March 1, 2014, obamawhitehouse.archives.gov/the-press-office/2014/03/01/readout-president-obama-s-call-president-putin; Ben Rhodes, *The World as It Is: A Memoir of the Obama White House* (New York: Random House, 2018), 271.

158 **"right to protect its interests":** "Telephone Conversation with US President Barack Obama," The Kremlin, March 2, 2014, http://en.kremlin.ru/events/president/news/20355.

158 **lobbied the White House:** Peter Baker, "Obama Team Debates How to Punish Russia," *The New York Times*, March 11, 2014, www.nytimes.com/2014/03/12/world/europe/obama-team-debates-how-to-punish-russia.html.

158 **The Obama administration was divided:** Baker, "Obama Team Debates."

159 **"new and scary stuff":** Author interview with Dan Fried, 2022.

160 **working the phones:** Doug Palmer, "Lew Talks Sanctions on Russia," *Politico*, March 2, 2014, www.politico.com/story/2014/03/russia-sanctions-ukraine-104164.

160 **bugged Angela Merkel's phone:** "The NSA's Secret Spy Hub in Berlin," *Spiegel International*, November 10, 2013, www.spiegel.de/international/germany/cover-story-how-nsa-spied-on-merkel-cell-phone-from-berlin-embassy-a-930205.html.

160 **a "trustworthy partner":** Adam Tooze, *Crashed: How a Decade of Financial Crises Changed the World* (New York: Viking, 2018), 499.

160 **"Aim first, then shoot":** Rhodes, *The World as It Is*, 271, 272.

160 **"theory of the case":** Author interview with Victoria Nuland, 2022.

161 **"knife in his back":** Author interview with Rory MacFarquhar, 2022.

161 **men like Arkady Rotenberg:** Joshua Yaffa, "Putin's Shadow Cabinet and the Bridge to Crimea," *The New Yorker*, May 22, 2017, www.newyorker.com/magazine/2017/05/29/putins-shadow-cabinet-and-the-bridge-to-crimea.

161 **managed construction projects for Putin:** "Russian Billionaire Arkady Rotenberg Says 'Putin Palace' Is His," *BBC News*, January 30, 2021, www.bbc.com/news/world-europe-55872249.

162 **John Kerry was in constant contact:** John Kerry, "Press Availability in London" (speech, London, UK, March 14, 2014), U.S. Department of State, 2009-2017.state.gov/secretary/remarks/2014/03/223523.htm.

162 **he authorized sanctions:** "Executive Order 13661 of March 16, 2014: Blocking Property of Additional Persons Contributing to the Situation in Ukraine," *Code of Federal Regulations*, titles 50 and 3 (2014),

www.federalregister.gov/documents/2014/03/19/2014-06141/blocking-property-of-additional-persons-contributing-to-the-situation-in-ukraine.

162 **hawkish aides and facilitators:** "Fact Sheet: Ukraine-Related Sanctions," The White House, March 17, 2014, obamawhitehouse.archives.gov/the-press-office/2014/03/17/fact-sheet-ukraine-related-sanctions.

162 **EU followed suit with a similar list:** "Council Condemns the Illegal Referendum in Crimea," European Foreign Affairs Council, March 17, 2014, www.consilium.europa.eu/media/28722/141614.pdf.

162 **"inseparable part of Russia":** Vladimir Putin, "Address by President of the Russian Federation" (speech, Moscow, Russia, March 18, 2014), The Kremlin, http://en.kremlin.ru/events/president/news/20603; Steven Lee Myers and Ellen Barry, "Putin Reclaims Crimea for Russia and Bitterly Denounces the West," The New York Times, March 18, 2014, www.nytimes.com/2014/03/19/world/europe/ukraine.html.

163 **New York for the premiere:** Michael Schulman, "At the 'Game of Thrones' Premiere, Even the Dragons Behaved," The New York Times, March 19, 2014, www.nytimes.com/2014/03/20/fashion/game-of-thrones-premiere-party.html.

163 **cameo as a ragged resident:** Jayme Deerwester, "'Game of Thrones': Former CIA Deputy Director David Cohen Cameos in Winterfell Soup Line," USA Today, April 22, 2019, www.usatoday.com/story/life/tv/2019/04/22/game-thrones-cia-deputy-david-cohen-cameo-winterfell-soup-line/3536782002.

163 **Lew, had been hospitalized:** Kate Davidson, "Lew Treated at Hospital on Mexico Trip," Politico, March 18, 2014, www.politico.com/story/2014/03/jack-lew-treated-at-hospital-on-mexico-trip-104773; "Treasury Says Lew Leaves Hospital after Surgery," Reuters, March 26, 2014, www.reuters.com/article/us-usa-treasury-lew/treasury-says-lew-leaves-hospital-after-surgery-idUSBREA2P1DV20140326.

163 **"investments in Gunvor":** "Treasury Sanctions Russian Officials, Members of the Russian Leadership's Inner Circle, and an Entity for Involvement in the Situation in Ukraine," U.S. Department of the Treasury, March 20, 2014, home.treasury.gov/news/press-releases/jl23331.

163 **one of Putin's "cashiers":** "Treasury Sanctions Russian Officials," U.S. Department of the Treasury, March 20, 2014.

164 **Marine One, the president's helicopter:** Rhodes, The World as It Is, 271, 272.

164 **"on key sectors of the Russian economy":** Barack Obama, "Statement by the President on Ukraine" (speech, Washington, D.C., March 20, 2014), The White House, obamawhitehouse.archives.gov/realitycheck/the-press-office/2014/03/20/statement-president-ukraine.

CHAPTER 26: THE CONTACT GROUP

165 **sold his shares in Gunvor:** Sarah Kent, "Russian Target of U.S. Sanctions Sells Gunvor Stake," The Wall Street Journal, March 20, 2014, www.wsj.com/articles/SB10001424052702303802104579451642197912718.

166 **"It's New Russia":** David M. Herszenhorn, "What Is Putin's 'New Russia'?" The New York Times, April 18, 2014, www.nytimes.com/2014/04/19/world/europe/what-is-putins-new-russia.html.

166 **"Dan Fried containment strategy":** Author interview with Rory MacFarquhar, 2022.

166 **"just wanted to do more, more, more":** Author interview with Rory MacFarquhar, 2022.

166 **"isn't a brick wall":** Author interview with Dan Fried, 2022.

166 **"whatever we can get the Europeans to agree to":** Author interview with Dan Fried, 2022.

167 **"a negotiating mandate":** Author interview with Dan Fried, 2022.

167 **met in the Dutch city of The Hague:** Julian Borger, "G7 Countries Snub Putin and Refuse to Attend Planned G8 Summit in Russia," The Guardian, March 24, 2014, www.theguardian.com/world/2014/mar/24/g7-countries-snub-putin-refuse-attend-g8-summit-russia.

167 **"coordinated sectoral sanctions":** "G7: The Hague Declaration," March 24, 2014, G7 Research Group at the University of Toronto, www.g7.utoronto.ca/summit/2014brussels/hague_140324.html; "The Hague Declaration Following the G7 Meeting on 24 March," European Commission, March 24, 2014, ec.europa.eu/commission/presscorner/detail/de/STATEMENT_14_82.

167 **twenty-eight member states:** On July 1, 2013, Croatia became a member of the EU, increasing the membership total from twenty-seven to twenty-eight. See "Croatia," European Neighbourhood Policy and Enlargement Negotiations, European Commission, accessed July 14, 2024, neighbourhood-enlargement.ec.europa.eu/croatia_en.

169 **nearly half of global economic output:** Martin Wolf, "The G7 Must Accept That It Cannot Run the World," Financial Times, May 23, 2023, www.ft.com/content/c8cf024d-87b7-4e18-8fa2-1b8a3f3fbba1; "What Does the G7 Do?" Council on Foreign Relations, June 28, 2023, www.cfr.org/backgrounder/what-does-g7-do.

169 **full percentage point of GDP:** Justin Huggler and Bruno Waterfield, "Ukraine Crisis: Russia Sanctions Would Hurt Germany's Growth," The Telegraph, May 9, 2014, www.telegraph.co.uk/news/worldnews/europe/ukraine/10820180/Ukraine-crisis-Russia-sanctions-would-hurt-Germanys-growth.html.

CHAPTER 27: THE SCALPEL

171 **fall by 10 percent:** David M. Herszenhorn, "Russia Economy Worsens Even Before Sanctions Hit," The New York Times, April 16, 2014, www.nytimes.com/2014/04/17/world/europe/russia-economy-worsens-even-before-sanctions-hit.html; Peter Baker and Andrew E. Kramer, "So Far, U.S. Sanctions over Ukraine May Be Inflicting Only Limited Pain on Russia," The New York Times, May 2, 2014, www.nytimes.com

/2014/05/02/world/europe/so-far-us-sanctions-over-ukraine-may-be-inflicting-only-limited-pain-on
-russia.html.

171 **Russia's economy stabilized:** Baker and Kramer, "U.S. Sanctions."

171 **reiterate the threat:** Kate Davidson, "Lew Warns Russia of More Sanctions," *Politico*, April 10, 2014, www.politico.com/story/2014/04/jack-lew-russia-sanctions-105589.

172 **faithfully observed Shabbat:** Jacob Kornbluh, "Jack Lew on Shabbat during White House years," *Jewish Insider*, December 12, 2017, jewishinsider.com/2017/12/jack-lew-on-shabbat-during-white-house-years.

173 **traveled to Kyiv:** "Minister of Finance of Ukraine Meets with Representatives of the U.S. Department of the Treasury and U.S. National Security Council," Government of Ukraine, February 26, 2014, www.kmu.gov.ua/en/news/247056979.

174 **big but not all that complicated:** For a thorough analysis of Russia's economic policy and performance during the Putin era, see Chris Miller, *Putinomics: Money and Power in Resurgent Russia* (Chapel Hill: University of North Carolina Press, 2018).

174 *half* **of Russia's federal budget:** Richard Connolly, *Russia's Response to Sanctions: How Western Economic Statecraft Is Reshaping Political Economy in Russia* (Cambridge: Cambridge University Press, 2018), 41, 50.

174 **largest exporter of fossil fuels—by far:** *World Energy Outlook 2022* (Paris: International Energy Agency, 2022), www.iea.org/reports/world-energy-outlook-2022.

174 **25 percent of its total federal budget:** Connolly, *Russia's Response to Sanctions*, 123.

174 **dependent on foreign trade:** Connolly, *Russia's Response to Sanctions*, 49.

174 **well over $700 billion:** Adam Tooze, *Crashed: How a Decade of Financial Crises Changed the World* (New York: Viking, 2018), 499; Connolly, *Russia's Response to Sanctions*, 164.

175 **Obama had already approved such penalties:** "Announcement of Additional Treasury Sanctions on Russian Government Officials and Entities," U.S. Department of the Treasury, April 28, 2014, home.treasury.gov/news/press-releases/jl2369.

175 **$600 million of Bank Rossiya's assets:** Philip Shishkin, "U.S. Sanctions over Ukraine Hit Two Russian Banks Hardest," *The Wall Street Journal*, March 5, 2015, www.wsj.com/articles/u-s-sanctions-over-ukraine-hit-two-russian-banks-hardest-1425597150.

175 **Visa and MasterCard shut down service:** Robin Sidel, "Visa, MasterCard Say New Russian Sanctions Hit Two More Banks," *The Wall Street Journal*, April 28, 2014, www.wsj.com/articles/SB10001424052702304163604579529942428713458.

175 **"Death Star blowing up Tatooine":** Author interview with Daleep Singh, 2022.

175 **"right for the jugular":** Author interview with Brad Setser, 2022.

176 **"velocity of the negative feedback loop":** Author interview with Daleep Singh, 2022.

176 **"scalpel" rather than a "sledgehammer":** Anne Gearan, "Further Sanctions against Russia Are Outlined, Tied to Ukraine's Presidential Election," *The Washington Post*, May 8, 2014, www.washingtonpost.com/world/national-security/further-sanctions-against-russia-are-outlined-tied-to-ukraines-presidential-election/2014/05/08/c1841320-d6de-11e3-95d3-3bcd77cd4e11_story.html; Victoria Nuland in "Russia's Destabilization of Ukraine: Hearing Before the House Committee on Foreign Affairs," 113th Cong., 2nd sess., May 8, 2014, docs.house.gov/meetings/FA/FA00/20140508/102206/HHRG-113-FA00-Transcript-20140508.pdf.

177 **80 percent of the equipment and software:** Connolly, *Russia's Response to Sanctions*, 89.

177 **Even Angela Merkel:** Christian Oliver, Stefan Wagstyl, and Richard McGregor, "Ukraine Crisis: Merkel Toughens Sanctions Talk against Russia," *Financial Times*, June 25, 2014, www.ft.com/content/9bb98d0a-fc7c-11e3-98b8-00144feab7de.

177 **Poroshenko joined Obama, Putin, Merkel:** "Background Briefing by Senior Administrative Officials on Ukraine," July 16, 2014, The American Presidency Project, www.presidency.ucsb.edu/documents/background-briefing-senior-administration-officials-ukraine; Peter Baker, "Awkward Diplomacy as Leaders Gather," *The New York Times*, June 6, 2014, www.nytimes.com/2014/06/07/world/europe/obama-honors-moment-of-liberation-in-normandy.html

178 **as the Normandy Format:** Andrew Lohsen and Pierre Morcos, "Understanding the Normandy Format and Its Relation to the Current Standoff with Russia," Center for International and Strategic Studies, February 9, 2022, www.csis.org/analysis/understanding-normandy-format-and-its-relation-current-standoff-russia.

178 **fifteen-point peace plan:** Lidia Kelly and Richard Balmforth, "Poroshenko's Ukraine Peace Plan Gets Limited Support from Putin," Reuters, June 21, 2014, www.reuters.com/article/idUSKBN0EW0EG; "Peace Plan, Unilateral Ceasefire Offer Hope for Resolving Conflict in Ukraine, Political Affairs Official Tells Security Council," United Nations, June 29, 2014, press.un.org/en/2014/sc11448.doc.htm; "Ukraine's Peace Plan Unveiled," *Deutsche Welle*, June 20, 2014, www.dw.com/en/ukraines-poroshenko-unveils-peace-plan-as-russia-defends-border-troop-deployment/a-17725021.

CHAPTER 28: THE OPENING SALVO

179 **prepared to sign an association agreement with the EU:** Shaun Walker, "Ukraine Set to Sign EU Pact That Sparked Revolution," *The Guardian*, June 26, 2014, www.theguardian.com/world/2014/jun/26/ukraine-european-union-trade-pact.

179 **A fragile ceasefire:** "Week-long Truce in Ukraine," *Deutsche Welle*, June 20, 2014, www.dw.com/en /ukrainian-president-poroshenko-announces-week-long-cease-fire-in-eastern-ukraine/a-17725729.

179 **"Progress has not been as clear":** Christian Oliver and Guy Dinmore, "Italy Leads Calls to Slow Sanctions against Russia," *Financial Times*, June 27, 2014, www.ft.com/content/6b191cca-fd39-11e3-bc93 -00144feab7de.

179 **Italy's new prime minister, Matteo Renzi:** Sam Frizell, "Italy's Youngest Ever Prime Minister Takes the Reins," *Time*, February 22, 2014, time.com/9452/italy-prime-minister-matteo-renzi.

179 **Eni and UniCredit:** Oliver and Dinmore, "Italy Leads Calls."

180 **by June 30:** "EU Leaders Choose Juncker to Lead the Future of the Union," European Council, June 27, 2014, www.consilium.europa.eu/en/meetings/european-council/2014/06/26-27.

180 **plan for sectoral sanctions:** Richard McGregor and Ed Crooks, "Ukraine Crisis: US Considers New Round of Sanctions on Russia," *Financial Times*, June 25, 2014, www.ft.com/content/e902ae62-fc1c -11e3-9a03-00144feab7de.

180 **warning about the risks of sanctions:** Mike Dorning, "Business at Odds with Obama over Russia Sanctions Threat," *Bloomberg*, June 25, 2014, www.bloomberg.com/news/articles/2014-06-25/business -at-odds-with-obama-over-russia-sanctions-threat.

180 **"pro-trade policies and multilateral diplomacy":** Richard McGregor, "US Business Groups Attack Russia Sanctions," *Financial Times*, June 26, 2014, www.ft.com/content/e76ed66a-fcbd-11e3-81f5 -00144feab7de.

180 **EU leaders chose to wait:** Andrew Gardner, "Deadline Passes without EU Sanctions on Russia," *Politico*, July 3, 2014, www.politico.eu/article/deadline-passes-without-eu%e2%80%88sanctions-on-russia.

181 **"system would bear this kind of leadership":** Author interview with Dan Fried, 2022.

181 **a whopping $40 billion:** Vladimir Soldatkin and Andrew Callus, "Rosneft Pays Out in Historic TNK-BP Deal Completion," Reuters, March 21, 2013, www.reuters.com/article/us-rosneft-tnkbp-deal/rosneft -pays-out-in-historic-tnk-bp-deal-completion-idUSBRE92K0IZ20130321.

181 **"dominance of the dollar":** Author interview with Daleep Singh, 2022.

181 **United States pulled the trigger:** "Background Briefing by Senior Administrative Officials on Ukraine," July 16, 2014; Andrew Gardner, "US and EU Strengthen Russian Sanctions," *Politico*, July 17, 2014, www.politico.eu/article/us-and-eu-strengthen-russian-sanctions.

181 **paltry set of sanctions:** Gardner, "Russian Sanctions."

181 **"dilute the impact of the American actions":** Peter Baker and James Kanter, "Raising Stakes on Russia, U.S. Adds Sanctions," *The New York Times*, July 16, 2014, www.nytimes.com/2014/07/17/world /europe/obama-widens-sanctions-against-russia.html.

182 **"frustration with Europe's reluctance":** Julie Pace, "US Preparing Unilateral Sanctions on Russia," The Associated Press, July 16, 2014, apnews.com/article/f5b5f816b4e047a783fabc84ad9fcaa2.

182 **Morgan Stanley had helped:** Alan Katz, Jesse Drucker, and Irina Reznik, "Morgan Stanley Enabled Rosneft as No. 1 until Crimea Grab," *Bloomberg*, August 18, 2014, www.bloomberg.com/news/articles /2014-08-18/morgan-stanley-enabled-rosneft-as-no-1-until-crimea-grab.

CHAPTER 29: MH17

183 **bodies of victims still wrapped in seat belts:** Sabrina Tavernise, "Fallen Bodies, Jet Parts, and a Child's Pink Book," *The New York Times*, July 17, 2014, www.nytimes.com/2014/07/18/world/europe/malaysia -airlines-plane-leaves-trail-of-debris.html.

183 **"end of the world":** Terry Gross, "Malaysia Flight Wreckage Was 'Like the End of the World,'" *Fresh Air* (podcast), NPR, August 6, 2014, www.npr.org/2014/08/06/338197374/malaysia-flight-wreckage-was -like-the-end-of-the-world.

183 **did not have them deployed:** "Photographs of Ukrainian Buks Geolocated in Poltava Oblast, Nearly Three Years Later," *Bellingcat*, April 4, 2017, www.bellingcat.com/news/uk-and-europe/2017/04/04 /photographs-ukrainian-buks-geolocated-nearly-three-years-later.

184 **thinking they had downed a Ukrainian military jet:** Heather Saul, "MH17 Malaysia Airlines Crash: Pro-Russian Separatists 'Discuss Downing of Flight' in Leaked Audio Released by Ukraine Security Service," *The Independent*, July 18, 2014, www.independent.co.uk/news/world/europe/malaysia-airlines-crash -prorussian-separatists-discuss-downing-of-flight-mh17-in-leaked-audio-released-by-ukraine-security -service-9613893.html; Mariano Castillo, "Alleged Phone Call: 'We Have Just Shot Down a Plane,'" CNN, July 18, 2014, www.cnn.com/2014/07/18/world/europe/ukraine-mh17-intercepted-audio/index.html.

184 **"It's a civilian!":** "Damning Video Shows Pro-Russian Rebels Surprised MH17 Was Civilian," Radio Free Europe/Radio Liberty, July 17, 2015, www.rferl.org/a/ukraine-video-shows-rebels-surprised-mh17 -wreckage-civilian/27133474.html.

184 **Russian-backed separatists fired the Buk:** Luke Harding, "Q&A: What We Know and Don't about the Downing of MH17," *The Guardian*, May 24, 2018, www.theguardian.com/world/2018/may/24/qa -mh17-investigation-russian-missile-aircraft-ukraine.

184 **Buk was spotted in separatist-held territory:** John Kerry, interview by David Gregory, *Meet the Press*, NBC News, July 20, 2014, www.nbcnews.com/storyline/ukraine-plane-crash/kerry-says-evidence-shows -russian-backed-separatists-downed-mh17-n160526.

185 **"wake-up call for Europe":** Jeff Mason and Steve Holland, "Obama Says Europe Should See Downed Jet as 'Wake-up Call,'" Reuters, July 18, 2014, www.reuters.com/article/ukraine-crisis-obama/obama-says-europe-should-see-downed-jet-as-wake-up-call-idINKBN0FN2PU20140718.

185 **looted the ghastly rubble:** Polly Mosendz, "Looters Stole Cash, Credit Cards, and Jewelry from Flight MH17 Crash Victims," *The Atlantic*, July 18, 2014, www.theatlantic.com/international/archive/2014/07/flight-mh17-crash-site-has-been-heavily-looted/374707.

185 **196 Dutch nationals:** "MH17 Incident," Government of the Netherlands, updated January 1, 2023, www.government.nl/topics/mh17-incident.

185 **"human remains should be used in a political game":** Justyna Pawlak, "Grieving Dutch Minister Made Europe Re-think Russia Sanctions," Reuters, July 25, 2014, www.reuters.com/article/us-ukraine-crisis-eu-insight/grieving-dutch-minister-made-europe-re-think-russia-sanctions-idUSKBN0FU1M520140726.

185 **"He carried the room":** Author interview with Radek Sikorski, 2023.

185 **"possible to speak against that":** Pawlak, "Grieving Dutch Minister."

185 **"Restricting access to capital markets":** Peter Spiegel, "Ukraine Crisis: EU to Weigh Far-reaching Sanctions on Russia," *Financial Times*, July 24, 2014, www.ft.com/content/15ecc35c-12a4-11e4-a6d4-00144feabdc0.

186 **"Russia needs EU technologies":** Spiegel, "Ukraine Crisis."

186 **one in two Russians held an account there:** Matthew Rocco et al., "Shares in Banks Exposed to Russia Hit on Sanctions Fears," *Financial Times*, February 24, 2022, www.ft.com/content/5b423554-6ce9-49fe-b74c-da41298b565f.

186 **sanctions had already left their mark:** Indira A. R. Lakshmanan, "U.S. Sanctions Squeeze Putin, Stop Short of Economic War," *Bloomberg*, July 17, 2014, www.bloomberg.com/news/articles/2014-07-18/u-s-sanctions-squeeze-putin-stop-short-of-economic-war.

186 **joint U.S.-European strike:** "Statement by the President of the European Council Herman Van Rompuy and the President of the European Commission in the Name of the European Union on the Agreed Additional Restrictive Measures Against Russia," European Council and European Commission, July 29, 2014, www.consilium.europa.eu/uedocs/cms_data/docs/pressdata/en/ec/144158.pdf; "Announcement of Additional Treasury Sanctions on Russian Financial Institutions and on a Defense Technology Entity," U.S. Department of the Treasury, July 29, 2014, home.treasury.gov/news/press-releases/jl2590.

186 **$9 billion for sanctions violations:** "BNP Paribas Agrees to Plead Guilty and to Pay $8.9 Billion for Illegally Processing Financial Transactions for Countries Subject to U.S. Economic Sanctions," U.S. Department of Justice, June 30, 2014, www.justice.gov/opa/pr/bnp-paribas-agrees-plead-guilty-and-pay-89-billion-illegally-processing-financial.

186 **significant exposure to Russia:** Anna Baraulina and Elena Popina, "Calpers Joins BlackRock's Goldberg Ramping Up on Russian Debt," *Bloomberg*, October 15, 2015, www.bloomberg.com/news/articles/2015-10-15/calpers-joins-blackrock-s-goldberg-ramping-up-on-russian-debt.

186 **Half of Sberbank's openly traded shares:** Neil Buckley and Martin Arnold, "Herman Gref, Sberbank's modernising sanctions survivor," *Financial Times*, January 31, 2016, www.ft.com/content/4abbcba6-c413-11e5-808f-8231cd71622e.

186 **applied only to *new* debt and equity:** "Directive 1 Pursuant to Executive Order 13662," U.S. Department of the Treasury, July 16, 2014, ofac.treasury.gov/media/8681/download?inline; "General License No. 1B," November 28, 2017, U.S. Department of the Treasury, ofac.treasury.gov/media/8971/download?inline.

CHAPTER 30: ESCALATION

188 **banning Western food imports:** Fred Weir, "Sour Apples in Russia? Putin Moves to Ban Food Imports from West," *Christian Science Monitor*, August 6, 2014, www.csmonitor.com/World/Europe/2014/0806/Sour-apples-in-Russia-Putin-moves-to-ban-food-imports-from-West.

188 **fifth-largest food importer:** Ivana Kottasova and Inez Torre, "Which Foods Are off Russian Menus?" CNN, August 18, 2014, www.cnn.com/2014/08/14/business/russia-eu-food-embargo/index.html.

188 **ordered all illegally imported food to be seized:** Sarah Rainsford, "Russians Shocked as Banned Western Food Destroyed," *BBC News*, August 7, 2015, www.bbc.com/news/world-europe-33818186.

188 **meats set ablaze:** "The Bonfire of the Vans of Cheese," *The Economist*, August 15, 2015, www.economist.com/europe/2015/08/15/the-bonfire-of-the-vans-of-cheese.

188 **"different kind of pizza":** "Flexing Its Mussels," *The Economist*, August 20, 2014, www.economist.com/europe/2014/08/20/flexing-its-mussels.

188 **recaptured the town of Ilovaisk:** Michael Cohen, "Ukraine's Battle at Ilovaisk, August 2014: The Tyranny of Means," *Military Review*, June 10, 2016, www.armyupress.army.mil/Journals/Military-Review/Online-Exclusive/2016-Online-Exclusive-Articles/Ukraines-Battle-at-Ilovaisk.

189 **hundreds of Ukrainian troops dead:** Alec Luhn, "Anatomy of a Bloodbath," *Foreign Policy*, September 6, 2014, foreignpolicy.com/2014/09/06/anatomy-of-a-bloodbath.

189 **"I'll take Kyiv in two weeks":** Ian Traynor, "Putin Claims Russian Forces 'Could Conquer Ukraine Capital in Two Weeks," *The Guardian*, September 2, 2014, www.theguardian.com/world/2014/sep/02/putin-russian-forces-could-conquer-ukraine-capital-kiev-fortnight.

189 **thousands of Russian troops in the Donbas:** Igor Sutyagin, "Russian Forces in Ukraine," Royal United Services Institute, March 1, 2015, www.jstor.org/stable/resrep37229.

189 **"repeating the mistakes made in Munich in 1938":** Traynor, "Putin Claims."

189 **"paying double later":** Anthony Luzzatto Gardner, *Stars with Stripes: The Essential Partnership between the European Union and the United States* (London: Springer Nature, 2020), 256.

189 **start sending weapons to Ukraine:** "Ukraine Crisis: US Senators Urge Arms 'to Fight Russia,'" *BBC News*, September 1, 2014, www.bbc.com/news/world-europe-29007631.

189 **"can't we help these people defend themselves?":** John McCain, interview by Major Garrett, *Face the Nation*, CBS News, August 31, 2014, www.youtube.com/watch?v=z9tcmpbcIj8.

189 **"cannot win the war with blankets":** Al Kamen, "State Department Failed to Keep Ukraine President on Message?" *The Washington Post*, October 6, 2014, www.washingtonpost.com/blogs/in-the-loop/wp/2014/10/06/state-department-failed-to-keep-ukraine-president-on-message.

190 **most significant achievement:** Michael McFaul, *From Cold War to Hot Peace: An American Ambassador in Putin's Russia* (Boston: Houghton Mifflin Harcourt, 2018), 286.

190 **overseen his company's business in Russia:** Daniel Gilbert, "Sanctions over Ukraine Put Exxon at Risk," *The Wall Street Journal*, September 11, 2014, www.wsj.com/articles/sanctions-over-ukraine-put-exxon-at-risk-1410477455.

190 **Order of Friendship:** Ed Crooks, "Rex Tillerson: From Exxon's Interests to America's," *Financial Times*, December 13, 2016, www.ft.com/content/7fdfd440-c15a-11e6-81c2-f57d90f6741a.

190 **stance against sanctions:** Andrew E. Kramer and Stanley Reed, "For Western Oil Companies, Expanding in Russia Is a Dance Around Sanctions," *The New York Times*, June 9, 2014, www.nytimes.com/2014/06/10/business/international/for-western-oil-companies-expanding-in-russia-is-a-dance-around-sanctions.html; Clifford Krauss, "Potential Crackdown on Russia Risks Also Punishing Western Oil Companies," *The New York Times*, March 27, 2014, www.nytimes.com/2014/03/28/business/energy-environment/potential-crackdown-on-russia-risks-also-punishing-western-oil-companies.html.

190 **Exxon was pushing forward:** Daniel Gilbert, "Exxon Sticks with Russia Despite Ukraine Sanctions," *The Wall Street Journal*, May 1, 2014, www.wsj.com/articles/SB10001424052702303678404579535423153883250.

190 **contracts with Igor Sechin:** *Exxon Mobil Corp. v. Mnuchin*, 430 F. Supp. 3d 220 (N.D. Tex. 2019).

190 **then sued OFAC:** John P. Barker et al., "Exxon Mobil Challenged a $2 Million OFAC Penalty—and the District Court Agreed," Arnold & Porter, January 7, 2020, www.arnoldporter.com/en/perspectives/advisories/2020/01/exxon-challenged-a-2-million-ofac.

191 **prohibit the provision of *all* services:** Stanley Reed and Clifford Krauss, "New Sanctions to Stall Exxon's Arctic Oil Plans," *The New York Times*, September 12, 2014, www.nytimes.com/2014/09/13/business/energy-environment/new-sanctions-to-stall-exxons-arctic-oil-plans.html.

191 **dog tags from Russian soldiers:** "Battle for Ukraine: How a Diplomatic Success Unravelled," *Financial Times*, February 3, 2015, www.ft.com/content/7cfc8ac6-ab17-11e4-91d2-00144feab7de.

191 **signed a ceasefire deal:** "Chairperson-in-Office Welcomes Minsk Agreement, Assures President Poroshenko of OSCE Support," Organization for Security and Cooperation in Europe, September 5, 2014, www.osce.org/cio/123245.

191 **known as the Minsk agreement:** Duncan Allan, "The Minsk Conundrum: Western Policy and Russia's War in Eastern Ukraine," Chatham House, May 22, 2020, www.chathamhouse.org/2020/05/minsk-conundrum-western-policy-and-russias-war-eastern-ukraine-0/minsk-1-agreement.

192 **would not deliver the Mistral warships:** Before France canceled it, the Mistral deal was set to be the largest-ever sale of Western military hardware to Russia—and the largest Western military transfer of any kind to Moscow since the United States sent the Soviet Union 149 naval vessels under Project Hula during World War II. Dan Lamothe, "France Backs off Sending Mistral Warship to Russia in $1.7 Billion Deal," *The Washington Post*, September 3, 2014, www.washingtonpost.com/news/checkpoint/wp/2014/09/03/france-backs-off-sending-mistral-warship-to-russia-in-1-7-billion-deal; Sebastien Roblin, "How France Almost Sold Russia Two Powerful Aircraft Carriers," *The National Interest*, September 1, 2019, nationalinterest.org/blog/buzz/how-france-almost-sold-russia-two-powerful-aircraft-carriers-77241; Sebastien Roblin, "Your History Book Missed This: In 1945, the U.S. Navy Gave Russia a Fleet of Ships," *The National Interest*, August 23, 2019, nationalinterest.org/blog/buzz/your-history-book-missed-1945-us-navy-gave-russia-fleet-ships-75696.

192 **meet with top officials:** Matthew Campbell and Dawn Kopecki, "Trent Lott's Firm Made a Fortune Lobbying for the Kremlin," *Bloomberg*, May 15, 2015, www.bloomberg.com/news/articles/2015-05-15/washington-insiders-reap-windfall-peddling-influence-for-kremlin; Nick Wadhams and Margaret Talev, "CEO No Stranger in D.C.," *Arkansas Democrat-Gazette*, December 14, 2016, www.arkansasonline.com/news/2016/dec/14/ceo-no-stranger-in-d-c-20161214; The White House, "Visitor Access Records," March 12, 2014, obamawhitehouse.archives.gov/briefing-room/disclosures/visitor-records.

192 **granted a short extension:** Andrew E. Kramer, "The 'Russification' of Oil Exploration,'" *The New York Times*, October 29, 2014, www.nytimes.com/2014/10/30/business/energy-environment/russia-oil-exploration-sanctions.html.

192 **suspended its joint venture with Rosneft:** Clifford Krauss, "Exxon Halts Oil Drilling in Waters of
Russia," *The New York Times*, September 19, 2014, www.nytimes.com/2014/09/20/business/exxon
-suspending-700-million-drilling-operation-in-russian-waters.html.
192 **930 million barrels of oil:** Steve LeVine, "ExxonMobil Reportedly Finds Oil in the Russian Arctic,"
Quartz, September 26, 2014, qz.com/272140/exxonmobil-reportedly-finds-oil-in-the-russian-arctic.

CHAPTER 31: "ECONOMY IN TATTERS"

193 **like Elvira Nabiullina:** Natalie Sportelli, "The Most Powerful Women in Politics for 2014," *Forbes*, May
28, 2014, www.forbes.com/sites/nataliesportelli/2014/05/28/the-most-powerful-women-in-politics
-for-2014/?sh=71a8c194595b; Paddy Hirsch, "Who Is the Real Elvira Nabiullina?" NPR, April 19, 2022,
www.npr.org/sections/money/2022/04/19/1093339972/who-is-the-real-elvira-nabiullina; "Yale University
President Levin Announces Selection of 2007 Yale World Fellows," *YaleNews*, May 3, 2007, news.yale.edu
/2007/05/03/yale-university-president-levin-announces-selection-2007-yale-world-fellows; Jane Lewis,
"Elvira Nabiullina: Putin's Central Bank Chief Blindsided by Russia's War on Ukraine," *MoneyWeek*,
April 3, 2022, moneyweek.com/investments/stockmarkets/emerging-markets/604656/meet-putins
-central-bank-chief-who-was-blindsided.
194 **hat in hand to China:** Alexander Gabuev, "A 'Soft Alliance'? Russia-China Relations after the Ukraine
Crisis," European Council on Foreign Relations, February 10, 2015, 3, ecfr.eu/publication/a_soft_alliance
_russia_china_relations_after_the_ukraine_crisis331.
194 **"Power of Siberia":** Zachary Keck, "China and Russia Sign Massive Natural Gas Deal," *The Diplomat*,
May 21, 2014, thediplomat.com/2014/05/china-and-russia-sign-massive-natural-gas-deal.
195 **separate trip to China:** Gabuev, "A 'Soft Alliance'?," 5.
195 **create a $25 billion currency swap line:** "Russia Signs Deal with China to Help Weather Sanctions,"
CNBC, October 13, 2014, www.cnbc.com/2014/10/13/russia-signs-deals-with-china-to-help-weather
-sanctions.html.
195 **launch of SPFS:** Natasha Turak, "Russia's Central Bank Governor Touts Moscow Alternative to SWIFT
Transfer System as Protection from US Sanctions," CNBC, May 24, 2018, www.cnbc.com/2018/05/23
/russias-central-bank-governor-touts-moscow-alternative-to-swift-transfer-system-as-protection-from
-us-sanctions.html.
195 **regulation forcing Visa and MasterCard:** Alec Luhn, "Russia Demands $3.8bn Security Deposit from
Visa and Mastercard," *The Guardian*, May 6, 2014, www.theguardian.com/world/2014/may/06/russia
-security-deposit-visa-mastercard-sanctions-ukraine.
195 **"free from external factors":** Richard Connolly, *Russia's Response to Sanctions: How Western Economic Statecraft is Reshaping Political Economy in Russia* (Cambridge: Cambridge University Press,
2018), 184.
195 **depend on food from the West:** Michael Birnbaum, "Russia Bans Food Imports from U.S., E.U.," *The
Washington Post*, August 7, 2014, www.washingtonpost.com/world/russia-bans-food-imports-from-us
-eu/2014/08/07/a29f5bea-1e14-11e4-82f9-2cd6fa8da5c4_story.html.
196 **limited economic sovereignty:** Connolly, *Russia's Response to Sanctions*, 50.
196 **$90 per barrel:** Anjali Raval and Gregory Meyer, "Oil Hits Lows as Market Chokes on Oversupply,"
Financial Times, October 6, 2014, www.ft.com/content/583e408c-4d19-11e4-bf60-00144feab7de.
196 **faced some $20 billion in debt repayments:** John Aglionby, Harriet Agnew, and Christopher Adams,
"Rosneft Changes Accounting Policy to Ease Effect of Rouble's Fall," *Financial Times*, February 3, 2015,
www.ft.com/content/6610a368-ab7d-11e4-8070-00144feab7de; Kathrin Hille and Ralph Atkins, "Russian
Companies Face Credit Crunch Danger," *Financial Times*, October 7, 2014, www.ft.com/content
/70a578b4-4d70-11e4-9683-00144feab7de; Ksenia Galouchko and Stephen Bierman, "Putin Readies
Aid as Rosneft's $21 Billion of Debt Looms," *Bloomberg*, November 16, 2014, www.bloomberg.com
/news/articles/2014-11-16/putin-readies-aid-as-rosneft-s-21-billion-looms-russia-credit.
196 **government nationalized Bashneft:** Darya Korsunskaya and Oksana Kobzeva, "Russia's Rosneft Seeks
to Increase Stake in Bashneft," Reuters, October 28, 2016, www.reuters.com/article/us-russia-bashneft
-rosneft-oil/russias-rosneft-seeks-to-increase-stake-in-bashneft-idUSKCN12S12J; Dina Khrennikova
and Jake Rudnitsky, "Moscow Court Rules to Nationalize Sistema's Bashneft Shares," *Bloomberg*, October 30, 2014, www.bloomberg.com/news/articles/2014-10-30/russia-keeps-sistema-claims-to-bashneft
-shares-as-decision-looms.
196 **40 rubles to the dollar:** "On the Edge of Recession," *The Economist*, October 4, 2014, www.economist
.com/europe/2014/10/04/on-the-edge-of-recession.
196 **"no capital controls":** Kathrin Hille, "Putin Seeks to Calm Investor Jitters over Russia," *Financial
Times*, October 2, 2014, www.ft.com/content/c70c8060-4a2f-11e4-bc07-00144feab7de.
196 **"All I have to do is smile":** Andrew E. Kramer, "Putin Trumpets Economic Strength, but Advisers
Seem Less Certain," *The New York Times*, October 2, 2014, www.nytimes.com/2014/10/03/world/europe
/putin-russia-economy.html.
196 **$500 billion in foreign exchange reserves:** Connolly, *Russia's Response to Sanctions*, 182.
197 **$6 billion to prop up the ruble:** Tomas Hirst, "The Russian Central Bank Admits Defeat," *Business

Insider, October 13, 2014, www.businessinsider.com/russian-central-bank-admits-defeat-over-defending-the-ruble-2014-10.

197 **end of quantitative easing:** James Kynge, "Fed Leaves Emerging Markets Exposed," *Financial Times*, October 29, 2014, www.ft.com/content/eee96c0e-5f8a-11e4-8c27-00144feabdc0.

197 **the dollar appreciated:** Alice Ross, "Dollar Surges in 2014 on Rate Rise Hopes," *Financial Times*, December 31, 2014, www.ft.com/content/5f6be486-9111-11e4-914a-00144feabdc0.

197 **ruble continued to drop:** Kathrin Hille and Roman Olearchyk, "Plunging Rouble Raises Spectre of Fresh Financial Crisis for Russia," *Financial Times*, November 9, 2014, www.ft.com/content/6c059328-666d-11e4-9c0c-00144feabdc0.

197 **$10 billion before the end of the year:** Ksenia Galouchko and Stephen Bierman, "Putin Readies Aid as Rosneft's $21 Billion of Debt Looms," *Bloomberg*, November 16, 2014, www.bloomberg.com/news/articles/2014-11-16/putin-readies-aid-as-rosneft-s-21-billion-looms-russia-credit.

197 **$32 billion in debt repayments:** Hille and Atkins, "Credit Crunch Danger."

197 **desperate for dollars:** Delphine Strauss, "Moscow Boosts Efforts to Ease Shortage of Dollars," *Financial Times*, October 15, 2014, www.ft.com/content/1ae5eb0a-5484-11e4-b2ea-00144feab7de.

197 **$50 billion bailout:** Delphine Strauss, "Russia's Rouble Falls to New Dollar Lows," *Financial Times*, October 23, 2014, www.ft.com/content/10ac6f1e-5acf-11e4-b449-00144feab7de.

197 **Russians hoarded foreign currency:** "The Rouble's Rout," *The Economist*, November 15, 2014, www.economist.com/finance-and-economics/2014/11/15/the-roubles-rout.

197 **approval rating hit an all-time high:** Kathrin Hille, "Rouble's Wobbles Send Tremors through Putin's Kremlin," *Financial Times*, November 7, 2014, www.ft.com/content/37ea9682-6696-11e4-9c0c-00144feabdc0.

197 **Putin charged Elvira Nabiullina:** Hille, "Rouble's Wobbles."

197 **interest rates to 9.5 percent:** "The Rouble's Rout," *The Economist*.

197 **"at any moment":** Hille and Olearchyk, "Plunging Rouble."

198 **OPEC decided to keep production flat:** Dave Mead and Porscha Stiger, "The 2014 Plunge in Import Petroleum Prices: What Happened?" *Beyond the Numbers* 4, no. 9 (May 2015), www.bls.gov/opub/btn/volume-4/pdf/the-2014-plunge-in-import-petroleum-prices-what-happened.pdf; Matt Clinch, "Oil Falls as OPEC Opts Not to Cut Production," CNBC, November 27, 2014, www.cnbc.com/2014/11/27/saudi-oil-minister-says-opec-will-not-cut-oil-production-reuters.html; Summer Said and Benoît Faucon, "Al-Naimi Likely to Remain Saudi Oil Minister Until Market Calms," *The Wall Street Journal*, January 23, 2015, www.wsj.com/articles/al-naimi-likely-to-remain-saudi-oil-minister-until-market-calms-1422042242.

198 **sliced in half:** Rabah Arezki and Olivier Blanchard, "Seven Questions about the Recent Oil Price Slump," *IMF Blog*, International Monetary Fund, December 22, 2014, www.imf.org/en/Blogs/Articles/2014/12/22/seven-questions-about-the-recent-oil-price-slump.

198 **canceled holiday travel:** Courtney Weaver, "Sun Sets on Russians' Upmarket Trips Abroad," *Financial Times*, December 9, 2014, www.ft.com/content/1f92b224-7edb-11e4-a828-00144feabdc0.

198 **"enemy of the nation":** Kathrin Hille, "The Woman Trying to Tame the Rouble," *Financial Times*, December 3, 2014, www.ft.com/content/ba20c594-7abf-11e4-b630-00144feabdc0.

198 **raised interest rates again:** Kathrin Hille, "Russia Raises Interest Rates to 10.5%," *Financial Times*, December 11, 2014, www.ft.com/content/5a17833e-8129-11e4-896c-00144feabdc0.

198 **Rosneft issued 625 billion rubles worth of bonds:** Vladimir Kuznetsov, "Rosneft Gets Central Bank Help Refinancing $7 Billion Loan," *Bloomberg*, December 12, 2014, www.bloomberg.com/news/articles/2014-12-12/rosneft-s-10-8-billion-refinancing-driven-by-central-bank-cash.

198 **bailout of Rosneft:** "Russia: Fault in our Tsars," *Financial Times*, December 16, 2014, www.ft.com/content/65b40e20-850b-11e4-bb63-00144feabdc0.

198 **worst single-day rout:** R.D., "Going over the Edge," *The Economist*, December 16, 2014, www.economist.com/finance-and-economics/2014/12/16/going-over-the-edge.

198 **the ruble nosedived:** R.D., "Going over the Edge."

199 **Volvo stopped selling cars:** Andrew E. Kramer, "Russia's Steep Rate Increase Fails to Stem Ruble's Decline," *The New York Times*, December 16, 2014, www.nytimes.com/2014/12/17/business/russia-ruble-interest-rates.html.

199 **anonymous text messages:** Neil Buckley and Martin Arnold, "Herman Gref, Sberbank's Modernising Sanctions Survivor," *Financial Times*, January 31, 2016, www.ft.com/content/4abbcba6-c413-11e5-808f-8231cd71622e.

199 **customers withdrew 1.3 trillion rubles:** Buckley and Arnold, "Herman Gref."

199 **inserted a handful of Kremlin insiders:** Connolly, *Russia's Response to Sanctions*, 174–75.

199 **informal capital controls:** Kathrin Hille, "Russia's Strong-arm Tactics Restore Fragile Calm to Banks," *Financial Times*, December 30, 2014, www.ft.com/content/85c3c432-9017-11e4-8f09-00144feabdc0.

199 **nearly a trillion and a half rubles:** Connolly, *Russia's Response to Sanctions*, 175.

199 **worst year of capital flight:** "Russia's Capital Outflows Reach Record $151.5 bln in 2014 as Sanctions, Oil Slump Hit," Reuters, January 16, 2015, www.reuters.com/article/russia-capital-outflows/update-1-russias-capital-outflows-reach-record-151-5-bln-in-2014-as-sanctions-oil-slump-hit-idUSL6N0UV3S320150116.

199 **S&P downgraded Russia's credit rating:** Jill Treanor, "Russia Downgraded to Junk Status for First Time in Decade," *The Guardian*, January 26, 2015, www.theguardian.com/business/2015/jan/26/russia-downgraded-junk-status-decade-credit-rating.

199 **cost of credit default swaps:** Sujata Rao, "More Losses Loom for Russian Bonds as Credit Rating Heads Back to Junk," Reuters, January 11, 2015, www.reuters.com/article/us-russia-crisis-ratings-implications/more-losses-loom-for-russian-bonds-as-credit-rating-heads-back-to-junk-idUSKBN0KK06Y20150111.

200 **more painful than the 2008 financial crisis:** Adam Tooze, *Crashed: How a Decade of Financial Crises Changed the World* (New York: Viking, 2018), 506.

200 **Real incomes were down:** "Russia Real Wage Growth," *Trading Economics*, tradingeconomics.com/russia/wage-growth.

200 **closer to 40 percent:** Jack Farchy, "Russia Faces Full Blown Crisis, Says Kudrin," *Financial Times*, December 22, 2014, www.ft.com/content/d8bf5266-89cb-11e4-9dbf-00144feabdc0.

201 **"Russia is isolated with its economy in tatters":** Barack Obama, "State of the Union Address" (speech, Washington, D.C., January 20, 2015), The White House, obamawhitehouse.archives.gov/the-press-office/2015/01/20/remarks-president-state-union-address-January-20-2015.

CHAPTER 32: BACK FROM THE EDGE

202 **barely contained economic slump:** Shaun Walker and Alberto Nardelli, "Russians Mark Less Than Merry Orthodox Christmas amid Rouble Fears," *The Guardian*, January 7, 2015, www.theguardian.com/world/2015/jan/07/russians-orthodox-christmas-rouble-2015-oil-price.

202 **a "false start":** "Игорь Бес Безлер Александр Бородай Новоросия это фальстарт!" ("Igor 'Bes' Bezler, Alexander Borodai: 'Novorossiya is a false start!'"), YouTube, January 1, 2015, www.youtube.com/watch?v=nKfCIFl6ivg#t=59.

202 **suspended their plans to build *Novorossiya*:** The leaders of the self-proclaimed Donetsk People's Republic and the Luhansk People's Republic formally suspended the *Novorossiya* project in May 2015. Andrei Kolesnikov, "Why the Kremlin Is Shutting Down the Novorossiya Project," Carnegie Endowment for International Peace, May 29, 2015, carnegiemoscow.org/commentary/60249; Steven Pifer, "Putin and Ukraine's East/West Divide," The Brookings Institution, May 14, 2015, www.brookings.edu/articles/putin-and-ukraines-eastwest-divide.

202 **occupied less than 5 percent:** Pifer, "Putin and Ukraine."

202 **"substantial collateral risks in Europe":** Author interview with Jack Lew, 2022.

203 **"We survived Leningrad, we could survive this":** Author interview with Jack Lew, 2022.

203 **targeted narrowly at Russian-occupied Crimea:** "Crimea and Sevastopol: Further EU Sanctions Approved," Council of the European Union, December 18, 2014, www.consilium.europa.eu/media/23879/146392.pdf; "Executive Order 13685—Blocking Property of Certain Persons and Prohibiting Certain Transactions with Respect to the Crimea Region of Ukraine," *Code of Federal Regulations*, titles 3 and 50 (2014), December 19, 2014, www.govinfo.gov/content/pkg/DCPD-201400947/pdf/DCPD-201400947.pdf.

203 **"bite off a piece of another country":** Victoria Nuland, "U.S. Policy in Ukraine: Countering Russia and Driving Reform: Hearing Before the Senate Committee on Foreign Relations," 114th Cong., 1st sess., March 10, 2015, www.govinfo.gov/content/pkg/CHRG-114shrg96831/html/CHRG-114shrg96831.htm.

204 **Putin's fighters took the airport:** Shaun Walker and Oksana Grytsenko, "Ukraine Forces Admit Loss of Donetsk Airport to Rebels," *The Guardian*, January 21, 2015, www.theguardian.com/world/2015/jan/21/russia-ukraine-war-fighting-east.

204 **The Minsk agreement was dead:** Rick Lyman and Andrew E. Kramer, "War Is Exploding Anew in Ukraine; Rebels Vow More," *The New York Times*, January 23, 2015, www.nytimes.com/2015/01/24/world/europe/ukraine-violence.html.

204 **offensive to take Debaltseve:** Nick Paton Walsh, "Inside the Ghost Town That's Key to Ukraine Conflict," CNN, February 18, 2015, www.cnn.com/2015/02/18/europe/debaltseve-strategic-ukraine/index.html.

204 **So did Vice President Joe Biden:** Glenn Thrush and Kenneth P. Vogel, "What Joe Biden Actually Did in Ukraine," *The New York Times*, November 10, 2019, www.nytimes.com/2019/11/10/us/politics/joe-biden-ukraine.html.

205 **regular calls with Putin and Poroshenko:** Shaun Walker, Julian Borger, Ian Traynor, "Putin and Ukraine Leader to Hold Phone Talks after Inconclusive End to Summit," *The Guardian*, February 6, 2015, www.theguardian.com/world/2015/feb/06/merkel-hollande-putin-ukraine-talks-moscow.

205 **"risk a conflagration":** "Germany Warns on Russia Sanctions," *Deutsche Welle*, January 4, 2015, www.dw.com/en/germany-warns-against-tougher-sanctions-on-russia/a-18169784; "Steinmeier Urges Caution over Russia Sanctions," *Deutsche Welle*, December 19, 2014, www.dw.com/en/german-foreign-minister-steinmeier-urges-caution-over-russia-sanctions/a-18143066.

205 **"He told me that":** "France Seeks End to Russia Sanctions over Ukraine," *BBC News*, January 5, 2015, www.bbc.com/news/world-europe-30679176.

205 **held a conference call:** "Ukraine Crisis: 'Last Chance' for Peace Says Hollande," *BBC News*, February 7, 2015, www.bbc.com/news/world-europe-31185027.

205 **"How many people have to die":** Soraya Sarhaddi Nelson, "Merkel's U.S. Visit Could Turn Testy," NPR, February 8, 2015, www.npr.org/2015/02/08/384695813/merkels-u-s-visit-could-turn-testy.

206 **inauspicious name "Minsk II":** "Ukraine Ceasefire: New Minsk Agreement Key Points," *BBC News*, February 12, 2015, www.bbc.com/news/world-europe-31436513.

207 **"There's no city left":** Alec Luhn and Oksana Grytsenko, "Ukrainian Soldiers Share Horrors of Debaltseve Battle after Stinging Defeat," *The Guardian*, February 18, 2015, www.theguardian.com/world/2015/feb/18/ukrainian-soldiers-share-horrors-of-debaltseve-battle-after-stinging-defeat.

207 **drained Ukraine of blood and treasure:** Duncan Allan, *The Minsk Conundrum: Western Policy and Russia's War in Eastern Ukraine* (London: Chatham House, May 22, 2020), www.chathamhouse.org/2020/05/minsk-conundrum-western-policy-and-russias-war-eastern-ukraine-0/minsk-1-agreement.

CHAPTER 33: FROM RUSSIA WITH BRIBES

208 **"I won't fail":** Anthony Luzzatto Gardner, *Stars with Stripes: The Essential Partnership between the European Union and the United States* (London: Springer Nature, 2020), 249.

209 **27 percent unemployment:** Adam Tooze, *Crashed: How a Decade of Financial Crises Changed the World* (New York: Viking, 2018), 515–16.

209 **Putin associates began cultivating members:** Sam Jones, Kerin Hope, Courtney Weaver, "Alarm Bells Ring over Syriza's Russian Links," *Financial Times*, January 28, 2015, www.ft.com/content/a87747de-a713-11e4-b6bd-00144feab7de.

209 **"no interest in imposing sanctions on Russia":** Andrew Higgins, "Greece Steps Back into Line with European Union Policy on Russia Sanctions," *The New York Times*, January 29, 2015, www.nytimes.com/2015/01/30/world/europe/european-union-russia-sanctions-greece.html.

209 **"could not have come at a better time":** David M. Herszenhorn and Liz Alderman, "Putin Meets with Alexis Tsipras of Greece, Raising Eyebrows in Europe," *The New York Times*, April 8, 2015, www.nytimes.com/2015/04/09/world/europe/putin-russia-alexis-tsipras-greece-financial-crisis.html.

209 **"repeatedly declared our disagreement":** Herszenhorn and Alderman, "Putin Meets with Alexis Tsipras of Greece, Raising Eyebrows in Europe."

209 **potential pipeline deal:** "Greece Poised to Sign Gas Deal with Russia: Spiegel," Reuters, April 18, 2015, www.reuters.com/article/eurozone-greece-russia-gas/greece-poised-to-sign-gas-deal-with-russia-spiegel-idINL5N0XF07E20150418.

209 **secured a commitment from Putin:** Yanis Varoufakis, *Adults in the Room: My Battle with the European and American Deep Establishment* (New York: Farrar, Straus and Giroux, 2017), 529.

209 **Alexey Miller flew to Athens:** Niki Kitsantonis, "As Cash Dwindles, Greece Negotiates with Gazprom on 'Energy Cooperation,'" *The New York Times*, April 21, 2015, www.nytimes.com/2015/04/22/business/international/greece-tsipras-russia-gazprom-pipeline.html.

210 **St. Petersburg International Economic Forum:** Kathrin Hille and Courtney Weaver, "As Greece Teeters, Alexis Tsipras Is Feted in St. Petersburg," *Financial Times*, June 18, 2015, www.ft.com/content/1e38db54-15d7-11e5-be54-00144feabdc0.

210 **"must strike a deal with the Germans":** Varoufakis, *Adults in the Room*, 348.

210 **"depleting Moscow's coffers":** Varoufakis, *Adults in the Room*, 529.

210 **extend sectoral sanctions on Russia:** "Russia: EU Extends Economic Sanctions by Six Months," European Council, June 22, 2015, www.consilium.europa.eu/en/press/press-releases/2015/06/22/russia-sanctions.

210 **€86 billion bailout from the EU:** Duncan Robinson and Christian Oliver, "Eurozone Approves €86bn Greek Bailout," *Financial Times*, August 14, 2015, www.ft.com/content/b01103d4-42bf-11e5-9abe-5b335da3a90e.

210 **Cypriot President Nicos Anastasiades:** Andrew Higgins, "Waving Cash, Putin Sows E.U. Divisions in an Effort to Break Sanctions," *The New York Times*, April 6, 2015, www.nytimes.com/2015/04/07/world/europe/using-cash-and-charm-putin-targets-europes-weakest-links.html.

210 **Viktor Orbán two Russian-made nuclear reactors:** Krisztina Than, "Special Report: Inside Hungary's $10.8 Billion Nuclear Deal with Russia," Reuters, March 30, 2015, www.reuters.com/article/us-russia-europe-hungary-specialreport/special-report-inside-hungarys-10-8-billion-nuclear-deal-with-russia-idUSKBN0MQ0MP20150330.

210 **plied Slovakia's Prime Minister Robert Fico:** Peter Green, "Energy, Politics and Putin: Russia's Gas Power Play Traps Europe," *TheStreet*, October 30, 2014, www.thestreet.com/politics/energy-politics-and-putin-russias-gas-power-play-traps-europe-12907434.

210 **"This is policy, this isn't purity":** Author interview with Dan Fried, 2022.

211 **Known as Nord Stream 2:** "Russia's Gazprom to Expand Nord Stream Gas Pipeline with E.ON, Shell, OMV," Reuters, June 18, 2015, www.reuters.com/article/energy-gazprom-pipeline/update-2-russias-gazprom-to-expand-nord-stream-gas-pipeline-with-e-on-shell-omv-idUKL5N0Z42OB20150618.

211 **depriving Kyiv of critical gas transit fees:** "Nord Stream-2 Pipeline to Kill Ukraine's Gas Transit Business—Naftogaz CEO," Reuters, November 6, 2015, www.reuters.com/article/naftogaz-gas/nord-stream-2-pipeline-to-kill-ukraines-gas-transit-business-naftogaz-ceo-idUSL8N13126H20151106.

211 **Italy's prime minister, was incensed:** Peter Spiegel and James Politi, "Italy's Renzi Joins Opposition to Nord Stream 2 Pipeline Deal," *Financial Times*, December 15, 2015, www.ft.com/content/cebd679c-a281-11e5-8d70-42b68cfae6e4.

211 **force a debate over the pipeline:** Alberto Mucci, "Matteo Renzi's Pipeline Politics," *Politico*, December 16, 2015, www.politico.eu/article/matteo-renzi-pipeline-politics-energy-south-stream-germany-russia-dependency.

211 **eventually renewed the sanctions:** Michael Birnbaum, "E.U. Extends Sanctions against Russia amid a Growing Split over Their Future," *The Washington Post*, December 21, 2015, www.washingtonpost.com/world/eu-extends-sanctions-against-russia-amid-growing-splits-over-their-future/2015/12/21/16157de6-a381-11e5-8318-bd8caed8c588_story.html.

212 **intended to use the turbines in Crimea:** Anton Zverev and Gleb Stolyarov, "Exclusive: Crimea Power Project Finalizes Plan to Use Turbines from Siemens—Sources," Reuters, August 5, 2016, www.reuters.com/article/us-ukraine-crisis-crimea-power-exclusive/exclusive-crimea-power-project-finalizes-plan-to-use-turbines-from-siemens-sources-idUSKCN10G22G.

212 **news story revealing Russia's plans:** Zverev and Stolyarov, "Crimea Power Project."

212 **"We want to maintain the conversation":** William Boston, "Siemens Chief Meets Putin in Russia," *The Wall Street Journal*, March 26, 2014, www.wsj.com/articles/siemens-boss-reaffirms-ties-with-russia-despite-crimea-1395848905?tesla=y.

CHAPTER 34: "DARK THOUGHT"

213 **"we request they leave":** Jennifer Griffin and Lucas Tomlinson, "Russia Launches Airstrikes in Northern Syria, Senior Military Official Says," *Fox News*, September 30, 2015, www.foxnews.com/world/russia-launches-airstrikes-in-northern-syria-senior-military-official-says.

213 **Russian bombs smashed targets across Syria:** Andrew Roth, Brian Murphy, and Missy Ryan, "Russia Begins Airstrikes in Syria; U.S. Warns of New Concerns in Conflict," *The Washington Post*, September 30, 2015, www.washingtonpost.com/world/russias-legislature-authorizes-putin-to-use-military-force-in-syria/2015/09/30/f069f752-6749-11e5-9ef3-fde182507eac_story.html.

213 **aimed at the various opponents of brutal Syrian dictator:** Henry Meyer, Donna Abu-Nasr, and Ilya Arkhipov, "Russian Strikes in Syria Draw Ire From Anti-Assad Opposition," *Bloomberg*, October 1, 2015, www.bloomberg.com/news/articles/2015-10-01/russia-pledges-to-continue-air-strikes-to-back-assad-offensive.

213 **Putin met with Obama:** Lesley Wroughton and Arshad Mohammed, "Obama Ends up Dealing with Russia and Living with Assad, for Now," Reuters, September 29, 2015, www.reuters.com/article/us-un-assembly-syria-obama/obama-ends-up-dealing-with-russia-and-living-with-assad-for-now-idUKKCN0RU01O20150930.

214 **over a million people sought asylum:** Jonathan Clayton and Hereward Holland, "Over One Million Sea Arrivals Reach Europe in 2015," Office of the United Nations High Commissioner for Refugees, December 30, 2015, www.unhcr.org/us/news/stories/over-one-million-sea-arrivals-reach-europe-2015; Jean-Christophe Dumont and Stefano Scarpetta, "Is This Humanitarian Migration Crisis Different?" *Migration Policy Debates*, OECD, No. 7, September 2015, www.oecd.org/migration/Is-this-refugee-crisis-different.pdf.

214 **"have not been able to develop over the past year":** "Report: Juncker Wants Closer Ties with Putin," *Deutsche Welle*, November 19, 2015, www.dw.com/en/eu-commission-kremlin-confirm-juncker-letter-to-putin/a-18863225.

214 **propose a trade pact:** Andrius Sytas, "Exclusive: EU's Juncker Dangles Trade Ties with Russia-led Bloc to Putin," Reuters, November 19, 2015, www.reuters.com/article/us-eu-juncker-russia/exclusive-eus-juncker-dangles-trade-ties-with-russia-led-bloc-to-putin-idUSKCN0T821T20151119.

214 **"broad coalition" to fight ISIS:** Andrey Biryukov, Helene Fouquet, and Henry Meyer, "Hollande, Putin Call for 'Broad' Coalition to Fight Terrorism," *Bloomberg*, November 26, 2015, www.bloomberg.com/news/articles/2015-11-26/hollande-putin-call-for-broad-coalition-to-fight-terrorism.

214 **hadn't mentioned Russian aggression in Ukraine:** Sytas, "EU's Juncker Dangles Trade Ties."

214 **"litmus test of Russian behavior":** Alex Barker, "NATO Prepares to Revive Russia Contacts," *Financial Times*, December 2, 2015, www.ft.com/content/874b5bd8-9923-11e5-9228-87e603d47bdc.

214 **"clear or a constructive change in policy":** Barker, "NATO Prepares."

215 **"if the dark thought":** Barker, "NATO Prepares."

215 **some "common ground":** Carol Morello and Andrew Roth, "Kerry and Putin Meet in Moscow, Seek Way Forward on Ending Syrian War," *The Washington Post*, December 15, 2015, www.washingtonpost.com/world/russian-support-for-syrian-government-and-ukrainian-separatists-top-agenda/2015/12/15/a84f89d6-9ea9-11e5-9ad2-568d814bbf3b_story.html.

215 **"Russia has a simple choice":** John Kerry, "Remarks by Secretary of State John Kerry at the 2016

Munich Security Conference" (speech, Munich, Germany, February 13, 2016), ua.usembassy.gov/remarks
-secretary-state-john-kerry-2016-munich-security-conference-021316.

CHAPTER 35: A WAY OUT VIA GOLDEN ESCALATOR

217 **Unless Washington was careful, "overuse of sanctions could undermine":** Jack Lew, "The Evolution of Sanctions and Lessons for the Future, (speech, Washington, D.C., March 30, 2016), Carnegie Endowment for International Peace, https://carnegieendowment.org/2016/03/30/u.s.-treasury-secretary-jacob-j.-lew-on-evolution-of-sanctions-and-lessons-for-future-event-5191."

217 **Italian authorities seized several villas:** "Italy Seizes Assets of Putin Ally and Judo Partner Rotenberg," Reuters, September 23, 2014, www.reuters.com/article/uk-ukraine-crisis-italy-idAFKCN0HI12H20140923.

217 **Timchenko liquidated his shares in Gunvor:** Jack Farchy, "Sanctioned Timchenko Sells Gunvor Stake," *Financial Times*, March 20, 2014, www.ft.com/content/72ac6954-b06a-11e3-8efc-00144feab7de.

217 **Rotenberg was handed a multibillion-dollar deal:** Joshua Yaffa, "Putin's Shadow Cabinet and the Bridge to Crimea," *The New Yorker*, May 22, 2017, www.newyorker.com/magazine/2017/05/29/putins-shadow-cabinet-and-the-bridge-to-crimea.

217 **given juicy, no-bid contracts:** Karina Orlova, "Putin Looks Out for His Friends," *The American Interest*, May 22, 2016, www.the-american-interest.com/2016/05/22/putin-looks-out-for-his-friends.

218 **world's worst-performing economies:** Mark Thompson, "Russia: One of the 10 Worst Economies in 2015," CNN, January 26, 2016, money.cnn.com/2016/01/25/news/economy/russia-10-worst-emerging-economies/index.html.

218 **Inflation spiked to more:** Holly Ellyat and Geoff Cutmore, "Why Russian Inflation Will Fall 'Abruptly' Next Year," CNBC, October 13, 2015, www.cnbc.com/2015/10/13/russian-inflation-nabiullina-forecast.html.

218 **dipped below $400 billion:** "Russian Reserves Fall below $400 billion, First Time Since 2009," Reuters, December 25, 2014, www.reuters.com/article/us-russia-reserves/russian-reserves-fall-below-400-billion-first-time-since-2009-idUKKBN0K30HC20141225.

218 **economic growth "virtually stopped":** "IMF Country Report No. 2019/260: Russian Federation," International Monetary Fund, August 2, 2019, www.imf.org/en/Publications/CR/Issues/2019/08/01/Russian-Federation-2019-Article-IV-Consultation-Press-Release-Staff-Report-48549.

218 **Russia missed out on hundreds of billions:** Anders Åslund and Maria Snegovaya, "The Impact of Western Sanctions on Russia and How They Can Be Made Even More Effective," The Atlantic Council, May 3, 2021, www.atlanticcouncil.org/in-depth-research-reports/report/the-impact-of-western-sanctions-on-russia.

218 **a blip in Europe's economic performance:** "Russia's and the EU's Sanctions: Economic and Trade Effects, Compliance and the Way Forward," Directorate-General for External Policies, European Parliament, European Union, October 2017, www.europarl.europa.eu/RegData/etudes/STUD/2017/603847/EXPO_STU(2017)603847_EN.pdf.

218 **40 percent of their exports to Russia:** "Russia's and the EU's Sanctions," European Union.

218 **Lithuania's dairy industry:** Jack Ewing, "Lithuania Feels Squeeze in Sanctions War with Russia," *The New York Times*, September 24, 2014, www.nytimes.com/2014/09/25/business/international/lithuania-feels-squeeze-in-sanctions-war-with-moscow.html.

220 **"Central Bank Governor of the Year":** Sid Werma, "Central Bank Governor of the Year 2015: Nabiullina Displays Crisis-fighting Skills," *Euromoney*, September 16, 2015, www.euromoney.com/article/b12klw38gh82lt/central-bank-governor-of-the-year-2015-nabiullina-displays-crisis-fighting-skills.

220 **reduced its dependence on the dollar:** "De-Dollarization Efforts in China and Russia," IF11885, Congressional Research Service, U.S. Library of Congress, July 23, 2021, crsreports.congress.gov/product/pdf/IF/IF11885.

221 **annexation of Crimea was "so smart":** Christopher Massie and Andrew Kaczynski, "Trump Called Russia's Invasion of Ukraine 'So Smart' in 2014," *BuzzFeed News*, August 1, 2016, www.buzzfeednews.com/article/christophermassie/trump-called-russias-invasion-of-ukraine-so-smart-in-2014.

221 **"great relationship with Putin":** Donald Trump, "Presidential Candidate Donald Trump Primary Night Speech" (speech, New York, New York, April 28, 2016), *C-SPAN*, www.c-span.org/video/?408719-1/presidential-candidate-donald-trump-primary-night-speech&start=1889&transcriptQuery=putin. Trump also said, "I think I'd get along very well with Vladimir Putin." See Andrew Kaczynski, Chris Massie, and Nathan McDermott, "80 Times Trump Talked about Putin," CNN, March 2017, www.cnn.com/interactive/2017/03/politics/trump-putin-russia-timeline.

221 **Paul Manafort, whose most recent job:** "Donald Trump Hires Paul Manafort to Lead Delegate Effort," *The New York Times*, March 28, 2016, archive.nytimes.com/www.nytimes.com/politics/first-draft/2016/03/28/donald-trump-hires-paul-manafort-to-lead-delegate-effort/; "Timeline of Paul Manafort's Role in the Trump Campaign," *ABC News*, October 30, 2017, abcnews.go.com/Politics/timeline-paul-manaforts-role-trump-campaign/story?id=50808957.

221 **Russia was behind the attack:** Michael Isikoff and David Corn, *Russian Roulette: The Inside Story of Putin's War on America and the Election of Donald Trump* (New York: Twelve Books, 2018), 67–70.

221 **handed over his emails to the Russians:** Eric Lipton, David E. Sanger, and Scott Shane, "The Perfect

Weapon: How Russian Cyberpower Invaded the U.S.," *The New York Times*, December 13, 2016, www .nytimes.com/2016/12/13/us/politics/russia-hack-election-dnc.html.

221 **like run-of-the-mill espionage:** Ellen Nakashima, "Russian Government Hackers Penetrated DNC, Stole Opposition Research on Trump," *The Washington Post*, June 14, 2016, www.washingtonpost.com/world /national-security/russian-government-hackers-penetrated-dnc-stole-opposition-research-on-trump /2016/06/14/cf006cb4-316e-11e6-8ff7-7b6c1998b7a0_story.html.

222 **resign hours before the start of the convention:** Dana Roberts, Ben Jacobs, Alan Yuhas, "Debbie Wasserman Schultz to Resign as DNC Chair as Email Scandal Rocks Democrats," *The Guardian*, July 25, 2016, www.theguardian.com/us-news/2016/jul/24/debbie-wasserman-schultz-resigns-dnc-chair -emails-sanders.

222 **ordered the interference in America's election:** Isikoff and Corn, *Russian Roulette*, 193.

222 **secretive discussions in the Situation Room:** Isikoff and Corn, *Russian Roulette*, 187–90.

222 **"tit-for-tat escalatory cycle":** David Shimer, *Rigged: America, Russia, and One Hundred Years of Covert Electoral Interference* (New York: Alfred A. Knopf, 2020), 176.

222 **alter actual vote tallies:** Shimer, *Rigged*, 176.

222 **far ahead of Trump in the polls:** Isikoff and Corn, *Russian Roulette*, 191.

223 **"the influence campaign, changing public opinion":** Shimer, *Rigged*, 5.

223 **"cut it out":** Louis Nelson, "Obama Says He Told Putin to 'Cut It Out' on Russia Hacking," *Politico*, December 16, 2016, www.politico.com/story/2016/12/obama-putin-232754.

223 **"we'll crash your economy":** David Corn and Michael Isikoff, "Why the Hell Are We Standing Down?" *Mother Jones*, March 9, 2018, www.motherjones.com/politics/2018/03/why-the-hell-are-we-standing -down.

223 **"deter with a strong set of measures up front":** Shimer, *Rigged*, 3.

223 **"should have dropped the hammer on them":** Author interview with Dan Fried, 2022.

223 **leak John Podesta's emails:** Matthew Nussbaum, "The Definitive Trump-Russia Timeline of Events," *Politico*, March 3, 2017, www.politico.com/trump-russia-ties-scandal-guide/timeline-of-events.

223 **just 77,000 votes:** "America's Electoral College and the Popular Vote," *The Economist*, December 28, 2016, www.economist.com/graphic-detail/2016/12/28/americas-electoral-college-and-the-popular-vote.

223 **spark a crisis:** Isikoff and Corn, *Russian Roulette*, 290–91.

223 **rescind such sanctions with the stroke of a pen:** Shimer, *Rigged*, 207.

224 **sanctions on two Russian intelligence agencies:** The White House, "Fact Sheet: Actions in Response to Russian Malicious Cyber Activity and Harassment," December 29, 2016, obamawhitehouse.archives .gov/the-press-office/2016/12/29/fact-sheet-actions-response-russian-malicious-cyber-activity-and.

224 **"cool heads to prevail":** Michael Flynn transcripts, Office of the Director of National Intelligence, May 29, 2020, d3i6fh83elv35t.cloudfront.net/static/2020/05/FlynnTranscripts.pdf.

224 **"Great move on delay":** Andrew Roth, "Putin Says He Won't Deport U.S. Diplomats as He Looks to Cultivate Relations with Trump," *The Washington Post*, December 30, 2016, www.washingtonpost .com/world/russia-plans-retaliation-and-serious-discomfortoverus-hacking-sanctions/2016/12/30 /4efd3650-ce12-11e6-85cd-e66532e35a44_story.html.

CHAPTER 36: THE INTERPRETER

227 **Known as 5G:** Sue Halpern, "The Terrifying Potential of the 5G Network," *The New Yorker*, April 26, 2019, www.newyorker.com/news/annals-of-communications/the-terrifying-potential-of-the-5g-network.

227 **Beijing's "peaceful rise":** Esther Pan, "The Promise and Pitfalls of China's 'Peaceful Rise,'" Council on Foreign Relations, April 14, 2006, www.cfr.org/backgrounder/promise-and-pitfalls-chinas-peaceful -rise.

227 **Huawei was a private Chinese tech company:** For a comprehensive history of Huawei, see Eva Dou, *House of Huawei: The Secret History of China's Most Powerful Company* (New York: Portfolio, 2025).

228 **"couldn't persuade the Brits":** Author interview with John Bolton, 2023.

228 **taste of life as a journalist under CCP rule:** Matt Pottinger, "Mightier Than the Pen," *The Wall Street Journal*, December 15, 2005, www.wsj.com/articles/SB113461636659623128.

229 **secretly communicated with Sergei Kislyak:** Maggie Haberman, Matthew Rosenberg, Matt Apuzzo, and Glenn Thrush, "Michael Flynn Resigns as National Security Adviser," *The New York Times*, February 13, 2017, www.nytimes.com/2017/02/13/us/politics/donald-trump-national-security-adviser -michael-flynn.html; Derek Hawkins, "Flynn Sets Record with Only 24 Days as National Security Adviser. The Average Tenure Is About 2.6 Years," *The Washington Post*, February 14, 2017, www.washingtonpost .com/news/morning-mix/wp/2017/02/14/flynn-sets-record-with-only-24-days-as-nsc-chief-the-average -tenure-is-about-2-6-years.

229 **NSC's top China official:** Mark Landler and Jane Perlez, "A Veteran and China Hand Advises Trump for Xi's Visit," *The New York Times*, April 4, 2017, www.nytimes.com/2017/04/04/world/asia/matthew -pottinger-trump-china.html; Michael Crowley, "The White House Official Trump Says Doesn't Exist," *Politico*, May 30, 2018, www.politico.com/magazine/story/2018/05/30/donald-trump-matthew -pottinger-asia-218551.

230 **"swallowing sawdust by the bucketful":** Matt Pottinger, Matthew Johnson, and David Feith, "Xi Jinping

in His Own Words," *Foreign Affairs*, November 30, 2022, www.foreignaffairs.com/china/xi-jinping -his-own-words.

230 **urging their British counterparts to keep Huawei out:** David Bond, George Parker, and Nic Fildes, "Theresa May Approves Huawei for UK 5G in Snub to US," *Financial Times*, April 24, 2019, www.ft .com/content/fca902a4-6657-11e9-a79d-04f350474d62.

230 **stop sharing intelligence:** Bill Bishop, "Allies Question U.S. Hardline on Huawei," *Axios*, February 22, 2019, www.axios.com/2019/02/23/allies-question-us-hardline-huawei.

230 **Theresa May greenlit Huawei's involvement:** Steven Swinford and Charles Hymas, "Theresa May Defies Security Warnings of Ministers and US to Allow Huawei to Help Build Britain's 5G Network," *The Telegraph*, April 24, 2019, www.telegraph.co.uk/politics/2019/04/23/theresa-may-defies-security-warnings -ministers-us-allow-huawei.

230 **courtesy of a heads-up:** "Defence Secretary Gavin Williamson Sacked over Huawei Leak," *BBC News*, May 1, 2019, www.bbc.com/news/uk-politics-48126974.

230 **"extraordinary, ambitious vision":** Philip Hammond, "Belt and Road Forum: Philip Hammond's Speech" (speech, Beijing, China, April 26, 2019), Government of the UK, www.gov.uk/government /speeches/belt-and-road-forum-philip-hammonds-speech.

231 **"Pottinger just shouted":** Richard Kerbaj, "5G Wars: The US Plot to Make Britain Ditch Huawei," *The Times of London*, August 21, 2022, www.thetimes.co.uk/article/5g-wars-the-us-plot-to-make-britain -ditch-huawei-mcqdld8sx.

231 **"if you can't beat 'em, join 'em":** Author interview with Matt Pottinger, 2023.

CHAPTER 37: IRRESPONSIBLE STAKEHOLDER

232 **fear of a rising rival superpower:** See Graham Allison, *Destined for War: Can America and China Escape Thucydides's Trap?* (Boston: Houghton Mifflin Harcourt, 2017) for the argument that the international system faces a "Thucydides trap" in which China's rise, and the fear it has elicited in the United States, has heightened the risk of war.

232 **"We were already at war":** Author interview with Robert Lighthizer, 2023.

233 **$5,000 in seed money:** Chris Miller, *Chip War: The Fight for the World's Most Critical Technology* (New York: Scribner, 2022), 271.

233 **Huawei started making its own switches:** Nathaniel Ahrens, "China's Competitiveness: Myth, Reality, and Lessons for the United States and Japan: Case Study: Huawei," Center for Strategic & International Studies, February 2013, csis-website-prod.s3.amazonaws.com/s3fs-public/legacy_files/files /publication/130215_competitiveness_Huawei_casestudy_Web.pdf.

233 **technology critical to China's national security:** Jonathan E. Hillman, *The Digital Silk Road: China's Quest to Wire the World and Win the Future* (New York: HarperCollins, 2021), 31.

233 **tune of $75 billion:** Chuin-Wei Yap, "State Support Helped Fuel Huawei's Global Rise," *The Wall Street Journal*, December 25, 2019, www.wsj.com/articles/state-support-helped-fuel-huaweis-global-rise -11577280736.

233 **insulate Huawei from foreign competition:** Hillman, *Digital Silk Road*, 33.

233 **team dedicated to copying foreign technologies:** Hillman, *Digital Silk Road*, 35–38.

234 **illegally copied code:** Miller, *Chip War*, 271–72.

234 **"the greatest transfer of wealth":** Josh Rogin, "NSA Chief: Cybercrime Constitutes the 'Greatest Transfer of Wealth in History,'" *Foreign Policy*, July 9, 2012, foreignpolicy.com/2012/07/09/nsa-chief -cybercrime-constitutes-the-greatest-transfer-of-wealth-in-history.

234 **"competitor out of business":** Author interview with Matt Pottinger, 2023.

234 **Nortel had filed for bankruptcy:** Natalie Obiko Pearson, "Did a Chinese Hack Kill Canada's Greatest Tech Company?" *Bloomberg*, July 1, 2020, www.bloomberg.com/news/features/2020-07-01/did-china -steal-canada-s-edge-in-5g-from-nortel.

234 **second-largest manufacturer of smartphones:** Samuel Gibbs, "Huawei Beats Apple to Become Second -largest Smartphone Maker," *The Guardian*, August 1, 2018, www.theguardian.com/technology/2018 /aug/01/huawei-beats-apple-smartphone-manufacturer-samsung-iphone.

234 **second-largest customer of TSMC:** Miller, *Chip War*, 275.

234 **rules of the international trading system:** "The International Trading System and Trade Negotiations," United Nations Conference on Trade and Development, unctad.org/topic/trade-agreements/the -international-trading-system.

235 **a "traumatic trifecta":** Rush Doshi, *The Long Game: China's Grand Strategy to Displace American Order* (New York: Oxford University Press, 2021), 48.

235 **China's chief adversary:** Doshi, *Long Game*, 54.

235 **hide its strength and bide its time:** Doshi, *Long Game*, 48.

236 **access to foreign industrial secrets:** Tim Morrison, "U.S.-China: Winning the Economic Competition" (speech, July 21, 2020), Subcommittee on Economic Policy, U.S. Senate Committee on Banking, Housing, and Urban Affairs, 116th Cong., 2nd sess., www.banking.senate.gov/imo/media/doc/Morrison %20Testimony%207-22-20.pdf.

236 **permanent normal trading privileges:** Collectively, U.S. businesses spent more than $100 million

lobbying to grant China permanent normal trading relations and to support China's entry into the WTO. See Bob Davis and Lingling Wei, *Superpower Showdown: How the Battle Between Trump and Xi Threatens a New Cold War* (New York: Harper Business, 2020), 70, 91; Eric Schmitt and Joseph Kahn, "The China Trade Vote: A Clinton Triumph; House in 237–197 Vote, Approves Normal Trade Rights for China," *The New York Times*, May 25, 2000, www.nytimes.com/2000/05/25/world/china-trade-vote-clinton-triumph-house-237-197-vote-approves-normal-trade-rights.html.

236 **"import one of democracy's most cherished values":** William J. Clinton, "Speech on China Trade Bill" (speech, Washington, D.C., March 9, 2000), *The New York Times*, archive.nytimes.com/www.nytimes.com/library/world/asia/030900clinton-china-text.html.

237 **$15 billion annually to almost $120 billion:** "Trade Goods with China," United States Census Bureau, www.census.gov/foreign-trade/balance/c5700.html.

237 **approached $300 billion:** "Trade Goods with China," United States Census Bureau.

237 **second-largest trading partner:** "Timeline of U.S. China Relations: 1949–2023," Council on Foreign Relations, www.cfr.org/timeline/us-china-relations.

237 **"strike at the heart of America's knowledge economy":** Robert B. Zoellick, "Whither China: From Membership to Responsibility: Remarks to National Committee on U.S.-China Relations" (speech, New York, NY, September 21, 2005), U.S. Department of State, 2001-2009.state.gov/s/d/former/zoellick/rem/53682.htm.

237 **"responsible stakeholder in that system":** Zoellick, "Whither China."

CHAPTER 38: THE AWAKENING

239 **joint venture in China:** "Goldman Sachs Announces Joint Venture in China," Goldman Sachs, December 2, 2004, www.goldmansachs.com/media-relations/press-releases/archived/2004/2004-12-02.html; "With Gao Hua Joint Venture, the Firm Establishes a Foothold in China's Domestic Financial Markets," Goldman Sachs, 2019, www.goldmansachs.com/our-firm/history/moments/2004-gao-hua.html.

239 **visited China some seventy times:** "China Telecom Privatization Shines through the Shadow of the Financial Crisis," Goldman Sachs, www.goldmansachs.com/our-firm/history/moments/1997-china-telecom-privatization.html; "Hank Paulson and Wang Qishan Illustrate a Superpower Divide," *The Economist*, November 17, 2018, www.economist.com/business/2018/11/17/hank-paulson-and-wang-qishan-illustrate-a-superpower-divide.

239 **a "born leader":** Henry M. Paulson, *Dealing with China: An Insider Unmasks the New Economic Superpower* (New York: Grand Central Publishing, 2015), 95.

239 **"You were my teacher":** Paulson, *Dealing with China*, 240.

239 **"most humbling moments":** Paulson, *Dealing with China*, 240.

239 **three times the size of the United States' own:** Christine Wong, "The Fiscal Stimulus Programme and Public Governance Issues in China," *OECD Journal on Budgeting*, October 19, 2011, www.oecd-ilibrary.org/governance/the-fiscal-stimulus-programme-and-public-governance-issues-in-china_budget-11-5kg3nhljqrjl.

239 **buoyed growth across Asia:** Karishma Vaswani, "Why Asia Turned to China during the Global Financial Crisis," *BBC News*, September 12, 2018, www.bbc.com/news/business-45493147.

240 **"actively accomplish something":** Rush Doshi, "Hu's to Blame for China's Foreign Assertiveness?" The Brookings Institution, January 22, 2019, www.brookings.edu/articles/hus-to-blame-for-chinas-foreign-assertiveness; Rush Doshi, *The Long Game: China's Grand Strategy to Displace American Order* (New York: Oxford University Press, 2021), 160–62.

240 **Chinese fishing trawler:** "Boat Collisions Spark Japan-China Diplomatic Row," *BBC News*, September 8, 2010, www.bbc.com/news/world-asia-pacific-11225522.

240 **cut off exports of rare-earth minerals to Japan:** Keith Bradsher, "Amid Tension, China Blocks Vital Exports to Japan," *The New York Times*, September 22, 2010, www.nytimes.com/2010/09/23/business/global/23rare.html; Mari Yamaguchi, "China Rare Earth Exports to Japan Still Halted," *Bloomberg Businessweek*, October 21, 2010, web.archive.org/web/20110909131412/http://www.businessweek.com/ap/financialnews/D9J02PF01.htm; "What Are 'Rare Earths' Used For?" *BBC News*, March 13, 2012, www.bbc.com/news/world-17357863.

240 **secure supplies of rare earths:** "FACTBOX-Japan budgets $650 mln for Rare Earths, Resources," Reuters, January 5, 2011, www.reuters.com/article/idUSTOE70404220110105.

240–41 **denounce his father:** Evan Osnos, "Born Red," *The New Yorker*, March 30, 2015, www.newyorker.com/magazine/2015/04/06/born-red.

241 **His sister died:** Austin Ramzy, "In Xi Jinping's Tears, a Message for China's People," *The New York Times*, March 3, 2016, www.nytimes.com/2016/03/04/world/asia/china-xi-jinping-tears.html; Chris Buckley and Didi Kirsten Tatlow, "Cultural Revolution Shaped Xi Jinping, From Schoolboy to Survivor," *The New York Times*, September 24, 2015, www.nytimes.com/2015/09/25/world/asia/xi-jinping-china-cultural-revolution.html.

241 **"Reddest leader of his generation":** Richard McGregor, "Party Man: Xi Jinping's Quest to Dominate China," *Foreign Affairs*, August 14, 2019, www.foreignaffairs.com/china/party-man.

241 **Document No. 9:** "Document 9: A *ChinaFile* Translation," *ChinaFile*, November 8, 2013, www.chinafile .com/document-9-chinafile-translation; Matt Pottinger, Matthew Johnson, and David Feith, "Xi Jinping in His Own Words," *Foreign Affairs*, November 30, 2022, www.foreignaffairs.com/china/xi-jinping -his-own-words.

241 **achieve "national rejuvenation":** Rosh Doshi, "Xi Jinping Just Made Clear Where China's Foreign Policy is Headed," *Washington Post*, October 25, 2017, www.washingtonpost.com/news/monkey-cage /wp/2017/10/25/xi-jinping-just-made-it-clear-where-chinas-foreign-policy-is-headed.

241 **kept out American tech firms:** Matt Sheehan, "How Google Took on China—and Lost," *MIT Technology Review*, December 19, 2018, www.technologyreview.com/2018/12/19/138307/how-google-took -on-china-and-lost; Ryan McMorrow and Sun Yu, "The Vanishing Billionaire: How Jack Ma Fell Foul of Xi Jinping," *Financial Times*, April 15, 2021, www.ft.com/content/1fe0559f-de6d-490e-b312-abba 0181da1f.

241 **detaining more than a million Uyghurs:** Lindsay Maizland, "China's Repression of Uyghurs in Xinjiang," Council on Foreign Relations, September 22, 2022, www.cfr.org/backgrounder/china-xinjiang -uyghurs-muslims-repression-genocide-human-rights.

241 **providing the facial recognition technology:** Darren Byler, *In the Camps: Life in China's High-Tech Penal Colony* (New York: Columbia Global Reports, 2021); Emma Graham-Harrison and Juliette Garside, "'Allow No Escapes': Leak Exposes Reality of China's Vast Prison Camp Network," *The Guardian*, November 24, 2019, www.theguardian.com/world/2019/nov/24/china-cables-leak-no-escapes-reality -china-uighur-prison-camp; Eva Dou, "Documents Link Huawei to China's Surveillance Programs," *The Washington Post*, December 14, 2021, www.washingtonpost.com/world/2021/12/14/huawei-surveillance -china; Vincent Ni, "Documents Link Huawei to Uyghur Surveillance Projects, Report Claims," *The Guardian*, December 15, 2021, www.theguardian.com/technology/2021/dec/15/documents-link-huawei -uyghur-surveillance-projects-report-claims.

242 **launched the Belt and Road Initiative:** Sheridan Prasso, "China's Digital Silk Road Is Looking More Like an Iron Curtain," *Bloomberg*, January 10, 2019, www.bloomberg.com/news/features/2019-01-10/china -s-digital-silk-road-is-looking-more-like-an-iron-curtain; Stefan Vladisavljev, "Surveying China's Digital Silk Road in the Western Balkans," *War on the Rocks*, August 3, 2021, warontherocks.com /2021/08/surveying-chinas-digital-silk-road-in-the-western-balkans; Joe Parkinson, Nicholas Bariyo, and Josh Chin, "Huawei Technicians Helped African Governments Spy on Political Opponents," *The Wall Street Journal*, August 15, 2019, www.wsj.com/articles/huawei-technicians-helped-african -governments-spy-on-political-opponents-11565793017.

242 **drowning in debt:** Ishaan Tharoor, "China Has a Hand in Sri Lanka's Economic Calamity," *The Washington Post*, July 20, 2022, www.washingtonpost.com/world/2022/07/20/sri-lanka-china-debt-trap; Marwaan Macan-Markar, "China Debt Trap Fear Haunts Maldives Government," *Nikkei Asia*, September 15, 2020, asia.nikkei.com/Spotlight/Belt-and-Road/China-debt-trap-fear-haunts-Maldives-government.

242 **interest rates several times higher:** Kai Wang, "China: Is It Burdening Poor Countries with Unsustainable Debt?" *BBC News*, January 2, 2022, www.bbc.com/news/59585507.

242 **ninety-nine-year lease on Sri Lanka's Hambantota port:** Maria Abi-Habib, "How China Got Sri Lanka to Cough Up a Port," *The New York Times*, June 25, 2018, www.nytimes.com/2018/06/25/world /asia/china-sri-lanka-port.html.

242 **Asian Infrastructure Investment Bank:** Doshi, *Long Game*, 217–25.

242 **Ernest Hemingway described:** Ernest Hemingway, *The Sun Also Rises* (New York: Warbler Classics, 2022), 110.

242 **also large Western countries:** Jamil Anderlini, "Big Nations Snub Beijing Bank Launch after US Lobbying," *Financial Times*, October 22, 2014, www.ft.com/content/41c3c0a0-59cd-11e4-9787-00144feab7de.

243 **"seek to join the AIIB":** George Osborne, "UK Announces Plans to Join Asian Infrastructure Investment Bank," His Majesty's Treasury, Government of the UK, March 12, 2015, www.gov.uk/government /news/uk-announces-plans-to-join-asian-infrastructure-investment-bank.

243 **"constant accommodation of China":** George Parker, Anne-Sylvaine Chassany, and Geoff Dyer, "Europeans Defy US to Join China-led Development Bank," *Financial Times*, March 16, 2015, www.ft.com /content/0655b342-cc29-11e4-beca-00144feab7de.

243 **produced by the U.S. private sector:** Michael Brown and Pavneet Singh, "China's Technology Transfer Strategy: How Chinese Investments in Emerging Technology Enable a Strategic Competitor to Access the Crown Jewels of U.S. Innovation," Defense Innovation Unit Experimental, January 2018, nationalsecurity.gmu.edu/wp-content/uploads/2020/02/DIUX-China-Tech-Transfer-Study-Selected -Readings.pdf.

243 **an "inherent contradiction":** Author interview with Matt Turpin, 2023.

244 **as "military-civil fusion":** H. R. McMaster, "How China Sees the World," *The Atlantic*, May 2020, www.theatlantic.com/magazine/archive/2020/05/mcmaster-china-strategy/609088; Hal Brands and Michael Beckley, *Danger Zone: The Coming Conflict with China* (New York: W. W. Norton & Company, 2022), 113.

244 **"Made in China 2025" was:** "China Unveils Blueprint to Upgrade Manufacturing Sector," *The Wall Street Journal*, May 19, 2015, www.wsj.com/articles/china-unveils-blueprint-to-upgrade-manufacturing-sector -1432009189.

244 **70 percent share by 2025:** Enda Curran, "From 'Made in China' to 'Made by China for China,'" *Bloomberg*, February 15, 2017, www.bloomberg.com/news/articles/2017-02-15/from-made-in-china-to-made-by-china-for-china; Davis and Wei, *Superpower Showdown*, 123–24.

244 **promoting "win-win cooperation":** "China's Xi Wants 'Win-win' Cooperation with US," *BBC News*, September 25, 2015, www.bbc.com/news/world-asia-china-34355581.

244 **imported some 85 percent of its semiconductors:** Chris Miller, *Chip War: The Fight for the World's Most Critical Technology* (New York: Scribner, 2022), 251–53.

244 **known as the Big Fund:** Edward White and Qianer Liu, "China's Big Fund Corruption Probe Casts Shadow over Chip Sector," *Financial Times*, September 28, 2022, www.ft.com/content/8358e81b-f4e7-4bad-bc08-19a77035e1b4.

245 **"fear in his eyes":** Miller, *Chip War*, 295.

245 **belated efforts by the U.S. government:** David Lawder and Ruby Lian, "U.S. Panel Launches Trade Secret Theft Probe into China Steel," Reuters, May 29, 2016, www.reuters.com/article/us-usa-china-steel-idUSKCN0YH2KX; "U.S. Launches Second WTO Complaint in China Chicken Trade Dispute," Reuters, May 10, 2016, www.yahoo.com/lifestyle/u-launches-second-wto-complaint-164154159.html.

245 **"cannot afford to cede our leadership":** Penny Pritzker, "U.S. Secretary of Commerce Penny Pritzker Delivers Major Policy Address on Semiconductors at Center for Strategic and International Studies" (speech, Washington, D.C.. November 2, 2016), U.S. Department of Commerce, 2014-2017.commerce.gov/news/secretary-speeches/2016/11/us-secretary-commerce-penny-pritzker-delivers-major-policy-address.html.

245 **"if it innovates faster":** "Report to the President: Ensuring Long-Term U.S. Leadership in Semiconductors," President's Council of Advisors on Science and Technology, January 2017, obamawhitehouse.archives.gov/sites/default/files/microsites/ostp/PCAST/pcast_ensuring_long-term_us_leadership_in_semiconductors.pdf.

245 **"Unilateral action is increasingly ineffective":** "Report to the President," President's Council of Advisors on Science and Technology.

CHAPTER 39: LET A HUNDRED CHINA POLICIES BLOOM

247 **"at the expense of American industry":** Donald J. Trump, "Inaugural Address" (speech, Washington, D.C., January 20, 2017), CNBC, www.cnbc.com/2017/01/20/transcript-of-president-trumps-inauguration-speech.html.

247 **"allow China to rape our country":** Nick Gas, "Trump: 'We Can't Continue to Allow China to Rape Our Country,'" *Politico*, May 2, 2016, www.politico.com/blogs/2016-gop-primary-live-updates-and-results/2016/05/trump-china-rape-america-222689.

247 **won 89 of the 100 counties:** Bob Davis and Lingling Wei, *Superpower Showdown: How the Battle Between Trump and Xi Threatens a New Cold War* (New York: Harper Business, 2020), 133.

247 **Trump declared "America first":** Donald J. Trump, "Inaugural Address" (speech, Washington, D.C., January 20, 2017), CNBC, www.cnbc.com/2017/01/20/transcript-of-president-trumps-inauguration-speech.html.

247 **"treasure cave found by Ali Baba":** Xi Jinping, "Keynote at the World Economic Forum: Jointly Shoulder Responsibility of Our Times, Promote Global Growth" (speech, Davos, Switzerland, January 17, 2017), *China Global Television Network America*, america.cgtn.com/2017/01/17/full-text-of-xi-jinping-keynote-at-the-world-economic-forum.

248 **ballooned to 70 percent:** Rush Doshi, *The Long Game: China's Grand Strategy to Displace American Order* (New York: Oxford University Press, 2021), 156.

248 **so close to equaling America's economic might:** Andrew F. Krepinevich, "Preserving the Balance: A U.S. Eurasia Defense Strategy," Center for Strategic and Budgetary Assessments, csbaonline.org/uploads/documents/Preserving_the_Balance_%2819Jan17%29HANDOUTS.pdf.

248 **"get along very well":** Andrew Kaczynski, Chris Massie, and Nathan McDermott, "80 Times Trump Talked about Putin," CNN, March 2017, www.cnn.com/interactive/2017/03/politics/trump-putin-russia-timeline.

248 **a "reverse Nixon":** Josh Rogin, *Chaos under Heaven: Trump, Xi, and the Battle for the 21st Century* (Boston: Houghton Mifflin Harcourt, 2021), 22, 29.

248 **lifting sanctions on Russia unconditionally:** Michael Isikoff, "How the Trump Administration's Secret Efforts to Ease Russia Sanctions Fell Short," *Yahoo News*, June 1, 2017, www.yahoo.com/news/trump-administrations-secret-efforts-ease-russia-sanctions-fell-short-231301145.html.

248 **informed members of Congress:** Isikoff, "Trump Administration's Secret Efforts."

248 **Countering America's Adversaries Through Sanctions Act:** U.S. Congress, House, "Countering America's Adversaries through Sanctions Act of 2017," HR 3364, 115th Cong., 1st sess., introduced in House July 24, 2017, www.congress.gov/bill/115th-congress/house-bill/3364.

248 **as "significantly flawed":** Emily Tamkin, "Trump Finally Signs Sanctions Bill, Then Adds Bizarre Statements," *Foreign Policy*, August 2, 2017, foreignpolicy.com/2017/08/02/trump-finally-signs-sanctions-bill-then-adds-bizarre-statements.

248 **"worst deal ever negotiated":** Carol Morello, "Iran Nuclear Deal Could Collapse under Trump," *The Washington Post*, November 9, 2016, www.washingtonpost.com/world/national-security/iran-nuclear-deal-could-collapse-under-trump/2016/11/09/f2d2bd02-a68c-11e6-ba59-a7d93165c6d4_story.html; Yeganeh Torbati, "Trump Election Puts Iran Nuclear Deal on Shaky Ground," Reuters, November 9, 2016, www.reuters.com/article/us-usa-election-trump-iran/trump-election-puts-iran-nuclear-deal-on-shaky-ground-idUSKBN13427E.

249 **Better to press Iran:** H. R. McMaster, *Battlegrounds: The Fight to Defend the Free World* (New York: HarperCollins, 2021), 295–96; Josh Rogin, "How Trump Can Confront Iran without Blowing up the Nuclear Deal," *The Washington Post*, August 6, 2017, www.washingtonpost.com/opinions/global-opinions/how-trump-can-confront-iran-without-blowing-up-the-nuclear-deal/2017/08/06/0cc021ae-7960-11e7-8f39-eeb7d3a2d304_story.html.

249 **most urgent national security matter:** Gerald F. Seib, Jay Solomon, and Carol E. Lee, "Barack Obama Warns Donald Trump on North Korea Threat," *The Wall Street Journal*, November 22, 2016, www.wsj.com/articles/trump-faces-north-korean-challenge-1479855286.

249 **90 percent of North Korea's foreign trade:** John Kruzel, "Does China Account for 90% of North Korean Trade, as Rex Tillerson Said?" *PolitiFact*, May 1, 2017, www.politifact.com/factchecks/2017/may/01/rex-tillerson/does-china-account-90-north-korean-trade-rex-tille.

249 **assistance in curbing North Korea's nuclear program:** Yeganeh Torbati and Ben Blanchard, "U.S., China Soften Tone, Say to Work Together on North Korea," Reuters, March 18, 2017, www.reuters.com/article/us-tillerson-asia-china/u-s-china-soften-tone-say-to-work-together-on-north-korea-idUSKBN16O2V9.

249 **need for "win-win solutions":** Mark Landler and Jane Perlez, "A Veteran and China Hand Advises Trump for Xi's Visit," *The New York Times*, April 4, 2017, www.nytimes.com/2017/04/04/world/asia/matthew-pottinger-trump-china.html.

249 **being "really rich":** Dominic Rushe, "'I'm Really Rich': Donald Trump Claims $9bn Fortune During Campaign Launch," *The Guardian*, June 16, 2015, www.theguardian.com/us-news/2015/jun/16/donald-trump-reveals-net-worth-presidential-campaign-launch.

249 **originally left off the manifest:** Rogin, *Chaos under Heaven*, 53.

249 **slew of trademarks for Ivanka:** Benjamin Haas, "Ivanka Trump Brand Secures China Trademarks on Day US President Met Xi Jinping," *The Guardian*, April 19, 2017, www.theguardian.com/us-news/2017/apr/19/ivanka-trump-brand-china-trademarks-day-us-president-met-xi-jinping.

249 **"most beautiful piece of chocolate cake":** Dan Merica, "Trump, Xi talked Syria Strike over 'Beautiful Chocolate Cake,'" CNN, April 12, 2017, www.cnn.com/2017/04/12/politics/donald-trump-xi-jingping-syria-chocolate-cake/index.html.

250 **"Solve the problem in North Korea":** Gerard Baker, Carol E. Lee, and Michael C. Bender, "Trump Says He Offered China Better Trade Terms in Exchange for Help on North Korea," *The Wall Street Journal*, April 12, 2017, www.wsj.com/articles/trump-says-he-offered-china-better-trade-terms-in-exchange-for-help-on-north-korea-1492027556; Rogin, *Chaos under Heaven*, 51–54.

250 **ways to boost U.S. exports to China:** Davis and Wei, *Superpower Showdown*, 172–74; Rogin, *Chaos under Heaven*, 51.

250 **"lost" to China:** Jim Tankersley, "Trump Hates the Trade Deficit. Most Economists Don't," *The New York Times*, March 5, 2018, www.nytimes.com/2018/03/05/us/politics/trade-deficit-tariffs-economists-trump.html.

250 **a whopping $350 billion:** U.S. Census Bureau, "Trade in Goods with China," www.census.gov/foreign-trade/balance/c5700.html.

251 **engaging in "economic aggression":** "U.S. Strategic Framework for the Indo-Pacific," National Security Council, October 2017, trumpwhitehouse.archives.gov/wp-content/uploads/2021/01/IPS-Final-Declass.pdf.

251 **America should use its own economic arsenal:** Rogin, *Chaos under Heaven*, 77.

251 **first official China strategy:** Rogin, *Chaos under Heaven*, 78.

251 **Lighthizer was rich:** Dan Alexander, Chase Peterson-Withorn and Michela Tindera, "The Definitive Net Worth of Donald Trump's Cabinet," *Forbes*, July 25, 2019, www.forbes.com/sites/michelatindera/2019/07/25/the-definitive-net-worth-of-donald-trumps-cabinet.

252 **forgotten more about trade policy:** Lydia DePillas, "Robert Lighthizer Blew Up 60 Years of Trade Policy. Nobody Knows What Happens Next," *ProPublica*, October 13, 2020, www.propublica.org/article/robert-lighthizer-blew-up-60-years-of-trade-policy-nobody-knows-what-happens-next.

252 **"China wants to join the WTO to achieve a dominant position":** Robert E. Lighthizer, "What Did Asian Donors Want?" *The New York Times*, February 25, 1997, www.nytimes.com/1997/02/25/opinion/what-did-asian-donors-want.html.

252 **"Tariffs were the only way":** Author interview with Robert Lighthizer, 2023.

252 **levy taxes on American firms:** Howard Gleckman, "What Is a Tariff and Who Pays It?" Tax Policy Center, September 25, 2018, www.taxpolicycenter.org/taxvox/what-tariff-and-who-pays-it.

252 **"unjustifiable" acts that burden or restrict U.S. commerce:** "Section 301 of the Trade Act of 1974," IF11346, Congressional Research Service, U.S. Library of Congress, September 22, 2023, crsreports.congress.gov/product/pdf/IF/IF11346.

252 **a 301 investigation into China's trade practices:** Scott Lincicome, Inu Manak, and Alfredo Carrillo Obregon, "Unfair Trade or Unfair Protection? The Evolution and Abuse of Section 301," *CATO Institute*, June 14, 2022, www.cato.org/policy-analysis/unfair-trade-or-unfair-protection-evolution-abuse-section-301.

253 **"harming American intellectual property":** Office of the U.S. Trade Representative, "USTR Announces Initiation of Section 301 Investigation of China," August 18, 2017, ustr.gov/about-us/policy-offices/press-office/press-releases/2017/august/ustr-announces-initiation-section.

253 **H. R. McMaster realized:** McMaster, *Battlegrounds*, 90–93.

253 **"Premier Li's long monologue":** McMaster, *Battlegrounds*, 126.

CHAPTER 40: THE CLUE: ZTE

254 **findings of his Section 301 investigation:** "Findings of the Investigation into China's Acts, Policies, and Practices Related to Technology Transfer, Intellectual Property, and Innovation under Section 301 of the Trade Act of 1974," Office of the United States Trade Representative, March 22, 2018, ustr.gov/sites/default/files/Section%20301%20FINAL.PDF.

254 **playbook for stealing American technology:** "Section 301 Investigation: China's Acts, Policies, and Practices Related to Technology Transfer, Intellectual Property, and Innovation," U.S. International Trade Commission, October 10, 2017, ustr.gov/sites/default/files/enforcement/301Investigations/China%20Technology%20Transfer%20Hearing%20Witness%20List.pdf.

254 **"requirement to transfer technology":** "Section 301 Investigation: China's Acts, Policies, and Practices related to Technology Transfer, Intellectual Property, and Innovation," Docket No. USTR-2017-0016, U.S.–China Business Council, September 28, 2017, www.uschina.org/sites/default/files/uscbc_submission_on_section_301_investigation_-_chinas_acts_politics_and_practices_related_to_technology_transfer_intellectual_property_and_innovation.pdf; Bob Davis and Lingling Wei, *Superpower Showdown: How the Battle Between Trump and Xi Threatens a New Cold War* (New York: Harper Business, 2020), 210.

254 **"seeks to attain domestic dominance and global leadership":** "China's Acts, Policies, and Practices Related to Technology Transfer," Office of the United States Trade Representative.

255 **"Huawei and ZTE cannot be trusted":** "Investigative Report on the U.S. National Security Issues Posed by Chinese Telecommunications Companies Huawei and ZTE," U.S. Congress, House, Permanent Select Committee on Intelligence, 112th Cong., 2nd sess., H. Rep., October 8, 2012, stacks.stanford.edu/file/druid:rm226yb7473/Huawei-ZTE%20Investigative%20Report%20%28FINAL%29.pdf.

255 **stopped procuring base stations:** Upon the release of the report, Representative Mike Rogers, chair of the House Intelligence Committee, said, "If I were an American company today . . . and you are looking at Huawei, I would find another vendor if you care about your intellectual property; if you care about your consumers' privacy and you care about the national security of the United States of America." See Jim Wolf, "U.S. House Intelligence Panel Head Blackballs China's Huawei," Reuters, October 5, 2012, www.reuters.com/article/usa-china-huawei/u-s-house-intelligence-panel-head-blackballs-chinas-huawei-idUSL1E8L5GYT20121005.

255 **a gentlemen's agreement with Congress:** Andrew Small, *No Limits: The Inside Story of China's War with the West* (London: C. Hurst & Co., 2022), 44.

255 **Spalding's proposed solution:** Sue Halpern, "The Terrifying Potential of the 5G Network," *The New Yorker*, April 26, 2019, www.newyorker.com/news/annals-of-communications/the-terrifying-potential-of-the-5g-network.

256 **"nationalizing 5G network":** Jonathan Swan et al., "Scoop: Trump Team Considers Nationalizing 5G Network," *Axios*, January 28, 2018, www.axios.com/2018/01/28/trump-team-debates-nationalizing-5g-network.

256 **"market, not government":** Maegan Vazquez, Joshua Berlinger, and Betsy Klein, "FCC Chief Opposes Trump Administration 5G Network Plan," CNN, January 29, 2018, edition.cnn.com/2018/01/28/politics/trump-nationalize-5g/index.html; Ajit Pai, "Remarks of FCC Chairman Ajit Pai at the Mobile World Congress" (speech, Barcelona, Spain, February 26, 2018), Federal Communications Commission, docs.fcc.gov/public/attachments/DOC-349432A1.docx.

256 **"It was just 'Get out'":** Halpern, "Terrifying Potential."

256 **"'You can't stop Huawei'":** Author interview with Ivan Kanapathy, 2023.

256 **a "treasure trove":** Karen Freifeld, "Exclusive: U.S. Probe of China's Huawei Includes Bank Fraud Accusations: Sources," Reuters, December 6, 2018, www.reuters.com/article/idUSKBN1O528D; Karen Freifeld, "Long Before Trump's Trade War with China, Huawei's Activities Were Secretly Tracked," Reuters, March 6, 2019, www.reuters.com/article/usa-china-huawei-tech/insight-long-before-trumps-trade-war-with-china-huaweis-activities-were-secretly-tracked-idINL1N1ZW0PD.

256 **red-handed violating American sanctions:** "ZTE Corporation Agrees to Plead Guilty and Pay Over $430.4 Million for Violating U.S. Sanctions by Sending U.S.-Origin Items to Iran," U.S. Department of Justice, March 7, 2017, www.justice.gov/opa/pr/zte-corporation-agrees-plead-guilty-and-pay-over-4304-million-violating-us-sanctions-sending.

256 **restricting U.S. companies from selling to ZTE:** "Additions to the Entity List: Final Rule," *Code of*

Federal Regulations, title 15 (March 8, 2016): 744, s3.amazonaws.com/public-inspection.federalregister.gov/2016-05104.pdf.

257 **ZTE pleaded guilty:** Shawn Donnan, "Chinese Telecom Giant ZTE to Pay up to $1.2bn, Plead Guilty in US Sanctions Case," *Financial Times*, March 7, 2017, www.ft.com/content/a44cf291-3f6f-3ac6-8f67-7cf40c68d5e4; Eunkyung Kim Shin et al., "US Government Imposes $1.19 Billion Fine Against ZTE for Violating US Sanctions and Export Controls," *Baker McKenzie*, March 23, 2017, sanctionsnews.bakermckenzie.com/us-government-imposes-1-19-billion-fine-against-zte-for-violating-us-sanctions-and-export-controls.

257 **violating the terms of the settlement:** David J. Lynch, "U.S. Companies Banned from Selling to China's ZTE Telecom Maker," *The Washington Post*, April 16, 2018, www.washingtonpost.com/news/business/wp/2018/04/16/u-s-companies-banned-from-selling-to-chinas-zte-telecom-maker; Pan Kwan Yuk, "US Hits China's ZTE with Denial of Export Privileges," *Financial Times*, April 16, 2018, www.ft.com/content/77bc02d4-4174-11e8-803a-295c97e6fd0b; Melissa M. Proctor, "Commerce Department and ZTE Reach New Agreement on U.S. Export Violations," Miller Proctor Law, June 12, 2018, millerproctorlaw.com/commerce-department-and-zte-reach-new-agreement-on-u-s-export-violations.

257 **"denial order" on ZTE:** "Order Activating Suspended Denial Order Relating to Zhongxing Telecommunications Equipment Corporation and ZTE Kangxun Telecommunications Ltd.," Bureau of Industry and Security, U.S. Department of Commerce, April 15, 2018, www.commerce.gov/sites/default/files/zte_denial_order.pdf.

257 **"full range of implications":** Louise Lucas, "ZTE Suspends Trading in HK and Shenzhen after US Ban," *Financial Times*, April 17, 2018, www.ft.com/content/e4440408-4221-11e8-93cf-67ac3a6482fd.

257 **"major operating activities of the company have ceased":** Sijia Jiang, "China's ZTE Says Main Business Operations Cease Due to U.S. Ban," Reuters, May 9, 2018, www.reuters.com/article/idUSKBN1IA1WF.

257 **emergency phone call:** The White House, "Readout of President Donald J. Trump's Call with President Xi Jinping of China," May 8, 2018, trumpwhitehouse.archives.gov/briefings-statements/readout-president-donald-j-trumps-call-president-xi-jinping-china-5.

257 **Xi would owe him one:** John Bolton, *The Room Where It Happened* (New York: Simon & Schuster, 2020), 291; Davis and Wei, *Superpower Showdown*, 225.

258 **"Too many jobs in China lost":** Donald J. Trump (@realDonaldTrump), "President Xi of China, and I, are working together," Twitter, May 13, 2018, twitter.com/realDonaldTrump/status/995680316458262533.

258 **"big percentage of individual parts from U.S. companies":** Donald J. Trump (@realDonaldTrump), "ZTE, the large Chinese phone company," Twitter, May 13, 2018, twitter.com/realDonaldTrump/status/996119678551552000.

258 **failed to reverse Trump's concession:** Kate O'Keeffe and Siobhan Hughes, "Congress Ends Bid to Undo Trump Deal to Save China's ZTE," *The Wall Street Journal*, July 20, 2018, www.wsj.com/articles/congress-ends-bid-to-undo-trump-deal-to-save-chinas-zte-1532110708.

258 **additional $1 billion fine:** David J. Lynch, Simon Denyer, and Heather Long, "U.S. Reaches Deal with China's ZTE That Includes $1 Billion Fine, Commerce Secretary Says," *The Washington Post*, June 7, 2018, www.washingtonpost.com/business/economy/us-reaches-deal-with-chinas-zte-that-includes-1-billion-fine-commerce-secretary-says/2018/06/07/ccffa4b0-6a52-11e8-9e38-24e693b38637_story.html.

258 **company resumed operations:** Hudson Lockett, "ZTE Shares Jump as US Awaits $400m Escrow Payment to Lift Ban," *Financial Times*, July 11, 2018, www.ft.com/content/6975240c-856d-11e8-96dd-fa565ec55929.

258 **"grasp the historical opportunity":** Rogier Creemers, Graham Webster, and Paul Triolo, "Translation: Xi Jinping's April 20 Speech at the National Cybersecurity and Informatization Work Conference," *DigiChina*, April 30, 2018, digichina.stanford.edu/work/translation-xi-jinpings-april-20-speech-at-the-national-cybersecurity-and-informatization-work-conference.

258 **seeking to end China's dependence:** Davis and Wei, *Superpower Showdown*, 391–92.

259 **U.S.-controlled "chokepoints":** Ben Murphy, "Chokepoints: China's Self-Identified Strategic Technology Import Dependencies," Center for Security and Emerging Technology, May 2022, cset.georgetown.edu/wp-content/uploads/CSET-Chokepoints.pdf.

259 **poisoned with Novichok:** "Russian Spy: What Happened to Sergei and Yulia Skripal?" *BBC News*, September 27, 2018, www.bbc.com/news/uk-43643025.

259 **linking the attack to Moscow:** David Bond, "Britain Shares 'Unprecedented' Skripal Intelligence with Allies," *Financial Times*, March 27, 2018, www.ft.com/content/7cb3440c-31d2-11e8-b5bf-23cb17fd1498.

259 **expelled sixty Russian officials:** Laurel Wamsley, "U.S. Expels 60 Russian Officials, Closes Consulate in Seattle," NPR, March 26, 2018, www.npr.org/sections/thetwo-way/2018/03/26/596966272/us-expels-dozens-of-russian-diplomats-closes-consulate-in-seattle.

259 **Rusal was hit with blocking sanctions:** "Treasury Designates Russian Oligarchs, Officials, and Entities in Response to Worldwide Malign Activity," U.S. Department of the Treasury, April 6, 2018, home.treasury.gov/news/press-releases/sm0338.

259 **refused to accept trades in Russian aluminum:** Agathe Demarais, *Backfire: How Sanctions Reshaped the World Against U.S. Interests* (New York: Columbia University Press, 2022), 90–93.

259 **Aluminum prices skyrocketed:** Thomas Biesheuvel and Mark Burton, "Why Aluminum Bears Brunt

of U.S. Sanctions on Russia," *Bloomberg*, April 20, 2018, www.bloomberg.com/news/articles/2018-04
-20/why-aluminum-bears-brunt-of-u-s-sanctions-on-russia-quicktake.

259 **waived the sanctions on Rusal:** Victoria Guida, "U.S. Eases Sanctions on Aluminum Firm Tied to
Russian Oligarch," *Politico*, April 23, 2018, www.politico.com/story/2018/04/23/us-sanctions-russia
-rusal-oleg-deripaska-545660.

260 **was leaving the Iran nuclear deal:** The White House, "President Donald J. Trump Is Ending United States
Participation in an Unacceptable Iran Deal," May 8, 2018, trumpwhitehouse.archives.gov/briefings
-statements/president-donald-j-trump-ending-united-states-participation-unacceptable-iran-deal.

CHAPTER 41: THE VALIDATION: FUJIAN JINHUA

261 **"mutual respect and win-win cooperation":** Keegan Elmer, "U.S. Tells China: We Want Competition . . .
But Also Cooperation," *Politico*, October 1, 2018, www.politico.com/story/2018/10/01/us-china-com
petition-not-cooperation-854874.

261 **"competition is not a four-letter word":** Elmer, "We Want Competition."

261 **"If names cannot be correct":** "Dealing with China, America Goes for Confucian Honesty," *The Economist*, October 4, 2018, www.economist.com/china/2018/10/04/dealing-with-china-america-goes-for
-confucian-honesty.

261 **launched his much-anticipated trade war:** Bob Davis and Lingling Wei, *Superpower Showdown: How
the Battle Between Trump and Xi Threatens a New Cold War* (New York: Harper Business, 2020), 238;
David J. Lynch, Danielle Paquette, and Emily Rauhala, "U.S. Levies Tariffs on $34 billion Worth of
Chinese Imports," *The Washington Post*, July 6, 2018, www.washingtonpost.com/world/trumps-trade
-war-with-china-is-finally-here--and-it-wont-be-pretty/2018/07/05/0e43048c-802c-11e8-b9f0
-61b08cdd0ea1_story.html.

262 **half of the $500 billion-plus:** President Donald J. Trump, "Statement from the President on Chinese
Tariffs" (speech, Washington, D.C., September 17, 2018), The White House, trumpwhitehouse.archives.gov
/briefings-statements/statement-from-the-president-4.

262 **shed some 1,000 points:** Davis and Wei, *Superpower Showdown*, 298.

262 **living in small-town Illinois:** Edward Luce, "Hank Paulson: 'I Think It's Pretty Likely We Will See a
Recession,'" *Financial Times*, April 14, 2023, www.ft.com/content/a101d2c1-13b7-4a20-9e8e-38fb1d54723d.

262 **"economic Iron Curtain":** Jeff Cox, "A New Cold War Is Brewing between China and the US, Says
Former Treasury Secretary Paulson," CNBC, November 7, 2018, www.cnbc.com/2018/11/07/economic
-iron-curtain-looms-for-us-and-china-former-treasury-chief-paulsonsays-.html.

262 **bolstered the authority of the Committee on Foreign Investment in the United States:** Christian C.
Davis, Tatman R. Savio, Kevin J. Wolf, "Treasury Releases Proposed CFIUS Regulations to Implement
FIRRMA," Akin Gump Strauss Hauer & Feld, September 20, 2019, www.akingump.com/en/insights
/alerts/treasury-releases-proposed-cfius-regulations-to-implement-firrma.

262 **"and it's China":** John Cornyn, "CFIUS Reform: Examining the Essential Elements, Before the U.S.
Senate Committee on Banking, Housing, and Urban Affairs," 115th Cong., 2nd sess., January 18, 2018,
www.banking.senate.gov/download/cornyn-testimony-1-18-18docx; Josh Rogin, *Chaos under Heaven:
Trump, Xi, and the Battle for the 21st Century* (Boston: Houghton Mifflin Harcourt, 2021), 132–34.

262 **U.S. International Development Finance Corporation:** "The U.S. Export Control System and the
Export Control Reform Act of 2018," R46814, Congressional Research Service, U.S. Library of Congress, June 7, 2021, crsreports.congress.gov/product/pdf/R/R46814; Daniel F. Runde and Romina Ban-
dura, "The BUILD Act Has Passed: What's Next?" Center for Strategic & International Studies, October 12,
2018, www.csis.org/analysis/build-act-has-passed-whats-next.

262 **prohibit all federal agencies from buying Huawei and ZTE:** "Huawei and U.S. Law," R46693, Congressional Research Service, U.S. Library of Congress, February 23, 2021, crsreports.congress.gov
/product/pdf/R/R46693.

263 **dominated by just three companies:** Chris Miller, *Chip War: The Fight for the World's Most Critical
Technology* (New York: Scribner, 2022), 305.

263 **homegrown memory chip company:** Michael Herh, "What Has Forced Fujian Jinhua Integrated Cir-
cuit to Stop DRAM Development?" *BusinessKorea*, January 28, 2019, www.businesskorea.co.kr/news
/articleView.html?idxno=28696.

263 **poached the president of Micron's Taiwanese subsidiary:** Masood Farivar, "US Launches Initiative to
Fight Chinese Economic Espionage," *VOA News*, November 1, 2018, www.voanews.com/a/us-launches
-initiative-to-fight-chinese-economic-espionage/4639587.html; "PRC State-Owned Company, Taiwan
Company, and Three Individuals Charged with Economic Espionage," U.S. Department of Justice, November 1, 2018, www.justice.gov/opa/pr/prc-state-owned-company-taiwan-company-and-three-individuals
-charged-economic-espionage.

263 **transfer memory chip technology to Fujian Jinhua:** "Taiwan Company Pleads Guilty to Trade Secret
Theft in Criminal Case Involving PRC State-Owned Company," U.S. Department of Justice, October 28,
2020, www.justice.gov/opa/pr/taiwan-company-pleads-guilty-trade-secret-theft-criminal-case-involving
-prc-state-owned.

263 **trade secrets belonging to Micron:** Miller, *Chip War*, 307; Scott Tong, "'Amateur' Mistakes Sink Thieves of U.S. Technology Working for China," *Marketplace*, December 22, 2020, www.marketplace .org/2020/12/22/amateur-mistakes-sink-thieves-of-u-s-technology-working-for-china.

263 **Micron sued Fujian Jinhua in California:** In November 2018, the Justice Department also filed criminal charges against UMC and Fujian Jinhua. In October 2020, UMC pleaded guilty to criminal charges of stealing trade secrets from Micron and was sentenced to pay a $60 million fine. Micron and Fujian Jinhua eventually reached a confidential settlement in the civil case following a May 2023 move by the Chinese government to ban Chinese firms from buying Micron's products. In February 2024, a California judge acquitted Fujian Jinhua of criminal charges, citing a lack of evidence that the former Micron employees had acted at its direction. See "Taiwan Company Pleads Guilty," U.S. Department of Justice; Lingling Wei, "Beijing Bans Micron as Supplier to Big Chinese Firms, Citing National Security," *The Wall Street Journal*, May 21, 2023, www.wsj.com/articles/beijing-bans-micron-as-supplier -to-big-chinese-firms-citing-national-security-5f326b90; Kanishka Singh, "Chinese Firm Fujian Jinhua Cleared of U.S. Allegations that It Stole Trade Secrets," Reuters, February 28, 2024, www.reuters. com/technology/chinese-firm-fujian-jinhua-cleared-us-allegations-that-it-stole-trade-secrets -2024-02-28; Aruna Viswanatha and Heather Somerville, "U.S. Defeat in Micron Trade-Secrets Case Reveals Struggle Countering Beijing," *The Wall Street Journal*, March 3, 2024, www.wsj.com/tech/micron -chipmaker-ip-theft-trial-verdict-6f839f15.

264 **Micron was nervous:** Davis and Wei, *Superpower Showdown*, 265–66.

264 **opposition from Steven Mnuchin:** Davis and Wei, *Superpower Showdown*, 266–67.

264 **impossible to produce advanced chips:** Miller, *Chip War*, 309.

264 **months away from full-scale production:** Joel Rosenblatt and Debby Wu, "Blacklisted Chinese Chipmaker on Trial for Alleged Theft," *Bloomberg*, February 27, 2022, www.bloomberg.com/news/articles /2022-02-28/blacklisted-chinese-chipmaker-seeks-vindication-in-u-s-trial?sref=uFaJcogC.

264 **adding Fujian Jinhua to the Entity List:** David Lawder, "U.S. Restricts Exports to Chinese Semiconductor Firm Fujian Jinhua," Reuters, October 30, 2018, www.reuters.com/article/us-usa-trade-china -semiconductors/u-s-restricts-exports-to-chinese-semiconductor-firm-fujian-jinhua-idUSKCN1N328E.

264 **criminal charges against Fujian Jinhua:** "PRC State-Owned Company," U.S. Department of Justice; Kadhim Shubber and James Politi, "US Charges Chinese Group with Theft of Micron Trade Secrets," *Financial Times*, November 1, 2018, www.ft.com/content/d34d9b58-ddff-11e8-8f50-cbae5495d92b.

265 **forced to halt production:** Kathrin Hille, "Trade War Forces Chinese Chipmaker Fujian Jinhua to Halt Output," *Financial Times*, January 28, 2019, www.ft.com/content/87b5580c-22bf-11e9-8ce6-5db4543da632.

CHAPTER 42: THE FIRST SHOT AT HUAWEI

266 **Donald Trump and Xi Jinping were in Buenos Aires:** Bob Davis and Lingling Wei, *Superpower Showdown: How the Battle Between Trump and Xi Threatens a New Cold War* (New York: Harper Business, 2020), 304–5; John Bolton, *The Room Where it Happened* (New York: Simon & Schuster, 2020), 297–99.

266 **delay the next round of U.S. tariffs:** Doug Palmer and Andrew Restuccia, "Trump, Xi Declare Truce on New Tariffs as Trade Talks Continue," *Politico*, December 1, 2018, www.politico.com/story/2018 /12/01/trump-china-xi-jinping-trade-1004954.

266 **push for a U.S.-China trade deal:** Davis and Wei, *Superpower Showdown*, 305–6; Bolton, *The Room*, 297–99.

266 **arrested by Canadian authorities:** Daisuke Wakabayashi and Alan Rappeport, "Huawei C.F.O. Is Arrested in Canada for Extradition to the U.S.," *The New York Times*, December 5, 2018, www.nytimes .com/2018/12/05/business/huawei-cfo-arrest-canada-extradition.html.

267 **Huawei may have evaded American sanctions:** Steve Stecklow, "Exclusive: Huawei CFO Linked to a Firm That Offered HP Gear to Iran," Reuters, January 31, 2013, www.reuters.com/article/uk-huawei-skycom /exclusive-huawei-cfo-linked-to-firm-that-offered-hp-gear-to-iran-idUKBRE90U0CA20130131; Matthew Goldstein et al, "How a National Security Investigation of Huawei Set Off an International Incident," *The New York Times*, December 14, 2018, www.nytimes.com/2018/12/14/business/huawei-meng-hsbc -canada.html.

267 **used "cut-off companies":** Paul Mozur, "ZTE Document Raises Questions about Huawei and Sanctions," *The New York Times*, March 18, 2016, www.nytimes.com/2016/03/19/technology/zte-document -raises-questions-about-huawei-and-sanctions.html?module=inline.

267 **warrant for Meng's arrest:** Goldstein et al, "National Security Investigation of Huawei."

267 **moved to house arrest:** Dan Bilefsky, "Massages and Private Shopping Trips Cushion Tycoon's Detention," *The New York Times*, January 14, 2021, www.nytimes.com/2021/01/14/world/canada/canada-meng -huawei-detention.html.

267 **"seriously harmed" Meng's human rights:** Louise Lucas et al., "China Demands Release of Huawei CFO Held on US charges," *Financial Times*, December 6, 2018, www.ft.com/content/10065056-f8e2 -11e8-af46-2022a0b02a6c.

268 **arrested two Canadian nationals:** Steven Lee Myers and Dan Bilefsky, "Second Canadian Arrested in China, Escalating Diplomatic Feud," *The New York Times*, December 12, 2018, www.nytimes.com /2018/12/12/world/asia/michael-spavor-canadian-detained-china.html.

268 **"small nuclear weapon":** Emily Fend, "Huawei's 5G Ambitions Threatened by US Export Ban," *Financial Times*, December 9, 2018, www.ft.com/content/323abb62-f9e1-11e8-af46-2022a0b02a6c.

268 **$11 billion buying components:** Louise Lucas, James Kynge, and Sue-Lin Wong, "Huawei Warns Ban Set to Hurt 1,200 US suppliers," *Financial Times*, May 29, 2019, www.ft.com/content/84603f22-81d9-11e9-9935-ad75bb96c849.

268 **$120 billion of total U.S. exports:** "U.S. Trade with China," Office of Technology Evaluation, Bureau of Industry and Security, U.S. Department of Commerce, 2018, www.bis.doc.gov/index.php/country-papers/2441-2018-statistical-analysis-of-us-trade-with-china-pdf/file.

268 **exempted from its retaliatory tariffs:** Davis and Wei, *Superpower Showdown*, 296–97.

268 **hundreds of billions of dollars' worth of American chips:** Davis and Wei, *Superpower Showdown*, 321–23.

269 **pushing the UK, Germany, and others to ban Huawei:** James Kynge et al., "UK and Germany Grow Wary of Huawei as US Turns Up Pressure," *Financial Times*, November 29, 2018, www.ft.com/content/6719b6b2-f33d-11e8-9623-d7f9881e729f.

269 **implemented official or de facto bans:** Vicky Xiuzhong Xu, "New Zealand Blocks Huawei, in Blow to Chinese Telecom Giant," *The New York Times*, November 28, 2018, www.nytimes.com/2018/11/28/business/huawei-new-zealand-papua-new-guinea.html.

269 **"Actions speak louder":** Louise Lucas and James Kynge, "Huawei Continues Global Push Despite Setbacks in West," *Financial Times*, December 16, 2018, www.ft.com/content/2d86836a-fd2b-11e8-aebf-99e208d3e521.

269 **Christopher Ford, the assistant secretary:** "About Dr. Christopher Ashley Ford," New Paradigms Forum, www.newparadigmsforum.com/about.

269 **"China's predatory economic tactics":** Author interview with Nazak Nikakhtar, 2023.

270 **filing disputes at the WTO:** "2021 Report to Congress on China's WTO Compliance," United States Trade Representative, February 2022, ustr.gov/sites/default/files/files/Press/Reports/2021USTR%20ReportCongressChinaWTO.pdf.

270 **"assault on our industries":** Author interview with Nazak Nikakhtar, 2023.

270 **a 150-page agreement:** Davis and Wei, *Superpower Showdown*, 14–20.

271 **"wolf culture" at Huawei:** Raymond Zhong, "Huawei's 'Wolf Culture' Helped It Grow, and Got It into Trouble," *The New York Times*, December 18, 2018, www.nytimes.com/2018/12/18/technology/huawei-workers-iran-sanctions.html.

271 **"never do anything to harm any country":** Raymond Zhong, "Huawei's Reclusive Founder Rejects Spying and Praises Trump," *The New York Times*, January 15, 2019, www.nytimes.com/2019/01/15/technology/huawei-ren-zhengfei.html.

271 **"Don't believe everything you hear":** Kate Fazzini, "Huawei Takes Out Full-Page WSJ Ad: 'Don't Believe Everything You Hear,'" CNBC, February 28, 2019, www.cnbc.com/2019/02/28/huawei-wsj-full-page-ad-dont-believe-everything-you-hear.html.

271 **no mention of "Made in China 2025":** Lingling Wei, "China Expects 2019 Economic Growth of 6% to 6.5%," *The Wall Street Journal*, March 4, 2019, www.wsj.com/articles/china-expects-2019-economic-growth-of-6-to-6-5-11551748675; Lingling Wei, "Beijing Drops Contentious 'Made in China 2025' Slogan, but Policy Remains," *The Wall Street Journal*, March 5, 2019, www.wsj.com/articles/china-drops-a-policy-the-u-s-dislikes-at-least-in-name-11551795370.

271 **China a "systemic rival":** "EU-China: A Strategic Outlook," European Commission and HR/VP contribution to the European Council, March 12, 2019, commission.europa.eu/system/files/2019-03/communication-eu-china-a-strategic-outlook.pdf.

271 **first major democracy to join the Belt and Road Initiative:** Colleen Barry, "China's Xi Visits Italy with Belt and Road Deal as Prize," The Associated Press, March 21, 2019, apnews.com/general-news-d3067d9eaf5346ee945f0a043197929d.

271 **would not ban Huawei:** Bojan Pancevski and Sara Germano, "Drop Huawei or See Intelligence Sharing Pared Back, U.S. Tells Germany," *The Wall Street Journal*, March 11, 2019, www.wsj.com/articles/drop-huawei-or-see-intelligence-sharing-pared-back-u-s-tells-germany-11552314827; Guy Chazan, "US Setback as Germany Fails to Ban Huawei in 5G Guidelines," *Financial Times*, March 7, 2019, www.ft.com/content/3dae0df4-40eb-11e9-9bee-efab61506f44.

271 **Crossed out in red:** Robert Lighthizer, *No Trade Is Free: Changing Course, Taking on China, and Helping America's Workers* (New York: HarperCollins, 2023), 176–77; Chris Buckley and Keith Bradsher, "How Xi's Last-Minute Switch on U.S.-China Trade Deal Upended It," *The New York Times*, May 16, 2019, www.nytimes.com/2019/05/16/world/asia/trade-xi-jinping-trump-china-united-states.html; Davis and Wei, *Superpower Showdown*, 21, 332.

272 **a bridge too far:** Davis and Wei, *Superpower Showdown*, 17–18.

272 **"The Trade Deal with China continues":** Donald J. Trump (@realDonaldTrump), ". . . of additional goods sent to us by China," Twitter, May 5, 2019, twitter.com/realDonaldTrump/status/1125069836088950784.

272 **new tariffs went into effect:** Sherisse Pham, "The US Just Raised Tariffs on Chinese Goods. China Says It Will Hit Back," CNN, May 10, 2019, www.cnn.com/2019/05/10/business/china-us-tariffs-trade/index.html.

272 **Steven Mnuchin once again:** Davis and Wei, *Superpower Showdown*, 27; Bolton, *The Room*, 308.
272 **"Add 'with the approval of the President'":** Bolton, *The Room*, 308.

CHAPTER 43: A FALSE START

273 **where Mao Zedong and his followers hid:** Victor C. Falkenheim, "Jiangxi Province, China," *Encyclopedia Britannica*, November 23, 2023, www.britannica.com/place/Jiangxi; "Jiangxi Soviet," *Encyclopedia Britannica*, November 23, 2023, www.britannica.com/topic/Jiangxi-Soviet.
273 **also the starting point of the Long March:** "Long March: Chinese History," *Encyclopedia Britannica*, November 30, 2023, www.britannica.com/event/Long-March.
273 **Xi Jinping traveled to Jiangxi:** James Griffiths, "China's Latest Trade War Card Isn't as Strong as Beijing Thinks," CNN, May 30, 2019, www.cnn.com/2019/05/21/politics/china-us-trade-war-rare-earths-intl/index.html.
273 **"embarking on a new Long March":** Zhou Xin, "Xi Jinping Calls for 'New Long March' in Dramatic Sign That China Is Preparing for Protracted Trade War," *South China Morning Post*, May 21, 2019, www.scmp.com/economy/china-economy/article/3011186/xi-jinping-calls-new-long-march-dramatic-sign-china-preparing; Yun Li, "Xi Jinping Says China Is Embarking on a 'New Long March,' Signaling No End to Trade War Soon," CNBC, May 21, 2019, www.cnbc.com/2019/05/21/xi-jinping-says-china-is-embarking-on-a-new-long-march-signaling-no-end-to-trade-war-soon.html.
273 **rare-earth processing facilities:** James T. Areddy, "Xi Jinping Flexes China's Trade Muscle with Visit to Rare-Earths Hub," *The Wall Street Journal*, May 21, 2019, www.wsj.com/articles/xi-jinping-flexes-china-s-trade-muscle-with-visit-to-rare-earths-hub-11558442724.
273 **largest known reserves of rare earths:** Areddy, "Xi Jinping"; M. Garside, "Rare Earth Elements—Statistics & Facts," Statista, accessed December 18, 2023, www.statista.com/topics/1744/rare-earth-elements/#topicOverview; Xianbin Yao, "China Is Moving Rapidly Up the Rare Earth Value Chain," *Brink News*, August 7, 2022, www.brinknews.com/china-is-moving-rapidly-up-the-rare-earth-value-chain.
273 **Lockheed Martin depended on rare earths:** Lara Seligman, "China Dominates the Rare Earths Market. This U.S. Mine is Trying to Change That," *Politico*, December 14, 2022, www.politico.com/news/magazine/2022/12/14/rare-earth-mines-00071102.
273 **"China has rare earths":** Lucy Hornby and Henry Sanderson, "Rare Earths: Beijing Threatens a New Front in the Trade War," *Financial Times*, June 3, 2019, www.ft.com/content/3cd18372-85e0-11e9-a028-86cea8523dc2.
274 **"rare earths become China's counter-weapon":** Lucy Hornby and Archie Zhang, "China's State Planner Suggests Using Rare Earths in US Trade War," *Financial Times*, May 29, 2019, www.ft.com/content/a0125e6a-8168-11e9-b592-5fe435b57a3b.
274 **"Don't say you were not warned":** Hornby and Sanderson, "Rare Earths."
274 **"keep China from becoming stronger":** Bob Davis and Lingling Wei, *Superpower Showdown: How the Battle Between Trump and Xi Threatens a New Cold War* (New York: Harper Business, 2020), 28.
274 **its own "Unreliable Entity List":** "China's 'Unreliable Entity List' Creates New Countervailing Risks for Companies Navigating U.S. Sanctions and Long-Arm Enforcement," Morrison & Foerster, October 7, 2020, www.mofo.com/resources/insights/201007-china-mofcom-unreliable-entity-list; Sue-Lin Wong and Nian Liu, "China Threatens to Blacklist 'Non-reliable' Foreign Companies," *Financial Times*, May 31, 2019, www.ft.com/content/a780050e-8392-11e9-9935-ad75bb96c849.
275 **"jeopardizing China's national security":** Tom Mitchell, "News of China's 'Unreliables List' Spooks Foreign Business," *Financial Times*, June 4, 2019, www.ft.com/content/80d7909c-86a4-11e9-a028-86cea8523dc2.
275 **warning of dire consequences:** Kate Conger, "China Summons Tech Giants to Warn Against Cooperating with Trump Ban," *The New York Times*, June 8, 2019, www.nytimes.com/2019/06/08/business/economy/china-huawei-trump.html.
275 **cut Huawei loose was Google:** Angela Moon, "Exclusive: Google Suspends Some Business with Huawei after Trump Blacklist: Source," Reuters, May 20, 2019, www.reuters.com/article/us-huawei-tech-alphabet-exclusive/exclusive-google-suspends-some-business-with-huawei-after-trump-blacklist-source-idUSKCN1SP0NB.
275 **"attack Huawei with such great strategy":** Yuen Yang and Siddarth Shrikanth, "Huawei Smartphone Sales Fall as Company Cuts Revenue Forecasts," *Financial Times*, June 17, 2019, www.ft.com/content/cc0563ae-90c8-11e9-aea1-2b1d33ac3271.
275 **"ready to prepare a Plan B":** Louise Lucas, James Kynge, and Sue-Lin Wong, "Huawei Warns Ban Set to Hurt 1,200 US Suppliers," *Financial Times*, May 29, 2019, www.ft.com/content/84603f22-81d9-11e9-9935-ad75bb96c849.
275 **year's worth of the chips:** Lucas, Kynge, and Wong, "Ban Set to Hurt."
275 **eleven contracts for 5G networks:** Yuan Yang, "Huawei's Sales Rise 23% Despite US Blacklisting," *Financial Times*, July 30, 2019, www.ft.com/content/a15af2e8-b29e-11e9-8cb2-799a3a8cf37b.
275 **feel the ripple effects of the move:** Alexandra Alper and David Shepardson, "Trump Agrees to Prompt Responses to License Requests for Huawei Sales," Reuters, July 22, 2019, www.reuters.com/article/uk

-huawei-tech-usa-idUKKCN1UH1Y0; "Micron Resumes Some Huawei Shipments Despite Trade Blacklist," *South China Morning Post*, June 26, 2019, www.scmp.com/news/china/article/3016079/micron -resumes-some-huawei-shipments-despite-trade-blacklist.

276 **arguing against, not for, export controls:** Stephen Nellis and Alexandra Alper, "U.S. Chipmakers Quietly Lobby to Ease Huawei Ban," Reuters, June 17, 2019, www.reuters.com/article/us-huawei-tech -usa-lobbying/u-s-chipmakers-quietly-lobby-to-ease-huawei-ban-idUSKCN1TH0VA.

276 **from the board of the Semiconductor Industry Association:** Dan Rosso, "Micron President and CEO Sanjay Mehrotra Elected Chair of Semiconductor Industry Association," Semiconductor Industry Association, November 29, 2018, www.semiconductors.org/micron-president-and-ceo-sanjay-mehrotra -elected-chair-of-semiconductor-industry-association. Mehrotra and other U.S. semiconductor CEOs later met with Trump, Ross, Mnuchin, and other top economic officials at the White House. Alexandra Alper and David Shepardson, "Trump Agrees to Prompt Responses to License Requests for Huawei Sales," Reuters, July 22, 2019, www.reuters.com/article/idUSKCN1UH1XW.

276 **Chinese supercomputer manufacturer, Sugon:** Kate O'Keeffe and Asa Fitch, "U.S. Targets China's Supercomputing Push with New Export Restrictions," *The Wall Street Journal*, June 21, 2019, www .wsj.com/articles/u-s-targets-chinas-supercomputing-push-with-new-export-restrictions -11561129547.

276 **Xi implored Trump to cut Huawei a break:** John Bolton, *The Room Where it Happened* (New York: Simon & Schuster, 2020), 308–9.

277 **Trump was ready to throw Xi a bone:** Davis and Wei, *Superpower Showdown*, 347–48; Bolton, *The Room*, 309; Josh Rogin, *Chaos under Heaven: Trump, Xi, and the Battle for the 21st Century* (Boston: Houghton Mifflin Harcourt, 2021), 163–64.

277 **"U.S. companies can sell their equipment to Huawei," the president affirmed:** Jon Russell, "Huawei Can Buy from US Suppliers Again—but Things Will Never Be the Same," *TechCrunch*, June 29, 2019, techcrunch.com/2019/06/29/huawei-us-supplier-ban-lifted; "Trump Reverses Course, Lifts Some Sanctions Against Chinese Telecom Firm Huawei," NPR, July 1, 2019, www.npr.org/2019/07/01/737761412 /trump-reverses-course-lifts-some-sanctions-against-chinese-telecom-firm-huawei.

277 **American companies "were not exactly happy":** David Phelan, "Trump Surprises G20 with Huawei Concession: U.S. Companies Can Sell to Huawei," *Forbes*, June 29, 2019, www.forbes.com/sites /davidphelan/2019/06/29/trump-surprises-g20-with-huawei-concession-u-s-companies-can-sell-to -huawei/?sh=608491311e21.

277 **Huawei rejoiced anyway:** Huawei Facts (@HuaweiFacts), "U-turn? Donald Trump Suggests He Would Allow #Huawei to Once Again Purchase U.S. technology! #HuaweiFacts," Twitter, June 29, 2019, twitter .com/HuaweiFacts/status/1144882620804689921?lang=en.

277 **national security officials were furious:** Rogin, *Chaos under Heaven*, 163–64.

277 **"where there is no threat to U.S. national security":** Dan Strumpf, "Ross Spells Out Reprieve for Huawei," *The Wall Street Journal*, July 9, 2019, www.wsj.com/articles/ross-spells-out-reprieve-for-huawei -11562695409.

277 **hundreds of license applications:** Jeanne Whalen, Joseph Marks, and Ellen Nakashima, "U.S. Approves First Licenses for Tech Sales to Huawei," *The Washington Post*, November 20, 2019, www.washingtonpost .com/technology/2019/11/20/us-said-approve-first-licenses-tech-sales-huawei.

277 **legal ways to get around the export controls:** Paul Mozur and Cecilia Kang, "U.S. Tech Companies Sidestep a Trump Ban, to Keep Selling to Huawei," *The New York Times*, June 25, 2019, www.nytimes .com/2019/06/25/technology/huawei-trump-ban-technology.html.

277 **Micron resumed sales of memory chips:** "Micron Resumes Some Huawei Shipments," *South China Morning Post*.

277 **were "UK-origin technologies":** Madhumita Murgia and Nic Fildes, "Huawei Chip Unit Hit as Arm Withdraws Licences," *Financial Times*, May 22, 2019, www.ft.com/content/a566bb84-7c88-11e9-81d2 -f785092ab560; Chaim Gartenberg, "ARM Will Continue to License Chip Architecture to Huawei After All," *The Verge*, October 25, 2019, www.theverge.com/2019/10/25/20932096/arm-license-chip -architecture-huawei-trump-trade-ban-uk-us.

278 **sixty commercial contracts:** Yuan Yang and Daniel Shane, "Huawei Sees Growth in Revenues and 5G Contracts Despite US Ban," *Financial Times*, October 16, 2019, www.ft.com/content/5f3c7f68-efdd-11e9 -ad1e-4367d8281195.

278 **hit $86 billion:** Yang and Shane, "Huawei sees growth"; Jill Disis, "Huawei's Smartphone Sales and 5G Business Stay Strong Despite US Hostility," CNN, www.cnn.com/2019/10/16/tech/huawei-earnings -us-china-trade-war/index.html.

CHAPTER 44: "BACKDOORS" AND "BETRAYAL"

279 **met with members of the Semiconductor Industry Association:** Bob Davis and Lingling Wei, *Superpower Showdown: How the Battle Between Trump and Xi Threatens a New Cold War* (New York: Harper Business, 2020), 360–61.

279 **siphon data from the building's servers:** Karishma Vaswani, "Huawei: The Story of a Controversial Company," *BBC News*, March 6, 2019, www.bbc.co.uk/news/resources/idt-sh/Huawei; Ghalia Kadiri

and Joan Tilouine, "A Addis-Abeba, le siège de l'Union africaine espionné par Pékin," *Le Monde*, January 26, 2018, www.lemonde.fr/afrique/article/2018/01/26/a-addis-abeba-le-siege-de-l-union-africaine -espionne-par-les-chinois_5247521_3212.html; John Aglionby, Emily Feng, and Yuan Yang, "African Union Accuses China of Hacking Headquarters," *Financial Times*, January 29, 2018, www.ft.com/content /c26a9214-04f2-11e8-9650-9c0ad2d7c5b5; Nick Statt, "China Denies Claims It Built Backdoors into Africa Union's Headquarters for Spying," *The Verge*, July 29, 2018, www.theverge.com/2018/1/29/16946802 /china-african-union-spying-hq-cybersecurity-computers-backdoors-espionage.

279 **access telecom networks around the world:** Bojan Pancevski, "U.S. Officials Say Huawei Can Covertly Access Telecom Networks," *The Wall Street Journal*, February 12, 2020, www.wsj.com/articles/u-s -officials-say-huawei-can-covertly-access-telecom-networks-11581452256; Bethany Allen-Ebrahimian, "Huawei Equipment Has Secret 'Back Doors,' U.S. Officials Claim," *Axios*, February 11, 2020, www .axios.com/2020/02/11/huawei-equipment-has-secret-back-doors-us-says.

279 **a kill switch that Beijing:** Jason Healey, "Five Jeez: Five Security Arguments Against Huawei 5G," Council on Foreign Relations, September 4, 2019, www.cfr.org/blog/five-security-arguments-against -huawei-5g; Andreas Becker, "Huawei Technology Is a Matter of Faith," *Deutsche Welle*, February 6, 2019, www.dw.com/en/using-huawei-technology-is-a-matter-of-faith/a-47390624.

280 **"conscience of everyone":** Davis and Wei, *Superpower Showdown*, 360–61.

280 **letting the KGB build U.S. telecommunications:** Davis and Wei, *Superpower Showdown*, 360–61. Pottinger would later reiterate this comparison in public remarks. See Raisina Dialogue (@raisinadialogue), "Matthew Pottinger of @WHNSC on the Tech Wars and Huawei," Twitter, January 16, 2020, twitter .com/raisinadialogue/status/1217814743823466497.

280 **closely linked to America's:** Davis and Wei, *Superpower Showdown*, 361.

280 **50 percent of sites in Germany's:** Anne Morris, "Huawei Faces an Uncertain 5G Future in Germany," *Fierce Wireless*, September 26, 2023, www.fiercewireless.com/5g/huawei-faces-uncertain-5g-future -germany.

280 **"U.S. companies can sell their equipment to Huawei" as long as:** Jon Russell, "Huawei Can Buy from US Suppliers Again—but Things Will Never Be the Same," *TechCrunch*, June 29, 2019, https://techcrunch .com/2019/06/29/huawei-us-supplier-ban-lifted.

281 **Coordinating Committee for Multilateral Export Controls:** John H. Henshaw, "The Origins of CoCom: Lessons for Contemporary Proliferation Control Regimes," Henry L. Stimson Center, May 1993, www.stimson.org/wp-content/files/file-attachments/Report7_1.pdf.

281 **being "worse than China":** Jonathan Swan, "Scoop: Trump Tells Macron the EU Is 'Worse' Than China," *Axios*, June 10, 2018, www.axios.com/2018/06/10/donald-trump-emmanuel-macron-eu-worse-than -china-trade-tariffs.

281 **called the Foreign Direct Product Rule:** "The History and Limits of America's Favourite New Economic Weapon," *The Economist*, February 8, 2023, www.economist.com/united-states/2023/02/08/the-history- and-limits-of-americas-favourite-new-economic-weapon.

282 **39 percent of the total value:** Saif M. Khan, "The Semiconductor Supply Chain: Assessing National Competitiveness," Center for Security and Emerging Technology, January 2021, cset.georgetown.edu /publication/the-semiconductor-supply-chain.

282 **Huawei as its second-biggest customer:** Cheng Ting-Fang and Lauly Li, "TSMC Halts New Huawei Orders after US Tightens Restrictions," *Nikkei Asia*, May 18, 2020, https://asia.nikkei.com/Spotlight /Huawei-crackdown/TSMC-halts-new-Huawei-orders-after-US-tightens-restrictions.

282 **15 percent of TSMC's revenue:** Ting-Fang and Li, "TSMC Halts New Huawei Orders."

282 **embedding secret "backdoors":** Pancevski, "Huawei Can Covertly Access Telecom Networks"; Allen-Ebrahimian, "Huawei Equipment Has Secret 'Back Doors.'"

282 **a "smoking gun":** Pancevski, "Huawei Can Covertly Access Telecom Networks."

282 **"maximal loss of control":** Katrin Bennhold and Jack Ewing, "In Huawei Battle, China Threatens Germany 'Where It Hurts': Automakers," *The New York Times*, January 16, 2020, www.nytimes.com /2020/01/16/world/europe/huawei-germany-china-5g-automakers.html.

282 **were heavily dependent on Huawei:** Pancevski, "Huawei Can Covertly Access Telecom Networks."

282 **Deutsche Telekom, the market leader:** Andrew Small, *No Limits: The Inside Story of China's War with the West* (London: C. Hurst & Co., 2022), 76.

283 **tens of thousands of German jobs:** Bennhold and Ewing, "China Threatens Germany."

283 **"Stand with Hong Kong":** "A Tweet from the Houston Rockets GM—'Fight for Freedom. Stand with Hong Kong.'—Angers China," *Chicago Tribune*, October 7, 2019, www.chicagotribune.com /sports/breaking/ct-houston-rockets-gm-tweet-china-20191006-qv2y4m7xvvhopafbnlvkrxb7cu-story .html.

283 **canceled the broadcast of NBA games:** Daniel Victor, "Hong Kong Protests Put N.B.A. on Edge in China," *The New York Times*, October 7, 2019, www.nytimes.com/2019/10/07/sports/basketball/nba -china-hong-kong.html.

283 **costing the NBA hundreds of millions:** Kurt Helin, "NBA Loses Hundreds of Millions of Dollars in China, May Return to Play Preseason Games in 2020," *NBC Sports*, February 16, 2020, www.nbcsports .com/nba/news/nba-loses-hundreds-of-millions-of-dollars-in-china-may-return-to-play-preseason -games-in-2020.

283 **share the same intelligence:** "Using Huawei in UK 5G Network 'Madness,' Says US," *BBC News*, January 13, 2020, www.bbc.com/news/business-51097474.

283 **"fantastic full-fiber broadband":** Natasha Lomas, "Freshly Elected as UK's Next PM, Boris Johnson Pledges Full Fiber Broadband Bonanza," *Tech Crunch*, July 23, 2019, techcrunch.com/2019/07/23/freshly-elected-as-uks-next-pm-boris-johnson-pledges-full-fiber-broadband-bonanza.

283 **promise would be impossible to keep:** Small, *No Limits*, 118.

283 **"genuine plea from one ally to another":** Josh Rogin, "Congress Warns Britain to Stay Away from Huawei," *The Washington Post*, January 27, 2020, www.washingtonpost.com/opinions/2020/01/27/congress-warns-britain-stay-away-huawei.

283 **hailed as "Britain Trump":** Daniel Lippman and Nahal Toosi, "Boris and Donald: A Very Special Relationship," *Politico*, December 12, 2019, www.politico.com/news/2019/12/12/trump-boris-johnson-relationship-083732; David Smith, "Trump Hails 'Good Man' Boris Johnson and Says of UK: 'They Like Me over There,'" *The Guardian*, July 23, 2019, www.theguardian.com/us-news/2019/jul/23/trump-boris-johnson-britain-trump-uk-prime-minister; "Trump Speaks with British PM Johnson about Telecoms Security—White House," Reuters, January 24, 2020, www.reuters.com/article/usa-trump-johnson-idCNW1N28T00D.

283 **Johnson of "betrayal":** John T. Bennett, "White House Refuses to Deny Trump Accused Boris Johnson of 'Betrayal' in Angry Phone Call over Huawei Decision," *The Independent*, February 24, 2020, www.independent.co.uk/news/world/americas/us-politics/trump-boris-johnson-huawei-5g-phone-call-white-house-a9355506.html.

284 **capped the amount of equipment:** Arjun Kharpal, "Huawei Allowed Limited Access to UK's 5G Networks as Britain Defies US Pressure," CNBC, January 28, 2020, www.cnbc.com/2020/01/28/huawei-uk-chinese-firm-allowed-limited-access-to-uk-5g-network.html.

CHAPTER 45: THE SECOND SHOT AT HUAWEI

285 **overseen Trump's impeachment:** Nicholas Fandos and Michael D. Shear, "Trump Impeachment for Abuse of Power and Obstruction of Congress," *The New York Times*, December 18, 2019, www.nytimes.com/2019/12/18/us/politics/trump-impeached.html.

286 **"autocracy over democracy":** Nancy Pelosi, "Remarks at Munich Security Conference" (speech, Munich, Germany, February 14, 2020), Office of Congresswoman Pelosi, pelosi.house.gov/news/press-releases/speaker-pelosi-remarks-at-munich-security-conference.

286 **"We have agreement in that regard":** Pelosi, "Remarks at Munich Security Conference."

286 **"Trojan horses for Chinese intelligence":** Michael R. Pompeo, "Remarks at the Munich Security Conference" (speech, Munich, Germany, February 15, 2020), U.S. Mission to the European Union, useu.usmission.gov/secretary-pompeo-remarks-at-the-munich-security-conference.

286 **"developing our own secure 5G":** Mark T. Esper, "Remarks by Secretary of Defense Mark T. Esper at the Munich Security Conference" (speech, Munich, Germany, February 15, 2020), U.S. Department of Defense, www.defense.gov/News/Speeches/Speech/Article/2085577/as-prepared-remarks-by-secretary-of-defense-mark-t-esper-at-the-munich-security.

286 **"Are you offering an alternative?":** David E. Sanger and David McCabe, "Huawei Is Winning the Argument in Europe, as the U.S. Fumbles to Develop Alternatives," *The New York Times*, February 17, 2020, www.nytimes.com/2020/02/17/us/politics/us-huawei-5g.html; Rob Schmitz, hosted by Leila Fadel, "U.S. Pressures Europe to Find Alternatives to Huawei," *All Things Considered* (podcast), NPR, February 15, 2020, www.npr.org/2020/02/15/806366021/europe-pressures-u-s-to-back-low-cost-alternative-to-huawei.

287 **"eighteen months ahead":** Lauly Li and Cheng Ting-Fang, "Huawei Claims over 90 Contracts for 5G, Leading Ericsson," *Nikkei Asia*, February 21, 2020, asia.nikkei.com/Business/China-tech/Huawei-claims-over-90-contracts-for-5G-leading-Ericsson.

287 **"Prism, prism on the wall":** Kelvin Chan, "US Suffers Setbacks in Effort to Ban Chinese Tech Company," *Yahoo News*, February 26, 2019, www.yahoo.com/lifestyle/huawei-exec-pokes-fun-us-093808388.html.

287 **PRISM, an American program:** Alicia Parlapiano, "Comparing Two Secret Surveillance Programs," *The New York Times*, June 7, 2013, archive.nytimes.com/www.nytimes.com/interactive/2013/06/07/us/comparing-two-secret-surveillance-programs.html; Richard Lempert, "PRISM and Boundless Informant: Is NSA Surveillance a Threat?" The Brookings Institution, June 13, 2013, www.brookings.edu/articles/prism-and-boundless-informant-is-nsa-surveillance-a-threat.

287 **Keith Krach, the State Department's undersecretary:** Andrea Huspeni, "At DocuSign, Keith Krach Continues His Epic 16-Year Quest to Reinvent the Business World," *Business Insider*, July 13, 2012, www.businessinsider.com/keith-krach-docusign-future-2012-7.

287 **CEO of DocuSign:** John D. Stoll, "Goodbye Lee Iacocca and the Era When Car Business Was King," *The Wall Street Journal*, July 4, 2019, www.wsj.com/articles/goodbye-lee-iacocca-and-the-era-when-car-business-was-king-11562248810.

288 **industry standard for secure 5G:** "The Clean Network," Keith Krach, November 2020, keithkrach.com/presentation/clean-network-overview-public-version.

288 **"Clean Network" principles:** Meg Rithmire and Courtney Han, "The Clean Network and the Future of Global Technology Competition," *Harvard Business School*, April 2021, www.hbs.edu/faculty/Pages /item.aspx?num=60084.

288 **Chinese authorities hid behind a wall of lies:** Lawrence Wright, "The Plague Year," *The New Yorker*, December 28, 2020, www.newyorker.com/magazine/2021/01/04/the-plague-year.

288 **ban travelers from China:** Josh Rogin, *Chaos under Heaven: Trump, Xi, and the Battle for the 21st Century* (Boston: Houghton Mifflin Harcourt, 2021), 257–59.

289 **sparing no effort to contain the outbreak:** "China's Xi Tells Trump No Effort Spared in Coronavirus Fight," Reuters, February 6, 2020, www.reuters.com/article/us-china-health-xi-trump/chinas-xi-tells -trump-no-effort-spared-in-coronavirus-fight-idINKBN2010CZ.

289 **"Fifteen days to slow the spread":** Will Feuer and Noah Higgins-Dunn, "A Year Later, Trump's '15 Days to Slow the Spread' Campaign Shows How Little We Knew about Covid," CNBC, March 16, 2021, www.cnbc.com/2021/03/16/covid-a-year-later-trumps-15-days-to-slow-the-spread-pledge-shows -how-little-we-knew.html.

289 **China produced 85 percent:** Nathaniel Taplin, "Why the Richest Country on Earth Can't Get You a Face Mask," *The Wall Street Journal*, April 1, 2020, www.wsj.com/articles/why-the-richest-country-on -earth-cant-get-you-a-face-mask-11585741254.

289 **confusing and false message:** Zeynep Tufekci, "Why Telling People They Don't Need Masks Back-fired," *The New York Times*, March 17, 2020, www.nytimes.com/2020/03/17/opinion/coronavirus-face -masks.html.

289 **controlled its own COVID outbreak:** Peter Hessler, "How China Controlled the Coronavirus," *The New Yorker*, August 10, 2020, www.newyorker.com/magazine/2020/08/17/how-china-controlled-the -coronavirus.

289 **terms like "Wuhan virus":** Rogin, *Chaos under Heaven*, 265–66.

289 **risked its access to Chinese-made masks:** "US Warned Not to Squeeze Huawei," *Global Times*, March 11, 2020, www.globaltimes.cn/content/1182273.shtml.

289 **blocking imports of Australian beef:** "China Punishes Australia for Promoting an Inquiry into COVID-19," *The Economist*, May 21, 2020, www.economist.com/asia/2020/05/21/china-punishes-australia -for-promoting-an-inquiry-into-covid-19.

289 **"for our enemies, we have shotguns":** "How Sweden Copes with Chinese Bullying," *The Economist*, February 20, 2020, www.economist.com/europe/2020/02/20/how-sweden-copes-with-chinese-bullying; Rush Doshi, *The Long Game: China's Grand Strategy to Displace American Order* (New York: Oxford University Press, 2021), 277–78.

290 **Tariffs had not plugged:** Benn Steil and Benjamin Della Rocca, "Tariffs and the Trade Balance: How Trump Validated His Critics," Council on Foreign Relations, April 21, 2021, www.cfr.org/blog/tariffs -and-trade-balance-how-trump-validated-his-critics.

290 **disrupt communications related to U.S. nuclear weapons:** Katie Bo Lillis, "CNN Exclusive: FBI Investigation Determined Chinese-made Huawei Equipment Could Disrupt US Nuclear Arsenal Communications," CNN, July 25, 2022, www.cnn.com/2022/07/23/politics/fbi-investigation-huawei -china-defense-department-communications-nuclear/index.html.

290 **"unprecedented economic leverage":** William P. Barr, "Keynote Address at the Department of Jus-tice's China Initiative Conference," U.S. Department of Justice, February 6, 2020, www.justice.gov /opa/speech/attorney-general-william-p-barr-delivers-keynote-address-department-justices-china.

291 **unleashed the FDPR:** Ana Swanson, "U.S. Delivers Another Blow to Huawei with New Tech Restric-tions," *The New York Times*, May 15, 2020, www.nytimes.com/2020/05/15/business/economy/commerce -department-huawei.html; U.S. Department of Commerce, "Commerce Addresses Huawei's Efforts to Undermine Entity List, Restricts Products Designed and Produced with U.S. Technologies," May 15, 2020, 2017-2021.commerce.gov/news/press-releases/2020/05/commerce-addresses-huaweis-efforts -undermine-entity-list-restricts.html.

CHAPTER 46: THE DOMINOES FALL

292 **TSMC also relied on American technologies:** Chris Miller, "Just How Badly Does Apple Need China?" *The Atlantic*, December 28, 2022, www.theatlantic.com/technology/archive/2022/12/tsmc-apple-memory -chip-production-us-china-taiwan-relations/672593.

292 **but rather cut ties with Huawei:** Kathrin Hille and Kiran Stacey, "TSMC Falls into Line with US Export Controls on Huawei," *Financial Times*, June 9, 2020, www.ft.com/content/bad129d1-4543 -4fe3-9ecb-15b3c917aca4.

292 **new chip factory in Arizona:** Don Clark and Ana Swanson, "T.S.M.C. Is Set to Build a U.S. Chip Fa-cility, a Win for Trump," *The New York Times*, May 14, 2020, www.nytimes.com/2020/05/14/technology /trump-tsmc-us-chip-facility.html; Debby Wu, "TSMC Scores Subsidies and Picks Site for $12 Billion U.S. Plant," *Bloomberg*, June 9, 2020, www.bloomberg.com/news/articles/2020-06-09/tsmc-confident-of -replacing-any-huawei-orders-lost-to-u-s-curbs; Virginia Heffernan, "I Saw the Face of God in a Semicon-ductor Factory," *Wired*, March 21, 2023, www.wired.com/story/i-saw-the-face-of-god-in-a-tsmc-factory.

292–93 **UK government launched an emergency review:** Helen Warrell and Nic Fildes, "UK Review of Huawei Eyes Impact of US Sanctions," *Financial Times*, May 31, 2020, www.ft.com/content/9e581ace-69ec-4a42-81c3-c28d2bb40aa1.

293 **a man he admired:** Matt Mathers, "What Has Boris Johnson Said about Trump?" *The Independent*, January 19, 2021, www.independent.co.uk/news/uk/politics/boris-johnson-donald-trump-comments-b1789384.html.

293 **"very, very serious" ramifications:** Nic Fildes and Helen Warrell, "Huawei Calls for UK to Grant Stay of Execution," *Financial Times*, July 8, 2020, www.ft.com/content/305692fe-661f-4125-a6ed-9365ac7359a2.

293 **"Our long-standing understanding":** Fildes and Warrell, "Huawei Calls."

293 **"months" before the company could provide reassurance:** Fildes and Warrell, "Huawei Calls."

293 **"arbitrary and pernicious":** "Media Statement on Foreign Direct Product Rule Changes Made by US Government," Huawei, May 2019, www.huawei.com/nl/facts/voices-of-huawei/media-statement-on-foreign-direct-product-rule-changes-made-by-us-government.

293 **"Survival is the keyword":** Kathrin Hille, "Huawei Says New US Sanctions Put Its Survival at Stake," *Financial Times*, May 18, 2020, www.ft.com/content/3c532149-94b2-4023-82e0-b51190dc2c46.

293 **currency swap line with China:** "Russia Signs Deals with China to Help Weather Sanctions," CNBC, October 13, 2014, www.cnbc.com/2014/10/13/russia-signs-deals-with-china-to-help-weather-sanctions.html.

293 **Cross-Border Interbank Payment System (CIPS):** Gabriel Wildau, "China Launch of Renminbi Payments System Reflects Swift Spying Concerns," *Financial Times*, October 8, 2015, www.ft.com/content/84241292-66a1-11e5-a155-02b6f8af6a62.

294 **"crush companies outside its own borders":** "Media Statement," Huawei.

294 **expressed their support for Huawei:** Arjun Kharpal, "Chinese Social Media Users Are Rallying Behind Huawei. Some Say They're Switching from Apple," CNBC, May 21, 2019, www.cnbc.com/2019/05/22/chinese-social-media-users-are-rallying-behind-huawei.html.

294 **the "princess of Huawei":** Helen Davidson, Vincent Ni, and Leyland Cecco, "Meng Wanzhou: 'Princess of Huawei' Who Became the Face of a High-Stakes Dispute," *The Guardian*, August 19, 2021, www.theguardian.com/technology/2021/aug/19/meng-wanzhou-huawei-profile-china-canada-us-dispute.

294 **"Chinese government will not just stand by":** David Kirton, "Huawei Warns China Will Strike Back Against New U.S. Restrictions," Reuters, March 31, 2020, www.reuters.com/article/us-huawei-results/huawei-warns-china-will-strike-back-against-new-u-s-restrictions-idUSKBN21I0YS.

295 **quest for technological self-sufficiency:** Kevin Yao, "What We Know about China's 'Dual Circulation' Economic Strategy," Reuters, September 8, 2020, www.reuters.com/article/china-economy-transformation-explainer-idUSKBN2600B5.

295 **anodyne name "dual circulation":** "China's Got a New Plan to Overtake the U.S. in Tech," *Bloomberg*, May 20, 2020, www.bloomberg.com/news/articles/2020-05-20/china-has-a-new-1-4-trillion-plan-to-overtake-the-u-s-in-tech; Hal Brands and Michael Beckley, *Danger Zone: The Coming Conflict with China* (New York: W. W. Norton & Company, 2022), 111–12.

295 **"We want to be your friend":** Laura Hughes and Helen Warrell, "China Envoy Warns of 'Consequences' if Britain Rejects Huawei," *Financial Times*, July 6, 2020, www.ft.com/content/3d67d1c1-98ff-439a-90a1-099c18621ee9.

295 **"China business community are all watching":** Hughes and Warrell, "China Envoy Warns."

295 **how well Huawei's products would function:** Small, *No Limits*, 124.

295 **sign on to Keith Krach's Clean Network:** Linda Hardesty, "U.S. Secretary of State Names Non-Huawei Telcos He Considers 'Clean,'" *Fierce Wireless*, June 25, 2020, www.fiercewireless.com/operators/u-s-secretary-state-names-non-huawei-telcos-he-considers-clean.

295 **new national security law for Hong Kong:** Chris Buckley, Keith Bradsher, and Tiffany May, "New Security Law Gives China Sweeping Powers over Hong Kong," *The New York Times*, June 29, 2020, www.nytimes.com/2020/06/29/world/asia/china-hong-kong-security-law-rules.html.

295 **"one country, two systems":** "Hong Kong National Security Law: What Is It and Is It Worrying?" *BBC News*, June 28, 2022, www.bbc.com/news/world-asia-china-52765838.

296 **barred completely from Britain's 5G:** Ryan Browne, "UK Says It Will Ban China's Huawei from 5G Networks in Major U-turn," CNBC, July 14, 2020, www.cnbc.com/2020/07/14/uk-says-it-will-phase-out-huawei-from-5g-networks-in-major-u-turn.html.

296 **cost the United Kingdom some £2 billion:** George Parker et al., "UK Orders Ban of New Huawei Equipment from End of Year," *Financial Times*, July 14, 2020, www.ft.com/content/997da795-e088-467e-aa54-74f76c321a75.

296 **closed the loopholes:** Dan Strumpf, "U.S. Tightens Restrictions on Huawei's Access to Chips," *The Wall Street Journal*, August 17, 2020, www.wsj.com/articles/commerce-department-tightens-restrictions-on-huaweis-access-to-chips-11597671747; "Addition of Huawei Non-U.S. Affiliates to the Entity List, the Removal of Temporary General License, and Amendments to General Prohibition Three (Foreign-Produced Direct Product Rule)," Bureau of Industry and Security, U.S. Department of Commerce, *Federal Register* 85 (August 20, 2020): 51596–629, www.federalregister.gov/documents/2020/08/20

/2020-18213/addition-of-huawei-non-us-affiliates-to-the-entity-list-the-removal-of-temporary-general
-license-and.

296 **"source any semiconductor from anyone":** Kathrin Hille, Edward White, and Kana Inagaki, "Chip
and Phone Supply Chain Shaken as Huawei Faces Mortal Threat," *Financial Times*, August 18, 2020,
www.ft.com/content/bdd2a70f-ecd2-4aff-b6c7-c0624bfdeebb.

296 **slew of Asian chipmaking powerhouses announced:** "Taiwan's MediaTek Pushes for Permission to Supply
Huawei after U.S. Curbs," Reuters, August 28, 2020, www.reuters.com/article/us-usa-huawei-mediatek
/taiwans-mediatek-pushes-for-permission-to-supply-huawei-after-u-s-curbs-idUSKBN25O0SG; Adi Rob-
ertson, "Samsung Reportedly Cutting off Chip Sales to Huawei," *The Verge*, September 8, 2020, www
.theverge.com/2020/9/8/21427769/samsung-huawei-trump-us-sanctions-end-trade-chip-semiconductors;
Andrew Salmon, "Samsung Turns Away from Huawei," *Asia Times*, September 9, 2020, asiatimes
.com/2020/09/samsung-turns-away-from-huawei.

296 **"will the layoffs finally land on me?":** Ryan McMorrow and Qianer Liu, "Huawei Employees Worry
about Lay-offs after Tougher US Sanctions," *Financial Times*, August 20, 2020, www.ft.com/content
/1fccedf5-bf88-45fe-9a39-2ac378571693.

297 **"Death Sentence for Huawei":** Hille, White, and Inagaki, "Chip and Phone Supply Chain Shaken."

297 **Huawei's growth ground to a halt:** Yuan Yang, "Huawei's Revenue Growth Slows as US Tightens Sanctions," *Financial Times*, October 23, 2020, www.ft.com/content/8e97a705-026b-4f7c-a2f5-408b4af98dd6.

297 **revenue plummeted by almost 30 percent:** James Kynge, "Huawei Suffers Biggest-Ever Decline in
Revenue after US Blacklisting," *Financial Times*, August 6, 2021, www.ft.com/content/dc170be7-262e
-4616-9ef9-2a49c611c26b; Kathrin Hille, Eleanor Olcott, and James Kynge, "US-China Business: The
Necessary Reinvention of Huawei," *Financial Times*, September 28, 2021, www.ft.com/content/9e98a0db
-8d0a-4f78-90d3-25bfebcf3ac9.

297 **delayed the production:** Mercedes Ruehl, Eli Meixler, and Kenji Kawase, "Huawei Delays Production
of Flagship Phone after US Sanctions," *Financial Times*, June 17, 2020, www.ft.com/content/38a50d25
-5604-4a14-bf54-d8942dec5e69; Lauly Li and Kenji Kawase, "Huawei and ZTE Slow Down China 5G
Rollout as US Curbs Start to Bite," *Financial Times*, August 23, 2020, www.ft.com/content/797e7ee3
-f8a1-4f31-bfa4-5d7c1b727172.

297 **pivot to new business lines:** Kathrin Hille, Qianer Liu, and Kiran Stacey, "Huawei Focuses on Cloud
Computing to Secure Its Survival," *Financial Times*, August 30, 2020, www.ft.com/content/209aa050
-6e9c-4ba0-b83c-ac8df0bb4f86.

CHAPTER 47: IRON CURTAIN

298 **"a conversation about China's relationship":** Matt Pottinger, "Remarks by Deputy National Security
Advisor Matt Pottinger to London-based Policy Exchange" (videoconference, Washington, D.C., October 23, 2020), National Security Council, trumpwhitehouse.archives.gov/briefings-statements/remarks
-deputy-national-security-advisor-matt-pottinger-london-based-policy-exchange; Matt Pottinger, "The
Importance of Being Candid: On China's Relationship with the Rest of the World" (videoconference,
Washington, D.C., October 23, 2020), *Policy Exchange*, policyexchange.org.uk/events/the-importance
-of-being-candid-on-chinas-relationship-with-the-rest-of-the-world.

298 **reciprocity and candor:** Pottinger, "Remarks by Deputy National Security Advisor Matt Pottinger."

299 **"speak honestly and publicly":** Pottinger, "Remarks by Deputy National Security Advisor Matt Pottinger."

299 **a deal that came together:** "United States–China Phase One Trade Agreement," Office of the United
States Trade Representative, January 15, 2020, ustr.gov/phase-one; "What's in the U.S. China Phase 1
Trade Deal," Reuters, January 15, 2020, www.reuters.com/article/idUSKBN1ZE21F.

299 **Beijing failed to honor its commitments:** Yen Nee Lee, "China Failed to Buy Agreed Amounts of U.S.
Goods under 'Phase One' Trade Deal, Data Shows," CNBC, January 22, 2021, www.cnbc.com/2021/01
/22/china-failed-to-buy-agreed-amounts-of-us-goods-in-phase-one-trade-deal-data.html; Chad P. Bown,
"Anatomy of a Flop: Why Trump's US-China Phase One Trade Deal Fell Short," Peterson Institute for
International Economics, February 8, 2021, www.piie.com/blogs/trade-and-investment-policy-watch
/anatomy-flop-why-trumps-us-china-phase-one-trade-deal-fell; Chad P. Bown, "US-China Phase One
Tracker: China's Purchases of US Goods," Peterson Institute for International Economics, July 19, 2022,
www.piie.com/research/piie-charts/us-china-phase-one-tracker-chinas-purchases-us-goods; "Trade
in Goods with China," U.S. Census Bureau, www.census.gov/foreign-trade/balance/c5700.html.

299 **sell Huawei tens of billions:** "Export Control Licensing Decisions for Huawei (November 9, 2020–
April 20, 2021)," Committee on Foreign Relations, House of Representatives, U.S. Congress, 117th
Cong., 1st sess., foreignaffairs.house.gov/wp-content/uploads/2021/10/Huawei-Licensing-Information
.pdf.

299 **the idea of banning TikTok:** Joe McDonald and Zen Soo, "Why Does US See Chinese-owned TikTok
as a Security Threat?" The Associated Press, March 24, 2023, apnews.com/article/tiktok-bytedance
-shou-zi-chew-8d8a6a9694357040d484670b7f4833be; John D. McKinnon and Stu Woo, "The Billionaire Keeping TikTok on Phones in the U.S.," *The Wall Street Journal*, September 20, 2023, www.wsj
.com/politics/policy/jeff-yass-tiktok-bytedance-ban-congress-15a41ec4.

300 **hand over intimate data:** Kelvin Chan and Haleluya Hadero, "Why TikTok's Security Risks Keep Raising Fears," The Associated Press, March 23, 2023, apnews.com/article/tiktok-ceo-shou-zi-chew-security-risk-cc36f36801d84fc0652112fa461ef140.

300 **divest its American assets:** Nicole Sperling, "Trump Officially Orders TikTok's Chinese Owner to Divest," The New York Times, August 14, 2020, www.nytimes.com/2020/08/14/business/tiktok-trump-bytedance-order.html.

300 **sale of the app to Oracle:** Erin Griffith and David McCabe, "'There's No There There': What the TikTok Deal Achieved," The New York Times, September 20, 2020, www.nytimes.com/2020/09/20/technology/tiktok-trump-victory.html.

300 **ban TikTok outright:** Donald J. Trump, "Executive Order 13942, Addressing the Threat Posed by TikTok, and Taking Additional Steps to Address the National Emergency with Respect to the Information and Communications Technology and Services Supply Chain," The White House, August 6, 2020, www.federalregister.gov/documents/2020/08/11/2020-17699/addressing-the-threat-posed-by-tiktok-and-taking-additional-steps-to-address-the-national-emergency.

300 **federal judge blocked it:** Bobby Allyn, "U.S. Judge Halts Trump's TikTok Ban, Hours Before It Was Set to Start," NPR, September 27, 2020, www.npr.org/2020/09/27/917452668/u-s-judge-halts-trumps-tiktok-ban-hours-before-it-was-set-to-start.

300 **sanctioning "informational materials":** Marland v. Trump, 498 F. Supp. 3d 624 (E.D. Pa. 2020).

300 **TikTok was thus protected:** John D. McKinnon, "TikTok Ban Faces Obscure Hurdle: The Berman Amendments," The Wall Street Journal, January 29, 2023, www.wsj.com/articles/tiktok-ban-faces-obscure-hurdle-the-berman-amendments-11674964611.

300 **China's answer to the world-class Taiwanese chip foundry:** Kathrin Hille and Robin Kwong, "Richard Chang Quits as SMIC Chief," Financial Times, November 10, 2009, www.ft.com/content/ad029ec2-cda5-11de-8162-00144feabdc0; Chris Miller, Chip War: The Fight for the World's Most Critical Technology (New York: Scribner, 2022), 180–81.

300 **$8 billion in its Shanghai debut:** Yuan Yang and Nian Liu, "SMIC Scores Mainland China's Biggest Listing in a Decade," Financial Times, July 16, 2020, www.ft.com/content/6a87d390-fdad-43c7-8ff9-c99f3b94294c.

300 **America's "technology blockade":** Edward White and Kana Inagaki, "China Starts 'Surgical' Retaliation against Foreign Companies after US-led Tech Blockade," Financial Times, April 16, 2023, www.ft.com/content/fc2038d2-3e25-4a3f-b8ca-0ceb5532a1f3.

301 **SMIC's ties to China's military:** "Blue Heron: Semiconductor Manufacturing International Corporation," SOS International, August 2020, www.jcapitalresearch.com/uploads/2/0/0/3/20032477/blue_heron_smic_footnoted.pdf.

301 **"unacceptable risk" of being diverted:** Yuan Yang, Kathrin Hille, Qianer Liu, "China's Biggest Chipmaker SMIC Hit by US Sanctions," Financial Times, September 27, 2020, www.ft.com/content/7325dcea-e327-4054-9b24-7a12a6a2cac6.

301 **$2 billion of equipment:** Ryan McMorrow and Nian Liu, "Shares in China's Top Chipmaker SMIC Fall after US Blacklisting," Financial Times, September 28, 2020, www.ft.com/content/6f513d88-1aad-4195-889e-d909411da0f4.

301 **most expensive mass-produced machine tool:** Miller, Chip War, 230.

301 **ASML had agreed to sell the machine to SMIC:** Cheng Ting-Fang and Lauly Li, "Exclusive: ASML Chip Tool Delivery to China Delayed amid US Ire," Nikkei Asia, November 6, 2019, asia.nikkei.com/Economy/Trade-war/Exclusive-ASML-chip-tool-delivery-to-China-delayed-amid-US-ire; Toby Sterling, "ASML Sees No Financial Impact from Delay to Chinese Order for EUV Machine," Reuters, January 22, 2020, www.reuters.com/article/asml-china/asml-sees-no-financial-impact-from-delay-to-chinese-order-for-euv-machine-idUKA5N29400B.

301 **added SMIC to the Entity List:** James Politi, Demetri Sevastopulo, and Hudson Lockett, "US Adds China's Largest Chipmaker to Export Blacklist," Financial Times, December 18, 2020, www.ft.com/content/7dcc105e-986b-4768-9239-9f8fa9073b53.

301 **export controls targeted DJI:** "Addition of Entities to the Entity List, Revision of Entry on the Entity List, and Removal of Entities from the Entity List," Bureau of Industry and Security, U.S. Department of Commerce, Federal Register 85 (December 22, 2020): 83416–32, www.federalregister.gov/documents/2020/12/22/2020-28031/addition-of-entities-to-the-entity-list-revision-of-entry-on-the-entity-list-and-removal-of-entities.

301 **banned from investing:** Donald J. Trump, "Executive Order Addressing the Threat from Securities Investments That Finance Communist Chinese Military Companies," The White House, November 12, 2020, trumpwhitehouse.archives.gov/presidential-actions/executive-order-addressing-threat-securities-investments-finance-communist-chinese-military-companies; Gordon Lubold and Dawn Lim, "Trump Bars Americans from Investing in Firms That Help China's Military," The Wall Street Journal, November 12, 2020, www.wsj.com/articles/trump-bars-americans-from-investing-in-firms-that-help-chinas-military-11605209431; U.S. Secretary of Defense, "Qualifying Entities Prepared in Response to Section 1237 of the National Defense Authorization Act for Fiscal Year 1999 (Public Law 105-261)," June 12, 2020, media.defense.gov/2020/Aug/28/2002486659/-1/-1/1/LINK_2_1237_TRANCHE_1_QUALIFIYING_ENTITIES.PDF.

301 **targeted China National Offshore Oil Corporation:** "Commerce Adds China National Offshore Oil Corporation to the Entity List and Skyrizon to the Military End-User List," U.S. Department of Commerce, January 14, 2021, 2017-2021.commerce.gov/news/press-releases/2021/01/commerce-adds-china-national-offshore-oil-corporation-entity-list-and.html.

302 **Pottinger resigned in protest:** Kaitlan Collins et al., "Trump's Deputy National Security Adviser Resigns as Other Top Officials Consider Quitting over Capitol Riot," CNN, January 7, 2021, www.cnn.com/2021/01/06/politics/national-security-adviser-resigns-trump-protest/index.html.

302 **plan was ultimately dropped:** Alexandra Alper and Humeyra Pamuk, "Trump Administration Shelves Planned Investment Ban on Alibaba, Tencent, Baidu: Sources," Reuters, January 13, 2021, www.reuters.com/article/us-usa-trump-china-tech/trump-administration-shelves-planned-investment-ban-on-alibaba-tencent-baidu-sources-idUSKBN29I2RW.

302 **more than 120 countries:** Iman Ghosh, "How China Overtook the U.S. as the World's Major Trading Partner," *Visual Capitalist*, January 22, 2020, www.visualcapitalist.com/china-u-s-worlds-trading-partner.

302 **"We had psyched ourselves out":** Author interview with Matt Pottinger, 2023.

302 **U.S. economy hummed along:** "US 2020 Election: The Economy under Trump in Six Charts," *BBC News*, November 3, 2020, www.bbc.com/news/world-45827430.

302 **balked at adding American companies to its Unreliable Entity List:** Lingling Wei, "Chinese Leaders Split over Releasing Blacklist of U.S. Companies," *The Wall Street Journal*, September 21, 2020, www.wsj.com/articles/chinese-leaders-split-over-releasing-blacklist-of-u-s-companies-11600708688.

302 **slapping individual sanctions:** "Foreign Ministry Spokesperson Announces Sanctions on Pompeo and Others," Ministry of Foreign Affairs of the People's Republic of China, January 20, 2021, www.fmprc.gov.cn/mfa_eng/xwfw_665399/s2510_665401/2535_665405/202101/t20210120_697094.html.

302 **"use the leverage while we've still got it":** Author interview with Matt Pottinger, 2023.

303 **company's violation of Iran sanctions:** "ZTE Corporation Pleads Guilty for Violating U.S. Sanctions by Sending U.S.-Origin Items to Iran," U.S. Department of Justice, March 22, 2017, www.justice.gov/opa/pr/zte-corporation-pleads-guilty-violating-us-sanctions-sending-us-origin-items-iran.

303 **"economic growth" was its official mission:** "About Commerce," U.S. Department of Commerce, www.commerce.gov/about.

304 **number-one trading partner in 2020:** "The People's Republic of China: China Trade & Investment Summary," Office of the United States Trade Representative, ustr.gov/countries-regions/china-mongolia-taiwan/peoples-republic-china; Ken Roberts, "China Is No. 1 Trade Partner Again Thanks to (Wait for It) U.S. Exports," *Forbes*, February 25, 2021, www.forbes.com/sites/kenroberts/2021/02/25/china-is-no-1-trade-partner-again-thanks-to-wait-for-it-us-exports.

305 **eliminated the office:** Robbie Gramer and Dan De Luce, "State Department Scraps Sanctions Office," *Foreign Policy*, October 26, 2017, foreignpolicy.com/2017/10/26/state-department-scraps-sanctions-office; In December 2020, Congress reestablished the State Department's Office of Sanctions Coordination by including it in a COVID-19 relief and omnibus spending bill that was signed into law by President Donald Trump. See "Consolidated Appropriations Act, 2021," H.R. 133, 116th Cong., 2nd sess., sec. 361, Office of Sanctions Coordination, accessed July 10, 2024, www.congress.gov/bill/116th-congress/house-bill/133/text; Daniel Fried and Edward Fishman, "The Rebirth of the State Department's Office of Sanctions Coordination: Guidelines for Success," *New Atlanticist* (blog), Atlantic Council, February 12, 2021, accessed July 10, 2024, www.atlanticcouncil.org/blogs/new-atlanticist/the-rebirth-of-the-state-departments-office-of-sanctions-coordination-guidelines-for-success.

305 **"independent of the United States":** "EU Needs Payment Systems Independent of U.S. to Keep Iran Deal Alive—Germany," Reuters, August 21, 2018, www.reuters.com/article/iran-nuclear-germany/eu-needs-payment-systems-independent-of-u-s-to-keep-iran-deal-alive-germany-idUSL8N1VC42N.

305 **"a sovereign continent, not a vassal":** Justin Scheck and Bradley Hope, "The Dollar Underpins American Power. Rivals Are Building Workarounds," *The Wall Street Journal*, May 29, 2019, www.wsj.com/articles/the-dollar-powers-american-dominance-rivals-are-building-workarounds-11559155440.

305 **Instrument in Support of Trade Exchanges:** John Irish and Riham Alkousaa, "Skirting U.S. Sanctions, Europeans Open New Trade Channel to Iran," Reuters, January 31, 2019, www.reuters.com/article/us-iran-usa-sanctions-eu/european-powers-launch-mechanism-for-trade-with-iran-idUSKCN1PP0K3; Annalisa Girardi, "INSTEX, A New Channel to Bypass U.S. Sanctions and Trade with Iran," *Forbes*, April 9, 2019, www.forbes.com/sites/annalisagirardi/2019/04/09/instex-a-new-channel-to-bypass-u-s-sanctions-and-trade-with-iran/?sh=94a4414270f7.

305 **INSTEX struggled to get off the ground:** Esfandyar Batmanghelidj, "Iran Trade Mechanism INSTEX Is Shutting Down," Bourse & Bazaar Foundation, February 3, 2023, www.bourseandbazaar.com/articles/2023/2/2/instex-shuts-down-in-a-loss-for-european-economic-sovereignty; Anna Sauerbrey, "The Failure of Europe's Feeble Muscle Flexing," *The New York Times*, February 10, 2020, www.nytimes.com/2020/02/10/opinion/europe-iran-nuclear-deal.html.

305 **concerned about the EU-China talks:** Demetri Sevastopulo et al., "Biden Team Voices Concern over EU-China Investment Deal," *Financial Times*, December 22, 2020, www.ft.com/content/2f0212ab-7e69-4de0-8870-89dd0d414306.

305 **"early consultations with our European partners":** Jake Sullivan (@jakejsullivan), "The Biden-Harris Administration Would Welcome Early Consultations," Twitter, December 21, 2020, twitter.com/jakejsullivan/status/1341180109118726144?s=20.

305 **close the deal:** Jack Ewing and Steven Lee Myers, "China and E.U. Leaders Strike Investment Deal, but Political Hurdles Await," *The New York Times*, December 30, 2020, www.nytimes.com/2020/12/30/business/china-eu-investment-deal.html.

305 **"most ambitious agreement that China has ever concluded":** European Commission, "Key Elements of the EU-China Comprehensive Agreement on Investment," December 30, 2020, ec.europa.eu/commission/presscorner/detail/en/ip_20_2542.

306 **crowning achievement for Xi:** Steven Erlanger, "Will the Sudden E.U.-China Deal Damage Relations with Biden?" *The New York Times*, January 6, 2021, www.nytimes.com/2021/01/06/world/europe/eu-china-deal-biden.html.

CHAPTER 48: THE PRACTITIONER

309 **banned following the 2008 financial crisis:** "Volcker Rule," Board of Governors of the Federal Reserve System, January 30, 2020, www.federalreserve.gov/supervisionreg/volcker-rule.htm.

310 **"*The Economist* personified":** Max Tani and Alex Thompson, "The Daleep Doctrine," *Politico*, February 24, 2022, www.politico.com/newsletters/west-wing-playbook/2022/02/24/the-daleep-doctrine-00011437.

310 **With more than $630 billion:** Valentina Pop, Sam Fleming, and James Politi, "Weaponisation of Finance: How the West Unleashed 'Shock and Awe' on Russia," *Financial Times*, April 6, 2022, www.ft.com/content/5b397d6b-bde4-4a8c-b9a4-080485d6c64a; World Bank, "GDP Growth (Annual %): Iran, Islamic Rep," 2020, data.worldbank.org/indicator/NY.GDP.MKTP.KD.ZG?end=2020&locations=IR&start=1960&view=chart.

310 **dollars, euros, pounds, and yen:** Gian Maria Milesi-Ferretti, "Russia's External Position: Does Financial Autarky Protect against Sanctions?" The Brookings Institution, March 3, 2022, www.brookings.edu/articles/russias-external-position-does-financial-autarky-protect-against-sanctions.

310 **most of Russia's foreign exchange reserves in euros:** Globally, central banks hold about 60 percent of all foreign exchange reserves in dollars and 20 percent in euros. Russia was an outlier in holding more of its reserves in euros than in dollars. See "Currency Composition of Official Foreign Exchange Reserves," International Monetary Fund; Milesi-Ferretti, "Russia's External Position."

311 **spent over $100 billion of reserves:** "Russia's Capital Outflows Reach Record $151.5 bln in 2014 as Sanctions, Oil Slump Hit," Reuters, January 16, 2015, www.reuters.com/article/russia-capital-outflows/update-1-russias-capital-outflows-reach-record-151-5-bln-in-2014-as-sanctions-oil-slump-hit-idUSL6N0UV3S320150116.

311 **"want to call Europe?":** David Brunnstrom, "EU Says It Has Solved the Kissinger Question," Reuters, November 19, 2009, www.reuters.com/article/us-eu-president-kissinger/eu-says-it-has-solved-the-kissinger-question-idUSTRE5AJ00B20091120.

CHAPTER 49: THE BEST-LAID PLANS

313 **abandoning decades of neoliberal dogma:** Jennifer Harris and Jake Sullivan, "America Needs a New Economic Philosophy. Foreign Policy Experts Can Help," *Foreign Policy*, February 7, 2020, foreignpolicy.com/2020/02/07/america-needs-a-new-economic-philosophy-foreign-policy-experts-can-help.

313 **"some humility about their use":** Author interview with Jon Finer, 2023.

313 **sanctions on more individuals and companies:** "2020 Year-End Sanctions and Export Controls Update," Gibson Dunn, February 5, 2021, www.gibsondunn.com/wp-content/uploads/2021/02/2020-year-end-sanctions-and-export-controls-update.pdf.

314 **reintroduced aggressive sanctions:** U.S. Department of State, "Maximum Pressure Campaign on the Regime in Iran," April 4, 2019, 2017-2021.state.gov/maximum-pressure-campaign-on-the-regime-in-iran.

314 **triggering a recession:** World Bank, "GDP Growth (Annual %): Iran, Islamic Rep," 2020, data.worldbank.org/indicator/NY.GDP.MKTP.KD.ZG?end=2020&locations=IR&start=1960&view=chart.

314 **restarting its nuclear program:** "Iran to Restart Some Nuclear Activity in Response to U.S. Withdrawal from Nuclear Deal," Reuters, January 6, 2019, www.reuters.com/article/us-usa-iran-actions/iran-to-restart-some-nuclear-activity-in-response-to-u-s-withdrawal-from-nuclear-deal-idUSKCN1SC1FP; "Timeline: Iran's Nuclear Program Since 2018," The Iran Primer, May 3, 2023, iranprimer.usip.org/blog/2023/may/03/timeline-iran%E2%80%99s-nuclear-program-2018.

314 **joined forces to create a financial channel:** John Irish and Riham Alkousaa, "Skirting U.S. Sanctions, Europeans Open New Trade Channel to Iran," Reuters, January 31, 2019, www.reuters.com/article/us-iran-usa-sanctions-eu/european-powers-launch-mechanism-for-trade-with-iran-idUSKCN1PP0K3."

314 **an ultraconservative hard-liner:** Vivian Yee, "Iranian Hard-Liner Ebrahim Raisi Wins Presidential

Vote," *The New York Times*, June 19, 2021, www.nytimes.com/2021/06/19/world/middleeast/iran-election -president-raisi.html.

314 **overthrow the autocratic president of Venezuela:** Agathe Demarais, *Backfire: How Sanctions Reshaped the World Against U.S. Interests* (New York: Columbia University Press, 2022), 27–34; "Venezuela: Overview of U.S. Sanctions," IF10715, Congressional Research Service, U.S. Library of Congress, November 1, 2023, crsreports.congress.gov/product/pdf/IF/IF10715.

314 **economic assistance from Russia and China:** Daniel McDowell, *Bucking the Buck: US Financial Sanctions & the International Backlash Against the Dollar* (New York: Oxford, 2023), 102; Luc Cohen and Marianna Parraga, "Special Report: How China Got Shipments of Venezuelan Oil Despite U.S. Sanctions," Reuters, June 12, 2020, www.reuters.com/article/us-venezuela-oil-deals-specialreport/special -report-how-china-got-shipments-of-venezuelan-oil-despite-u-s-sanctions-idUSKBN23J1N1.

314 **severe humanitarian crisis:** Diana Roy, "Do U.S. Sanctions on Venezuela Work?" Council on Foreign Relations, November 4, 2022, www.cfr.org/in-brief/do-us-sanctions-venezuela-work; "Venezuela's Refugee Crisis Needs a Proper Response," *Financial Times*, January 2, 2020, www.ft.com/content/af000cac -2d51-11ea-bc77-65e4aa615551.

314 **sanctioning Fatou Bensouda:** Julian Borger, "Trump Targets ICC with Sanctions after Court Opens War Crimes Investigation," *The Guardian*, June 11, 2020, www.theguardian.com/us-news/2020/jun /11/trump-icc-us-war-crimes-investigation-sanctions; "Blocking Property of Certain Persons Associated with the International Criminal Court Designations," Office of Foreign Assets Control, U.S. Department of the Treasury, September 2, 2020, ofac.treasury.gov/recent-actions/20200902; "US Sanctions on the International Criminal Court," Human Rights Watch, December 14, 2020, www.hrw.org/news /2020/12/14/us-sanctions-international-criminal-court.

314 **pushed to amend IEEPA:** Andrew Boyle and Tim Lau, "The President's Extraordinary Sanctions Powers," Brennan Center for Justice, July 20, 2021, www.brennancenter.org/our-work/research-reports /presidents-extraordinary-sanctions-powers; Andrew Boyle, "Congress Must Reform Sanctions Law to Avoid ICC Penalties from Happening Again," Just Security, April 13, 2021, justsecurity.org/75748 /congress-must-reform-sanctions-law-to-avoid-icc-penalties-from-happening-again; Elizabeth Goitein, "2022 Update: Reforming Emergency Powers," Brennan Center for Justice, February 2, 2022, brennancenter.org/our-work/analysis-opinion/2022-update-reforming-emergency-powers; Elizabeth Goitein, "The Alarming Scope of the President's Emergency Powers," *The Atlantic*, January/February 2019, theatlantic.com/magazine/archive/2019/01/presidential-emergency-powers/576418; Peter E. Harrell, "How to Reform IEEPA," Lawfare, August 28, 2019, lawfaremedia.org/article/how-reform-ieepa.

314–15 **a top-to-bottom review:** Saleha Mohsin and Nick Wadhams, "Treasury Sanctions Programs Face Broad Review from Biden Team," *Bloomberg*, December 8, 2020, www.bloomberg.com/news/articles /2020-12-09/treasury-sanctions-programs-face-broad-review-from-biden-team; "Readout: Treasury Deputy Secretary Wally Adeyemo Meeting with Thought Leaders on U.S. Economic and Financial Sanctions," U.S. Department of the Treasury, April 1, 2021, home.treasury.gov/news/press-releases /jy0098.

315 **against the "overuse of sanctions":** Jacob J. Lew, "The Evolution of Sanctions and Lessons for the Future" (speech, Washington, D.C., March 30, 2016), Carnegie Endowment for International Peace, https:// carnegieendowment.org/2016/03/30/u.s.-treasury-secretary-jacob-j.-lew-on-evolution-of-sanctions-and -lessons-for-future/ivpl.

315 **"pay in blood and money":** Glenn Thrush and Kenneth P. Vogel, "What Joe Biden Actually Did in Ukraine," *The New York Times*, November 10, 2019, www.nytimes.com/2019/11/10/us/politics/joe -biden-ukraine.html

315 **long list of further misdeeds:** Michael Schwirtz and Melissa Eddy, "Aleksei Nalvany Was Poisoned with Novichok, Germany Says," *The New York Times*, September 2, 2020, www.nytimes.com/2020/09 /02/world/europe/navalny-poison-novichok.html; Ellen Nakashima and Craig Timberg, "Russian Government Hackers Are Behind a Broad Espionage Campaign That Has Compromised U.S. Agencies, Including Treasury and Commerce," *The Washington Post*, December 14, 2020, www.washingtonpost .com/national-security/russian-government-spies-are-behind-a-broad-hacking-campaign-that-has -breached-us-agencies-and-a-top-cyber-firm/2020/12/13/d5a53b88-3d7d-11eb-9453-fc36ba051781 _story.html; Charlie Savage, Eric Schmitt, and Michael Schwirtz, "Russia Secretly Offered Afghan Militants Bounties to Kill U.S. Troops, Intelligence Says," *The New York Times*, June 26, 2020, www .nytimes.com/2020/06/26/us/politics/russia-afghanistan-bounties.html.

315 **Trump as "Putin's puppy":** Joseph R. Biden, "Presidential Debate at Case Western Reserve University and Cleveland Clinic" (speech, Cleveland, OH, September 29, 2020), The Commission on Presidential Debates, www.debates.org/voter-education/debate-transcripts/september-29-2020-debate-transcript.

315 **"stable and predictable relationship":** The White House, "Readout of President Joseph R. Biden, Jr. Call with President Vladimir Putin of Russia," April 13, 2021, www.whitehouse.gov/briefing-room /statements-releases/2021/04/13/readout-of-president-joseph-r-biden-jr-call-with-president-vladimir -putin-of-russia-4-13.

315 **new sanctions on Russia:** U.S. Department of the Treasury, "Treasury Sanctions Russia with Sweeping New Sanctions Authority," April 15, 2021, home.treasury.gov/news/press-releases/jy0127.

315 **"didn't want to be so heavy-hitting early on":** Author interview with Peter Harrell, 2023.
316 **some 100,000 troops:** "Official: Russian Military Build-up Near Ukraine Numbers More Than 100,000 troops, EU Says," Reuters, April 19, 2021, www.reuters.com/world/europe/russian-military-build-up-near-ukraine-numbers-more-than-150000-troops-eus-2021-04-19.
316 **Putin's largest military buildup:** Andrew E. Kramer, "In Russia, a Military Buildup That Can't Be Missed," *The New York Times*, April 16, 2021, www.nytimes.com/2021/04/16/world/europe/russia-ukraine-troops.html.
316 **"clearly considering military action":** Erin Banco et al., "'Something Was Badly Wrong': When Washington Realized Russia Was Actually Invading Ukraine," *Politico*, February 24, 2023, www.politico.com/news/magazine/2023/02/24/russia-ukraine-war-oral-history-00083757.
316 **offered to meet him face-to-face:** The White House, "President Joseph R. Biden, Jr. Call with President Vladimir Putin."
316 **"cycle of escalation and conflict with Russia":** Alexander Smith et al., "Biden Calls for De-escalation with Russia Following Sanctions, Proposes Meeting with Putin," *NBC News*, April 15, 2021, www.nbcnews.com/news/world/u-s-sanction-russia-alleged-election-interference-solarwinds-hack-n1264142.
316 **Russian troops pulled back:** Zahra Ullah, Anna Chernova, and Eliza Mackintosh, "Russia Pulls Back Troops after Massive Buildup Near Ukraine Border," CNN, April 23, 2021, www.cnn.com/2021/04/22/europe/russia-military-ukraine-border-exercises-intl/index.html.
316 **Biden's promised summit with Putin:** Matthew Lee, Jonathan Lemire, and Jamey Keaten, "White House, Kremlin Aim for Biden-Putin Summit in Geneva," The Associated Press, May 24, 2021, apnews.com/article/geneva-europe-summits-government-and-politics-93dbab09cac22047a7b2f9fb61682c94.

CHAPTER 50: "AMERICA IS BACK"

317 **cyberattacks by Russian hackers:** David E. Sanger, Clifford Krauss, Nicole Perlroth, "Cyberattack Forces a Shutdown of a Top U.S. Pipeline," *The New York Times*, May 8, 2021, www.nytimes.com/2021/05/08/us/politics/cyberattack-colonial-pipeline.html; David E. Sanger, Michael D. Shear, and Anton Troianovski, "Biden and Putin Express Desire for Better Relations at Summit Shaped by Disputes," *The New York Times*, June 16, 2021, www.nytimes.com/2021/06/16/world/europe/biden-putin-geneva-meeting.html.
317 **"last thing he wants now is a Cold War":** Joseph R. Biden, "Remarks by President Biden in Press Conference (speech, Geneva, Switzerland, June 16, 2021), The White House, www.whitehouse.gov/briefing-room/speeches-remarks/2021/06/16/remarks-by-president-biden-in-press-conference-4.
317 **"'There is no happiness in life'":** Sanger, Shear, and Troianovski, "Biden and Putin."
317 **double the capacity of the existing pipeline:** David McHugh, "Explainer: What's Russia's Nord Stream 2 Pipeline to Europe," The Associated Press, February 8, 2022, apnews.com/article/russia-ukraine-nord-stream-2-oil-pipeline-779970ee17f6fa9d0fa2996e45cbeab9.
317 **without first crossing Eastern Europe:** Mark Temnycky, "The Security Implications of Nord Stream 2 for Ukraine, Poland, and Germany," The Wilson Center, March 17, 2021, www.wilsoncenter.org/blog-post/security-implications-nord-stream-2-ukraine-poland-and-germany.
318 **both Trump and Biden had threatened:** "Russia's Nord Stream 2 Natural Gas Pipeline to Germany Halted," IF11138, Congressional Research Service, U.S. Library of Congress, March 10, 2022, crsreports.congress.gov/product/pdf/IF/IF11138.
318 **Berlin committed to back tougher penalties:** "Joint Statement of the US and Germany on Support for Ukraine, European Energy Security, and Our Climate Goals," Federal Foreign Office, Government of Germany, July 21, 2021, www.auswaertiges-amt.de/en/newsroom/news/joint-statement-usa-and-germany/2472084; Simon Lewis and Andrea Shalal, "U.S., Germany Strike Nord Stream 2 Pipeline Deal to Push Back on Russian 'Aggression,'" Reuters, July 21, 2021, www.reuters.com/business/energy/us-germany-deal-nord-stream-2-pipeline-draws-ire-lawmakers-both-countries-2021-07-21.
318 **"America is back":** Joseph R. Biden, "Remarks by President Biden on America's Place in the World" (speech, Washington, D.C., February 4, 2021), The White House, www.whitehouse.gov/briefing-room/speeches-remarks/2021/02/04/remarks-by-president-biden-on-americas-place-in-the-world.
318 **"inalienable part of Russia":** Vladimir Putin, "On the Historical Unity of Russians and Ukrainians" (speech, Moscow, Russia, July 12, 2021), The Kremlin, http://en.kremlin.ru/events/president/news/66181.
318 **"Russia was robbed":** Peter Dickinson, "Putin's New Ukraine Essay Reveals Imperial Ambitions," The Atlantic Council, July 15, 2021, www.atlanticcouncil.org/blogs/ukrainealert/putins-new-ukraine-essay-reflects-imperial-ambitions.
318 **"final ultimatum to Ukraine":** Steve Rosenberg (@BBCSteveR), "This week Vladimir Putin published a controversial article on Russia & Ukraine," Twitter, July 14, 2021, twitter.com/BBCSteveR/status/1415213223779913733; "Putin issued the final ultimatum to Ukraine: 'Kyiv Simply Does Not Need Donbas'" *Moscow Komsomol*, July 12, 2021, www.mk.ru/politics/2021/07/12/putin-vykatil-ukraine-posledniy-ultimatum-kievu-donbass-prosto-ne-nuzhen.html.
318 **raised antennae in the White House:** Banco et al., "'Something Was Badly Wrong.'"

318 **"end America's longest war"**: Joseph R. Biden, "Remarks by President Biden on the Way Forward in Afghanistan" (speech, Washington, D.C., April 14, 2021), The White House, www.whitehouse.gov /briefing-room/speeches-remarks/2021/04/14/remarks-by-president-biden-on-the-way-forward -in-afghanistan; Ruby Mellen, "The Shocking Speed of the Taliban's Advance: A Visual Timeline," The Washington Post, August 16, 2021, www.washingtonpost.com/world/2021/08/16/taliban-timeline.

318 **killing more than 180 people**: Shawn Boburg et al., "The 13 U.S. Service Members Killed in the Kabul Airport Attack," The Washington Post, August 29, 2021, www.washingtonpost.com/national-security /2021/08/27/us-service-members-killed-kabul-airport-names.

318 **calls to resign**: Julian Borger, "Jake Sullivan: The Biden Insider at the Center of the Afghanistan Crisis," The Guardian, September 26, 2021, www.theguardian.com/us-news/2021/sep/26/jake-sullivan-national -security-adviser-profile-afghanistan.

319 **"once-in-a-generation intellect"**: Mark Leibovich, "Jake Sullivan, Biden's Adviser, a Figure of Fascination and Schadenfreude," The New York Times, November 30, 2021, www.nytimes.com/2021/11/30 /us/politics/jake-sullivan-biden.html.

319 *Zapad* **exercise was much bigger**: Banco et al., "'Something Was Badly Wrong.'"

CHAPTER 51: STANDING ATHWART HISTORY, YELLING STOP

320 **logistical resources and ammunition stocks**: Erin Banco et al., "'Something Was Badly Wrong': When Washington Realized Russia Was Actually Invading Ukraine," Politico, February 24, 2023, www.politico.com/news/magazine/2023/02/24/russia-ukraine-war-oral-history-00083757.

320 **piece together Putin's intentions**: Banco et al., "'Something Was Badly Wrong.'"

320 **total victory over a country**: Shane Harris et al., "Road to War: U.S. Struggled to Convince Allies, and Zelensky, of Risk of Invasion," The Washington Post, August 16, 2023, www.washingtonpost.com/national -security/interactive/2022/ukraine-road-to-war.

320 **"most horrific combat operations"**: Banco et al., "'Something Was Badly Wrong.'"

320 **intelligence agencies failed to connect the dots**: Uri Friedman, "The Ten Biggest American Intelligence Failures," Foreign Policy, January 3, 2012, foreignpolicy.com/2012/01/03/the-ten-biggest-american -intelligence-failures.

321 **Taliban were much further from taking Kabul**: Jacqueline Alemany, "Power Up: Inside Biden's 72 Hours at Camp David During the Taliban Takeover," The Washington Post, August 17, 2021, www .washingtonpost.com/politics/2021/08/17/power-up-inside-bidens-72-hours-camp-david-during -taliban-takeover; Ruby Mellen, "The Shocking Speed of the Taliban's Advance." The Washington Post, August 16, 2021, www.washingtonpost.com/world/2021/08/16/taliban-timeline.

321 **Putin expected the costs of war**: Harris et al., "Road to War."

321 **pain would be short-lived**: Harris et al., "Road to War."

321 **multiyear modernization program**: Anton Troianovski, Michael Schwirtz, and Andrew E. Kramer, "Russia's Military, Once Creaky, Is Modern and Lethal," The New York Times, January 27, 2022, www .nytimes.com/2022/01/27/world/europe/russia-military-putin-ukraine.html.

321 **"comparative military advantage over Russia"**: Author interview with Jon Finer, 2023.

321 **European reliance on Russian energy**: In 2014, Russia accounted for 39 percent of EU natural gas imports. By 2021, that number eclipsed 50 percent. See "European Energy Security Strategy," European Commission, May 28, 2014, eur-lex.europa.eu/legal-content/EN/TXT/PDF/?uri=CELEX:52014D C0330&from=EN and "Infographic: Where Does the EU's Gas Come From?" European Council, www.consilium.europa.eu/en/infographics/eu-gas-supply.

322 **EU's fifth-largest trading partner**: "Trade: Russia," European Commission, policy.trade.ec.europa .eu/eu-trade-relationships-country-and-region/countries-and-regions/russia_en; "Russia's Trade and Investment Role in the Global Economy," IF12066, Congressional Research Service, U.S. Library of Congress, January 17, 2023, crsreports.congress.gov/product/pdf/IF/IF12066.

CHAPTER 52: PANIC AT THE PUMP

324 **unexpected change of protocol**: David E. Sanger with Mary K. Brooks, New Cold Wars: China's Rise, Russia's Invasion, and America's Struggle to Defend the West (New York: Crown, 2024), 5.

325 **highest point in seven years**: Stanley Reed, "Oil Producers Aren't Keeping Up with Demand, Causing Prices to Stay High," The New York Times, January 14, 2022, www.nytimes.com/2022/01/14/business /energy-environment/oil-prices-opec.html.

325 **levels unseen in four decades**: Gwynn Guilford, "U.S. Inflation Hit a 39-Year High in November," The Wall Street Journal, December 10, 2021, www.wsj.com/articles/us-inflation-consumer-price-index -november-2021-11639088867.

325 **checked the average national gasoline**: Jeff Stein, "Inside the Biden Team's Fixation on Gas Prices," The Washington Post, November 2, 2022, www.washingtonpost.com/us-policy/2022/11/02/biden-klain -gas-prices.

325 **Russia's economy lacked diversification**: "Country & Product Complexity Rankings," Harvard Kennedy School Growth Lab, atlas.cid.harvard.edu/rankings.

325 **dependent on sales of fossil fuels:** "Energy Fact Sheet: Why Does Russian Oil and Gas Matter?" International Energy Agency, March 21, 2022, www.iea.org/articles/energy-fact-sheet-why-does-russian-oil-and-gas-matter.

325 **The U.S.-Saudi relationship:** Iain Marlow, "How US-Saudi Relations Are Strained by Oil and Distrust," *The Washington Post*, April 3, 2023, www.washingtonpost.com/business/energy/2023/04/03/what-opec-oil-cuts-mean-for-us-saudi-arabia-relations/b8095820-d24f-11ed-ac8b-cd7da05168e9_story.html.

326 **Most European governments still doubted:** When Avril Haines, the U.S. director of national intelligence, briefed all NATO members in November 2021 on the latest U.S. intelligence, she was met with skepticism from representatives of both Germany and France, who saw an invasion as irrational and believed Putin was engaging in coercive diplomacy. See Shane Harris et al., "Road to War: U.S. Struggled to Convince Allies, And Zelensky, of Risk of Invasion," *The Washington Post*, August 16, 2023, www.washingtonpost.com/national-security/interactive/2022/ukraine-road-to-war.

326 **continued diplomacy with Moscow:** Harris et al., "Road to War."

326 **offering a path out of the standoff:** The White House, "Readout of President Biden's Video Call with President Vladimir Putin of Russia," December 7, 2021, www.whitehouse.gov/briefing-room/statements-releases/2021/12/07/readout-of-president-bidens-video-call-with-president-vladimir-putin-of-russia; Paul Sonne, Ashley Parker, and Isabelle Khurshudyan, "Biden Threatens Putin with Economic Sanctions If He Further Invades Ukraine," *The Washington Post*, December 7, 2021, www.washingtonpost.com/politics/biden-putin-to-discuss-ukraine-in-video-call-amid-growing-tensions/2021/12/06/e089e36a-5707-11ec-a219-9b4ae96da3b7_story.html.

326 **Olaf Scholz succeeded Angela Merkel:** "Scholz Succeeds Merkel as Chancellor," *The New York Times*, December 8, 2021, www.nytimes.com/live/2021/12/08/world/germany-scholz-merkel.

326 **all twenty-seven EU leaders:** On January 31, 2020, the United Kingdom formally exited the EU, decreasing the membership total from twenty-eight to twenty-seven. See "Timeline—EU-UK Withdrawal Agreement," Council of the European Union, accessed July 14, 2024, consilium.europa.eu/en/policies/eu-relations-with-the-united-kingdom/the-eu-uk-withdrawal-agreement/timeline-eu-uk-withdrawal-agreement.

326 **"massive consequences and severe cost":** "European Council Meeting (16 December 2021)—Conclusions," General Secretariat of the Council, European Council, December 16, 2021, www.consilium.europa.eu/media/53575/20211216-euco-conclusions-en.pdf.

CHAPTER 53: "AN INVASION IS AN INVASION"

327 **type of office:** Michael Sauga, "How Well Are Sanctions Against Russia Working?" *Spiegel International*, July 1, 2022, www.spiegel.de/international/europe/how-well-are-european-sanctions-against-russia-working-a-2c83502d-e64f-43a7-98c8-a8076e5746fc.

327 **Ursula von der Leyen, the Commission's president:** Mark Landler, "Quoth the Raven: I Bake Cookies, Too," *The New York Times*, April 23, 2006, www.nytimes.com/2006/04/23/weekinreview/quoth-the-raven-i-bake-cookies-too.html; Nicki Peter Petrikowski, "Ursula von der Leyen," *Encyclopedia Britannica*, December 21, 2023, www.britannica.com/biography/Ursula-von-der-Leyen; "Ursula von der Leyen: Merkel Loyalist, Mother of Seven," *France24*, July 2, 2019, www.france24.com/en/20190702-ursula-von-der-leyen-merkel-loyalist-mother-seven.

327 **Merkel's heir apparent:** David Charter, "Merkel Anoints Popular Rival as Heir Apparent," *The Times*, December 16, 2013, www.thetimes.co.uk/article/merkel-anoints-popular-rival-as-heir-apparent-8ff09z6c6np.

327 **elected president of the European Commission:** "Parliament Elects Ursula von der Leyen as First Female Commission President," European Parliament, July 16, 2019, www.europarl.europa.eu/news/en/press-room/20190711IPR56824/parliament-elects-ursula-von-der-leyen-as-first-female-commission-president.

327 **roughly 250-square-foot quarters:** David M. Herszenhorn and Maïa de la Baume, "Von der Leyen's Plan to Sleep on the Job," *Politico*, October 3, 2019, www.politico.eu/article/european-commission-president-elect-von-der-leyens-plan-to-sleep-on-the-job; Jennifer Rankin, "New EU Commission President to Live, Work and Sleep at the Office," *The Guardian*, October 3, 2019, www.theguardian.com/world/2019/oct/03/eu-new-commission-president-will-live-work-and-sleep-at-the-office.

328 **nothing down on paper:** Matina Stevis-Gridneff, hosted by Michael Barbaro, "How Europe Came Around on Sanctions," *The Daily* (podcast), The New York Times, March 2, 2022, www.nytimes.com/2022/03/02/podcasts/the-daily/russia-ukraine-invasion-eu-sanctions.html?showTranscript.

328 **sway the discussion in a more hawkish direction:** Stevis-Gridneff, "How Europe Came Around on Sanctions"; Sauga, "How Well Are Sanctions Against Russia Working?"

329 **series of elaborate tabletop exercises:** Ellen Nakashima and Ashley Parker, "Inside the White House Preparations for a Russian Invasion," *The Washington Post*, February 14, 2022, www.washingtonpost.com/national-security/2022/02/14/white-house-prepares-russian-invasion.

330 **"An invasion is an invasion," period:** David E. Sanger, "Biden Predicts Putin Will Order Ukraine Invasion, but 'Will Regret Having Done It,'" *The New York Times*, January 19, 2022, www.nytimes.com/2022/01/19/us/politics/biden-putin-russia-ukraine.html.

330 **blood supplies and equipment:** Phil Stewart, "Exclusive: Russia Moves Blood Supplies Near Ukraine, Adding to U.S. Concern, Officials say," Reuters, January 29, 2022, www.reuters.com/world/europe

/exclusive-russia-moves-blood-supplies-near-ukraine-adding-us-concern-officials-2022-01-28; Erin Banco et al., "'Something Was Badly Wrong': When Washington Realized Russia Was Actually Invading Ukraine," *Politico*, February 24, 2023, www.politico.com/news/magazine/2023/02/24/russia-ukraine -war-oral-history-00083757.

330 **a deal with Russian deputy foreign minister:** Isabelle Khurshudyan, Missy Ryan, and Paul Sonne, "Russia-U.S. Talks Hit Impasse over NATO Expansion as Moscow Denies Plans to Invade Ukraine," *The Washington Post*, January 10, 2022, www.washingtonpost.com/world/2022/01/10/us-russia-delegations -meet-geneva.

330 **permanent end to NATO:** These demands were put forward by Russia in two draft treaties on December 17, 2021. See Steven Pifer, "Russia's Draft Agreements with NATO and the United States: Intended for Rejection?" The Brookings Institution, December 21, 2021, www.brookings.edu/articles/russias-draft -agreements-with-nato-and-the-united-states-intended-for-rejection.

330 **going through the motions:** Harris et al., "Road to War."

330 **Some members of Congress:** Scott Wong and Julie Tsirkin, "Congress Runs Out of Time on Preemptive Russia Sanctions," *NBC News*, February 14, 2022, www.nbcnews.com/politics/congress/congress -runs-time-pre-emptive-russia-sanctions-rcna16229; Andrew Desiderio, "Why Congress' Sanctions Push Cooled Even as Russia's Aggression Didn't," *Politico*, February 18, 2022, www.politico.com/news /2022/02/18/congress-sanctions-russias-aggression-00010051.

330 **"The purpose of the sanctions":** Antony J. Blinken, interview by Dana Bash, *State of the Union*, CNN, February 20, 2022, www.state.gov/secretary-antony-j-blinken-with-state-of-the-union-on-cnn-with -dana-bash.

330 **including sending weapons to Ukraine:** Annie Karni, "Biden Affirms Support Against 'Russian Aggression' in Meeting with Ukraine's Leader," *The New York Times*, September 1, 2021, www.nytimes .com/2021/09/01/us/politics/biden-ukraine-zelensky-russia.html; Serhii Plokhy, *The Russo-Ukrainian War: The Return of History* (New York: W.W. Norton & Company, 2023), 248–49.

330 **"face swift and severe consequences":** Joseph R. Biden, "Statement from President Biden on United Nations Security Council Meeting" (speech, Washington, D.C., January 31, 2022), www.whitehouse.gov /briefing-room/statements-releases/2022/01/31/statement-from-president-biden-on-united-nations -security-council-meeting.

331 **"Friendship between the two States has no limits":** Tony Munroe, Andrew Osborn, and Humeyra Pamuk, "China, Russia Partner Up Against West at Olympics Summit," Reuters, February 4, 2022, www.reuters.com/world/europe/russia-china-tell-nato-stop-expansion-moscow-backs-beijing-taiwan -2022-02-04.

331 **delay any invasion until after the Olympics:** Edward Wong and Julian E. Barnes, "China Asked Russia to Delay Ukraine War Until After Olympics, U.S. Officials Say," *The New York Times*, March 2, 2022, www.nytimes.com/2022/03/02/us/politics/russia-ukraine-china.html.

332 **little interest in foreign policy:** Ulrich Speck, "Scholz's Views," German Marshall Fund, October 28, 2021, www.gmfus.org/news/scholzs-views.

332 **publicly critical of sanctions on Russia:** Hans von der Burchard, "'We Failed' on Russia: Top German Social Democrat Offers Mea Culpa," *Politico*, October 19, 2022, www.politico.eu/article/we-failed-germany -depended-on-russia-social-democrat-said; "Germany Warns on Russia Sanctions," *Deutsche Welle*, April 1, 2015, www.dw.com/en/germany-warns-against-tougher-sanctions-on-russia/a-18169784.

332 **Scholz's own views remained murky:** Katrin Bennhold, "Germany's 'Invisible' Chancellor Heads to Washington amid Fierce Criticism," *The New York Times*, February 6, 2022, www.nytimes.com/2022 /02/06/world/europe/olaf-scholz-biden-ukraine-russia.html.

332 **"Berlin, we have a problem":** Matthias Gebauer et al., "The Price of Berlin's Hesitancy on Ukraine," *Spiegel International*, January 28, 2022, www.spiegel.de/international/germany/an-unreliable-partner -the-price-of-berlin-s-hesitancy-on-ukraine-a-3bf5a21e-c37e-4ab0-af8d-c75bf6d2c99b.

332 **support for "severe sanctions":** Joseph R. Biden and Olaf Scholz, "Remarks by President Biden and Chancellor Scholz of the Federal Republic of Germany at Press Conference" (speech, Washington, D.C., February 7, 2022), The White House, www.whitehouse.gov/briefing-room/statements-releases/2022/02 /07/remarks-by-president-biden-and-chancellor-scholz-of-the-federal-republic-of-germany-at-press -conference.

333 **"there will no longer be a Nord Stream 2":** Biden and Scholz, "Remarks by President Biden and Chancellor Scholz."

333 **60 percent of household deposits:** Bofit Viikkokatsaus, "State Banks Dominate Russian Banking Sector," The Bank of Finland Institute for Emerging Economies, January 4, 2019, www.bofit.fi/en/monitoring /weekly/2019/vw201901_2.

333 **payments for Russian energy sales:** Dan De Luce, "Too Big to Sanction? A Large Russian Bank Still Operates Freely Because It Helps Europe Get Russian Gas," *NBC News*, June 18, 2022, www.nbcnews .com/news/world/big-sanction-big-russian-bank-still-operates-freely-global-economy-hel-rcna 34123.

333 **heavily reliant on foreign chips:** Alena Popova, "How to Exploit Russia's Addiction to Western Technology," *Foreign Affairs*, November 3, 2023, www.foreignaffairs.com/china/how-exploit-russias-addiction -western-technology.

333 **"isolated from global financial markets":** Jen Psaki, Anne Neuberger, Daleep Singh, "Press Briefing by Press Secretary Jen Psaki, Deputy National Security Advisor for Cyber and Emerging Technology Anne Neuberger, and Deputy National Security Advisor for International Economics and Deputy NEC Director Daleep Singh" (press conference, Washington, D.C., February 18, 2022), The American Presidency Project, www.presidency.ucsb.edu/documents/press-briefing-press-secretary-jen-psaki-deputy -national-security-advisor-for-cyber-and.

334 **emergency meeting of the National Security Council:** Christina Wilkie, "Biden Abruptly Cancels Delaware Trip after Top Level Meeting on Ukraine Crisis," CNBC, February 20, 2022, www.cnbc.com /2022/02/20/biden-abruptly-cancels-delaware-trip-after-top-level-calls-on-ukraine.html.

334 **bar Sberbank and VTB from banking services:** The plan as of February 20 was to ban the large Russian banks from correspondent and payable-through accounts in the United States. See Alexandra Alper and Karen Freifeld, "Exclusive: U.S. Plans to Cut Ties with Targeted Russian Banks if Ukraine Is Invaded: Sources," Reuters, February 21, 2022, www.reuters.com/world/exclusive-us-plans-cut-ties -with-targeted-russian-banks-if-ukraine-is-invaded-2022-02-21.

CHAPTER 54: THE SCHOLZ JOLT

335 **"Speak directly!" he barked:** Shaun Walker, "Putin's Absurd, Angry Spectacle Will Be a Turning Point in His Long Reign," The Guardian, February 21, 2022, www.theguardian.com/world/2022/feb /21/putin-angry-spectacle-amounts-to-declaration-war-ukraine.

335 **"keep the peace" in the Donbas:** Andrew Osborn and Dmitry Antonov, "Putin Orders Troops to Ukraine after Recognizing Breakaway Regions," Reuters, February 21, 2022, www.reuters.com/markets /europe/kremlin-says-no-concrete-plans-summit-with-biden-over-ukraine-2022-02-21.

336 **Putin's only real advisors:** Max Seddon, Christopher Miller, and Felicia Schwartz, "How Putin Blundered into Ukraine—Then Doubled Down," Financial Times, February 23, 2023, www.ft.com/content/80002564 -33e8-48fb-b734-44810afb7a49.

336 **Russian armored vehicles were plowing through:** Andrew Roth and Julian Borger, "Putin Orders Troops into Eastern Ukraine on 'Peacekeeping Duties,'" The Guardian, February 21, 2022, www.theguardian .com/world/2022/feb/21/ukraine-putin-decide-recognition-breakaway-states-today.

336 **trade embargo on Donetsk and Luhansk:** Joseph R. Biden, "Executive Order 14065 of February 21, 2022, Blocking Property of Certain Persons and Prohibiting Certain Transactions with Respect to Continued Russian Efforts to Undermine the Sovereignty and Territorial Integrity of Ukraine," Code of Federal Regulations, titles 3 and 50 (2022), www.federalregister.gov/documents/2022/02/23/2022 -04020/blocking-property-of-certain-persons-and-prohibiting-certain-transactions-with-respect -to-continued.

336 **"that is what is underway":** Quint Forgey, "White House Official: 'This Is the Beginning of an Invasion,'" Politico, February 22, 2022, www.politico.com/news/2022/02/22/white-house-beginning-invasion -russia-ukraine-00010589.

336 **rescinded the German government's certification:** Melissa Eddy, "Germany Puts a Stop to Nord Stream 2, a Key Russian Natural Gas Pipeline," The New York Times, February 22, 2022, www.nytimes .com/2022/02/22/business/nord-stream-pipeline-germany-russia.html.

337 **EU agreed to match the U.S. sanctions:** "EU Adopts Package of Sanctions in Response to Russian Recognition of the Non-government Controlled Areas of the Donetsk and Luhansk Oblasts of Ukraine and Sending of Troops into the Region," European Council, February 23, 2022, www.consilium.europa .eu/en/press/press-releases/2022/02/23/russian-recognition-of-the-non-government-controlled-areas -of-the-donetsk-and-luhansk-oblasts-of-ukraine-as-independent-entities-eu-adopts-package-of -sanctions.

337 **Japan and the rest of the G7:** "Sanction Measures following Russia's Recognition of the 'Independence' of the 'Donetsk People's Republic' and the 'Luhansk People's Republic' and the Ratification of Treaties with the Two 'Republics' (Statement by Foreign Minister Hayashi Yoshimasa)," Ministry of Foreign Affairs of Japan, February 24, 2022, www.mofa.go.jp/press/release/press4e_003085.html.

337 **sanctions would "really bite":** George Parker, Stephen Morris, and Laura Hughes, "Boris Johnson Tells City of London to Prepare for Tough New Sanctions on Russia," Financial Times, February 23, 2022, www.ft.com/content/267b7b4b-7992-4262-a0d7-d7894d8300ae.

CHAPTER 55: BANKS VS. TANKS

338 **"demilitarization and de-Nazification of Ukraine":** Vladimir Putin, "Declaration of War on Ukraine" (speech, Moscow, February 24, 2022), The Spectator, www.spectator.co.uk/article/full-text-putin-s -declaration-of-war-on-ukraine; Jake Epstein, "Putin Announced Attacks Against Ukraine on Thursday in the Same Suit he Wore for his Monday Speech, Prompting Speculation That His War Declaration was Pretaped," Business Insider, February 24, 2022, www.businessinsider.com/putins-suit-war-declaration -ukraine-possibly-pre-taped-2022-2.

338 **missiles rained down:** Alexander Ward, Nahal Toosi, and Paul McLeary, "Russia Attacks Ukraine," Politico, February 23, 2022, www.politico.com/news/2022/02/23/russia-invasion-ukraine-00011238.

338 **pre-recorded the war speech:** Philippe Naughton, "Putin's Declaration of War on Ukraine Was Filmed Three Days Ago, Says Russian Newspaper," *The Daily Beast*, February 24, 2022, www.thedailybeast .com/putins-declaration-of-war-on-ukraine-was-filmed-three-days-ago-says-russian-newspaper -novaya-gazeta.

339 **140 miles away from the Belarusian border:** Evan Gershkovich, "Russia's Massive Military Drills on Ukraine Border Stir Invasion Fears," *The Wall Street Journal*, February 10, 2022, www.wsj.com/articles /massive-russian-military-drills-on-ukraine-border-ratchet-up-threat-11644496231.

339 **"decapitate" Ukraine's government:** Phil Stewart and Idrees Ali, "Russia Plans to 'Decapitate' Ukraine Government—U.S. Defense Official," Reuters, February 24, 2022, www.reuters.com/world/us-believes -russia-planning-decapitate-ukraines-government-2022-02-24.

339 **Russian soldiers packed parade uniforms:** Zach Beauchamp, "Why the First Few Days of War in Ukraine Went Badly for Russia," *Vox*, February 28, 2022, www.vox.com/22954833/russia-ukraine-invasion -strategy-putin-kyiv; Serhii Plokhy, *The Russo-Ukrainian War: The Return of History* (New York: W.W. Norton & Company, 2023), 153; Sinéad Baker, "Ukraine Said Russian Troops Brought Parade Uniforms to Kyiv, Expecting a Quick Triumph That Never Came," *Business Insider*, April 7, 2022, www .businessinsider.com/ukraine-said-found-russian-parade-uniforms-left-behind-in-kyiv-2022-4.

339 **VTB held 20 percent of all assets:** "U.S. Treasury Announces Unprecedented & Expansive Sanctions Against Russia, Imposing Swift and Severe Economic Costs," U.S. Department of the Treasury, February 24, 2022, home.treasury.gov/news/press-releases/jy0608.

340 **$40 billion every single day:** "U.S. Treasury Announces Unprecedented & Expansive Sanctions," February 24, 2022.

340 **Commerce issued its FDPR on Russia:** "Commerce Implements Sweeping Restrictions on Exports to Russia in Response to Further Invasion of Ukraine," U.S. Department of Commerce, February 24, 2022, www.commerce.gov/news/press-releases/2022/02/commerce-implements-sweeping-restrictions -exports-russia-response.

340 **TSMC and other big chipmakers:** Jeanne Whalen, "Computer Chip Industry Begins Halting Deliveries to Russia in Response to U.S. Sanctions," *The Washington Post*, February 25, 2022, www.washingtonpost .com/technology/2022/02/25/ukraine-russia-chips-sanctions-tsmc.

340 **Russian financial markets:** George Steer and Tommy Stubbington, "Russian Stocks Swing Higher as Investors Weigh Sanctions Risks," *Financial Times*, February 22, 2022, www.ft.com/content/9b6d0a0c -e95f-4e3a-af96-d5adbfa57b56.

340 **lost a third of its value:** George Steer and Tommy Stubbington, "Russian Stocks Plunge and Rouble Hits Record Low after Ukraine Invasion," *Financial Times*, February 24, 2022, www.ft.com/content /b9b860f6-912d-4758-a61e-16407f76f878.

340 **killed untold numbers of civilians:** Natalia Zinets and Aleksandar Vasovic, "Missiles Rain Down around Ukraine," Reuters, February 24, 2022, www.reuters.com/world/europe/putin-orders-military -operations-ukraine-demands-kyiv-forces-surrender-2022-02-24; "On the Ground in Kyiv: Citizens Flee as Russia Bombs the City," *Politico*, February 24, 2022, www.politico.com/news/2022/02/24/citizens -flee-as-russia-bombs-ukraine-00011393.

340 **Zelensky declared martial law:** "President Signs a Decree on the Imposition of Martial Law in Ukraine, the Verkhovna Rada Approved It," February 24, 2022, Office of President of Ukraine Volodymyr Zel-enskyy, www.president.gov.ua/en/news/prezident-pidpisav-ukaz-pro-zaprovadzhennya-voyennogo-stanu -73109; Tamara Qiblawi and Caroll Alvarado, "Ukrainian Males Aged 18–60 Are Banned from Leaving the Country, Zelensky Says in New Declaration," CNN, February 24, 2022, www.cnn.com/europe /live-news/ukraine-russia-news-02-24-22-intl#h_4309a4916d57670f85519210a07fb2c9.

341 **"only goal they have is to contain":** Max Fisher, "Word by Word and Between the Lines: A Close Look at Putin's Speech," *The New York Times*, February 23, 2022, www.nytimes.com/2022/02/23/world/europe /putin-speech-russia-ukraine.html.

341 **unassuming title General License 8:** "Publication of Russian Foreign Activities Sanctions Regula-tions Web General Licenses 8, 8A, 8B, and 8C," Office of Foreign Assets Control, U.S. Department of the Treasury, *Federal Register* 87 (September 8, 2022)" 54890–92, www.federalregister.gov/documents /2022/09/08/2022-19312/publication-of-russian-harmful-foreign-activities-sanctions-regulations -web-general-licenses-8-8a-8b.

341 **"specifically designed to allow energy payments":** Joseph R. Biden, "Remarks by President Biden on Russia's Unprovoked and Unjustified Attack on Ukraine" (speech, Washington, D.C., February 24, 2022), www.whitehouse.gov/briefing-room/speeches-remarks/2022/02/24/remarks-by-president-biden-on -russias-unprovoked-and-unjustified-attack-on-ukraine.

341 **a major gap:** For example, in a blog post, the economic historian Adam Tooze delivered the following verdict on the sanctions: "Biden has clearly kept his promise. America has introduced sweeping sanc-tions against all the major banks of Russia that do everything but block the most important transac-tions that might actually impose severe costs on Russia and America's major European allies." See Adam Tooze, "Chartbook #86: About Those Sanctions: SWIFT, Correspondent Banking, and the GL 8 Energy Carve-out," Substack, February 24, 2022, adamtooze.substack.com/p/chartbook-86-about-those -sanctions?utm_source=url.

341 **$350 million for oil:** Javier Blas, "Oil, Gas and Commodities Aren't Being Weaponized—for Now," *Bloomberg*, February 23, 2022, www.bloomberg.com/opinion/articles/2022-02-23/commodities-aren-t-being-weaponized-in-confrontation-over-ukraine-for-now.

341 **oil prices topped $100 per barrel:** Stephanie Kelly, "Oil Tops $105/bbl after Russia Attacks Ukraine," Reuters, February 24, 2022, www.reuters.com/business/energy/oil-rises-us-says-russian-attack-ukraine-may-occur-soon-2022-02-24; Sam Meredith, Joanna Tan, and Abigail Ng, "Oil Surges Above $100 for the First Time Since 2014, before Paring Gains," CNBC, February 23, 2022, www.cnbc.com/2022/02/24/oil-prices-jump-as-russia-launches-attack-on-ukraine.html.

342 **"last time you see me alive":** Mark Landler, Katrin Bennhold, and Matina Stevis-Gridneff, "How the West Marshaled a Stunning Show of Unity Against Russia," *The New York Times*, March 5, 2022, www.nytimes.com/2022/03/05/world/europe/russia-ukraine-invasion-sanctions.html.

342 **dying in pursuit of European values:** Matina Stevis-Gridneff, hosted by Michael Barbaro, "How Europe Came Around on Sanctions," *The Daily* (podcast), *The New York Times*, March 2, 2022, www.nytimes.com/2022/03/02/podcasts/the-daily/russia-ukraine-invasion-eu-sanctions.html; Paul Sonne et al., "Battle for Kyiv: Ukrainian Valor, Russia Blunders Combined to Save the Capital," *The Washington Post*, August 24, 2022, www.washingtonpost.com/national-security/interactive/2022/kyiv-battle-ukraine-survival.

342 **broke down in tears:** Sonne et al., "Battle for Kyiv."

CHAPTER 56: PANDORA'S BOX

343 **signs reading BAN RUSSIA FROM SWIFT!:** Nick Wadhams, Saleha Mohsin, and Josh Wingrove, "U.S. Puts Banning Russia from SWIFT Global System Back in Play," *The Japan Times*, February 26, 2022, www.japantimes.co.jp/news/2022/02/26/world/us-russia-ukraine-swift-finance.

343 **The idea quickly took hold:** Nadine Schmidt, "German Lawmakers Call on Leader to Cut Russia from Vital SWIFT Payments System," CNN, February 25, 2022, www.cnn.com/europe/live-news/ukraine-russia-news-02-25-22/h_9136dff3348e8b6a88916ef495ed807e.

343 **more than 40 million messages each day:** "Monthly FIN Traffic Evolution," Swift, December 2022, www.swift.com/about-us/discover-swift/fin-traffic-figures; "Swift Usership," Swift, www.swift.com/join-swift/swift-usership.

343 **Russia's own SPFS:** Natasha Turak, "Russia's Central Bank Governor Touts Moscow Alternative to SWIFT Transfer System as Protection from US Sanctions," CNBC, May 23, 2018, www.cnbc.com/2018/05/23/russias-central-bank-governor-touts-moscow-alternative-to-swift-transfer-system-as-protection-from-us-sanctions.html.

344 **more than $630 billion in hard currency:** Valentina Pop, Sam Fleming, and James Politi, "Weaponisation of Finance: How the West Unleashed 'Shock and Awe' on Russia," *Financial Times*, April 6, 2022, www.ft.com/content/5b397d6b-bde4-4a8c-b9a4-080485d6c64a.

344 **consisted of dollars, euros, and other G7 currencies:** Gian Maria Milesi-Ferretti, "Russia's External Position: Does Financial Autarky Protect Against Sanctions?" The Brookings Institution, March 3, 2022, www.brookings.edu/articles/russias-external-position-does-financial-autarky-protect-against-sanctions.

344 **six times larger than Iran's:** At the start of 2012, Iran possessed roughly $100 billion in foreign exchange reserves. See Yeganeh Torbati, "Iran Central Bank under Fire as Rial Hits New Lows," Reuters, September 10, 2012, www.reuters.com/article/iran-economy-rial/iran-central-bank-under-fire-as-rial-hits-new-lows-idUSL5E8KA7LI20120910.

344 **pushed for it was Chrystia Freeland:** David Lawder and Andrea Shalal, "Canada's Freeland Strays from G20 Economic Script to Warn Russia on Ukraine—Sources," Reuters, February 18, 2022, www.reuters.com/world/canadas-freeland-strays-g20-economic-script-warn-russia-ukraine-sources-2022-02-19; Pop, Fleming, and Politi, "Weaponisation of Finance"; Justin Ling, "Behind the Push to Freeze Moscow's Foreign Case," *Politico*, February 27, 2022, www.politico.com/news/2022/02/27/canada-russia-cash-freeze-freeland-00012139.

345 **60 percent of global foreign exchange reserves:** "Currency Composition of Official Foreign Exchange Reserves," International Monetary Fund.

346 **"whatever it takes":** Mario Draghi, "Speech by Mario Draghi, President of the European Central Bank at the Global Investment Conference in London 26 July 2012" (speech, London, UK, July 26, 2012), www.ecb.europa.eu/press/key/date/2012/html/sp120726.en.html.

346 **"Big nations don't bluff":** For an example of Biden's use of this mantra, see Jeffrey Goldberg, "The Obama Doctrine," *The Atlantic*, April 2016, www.theatlantic.com/magazine/archive/2016/04/the-obama-doctrine/471525; Joseph R. Biden, "Remarks by President Biden on Russia's Unprovoked and Unjustified Attack on Ukraine," (speech, Washington, D.C., February 24, 2022), www.whitehouse.gov/briefing-room/speeches-remarks/2022/02/24/remarks-by-president-biden-on-russias-unprovoked-and-unjustified-attack-on-ukraine.

346 **"deploying its international reserves":** This was the language that was ultimately used in the G7 leaders' statement. See The White House, "Joint Statement on Further Restrictive Economic Measures,"

February 26, 2022, www.whitehouse.gov/briefing-room/statements-releases/2022/02/26/joint-statement
-on-further-restrictive-economic-measures.

346 **they would be "immobilized":** In its FAQs, OFAC noted that the prohibitions "effectively immobilize
any assets of the Central Bank of the Russian Federation" but clarified that the central bank was not
subject to blocking sanctions. The penalties had a similar effect to blocking sanctions, with the one key
difference that financial institutions initially did not have to disclose to OFAC whether they held assets
of the Central Bank of Russia. OFAC later added a reporting requirement in May 2023. See "Russia
Harmful Activities Sanctions: FAQ 1004," Office of Foreign Assets Control, March 2, 2022, ofac.treasury
.gov/faqs/1004, and "Russia Harmful Activities Sanctions: FAQ 998," Office of Foreign Assets Control,
May 19, 2023, ofac.treasury.gov/faqs/998.

347 **conference call with the boss:** Jen Psaki, "Press Briefing by Press Secretary Jen Psaki, February 25,
2022" (speech, Washington, D.C., February 25, 2022), The White House, www.whitehouse.gov/briefing
-room/press-briefings/2022/02/25/press-briefing-by-press-secretary-jen-psaki-february-25-2022.

348 **tandem with the issuers of the world's other reserve currencies:** "The U.S. Dollar as the World's
Dominant Reserve Currency," IF11707, Congressional Research Service, U.S. Library of Congress,
September 15, 2022, crsreports.congress.gov/product/pdf/IF/IF11707.

348 **loitering outside their house:** Carol D. Leonnig and Tyler Pager, "Police Investigated 'Unlawful Entry'
onto Property of White House National Security Aide," The Washington Post, March 12, 2022, www
.washingtonpost.com/politics/2022/03/12/police-investigated-unlawful-entry-onto-property-white
-house-national-security-aide.

349 **committing themselves to target Russia's central bank:** The statement also committed to remove
"selected Russian banks" from SWIFT and to create a joint task force to "ensure the effective implementation" of the sanctions. See The White House, "Joint Statement on Further Restrictive Economic
Measures."

349 **"You heard about Fortress Russia":** The White House, "Background Press Call by a Senior Administration Official on Imposing Additional Severe Costs on Russia," February 26, 2022, www.whitehouse
.gov/briefing-room/press-briefings/2022/02/27/background-press-call-by-a-senior-administration
-official-on-imposing-additional-severe-costs-on-russia.

349 **"Nobody saw that coming":** Michael Sauga, "How Well Are Sanctions Against Russia Working?" Spiegel International, July 1, 2022, www.spiegel.de/international/europe/how-well-are-european-sanctions
-against-russia-working-a-2c83502d-e64f-43a7-98c8-a8076e5746fc.

CHAPTER 57: MONETARY POLICY AT THE POINT OF A GUN

350 **100 rubles to the dollar:** Natasha Turak, "Russia Central Bank More Than Doubles Key Interest Rate
to 20% to Boost Sinking Ruble," CNBC, February 28, 2022, www.cnbc.com/2022/02/28/russia-central
-bank-hikes-interest-rates-to-20percent-from-9point5percent-to-bolster-ruble.html.

350 **immobilization of Russia's central bank reserves:** "Treasury Prohibits Transactions with Central
Bank of Russia and Imposes Sanctions on Key Sources of Russia's Wealth," U.S. Department of the
Treasury, February 28, 2022, home.treasury.gov/news/press-releases/jy0612.

350 **giant bank run:** Natasha Turak, "Long Lines at Russia's ATMs as Bank Run Begins—with More Pain
to Come," CNBC, February 28, 2022, www.cnbc.com/2022/02/28/long-lines-at-russias-atms-as-bank
-run-begins-ruble-hit-by-sanctions.html; Nastassia Astrasheuskaya and Max Seddon, "Russians Search
for Cash as West Imposes Sanctions on Banks," Financial Times, February 27, 2022, www.ft.com/content
/0bd34bcd-52d9-4cff-9f81-33069a1851a3.

350 **chasing cash trucks around the city:** "'This Is a Mess': Anxious Russians Grab Cash and Plot Emigration," Financial Times, February 28, 2022, www.ft.com/content/424d8ed3-34ce-4729-8d9c-eebf0c
7f5d4d.

351 **"unfriendly measures against our country":** Maria Tsvetkova, "Putin Puts Nuclear Deterrent on Alert;
West Squeezes Russian Economy," Reuters, February 27, 2022, www.reuters.com/world/india/war-with
-ukraine-putin-puts-nuclear-deterrence-forces-alert-2022-02-27.

351 **"emigration" spiked by a factor of five:** "'This Is a Mess,'" Financial Times.

351 **Sberbank's subsidiaries in Europe:** European Central Bank, "ECB Assesses That Sberbank Europe
AG and Its Subsidiaries in Croatia and Slovenia Are Failing or Likely to Fail," February 28, 2022, www
.bankingsupervision.europa.eu/press/pr/date/2022/html/ssm.pr220228~3121b6aec1.en.html.

351 **seven Russian banks it had barred from SWIFT:** The seven banks that the EU kicked out of SWIFT
were VTB Bank, Bank Otkritie, Novikombank, Promsvyazbank, Bank Rossiya, Sovcombank, and VEB;
see "Ukraine: EU Agrees to Exclude Key Russian Banks from SWIFT," European Commission, March 2,
2022, ec.europa.eu/commission/presscorner/detail/en/ip_22_1484.

351 **Putin convened a secret meeting:** Max Seddon and Polina Ivanova, "How Putin's Technocrats Saved
the Economy to Fight a War They Opposed," Financial Times, December 16, 2022, www.ft.com/content
/fe5fe0ed-e5d4-474e-bb5a-10c9657285d2.

351 **"kingdom of the antichrist":** Sergei Glazyev, "Artificially Created Obsession," Izborsky Club, November 7, 2013, izborsk-club.ru/2121; Paul D'Anieri, Ukraine and Russia: From Civilized Divorce to Uncivil
War (Cambridge: Cambridge University Press, 2019), 201.

351 **brooch to symbolize her outlook:** Ashutosh Pandey, "The Central Banker Cleaning Up Putin's Mess," *Deutsche Welle*, April 29, 2022, www.dw.com/en/elvira-nabiullina-the-central-banker-vladimir-putin-is-relying-on-to-clean-up-russias-economic-mess/a-61634244.

351 **she wore no brooch:** Max Seddon, "Elvira Nabiullina, a Technocrat Plunged into Chaos at Russia's Central Bank," *Financial Times*, March 4, 2022, www.ft.com/content/874e18e6-b97c-4508-b43c-4454466a2c3c.

352 **first learned of the invasion on television:** Seddon and Ivanova, "Putin's Technocrats."

352 **doubled interest rates:** Katie Martin et al., "Russia Doubles Interest Rates after Sanctions Send Rouble Plunging," *Financial Times*, February 28, 2022, www.ft.com/content/f7148532-36cd-4683-8f1b-ea79428488c4.

352 **exchange 80 percent of all the money:** Paddy Hirsch, "How Russia Rescued the Ruble," NPR, April 5, 2022, www.npr.org/sections/money/2022/04/05/1090920442/how-russia-rescued-the-ruble.

352 **big exporters as a de facto central bank:** Tommy Stubbington and Polina Ivanova, "Russia Steadies Rouble with Harsh Capital Controls and Investment Curbs," *Financial Times*, April 1, 2022, www.ft.com/content/4ebde1bf-674c-468d-a8f0-2b306496962d.

352 **abandon its roughly 20 percent stake in Rosneft:** "BP to Exit Rosneft Shareholding," BP, February 27, 2022, www.bp.com/en/global/corporate/news-and-insights/press-releases/bp-to-exit-rosneft-shareholding.html; Ron Bousso and Dmitry Zhdannikov, "BP Quits Russia in up to $25 Billion Hit after Ukraine Invasion," Reuters, February 28, 2022, www.reuters.com/business/energy/britains-bp-says-exit-stake-russian-oil-giant-rosneft-2022-02-27.

352 **banned foreigners from selling their Russian assets:** Nastassia Astrasheuskaya and Tom Wilson, "Moscow to Ban Foreign Investors from Selling Russian Assets," *Financial Times*, March 1, 2022, www.ft.com/content/1a04fd70-1a64-4277-8c0d-00e49402c3be.

352 **no longer transfer money abroad:** Caitlin Ostroff, "How Russia's Central Bank Engineered the Ruble's Rebound," *The Wall Street Journal*, March 28, 2022, www.wsj.com/articles/how-russias-central-bank-engineered-the-rubles-rebound-11648458200; Stubbington and Ivanova, "Russia Steadies Rouble."

352 **closure of cash-based exchanges:** Stubbington and Ivanova, "Russia Steadies Rouble."

352 **rather resign than oversee currency controls:** Seddon and Ivanova, "Putin's Technocrats."

353 **"backed by riot police":** Seddon and Ivanova, "Putin's Technocrats."

353 **contract by 10 to 15 percent:** For example, Goldman Sachs projected a GDP decline of 10 percent, J.P. Morgan projected a GDP decline of 11 percent, and the Institute of International Finance projected a GDP decline of 15 percent. See "Goldman, Barclays Cut 2022 Russia Outlook, See Double-Digit Drop," *Bloomberg*, March 21, 2022, www.bloomberg.com/news/articles/2022-03-21/goldman-barclays-cut-2022-russia-outlook-see-double-digit-drop; Jason Laljee, "Russia's Economy Could Suffer a 'Deep' Recession That Cuts GDP by 11% as Sanctions Sharpen, JPMorgan Says," *Business Insider*, March 4, 2022, www.businessinsider.com/russia-economy-recession-sanctions-nato-swift-putin-ukraine-biden-debt-2022-3; "Russia's GDP to Fall 15% This Year on Ukraine-linked Sanctions—IIF," Reuters, March 10, 2022, www.reuters.com/markets/rates-bonds/russias-gdp-fall-15-this-year-ukraine-linked-sanctions-iif-2022-03-10.

353 **grow by 3 percent or more:** "Russia's GDP to Fall," Reuters.

353 **Putin "has no idea what's coming":** Joseph R. Biden, "State of the Union Address" (speech, Washington, D.C., March 1, 2022), The White House, www.whitehouse.gov/state-of-the-union-2022.

CHAPTER 58: A POTEMKIN CURRENCY

354 **deliver a shipment of Russian crude:** "Tanker with Cargo of Russian Oil Berths at Tranmere Oil Terminal," *Birkenhead News*, March 3, 2022, www.birkenhead.news/tanker-with-cargo-of-russian-oil-berths-at-tranmere-oil-terminal; "Essar Statement on Compliance with Sanctions Affecting Russia-Related Entities," Essar Oil, March 4, 2022, www.essaroil.co.uk/news/essar-statement-on-compliance-with-sanctions-affecting-russia-related-entities.

354 **"under no circumstances unload any Russian oil":** Matt Clinch, "Angry Dock Workers in the UK Are Refusing to Unload Any Russian Oil Due to Ukraine Invasion," CNBC, March 6, 2022, www.cnbc.com/2022/03/06/ukraine-angry-dock-workers-in-the-uk-are-refusing-to-unload-russian-oil.html.

354 **"blood on this oil":** "Dutch Dockers Prepare for Legal Battle over Russia Oil," *SourceMaterial*, March 4, 2022, www.source-material.org/dutch-dockers-prepare-for-legal-battle-over-russia-oil.

354 **largest exporter of fossil fuels, arguably held:** "World Energy Outlook 2022," International Energy Agency, 2022, iea.blob.core.windows.net/assets/fe7c251b-8651-4d3a-8362-0ffe3e50d37b/Executive summary_WorldEnergyOutlook2022.pdf.

355 **fended off elite Russian paratroopers:** Liam Collins, Michael Kofman, and John Spencer, "The Battle of Hostomel Airport: A Key Moment in Russia's Defeat in Kyiv," *War on the Rocks*, August 10, 2023, warontherocks.com/2023/08/the-battle-of-hostomel-airport-a-key-moment-in-russias-defeat-in-kyiv.

355 **deprived Russia of air superiority:** "Russia Crisis Military Assessment: Why Did Russia's Invasion Stumble?" The Atlantic Council, March 2, 2022, www.atlanticcouncil.org/blogs/new-atlanticist/russia-crisis-military-assessment-why-did-russias-invasion-stumble.

355 **stalled before it could reach Kyiv:** Claire Press and Svitlana Libet, "How Russia's 35-mile Armoured Convoy Ended in Failure," *BBC News*, February 22, 2023, www.bbc.com/news/world-europe-64664944.

355 **send Ukraine billions of dollars of weapons:** "Russian War in Ukraine: Timeline," U.S. Department of Defense, www.defense.gov/Spotlights/Support-for-Ukraine/Timeline.

355 **"purchase and delivery of weapons":** Maïa de la Baume and Jacopo Barigazzi, "EU Agrees to Give €500M in Arms, Aid to Ukrainian Military in 'Watershed' Move," *Politico*, February 27, 2022, www.politico.eu/article/eu-ukraine-russia-funding-weapons-budget-military-aid; "EU Doubles Military Aid to Ukraine," *Deutsche Welle*, March 23, 2022, www.dw.com/en/ukraine-eu-doubles-military-aid-to-1-billion-as-it-happened/a-61226171.

355 **declared a *Zeitenwende*:** Olaf Scholz, "Resolutely Committed to Peace and Security" (speech, Berlin, Germany, February 27, 2022), The Federal Government of Germany, www.bundesregierung.de/breg-en/news/policy-statement-by-olaf-scholz-chancellor-of-the-federal-republic-of-germany-and-member-of-the-german-bundestag-27-february-2022-in-berlin-2008378; Lukas Paul Schmelter, "It's Time for Olaf Scholz to Walk His Talk," *Foreign Policy*, August 9, 2022, foreignpolicy.com/2022/08/09/scholz-germany-zeitenwende-ukraine-russia-war-bundeswehr-nato-defense-military-security; Tony Barber, "Year in a Word: Zeitenwende," *Financial Times*, December 24, 2022, www.ft.com/content/3d0bfcab-d56c-4527-bf8f-7ed2c7020c7d.

355 **Even traditionally neutral Switzerland:** "Ukraine: Further Trade and Financial Sanctions Imposed Against Russia," The Federal Council of Switzerland, March 4, 2022, www.admin.ch/gov/en/start/documentation/media-releases.msg-id-87474.html.

355 **announced their exits from Russia:** Lauren Goode, "Apple Stops Sales in Russia—and Takes a Rare Stand," *Wired*, March 1, 2022, www.wired.com/story/apple-russia-iphone-ukraine-traffic-maps-rt-sputnik-app-store; "McDonald's to Exit from Russia," McDonald's, May 16, 2022, corporate.mcdonalds.com/corpmcd/our-stories/article/mcd-exit-russia.html; Jonathan Roeder, "Coca-Cola Announces Suspension of Operations in Russia," *Bloomberg*, March 8, 2022, www.bloomberg.com/news/articles/2022-03-08/coca-cola-announces-suspension-of-operations-in-russia; Jeffrey Sonnenfeld and Steven Tian, "Some of the Biggest Brands Are Leaving Russia. Others Just Can't Quit Putin. Here's a List," *The New York Times*, April 7, 2022, www.nytimes.com/interactive/2022/04/07/opinion/companies-ukraine-boycott.html.

355 **their superyachts were not:** Amanda Macias and Brian Schwartz, "World's Largest Yacht, Linked to Russian Billionaire Usmanov, Is Seized by Germany," CNBC, April 14, 2022, www.cnbc.com/2022/04/14/worlds-largest-yacht-linked-to-russian-billionaire-usmanov-seized-by-germany.html; Brian Schwartz and Amanda Macias, "Here Are the Russian Oligarch Yachts Being Seized as Sanctions Take Effect," CNBC, March 3, 2022, www.cnbc.com/2022/03/03/here-are-the-russian-oligarch-yachts-being-seized-as-sanctions-take-effect.html.

355 **vessel belonging to Rosneft CEO:** Belén Carreño and Joan Faus, "Spain Detains Yacht Thought to Be Owned by Rosneft CEO—Police Source," Reuters, March 16, 2022, www.reuters.com/world/europe/spain-detains-yacht-suspicion-it-belongs-russian-oligarch-ministry-2022-03-16.

356 **"visit Stamford Bridge one last time":** "Statement from Roman Abramovich," Chelsea FC, March 2, 2022, www.chelseafc.com/en/news/article/statement-from-roman-abramovich.

356 **forcing him to sell the team:** Adam Crafton, "Special Report: What Roman Abramovich Did Next," *The Athletic*, July 27, 2023, theathletic.com/4717198/2023/07/27/roman-abramovich-putin-chelsea.

356 **wheat prices soared:** Emiko Terazono and Michael Pooler, "Wheat Prices Hit Record Highs as War Halts Exports from Ukraine and Russia," *Financial Times*, March 4, 2022, www.ft.com/content/e6a28dd9-ecea-4d67-b6b5-a50301b731b2.

356 **stopping grain shipments via the Black Sea:** Nik Martin, "Ukraine War: Russia Blocks Shops Carrying Grain Exports," *Deutsche Welle*, March 17, 2022, www.dw.com/en/ukraine-war-russia-blocks-ships-carrying-grain-exports/a-61165985.

356 **warnings from the UN:** "Ukraine War: More Countries Will 'Feel the Burn' as Food and Energy Price Rises Fuel Hunger, Warns WFP," United Nations World Food Programme, March 11, 2022, www.wfp.org/stories/ukraine-war-more-countries-will-feel-burn-food-and-energy-price-rises-fuel-hunger-warns-wfp.

356 **damaged parts of the Caspian Pipeline:** "Russia Warns of Sharp Caspian Pipeline Oil Export Drop after Storm," Reuters, March 22, 2022, www.reuters.com/business/energy/russia-warns-sharp-caspian-pipeline-oil-export-drop-after-storm-2022-03-22.

356 **more than one million barrels of Kazakh oil:** Benoît Faucon, "Putin's Secret Weapon on Energy: An Ex-Morgan Stanley Banker," *The Wall Street Journal*, March 2, 2023, www.wsj.com/articles/russia-putin-oil-gas-sorokin-sanctions-e1189493; Derek Brower and Myles McCormick, "Major Russian Pipeline Fully Halts Oil Exports, Sending Crude Prices Higher," *Financial Times*, March 23, 2022, www.ft.com/content/9d6fe3e6-597f-4089-a553-3f8a0edc18e8.

356 **oil prices leapt to over $120 per barrel:** "Brent Crude Oil," *Trading Economics*, tradingeconomics.com/commodity/brent-crude-oil; David Gaffen, "Oil Jumps 5% as Caspian Pipeline Disruption Adds

to Supply Fears," Reuters, March 23, 2022, www.reuters.com/business/energy/oil-prices-resume-climb
-after-us-stockpiles-drop-tight-market-2022-03-23.

356 **all-time high of around $147, set in 2008:** Mohsin S. Khan, "The 2008 Oil Price 'Bubble,'" Peterson
International Institute of Economics, August 2009, www.piie.com/publications/policy-briefs/2008-oil
-price-bubble.

356 **nearly 80 percent of Americans:** "Vast Majority of Americans Say Ban Russian Oil, Quinnipiac Uni-
versity National Poll Finds; Nearly 8 in 10 Support U.S. Military Response if Putin Attacks a NATO
Country," Quinnipiac University Polling, March 7, 2022, poll.qu.edu/poll-release?releaseid=3838; Chris
Jackson, Mallory Newall, and Hailey Foster, "Americans Continue to Support Ban on Russian Oil,"
Ipsos, March 13, 2022, www.ipsos.com/en-us/news-polls/March-2022-ABC-news-poll.

356 **plans to cease all operations in Russia:** "Shell Announces Intent to Withdraw from Russian Oil and
Gas," Shell, March 8, 2022, shell.gcs-web.com/news-releases/news-release-details/shell-announces-intent
-withdraw-russian-oil-and-gas.

356 **leave behind some $4 billion:** Sabrina Valle, "Exxon to Exit Russia, Leaving $4 bln in Assets," Reuters,
March 2, 2022, www.reuters.com/business/energy/exxon-mobil-begins-removing-us-employees-its
-russian-oil-gas-operations-2022-03-01; in October 2022, after seven months of exit negotiations, the
Russian government unilaterally expropriated all of Exxon's assets in Russia. See Sabrina Valle,
"Exclusive: Exxon Exits Russia Empty-Handed with Oil Project Unilaterally Seized," Reuters, October 17, 2022, reuters.com/business/energy/exclusive-exxon-exits-russia-empty-handed-with-oil-project
-unilaterally-2022-10-17.

356 **"Popular opinion turned against Russian energy":** Author interview with Peter Harrell, 2023.

356 **Canada unilaterally banned oil imports:** "Government of Canada Moves to Prohibit Import of Russian
Oil," Natural Resources, Government of Canada, February 28, 2022, www.canada.ca/en/natural-resources
-canada/news/2022/02/government-of-canada-moves-to-prohibit-import-of-russian-oil.html.

356 **Biden administration soon did the same:** Andrew Desiderio, Burgess Everett, and Jonathan Lemire,
"Biden Bans Russian Oil under Pressure from Congress," *Politico*, March 7, 2022, www.politico.com
/news/2022/03/07/russia-oil-ukraine-biden-00014873.

356 **bought a small amount of oil from Russia:** "Weekly U.S. Imports from Russia of Crude Oil," U.S.
Energy Information Administration, www.eia.gov/dnav/pet/hist/LeafHandler.ashx?n=pet&s=w_epc0
_im0_nus-nrs_mbbld&f=w.

357 **UK and Australia joined:** Kwasi Kwarteng, "Statement on the Phasing Out of Russian Oil Imports"
(speech, London, UK, March 9, 2022), Government of the UK, www.gov.uk/government/speeches
/statement-on-the-phasing-out-of-russian-oil-imports; Marise Payne, "Autonomous Sanctions (Import Sanctioned Goods—Russia) Designation 2022," Australia Ministry for Foreign Affairs, March 10,
2022, www.legislation.gov.au/Details/F2022L00310.

357 **30 percent of the continent's total oil imports:** "In Focus: Reducing the EU's Dependence on Imported Fossil Fuels," European Commission, April 20, 2022, commission.europa.eu/news/focus-reducing
-eus-dependence-imported-fossil-fuels-2022-04-20_en; "Oil Market and Russian Supply," International
Energy Agency, www.iea.org/reports/russian-supplies-to-global-energy-markets/oil-market-and-russian
-supply-2.

357 **Weaning off Russian natural gas:** "In Focus: Reducing the EU's Dependence on Imported Fossil Fuels," European Commission, April 20, 2022, commission.europa.eu/news/focus-reducing-eus-dependence
-imported-fossil-fuels-2022-04-20_en.

357 **successfully defended their capital:** Aaron Steckelberg et al., "Why Russia Gave Up on Urban War in
Kyiv and Turned to Big Battles in the East," *The Washington Post*, April 15, 2022, www.washingtonpost
.com/world/interactive/2022/kyiv-urban-warfare-russia-siege-donbas?.

357 **continue servicing its debt instead:** Daniel Flatley, "U.S. Treasury Confirms Russia Not Barred from
Servicing Bonds," *Bloomberg*, March 16, 2022, www.bloomberg.com/news/articles/2022-03-16/u-s
-treasury-confirms-russia-not-barred-from-servicing-bonds; Tommy Stubbington and Philip Staf-
ford, "Russian Bond Interest Payments in Flow through Western Financial Systems," *Financial Times*,
March 18, 2022, www.ft.com/content/c381f620-1897-489a-81d1-956f01fb0bf0.

357 **credit cards kept working:** Kalyenna Makortoff, "Mastercard and Visa Block in Russia Does Not Stop
Domestic Purchases," *The Guardian*, March 6, 2022, www.theguardian.com/business/2022/mar/06
/russians-visa-mastercard-ban-domestic-purchases-mir.

357 **central bank stabilized the ruble:** Tommy Stubbington and Polina Ivanova, "Russia Steadies Rouble
with Harsh Capital Controls and Investment Curbs," *Financial Times*, April 1, 2022, www.ft.com/content
/4ebde1bf-674c-468d-a8f0-2b306496962d.

357 **blocking most avenues for selling it:** Paddy Hirsch, "How Russia Rescued the Ruble," NPR, April 5,
2022, www.npr.org/sections/money/2022/04/05/1090920442/how-russia-rescued-the-ruble.

357 **a "Potemkin currency":** Hirsch, "How Russia Rescued the Ruble."

357 **rubles into an account at Gazprombank:** Nastassia Astrasheuskaya and Leila Abboud, "Putin Issues
Decree Requesting 'Unfriendly' Countries Pay for Gas in Roubles," *Financial Times*, March 31, 2022,
www.ft.com/content/d8ee2429-7caf-4e1f-9c85-dd1f825d36e3.

358 **trade surplus rose to the highest level:** Stubbington and Ivanova, "Russia Steadies Rouble."

CHAPTER 59: SUPPLY AND DEMAND

359 **network of subterranean salt caverns:** "SPR Storage Sites," Office of Cybersecurity, Energy Security, and Emergency Response, U.S. Department of Energy, www.energy.gov/ceser/spr-storage-sites.

359 **site of the Strategic Petroleum Reserve:** "SPR Storage Sites," U.S. Department of Energy; Noah Berman, "How Does the U.S. Government Use the Strategic Petroleum Reserve?" Council on Foreign Relations, January 11, 2023, www.cfr.org/backgrounder/how-does-us-government-use-strategic-petroleum-reserve.

359 **emergency drawdowns on just three occasions:** Smaller releases had occurred a few dozen other times as part of exchange agreements with refineries and to comply with congressional mandates. See "History of SPR Releases," Office of Cybersecurity, Energy Security, and Emergency Response, U.S. Department of Energy, www.energy.gov/ceser/history-spr-releases; "Strategic Petroleum Reserve Oil Releases: October 2021 through October 2022," IN11916, Congressional Research Service, U.S. Library of Congress, April 22, 2022, crsreports.congress.gov/product/pdf/IN/IN11916.

359 **50 million barrels of oil from the SPR:** The White House, "President Biden Announces Release from the Strategic Petroleum Reserve as Part of Ongoing Efforts to Lower Prices and Address Lack of Supply around the World," November 23, 2021, www.whitehouse.gov/briefing-room/statements-releases/2021/11/23/president-biden-announces-release-from-the-strategic-petroleum-reserve-as-part-of-ongoing-efforts-to-lower-prices-and-address-lack-of-supply-around-the-world.

359 **attempt to tame prices:** Helima Croft, hosted by James M. Lindsay, "The Future of Energy, with Helima Croft," *The President's Inbox* (podcast), Council on Foreign Relations, December 7, 2021, www.cfr.org/podcasts/future-energy-helima-croft.

360 **full month's worth of Russian exports:** "Oil Market and Russian Supply," International Energy Agency, www.iea.org/reports/russian-supplies-to-global-energy-markets/oil-market-and-russian-supply-2.

360 **injecting freshwater into the bottom:** "SPR Storage Sites," U.S. Department of Energy.

360 **alter the shape of the caverns:** Robert McNally, *Crude Volatility: The History and the Future of Boom-Bust Oil Prices* (New York: Columbia University Press, 2017), 186; Ari Natter and Sheela Tobben, "Biden Oil Plan Hinges on 1970s Reserve with Troubled History," *Bloomberg*, March 31, 2022, www.bloomberg.com/news/articles/2022-03-31/biden-s-oil-gambit-hinges-on-1970s-reserve-with-troubled-history; Tristan Abbey, "Is Biden Breaking the Strategic Petroleum Reserve?" *The New Atlantis*, October 27, 2022, www.thenewatlantis.com/publications/did-biden-break-the-strategic-petroleum-reserve.

360 **legal authority for a withdrawal:** Heather L. Greenley, "The Strategic Petroleum Reserve: Background, Authorities, and Considerations," Congressional Research Service, U.S. Library of Congress, R46355, May 13, 2020, www.everycrsreport.com/files/20200513_R46355_a7b0f9897caa032cac61287f9bfc4d010f0b8dc0.pdf.

360 **remove regulatory barriers:** Timothy Puko, Tarini Parti, and Collin Eaton, "Biden to Draw Down Oil Reserves in Bid to Ease Gas Prices," *The Wall Street Journal*, March 31, 2022, www.wsj.com/articles/crude-oil-prices-drop-as-biden-plans-to-tap-strategic-oil-reserves-11648738097.

360 **U.S. producers were flush with cash:** Clifford Krauss, "Why U.S. Oil Companies Aren't Riding to Europe's Rescue," *The New York Times*, April 26, 2022, www.nytimes.com/2022/04/26/business/energy-environment/oil-us-europe-russia.html.

360 **30 million barrels of its own strategic stocks:** "IEA Confirms Member Country Contributions to Second Collective Action to Release Oil Stocks in Response to Russia's Invasion of Ukraine," International Energy Agency, April 7, 2022, www.iea.org/news/iea-confirms-member-country-contributions-to-second-collective-action-to-release-oil-stocks-in-response-to-russia-s-invasion-of-ukraine; "IEA Governing Board Concludes 2022 Collective Actions," International Energy Agency, June 22, 2023, www.iea.org/news/iea-governing-board-concludes-2022-collective-actions.

360 **surge supplies of LNG to Europe:** Joseph R. Biden and Ursula von der Leyen, "Remarks by President Biden and European Commission President Ursula von der Leyen in Joint Press Statement" (speech, Washington, D.C., March 25, 2022), The White House, www.whitehouse.gov/briefing-room/speeches-remarks/2022/03/25/remarks-by-president-biden-and-european-commission-president-ursula-von-der-leyen-in-joint-press-statement.

360 **"imposing a cost on America":** Joseph R. Biden, "Remarks by President Biden on Actions to Lower Gas Prices at the Pump for American Families" (speech, Washington, D.C., March 31, 2022), www.whitehouse.gov/briefing-room/speeches-remarks/2022/03/31/remarks-by-president-biden-on-actions-to-lower-gas-prices-at-the-pump-for-american-families; The White House, "Fact Sheet: President Biden's Plan to Respond to Putin's Price Hike at the Pump," March 31, 2022, www.whitehouse.gov/briefing-room/statements-releases/2022/03/31/fact-sheet-president-bidens-plan-to-respond-to-putins-price-hike-at-the-pump.

360 **largest-ever in U.S. history:** "When Have the United States and Others Previously Released Oil from Reserves?" Reuters, March 30, 2022, www.reuters.com/business/energy/when-have-united-states-others-previously-released-oil-reserves-2022-03-31.

361 **India's purchases of Russian oil shot up:** Weizhen Tan, "India Is Snapping Up Cheap Russian Oil, and China Could Be Next," CNBC, March 27, 2022, www.cnbc.com/2022/03/28/russia-india-india-buys-cheap-russian-oil-china-could-be-next.html; Harry Dempsey and Chloe Cornish, "Russian Oil Ex-

ports to India Surge as Europe Shuns Cargoes," *Financial Times*, March 18, 2022, www.ft.com/content /5efc6338-3f01-4015-aedf-53a4a1944ca8.

361 **Indian government refrained from picking a side:** Ashley J. Tellis, "'What Is in Our Interest': India and the Ukraine War," Carnegie Endowment for International Peace, April 25, 2022, carnegieendowment .org/2022/04/25/what-is-in-our-interest-india-and-ukraine-war-pub-86961; "Split Opinion in India on Whether Russia or Western Countries to Blame for Ukraine Conflict: Survey," *The Times of India*, October 25, 2022, timesofindia.indiatimes.com/india/split-opinion-in-india-on-whether-russia-or -western-countries-to-blame-for-ukraine-conflict-survey/articleshow/95050848.cms.

361 **a new rupee-ruble mechanism:** Chloe Cornish, "India Explores 'Rupee-Rouble' Exchange Scheme to Beat Russia Sanctions," *Financial Times*, March 16, 2022, www.ft.com/content/a5ee2d6b-693f-475d-80c6 -0036c2657ef1.

361 **warm relations and close military ties:** Rajan Menon and Eugene Rumer, "Russia and India: A New Chapter," Carnegie Endowment for International Peace, September 20, 2022, carnegieendowment .org/2022/09/20/russia-and-india-new-chapter-pub-87958.

361 **son of Indian immigrants:** Daleep Singh, "Op-Ed: Deputy National Security Advisor Daleep Singh on Supporting the Asian Americans and Pacific Islanders Community," The White House, June 4, 2021, www.whitehouse.gov/briefing-room/blog/2021/06/04/op-ed-deputy-national-security-advisor-daleep -singh-on-supporting-the-asian-americans-and-pacific-islanders-community.

361 **relative of Dalip Singh Saund:** Chidanand Rajghatta, "Biden's Sanctions Man Is Indian-American Daleep Singh," *The Times of India*, February 23, 2022, timesofindia.indiatimes.com/world/us/bidens -sanctions-man-is-indian-american-daleep-singh/articleshow/89768488.cms.

361 **He offered Washington's support:** The White House, "Readout of Senior Administration Travel to India," April 1, 2022, www.whitehouse.gov/briefing-room/statements-releases/2022/04/01/readout-of -senior-administration-travel-to-india.

362 **"consequences to countries that actively attempt to circumvent":** Rezaul H. Laskar, "US Deputy NSA Daleep Singh Raises War 'Consequences' in India," *Hindustan Times*, April 1, 2022, www.hindustantimes .com/india-news/us-deputy-nsa-raises-war-consequences-in-india-101648730876864.html.

362 **"clearly a bad diplomat":** Sreemoy Talukdar, "US Deputy NSA Daleep Singh's Threats of 'Conse-quences' Point to a Fissure within Joe Biden Administration on India," *Firstpost*, April 2, 2022, www .firstpost.com/opinion/us-deputy-nsa-daleep-singhs-threats-of-consequences-point-to-a-fissure-within -joe-biden-administration-on-india-10510802.html.

362 **Sergei Lavrov touched down:** "Russia's Lavrov to Visit India, Supportive Despite Ukraine Crisis," Reu-ters, March 30, 2022, www.reuters.com/world/russias-lavrov-visit-india-supportive-despite-ukraine -crisis-2022-03-30.

362 **"India must not be dependent":** "US Pressure Won't Affect India-Russia Partnership: Russian FM Lavrov," *The Economic Times*, April 1, 2022, economictimes.indiatimes.com/news/india/us-pressure -wont-affect-india-russia-partnership-russian-fm-lavrov/articleshow/90591533.cms.

CHAPTER 60: THE RUBIK'S CUBE

363 **leafy suburb northwest of the capital:** Serhii Plokhy, *The Russo-Ukrainian War: The Return of History* (New York: W.W. Norton & Company, 2023), 167–72; Tara John et al., "Bodies Tied Up, Shot and Left to Rot in Bucha Hint at Gruesome Reality of Russia's Occupation in Ukraine," CNN, April 5, 2022, edition.cnn.com/2022/04/05/europe/bucha-ukraine-russian-occupation-reality-intl-cmd/index.html.

363 **civilians, shot at point-blank range:** John et al., "Bodies Tied Up."

363 **deliberate war crimes:** Graeme Massie, "Ukraine Says 'Torture Room' Found after Russian Troops Withdrawal from Bucha," *The Independent*, April 5, 2022, www.independent.co.uk/news/world/europe /ukraine-russia-torture-room-bucha-b2050946.html; Laurel Wamsley, "Rape Has Reportedly Become a Weapon in Ukraine. Finding Justice May Be Difficult," NPR, April 30, 2022, www.npr.org/2022/04 /30/1093339262/ukraine-russia-rape-war-crimes.

363 **tightened penalties on Sberbank:** U.S Department of the Treasury, "U.S. Treasury Escalates Sanc-tions on Russia for Its Atrocities in Ukraine," April 6, 2022, home.treasury.gov/news/press-releases /jy0705.

363 **banned all new investment by American firms:** More than any other sanction, the ban on new invest-ment caused an influx of questions to OFAC, as companies scrambled to understand what "new invest-ment" meant and whether they could even spend money to wind down their operations in Russia. See Joseph R. Biden, "Executive Order 14071 of April 6, 2022, Prohibiting New Investment in and Certain Services to the Russian Federation in Response to Continued Russian Federation Aggression," *Code of Federal Regulations*, titles 3 and 50 (2022), www.federalregister.gov/documents/2022/04/08/2022-07757 /prohibiting-new-investment-in-and-certain-services-to-the-russian-federation-in-response-to; Andrew Edgecliff-Johnson and Matthew Rocco, "McDonald's Leads Fresh Exodus of Western Consumer Brands from Russia," *Financial Times*, March 8, 2022, www.ft.com/content/21e27317-5151-43c8-b0be-40f375 42698d.

363 **overturned Treasury's decision on Russian debt repayments:** The White House, "Fact Sheet: United States, G7 and EU Impose Severe and Immediate Costs on Russia," April 6, 2022, www.whitehouse

.gov/briefing-room/statements-releases/2022/04/06/fact-sheet-united-states-g7-and-eu-impose -severe-and-immediate-costs-on-russia; Alina Selyukh, "What's Happening with Russia's 1st Default on Foreign Debt in a Century," NPR, June 27, 2022, www.npr.org/2022/06/27/1107750231/russia-default -foreign-debt-payments-explained.

364 **recently defaulted on its domestic debt in 1998:** Rachel Pannett and Julian Duplain, "Russia Defaults on Foreign Debt for First Time Since 1918: What to Know," *The Washington Post*, June 27, 2022, www .washingtonpost.com/world/2022/06/27/russia-defaults-foreign-debt-ukraine-war.

364 **oil revenues had surged by 50 percent:** Grant Smith, "Russia Oil Revenue up 50% This Year Despite Boycott, IEA Says," *Bloomberg*, May 12, 2022, www.bloomberg.com/news/articles/2022-05-12/russia -oil-revenue-up-50-this-year-despite-boycott-iea-says; "India and China Increasingly Welcome Shunned Russian Oil," PBS, June 13, 2022, www.pbs.org/newshour/world/india-and-china-increasingly-welcome -shunned-russian-oil; Ricardo Hausmann, Agata Loskot-Strachota, Axel Ockenfels, Ulrich Schetter, Simone Tagliapietra, Guntram Wolff, and Georg Zachmann, "How to Weaken Russian Oil and Gas Strength," *Science* 469 (April 2022), www.hks.harvard.edu/publications/how-weaken-russian-oil-and -gas-strength.

364 **Indian imports of Russian oil kept climbing:** Stanley Reed, "Russia's Oil Output Rose Last Month, Despite Sanctions," *The New York Times*, June 15, 2022, www.nytimes.com/2022/06/15/business/russia -oil-sanctions.html; "India and China Increasingly Welcome Shunned Russian Oil," PBS.

365 **five million barrels of crude oil each day:** "Oil Market and Russian Supply," International Energy Agency, www.iea.org/reports/russian-supplies-to-global-energy-markets/oil-market-and-russian-supply-2.

365 **levy taxes on their purchases:** Ricardo Hausmann, "The Case for a Punitive Tax on Russian Oil," *Project Syndicate*, February 26, 2022, www.project-syndicate.org/commentary/case-for-punitive-tax -on-russian-oil-by-ricardo-hausmann-2022-02.

366 **"use sanctions to make oil cheaper":** Author interview with Andrea Gacki, 2023.

367 **"didn't need the importing countries":** Author interview with Peter Harrell, 2023.

CHAPTER 61: "WHAT OTHER OPTION DO WE HAVE?"

368 **5 percent of all global trade:** "Crude Petroleum," *Observatory of Economic Complexity*, oec.world/en /profile/hs/crude-petroleum.

369 **"Russia's supply is essentially 100 percent inelastic":** Author interview with Catherine Wolfram, 2023.

369 **plunged below $15 per barrel:** Ryan Chilcote, "Why Russia Just Torpedoed Global Oil Prices," PBS, March 10, 2020, www.pbs.org/newshour/economy/why-russia-just-torpedoed-global-oil-prices; "Russia: Petroleum and Other Liquids," U.S. Energy Information Administration, www.eia.gov/international /data/country/RUS/petroleum-and-other-liquids/monthly-petroleum-and-other-liquids-production; Anders Åslund, "Putin Concedes Defeat in the Oil Price War," The Atlantic Council, April 14, 2020, www.atlanticcouncil.org/blogs/new-atlanticist/putin-concedes-defeat-in-the-oil-price-war; "Urals Oil: Price," *Trading Economics*, tradingeconomics.com/commodity/urals-oil.

369 **leveled much of the city:** Holly Ellyatt, "Mariupol Hasn't Surrendered to Russia, PM Says; at Least 5 Dead, 20 Injured in Kharkiv Attack," CNBC, April 18, 2022, www.cnbc.com/2022/04/17/russia-ukraine -live-updates.html; Luke Harding, "'It's Like the USSR': Residents on Life in Mariupol a Year Since Russian Occupation," *The Guardian*, May 18, 2023, www.theguardian.com/world/2023/may/18/its -like-the-ussr-residents-on-life-in-mariupol-a-year-since-russian-occupation; Valerie Hopkins et al., "Ukrainian Holdouts in Mariupol Surrender to an Uncertain Fate," *The New York Times*, May 17, 2022, www.nytimes.com/2022/05/17/world/europe/ukraine-mariupol-fighters-surrender.html.

369 **"careful when we think about a complete European ban":** James Politi, "Janet Yellen Calls for EU Caution on Russian Energy Ban," *Financial Times*, April 21, 2022, www.ft.com/content/0738a816-cb3c -44f9-9257-7a8489bf4c9c.

370 **he would step down:** Tyler Pager, "Biden's Sanctions Coordinator to Take Leave of Absence from White House," *The Washington Post*, April 26, 2022, www.washingtonpost.com/politics/2022/04/26 /biden-sanctions-coordinator-white-house.

370 **"the future of the European Union":** Ursula von der Leyen, "Speech by President von der Leyen at the EP Plenary on the Social and Economic Consequences for the EU of the Russian War in Ukraine— Reinforcing the EU's Capacity to Act" (speech, Strasbourg, France, May 4, 2022), ec.europa.eu/commission /presscorner/detail/en/speech_22_2785.

370 **ban European companies from providing shipping:** Francesco Guarascio and John Chalmers, "EU's Toughest Russia Sanctions Yet Snag on Worries over Oil Ban," Reuters, May 4, 2022, www.reuters .com/world/europe/eu-lay-out-new-sanctions-russia-targeting-oil-imports-2022-05-04.

370 **Russian oil would come off the market:** Noah Browning, "Russian Oil Output to Fall 1.4 mn BPD Next Year as EU Ban Takes Effect: IEA," Reuters, November 15, 2022, www.reuters.com/business/energy /russian-oil-output-fall-14-mln-bpd-next-year-eu-ban-takes-effect-iea-2022-11-15; Scott Disavino, "Oil Edges Up on Supply Jitters as EU Plans Russian Oil Ban," Reuters, May 5, 2022, www.reuters.com /business/oil-extends-gains-after-news-eus-russian-oil-ban-proposal-2022-05-05.

371 **well above the all-time high:** "Brent Crude Oil," *Trading Economics*, https://tradingeconomics.com/commodity/brent-crude-oil; Mohsin S. Khan, "The 2008 Oil Price 'Bubble,'" Peterson International Institute of Economics, August 2009, www.piie.com/publications/policy-briefs/2008-oil-price-bubble.

372 **The International Group of P&I Clubs, the umbrella organization:** "Group Clubs," International Group of P&I Clubs, www.igpandi.org/group-clubs.

372 **all member clubs would immediately stop insuring:** Laurence Norman, Joe Wallace, and Georgi Kantchev, "EU Sets Harshest Russia Sanctions, Targeting Oil and Insurance," *The Wall Street Journal*, May 31, 2022, www.wsj.com/articles/eus-ban-on-russian-oil-adds-stress-to-regions-economies-11653993757.

372 **the twenty-seven EU leaders formally signed on:** "Special Meeting of the European Council, 30–31 May 2022," May 30–31, 2022, European Council, www.consilium.europa.eu/en/meetings/european-council/2022/05/30-31.

372 **phase out roughly 90 percent:** Leila Fadel and Rob Schmitz, "European Union Leaders Agree to Ban 90% of Russian Oil by the End of 2022," NPR, May 31, 2022, www.npr.org/2022/05/31/1102097085/european-union-leaders-agree-to-ban-90-of-russian-oil-by-the-end-of-2022.

372 **carve-out for shipping:** "Russia's War on Ukraine: EU Adopts Sixth Package of Sanctions against Russia," European Commission, June 3, 2022, ec.europa.eu/commission/presscorner/detail/en/IP_22_2802.

372 **"toughest sanctions yet":** Norman, Wallace, and Kantchev, "EU Sets Harshest Russia Sanctions."

372 **oil prices rocketed up to $120:** "European Brent Spot Price FOB," U.S. Energy Information Administration, www.eia.gov/dnav/pet/hist/LeafHandler.ashx?n=PET&s=RBRTE&f=M.

CHAPTER 62: THE SERVICE PROVIDERS' CARTEL

374 **relied on LNG from the Sakhalin-2 project:** Yuka Obayashi, "Explainer: How Can Japan Secure Enough Gas if Sakhalin Supply Is Cut," Reuters, July 8, 2022, www.reuters.com/business/energy/how-can-japan-secure-enough-gas-if-sakhalin-supply-is-cut-2022-07-08.

375 **"consider a range of approaches":** "G7 Leaders' Communiqué," G7, Elmau, Germany, June 26–28, 2022, www.g7germany.de/resource/blob/974430/2062292/fbdb2c7e996205aee402386aae057c5e/2022-07-14-leaders-communique-data.pdf.

375 **law banning European companies from complying:** Eytan J. Fisch et al., "Navigating the Future Landscape of EU Blocking Statute," Skadden, Arps, Slate, Meagher, & Flom, January 27, 2022, www.skadden.com/insights/publications/2022/01/navigating-the-future-landscape-of-the-eu-blocking-statute.

376 **"allergic to secondary sanctions":** Author interview with Elizabeth Rosenberg, 2023.

376 **underlying sale complied with the price cap:** Edward Fishman, "How the Price Cap on Russian Oil Will Work in Practice," Columbia School of International and Public Affairs, Center on Global Energy Policy, November 30, 2022, www.energypolicy.columbia.edu/publications/how-price-cap-russian-oil-will-work-practice.

376 **buyers' cartel as a counterweight to OPEC:** David E. Spiro, *The Hidden Hand of American Hegemony: Petrodollar Recycling and International Markets* (Ithaca: Cornell University Press, 1999), 27.

376 **95 percent of the global tanker fleet:** Andrea Shalal and Timothy Gardner, "As Clock Ticks on G7's Russia Oil Price Cap, Big Questions Remain," Reuters, November 4, 2022, www.reuters.com/business/energy/clock-ticks-g7s-russia-oil-price-cap-big-questions-remain-2022-11-04.

376 **traveled to Jakarta:** "Readout: Assistant Secretary Elizabeth Rosenberg's Visit to Indonesia," U.S. Department of the Treasury, August 9, 2022, home.treasury.gov/news/press-releases/jy0917.

377 **"30 percent lower than the international market price":** Kevin Whitelaw, "Russia Seen Floating Long-Term Oil Discounts Amid Price-Cap Push," *Bloomberg*, August 24, 2022, www.bloomberg.com/news/articles/2022-08-24/russia-seen-floating-long-term-oil-discounts-amid-price-cap-push.

377 **traveled together to Mumbai:** "Readout: Deputy Secretary of the Treasury Wally Adeyemo's Travel to Mumbai," U.S. Department of the Treasury, August 25, 2022, home.treasury.gov/news/press-releases/jy0928.

377 **implement the price cap policy by December 5:** "G7 Finance Ministers' Statement on the United Response to Russia's War of Aggression against Ukraine," G7, September 2, 2022, www.bundesfinanzministerium.de/Content/EN/Downloads/G7-G20/2022-09-02-g7-ministers-statement.pdf?__blob=publicationFile&v=7.

377 **"exactly what we needed":** David Lawder and Christian Kraemer, "G7 Ministers Forge Ahead with Russian Oil Price Cap, Details Thin," Reuters, September 2, 2022, www.reuters.com/business/energy/g7-finance-chiefs-seen-advancing-russian-oil-price-cap-plan-2022-09-02.

377 **gearing up for a counteroffensive:** Andrew E. Kramer, "Ukraine Launches Southern Offensive, as Inspectors Head to Nuclear Plant," *The New York Times*, August 29, 2022, www.nytimes.com/2022/08/29/world/europe/ukraine-russia-counteroffensive.html.

CHAPTER 63: AN ECONOMIC WAR OF ATTRITION

378 **$500 billion to over $1 trillion:** Steven Arons, "Ukraine Reconstruction May Cost $1.1 Trillion, EIB Head Says," *Bloomberg*, June 21, 2022, www.bloomberg.com/news/articles/2022-06-21/ukraine-reconstruction

-may-cost-1-1-trillion-eib-head-says; "Ukraine Sees Post-war Reconstruction Costs Nearing $750 billion -PM," Reuters, October 24, 2022, www.reuters.com/world/europe/ukraine-sees-post-war-reconstruction -costs-nearing-750-billion-pm-2022-10-24.

378 **move to seize Russian assets:** In June 2024, the leaders of the G7 agreed to use interest income stemming from Russia's immobilized sovereign assets to finance "Extraordinary Revenue Acceleration (ERA) Loans for Ukraine," with the initial disbursement expected to total approximately $50 billion. This policy did not preclude the possibility of seizing the underlying principal of Russia's sovereign assets sometime in the future. See The White House, "G7 Leaders' Statement," June 14, 2024, www .whitehouse.gov/briefing-room/statements-releases/2024/06/14/g7-leaders-statement-8. Notable commentators have advocated for confiscating Russian sovereign assets. See, for instance, Lawrence Summers, Philip Zelikow, and Robert Zoellick, "The Other Counteroffensive to Save Ukraine," *Foreign Affairs*, June 15, 2023, www.foreignaffairs.com/ukraine/other-counteroffensive-save-ukraine; Lawrence Summers, Philip Zelikow, and Robert Zoellick, "Why Russian Reserves Should Be Used to Help Ukraine," *The Economist*, July 27, 2023, www.economist.com/by-invitation/2023/07/27/lawrence-summers-philip -zelikow-and-robert-zoellick-on-why-russian-reserves-should-be-used-to-help-ukraine.

378 **They aimed at something simpler:** Edward Fishman and Chris Miller, "The New Russian Sanctions Playbook," *Foreign Affairs*, February 28, 2022, www.foreignaffairs.com/articles/russia-fsu/2022-02-28 /new-russian-sanctions-playbook.

378 **tool of attrition:** Edward Fishman, "A Tool of Attrition," *Foreign Affairs*, February 23, 2023, www .foreignaffairs.com/ukraine/tool-attrition.

378 **remarks that stirred controversy:** Emma Ashford and Matthew Kroenig, "Is Weakening Russia a Bad Idea?" *Foreign Policy*, April 29, 2022, foreignpolicy.com/2022/04/29/austin-blinken-ukraine-zelensky -weaken-russia-a-bad-idea.

379 **"We want to see Russia weakened":** Kylie Atwood and Jennifer Hansler, "Austin Says US Wants to See Russia's Military Capabilities Weakened," CNN, April 25, 2022, www.cnn.com/2022/04/25/politics /blinken-austin-kyiv-ukraine-zelensky-meeting/index.html; Natasha Bertrand et al., "Austin's Assertion That US Wants to 'Weaken' Russia Underlines Biden Strategy Shift," CNN, April 26, 2022, www .cnn.com/2022/04/25/politics/biden-administration-russia-strategy/index.html.

379 **ramped up military aid to Ukraine:** U.S. Department of Defense, "Russian War in Ukraine: Timeline," www.defense.gov/Spotlights/Support-for-Ukraine/Timeline.

379 **HIMARS, a truck-mounted weapons system:** Matthew Mpoke Bigg and Eric Schmitt, "A U.S.-made Long-Range Rocket System Has Helped Give Ukraine Momentum in the War," *The New York Times*, January 2, 2023, www.nytimes.com/2023/01/03/world/europe/himars-rockets-us-ukraine-war.html.

379 **pummel Russian supply lines:** Maria Varenikova and Matthew Mpoke Bigg, "Ukraine Hits a Key Bridge in Kherson as Russia Steps Up Missile Strikes across the South," *The New York Times*, July 27, 2022, www.nytimes.com/2022/07/27/world/europe/ukraine-kherson-missile-strikes.html; Serhii Plokhy, *The Russo-Ukrainian War: The Return of History* (New York: W.W. Norton & Company, 2023), 217–22.

380 **relied on imports of Western-made computer chips:** Zoya Sheftalovich and Laurens Cerulus, "The Chips Are Down: Putin Scrambles for High-Tech Parts as His Arsenal Goes Up in Smoke," *Politico*, September 5, 2022, www.politico.eu/article/the-chips-are-down-russia-hunts-western-parts-to-run-its -war-machines.

380 **refrigerators and dishwashers for chips:** Jeanne Whalen, "Sanctions Forcing Russia to Use Appliance Parts in Military Gear, U.S. Says," *The Washington Post*, May 11, 2022, www.washingtonpost.com /technology/2022/05/11/russia-sanctions-effect-military.

380 **devastated the country's car, truck, and locomotive industries:** Chris Miller, "Is Russia's Economy on the Brink?" *Foreign Affairs*, September 2, 2022, www.foreignaffairs.com/russian-federation/russia -economy-brink-moscow-war-ukraine.

380 **output was down 80 percent:** In 2022, the automotive sector in Russia directly or indirectly employed some 3.5 million people. See Vladimir Milov, "The Sanctions on Russia Are Working," *Foreign Affairs*, January 18, 2023, www.foreignaffairs.com/russian-federation/sanctions-russia-are-working; Russia's automotive production was down 80 percent in September 2022 compared with the same month in 2021. See Polina Ivanova and Max Seddon, "Russia's Wartime Economy: Learning to Live without Imports," *Financial Times*, December 14, 2022, www.ft.com/content/6c01e84b-5333-4024-aaf1-521cf1207eb4.

380 **Millions of workers were furloughed:** Milov, "Sanctions on Russia Are Working."

380 **imports for 50 percent or more of their inputs:** Ivanova and Seddon, "Russia's Wartime Economy."

380 **shortages of chicks for broiler hens:** Ivanova and Seddon, "Russia's Wartime Economy."

380 **vehicles without airbags and anti-lock brakes:** "Russian Cars Drop Airbags, Anti-lock Brakes Because of Sanctions," *Automotive News*, June 19, 2022, www.autonews.com/manufacturing/russian-cars -drop-airbags-anti-lock-brakes-because-sanctions.

380 **"more paper in the sausage":** Ivanova and Seddon, "Russia's Wartime Economy."

380 **front companies in neighboring states:** "Russia," Central Intelligence Agency, www.cia.gov/the-world -factbook/countries/russia/#geography; Ivanova and Seddon, "Russia's Wartime Economy."

380 **contraband was as small as computer chips:** Sheftalovich and Cerulus, "The Chips Are Down."

381 **Putin imposed a draft:** Zoya Sheftalovich, "Full Text of Putin's Mobilization Decree—Translated,"

Politico, September 21, 2022, www.politico.eu/article/text-vladimir-putin-mobilization-decree-war -ukraine-russia; Anton Troianovski et al., "Ukraine War Comes Home to Russians as Putin Imposes Draft," *The New York Times*, September 22, 2022, www.nytimes.com/2022/09/22/world/europe/putin -russia-military-ukraine-war.html.

381 **Russians fled the country:** "Over 1,000 Russian Protestors Arrested after Putin Mobilizes More Troops," *The New York Times*, September 21, 2022, www.nytimes.com/live/2022/09/21/world/russia-ukraine -war-putin; Pjotr Sauer, "'I Will Cross the Border Tonight': Russians Flee after News of Draft," *The Guardian*, September 22, 2022, www.theguardian.com/world/2022/sep/22/my-heart-sank-with-news -of-draft-russians-flee-in-droves; Charles Maynes, "Putin Signs a Tough New Military Draft Law, Banning Conscripts from Fleeing Russia," NPR, April 14, 2023, www.npr.org/2023/04/13/1169464889 /russia-military-draft-ukraine-war.

381 **remained part of Russia "forever":** Max Seddon, "Vladimir Putin Annexes Four Ukrainian Regions," *Financial Times*, September 30, 2022, www.ft.com/content/38a1ea78-5530-4eba-85e5-70c2e38024a9.

CHAPTER 64: A PARTITIONED MARKET

382 **"price cap on our local pub's beer":** Javier Blas (@JavierBlas), "My friends and I have agreed to impose a price cap," Twitter, September 2, 2022, twitter.com/JavierBlas/status/1565659185823580163.

382 **"more complicated than the local pub":** Ben Harris (@AsstSecEcon), "The global energy trade is a bit more complicated," Twitter, September 2, 2022, twitter.com/AsstSecEcon/status/1565738230154231808?s =20; Archived version: archive.is/4eTIP.

382 **"called an idiot by so many people":** Author interview with Ben Harris, 2023.

382 **Oil traders, in particular:** Javier Blas and Jack Farchy, *The World for Sale: Money, Power, and the Traders Who Barter the Earth's Resources* (New York: Oxford University Press, 2021), 222–32.

383 **production levels, creating OPEC+:** "What Is OPEC+ and How Is It Different from OPEC?" U.S. Energy Information Administration, May 9, 2023, www.eia.gov/todayinenergy/detail.php?id=56420.

383 **"pay the price":** Peter Baker and Ben Hubbard, "Biden to Travel to Saudi Arabia, Ending Its 'Pariah' Status," *The New York Times*, June 2, 2022, www.nytimes.com/2022/06/02/us/politics/biden-saudi-arabia .html.

383 **loose commitment from the Saudis:** The White House, "Fact Sheet: Results of Bilateral Meeting Between the United States and the Kingdom of Saudi Arabia," July 15, 2022, www.whitehouse.gov/briefing -room/statements-releases/2022/07/15/fact-sheet-results-of-bilateral-meeting-between-the-united-states -and-the-kingdom-of-saudi-arabia; Peter Baker and David E. Sanger, "Biden's Fraught Saudi Visit Garners Scathing Criticism and Modest Accords," *The New York Times*, July 15, 2022, www.nytimes .com/2022/07/15/world/middleeast/biden-mbs-saudi-visit.html.

383 **received assurances that Saudi Arabia:** Mark Mazzetti, Edward Wong, and Adam Entous, "U.S. Officials Had a Secret Oil Deal with the Saudis. Or So They Thought," *The New York Times*, October 25, 2022, www.nytimes.com/2022/10/25/us/politics/us-saudi-oil-deal.html.

383 **OPEC+ ministers agreed to slash oil production:** Organization of the Petroleum Exporting Countries, "33rd OPEC and non-OPEC Ministerial Meeting," October 5, 2022, www.opec.org/opec_web /en/press_room/7021.htm; Hanna Ziady, "OPEC Announces the Biggest Cut to Oil Production Since the Start of the Pandemic," CNN, October 5, 2022, www.cnn.com/2022/10/05/energy/opec-production -cuts/index.html.

383 **direct shot at the price cap:** Derek Brower et al., "The New Oil War: OPEC Moves Against the US," *Financial Times*, October 7, 2022, www.ft.com/content/70853af8-b7a4-4a28-bdfe-b4f3e375a1f0.

384 **"reduce OPEC's control over energy prices":** Jake Sullivan and Brian Deese, "Statement from National Security Advisor Jake Sullivan and NEC Director Brian Deese" (speech, Washington, D.C., October 5, 2022), The White House, www.whitehouse.gov/briefing-room/statements-releases/2022/10 /05/statement-from-national-security-advisor-jake-sullivan-and-nec-director-brian-deese.

384 **save the Global South billions:** James Politi, "Russian Oil Price Cap Would Save Emerging Markets Billions, US Says," *Financial Times*, October 4, 2022, www.ft.com/content/5f102e4e-e92b-482c-adb9 -86d66c919673.

384 **Moscow stood ready to make further cuts:** "Russia May Cut Oil Output if Price Caps Introduced— Deputy PM Novak," Reuters, October 5, 2022, www.reuters.com/markets/commodities/russia-may -cut-oil-output-if-price-caps-introduced-deputy-pm-novak-2022-10-05.

384 **shut down all Europe-bound gas supplies:** Sergey Vakulenko, "Shutting Down Nord Stream Marks the Point of No Return for Russian Gas," Carnegie Endowment for International Peace, September 7, 2022, carnegieendowment.org/politika/87837; Richard Milne, Henry Foy, and David Sheppard, "Sabotage of Gas Pipelines a Wake-up Call for Europe, Officials warn," *Financial Times*, September 28, 2022, www.ft.com/content/ad885fea-035f-4b93-98e7-c75da2c308f8.

384 **dropped by more than 80 percent:** Kong Chyong, Anne-Sophie Corbeau, and Ira Joseph, "Future Options for Russian Gas Exports," Columbia School for International and Public Affairs Center on Global Energy Policy, January 19, 2023, www.energypolicy.columbia.edu/publications/future-options -russian-gas-exports; "Nord Stream 1: How Russia Is Cutting Gas Supplies to Europe," *BBC News*, www .bbc.com/news/world-europe-60131520.

384 **more trouble sacrificing oil revenues:** Nastassia Astrasheuskaya, "Russia's Budget Surplus Evaporates as Energy Revenues Shrink," *Financial Times*, September 12, 2022, www.ft.com/content/d9cdc51f-5fe3-4f4a-b0e8-054ef21a2a6e.

384 **Democrats performed better than expected:** "Midterm News: Democrats Keep Control of Senate with Victory in Nevada," *The New York Times*, November 12, 2022, www.nytimes.com/live/2022/11/12/us/election-results-updates.

384 **sold another 15 million barrels:** Jasmin Melvin, "US to Complete 180-million Barrel SPR Drawdown, Lay Out Plan to Replenish Oil Reserves," S&P Global, October 19, 2022, www.spglobal.com/commodityinsights/en/market-insights/latest-news/oil/101922-us-to-complete-180-million-barrel-spr-drawdown-lay-out-plan-to-replenish-oil-reserve; "As Much as 15 Million Barrels of Crude Oil Sold from the U.S. Strategic Petroleum Reserve," U.S. Energy Information Administration, October 24, 2022, www.eia.gov/todayinenergy/detail.php?id=54359.

384 **massive wave of COVID infections:** Bernard Orr and Martin Quin Pollard, "China's COVID Infections Hit Record as Economic Outlook Darkens," Reuters, November 24, 2022, www.reuters.com/world/china/chinas-daily-covid-cases-hit-record-high-2022-11-24.

385 **Russia's marginal cost of production:** Notably, Rosneft's investor presentations showed that margins remained in the black even when market prices dipped under $20 during the early months of COVID. See "Financial Results for 4Q and 12M 2021," *Rosneft*, February 11, 2022, www.rosneft.com/upload/site2/document_cons_report/Q42021_Results_ENG_final.pdf; "Why Russian Oil Price Cap Is Easier Said Than Done," Reuters, June 28, 2022, www.reuters.com/business/energy/why-russian-oil-price-cap-is-easier-said-than-done-2022-06-28; Catherine Wolfram, Simon Johnson, and Lukasz Rachel, "The Price Cap on Russian Oil Exports, Explained," Harvard Kennedy School Belfer Center, December 2022, www.belfercenter.org/sites/default/files/files/publication/Brief_Russian%20Oil%20Price%20Cap_FINAL_0.pdf; Ricardo Hausmann, "The Case for a Punitive Tax on Russian Oil," *Project Syndicate*, February 26, 2022, www.project-syndicate.org/commentary/case-for-punitive-tax-on-russian-oil-by-ricardo-hausmann-2022-02.

385 **$45 per barrel:** Alena Yakushova, "The Ministry of Finance Revealed the First Losses from Falling Oil Prices," *Vedomosti*, April 3, 2020, www.vedomosti.ru/economics/articles/2020/04/03/827078-minfin-prodast-valyutu-na-778-mlrd-rublei; Nastassia Astrasheuskaya, Polina Ivanova, and Nick Peterson, "Russian Economy Could Weather Impact of EU Oil Ban, "*Financial Times*, May 5, 2022, www.ft.com/content/82dfa0f1-2a16-4358-ae67-29c69f6938c3.

385 **breakeven point had risen to at least $70:** "How Much Oil and Gas Revenue Will the New Oil Price Calculation Bring to the Budget," *RBC*, February 14, 2023, amp.rbc.ru/rbcnews/economics/14/02/2023/63ea2db49a794722ee2910ae; Lyubov Romanova, "The Ministry of Finance Expects the Share of Budget Revenues from the Sale of Oil and Gas in 2022 to Be Above 40%," *Vedomosti*, June 20, 2022, www.vedomosti.ru/economics/articles/2022/06/20/927599-minfin-byudzheta-prodazhi-nefti. Independent analysts projected that Russia's fiscal breakeven oil price in 2023 may even exceed $110 per barrel. See Craig Kennedy, "Measuring the Shadows: Chapter 7," *Navigating Russia*, Substack, August 23, 2023, navigatingrussia.substack.com/p/measuring-the-shadows#%C2%A7chapter-moscow-contrives-to-have-opec-solve-its-oil-price-problem.

385 **$55 and $65 per barrel:** Alan Rappeport, "What Price Is Right? Why Capping Russian Oil Is Complicated," *The New York Times*, September 16, 2022, www.nytimes.com/2022/09/16/business/russian-oil-price-cap.html.

385 **Kremlin warned would prompt Russia to cut off sales:** "Russia to Suspend Oil Supplies to States That Will Impose Restrictions on Price of Its Oil," Tass, September 1, 2022, tass.com/economy/1501249; "Russia Says It Will Stop Selling Oil to Countries That Set Price Caps," Reuters, September 2, 2022, www.reuters.com/business/energy/russia-says-it-will-stop-selling-oil-countries-that-impose-price-caps-2022-09-02.

386 **had just liberated Kherson:** Marc Santora et al., "Russia Orders Retreat from Kherson, a Serious Reversal in the Ukraine War," *The New York Times*, November 9, 2022, www.nytimes.com/2022/11/09/world/europe/ukraine-russia-kherson-retreat.html.

386 **cap north of $70:** Jan Strupczewski, "EU Split on Russian Oil Price Cap Level, Talks to Resume Thursday," Reuters, November 23, 2022, www.reuters.com/business/energy/g7-looking-russian-oil-price-cap-65-70-per-barrel-eu-diplomat-2022-11-23; "Urals Oil: Price," *Trading Economics*, https://tradingeconomics.com/commodity/urals-oil; Jorge Liboreiro and Efi Koutsokosta, "Following G7 Plan, EU Countries Agree to Cap Russian Oil at $60 per Barrel," *Euronews*, December 2, 2022, www.euronews.com/my-europe/2022/12/02/following-g7-plan-eu-countries-near-deal-to-cap-russian-oil-at-60-per-barrel.

386 **internal EU horse-trading:** Strupczewski, "EU Split on Russian Oil Price Cap."

386 **Warsaw agreed to relent:** Andrew Duehren, "How Washington Persuaded Europe to Put a Price Cap on Russian Oil," *The Wall Street Journal*, December 11, 2022, www.wsj.com/articles/how-washington-persuaded-europe-to-put-a-price-cap-on-russian-oil-11670715983.

386 **set just over forty-eight hours before:** Andrew Duehren and Laurence Norman, "G-7 Set Russian Oil Price Cap of $60 a Barrel," *The Wall Street Journal*, December 2, 2022, www.wsj.com/articles/eu-g-7-wait-on-poland-to-advance-with-russian-oil-price-cap-11669983529?mod=article_inline.

386 **traffic jam formed at the mouth of the Bosphorus:** Tom Wilson, "How the G7's Oil Price Cap Blocked the Bosphorus," *Financial Times*, December 6, 2022, www.ft.com/content/dc40a88f-7d20-4a17-a37c -332f35b65942.

386 **"remain in place under any circumstances":** "Turkey: Request from Authorities for Confirmatory Letters of P&I Cover for Ships Entering International Straits and Turkish Waters, Ports and Termi- nals," The London P&I Club, December 5, 2022, www.londonpandi.com/knowledge/news-alerts/turkey -request-from-authorities-for-confirmatory-letters-of-pi-cover-for-ships-entering-international-straits -and-turkish-waters-ports-and-terminals.

386 **requirement went "well beyond" the norm:** "Turkey: Request from Authorities," The London P&I Club.

386–87 **"catastrophic consequences for our country":** Wilson, "Price Cap."

387 **allowed the tankers to proceed:** Ian Smith, Tom Wilson, and Ayla Jean Yackley, "Insurance Dispute Blocking Oil Tankers in Turkish Waters Resolved," *Financial Times*, December 13, 2022, www.ft.com /content/dfe37d21-6462-43ae-8e3d-1263c0d82604.

387 **below $80 per barrel:** "European Brent Spot Price FOB," U.S. Energy Information Administration, www.eia.gov/dnav/pet/hist/LeafHandler.ashx?n=PET&s=RBRTE&f=M; Jimmy Troderman, "Crude Oil Prices Increased in First-Half 2022 and Declined in Second-Half 2022," U.S. Energy Information Administration, January 4, 2023, www.eia.gov/todayinenergy/detail.php?id=55079.

387 **price of Russian oil fell even further:** "Russia's Urals Oil Averaged $57.49/bbl in Past Month, Below Price Cap," Reuters, December 16, 2022, www.reuters.com/business/energy/russias-urals-oil-averaged -5749bbl-past-month-below-price-cap-2022-12-16.

387 **discounts of $30 or more:** "The Price Cap on Russian Oil: A Progress Report," U.S. Department of the Treasury, May 18, 2023, home.treasury.gov/news/featured-stories/the-price-cap-on-russian-oil-a -progress-report.

387 **took more than a month:** Nuran Erkul, "Oil Trade Routes That Take at Least 5 Times as Long after War Will Likely Result in More Pollution," *Anadolu Ajansi*, April 26, 2023, www.aa.com.tr/en/economy /oil-trade-routes-that-take-at-least-5-times-as-long-after-war-will-likely-result-in-more-pollution /2881764#.

387 **oil revenues were down by nearly 50 percent:** "Russian Oil and Gas Budget Revenues Almost Halved in the First Half of the Year," Reuters, July 5, 2023, www.reuters.com/business/energy/russian-oil-gas -budget-revenues-almost-halved-january-june-2023-07-05.

387 **lose over $1 trillion:** Laura Cozzi and Jason Bordoff, "World Energy Outlook 2022: An Insider's Look," Columbia Energy Exchange, November 29, 2022, www.energypolicy.columbia.edu/world-energy-outlook -2022-insider-s-look.

388 **"very difficult" undertaking:** Daniel Yergin, hosted by Michael Morrell, "Global Energy Expert Dan- iel Yergin," *Intelligence Matters* (podcast), *CBS News*, August 31, 2022, www.cbsnews.com/news/energy -daniel-yergin-on-energy-security-intelligence-matters.

388 **"the end of the global oil market":** Daniel Yergin, "Putin Can't Count on the Global Oil Market," *The Wall Street Journal*, December 26, 2022, www.wsj.com/articles/putin-cant-count-on-the-global-oil-market -price-cap-revenue-production-cut-friedman-biden-eu-russia-energy-11672065849.

CHAPTER 65: "SMALL YARD AND HIGH FENCE"

391 **a hefty stash of computer chips:** "Woman with Fake Baby Bump Caught Smuggling Computer Chips into China," *Bloomberg*, December 2, 2022, www.bloomberg.com/news/articles/2022-12-02/woman -with-fake-baby-bump-caught-smuggling-computer-chips-into-china.

391 **stockpile as many foreign-made semiconductors:** Che Pan, "Tech War: Chinese Chip Firms Stock- pile Equipment Ahead of US-Japan-Netherlands Agreement on Tightening Export Controls," *South China Morning Post*, February 24, 2023, www.scmp.com/tech/tech-war/article/3211416/tech-war -chinese-chip-firms-stockpile-equipment-ahead-us-japan-netherlands-agreement-tightening.

391 **new export controls on China:** "Commerce Implements New Export Controls on Advanced Comput- ing and Semiconductor Manufacturing Items to the People's Republic of China (PRC)," Bureau of In- dustry and Security, U.S. Department of Commerce, October 7, 2022, www.bis.doc.gov/index.php /documents/about-bis/newsroom/press-releases/3158-2022-10-07-bis-press-release-advanced-computing -and-semiconductor-manufacturing-controls-final/file.

391 **boilerplate press release:** "Commerce Implements New Export Controls," Bureau of Industry and Security.

392 **supremacy in frontier technologies:** As Secretary of State Tony Blinken said at a speech at Stanford University, "We are at an inflection point. The post–Cold War world has come to an end, and there is an intense competition underway to shape what comes next. And at the heart of that competition is technology. Technology will in many ways retool our economies. It will reform our militaries. It will reshape the lives of people across the planet. And so it's profoundly a source of national strength." See Antony J. Blinken, "Remarks to the Press" (speech, Stanford, CA, October 17, 2022), U.S. Department of State, www.state.gov/secretary-antony-blinken-remarks-to-the-press-3.

392 **Center for Security and Emerging Technology:** Nick Anderson, "Georgetown Launches Think Tank on Security and Emerging Technology," *The Washington Post*, February 28, 2019, www.washingtonpost.com/local/education/georgetown-launches-think-tank-on-security-and-emerging-technology/2019/02/27/d6dabc62-391f-11e9-a2cd-307b06d0257b_story.html.

392 **number-one trading partner in goods:** "The People's Republic of China: China Trade & Investment Summary," Office of the United States Trade Representative, ustr.gov/countries-regions/china-mongolia-taiwan/peoples-republic-china; "Trade Goods with China," United States Census Bureau, www.census.gov/foreign-trade/balance/c5700.html.

393 **extensive training by ASML personnel:** Jessica Timings, "Busting ASML Myths," *ASML*, February 23, 2022, www.asml.com/en/news/stories/2022/busting-asml-myths; Chris Miller, *Chip War: The Fight for the World's Most Critical Technology* (New York: Scribner, 2022), 229.

393 **size of a bus:** Timings, "Busting ASML Myths"; Will Knight, "The $150 Million Machine Keeping Moore's Law Alive," *Wired*, August 30, 2021, www.wired.com/story/asml-extreme-ultraviolet-lithography-chips-moores-law.

393 **continue withholding the license that ASML needed:** Stu Woo and Yang Jie, "China Wants a Chip Machine from the Dutch. The U.S. Said No," *The Wall Street Journal*, July 17, 2021, www.wsj.com/articles/china-wants-a-chip-machine-from-the-dutch-the-u-s-said-no-11626514513.

393 **warned that export controls could backfire:** Woo and Jie, "China Wants a Chip Machine."

393 **biggest buyer of semiconductor manufacturing equipment:** "2021 Global Semiconductor Equipment Sales Surge 44% to Industry Record $102.6 Billion, SEMI Reports," *PR Newswire*, April 12, 2022, www.prnewswire.com/news-releases/2021-global-semiconductor-equipment-sales-surge-44-to-industry-record-102-6-billion-semi-reports-301523886.html.

393 **Japan, whose semiconductor industry:** Julian Ryall, "Japan Strengthens Hold on Semiconductor Raw Materials amid Global Chip Shortage," *South China Morning Post*, September 28, 2021, www.scmp.com/week-asia/politics/article/3150323/japan-strengthens-hold-semiconductor-raw-materials-amid-global.

393 **FDPR against Russia:** "America Has a Plan to Throttle Chinese Chipmakers," *The Economist*, April 30, 2022, www.economist.com/business/america-has-a-plan-to-throttle-chinese-chipmakers/21808959.

393 **restrictions issued by almost forty other governments:** "Commerce Implements Sweeping Restrictions on Exports to Russia in Response to Further Invasion of Ukraine," Bureau of Industry and Security, U.S. Department of Commerce, February 24, 2022, www.bis.doc.gov/index.php/documents/about-bis/newsroom/press-releases/2914-2022-02-24-bis-russia-rule-press-release-and-tweets-final/file; "Fact Sheet: The Impact of Sanctions and Export Controls on the Russian Federation," U.S. Department of State, October 20, 2022, www.state.gov/the-impact-of-sanctions-and-export-controls-on-the-russian-federation.

393 **havoc on Russia's military-industrial complex:** "Impact of Sanctions and Export Controls," U.S. Department of State.

393 **maintain "as large of a lead as possible":** Jake Sullivan, "Remarks by National Security Advisor Jake Sullivan at the Special Competitive Studies Project Global Emerging Technologies Summit" (speech, Washington, D.C., September 16, 2022), The White House, www.whitehouse.gov/briefing-room/speeches-remarks/2022/09/16/remarks-by-national-security-advisor-jake-sullivan-at-the-special-competitive-studies-project-global-emerging-technologies-summit.

394 **"took advantage of our complacency and inherent openness":** Sullivan, "Remarks."

394 **Nancy Pelosi traveled to Taiwan:** David Rising, "China's Response to Pelosi Visit a Sign of Future Intentions," The Associated Press, August 19, 2022, apnews.com/article/taiwan-china-beijing-congress-8857910a1e44cefa70bc4dfd184ef880.

394 **dry run for an amphibious assault:** Alastair Gale and Nancy A. Youssef, "China's Military Exercises Showcase Modern Fighting Force Preparing for Possible War in the Taiwan Strait," *The Wall Street Journal*, August 7, 2022, www.wsj.com/articles/chinas-military-exercises-showcase-modern-fighting-force-preparing-for-possible-war-in-the-taiwan-strait-11659906152.

394 **commercial ships evacuated the waters around Taiwan:** Costas Paris, "China Military Drills Prompt Ships to Leave Taiwan Waters," *The Wall Street Journal*, August 5, 2022, www.wsj.com/articles/china-military-drills-prompt-ships-to-leave-taiwan-waters-11659712279.

394 **banned imports from more than a hundred Taiwanese brands:** Cindy Wang, "China Slaps Export Ban on 100 Taiwanese Brands Before Pelosi Visit," *Bloomberg*, August 2, 2022, www.bloomberg.com/news/articles/2022-08-02/china-slaps-export-ban-on-100-taiwan-brands-before-pelosi-visit; Akio Yaita and Sankei Shimbun, "China Begins to Exact Revenge on the People of Taiwan," *Japan Forward*, August 8, 2022, japan-forward.com/china-begins-to-exact-revenge-on-the-people-of-taiwan.

394 **ordered Nvidia to stop selling its marquee graphics processing units:** Liza Lin and Dan Strumpf, "Latest U.S. Chips Curbs Deliver Setback to China's AI Ambitions," *The Wall Street Journal*, September 1, 2022, www.wsj.com/articles/latest-u-s-chip-curbs-deliver-setback-to-chinas-ai-ambitions-11662037050.

394 **CHIPS and Science Act:** Justin Badlam et al., "The CHIPS and Science Act: Here's What's in It," McKinsey & Company, October 4, 2022, www.mckinsey.com/industries/public-sector/our-insights/the-chips-and-science-act-heres-whats-in-it; The White House, "Fact Sheet: CHIPS and Science Act Will Lower Costs, Create Jobs, Strengthen Supply Chains, and Counter China," August 9, 2022, www.whitehouse

.gov/briefing-room/statements-releases/2022/08/09/fact-sheet-chips-and-science-act-will-lower
-costs-create-jobs-strengthen-supply-chains-and-counter-china.

394 **90 percent of the world's most advanced chips:** "Taiwan's Dominance of the Chip Industry Makes It More Important," *The Economist*, March 6, 2023, www.economist.com/special-report/2023/03/06 /taiwans-dominance-of-the-chip-industry-makes-it-more-important; Jason Hsu, "Can the US Regain the Lead in the Microchip Race?," Ash Center for Democratic Governance and Innovation, Harvard Kennedy School, July 29, 2022, ash.harvard.edu/global-microchip-production-can-we-catch; David Sacks and Chris Miller, "The War over the World's Most Critical Technology: A Conversation with Chris Miller," Council on Foreign Relations, January 3, 2023, www.cfr.org/blog/war-over-worlds-most -critical-technology-conversation-chris-miller.

394 **as a "down payment":** Alan F. Estevez, interview by Martijn Rasser, Center for New American Security Technology and National Security Program, October 27, 2022, www.cnas.org/publications/transcript /a-conversation-with-under-secretary-of-commerce-alan-f-estevez.

394 **Applied Materials, Lam Research, and KLA:** Qianer Liu, Kathrin Hille, and Yuan Yang, "World's Top Chip Equipment Suppliers Halt Business with China," *Financial Times*, October 13, 2022, www .ft.com/content/51f9ec46-ec9e-43a1-ba64-45e0e6e6da71.

394 **halt dealings with Chinese customers:** Liu, Hille, and Yang, "World's Top Chip Equipment Suppliers."

395 **Chinese chip stocks lost almost $10 billion:** Hudson Lockett, "China Chip Stocks Lose $8.6bn in Wipeout Due to US Export Controls," *Financial Times*, October 10, 2022, www.ft.com/content/63a408cf -b4cc-4825-a6aa-ad829142e335.

395 **the Netherlands and Japan agreed:** Takashi Mochizuki, Cagan Koc, and Peter Elstrom, "Japan to Join US Effort to Tighten Chip Exports to China," *Bloomberg*, December 12, 2022, www.bloomberg.com /news/articles/2022-12-12/japan-is-said-to-join-us-effort-to-tighten-chip-exports-to-china; Andy Bounds and Demetri Sevastopulo, "Netherlands to Restrict Chip Exports after US Pressure Over China Threat," *Financial Times*, March 8, 2023, www.ft.com/content/e911774c-a048-4ed1-9f90-e4bb684a3156; Takahiko Hyuga and Yuki Furukawa, "Japan Tightens Chip Gear Exports as US Seeks to Contain China," *Bloomberg*, March 30, 2023, www.bloomberg.com/news/articles/2023-03-31/japan-tightens-chip-gear -exports-as-us-seeks-to-contain-china.

395 **through the Inflation Reduction Act:** The White House, "Fact Sheet: The Inflation Reduction Act Supports Workers and Families," August 19, 2022, www.whitehouse.gov/briefing-room/statements-releases /2022/08/19/fact-sheet-the-inflation-reduction-act-supports-workers-and-families.

395 **"de-risking and diversifying, not decoupling":** Jake Sullivan, "Remarks by National Security Advisor Jake Sullivan on Renewing American Economic Leadership at the Brookings Institution" (speech, Washington, D.C., April 27, 2023), The White House, www.whitehouse.gov/briefing-room/speeches -remarks/2023/04/27/remarks-by-national-security-advisor-jake-sullivan-on-renewing-american -economic-leadership-at-the-brookings-institution.

395 **a "small yard" of foundational technologies with a "high fence":** Sullivan, "Remarks."

395 **three technological "families":** Sullivan noted that "computing-related technologies" encompassed "microelectronics, quantum information systems, and artificial intelligence." Sullivan, "Remarks."

396 **restricting exports of gallium and germanium:** Hanna Ziady and Xiaofei Xu, "China Hits Back in the Chip War, Imposing Export Curbs on Crucial Raw Materials," CNN, July 3, 2023, www.cnn.com/2023 /07/03/business/germanium-gallium-china-export-restrictions/index.html; Zeyi Yang, "China Just Fought Back in the Semiconductor Exports War. Here's What You Need to Know," *MIT Technology Review*, July 10, 2023, www.technologyreview.com/2023/07/10/1076025/china-export-control-semiconductor -material.

396 **€140 million in cash:** Deborah Haynes, "Russia Flew €140m in Cash and Captured Western Weapons to Iran in Return for Deadly Drones, Source Claims," *Sky News*, July 13, 2022, news.sky.com/story /russia-gave-eur140m-and-captured-western-weapons-to-iran-in-return-for-deadly-drones-source -claims-12741742.

396 **Japanese kamikaze pilots:** Aamer Madhani, Colleen Long, and Zeke Miller, "Russia Is Seeking More Attack Drones from Iran after Depleting Stockpile, White House Says," PBS, May 15, 2023, www.pbs .org/newshour/world/russia-is-seeking-more-attack-drones-from-iran-after-depleting-stockpile -white-house-says.

396 **deepen their commercial ties:** As CIA Director Bill Burns said, "What's beginning to emerge is at least the beginnings of a full-fledged defense partnership between Russia and Iran." See William J. Burns, interview by Judy Woodruff, "CIA Director Bill Burns on War in Ukraine, Intelligence Challenges Posed by China," *News Hour*, PBS, December 16, 2022, www.pbs.org/newshour/show/cia-director -bill-burns-on-war-in-ukraine-intelligence-challenges-posed-by-china. Sino-Russian trade surged at the start of 2023 as China sent Russia microchips, trench-digging excavators, bulletproof vests, helmets, and myriad other equipment. See Philip Wang, "China Sees Biggest Trade Increase with Russia in 2023, Chinese Customs Data Shows," CNN, June 7, 2023, www.cnn.com/2023/06/07/business /china-russia-trade-increase-intl/index.html, Sarah Anne Aarup, Sergey Panov, and Douglas Busvine, "China Secretly Sends Enough Gear to Russia to Equip an Army," *Politico*, July 24, 2023, www.politico .eu/article/china-firms-russia-body-armor-bullet-proof-drones-thermal-optics-army-equipment

-shanghai-h-win, and Austin Ramzy and Jason Douglas, "Booming Trade with China Helps Boost Russia's War Effort," *The Wall Street Journal*, August 21, 2023, www.wsj.com/world/china/booming -china-russia-trade-sends-trench-digging-machines-to-ukraines-front-lines-85f5b5ff.

396 **helped break Tehran's diplomatic isolation:** Keith Bradsher, "China's Economic Stake in the Middle East: Its Thirst for Oil," *The New York Times*, October 11, 2023, www.nytimes.com/2023/10/11/business /china-oil-saudi-arabia-iran.html; Peter Baker, "Chinese-Brokered Deal Upends Mideast Diplomacy and Challenges U.S.," *The New York Times*, March 11, 2023, www.nytimes.com/2023/03/11/us/politics /saudi-arabia-iran-china-biden.html.

397 **"replaced by global market forces":** Quoted in Adam Tooze, "Beyond the Crash," *The Guardian*, July 29, 2018, www.theguardian.com/commentisfree/2018/jul/29/city-of-london-desperate-gamble -china-vulnerable-economy.

CHAPTER 66: THE SCRAMBLE FOR ECONOMIC SECURITY

398 **"Every night I ask myself":** Joe Leahy and Hudson Lockett, "Brazil's Lula Calls for End to Dollar Trade Dominance," *Financial Times*, April 13, 2023, www.ft.com/content/669260a5-82a5-4e7a-9bbf -4f41c54a6143.

399 **growing tensions between two of its members:** Jeffrey Gettleman, Hari Kumar, and Sameer Yasir, "Worst Clash in Decades on Disputed India-China Border Kills 20 Indian Troops," *The New York Times*, June 16, 2020, www.nytimes.com/2020/06/16/world/asia/indian-china-border-clash.html.

400 **The COVID pandemic and the attendant supply-chain:** Even before Russia's invasion of Ukraine, a McKinsey study found that a majority of companies across a wide range of industries were taking steps to protect their supply chains from disruption, motivated in large part by the pandemic. See Knut Alicke, Ed Barriball, and Vera Trautwein, "How COVID-19 Is Reshaping Supply Chains," McKinsey & Company, November 23, 2021, www.mckinsey.com/capabilities/operations/our-insights/how-covid-19 -is-reshaping-supply-chains.

400 **Overseeing this shift:** Governments might hope to wall off only select sectors of their economies, but many businesses have started moving at a faster pace than required by government policy. Businesses have done so owing to their changing assessment of risk: in a survey of 500 institutional investors about the top risks to the global economy in 2024, geopolitics ranked number one. See Chris Miller, "The West's De-Risking Strategy Towards China Will Fail, Says Chris Miller," *The Economist*, August 4, 2023, www.economist.com/by-invitation/2023/08/04/the-wests-de-risking-strategy-towards-china -will-fail-says-chris-miller; Jami Miscik, Peter Orszag, and Theodore Bunzel, "Geopolitics in the C-Suite," Foreign Affairs, March 11, 2024, foreignaffairs.com/united-states/geopolitics-c-suite.

400 **Beijing and Moscow had long waged economic wars:** Keith Bradsher, "Amid Tension, China Blocks Vital Exports to Japan," *The New York Times*, September 22, 2010, www.nytimes.com/2010/09/23 /business/global/23rare.html; Farah Master, "Empty Hotels, Idle Boats: What Happens When a Pacific Island Upsets China," Reuters, August 19, 2018, www.reuters.com/article/us-pacific-china-palau-insight /empty-hotels-idle-boats-what-happens-when-a-pacific-island-upsets-china-idUSKBN1L4036; for a comprehensive discussion of Chinese economic warfare, see Bethany Allen, *Beijing Rules: How China Weaponized Its Economy to Confront the World* (New York: HarperCollins, 2023).

400 **tactics grew more aggressive:** In recent years, Beijing has established the legal and bureaucratic machinery to wield sanctions and export controls resembling America's own. See Jeannette Chu, "The New Arms Race: Sanctions, Export Control Policy, and China," Center for Strategic & International Studies, March 25, 2022, www.csis.org/analysis/new-arms-race-sanctions-export-control-policy-and -china. Russia, for its part, openly weaponized its gas exports against Europe. See Samantha Gross and Constanze Stelzenmüller, "Europe's Messy Russian Gas Divorce," Brookings Institution, June 18, 2024, www.brookings.edu/articles/europes-messy-russian-gas-divorce.

400 **"This version of globalization":** Yuka Hayashi, "U.S. Trade Chief Outlines Policy Shift, Citing Ukraine War and Pandemic," *The Wall Street Journal*, March 30, 2023, www.wsj.com/articles/u-s-trade-chief -outlines-policy-shift-citing-ukraine-war-and-pandemic-11648667442.

400 **as Janet Yellen put it, was "friendshoring":** Janet L. Yellen, "The Way Forward for the Global Economy" (speech, Washington, D.C., April 13, 2022), U.S. Department of the Treasury, home.treasury.gov /news/press-releases/jy0714.

400 **but rather "secure trade":** Yellen, "The Way Forward."

400 **G7 issued a sweeping statement:** The White House, "G7 Hiroshima Leaders' Communiqué" (Hiroshima: G7, May 20, 2023), www.whitehouse.gov/briefing-room/statements-releases/2023/05/20/g7-hiroshima -leaders-communique; The White House, "G7 Leaders' Statement on Economic Resilience and Economic Security," May 20, 2023, www.whitehouse.gov/briefing-room/statements-releases/2023/05/20 /g7-leaders-statement-on-economic-resilience-and-economic-security.

400 **defend itself against "economic coercion":** The White House, "G7 Leaders' Statement," May 20, 2023.

401 **Japan, the summit's host:** "Japan's Economic Security Legislation," European Parliament, www.europarl .europa.eu/RegData/etudes/ATAG/2023/751417/EPRS_ATA(2023)751417_EN.pdf; "Japan's Economic Security Promotion Act and the Implications for Businesses," International Institute for Strategic

Studies, May 2022, www.iiss.org/publications/strategic-comments/2022/japans-economic-security
-promotion-act-and-the-implications-for-businesses; Shiela A. Smith, "Japan Turns Its Attention to
Economic Security," Council on Foreign Relations, May 16, 2022, www.cfr.org/blog/japan-turns-its
-attention-economic-security; "Summary of Economic Security Promotion Act," Council on Foreign Relations, www.cfr.org/sites/default/files/pdf/economic%20security%20promotion%20act%20%28summary
%29%28English%29.pdf?utm_source=sendupdatelogo.

401 **Economic Security Strategy:** "An EU Approach to Enhance Economic Security," European Commission, June 20, 2023, ec.europa.eu/commission/presscorner/detail/en/IP_23_3358.

401 **call a "security dilemma":** John H. Herz, "Idealist Internationalism and the Security Dilemma," *World
Politics* 2, no. 2 (1950), 157–80, www.jstor.org/stable/2009187.

CHAPTER 67: BREAKING THE CHOKEPOINTS

402 **uncovering the sanctions evasion scheme:** Steve Stecklow, "Exclusive: Huawei CFO Linked to Firm
That Offered HP Gear to Iran," Reuters, January 31, 2023, www.reuters.com/article/uk-huawei-skycom
/exclusive-huawei-cfo-linked-to-firm-that-offered-hp-gear-to-iran-idUKBRE90U0CA20130131; Kate
Conger, "Huawei Executive Took Part in Sanctions Fraud, Prosecutors Say," *The New York Times*, December 7, 2018, www.nytimes.com/2018/12/07/technology/huawei-meng-wanzhou-fraud.html.

402 **replace the dollar as the backbone:** "Libra: Facebook's Digital Currency," *Financial Times*, www.ft
.com/content/0c5c4012-9100-11e9-b7ea-60e35ef678d2.

402 **without passing through the intermediary infrastructure:** Timothy G. Massad, "Facebook's Libra
2.0," The Brookings Institution, June 22, 2020, www.brookings.edu/articles/facebooks-libra-2-0; Jahid
Elgarni and Isabelle Bufflier, "Is Facebook's Diem the Future of Cryptocurrency or a Financial Pipe
Dream?" Skema Business School, February 1, 2022, knowledge.skema.edu/is-facebooks-diem-the-future
-of-cryptocurrency-or-a-financial-pipe-dream.

402 **"move fast and break things":** Drake Baer, "Mark Zuckerberg Explains Why Facebook Doesn't 'Move
Fast and Break Things' Anymore," *Business Insider*, May 2, 2014, www.businessinsider.com/mark
-zuckerberg-on-facebooks-new-motto-2014-5.

402–3 **"I thought crypto was a threat":** Author interview with Stuart Levey, 2023.

403 **hoped that Levey could win over regulators:** Hannah Murphy and Kiran Stacey, "Facebook Libra: the
Inside Story of How the Company's Cryptocurrency Dream Died," *Financial Times*, March 10, 2022,
www.ft.com/content/a88fb591-72d5-4b6b-bb5d-223adfb893f3.

403 **creation of alternative intermediaries:** Barry Eichengreen, "Sanctions, SWIFT, and China's Cross-
Border Interbank System," Center for Strategic & International Studies, May 20, 2022, www.csis.org
/analysis/sanctions-swift-and-chinas-cross-border-interbank-payments-system.

403 **owing to American monetary policy:** Adam Tooze, "Is This the End of the American Century?" *London Review of Books* 42, no. 7 (April 4, 2019), www.lrb.co.uk/the-paper/v41/n07/adam-tooze/is-this
-the-end-of-the-american-century.

403 **global lender of last resort:** Adam Tooze, *Crashed: How a Decade of Financial Crises Changed the
World* (New York: Viking, 2018), 9–11.

403 **swap lines to distribute dollar funding:** Adam Tooze, *Shutdown: How Covid Shook the World's Economy* (New York: Viking, 2021), 122–26.

403 **shore up faith in the dollar:** Edoardo Saravalle, "How U.S. Sanctions Depend on the Federal Reserve,"
Center for New American Security, July 29, 2020, www.cnas.org/publications/commentary/how-u-s
-sanctions-depend-on-the-federal-reserve.

403 **Beijing devalued its currency:** Gabriel Wildau and Tom Mitchell, "China: Renminbi Stalls on Road to
Being a Global Currency," *Financial Times*, December 11, 2016, www.ft.com/content/e480fd92-bc6a
-11e6-8b45-b8b81dd5d080; Helen Thompson, *Disorder: Hard Times in the 21st Century* (Oxford: Oxford University Press, 2022), 124; Leslie Shaffer, "365 Days Later: China's Yuan Falls without the Horror
Show," CNBC, August 10, 2016, www.cnbc.com/2016/08/10/china-economy-news-one-year-after-yuan
-devaluation-renminbi-poised-to-fall-further.html.

403 **fell by more than half:** Gerard DiPippo and Andrea Leonard Palazzi, "It's All about Networking: The
Limits of Renminbi Internationalization," Center for Strategic & International Studies, April 18, 2023,
www.csis.org/analysis/its-all-about-networking-limits-renminbi-internationalization.

403–4 **less than 30 percent of its trade:** Gerard DiPippo (@gdp1985), "PBOC data for currency settlement
are out," Twitter, July 25, 2023, twitter.com/gdp1985/status/1683822144822579200; Gerard DiPippo
(@gdp1985), "China-Russia trade may have maxed out," Twitter, July 4, 2024, twitter.com/gdp1985
/status/1808923741147312319; "RMB Tracker Slides," Swift, August 2023, www.swift.com/our-solutions
/compliance-and-shared-services/business-intelligence/renminbi/rmb-tracker/rmb-tracker-document
-centre.

404 **e-CNY's adoption by hundreds of millions:** Jonathan Cheng, "China Rolls Out Pilot Test of Digital
Currency," *The Wall Street Journal*, April 20, 2020, www.wsj.com/articles/china-rolls-out-pilot-test
-of-digital-currency-11587385339; Rae Wee, "China's Digital Yuan Transactions Seeing Strong Momentum, Says Cbank Gov Yi," Reuters, July 19, 2023, www.reuters.com/markets/asia/chinas-digital
-yuan-transactions-seeing-strong-momentum-says-cbank-gov-yi-2023-07-19.

404 **standard setter in digital currencies:** Martin Chorzempa, "What China's Embrace of Digital Currency Means for the World," in *Rethinking the Power of Money* (Washington: Wilson Center, March 2023), www.wilsoncenter.org/sites/default/files/media/uploads/documents/GEO-230105%20-%20Rethinking%20Money%20report%20-%20combined.pdf.

404 **Beijing can monitor all transactions:** Eichengreen, "Sanctions, SWIFT, and China's Cross-Border Interbank System."

404 **more alarmed if China possessed the same capabilities:** "China Punishes Australia for Promoting an Inquiry into Covid-19," *The Economist*, May 21, 2020, www.economist.com/asia/2020/05/21/china-punishes-australia-for-promoting-an-inquiry-into-covid-19; Matthew Reynolds and Matthew P. Goodman, "China's Economic Coercion: Lessons from Lithuania," Center for Strategic & International Studies, May 6, 2022, www.csis.org/analysis/chinas-economic-coercion-lessons-lithuania; Michael Walsh, "Australia Called for a COVID-19 Probe. China Responded with a Trade War," *ABC News Australia*, January 2, 2021, www.abc.net.au/news/2021-01-03/heres-what-happened-between-china-and-australia-in-2020/13019242.

404 **payment apps, Alipay and WeChat:** Chorzempa, "China's Embrace."

405 **India banned dozens:** Sankalp Phartiyal, "India Bans 200-Plus Chinese Mobile Apps in Boon for Paytm," *Bloomberg*, February 7, 2020, www.bloomberg.com/news/articles/2023-02-07/ant-backed-paytm-soars-after-report-india-banned-chinese-rivals; Jacob Kastrenakes, "India Bans PUBG Mobile, Alipay, Baidu, and More Chinese Apps," *The Verge*, September 2, 2020, www.theverge.com/2020/9/2/21418120/pubg-mobile-india-ban-118-apps-china-alipay-baidu.

405 **it is WhatsApp:** Alex Heath and Shirin Ghaffary, "How India Runs on WhatsApp," *The Verge*, August 24, 2022, www.theverge.com/23320306/whatsapp-india-messaging-business-privacy-land-of-the-giants.

405 **Diem folded in 2022:** Murphy and Stacey, "Facebook Libra."

405 **pilot a digital dollar:** Lananh Nguyen, "Banking Giants and New York Fed Start 12-Week Digital Dollar Pilot," Reuters, November 15, 2022, www.reuters.com/markets/currencies/banking-giants-new-york-fed-start-12-week-digital-dollar-pilot-2022-11-15.

405 **speed up cross-border payments:** Michelle Neal, "Advances in Digital Currency Experimentation" (speech, Singapore, November 4, 2022), Bank for International Settlements, www.bis.org/review/r221104c.htm; "Project Cedar: Phase One Report" (New York: Federal Reserve Bank of New York, Fall 2022), www.newyorkfed.org/medialibrary/media/nyic/project-cedar-phase-one-report.pdf.

405 **renminbi remains a far riskier alternative:** Alan Beattie, "The Fundamental Reason China Will Struggle to Dethrone the Dollar," *Financial Times*, August 31, 2023, www.ft.com/content/daa1f8a6-3c49-426c-b08f-2c569837bd6d.

406 **a "shadow fleet":** Craig Kennedy, "Measuring the Shadows: Chapter 4: Can Russia Close Its 'Tanker Gap'?" *Navigating Russia*, Substack, August 23, 2023, navigatingrussia.substack.com/p/measuring-the-shadows#%C2%A7chapter-can-russia-close-its-tanker-gap.

406 **help of sovereign guarantees:** Nidhi Verma, "Iran Offers India $1 bln Sovereign Guarantee for Oil Shipments," Reuters, July 23, 2013, www.reuters.com/article/india-iran-shipment-guarantee/iran-offers-india-1-bln-sovereign-guarantee-for-oil-shipments-idINDEE96M09I20130723; Nidhi Verma and Rajesh Kumar Singh, "India Mulls Guarantee for Insuring Refiners That Use Iran Oil—Source," Reuters, August 8, 2013, www.reuters.com/article/us-india-iran-oil-insurance/india-mulls-guarantee-for-insuring-refiners-that-use-iran-oil-source-idUSBRE9770P220130808.

406 **China is already settling some of its energy bills:** Michael Stott and James Kynge, "China Capitalises on US Sanctions in Fight to Dethrone Dollar," *Financial Times*, August 24, 2023, www.ft.com/content/3888bdba-d0d6-49a1-9e78-4d07ce458f42; "China to Use Shanghai Exchange for Yuan Energy Deals with Gulf Nations," Reuters, December 9, 2022, www.reuters.com/business/energy/chinas-xi-tells-gulf-nations-use-shanghai-exchange-yuan-energy-deals-2022-12-09.

406–7 **demand similar arrangements for their own currencies:** Javier Blas, "The Myth of Inevitable Rise of a Petroyuan," *Bloomberg*, February 27, 2023, www.bloomberg.com/opinion/articles/2023-02-27/pricing-petroleum-in-china-s-yuan-sounds-inevitable-not-for-saudi-arabia.

407 **tens of billions of additional dollars:** Julie Zhu et al., "Exclusive: China to Launch $40 Billion State Fund to Boost Chip Industry," Reuters, September 5, 2023, www.reuters.com/technology/china-launch-new-40-bln-state-fund-boost-chip-industry-sources-say-2023-09-05.

407 **put Huawei in charge:** Gregory C. Allen, "In Chip Race, China Gives Huawei the Steering Wheel: Huawei's New Smartphone and the Future of Semiconductor Export Controls," Center for Strategic & International Studies, October 6, 2023, www.csis.org/analysis/chip-race-china-gives-huawei-steering-wheel-huaweis-new-smartphone-and-future; Ian King and Debby Wu, "Huawei Building Secret Network for Chips, Trade Group Warns," *Bloomberg*, August 22, 2023, www.bloomberg.com/news/articles/2023-08-23/huawei-building-secret-chip-plants-in-china-to-bypass-us-sanctions-group-warns.

407 **matched the latest iPhone:** Vlad Savov and Debby Wu, "Huawei Teardown Shows Chip Breakthrough in Blow to US Sanctions," September 4, 2023, www.bloomberg.com/news/features/2023-09-04/look-inside-huawei-mate-60-pro-phone-powered-by-made-in-china-chip.

407 **Known as the Mate 60 Pro:** Qianer Liu, "How Huawei Surprised the US with a Cutting-Edge Chip Made in China," *Financial Times*, November 30, 2023, www.ft.com/content/327414d2-fe13-438e-9767-333cdb94c7e1.

407 **coincide with a trip to Beijing:** Eva Dou, "New Phone Sparks Worry China Has Found a Way around U.S. Tech Limits," *The Washington Post*, September 2, 2023, www.washingtonpost.com/technology /2023/09/02/huawei-raimondo-phone-chip-sanctions; "China Secretly Transforms Huawei into Most Powerful Chip War Weapon," *Bloomberg*, December 1, 2023, www.bloomberg.com/graphics/2023-china -huawei-semiconductor.

407 **"Extreme suppression by the U.S.":** Quoted in Che Pan, "Tech War: Huawei Surprises Again with Low-Key Presales of Top-of-the-Line Mate 60 Pro+ as US-Blacklisted Firm Stays Mum over 'Break-through' 5G Mobile Chip," *South China Morning Post*, September 8, 2023, www.scmp.com/tech/big-tech /article/3233921/tech-war-huawei-surprises-again-low-key-presales-top-line-mate-60-pro-us-blacklisted -firm-stays-mum.

407 **It turned out the Chinese companies:** Cagan Koc and Mackenzie Hawkins, "Huawei Chip Break-through Used Tech from Two US Gear Suppliers," *Bloomberg*, March 7, 2024, www.bloomberg.com /news/articles/2024-03-08/huawei-chip-breakthrough-used-tech-from-two-us-gear-suppliers; Allen, "In Chip Race"; Qianer Liu, "Huawei Surprised the US."

407 **five years behind cutting-edge chip manufacturers:** Dan Wang, "China's Hidden Tech Revolution," *Foreign Affairs*, February 28, 2023, www.foreignaffairs.com/china/chinas-hidden-tech-revolution-how -beijing-threatens-us-dominance-dan-wang; Chris Miller, "What the Most 'Chinese' Smartphone Yet Tells Us about Politics," *Financial Times*, September 21, 2023, www.ft.com/content/e43949cb-bc76 -4a93-b0c5-c9c08af57b62.

407 **booming underground market:** Josh Ye, David Kirton, and Chen Lin, "Focus: Inside China's Under-ground Market for High-End Nvidia AI Chips," Reuters, June 20, 2023, www.reuters.com/technology /inside-chinas-underground-market-high-end-nvidia-ai-chips-2023-06-19; "How Huawei's Chipmaker Turned US Sanctions into a China Success Story," *Bloomberg*, November 21, 2023, www.bloomberg .com/news/articles/2023-11-21/china-huawei-semiconductor-maker-smic-broke-through-a-decade -of-us-sanctions.

408 **untold sums striving to catch up:** China's previous enormous investments in the chip sector were tainted by fraud and largely went to waste. See Edward White and Qianer Liu, "China's Big Fund Cor-ruption Probe Casts Shadow over Chip Sector," *Financial Times*, September 28, 2022, www.ft.com /content/8358e81b-f4e7-4bad-bc08-19a77035e1b4.

408 **ingredients for the clean-energy transition:** Jon Emont, "China Controls Minerals That Run the World—and It Just Fired a Warning Shot at U.S.," *The Wall Street Journal*, July 7, 2023, www.wsj.com /articles/china-controls-minerals-that-run-the-worldand-just-fired-a-warning-shot-at-u-s-5961d77b; Jackie Northam, "China Dominates the EV Battery Industry. Can the Rest of the World Catch up?" NPR, July 22, 2023, www.npr.org/2023/07/22/1189580644/china-dominates-the-ev-battery-industry-can -the-rest-of-the-world-catch-up; Christina Lu, "The Critical Minerals Club," *Foreign Policy*, April 14, 2023, foreignpolicy.com/2023/04/14/us-china-critical-mineral-security-europe-rare-earth-energy-transition.

408 **controls nearly *all* the world's supply:** Matthew P. Funiaole, Brian Hart, and Aidan Powers-Riggs, "Mineral Monopoly: China's Control over Gallium Is a National Security Threat," Center for Strategic & International Studies, July 18, 2023, features.csis.org/hiddenreach/china-critical-mineral-gallium.

408 **top car exporter in 2023:** "How China Became a Car-Exporting Juggernaut," *The Economist*, August 10, 2023, www.economist.com/graphic-detail/2023/08/10/how-china-became-a-car-exporting-juggernaut; Rita Liao, "Powered by Electric Vehicle Growth, China Overtakes Japan as Biggest Auto Exporter," *Tech-Crunch*, August 8, 2023, techcrunch.com/2023/08/08/powered-by-electric-vehicle-growth-china-over takes-japan-as-biggest-auto-exporter; Chris Miller, "As Chinese Cars Speed into Global Markets, Tensions Will Only Escalate," *Financial Times*, July 13, 2023, www.ft.com/content/a4eeda36-5e89-4d6f-93a9 -c3971580ed3d. Owing to the meteoric rise of China's auto industry—and the threat that Chinese electric vehicles could flood the U.S. market and decimate American carmakers—the Biden administration placed a 100 percent tariff on Chinese EVs in May 2024. See The White House, "Fact Sheet: President Biden Takes Action to Protect American Workers and Businesses from China's Unfair Trade Practices," May 14, 2024, www.whitehouse.gov/briefing-room/statements-releases/2024/05/14/fact-sheet-president-biden -takes-action-to-protect-american-workers-and-businesses-from-chinas-unfair-trade-practices.

408 **expertise in *processing* minerals:** Aaron Steckelberg, "The Underbelly of Electric Vehicles," *The Wash-ington Post*, April 27, 2023, www.washingtonpost.com/world/interactive/2023/electric-car-batteries-geography.

408 **subsidies for clean tech:** Bentley Allan, Noah Gordon, and Cathy Wang, "Friendshoring Critical Min-erals: What Could the U.S. and Its Partners Produce?" Carnegie Endowment for International Peace, May 3, 2023, carnegieendowment.org/2023/05/03/friendshoring-critical-minerals-what-could-u.s.-and -its-partners-produce-pub-89659; James Temple, "US Minerals Industries Are Booming. Here's Why," *MIT Technology Review*, March 13, 2023, www.technologyreview.com/2023/03/13/1069658/us-minerals -industries-are-booming-heres-why.

408 **"begin consequential diplomacy":** Bob Davis, "Kurt Campbell on Talking to China Again," *The Wire China*, July 16, 2023, www.thewirechina.com/2023/07/16/kurt-campbell-on-talking-to-china-again.

409 **spiraling economic war:** James Crabtree, "U.S.-China De-Risking Will Inevitably Escalate," *Foreign Policy*, August 20, 2023, foreignpolicy.com/2023/08/20/derisking-decoupling-us-china-biden-economy -trade-technology-semiconductors-chips-supply-chains-ai-geopolitics-escalation.

CHAPTER 68: STRATEGY AND SACRIFICE

410 **Iran revived its nuclear program:** "Timeline: Iran's Nuclear Program Since 2018," The Iran Primer, May 3, 2023, iranprimer.usip.org/blog/2023/may/03/timeline-iran%E2%80%99s-nuclear-program-2018.

410 **the art of the possible:** Jonathan Steinberg, *Bismarck: A Life* (New York: Oxford University Press, 2011), 8.

411 **regaining its prewar economic or military power:** Edward Fishman, "A Tool of Attrition," *Foreign Affairs*, February 23, 2023, www.foreignaffairs.com/ukraine/tool-attrition.

412 **almost half of global GDP:** "What Does the G7 Do?" Council on Foreign Relations, June 28, 2023, www.cfr.org/backgrounder/what-does-g7-do. This estimate includes the full EU as a G7 economy.

412 *away* **from the dollar and** *toward* **the euro:** After the Trump administration imposed sanctions on the Russian aluminum company Rusal in April 2018, the Central Bank of Russia reallocated over $100 billion in U.S. dollar holdings to the euro, renminbi, and yen. This shift resulted in the euro surpassing the dollar as the primary reserve currency of the Russian central bank. See Daniel McDowell, *Bucking the Buck: US Financial Sanctions & the International Backlash Against the Dollar* (New York: Oxford, 2023), 42–49; Natasha Doff and Anya Andrianova, "Russia Buys Quarter of World Yuan Reserves in Shift From Dollar," *Bloomberg*, January 9, 2019, updated January 10, 2019, www.bloomberg .com/news/articles/2019-01-09/russia-boosted-yuan-euro-holdings-as-it-dumped-dollars-in-2018; and Gian Maria Milesi-Ferretti, "Russia's External Position: Does Financial Autarky Protect Against Sanctions?" The Brookings Institution, March 3, 2022, www.brookings.edu/articles/russias-external -position-does-financial-autarky-protect-against-sanctions.

412 **dollar's usage in global payments has shot up:** The dollar's gains largely came at the expense of the euro. See "RMB Tracker Slides," Swift, August 2023, www.swift.com/our-solutions/compliance-and -shared-services/business-intelligence/renminbi/rmb-tracker/rmb-tracker-document-centre and Carter Johnson and Alexandre Tanzi, "Dollar Usage in Global Payments in July Rises to Record, Swift Says," *Bloomberg*, August 23, 2023, www.bloomberg.com/news/articles/2023-08-24/dollar-usage-in-global -payments-in-july-rises-to-record-swift-says.

412 **"steering committee of the free world":** Jake Sullivan, "Remarks by National Security Advisor Jake Sullivan on the Biden-Harris Administration's National Security Strategy" (speech, Washington, D.C., October 12, 2022), The White House, www.whitehouse.gov/briefing-room/speeches-remarks/2022/10 /13/remarks-by-national-security-advisor-jake-sullivan-on-the-biden-harris-administrations-national -security-strategy.

412 **buying two million barrels per day:** Nidhi Verma, "India's Russian Oil Buying Scales New Highs in May," Reuters, July 21, 2023, www.reuters.com/business/energy/indias-russian-oil-buying-scales-new -highs-may-trade-2023-06-21.

412 **largest source of foreign oil:** Lee Ying Shan, "India Importing Russian Oil Is a 'Win-Win' for the World Economy, Says India's No. 1 Oil Company," CNBC, September 6, 2023, www.cnbc.com/2023 /09/06/india-importing-russian-oil-is-win-win-for-global-economy-says-ongc.html.

412 **China massively ramped up trade with Russia:** Philip Wang, "China Sees Biggest Trade Increase with Russia in 2023, Chinese Customs Data Shows," CNN, June 7, 2023, www.cnn.com/2023/06/07/business /china-russia-trade-increase-intl/index.html.

412 **Turkey boosted imports:** "Turkey Doubles Russian Oil Imports, Filling EU Void," Reuters, August 22, 2022, www.reuters.com/business/energy/turkey-doubles-russian-oil-imports-filling-eu-void-2022-08-22; Henry Ridgwell, "Russian Trade Rises Despite Sanctions, as NATO Member Turkey Offers 'Critical Life-line,'" *VOA News*, June 8, 2023, www.voanews.com/a/russian-trade-rises-despite-sanctions-as-nato -member-turkey-offers-critical-lifeline-/7128651.html.

413 **haven for sanctioned Russian oligarchs:** Benoît Faucon and Rory Jones, "U.A.E. Cashes In on Russia's Economic Woes," *The Wall Street Journal*, August 21, 2023, www.wsj.com/world/russia/u-a-e-cashes -in-on-russias-economic-woes-52700157.

413 **contracted by just over 2 percent:** "Russian Federation: At a Glance," International Monetary Fund, December 14, 2023, www.imf.org/en/Countries/RUS#countrydata; "Infographic: Impact of Sanctions on the Russian Economy," European Council, December 10, 2023, www.consilium.europa.eu/en/infographics /impact-sanctions-russian-economy.

413 **returned to modest growth:** Darya Korsunskaya and Alexander Marrow, "Russia's GDP Boost from Military Spending Belies Wider Economic Woes," Reuters, February 7, 2024, www.reuters.com/world /europe/russias-gdp-boost-military-spending-belies-wider-economic-woes-2024-02-07.

413 **invited in six new members:** Argentina eventually declined the invitation to join the BRICS. See Far-naz Fassihi et al., "What to Know about the 6 Nations Invited to Join BRIC," *The New York Times*, August 23, 2023, www.nytimes.com/2023/08/23/world/asia/brics-nations-new-members-expansion.html; Robert Plummer, "Argentina Pulls Out of Plans to Join Brics Bloc," *BBC News*, December 29, 2023, www.bbc.com/news/world-latin-america-67842992.

413 **"cut off the head of the snake" and bomb:** Ross Colvin, "'Cut Off Head of Snake,' Saudis Told U.S. on Iran," Reuters, November 29, 2010, www.reuters.com/article/us-wikileaks-iran-saudis/cut-off-head-of -snake-saudis-told-u-s-on-iran-idUSTRE6AS02B20101129.

413 **Iran's diplomatic rehabilitation:** Farnaz Fassihi, "With BRICS Invite, Iran Shrugs Off Outcast Status in the West," August 25, 2023, www.nytimes.com/2023/08/25/world/middleeast/iran-brics.html.

413 **sanctioning two big oil producers:** Edward Fishman and Kevin Brunelli, "Putin Needs to Feel the Pain," *Politico*, February 28, 2024, www.politico.com/news/magazine/2024/02/28/biden-putin-sanctions-russia-ukraine-00143808.

414 **"nobody" in Moscow expected the G7:** Michael Sauga, "How Well Are Sanctions Against Russia Working?" *Spiegel International*, July 1, 2022, www.spiegel.de/international/europe/how-well-are-european-sanctions-against-russia-working-a-2c83502d-e64f-43a7-98c8-a8076e5746fc; Max Seddon and Polina Ivanova, "How Putin's Technocrats Saved the Economy to Fight a War They Opposed," *Financial Times*, December 16, 2022, www.ft.com/content/fe5fe0ed-e5d4-474e-bb5a-10c9657285d2.

415 **needed to see the "visuals" of the war:** Erin Banco et al., "'Something Was Badly Wrong': When Washington Realized Russia Was Actually Invading Ukraine," *Politico*, February 24, 2023, www.politico.com/news/magazine/2023/02/24/russia-ukraine-war-oral-history-00083757.

415 **$220 billion from oil exports in 2022:** Anatoly Kurmanaev and Stanley Reed, "How Russia Is Surviving the Tightening Grip on Its Oil Revenue," *The New York Times*, February 7, 2023, www.nytimes.com/2023/02/07/business/russia-oil-embargo.html; Statista Research Department, "Federal Budget's Oil and Gas Revenue in Russia from 2006 to 2022," Statista, April 3, 2023, www.statista.com/statistics/1028682/russia-federal-budget-oil-and-gas-revenue.

415 **try to conquer Taiwan:** For assessments of the very real risk of a U.S.–China conflict over Taiwan in the 2020s, see Hal Brands and Michael Beckley, *Danger Zone: The Coming Conflict with China* (New York: W. W. Norton & Company, 2022); Dmitri Alperovitch and Garrett M. Graff, *World on the Brink: How America Can Beat China in the Race for the 21st Century* (New York: PublicAffairs, 2024).

416 **the time to get ready is now:** Edward Fishman, "Challenges from Chinese Policy in 2022: Zero-COVID, Ukraine, and Pacific Diplomacy" (testimony, Washington, D.C., August 3, 2022), U.S.–China Economic and Security Review Commission, www.uscc.gov/sites/default/files/2022-08/Edward_Fishman_Testimony.pdf; Charles Edel and Edward Fishman, "The U.S. Needs an Economic War Council for China," *Foreign Policy*, April 6, 2023, foreignpolicy.com/2023/04/06/united-states-china-taiwan-war-sanctions.

416 **increasing gasoline prices:** Alan Rappeport, "Inflation Fears Could Limit the U.S. Sanctions Response to Russia's Ukraine Invasion," *The New York Times*, February 24, 2022, www.nytimes.com/2022/02/24/business/biden-sanctions-russia-ukraine.html.

CONCLUSION: IMPOSSIBLE TRINITY

417 **had "sanctioned ourselves out of influence":** George W. Bush, "President Holds Press Conference" (speech, Washington, D.C., December 20, 2004), The White House, georgewbush-whitehouse.archives.gov/news/releases/2004/12/20041220-3.html.

417 **"without firing a shot":** Barack Obama, "Remarks by the President in Commencement Address to the United States Air Force Academy" (speech, Colorado Springs, CO, June 2, 2016), The White House, obamawhitehouse.archives.gov/the-press-office/2016/06/02/remarks-president-commencement-address-united-states-air-force-academy.

418 **Trump was as sanctions-happy a president:** "2020 Year-End Sanctions and Export Controls Update" Gibson Dunn, February 5, 2021, www.gibsondunn.com/wp-content/uploads/2021/02/2020-year-end-sanctions-and-export-controls-update.pdf.

419 **Huawei into a tailspin:** Huawei reported annual revenue of ¥704.2 billion in 2023. This figure is 21 percent lower than its peak of ¥891.4 billion in 2020, the year the FDPR entered into force. While the company's performance has rebounded to some extent in recent years, Huawei's annual revenue in 2023 was still lower than it was as far back as 2018. See "Huawei Releases 2023 Annual Report: Performance in Line with Forecast," Huawei, March 29, 2024, www.huawei.com/en/news/2024/3/huawei-annual-report-2023.

419 **maintaining "as large of a lead as possible":** Jake Sullivan, "Remarks by National Security Advisor Jake Sullivan at the Special Competitive Studies Project Global Emerging Technologies Summit" (speech, Washington, D.C., September 16, 2022), The White House, www.whitehouse.gov/briefing-room/speeches-remarks/2022/09/16/remarks-by-national-security-advisor-jake-sullivan-at-the-special-competitive-studies-project-global-emerging-technologies-summit.

419 **"most severe sanctions":** Joseph R. Biden and Olaf Scholz, "Remarks by President Biden and Chancellor Scholz of the Federal Republic Germany at Press Conference" (speech, Washington, D.C., February 7, 2022), The White House, www.whitehouse.gov/briefing-room/statements-releases/2022/02/07/remarks-by-president-biden-and-chancellor-scholz-of-the-federal-republic-of-germany-at-press-conference.

420 **"On Iran, we were using machetes":** Valentina Pop, Sam Fleming, and James Politi, "Weaponisation of Finance: How the West Unleashed 'Shock and Awe' on Russia," *Financial Times*, April 6, 2022, www.ft.com/content/5b397d6b-bde4-4a8c-b9a4-080485d6c64a.

420 **create a permanent economic war council:** Edward Fishman, "How to Fix America's Failing Sanctions Policy," The Lawfare Institute, June 4, 2020, www.lawfaremedia.org/article/how-fix-americas-failing-sanctions-policy.

421 **planning for the economic wars of tomorrow:** Edward Fishman, "Even Smarter Sanctions," *Foreign Affairs*, October 16, 2017, www.foreignaffairs.com/united-states/even-smarter-sanctions; Edward

Fishman, "Challenges from Chinese Policy." in 2022: Zero-COVID, Ukraine, and Pacific Diplomacy" (testimony, Washington, D.C., August 3, 2022), U.S.–China Economic and Security Review Commission, www.uscc.gov/sites/default/files/2022-08/Edward_Fishman_Testimony.pdf.

421 *before* **crises start:** Edel and Fishman, "U.S. Needs an Economic War Council."

422 **70 percent of the AI chips:** Don Clark, "How Nvidia Built a Competitive Moat Around A.I. Chips," *The New York Times*, August 21, 2023, www.nytimes.com/2023/08/21/technology/nvidia-ai-chips-gpu .html.

422 **responsible use of AI:** Mustafa Suleyman, a well-known artificial intelligence entrepreneur and researcher, has argued that the U.S. government should use semiconductors as a "chokepoint" to enforce global standards for the safe and ethical use of AI. See Richard Waters, "US Should Use Chip Leadership to Enforce AI Standards, Says Mustafa Suleyman," *Financial Times*, September 1, 2023, www.ft.com/content/f828fef3-862c-4022-99d0-41efbc73db80.

422 **become an economic security alliance:** The White House, "G7 Hiroshima Leaders' Communiqué" (Hiroshima: G7, May 20, 2023), www.whitehouse.gov/briefing-room/statements-releases/2023/05/20 /g7-hiroshima-leaders-communique.

422 **regular sanctions-planning dialogues:** Fishman, "Fix America's Failing Sanctions Policy"; Edward Fishman, "The Death and Rebirth of American Internationalism," *Boston Review*, August 12, 2020, www.bostonreview.net/articles/edward-fishman-tk; Edward Fishman and Siddharth Mohandas, "A Council of Democracies Can Save Multilateralism," *Foreign Affairs*, August 3, 2020, www.foreignaffairs .com/articles/asia/2020-08-03/council-democracies-can-save-multilateralism.

423 **this era as *les trente glorieuses*:** Tony Judt, *Postwar: A History of Europe Since 1945* (New York: Penguin Books, 2005), 324–25.

423 **but the win-win logic:** See Robert Wright, *Nonzero: The Logic of Human Destiny* (New York: Vintage Books, 2001), which heralded the dawn of an interdependent global society. Bill Clinton said it had "a huge effect on me as the president" in an interview with *Foreign Policy*: "Bill Clinton's World," *Foreign Policy*, November 30, 2009, foreignpolicy.com/2009/11/30/bill-clintons-world.

424 **make conflict between states obsolete:** This perspective was memorably articulated by the columnist Thomas Friedman in his "Golden Arches Theory of Conflict Prevention," which asserted that countries with McDonald's franchises would not fight wars with one another. See Thomas L. Friedman, *The Lexus and the Olive Tree: Understanding Globalization* (New York: Picador, 2000), 248–275.

424 **the realm of "soft power":** See Joseph S. Nye, Jr., *Soft Power: The Means to Success in World Politics* (New York: PublicAffairs, 2005).

424 **by "mutual *independence*":** John Lewis Gaddis, "The Long Peace: Elements of Stability in the Postwar International System," *International Security* 10, no. 4 (1986): 112, doi.org/10.2307/2538951.

424 **Globalization's triumphant march first slowed:** Shekhar Aiyar and Anna Ilyina, "Charting Globalization's Turn to Slowbalization after Global Financial Crisis," *IMF Blog*, International Monetary Fund, February 8, 2023, www.imf.org/en/Blogs/Articles/2023/02/08/charting-globalizations-turn-to -slowbalization-after-global-financial-crisis; David H. Autor, David Dorn, and Gordon H. Hanson, "The China Shock: Learning from Labor Market Adjustment to Large Changes in Trade," National Bureau of Economic Research Working Paper No. 21906, National Bureau of Economic Research, January 2016, www.nber.org/system/files/working_papers/w21906/w21906.pdf.

List of Maps, Charts, and Illustrations

ILLUSTRATIONS

p. 15: Pericles (colaimages/Alamy Stock Photo), Napoleon (Adam Eastland Art + Architecture/ Alamy Stock Photo), and Woodrow Wilson (The White House via CC BY 3.0 US)

p. 30: William Simon (Charles Bennett/AP Photo)

p. 41: Stuart Levey (Ronald Zak/AP Photo)

p. 51: Adam Szubin (Stephen Voss/Bloomberg via Getty Images)

p. 60: Mahmoud Ahmadinejad (Julie Jacobson/AP Photo)

p. 66: Newspaper ad: "Invitation for Bid" (Courtesy of Christy Clark)

p. 97: David Cohen and Wendy Sherman (Susan Walsh/AP Photo)

p. 114: Hassan Rouhani (Kaveh Kazemi/Getty Images)

p. 128: John Kerry and Javad Zarif (Rick Wilking, Pool/AP Photo)

p. 134: John Kerry with bankers in London (Paul Hackett, Pool/AP Photo)

p. 142: Dan Fried (Alexey Vitvitsky/Sputnik via AP Photo)

p. 147: Vladimir Putin at the Munich Security Conference (Oliver Lang/DDP/AFP via Getty Images)

p. 153: Victoria Nuland (Andrew Kravchenko, Pool/AP Photo)

p. 173: Jack Lew (Andrew Harnik/AP Photo)

p. 184: Crash site of Malaysia Airlines Flight 17 (Dmitry Lovetsky/AP Photo)

p. 191: Rex Tillerson and Vladimir Putin (Alexei Druzhinin, Pool/RIA Novosti via AP Photo)

p. 194: Elvira Nabiullina (Mikhail Voskresenskiy/Sputnik via AP Photo)

p. 229: Matt Pottinger (Mark Schiefelbein, Pool/AP Photo)

p. 234: Ren Zhengfei (Kyodo via AP Images)

p. 250: Donald Trump and Xi Jinping (Alex Brandon/AP Photo)

p. 251: Robert Lighthizer and Steven Mnuchin (Andrew Harnik/AP Photo)

p. 274: Xi Jinping at rare-earth processing facility (Xinhua News Agency via Getty Images)

p. 294: Meng Wanzhou (Darryl Dyck/The Canadian Press via AP Photo)

p. 311: Daleep Singh (Sipa via AP Images)

p. 328: Ursula von der Leyen and Bjoern Seibert (T. Monasse/ANDBZ/Abaca via Sipa USA/ AP Images)

p. 331: Vladimir Putin and Xi Jinping (Alexei Druzhinin, Sputnik, Kremlin Pool Photo via AP)

p. 332: Olaf Scholz and Joe Biden (Alex Brandon/AP Photo)

p. 336: Vladimir Putin with his security council (Sputnik, Kremlin Pool Photo via AP Photo)

p. 348: Janet Yellen (Manuel Balce Ceneta/AP Photo)

p. 379: Volodymyr Zelensky and Jake Sullivan (Ukrainian Presidential Press Office via AP Images)

p. 399: BRICS leaders (Gianluigi Guercia, Pool/AP Photo)

Index

Page numbers in *italics* refer to illustrations.